Quattro Pro for Windows
Inside & Out

Stephen Cobb
Bryan Pfaffenberger

Quattro Pro for Windows Inside & Out

Osborne **McGraw-Hill**
Berkeley New York St. Louis San Francisco
Auckland Bogotá Hamburg London Madrid
Mexico City Milan Montreal New Delhi Panama City
Paris São Paulo Singapore Sydney
Tokyo Toronto

Osborne **McGraw-Hill**
2600 Tenth Street
Berkeley, California 94710 U.S.A.

For information on translations and book distributors outside of the U.S.A., please write to Osborne **McGraw-Hill** at the above address.

Quattro Pro for Windows Inside & Out

Copyright © 1992 by McGraw-Hill, Inc. All rights reserved. Printed in the United States of America. Except as permitted under the Copyright Act of 1976, no part of this publication may be reproduced or distributed in any form or by any means, or stored in a database or retrieval system, without the prior written permission of the publisher, with the exception that the program listings may be entered, stored, and executed in a computer system, but may not be reproduced for publication.

1234567890 DOC 998765432

ISBN 0-07-881-768-4

Publisher
Kenna S. Wood

Acquisitions Editor
Elizabeth Fisher

Associate Editor
Scott Rogers

Editorial Assistant
Hannah Raiden

Project Editors
Paul Medoff
Linda Medoff

Copy Editor
Paul Medoff

Proofreader
Linda Medoff

Indexer
Matthew Spence

Computer Designer
Peter Hancik

Cover Designer
Mason Fong

Quality Control Specialist
Bob Myren

Information has been obtained by Osborne **McGraw-Hill** from sources believed to be reliable. However, because of the possibility of human or mechanical error by our sources, Osborne **McGraw-Hill**, or others, Osborne **McGraw-Hill** does not guarantee the accuracy, adequacy, or completeness of any information and is not responsible for any errors or omissions or the results obtained from use of such information.

Contents at a Glance

1 Getting Started 1

2 Building Spreadsheet Models 51

3 Blocks and Names 121

4 Filing, Printing, and Styling 175

5 Mastering Functions 229

6 Database Commands 309

7 Views, Titles, and Defaults 353

8	Data Sharing and Transfer	**401**
9	Graphing Fundamentals	**437**
10	Presentation Graphics	**481**
11	Advanced Data Analysis	**507**
12	Managing Text	**537**
13	Macros	**567**
14	Creating Applications	**599**
A	Working with Windows	**621**
B	Installation	**631**
C	Questions and Support	**643**
	Index	**649**

Contents

Acknowledgments . . . . *xix*

Introduction . . . . *xxi*

1 Getting Started 1

What Is Quattro Pro? 2
   Basic Orientation 2
   Database Management 11
   Graphs and Charts 12
Starting Quattro Pro 14
   Hardware Requirements 15
   Software Requirements 17
   Screens and Printers 20
   Basic Installation 21
Spreadsheet Concepts 22
   Exploring the Workspace 23
   Navigating the Spreadsheet 28
   Types of Information 30
   Labels 32
   Entering and Editing 34
   Editing Cells 35
   Instructions and Formulas 36
   The Object Inspector 38

Using Functions	42
Saving and Ending	46
Keystroke Navigation	49

2 Building Spreadsheet Models ... 51

Making Cell Entries	52
The Sample Model	52
Properties, Defaults, and the Active Page	53
Labels, Columns, and the Active Block	58
The SpeedBar and Column Shortcuts	65
Anatomy of a SpeedBar	66
The Style Buttons	67
The Fit Button	67
Columns and Mice	69
Dragging, Dropping, and Undoing Entries	71
Entry Errors	71
Drag-and-Drop Feature	71
The Undo Feature	73
Cell Editing	74
Error Messages	80
Mixed Entries	81
Storing Information	81
Numbers, Numeric Formats, and Named Styles	84
Value Indicators	84
Long Numbers	85
Numbers, Formulas, and Formats	85
Named Styles	88
Styles and Numeric Formats	92
Dates and Date Formats	95
Spreadsheet Editing	97
Copy and Paste	97
Paste Special	101
Clear Contents	102
Cut and Paste	102
Using Formulas	103
Formulas and Blocks	103
Using SpeedSum	107

Group Work 110
    Temporary Groupings 110
    Named Groups 115
    Group Entries 116
Zooming Off 118

3 Blocks and Names 121

Absolutely Accurate 122
    Problems with Relatives 123
    Absolute Solutions 123
    Rounding Out 127
Block Editing 129
    Block Operations and Block | Move 130
    Block Coordinates and POINT Mode 131
    The Move Destination 134
    Block | Copy 135
    Block | Insert 140
    Block | Delete 151
Block | Fill and SpeedFill 152
    The SpeedFill Button 152
    Block | Fill 156
    Further Series Settings 159
Block | Names 161
    Naming Blocks 161
    Block Name Rules 163
    Deleting and Tracking Block Names ... 163
    Creating Names from Labels 166
Block Shapes and Values 167
    Block | Transpose 168
    Values on the Block 169
Search and Replace 170
    Basic Search and Replace 170

4 Filing, Printing, and Styling 175

Working with Files 176
    Of Files, Disks, and Directories 177

Paths and Names	181
File Saves and File Lists	182
Changing Directories and Drives	185
File Types and Wildcards	187
Further File Menu Commands	189
File	New	189
File	Open and File	Retrieve	190
File	Close	192
File	Save As	193
File	Save All	193
File	Close All	194
File	Workspace	194
File	Exit	195
Printing	196
The Print Block	196
The Print Process	199
Print Settings and Print Preview	201
Print Options	205
File	Page Setup	211
File	Printer Setup	217
Named Settings	218
Adding Style to Reports	219
Fonts	219
Lines	221
Shading	223
Hiding and Sizing Columns and Rows	224
Instant Formatting	226

5 Mastering Functions   229

Formulas as Instructions	230
The Format of Formulas	230
Acceptable Values	232
Operators and Priorities	233
Formulas and Blocks	234
Editing and Calculating Formulas	235
Named Blocks and Pages	236
Common Formula Errors	237
Functions as Built-in Formulas	241

Function Arguments	241
Function Syntax	242
The Functions Key, ALT-F3	242
Mastering Functions	244
Aggregate Functions	**245**
SUM	245
SUMPRODUCT: Sum of the Products	248
COUNT	249
AVG: Average Value	249
MAX: Maximum Value	250
MIN: Minimum Value	250
STD: Standard Deviation	251
VAR: Variance	251
Arithmetic Functions	**251**
ABS: Absolute Value	252
INT: Number as an Integer	252
MOD: Modulus, the Remainder	252
RND: Random Number	253
ROUND	254
EXP: Exponent	255
SQRT: Square Root	255
LN and LOG: Logarithms	256
Database Functions	**256**
DMAX: Maximum Value	258
DMIN: Minimum Value	258
DSTD: Standard Deviation Measure	259
DSUM: Sum Value	259
DVAR: Variance Measure	259
Financial Functions	**260**
Payment Functions	261
Investment Functions	270
Depreciation Functions	282
Logical Functions	**285**
IF	285
Lookup Tables, VLOOKUP, and HLOOKUP	289
CHOOSE	293
INDEX: More Complex Lookup Tables	293
Trigonometric Functions	**294**
PI	295
Degrees and Radians	295

SIN, COS, and TAN: Sine, Cosine, and Tangent	297
ASIN, ACOS, ATAN, and ATAN2: Inverse Trigonometric Functions	297
Trigonometric Applications	297
Date and Time Math	299
Entering Dates with DATE	299
DATEVALUE: Converting a Date Label to a Value	300
Date Deduction	301
Dynamic Date Series	301
YEAR, MONTH, and DAY: Date Part Functions	302
Time Functions	304
HOUR, MINUTE, and SECOND: Time Part Functions	306
Miscellaneous Functions	306
Special Functions	306
ERR: Error	307
NA	307
TRUE and FALSE	307
The IS Functions	307
String Functions	308

6 Database Commands — 309

Sorting and SpeedSort	310
Using SpeedSort	310
The Data	Sort Command	314
Sort Rules	316
Sorting Tips	316
All About Databases	319
Defining a Database	319
Creating a Database	322
Making Inquiries	325
Lines of Questioning	326
Locating Data	328
Repeating a Query	330
Additional Criteria	330
Multiple Criteria	330
Criteria Techniques	332
Naming Fields	333

Formulated Criteria	334
Matching Text	336
Query Extract	337
Setting Up an Extract	338
Unique Records	339
Working with Extracted Data	340
Deleting Records	340
Foreign Databases and Multiple Spreadsheets	341
Splitting Up Your Work	341
Working with Foreign Databases	342
Data Entry Techniques	343
Input Form	343
Data Control	344
Data Functions and Data Tables	345
Data Function Basics	345
Data Table Basics	346
Data Cross-Tabulation	348

7 Views, Titles, and Defaults ... 353

Viewing Options	354
The Window Menu	355
Hide and Show	356
Minimize and Maximize	356
Window Arrangements	358
New Views	360
Window Panes	361
Titles	365
Borders and Lines	367
Levels of Defaults	368
Application Settings	369
Display Settings	370
International Settings	371
Startup Settings	374
Macro Settings	380
SpeedBar Settings	381
Active Notebook Settings	382
Recalc Settings	382

Zoom Factor	385
Palette Settings	386
Notebook Display Settings	388
Macro Library	388
Active Page Settings	388
Name	389
Protection	390
Line Color	390
Conditional Color Settings	390
Label Alignment	392
Display Zeros	392
Default Width Settings	393
Border Settings	393
Grid Line Settings	393
Formats, Custom and Default	394
The Normal Style	395
User-Defined Numeric Formats	396

8 Data Sharing and Transfer 401

Safeguarding Your Data	402
Password Protection	403
Data Loss and Recovery	406
Foreign Files	407
Opening Foreign Files	407
Writing to Foreign Files	409
Extracting, Combining, Inserting, and Linking	413
Data Extraction	413
Combining Data	415
Inserting Files	417
Extracting from Foreign Files	418
The Database Desktop	421
What Database Desktop Does	422
Running Database Desktop	422
Answers into Notebooks	427
Querying by Example	429
Querying Two Tables	430
Using Queries	432

Formulated Criteria	334
Matching Text	336
Query Extract	337
Setting Up an Extract	338
Unique Records	339
Working with Extracted Data	340
Deleting Records	340
Foreign Databases and Multiple Spreadsheets	341
Splitting Up Your Work	341
Working with Foreign Databases	342
Data Entry Techniques	343
Input Form	343
Data Control	344
Data Functions and Data Tables	345
Data Function Basics	345
Data Table Basics	346
Data Cross-Tabulation	348

7 Views, Titles, and Defaults 353

Viewing Options	354
The Window Menu	355
Hide and Show	356
Minimize and Maximize	356
Window Arrangements	358
New Views	360
Window Panes	361
Titles	365
Borders and Lines	367
Levels of Defaults	368
Application Settings	369
Display Settings	370
International Settings	371
Startup Settings	374
Macro Settings	380
SpeedBar Settings	381
Active Notebook Settings	382
Recalc Settings	382

    Zoom Factor 385
    Palette Settings 386
    Notebook Display Settings 388
    Macro Library 388
Active Page Settings 388
    Name 389
    Protection 390
    Line Color 390
    Conditional Color Settings 390
    Label Alignment 392
    Display Zeros 392
    Default Width Settings 393
    Border Settings 393
    Grid Line Settings 393
Formats, Custom and Default 394
    The Normal Style 395
    User-Defined Numeric Formats 396

8   Data Sharing and Transfer 401

Safeguarding Your Data 402
    Password Protection 403
    Data Loss and Recovery 406
Foreign Files 407
    Opening Foreign Files 407
    Writing to Foreign Files 409
Extracting, Combining, Inserting, and Linking ... 413
    Data Extraction 413
    Combining Data 415
    Inserting Files 417
    Extracting from Foreign Files 418
The Database Desktop 421
    What Database Desktop Does 422
    Running Database Desktop 422
    Answers into Notebooks 427
    Querying by Example 429
    Querying Two Tables 430
    Using Queries 432

9 Graphing Fundamentals 437

- Understanding Graph Terminology 441
- Viewing the Graphs Page 442
- Working with Floating Graphs 445
- The Graph Window 445
- Choosing the Graph Type 447
  - Two-Dimensional Graphs 449
  - Three-Dimensional Graphs 453
  - Rotated Graphs 458
  - Combo and Multiple Graphs 458
- Data Series 461
- Special Series Considerations 464
- Titles 465
- Customizing Your Graph with Properties 466
  - Graph Properties Menus 468
- Plotting Data on a Secondary Y Axis 472
- Using Logarithmic Scales 475
- Adjusting the Y-Axis Scale 475
- Managing Graphs 478

10 Presentation Graphics 481

- Choosing the Aspect Ratio 483
- Customizing a Graph with Properties 484
- Copying Graphs 487
- Exploding a Pie Slice 490
- Adding Text 492
- Drawing Lines and Shapes 494
- Creating a Text Graph 496
- Managing Graphics Objects 498
  - Editing Objects 498
  - Grouping and Ungrouping Objects 499
  - Aligning Objects 499
  - Using Object Layers 499
- Slide Shows 501
  - Creating Slide Shows 501
  - Displaying a Slide Show 502

Editing a Slide Show 502
　　　Creating an Interactive Presentation with Graph
　　　　　Buttons 504

11 Advanced Data Analysis 507

　　Regression: Finding Relationships Between Variables 508
　　A Regression Example 509
　　　　Setting Up Regression 511
　　　　Interpreting Regression Results 513
　　　　Using Regression Results 514
　　　　Regression with Multiple Variables 516
　　Generating a Frequency Distribution 518
　　　　Performing a Distribution Analysis 519
　　Generating What-If Tables 521
　　　　A What-If Scenario 523
　　　　Two-Way What-If Tables 526
　　Creating XY Graphs 527
　　Plotting Data Series for an XY Graph 527
　　Goal Seeking with Solve For 530
　　The Optimizer 531

12 Managing Text 537

　　Entering and Reformatting Blocks of Text 538
　　Exchanging Data with Word Processing Programs 541
　　　　Data Exchange with the Clipboard 542
　　　　Importing Text with Hot Links 544
　　　　Importing Data by Embedding It 548
　　Parsing Text 551
　　Text in Formulas 556
　　　　Labels in Logical Functions 556
　　　　Combining Labels with Concatenation 557
　　　　String Functions 558

13 Macros 567

Using Macros 569
    Recording Your First Macro 569
    Naming the Macro 572
    Running the Macro 573
    Editing a Recorded Macro 574
    Recording Another Macro 575
    Assigning a Macro to a Key 575
    Assigning a Macro to a Button 576
    Organizing the Macros Page 578
    Creating an Autoload Macro 580
    Tips for Recording Macros 581
    Pausing a Macro for User Action 587
    Prompting the User for Input 587
    Using Conditional Instructions 588
Creating a Macro Library 595
Debugging Macros 596

14 Creating Applications 599

Introducing Quattro Pro's Application Development
    Tools 600
Using Macros to Hide Quattro Pro's Complexity 602
Introducing UI Builder 603
    Example: Creating a Dialog Box 609
Linking Controls to Commands 611
    Using Dialog | Connect 612
    Using Dialog | Links 613
Opening a Dialog Box 616
    Opening a Dialog Box with an Autoload Macro 617
    Opening a Dialog Box with a Menu 618
Developing Your Own Applications 620

A Working with Windows 621
GUIs and CLIs 622
    A Role for Windows 624
Using Windows 626
    Dialog Boxing 628
Conclusion 630

B Installation 631
Basic Installation 632
The Big Screen 635
Choosing a Printer 636
The Data Directory 637
An Autoload File 640
The PATH Statement 640

C Questions and Support 643
Getting Support 644
    Written Support 644
    Online Support 645
    Registration 645
Questions 646

Index 649

Acknowledgments

My sincere thanks to the readers and reviewers who have supported the Quattro Pro books through their previous incarnations and made suggestions for improvements, many of which were incorporated into this book.

Programs grow ever more powerful, and books that do justice to them take more and more effort to produce. Many thanks are due to the team at Osborne: Liz, Scott, Hannah, and Peter. Thanks as well to Michael, Paul, and Linda for their invaluable input. Hopefully, this book we built is suitable reward and justification for the patience shown and the care taken.

Many thanks are due to the folks at CompuServe for making California just an upload away from a cottage in Scotland (they don't do it for free, but they do it right). The book also benefited from the generous loan of a very reliable Tandon 486/33, courtesy of the good folks at Tandon plc.

As to the lasses in the front line, suffice it to say that without Erin and Chey there would be no book. Thanks to you once more yet for everything.

—Stephen Cobb

Many thanks are due to everyone involved in this project, especially Hannah, Scott, Paul, and Linda, who cheerfully expedited my chapters through the editorial process. Thanks to Nan Borreson of Borland International for keeping me well stocked with beta software, and thanks to Borland for creating such a terrific piece of software!

—Bryan Pfaffenberger

Introduction

This book is a complete guide to Quattro Pro for Windows, a graphically oriented spreadsheet with a wide range of potential applications, from budget projections to statistical analysis; loan amortization to database management. In this book we give you plenty of examples of what Quattro Pro can do, plus clear instructions on how to put the program to work. You will quickly learn how to enter information, perform calculations, format reports, and develop your own spreadsheet models. We then show you how the more advanced features of the program can be used to create impressive charts and presentations, perform detailed analysis, and even develop customized applications using the powerful macro language.

About This Book

If you are new to spreadsheets, the best approach is to read this book chapter by chapter. The features of the program are covered in a natural order of progression, based on many years of experience conducting training seminars and writing guides to other programs, including the DOS version of Quattro Pro. The first few chapters use step-by-step examples, so that learning the basic commands is made easy. More experienced users can go straight from the table of contents to the sections that interest them. The extensive index enables the book to be used as a complete reference to the program.

How This Book Is Organized

The first chapter, "Getting Started," tells you what to expect from Quattro Pro and Windows. By following the step-by-step instructions you'll learn how the basic commands work and how spreadsheet formulas are created. In the second chapter, "Spreadsheet Models," you'll learn how to tackle a typical spreadsheet model that extends across several pages of a Quattro Pro notebook. You'll learn cell editing, cell formatting, and formula copying. In Chapter 3, "Blocks and Names," you'll build on the basic knowledge about spreadsheet making that you acquired in Chapters 1 and 2. You'll learn to use the block commands and more advanced editing commands, such as search and replace. We also look at how you name blocks of cells and how you can fill them using the SpeedFill button.

Chapter 4, "Filing, Printing, and Styling," concentrates on commands used to open and close notebooks and print reports from them. You'll also learn how to embellish notebook reports using a variety of design elements such as fonts and shading. In Chapter 5, "Mastering Functions," you'll find details of the wide range of functions that Quattro Pro provides to help you build powerful formulas. You will see examples of how these are applied in everything from tax returns to trigonometry. In Chapter 6, "Database Commands," you will learn two further aspects of managing information in a spreadsheet: sorting and querying. This includes the SpeedSort button and commands that locate records in any collection of information assembled as a database.

Chapter 7, "Views, Titles, and Defaults," reviews basic assumptions made by Quattro Pro, known as default settings, and tells you how to change them. We tell you how to create custom numeric formats that can save a lot of time when you need to work with unusual units of measure, such as foreign currency. In Chapter 8, "Data Sharing and Transfer," you will learn how to bring data into Quattro Pro from other programs and export data from Quattro Pro so that other programs can read it. You will

Introduction   xxiii

also learn how to extract and combine sections of notebooks and query database files from the Database Desktop.

Chapter 9, "Graphing Fundamentals," introduces all the basics of creating a graph with Quattro Pro, including creating a floating graph, naming the graph, sizing and moving the floating graph, customizing the graph, choosing a graph type, and customizing your graph using graph properties. Chapter 10, "Presentation Graphics," shows you how to take full advantage of Quattro Pro's impressive features for creating presentation-quality graphs. You'll learn how to adjust the aspect ratio for transparencies, 35mm slides, and screen slides; how to individually format the properties of virtually every aspect of your graph; how to add lines, shapes, and text boxes to your graph; and how to create onscreen slide shows.

Chapter 11, "Advanced Data Analysis," introduces many of Quattro Pro's advanced data analysis capabilities. You'll learn how to use linear regression analysis to find relationships between variables, how to generate a frequency distribution, how to generate what-if tables that list all the possible "what-if" outcomes in an analysis, how to create XY graphs to display your analyses, how to use Solve For for goal-seeking, and how to use Quattro Pro's sophisticated Optimizer capabilities.

Chapter 12, "Managing Text," covers the many ways you can use text with Quattro Pro. You'll learn how to enter and reformat blocks of text, how to exchange data with word processing programs using Windows 3.1's Object Linking and Embedding capabilities, how to parse incoming text into separate cells, and how to use text in formulas.

Chapter 13, "Using Macros," introduces recorded and written Quattro Pro macros. Macros give you a way to store and retrieve a series of keystrokes, mouse actions, and command choices. In this chapter, you learn how to create macros the easy way (by recording), and how to write your own macros using Quattro Pro's version of the industry-standard spreadsheet macro language. You'll learn how to assign your macros to keys or buttons, how to create and organize a macros page in your notebooks, how to create a macro that starts automatically when you open the notebook containing the macro, how to pause a macro for user input, how to prompt the user for input, how to use conditional instructions, and much more.

Chapter 14, "Creating Applications," introduces one of Quattro Pro's most exciting features: the tools provided for application development (including UI Builder, link commands, and custom SpeedBars). In brief, an application is a customized Quattro Pro notebook that reduces Quattro Pro's complexity (for example, by hiding unneeded menu commands) at the same time that it presents menu options, dialog boxes, and SpeedBars appropriate to the task at hand—in other words, a make-your-own program that uses spreadsheet functions. These tools are so easy to use that anyone can quickly create an application with Quattro Pro. In this chapter, you'll learn how to create your own custom dialog boxes and menu commands, and you'll also learn how to link these commands with macros so that they accomplish custom tasks.

In Appendix A there are tips on using Windows for those who are new to this operating environment. Appendix B covers the installation of Quattro Pro, while Appendix C offers suggestions for those needing additional support, as well as some last-minute tips and tricks.

A Final Note

Besides being a powerful tool for calculation, analysis, and presentation, Quattro Pro is a lot of fun to work with and write about. We hope that our enthusiasm for the program will be infectious and that through these pages you will enjoy learning Quattro Pro inside and out.

CHAPTER 1

Getting Started

Chapter 1 tells you what Quattro Pro is and how to start using it for a variety of tasks. It introduces the basic concepts of Quattro Pro, helping you build a foundation for the procedures you will learn in the rest of the book. By the end of this chapter you will have learned how to enter data, create formulas, and store your work. The chapter begins with a look at the main features and benefits of Quattro Pro.

What Is Quattro Pro?

Quattro Pro can be described as a graphically oriented electronic spreadsheet program with integrated database management, presentation, and application development capabilities. This definition makes the program sound more complicated than it is. The terms "spreadsheet," "database management," and "presentation" simply refer to ways of organizing and analyzing information.

Basic Orientation

A *spreadsheet* arranges information in columns and rows like a columnar pad. You can see this on the left of Figure 1-1, which shows how a Quattro Pro spreadsheet used to tabulate yacht sales might appear. A *database management* program stores information in fields and records. For example, the yacht sales in Figure 1-1 can be sorted according to the values in the Total column or alphabetically according to the Model column. A *presentation* program treats information visually, as in pie charts, bar graphs, diagrams, and slide shows. In Figure 1-1, the table of yacht sales is displayed as a three-dimensional bar graph.

To understand why Quattro Pro is described as a *graphically oriented* spreadsheet, consider Figure 1-1. Apart from the fact that the spreadsheet includes both a graph and a drawing of the company logo that were created by Quattro Pro, the screen is full of icons and other objects that allow you to issue commands without using menus or typing function keys. For example, the third row of the screen contains a collection of icons known as the *SpeedBar*. This provides point-and-click access to commands like Cut, Copy, and Paste. However, Quattro Pro goes a step further and provides a visual metaphor for one of its most

Chapter 1: Getting Started 3

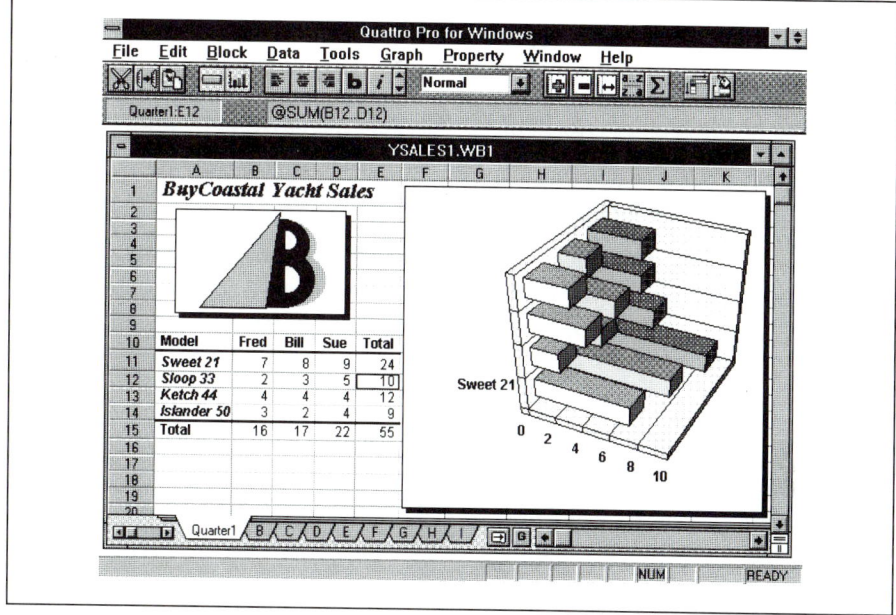

FIGURE 1-1 A typical Quattro Pro spreadsheet including chart and graphics

powerful features: multipage spreadsheets (in Figure 1-1, you see the Quarter 1 page), otherwise known as *notebooks*.

Notebook Computing

All spreadsheet programs work by adding computer power to the simple but effective method of arranging information used by accountants for centuries: the columnar pad. Instead of writing numbers on a paper pad, you enter them on a computer screen. Instead of calculating numbers on a calculator, you tell the spreadsheet program to calculate them for you. Instead of putting the columnar pad in a filing cabinet or desk drawer, you tell the program to store your work in a file on a computer's disk. When you want a paper report, you tell the program which columns and rows you want to send to your computer's printer.

When you load a Quattro Pro file on your computer, you immediately see how the column and row arrangement is translated into a screen image. This is shown in Figure 1-2, where you can see a spreadsheet and graph of the number of people taking flights on northern routes. The numbers are broken down according to Coach, Business, and First class for each of four quarters. The capital letters across the top of the worksheet identify the columns; the numbers down the left side of the worksheet identify the rows. The collection of words and numbers you see in Figure 1-2 is referred to as a *model* because it describes, or models, a particular set of circumstances—in this case, the passenger volume on certain routes flown by TOA (Take Over Airlines).

Each junction of a spreadsheet column and row produces a box, or *cell*, into which you can enter a number, a formula, or text. The column letters and row numbers are combined to give each cell a unique address. In Figure 1-2, you can see that the word "Northern" has been entered in column A, row 1, known as cell A1. The number 123 has been entered in cell C5. The rows extend off the bottom of the screen to 8192. The columns extend off the right of the screen, past Z to AA through AB, and so on to IV for a total of 256 columns.

FIGURE 1-2 A spreadsheet model of airline passenger volume

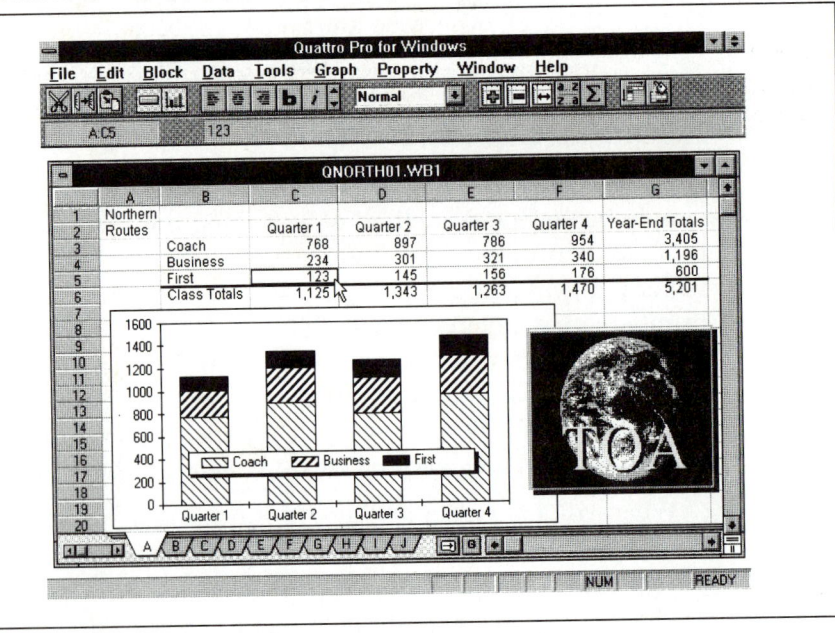

Chapter 1: Getting Started

Note There are also letters across the bottom of the screen on what appear to be notebook divider tabs. These do not refer to columns but to notebook pages, which will be described in a moment.

The numbers in row 6 are the results of calculations that add up the three figures for each quarter. The numbers in column G are totals of each of the three classes of travel. Because these totals are calculations, changing the number in C5 will cause the totals to change. In Figure 1-3, you can see that 123 has been altered to 231. You can also see that three other numbers changed: the total for Quarter 1, the total for First, and the grand total in cell G6.

Note The first bar in the graph in Figure 1-3 has changed to reflect the new value in C5. Graphs in Quattro Pro spreadsheets are "live," meaning that they immediately reflect changes in the underlying data.

With a single command, you can undo the change to the entry in C5. This allows you to perform "what-if" calculations, evaluating a model using many different values. You can see that the electronic spreadsheet is a major improvement over the pencil and columnar pad. However,

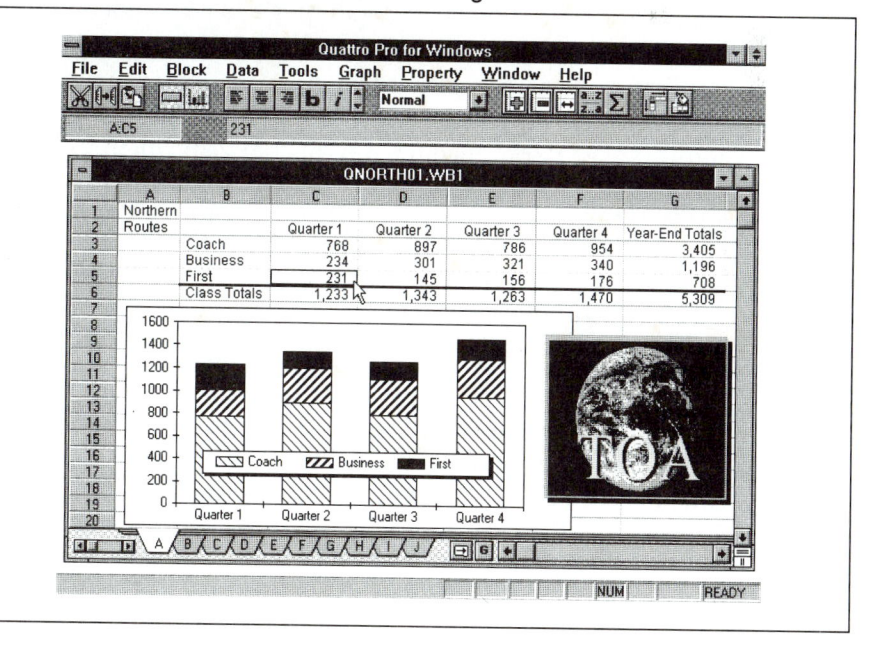

FIGURE 1-3 The spreadsheet updated to reflect a new figure

columnar pads have several benefits when it comes to organizing information. Because a single page is limited in size, large collections of information must be broken down into manageable parts. This imposes a structure on the data that keeps each part from getting too large or complex. Before Quattro Pro, other spreadsheet programs had attempted to emulate this aspect of the columnar pad, but with varying degrees of success.

When Lotus 1-2-3 was first introduced, it adopted the "giant sheet" approach, requiring all related information to be entered into the same spreadsheet. Commands were provided to allow data to be copied between spreadsheets but there was no provision for active links between separate sheets. This made it difficult to translate traditional multipage accounting schedules into spreadsheets and often led to single sheets reaching an unmanageable size. Improvements were made in 1-2-3 Release 2.2, which allowed active links between separate files. With Release 3, 1-2-3 enabled multiple-sheet spreadsheets to be created within a single file. This meant a group of sheets could be manipulated at the same time, and it was possible to create "three-dimensional" models.

A typical 3-D model consists of several supporting sheets plus a consolidation sheet. For example, the total passenger volume figures for TOA could be divided into northern and southern routes. A model of the total volume would then consist of a consolidation sheet that added together the figures from two supporting sheets, one for northern routes and the other for southern routes. You can create such an arrangement in 1-2-3, but the commands for navigating and viewing multiple-page spreadsheet files are cumbersome. Borland addressed this problem when designing Quattro Pro and came up with the concept of the *spreadsheet notebook*.

In the top left of Figure 1-3 you can see that cell C5 is actually referred to as A:C5, meaning cell C5 on page A of the notebook. Across the bottom of the screen you can see a series of lettered tabs that represent pages of the notebook. There are 256 pages in each file, lettered, like columns, from A to IV.

Borland realized that there is considerable potential for confusion if you use lettering both for pages and columns. That is why you can name each page. In Figure 1-4, you can see how this works for the TOA model. The page shown in Figure 1-3 has been called Northern. A second notebook page, called Southern, has been created. Figure 1-4 shows a

Chapter 1: Getting Started 7

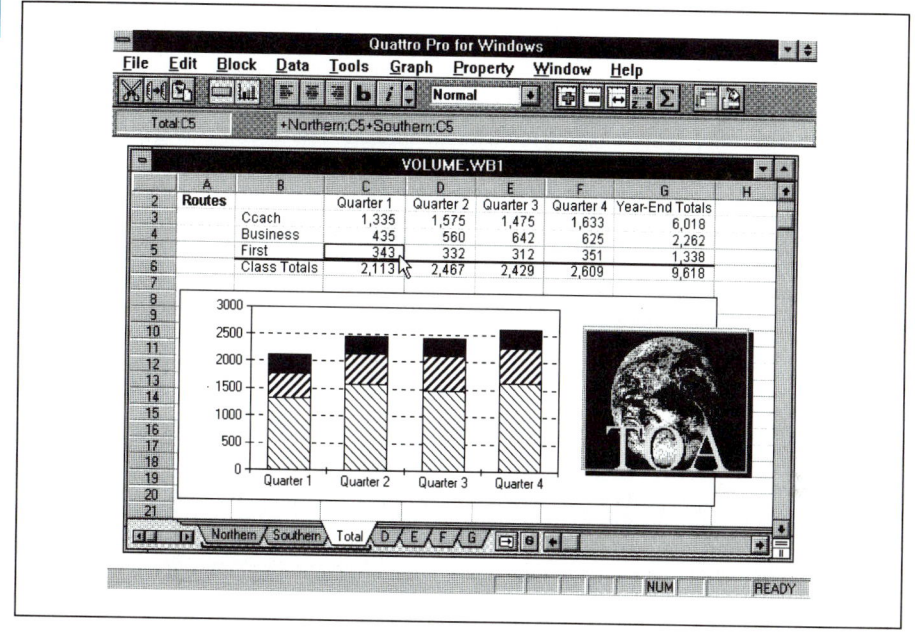

FIGURE 1-4 Using notebook pages with names instead of letters

third page, called Total, that adds together the volume from Northern and Southern. You can see that cell C5 of the page called Total is referred to as Total:C5. This cell contains a formula that adds together cells Northern:C5 and Southern:C5.

To further simplify notebook computing, Quattro Pro allows you to name groups of pages and apply commands to all of the pages at the same time. For example, the font used for the spreadsheet entries can be adjusted in several pages at the same time. You can even enter the same data into multiple sheets with a single command. You can open multiple views of the same spreadsheet file and view different pages in each one. The different views can be arranged by Quattro Pro, or you can adjust each one separately, as in Figure 1-5.

If you have used other spreadsheets before switching to Quattro Pro, it may take you a while to rethink how you organize your work. A notebook can accommodate a large amount of work, and so all related spreadsheets can be grouped together in the same notebook. Fortunately, Quattro Pro can insert spreadsheets created by other programs, such as

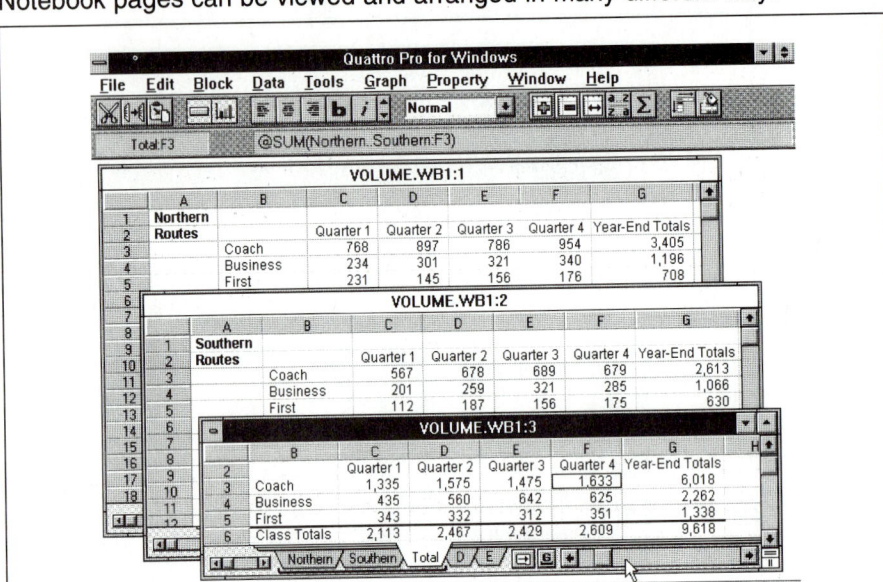

FIGURE 1-5 Notebook pages can be viewed and arranged in many different ways

1-2-3, as new pages in a notebook. This simplifies the process of converting your work to the notebook approach. You can see a diagram of the notebook concept in Figure 1-6, which, by the way, was drawn in Quattro Pro. Note that Quattro Pro supports links between notebooks, as well as between pages within a notebook. Quattro Pro also supports the Windows 3.1 data-sharing technologies known as DDE (Dynamic Data Exchange) and OLE (Object Linking and Embedding). The main spreadsheet features of Quattro Pro are summarized in Table 1-1.

What Is WYSIWYG?

Quattro Pro is sometimes described as a *WYSIWYG* spreadsheet. WYSIWYG is an acronym for "What You See Is What You Get," which refers to the ability to show on screen an exact image of what will be printed when the time comes to produce a report from the spreadsheet. Figure 1-7 shows a report printed from the spreadsheet that is shown in Figure 1-4.

Chapter 1: Getting Started

FIGURE 1-6 A diagram of the notebook concept drawn with Quattro Pro

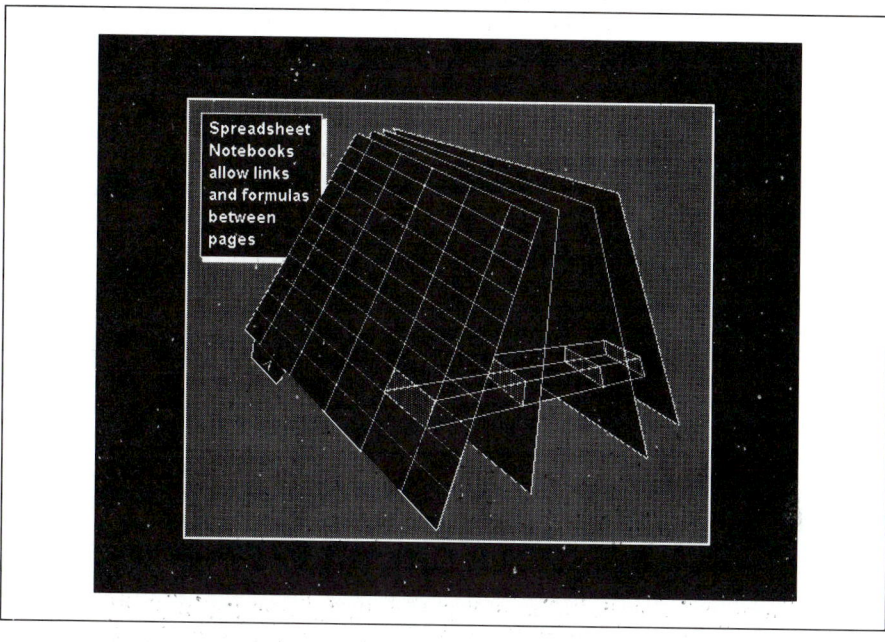

Spreadsheet Notebooks allow links and formulas between pages

FIGURE 1-7 A report printed from a Quattro Pro spreadsheet

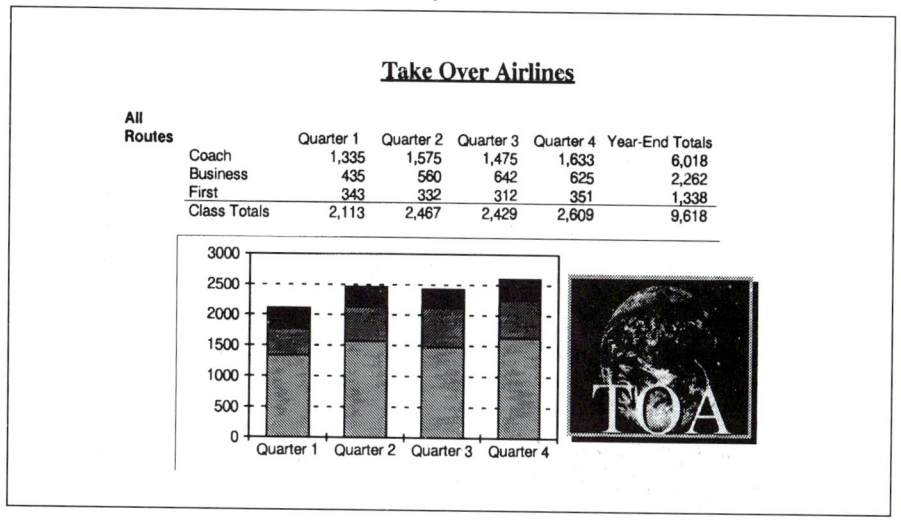

Take Over Airlines

All Routes

	Quarter 1	Quarter 2	Quarter 3	Quarter 4	Year-End Totals
Coach	1,335	1,575	1,475	1,633	6,018
Business	435	560	642	625	2,262
First	343	332	312	351	1,338
Class Totals	2,113	2,467	2,429	2,609	9,618

TABLE 1-1 Spreadsheet Features

Spreadsheet notebooks	You can create over 250 pages in each file, with over 2 million cells per page. Page names appear on page tabs. Page groups can be named and data entered simultaneously across groups.
SpeedBar	You get instant access to most commonly used spreadsheet commands via icon buttons on the SpeedBar, which change according to the task at hand. You can create your own custom SpeedBars.
Object inspectors	Simply click the right mouse button on any part of the spreadsheet to adjust its appearance and properties. Instead of digging through menus for commands, you can adjust most aspects of the program with this "object inspector" feature.
Intelligent commands	Many commands, such as the Insert button, respond according to the circumstances in which you use them, streamlining operations.
SpeedFill	Instantly fills a block of cells with appropriate formulas, values, or text entries.
SpeedSum	Instantly sums columns and rows. Use across a group of pages to consolidate figures.

Quattro Pro allows you to use a wide range of fonts. You can use any of the fonts you have installed in Windows, including TrueType, Adobe Type Manager, and BitStream FaceLift. To help you fit reports onto the page, there is a "center blocks" setting that spreads printed output evenly between borders and a "print to fit" setting that automatically shrinks reports to fit the page. The publishing features of Quattro Pro are summarized in Table 1-2.

TABLE 1-2 Publishing Features

Full WYSIWYG editing	Your spreadsheet appears exactly as it will when printed. Zoom in and out for detail work or an overview.
Named styles	Format cells and blocks using styles that you create, modify, and name. Quickly select styles from a pop-up list.
SpeedFormat	Format tables instantly with the SpeedFormat button that offers a selection of predefined table styles.
Fonts and lines	Full support for all fonts installed in Windows, including ATM and TrueType fonts. Line drawing around cells in any combination and a variety of styles.
Colors and shading	Full range of colors for text, background, and fills. Wash effects and bitmaps may also be used. Color output on color devices.
Print-to-fit	Proportional shrinking or enlargement of objects to fit neatly on the printed page.
Print preview	Accurate display of print block before committing to paper. Access page setup and print operations directly from preview mode.
Charts and pictures	Paste graphs, drawings, and imported art work directly into the spreadsheet to enhance and illustrate reports.

Database Management

As well as working as a spreadsheet, Quattro Pro offers database management facilities. A *database* is a collection of information organized in a meaningful way. Anything from a telephone directory to a filing cabinet of medical records can be considered a database. *Database management* is the electronic storage and organization of such information. A database involves grouping pieces of information as *records* and organizing the records into *fields*. For example, the figures for the three classes of travel in Figure 1-4 could be sorted alphabetically by name or numerically by the largest total.

Another aspect of database management is the ability to locate specific information. For example, you can see a list of employees in Figure 1-8. The columns in the table represent database fields, one for each category of information. The rows constitute records, one for each employee. Using the database commands in Quattro Pro also shown in Figure 1-8, you can find, for example, all the records for employees earning above a certain amount. You can even copy selected records to a separate page of the notebook and then sort them and format them into a report.

Because a lot of company data is handled by specialized database management software, Quattro Pro provides a table viewer utility that helps you search out records in database files created by programs other than Quattro Pro. You can search using query by example and SQL (Standard Query Language) commands. You can then bring the selected records into a spreadsheet notebook. The database features of Quattro Pro are summarized in Table 1-3.

Graphs and Charts

The value of pictures in conveying information has been appreciated for thousands of years. While a trend can be understood from a page full

TABLE 1-3 Database Features

Sorting	Sort rows based on up to five keys. Use the SpeedSort button for instant sorting of selected cells.
Query database tables	Create and query your own databases within spreadsheets, finding records that match your criteria. Copy matching records to separate pages of the same notebook.
Import and export data	Automatic translation of DBF and DB files in and out of spreadsheet tables. Import and export of delimited ASCII and other data formats.
Database desktop	Separate module permits browsing of foreign databases and querying by example to import selected data.
Paradox links	Directly load Paradox answer tables.

FIGURE 1-8 A typical spreadsheet database and the Data menu commands

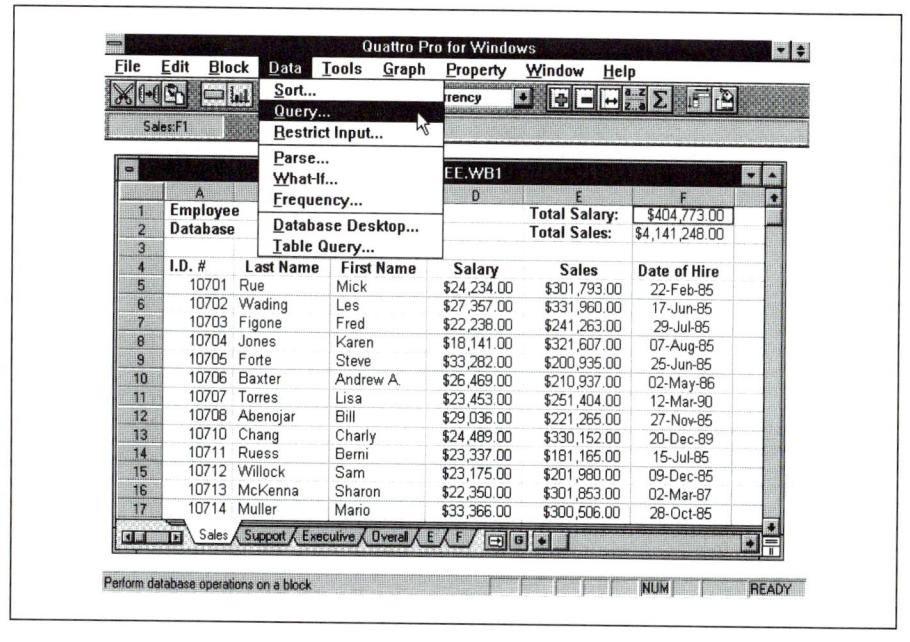

of numbers eventually, a graph can convey the same information at a glance. Computers make it easy to create such graphs and charts. In Quattro Pro, you can draw a graph from numbers and words with a single command. Whenever the numbers in the spreadsheet change, the graph is automatically updated. Graphs can be pasted into the spreadsheet, as shown in Figure 1-4, or viewed on a full screen, as in Figure 1-9. The graphs can be embellished with drawings and text, like the company logos seen earlier in Figures 1-1 and 1-3 or the arrows and notes added to Figure 1-9.

The limitations of black-and-white printing do not do justice to the vibrant colors that can be displayed on a computer monitor, but you can see that the use of an image is effective in conveying information, in this case, the trend in passenger volume figures shown in earlier examples. The type of graph in Figure 1-9, a three-dimensional ribbon chart, is one of more than a dozen chart styles Quattro Pro offers. Three-dimensional charts can be rotated and their perspective adjusted for a variety of interesting effects. Graphs are described in more detail in Chapter 9.

FIGURE 1-9 A full-screen chart annotated with text and drawn objects

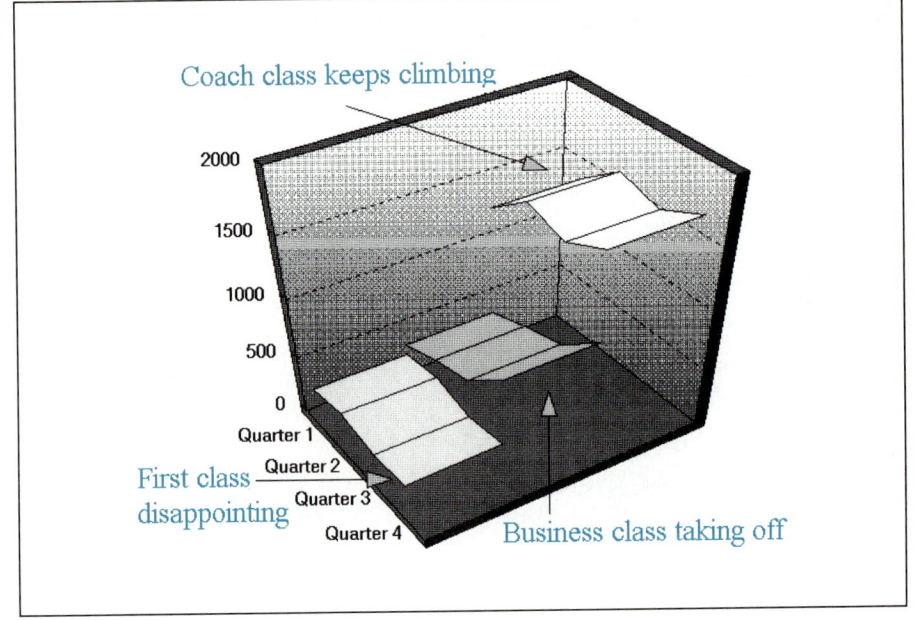

Coach class keeps climbing

2000
1500
1000
500
0
Quarter 1
Quarter 2
Quarter 3
Quarter 4

First class disappointing

Business class taking off

These days, computers are not only used to create paper illustrations and 35mm slides. They are also used to make presentations on a large screen or overhead display system. With Quattro Pro, you can put together a series of graphs that are then displayed, one after another, at your command or by simple user input. A variety of visual effects can be used to fade from one slide to another, and sound effects can be added to create a multimedia presentation environment. Presentation graphics are discussed in Chapter 10.

The graphics features in Quattro Pro are summarized in Table 1-4.

Starting Quattro Pro

There are two steps to getting started with Quattro Pro: installing (something you only need to do once—the program can't be run from the compressed files on the disks in the package) and launching, that is, issuing the command that begins the program (something you do at the

Chapter 1: Getting Started   15

TABLE 1-4   Graphics Features

Chart gallery	Wide range of chart types including 3-D wire frame and surface plots.
3-D rotation	Full control over rotation, elevation, and perspective of 3-D graphs.
Design features	Instant intelligent graphing of preselected data. Full control over type, coloring, and shading. Use wash effects and bitmaps to fill any part of a graph.
Instant access	Consistent use of object inspector eliminates complex and lengthy setting menus. All aspects of a graph can be adjusted with a few mouse strokes.
Graph annotation	Full range of drawing tools can embellish designs and add free-floating text.
Graph objects	Live charts and complex drawings can be pasted into the spreadsheet for attractive reports.
Graph buttons	Macros can be attached to pasted objects to create mouse-driven graphic interfaces.
Slides and slide shows	All graphs are stored as icons on special notebook page for easy management. Select slides and drag to the projector icon for instant slide shows.

start of every Quattro Pro session). Both steps are outlined here, but you can find more detailed information in Appendix B. Before you install Quattro Pro, however, you might want to review the program's hardware and software requirements.

Hardware Requirements

In order to provide so many features, Quattro Pro requires a fairly powerful *hardware configuration*—that is, collection of equipment. Quattro Pro can run on any Windows-compatible PC that has a hard disk with ten available megabytes and at least four megabytes of RAM (Random Access Memory). The expression "four megabytes of RAM" refers to the size of the memory area used by a PC to hold programs and data temporarily while they are being used.

Note Information and the space it takes up in a computer system is measured in bytes—one byte is roughly the amount required to hold one character. One kilobyte (1K) is 1024 bytes, while a megabyte (1Mb) is 1024K, or 1,048,576 bytes.

There is an important distinction to be made between disk storage and random access memory, or RAM. The RAM in your computer is the area that holds program files while you use them plus the data on which the program is working, such as the spreadsheet file you saw in Figure 1-4. The information in RAM constantly changes while you use your computer and is wiped out when you turn off the computer. The disks you use—either the removable floppy disks or the fixed disks, known as hard disks, within the computer—store information permanently. This means that when you turn off the computer, the information in disk files stays there, ready for the next time you need it. Unless there is a physical problem with the disk, the files should remain as you left them until the next time you need them.

Note Quattro Pro requires that you have ten megabytes of free disk space on your hard disk before it can be installed.

When information is being stored on a disk, it is being *written* into a file. When it is retrieved, the file is *read* from the disk. The process of reading and writing is known as *disk access*, and is one of the few aspects of computing that requires moving parts. This means that accessing information on disk is much slower than working with it in RAM, which is electronic. Hard disks, which spin very fast, access data quicker than floppy disks. You will find that the performance of Quattro Pro is improved by adding more RAM to your computer, rather than using a faster or larger hard disk.

The most important nonmoving part of your computer is the central processing unit, or CPU, the single chip that is at the heart of the PC's electronics. There are several levels of CPU, known by their Intel product codes, each one more powerful that its predecessor. Quattro Pro works well with 80386, 80486, and 80586 processors. It will not run on 8088

Chapter 1: Getting Started

processors and only runs slowly on 80286 processors. Quattro Pro will automatically take advantage of a math coprocessor if you have one installed in your computer. A math coprocessor improves the speed of recalculation.

Software Requirements

When you are working with Quattro Pro, your computer's RAM contains two other things as well as your spreadsheet and the Quattro Pro program: the disk operating system and the Windows operating environment. The disk operating system (DOS) is the piece of software that controls basic computer operations such as arranging files on disk. It is only after you have loaded DOS that a program like Windows can communicate with your hardware. When you tell your computer to load Windows, it is actually DOS that carries out this command.

When you load Windows it provides a "graphical user interface and mouse-driven operating environment." This means that all actions and operations are represented visually, using icons and dialog boxes, and you can use a mouse to issue commands. Mouse actions consist of pointing, clicking, dragging, and double-clicking. *Pointing* means placing the mouse pointer over a specific object on the screen. *Clicking* means pressing and quickly releasing the mouse button when you are pointing to an object. For most commands you use the button on the left; however, Quattro Pro makes extensive use of the right mouse button as well. *Dragging* means pointing to an object and holding down the mouse button while moving the mouse. *Double-clicking* means pressing and releasing the mouse button twice in quick succession while pointing to an object. For example, one way to start a program in Windows is to point to the program icon and double-click on it.

Consider the view of Windows shown in Figure 1-10. The rectangle entitled Desktop is a dialog box that allows you to alter the appearance and operation of the Windows desktop. To get to this dialog box, the user first double-clicked on the Control Panel icon in the Main program group, visible at the bottom left of the screen. When the Control Panel window appeared, the Desktop icon was double-clicked, resulting in the display seen in Figure 1-10.

FIGURE 1-10 Working with Windows dialog boxes

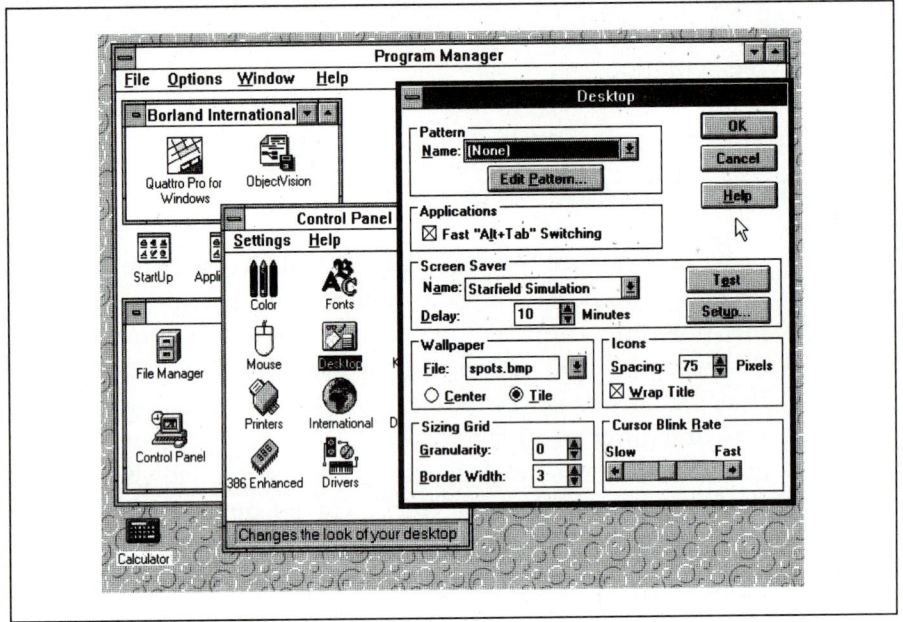

In Windows, each action is a logical progression from the previous command. The path that you have taken remains clearly visible, as are the current options. A variety of visual devices are used to get your input, including radio buttons, sliders, check boxes, and pop-up lists.

Suppose, for example, you want to adjust the Windows wallpaper. *Wallpaper* is the graphic design that is displayed behind all of the windows. The arrangement of circles in the background of Figure 1-10 is created by selecting a small picture file called SPOTS.BMP and repeating it across the desktop with the Tile option. When you select the File option in the Desktop dialog box a list pops up from which you can choose a file. Choosing between the Tile and Center options is done by clicking a radio button (this means that selecting Tile deselects Center and vice versa, since only one of the two buttons can be selected at once).

In the Icons section of the Desktop dialog box, a check box called Wrap Title determines whether the titles for icons are wrapped onto two lines, as is the case with the Quattro Pro for Windows icon in Figure 1-10. A check box can be checked, as in Figure 1-10, or unchecked. To determine how fast the Windows editing cursor flashes, you use a slider labeled Cursor Blink Rate. To register the current dialog box settings, click the OK button. You can also press ENTER to select OK, since this is the default button, the one that Windows assumes you want to press, as indicated by the thicker outline. You can select the Cancel button or press ESC to leave the dialog box without registering any changes. There is also a Help button that will summon up an explanation of the current dialog box.

Note If you are not yet clear on how to use your mouse with Windows, you might want to refer to Appendix A, which explains how to perform basic Windows operations.

Selecting icons and responding to dialog boxes is a lot easier than typing program names at the DOS prompt and responding to obscure DOS error messages when something goes wrong. Of course, even Windows takes time and effort to master, but the icon and dialog box interface is common to all Windows-based applications. This minimizes the number of commands and operations that you have to learn as you explore further applications.

Unlike some other graphical interfaces, Windows does not require you to use a mouse. All commands can be accessed from the keyboard. For example, in Figure 1-10, the Tile option can be selected by holding down the ALT key and typing the letter T (a keystroke that is typically described as ALT-T). This convention of parallel mouse and keyboard operation is carried over into Quattro Pro. In practice, a mouse is highly desirable for operating most Windows-based applications, but the presence of keyboard shortcuts enriches the user interface. You may well find that you use the keyboard for some operations, the mouse for others.

Note Look for key letters to be underlined in Windows menus and dialog boxes. Items with key letters can be selected by pressing ALT and the key letter.

To recap: Windows is an operating environment that sits between the application (Quattro Pro) and the operating system (DOS). Windows allows many different programs to share the same basic software components, such as printing and fonts. This makes for efficient use of your computer's resources and it allows the designers of programs like Quattro Pro to concentrate on features within the application itself.

Screens and Printers

Quattro Pro is not particularly concerned about the type of printer or display system you use. This is because all screen and printer activity is handled by Windows rather than Quattro Pro. When you install Windows, you have to tell it the type of display you have—equipment that meets one of the following standards: EGA, VGA, SuperVGA, XGA, 8514/a, Hercules, or something that can emulate one of these. It is possible to run Windows with a display system other than the ones listed here, but that usually requires a special program, called a *driver*, supplied with the display system.

With some display systems, you can choose between several different screen resolution and color settings. The resolution setting determines how sharp the screen appears and is measured as lines and rows, as in 640×480, which is the basic VGA setting. A higher resolution, such as 800×600, means that objects on the screen can be drawn smaller while retaining legibility. This allows Windows to "zoom out" and show you a larger work area. The color setting is often stated along with the resolution, as in 800×600×16, meaning that 16 colors are used. Many display systems can show more colors, as in 800×600×256. However, the more colors you use the longer it takes Windows to draw the screen.

Note Windows 3.1 comes with an 800×600×16 driver that is particularly fast and can be used with a wide range of Super VGA cards.

You can install a printer for Windows at any time using the Printers tool in the Control Panel, an icon that is usually found in the Main program group. Whatever models you install through the Printers dialog box will be available in Quattro Pro. If you use the Printers tool to select a default printer, one that Windows will assume you want to use all the time, it will be preselected as the default printer in Quattro Pro. However, you can use the Quattro Pro File menu's Printer Setup command to select a different printer.

Bear in mind that you cannot print charts or spreadsheets in color unless you have a color printer. Fortunately, Quattro Pro does a good job of converting colors to shades of gray during printing, particularly on higher-resolution devices such as laser printers. Quattro Pro can even show you what the converted results will look like before you actually print them.

As you probably know, one of the great advantages of Windows is that it can display text in a variety of different styles. A specific shape and size of letters and numbers is referred to as a font. A *font* consists of a typestyle or letter shape, such as Times or Helvetica; a point (1/72 inch) size, usually between 6 and 72; and an optional attribute, such as bold or italic. For example, the large text in the top left of Figure 1-9 is Arial 18-point bold. The text alongside the arrows is Times Roman 12 point. Quattro Pro can use all of the fonts you have installed in your version of Windows, including those supplied by Adobe and BitStream, and you can mix and match as many fonts as you like. Bear in mind that scalable fonts will give you a closer match between what you see on the screen and what is printed out. Examples of scalable fonts are the TrueType fonts supplied with Windows 3.1 and those supported by Adobe Type Manager and BitStream Facelift.

Basic Installation

To install Quattro Pro, you must first start Windows. This is typically done by typing WIN at the DOS prompt and then pressing ENTER. Once the Windows desktop appears, you can place disk 1 of the original Quattro Pro program disks into drive A (most PCs have a floppy disk drive that is called A and a hard disk drive called C). Now press ALT-F to activate the Program Manager File menu and type R for Run. A text box called Command Line appears containing the edit cursor. Type A:INSTALL and press ENTER to initiate the installation process.

When the installation program has copied the program files onto the hard disk, you will need to answer some questions about your system. When you have answered these, Quattro Pro will be installed and ready to use. The installation procedure creates a new program group called Quattro Pro for Windows and within that, a new icon, also called Quattro Pro for Windows. You can see the program icon in Figure 1-10. In this figure, however, the program group is called Borland International, as it contains several of that company's programs. If you would like advice on customizing the installation of Quattro Pro on your system, refer to Appendix B.

To load Quattro Pro, select (click once on) the Quattro Pro program icon and press ENTER or double-click on the icon. Quattro Pro presents you with a screen like the one shown in Figure 1-11. This figure has been annotated, and the various parts are described in the next section. At this point, you could begin entering new data or retrieve data you have previously stored. Exiting the program is discussed in the section "Saving and Ending," later in this chapter.

Spreadsheet Concepts

This section introduces the basic concepts of Quattro Pro spreadsheets and prepares you for the next chapter. Some brief examples will be used to demonstrate how to enter and calculate numbers with Quattro Pro. These examples will also familiarize you with the different ways of issuing commands in Quattro Pro.

FIGURE 1-11

When you start the program, you see a blank spreadsheet notebook

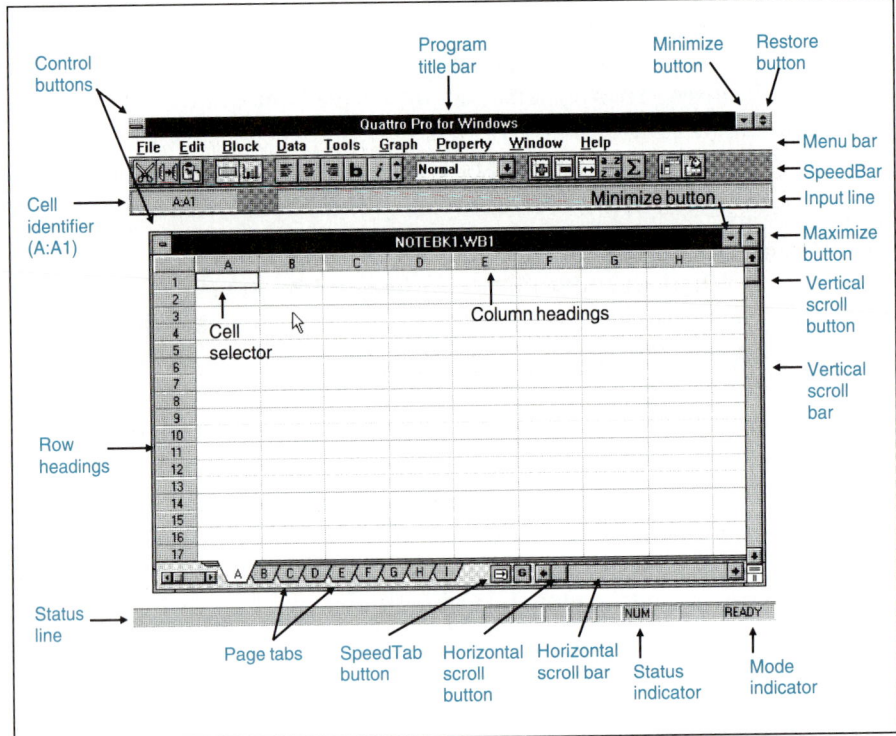

Exploring the Workspace

When you first load Quattro Pro, you are presented with an electronic workspace containing a blank notebook, as shown in Figure 1-11. There are four lines above the workspace and one below it. These lines provide a set of controls and instruments, much like the dashboard of a car, that enable you to operate the program.

The Program Title Bar

The first line of the screen in Figure 1-11 is referred to as the program title bar, since it displays the title of the program being displayed. This bar appears in all Windows applications, and it controls the way the applications are displayed. There are three possibilities: full-screen, otherwise known as *maximized*; *restored*, otherwise known as *windowed*; and *minimized*, otherwise known as *iconized*.

Quattro Pro is displayed full-screen in Figure 1-11, which is how the program normally appears the first time you load it. This maximized display means that no other programs or windows are visible. However, if you click on the double arrow button on the far right of the title bar, known as the Restore button, the program is displayed in a smaller window with a border. At the same time, the double arrows on the Restore button change to a single up arrow, and the button is now referred to as the Maximize button. Clicking the Maximize button will return the display to full-screen.

When a program is displayed in a window with borders, the location and size of the window can be adjusted. This allows you to see more than one program at the same time. In Figure 1-12, you can see Quattro Pro displayed in a window, allowing parts of the Program Manager and desktop to be viewed as well. The Notepad program is also running in a window. Note that the title bar of the current, or *active*, window is shown in a different color to distinguish it from the inactive windows. In this case, Notepad is the active window, and Quattro Pro is inactive.

Not only can you maximize a program or run it in a window, you can minimize it. This turns the program into a small icon, to free your screen for another program without closing the program or the document you are working on. The Minimize button is the one just to the left of the Maximize/Restore button with the single down arrow. Minimizing a program rather than closing it means you can return to your work without having to reload the program or the file. In Figure 1-12, the Paintbrush program, which is editing an untitled document, has been minimized. To restore a program that has been minimized, simply double-click on the icon.

The button on the left of the program title bar gives you menu and keyboard access to the Minimize, Maximize, and Restore functions, as well as window moving and sizing. The same button, known as the Control button, allows you to close the current window and the program running in it. You can also use the Control button to access the Task List, which allows you to switch directly to any other program that is running (such as Notepad and Paintbrush in Figure 1-12). All windows have Control buttons. You can see that there is one on the NOTEBK1.WB1 title bar. Along with Maximize and Minimize buttons, the notebook Control button gives you the ability to adjust the size and shape of the notebook window.

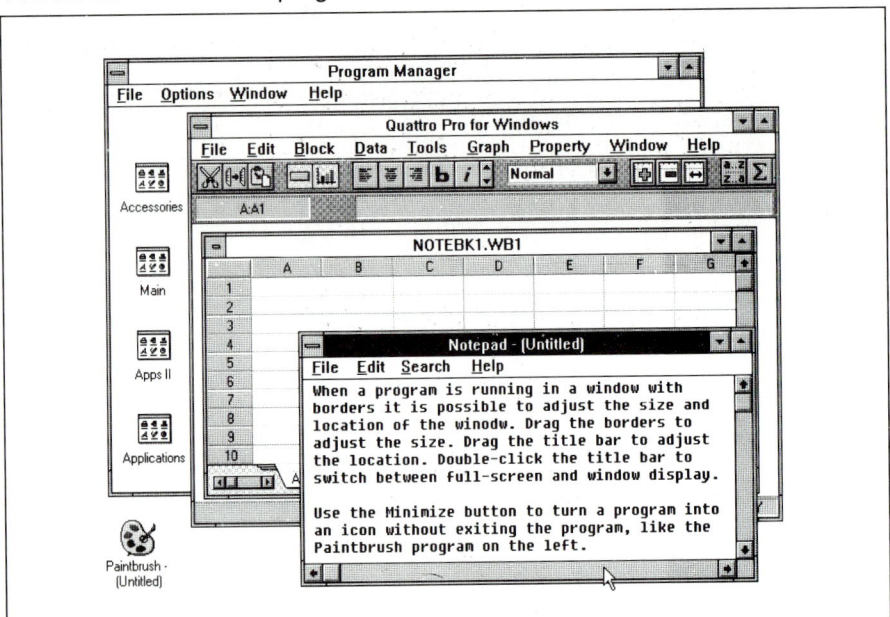

FIGURE 1-12 You can run a Windows program full-screen, in a window, or minimized

Chapter 1: Getting Started   **25**

Note Double-clicking the Control button on the program title bar is a shortcut to exit the current program. While Quattro Pro will not let you exit without saving your work, it is a good idea not to double-click the Control button by mistake.

The Menu Bar

The second line of the Quattro Pro screen is the menu bar, offering File, Edit, Block, and other menu headings. As you can see from Figure 1-13, the menu bar gives you access to *pull-down* menus. Click on any word in the menu bar, and you will pull down the corresponding menu below it. In Figure 1-13, the Tools menu is displayed.

Note that some items on the Tools menu have arrows to the right of them, while others are followed by three dots. The arrows mean that those items lead to further menus. Three dots, known as an ellipsis, after an item means that the item leads to a dialog box. At the bottom left of the screen, on the status line, you will find an explanation of the menu item that is highlighted. When a menu is displayed, you can either make a

FIGURE 1-13 A typical Windows-style pull-down menu

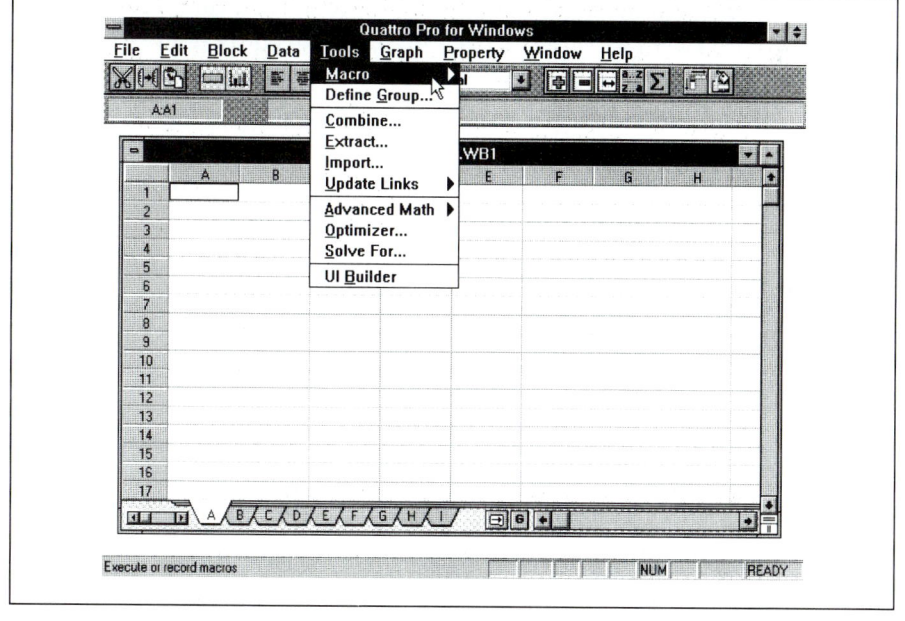

selection from it or put it away. You can put menus away by clicking outside the menu or by pressing ESC. You can make a selection from a menu by clicking on the item you want.

It is not necessary for you to use your mouse to use the Quattro Pro menu system. Each menu item has one letter underlined. This is referred to as the *key letter*. To select an item from the menu bar you hold down the ALT key and press the key letter, for example, T for Tools. This keystroke is referred to as ALT-T. This book will underline the key letters for commands whenever appropriate. To put the menu away, press ESC. Note that this still leaves the menu bar item highlighted, and a second press of ESC will be necessary to exit the menu system completely. You could, instead, simply click somewhere other than the menu bar.

Once a menu has been pulled down, you can select an item from it by typing the key letter alone. For example, to choose Define Group from the Tools menu you press **G**, not ALT-G. In this case, the result is a dialog box like the one shown in Figure 1-14. You can see that there are five different items in this dialog box that have key letters. To select any of these items, you must press ALT plus the key letter.

Note The rule of thumb is that key letters must be pressed with ALT unless they appear on a pull-down menu.

To put away the dialog box without recording or saving any changes or changed settings, press ESC, which is equivalent to clicking the Cancel button. However, if you want to record any information in the dialog box, you should choose OK, either by clicking on it or by pressing ENTER, when the OK button is selected (surrounded by bold outline), which is equivalent to selecting OK. The keyboard equivalent of selecting the Help button is the F1 key.

You can also navigate the menu system with the arrow keys. Pressing the slash (/) key highlights the first item on the menu bar, File. You can then press ENTER if you want to select the File menu or press RIGHT ARROW to highlight the next item on the menu bar (Edit). When you press ENTER to select a menu bar item, the menu is pulled down and the first item on the menu is highlighted. You can press ENTER to select this item or use DOWN ARROW to move the highlighting to another item. If you press LEFT ARROW or RIGHT ARROW while a pull-down menu is displayed, the pull-down menu for the next menu bar item will appear. You can press ESC once to put the menu away and a second time to exit the menu bar.

FIGURE 1-14 A typical dialog box

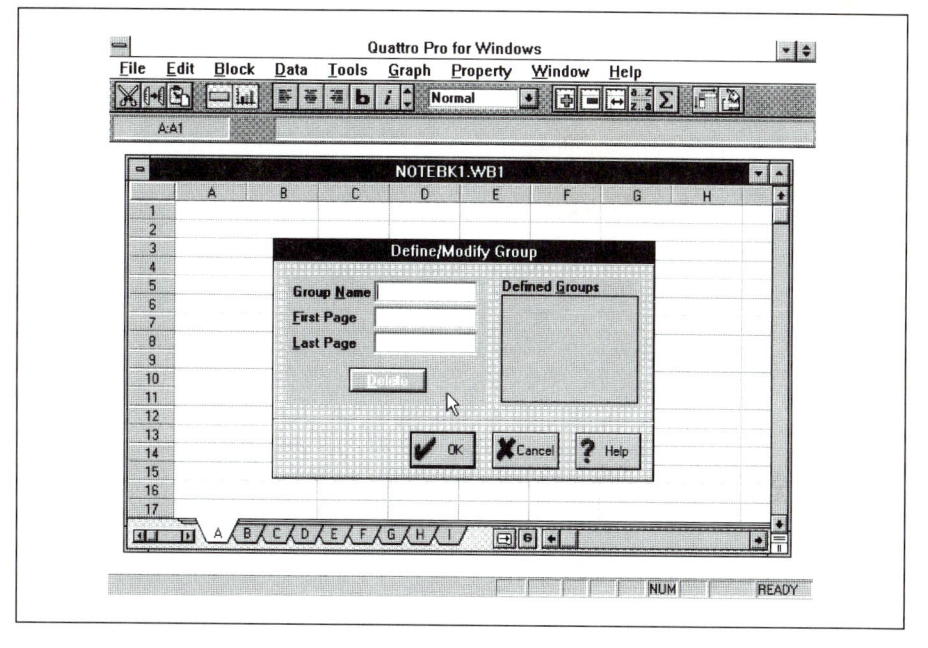

Note You can also activate the menu bar by pressing and then releasing ALT. If you do this and then keep pressing the RIGHT ARROW key to move the highlighting across the menu bar, you will eventually activate the Control button on the program title bar, and then the one that is on the notebook.

The SpeedBar

On the third line of the Quattro Pro screen is the SpeedBar. This is a series of tool icons that provide instant access to commonly used commands. This is part of what Borland calls Direct Drive technology, an approach to software design that favors immediate access to commands rather than menus and complex keystroke sequences. If you have already explored the menu system, you may have noticed that most of the menus are quite short. This is a result of Direct Drive technology. The first three tools on the SpeedBar are buttons for the Cut, Copy, and Paste commands on the Edit menu, but the SpeedBar makes them easier to access.

The other tools on the SpeedBar will be described later. They include graphing, formatting, and SpeedSum, a feature that automatically totals spreadsheet columns and rows. At this point, it is important to note that the selection of tools on the SpeedBar changes according to the task you are performing. The SpeedBar is said to be *context sensitive*. For example, when you are working with graphs, the SpeedBar includes a set of tools for graphing.

The Input Line

Below the SpeedBar is the input line. This is divided into two boxes. The box on the left is the cell identifier. This tells you which cell is currently selected. For example, in Figure 1-11, the cell identifier says A:A1. This means cell A1 on page A of the notebook. The larger box on the right is where you edit data entered into the spreadsheet. For this reason, the fourth line of the screen is sometimes called the edit line.

The Status Line

At the bottom of the Quattro Pro workspace is a line referred to as the status line. On the left of the line you will see descriptions of menu items when you are using the menu system and descriptions of buttons when using the SpeedBar. On the right of the line are boxes that show the status of the NUM LOCK, CAPS LOCK, and SCROLL LOCK keys on your keyboard. The box on the far right of the status line is referred to as the mode indicator. When you first start Quattro Pro it is in READY mode. This means that you are free to select a cell and make an entry. However, as you will see in a moment, the mode changes as you start to work with the program.

Navigating the Spreadsheet

Above the status line and below the input line is the workspace. When you load Quattro Pro a blank *notebook* is displayed in the workspace, into which you can place numbers, words, graphic objects, and instructions (formulas and calculations). The notebook has its own title bar. The default title, the one that Quattro Pro provides for you, is NOTEBK1.WB1. The notebook title bar has three buttons: Control, Minimize, and Maximize. These can be used to adjust the size and location of the notebook within the workspace, close the notebook, and switch between notebooks if more than one is open. There is a line of letters across the top of the spreadsheet and a list of numbers down the left side. The letters represent a series of columns and the numbers a series of rows. The intersection of each column and row forms a rectangle, a box into which you put information. These boxes are called *cells*.

One of the spreadsheet cells is highlighted when you start the program. This highlighted cell is called A1 because it is in column A on row 1. Every cell has a name based on its location, or *coordinates*, just like a map. You move from cell to cell to lay out information. When you first start Quattro Pro, you are in cell A1. If you were to enter information at this point, it would be placed in cell A1. The cell you are in is called the *current cell*. The highlighting that marks the cell you are in is called the *cell selector*. It can be moved with the *cursor* or *arrow* keys. These are located on the right of your keyboard. Alternatively, you can select a cell by moving the mouse pointer over the cell and clicking the left mouse button.

To explore the work area, press RIGHT ARROW once. You will see the highlighting move to the next cell to the right, B1. You are now in cell B1. Press DOWN ARROW once and you will be in cell B2. Notice that the cell identifier on the fourth line of the screen shows your current location. This is very helpful, as eyeballing your location is notably prone to error, particularly after several hours of staring at the screen.

Your keyboard has the ability to repeat keystrokes and will do so if you push and hold down, rather than just press, a key. Throughout the rest of this book you should take the term "press" to mean lightly tap rather than push and hold down. To see the keyboard repeat feature in action, press DOWN ARROW and hold it for two seconds. You will see the cell indicator move quickly down the screen, and the numbers at the left will scroll by rapidly. You can see that you are dragging the window with you to view a different area of the spreadsheet. Now try pressing HOME. It takes you back to A1.

The UP ARROW, DOWN ARROW, LEFT ARROW, and RIGHT ARROW keys move you one cell in each of their respective directions. CTRL-RIGHT ARROW and CTRL-LEFT ARROW move a screen at a time across the worksheet. (Hold down CTRL and press the arrow key.) The same effect can be achieved with TAB and SHIFT-TAB, respectively. PGUP and PGDN move you a screen at a time up and down the worksheet. HOME always places you in A1 (unless you are using locked titles, described in Chapter 6). END, followed by UP ARROW, DOWN ARROW, LEFT ARROW, or RIGHT ARROW, takes you to the last cell in that direction. The last cell means the last occupied cell in a row or column or the first occupied cell, if the next cell is empty.

Note   Do not hold the END key down like the CTRL key; you press END, release it, and then press the arrow key. If the cell selector is in a blank cell and there are no more entries in the direction you point, your cell selector will reach the very end of the spreadsheet. If this happens, just press HOME to return to the top of the spreadsheet.

A guide to your relative location within the worksheet is provided by the position of the elevator boxes (scroll buttons) on the vertical and horizontal scroll bars at the right and bottom of the worksheet. The scroll bars are particularly useful when you have built a model in the spreadsheet. Using your mouse to drag a scroll button along a scroll bar brings a different area of the spreadsheet into view. You can also click on the arrows at each end of the scroll bars to adjust the view up or down, left or right. However, pressing the HOME key is the quickest way to get back to A1.

Across the bottom of the notebook are a series of lettered tabs that represent separate pages of the notebook. There are 256 spreadsheet pages in each notebook. To move to another page, simply click on the page tab. For example, to move to page F, click on the tab labeled F. Alternatively, press CTRL-PGDN to move one page at a time from A to F. The screen will change very little, but you will see that the cell identifier reflects the new location. For example, if cell A1 is selected on page A and you move to page F, the cell identifier changes from A:A1 to F:A1. Use CTRL-PGUP to move back to page A, or click on the A tab.

Types of Information

Quattro Pro categorizes all information into one of two types of data: values or labels. Put simply, *values* are numbers and calculations, and *labels* are words or text. Quattro Pro treats the two categories of data differently. By looking at the first character of each new entry made into the worksheet, Quattro Pro guesses the appropriate category for that data—value or label.

Chapter 1: Getting Started 31

Values

To see how to enter information into Quattro Pro and how the program recognizes values, try the following exercise, making sure that you begin on page A.

1. Select cell B3. You can do this by moving the cell selector with the arrow keys, or you can point at cell B3 with your mouse and click the left mouse button. The cell identifier in the upper left of the screen changes to B3.

2. Type **789** using the row of numbers at the top of the keyboard. Do not press ENTER or any other key; just observe what has happened. The results can be seen in Figure 1-15.

   Notice that the number 789 has not yet been placed into the spreadsheet. Instead, it is on the input line. The cursor is flashing after the number 9. At this point, if you have made a mistake, you can use BACKSPACE to back over what you have typed and then change it.

FIGURE 1-15 Typing a spreadsheet entry

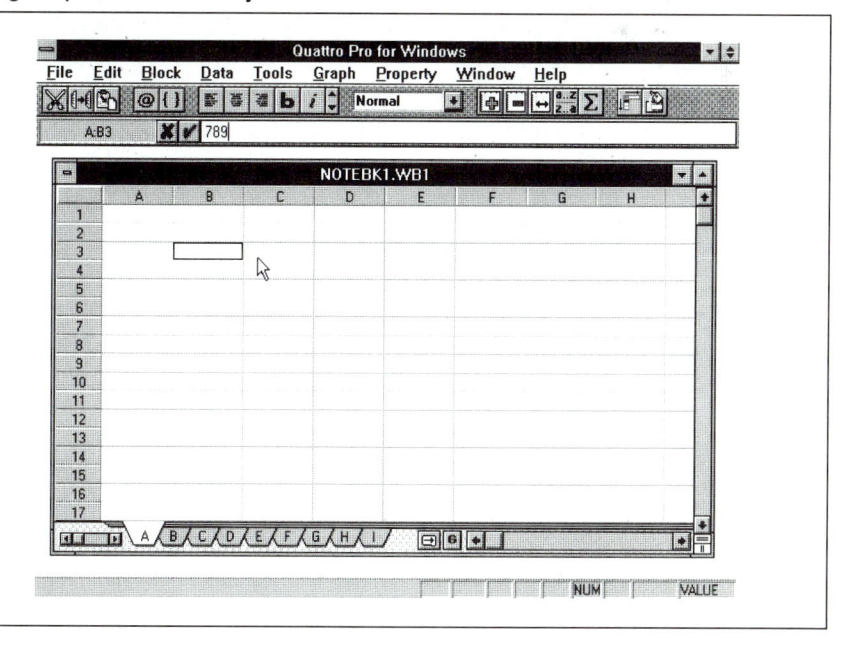

Also note that the mode indicator at the bottom right of the screen now says VALUE. This tells you that Quattro Pro is reading what you have typed as a value. In addition, two new buttons have appeared on the SpeedBar. They are marked @ and {}. The input line has also acquired two buttons, marked with a cross and a check.

3. To place the number 789 into the spreadsheet, you can either press ENTER or click on the check button. (If you were to decide that you didn't want to enter anything into cell B3, you could press ESC or click on the cross button—both actions return you to READY mode without entering the value and allow you to proceed.)

Note If you pressed ENTER prematurely or otherwise caused the number to leave the top line of the screen, just type 789 again and observe what happens before you press ENTER.

4. When you press ENTER or click on the check button, Quattro Pro enters what you have typed on the input line in the current cell of the spreadsheet, as shown in Figure 1-16. Notice that the numbers you have entered are placed on the right-hand side of the cell. Quattro Pro normally aligns numbers evenly with the right of the column. This is referred to as *right alignment.*

The mode indicator changes from VALUE back to READY, and the input line now lists the contents of the cell. This might seem like a duplication of effort. However, in a moment you will see that what Quattro Pro shows you in the input line is sometimes different from what is displayed in the worksheet. The input line shows the exact content of the cell as Quattro Pro reads it.

Labels

Now that you are back in READY mode, you can move to another cell. Press LEFT ARROW once, and you will be in cell A3. Here you will enter a label. Before you type, take a look at your keyboard and locate CAPS LOCK. This key enables you to type in capital letters without using SHIFT. You might find that it is convenient for you to type labels all in capitals. Press CAPS LOCK once and then notice that the bottom status area reflects this change with the message CAP. When you use locked capitals, the letters

Chapter 1: Getting Started 33

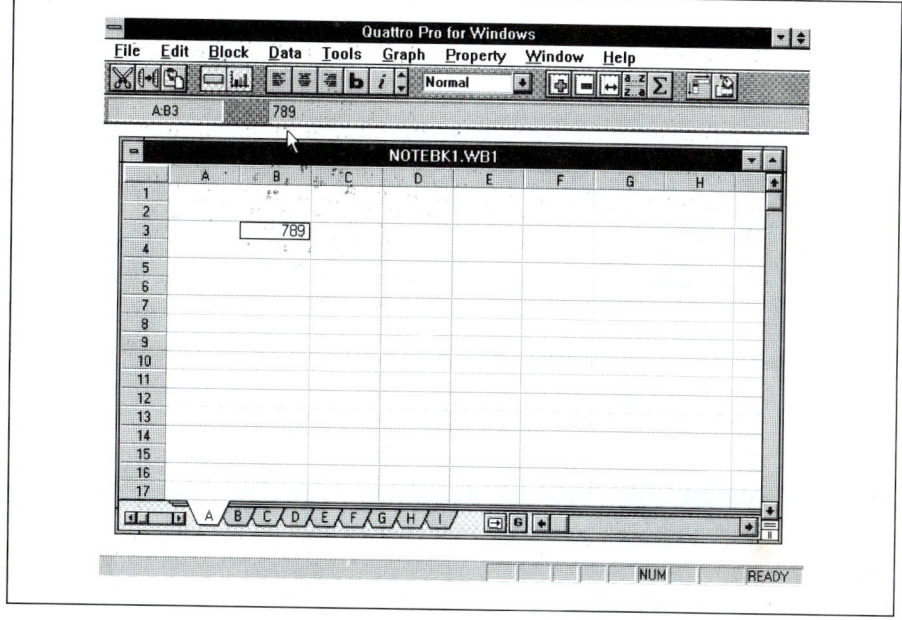

FIGURE 1-16 The value entered in the spreadsheet

A through Z are automatically typed as capitals. However, you must still use SHIFT to access symbols and commands that appear on the upper half of other keys.

You are now going to type **PRICE** because you will use this notebook page to figure out the cost of purchasing and financing a yacht. When you type **P**, notice that the mode indicator changes to LABEL. Also notice that what you type appears on the input line, so you can change it with BACKSPACE if you make an error. After you have typed **PRICE**, press ENTER or click the check button.

Now observe the input line. In front of the word you typed is an apostrophe ('). The apostrophe was automatically placed there by Quattro Pro as a reminder that this is a label. Although you are not likely to confuse this particular label with a number, later you will encounter instructions that look like labels, but are in fact values.

The apostrophe not only tells you that this is a label, but it also signifies that this is a left-aligned label. Labels can either be left-aligned, right-aligned, or centered in the column. Right-aligned labels are preceded by a quotation mark ("). Centered labels begin with a caret (^), which is the shifted 6 on the keyboard. Rather than make you type one of the three label align characters (',", or ^) before every label, Quattro Pro assumes one of them. This is the *default label alignment* and, as you can see, it is left-aligned. You can change the default, as described later, or change the alignment of a block of labels. To enter a new label aligned differently from the default, just type the desired alignment before the text of the label. If you want the actual text of the label to begin with one of the symbols used for alignment characters, use two of them. Thus, entering " "**Right On**" will actually produce a right-aligned label that reads "Right On" (with the quotes included).

Entering and Editing

You will now enter another label directly below PRICE. This will be DELIVERY, but you will use a slightly different method to enter it into the cell.

1. Press DOWN ARROW to select cell A4.
2. Type **DELIVERY**. It will appear on the edit line like 789 and PRICE did before.
3. Press DOWN ARROW again. Doing so enters the label and moves you down to the next row.

Note Entering with arrow keys is useful when you want to enter a lot of labels or numbers in a column or row. The arrow keys will enter what you are typing and move you in a particular direction with one keystroke. However, you should avoid pressing the arrow keys when typing fresh data until you are ready to enter the data.

4. Practice this method of entering by typing **TAX** and pressing DOWN ARROW, followed by typing **TOTAL** and pressing DOWN ARROW. The results will look like Figure 1-17.

Note that DELIVERY extends beyond column A of the spreadsheet in Figure 1-17. Don't worry about this for now. If you are using a different font than the one in Figure 1-17, it is possible that the word will fit within column A of your spreadsheet.

Chapter 1: Getting Started

FIGURE 1-17 A series of labels entered in a spreadsheet column

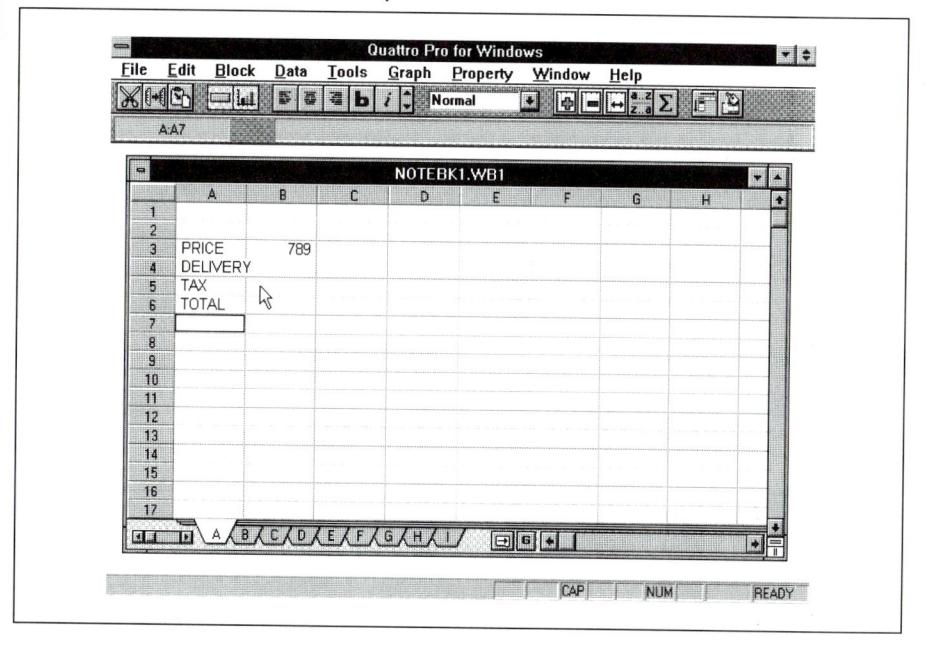

Editing Cells

Changing worksheet entries and correcting mistakes is one of the most important procedures you will need to know. In this example, 789 is a ridiculously low price for a yacht, so you need to change it. Use your mouse or the arrow keys to select cell B3, which contains the number 789. To change a cell entry completely, just type a new entry. For example, type **8000** and press ENTER. Note that the new number completely replaces the old one.

Note Do not put commas in the thousands when entering numbers in Quattro Pro. Commas are added to numbers by cell formatting, which will be discussed later.

What if you want to modify the contents of the cell, rather than completely replace them? For example, you might want to change 8000 to 8095 to reflect a price increase. When you do not need to completely change a cell, you can change part of it by selecting the cell and then pressing the Edit key, F2. Alternatively, you can click on the input line anywhere to the right of the current entry. In both cases the cursor appears, allowing you to edit the contents of the cell. For this example, press BACKSPACE twice to back over the last two zeros of 8000, and type **95**. Now press ENTER or click the check button to see the modified contents returned to the cell.

Note If you are a mouse user you can select text on the input line by dragging the edit cursor across the characters you want to select. When you have selected text like this, you can replace it with new text simply by typing the new text.

Instructions and Formulas

Suppose you now want to add the figure for delivery costs to the worksheet. Select cell B4, type **750**, and enter it into the cell by pressing DOWN ARROW (don't worry if the Y in DELIVERY disappears—this will be dealt with in a moment). You are now in cell B5 and ready to do some math with Quattro Pro. In cell B5, you want a figure for the tax that must be paid on the price of the yacht (but not the delivery costs). Assume that the tax rate is 10 percent or 0.1. This means that the figure you want in cell B5 is 8095×0.1. You want Quattro Pro to calculate this for you, so you will type an instruction (or *formula*) that will tell the program to multiply the number in cell B3 by 0.1 and place the answer in cell B5.

Note that you are not going to tell the program simply to multiply the number 8095 by 0.1. Quattro Pro can do that, but that is not the true power of a spreadsheet. What you want to do is establish a relationship between the cells so that, even if the price in B3 changes, the relationship will remain, and B5 will continue to give you 10 percent of the contents of B3. The instruction will be entered as **.1*B3**. Quattro Pro uses the asterisk for a multiplication sign. Note that the program considers the decimal point to be a *value indicator* and reads what follows it as a value. Having selected cell B5, type **.1*B3** and press ENTER. You will immediately see the tax figure calculated, as shown in Figure 1-18.

When you look at the input line, you can see that Quattro Pro is not concerned about the actual number in cell B5. It simply records the relationship between the two cells. This will remain the same, whatever number is in cell B5. Suppose that the price goes up. Select B3 and type **9125**, the new price, then press ENTER. Instantly, Quattro Pro updates

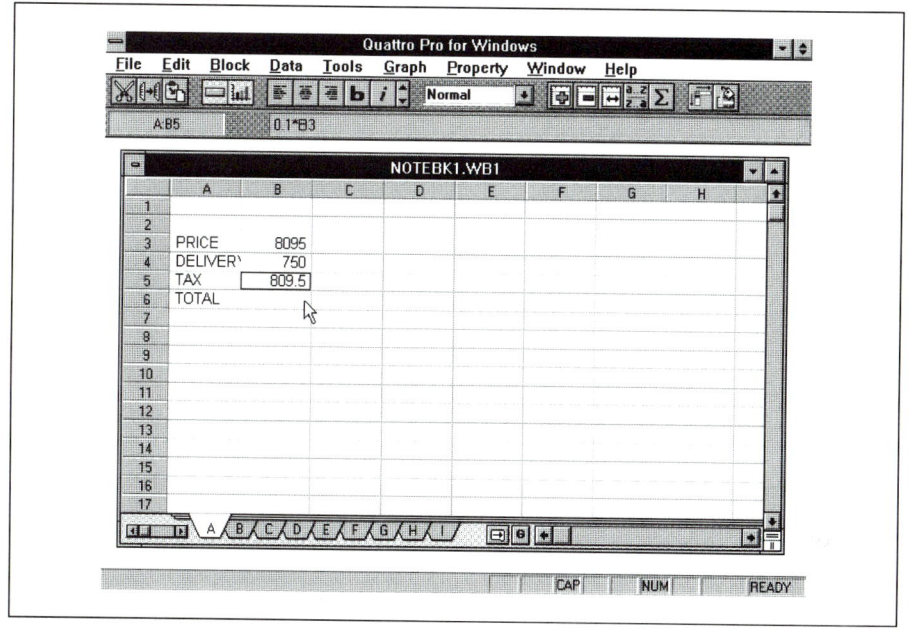

FIGURE 1-18 A formula, as it appears in the spreadsheet and the input line

cell B5. If you move the cell selector down to cell B5 and then look at the input line, you will see that the cell contents have not changed. They are still the same formula you entered before.

Now you want to calculate a total price for the yacht, including the price, delivery costs, and tax. You will need to add several cells together. To do this, first select the cell that is to contain the answer—in this case, B6. Now you will type an instruction that tells Quattro Pro that this cell will contain the sum of cells B3, B4, and B5. You might think that you could type **B3+B4+B5**, and this is almost correct. However, instructions involving only cell references need special treatment because Quattro Pro will read the letter B as a label.

To get around this problem and make sure that Quattro Pro knows that what you are typing is a value, type a plus sign first and then the cell reference. With cell B6 selected, type the formula **+B3+B4+B5** and press ENTER. The results can be seen in Figure 1-19. To test the calculation you have just created select cell B3 and enter a new value, **9995**, to replace 9125. You will see the TAX and TOTAL figures change.

Note There are other ways to add up values and other techniques for creating formulas. These will be discussed in Chapter 2.

Although the calculations in Figure 1-19 are correct, there are several problems with the appearance of the spreadsheet. The word DELIVERY has been truncated, and the values are displayed with differing degrees of precision. To correct these problems you will use a Quattro Pro feature, known as the *object inspector*, which provides a uniform technique for adjusting just about any aspect of the program. The first step is to decide what item or object you want to adjust. In this case, it is the cells that have been used so far, A3 through B6.

A rectangular group of cells is called a *block*. There are several ways to select a block. You can select the cell in the top-left corner, in this case A3, then hold down SHIFT while you click on the lower-right cell, in this case B6. This immediately selects all of the cells from A3 through B6.

FIGURE 1-19 The new TOTAL calculation

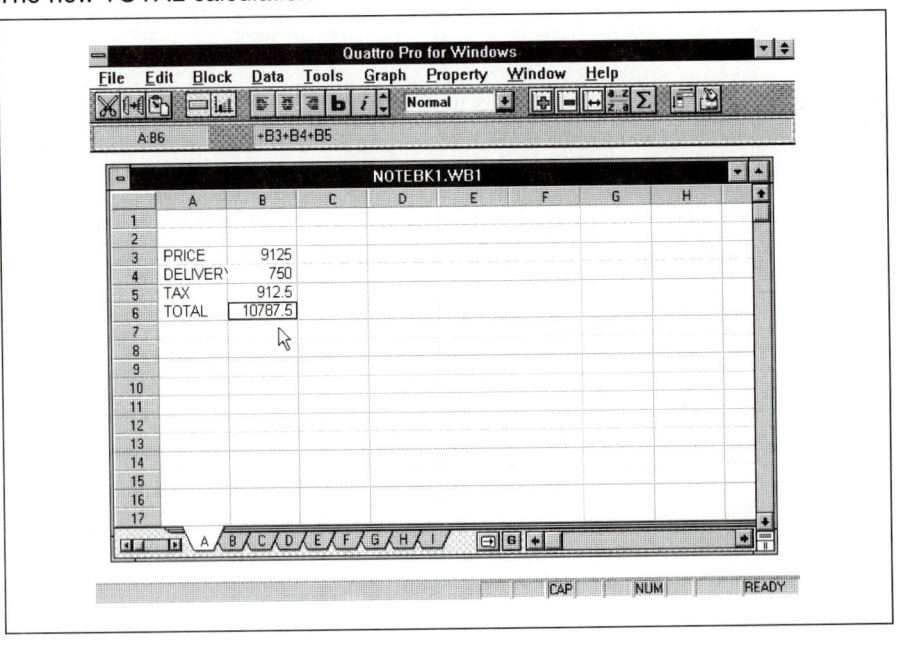

Chapter 1: Getting Started

You can also point to the top-left cell and hold down the left mouse button while you drag the pointer to the lower-right cell and release the button. If you want to select a block of cells with the keyboard, you begin by selecting the top left cell (A3). Then you press SHIFT-F7, the Extend key. The message EXT appears in the status area at the bottom right of the screen. Now you can use the arrow keys to extend the highlighting, in this case to B6.

When you have selected a block of cells, using any of the above techniques, you can change the appearance of the cells by pointing at the block and then clicking the right mouse button. This invokes the Active Block dialog box shown in Figure 1-20. Note that the coordinates of the selected cells appear in the title bar of the dialog box. To invoke the Active Block dialog box from the keyboard, you can press the Current Object key, F12. Alternatively, you can press ALT-P to activate the Property menu and press ENTER to select the first item on the menu, Current Object, or press ALT-P and then C.

The Active Block dialog box is known as a compound dialog box because it allows you to change several different settings. The settings or properties that you can change are listed on the left of the box, beginning with Numeric Format. You can select any item in the list by

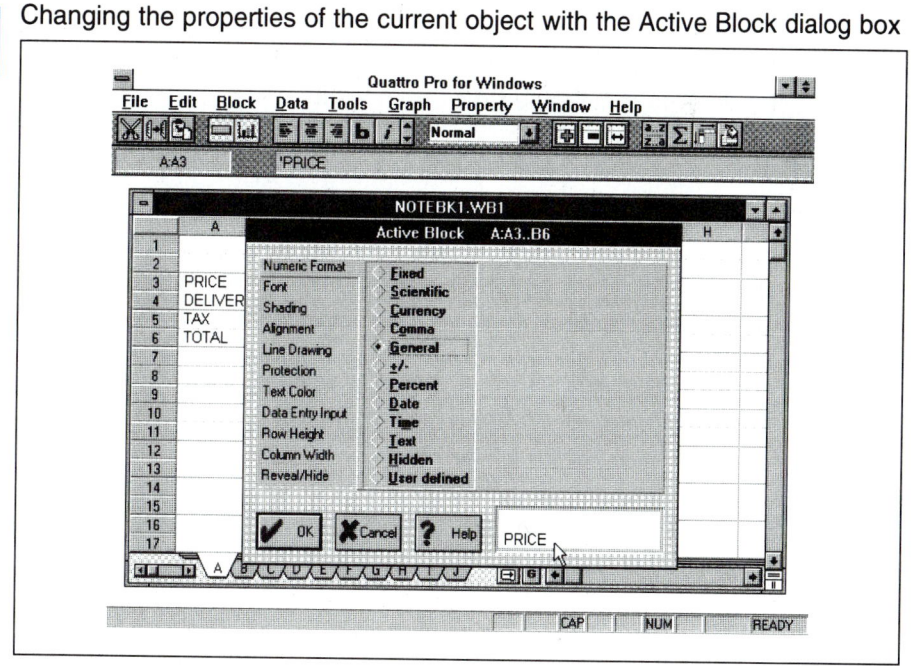

FIGURE 1-20 Changing the properties of the current object with the Active Block dialog box

clicking on it with the mouse or moving to it with CTRL-PGDN. The choices available on the right side will then change, to conform to the property that you are adjusting.

In the lower right of the Active Block dialog box, you can see an example of the current properties. Quattro Pro will attempt to preview any changes you make to the properties of the active block by altering the appearance of the word in the preview box. In this case PRICE appears in the preview because cell A3 was the active cell when you invoked the dialog box. Bear in mind that it is not always possible for the preview to show all changes. For example, the numeric format setting does not affect label entries, so this preview would not reflect a change to the numeric format. However, font and alignment changes, which affect both labels and values, will be shown in the dialog box.

To see how the Active Block dialog box works, select Font, the second item in the list. You can do this by clicking on Font or by pressing CTRL-PGDN. You will see the dialog box change to allow adjustments to the font, as shown in Figure 1-21. You can see that the current typeface is Arial. The point size is 10, and no options are selected. Do not worry if you are using a different typeface or point size. Point to the small box to the left of Bold under Options and click the left mouse button. You will see a check mark appear as Bold is activated. You will also see PRICE appear in bold. Click the Bold box again to turn off bold, since you don't need it at the moment. If you are using the keyboard, press ALT-B to turn bold on, and ALT-B again to turn it off.

There are two properties you do want to change for the active block in this example. The first is the column width. Click on Column Width or press CTRL-PGDN several times. When the Column Width settings are displayed, check Auto Width, as shown in Figure 1-22. This tells Quattro Pro to adjust the width of the columns within the active block so that they accommodate the widest entry in the active block. This will ensure that column A is made wide enough to display DELIVERY. Note the Extra Characters setting, which determines how many characters Quattro Pro leaves between the columns. The default setting is 1 character, which is fine for this example.

The second property to change is Numeric Format, so click on it or use the CTRL-PGUP key to select it. To display all of the numbers in the active block with two decimal places and a comma separating thousands and hundreds, check the Comma setting. If you are using the keyboard,

Chapter 1: Getting Started

FIGURE 1-21 The Font property settings

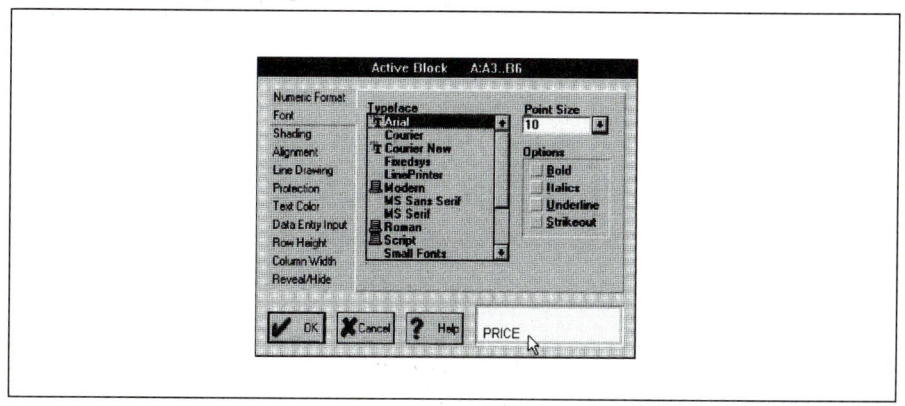

simply press UP ARROW once to move the setting from General to Comma. When you select Comma, a box appears to the right for you to tell Quattro Pro how many decimal places you want displayed. In this case, the default setting of 2 is fine. In fact, you are ready to click the OK button. To select OK from the keyboard make sure it is highlighted, then press ENTER (you can always click Cancel or press ESC to exit the properties dialog box

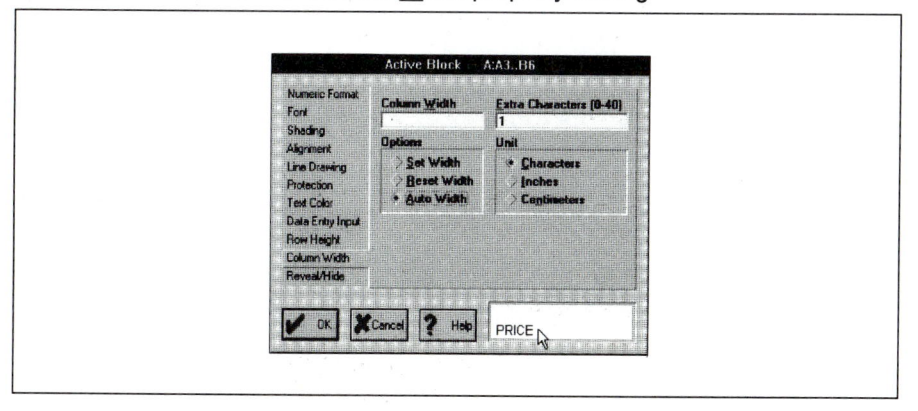

FIGURE 1-22 Using Auto Width as the Column Width property setting

without making any changes). The checkmark OK button, the X-mark Cancel button, and the question-mark Help button look like this:

The results are shown in Figure 1-23. Note that column A is now slightly wider, and all of the numbers have two decimal places. Also note that the block stays selected, allowing you to do further work with those cells without having to select the block again.

Using Functions

Suppose you want to take out a loan to finance the purchase of this yacht. You might want to calculate what your monthly payment would be. A loan payment calculation involves three pieces of information: principal—the amount of money being borrowed, interest—the charge for each period during which the money is borrowed, and term—the number

FIGURE 1-23 The results of adjusting the column width and setting the Numeric Format to Comma with two decimal places

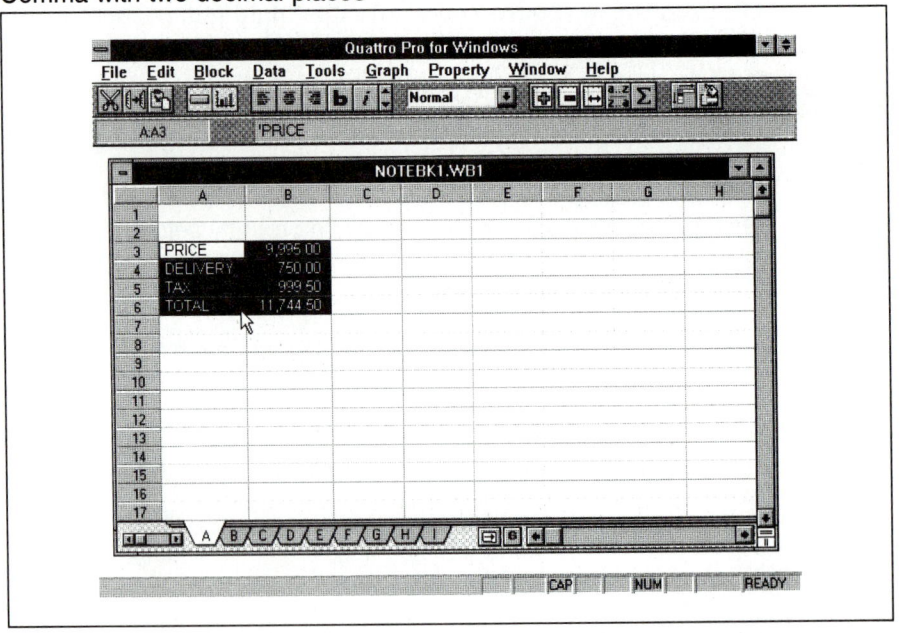

Chapter 1: Getting Started 43

of periods over which the loan is repaid. Follow these steps to create the loan payment calculation:

1. Select cell D3.

2. Type **AMOUNT**, press DOWN ARROW to enter it, and select D4.

3. Type **INTEREST** and enter it in D4 using DOWN ARROW. Enter **TERM** in D5 and **PAYMENT** in D6.

4. Select cell E3, ready to enter the amount of the loan principal.

5. The amount you want to finance is the total price from cell A6. Instead of typing the number again, type **+B6** and press ENTER. This establishes a relationship between these two cells, so that whatever is in cell B6 is also in cell E3.

6. Select cell E4. Here you want to enter the rate of interest you will pay. This needs to be expressed as a rate per period of the loan. If you are going to make monthly payments you need to enter the amount of interest you will pay in one month. If the bank is charging 12 percent annually, the rate is 0.01, or 1 percent per month. Type **.01** and enter it in cell E4.

7. Select cell E5. In this cell type the term, the number of months for the loan, in this case **36**, and press DOWN ARROW. The results so far are shown in Figure 1-24.

In cell E6 you will create a formula that calculates the loan payment. You do not need to know the details of the calculation because Quattro Pro knows exactly how to calculate a loan payment if it is given the principal, interest, and term. Payment calculation is one of the many built-in formulas, or *functions*, included in Quattro Pro. The complete formula will be as follows:

@PMT(E3,E4,E5)

This statement begins with the @ sign so that Quattro Pro will read the text that follows as a function name rather than a label. Within the parentheses are three cell references, separated by commas. These cells represent the principal, interest, and term, and are said to be function *arguments*. To create the entry in E6 with your mouse, follow these steps:

FIGURE 1-24 Initial entries for the loan payment calculation

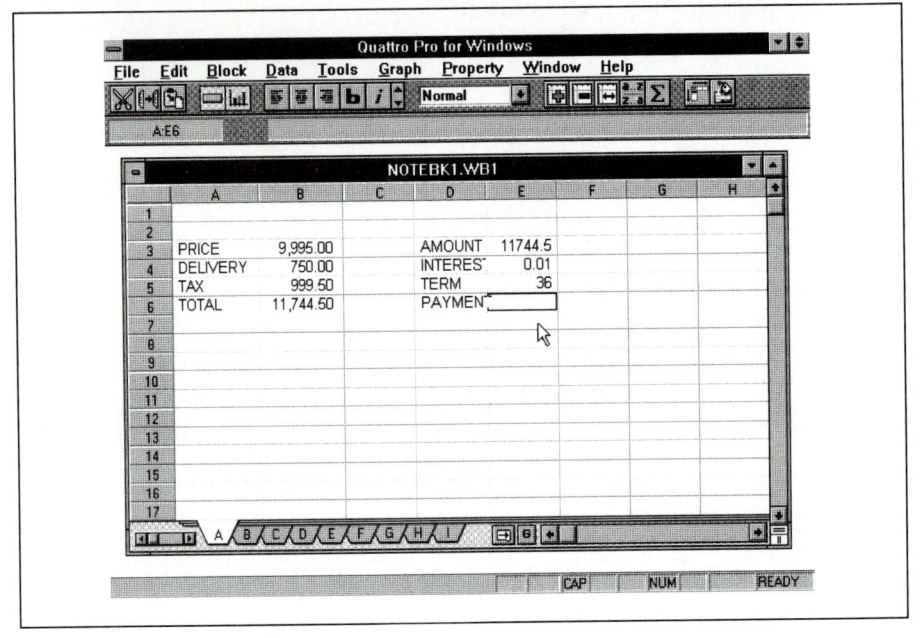

1. With cell E6 selected, point to the input line and click the left mouse button. The cross and check buttons should appear. Also, the SpeedBar will have changed to include a button marked @, the symbol for built-in functions.

2. Click on the @ button and a list called Functions will appear. Drag the elevator button down the scroll bar on the right of the Functions list until you can see the PMT function.

3. Click on the PMT function to highlight it and then click on OK. This will place the text **@PMT(** on the input line.

Note A handy shortcut is to double-click on the function instead of using a single click and the OK button.

4. Now click on the first cell you need in the formula, E3. Quattro Pro will add the cell reference to the formula.

5. Now type a comma and click on the next cell, E4.

Chapter 1: Getting Started

6. Type another comma and click on E5.

7. To complete the formula, type a closing parenthesis and click on the check button. The results can be seen in Figure 1-25.

You can see that the function statement has calculated the payment to several decimal places. Also, the column width could do with some adjusting. These items will be taken care of in a moment.

To create the formula using the keyboard, you can either type it in its entirety or use the Functions key, ALT-F3, and the arrow keys. To use the Functions key, select cell E6 and press ALT-F3. The Functions list appears, and you can press PGDN to bring the PMT function into view. Use UP ARROW or DOWN ARROW to highlight PMT and then press ENTER. Now you can either type **E3** or use the arrow keys to highlight E3. When you have selected E3, the coordinates will appear on the input line. Now type a comma and select the next cell, E4, or type **E4**. Follow this with a comma and select E5 or type **E5**. Finally, type a closing parenthesis and press ENTER. The results will be the same as in Figure 1-25.

FIGURE 1-25 The completed loan payment formula

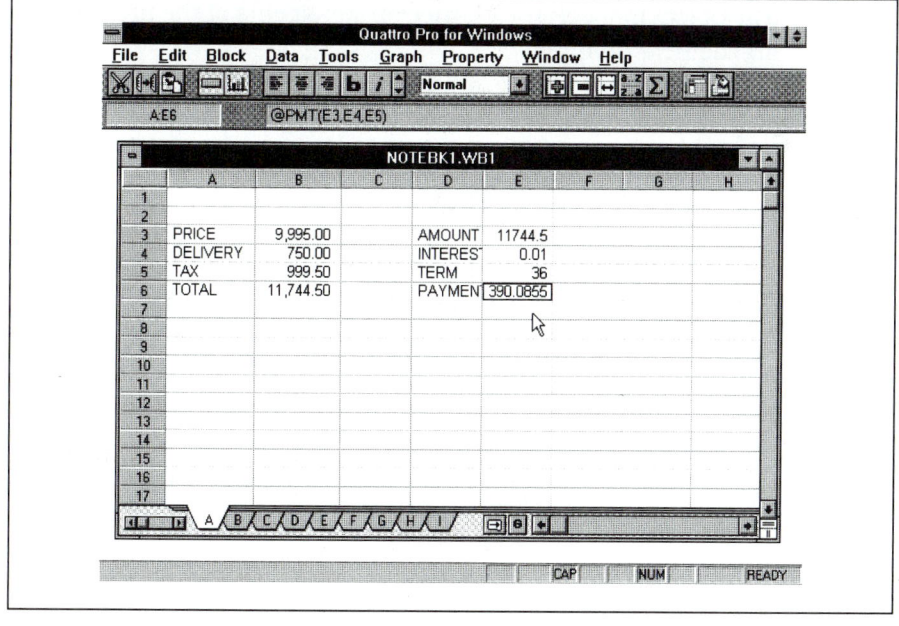

To give you an idea of how flexible a spreadsheet can be, you can make changes to the assumptions that produce the answer in E6. For example, if you were considering a more expensive model, you could type the new price in B3 and immediately see the new payment in E6. To reduce the amount of the monthly payment, enter a longer term, such as 48 months, into E5. Finally, to tidy up the payment calculation entries, do the following:

1. Select cells D3 through E6.
2. Point to the block and click the right mouse button or press F12. The Active Block dialog box will appear, showing the Numeric Format.
3. Click on Comma in the format list or use the arrow keys to make Comma the active setting.
4. Click on Column Width or use CTRL-PGDN to activate it.
5. Click on Auto Width or press ALT-A to select it.
6. Click on OK or press ENTER.

The results are shown in Figure 1-26, which shows one other change. The Numeric Format setting in E4 was changed to Percent. You can use the object inspector with a single cell or a block of cells. You can also use the object inspector to change other aspects of the program, as described in the next chapter.

Saving and Ending

Having completed this series of calculations, you may decide to take a break. You need to think about where the information you have created is located. So far, all of the work you have been doing is in the computer's memory. The only problem with this is that the memory is only as good as the power to your computer. If you accidentally pull the plug or your system suffers an electrical failure, the memory's contents are lost. You must transfer the data to permanent storage on disk. This is known as saving your work and has to be done on a regular basis and particularly when you leave your PC unattended.

Chapter 1: Getting Started

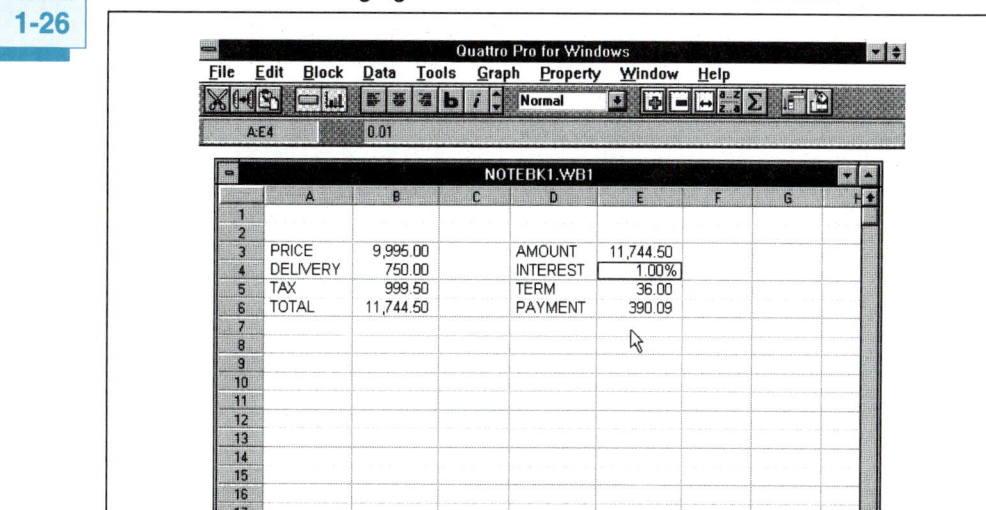

FIGURE 1-26 The results after changing the column width and numeric format

[Screenshot of Quattro Pro for Windows spreadsheet NOTEBK1.WB1 showing:
- A:E4 cell reference, value 0.01
- Row 3: PRICE 9,995.00, AMOUNT 11,744.50
- Row 4: DELIVERY 750.00, INTEREST 1.00%
- Row 5: TAX 999.50, TERM 36.00
- Row 6: TOTAL 11,744.50, PAYMENT 390.09]

Saving a file with Quattro Pro involves using the menu system. You can do this with the keyboard by typing **/** to bring up the menus and then **F** to activate the File menu. Alternatively, you can press ALT-F. Now type **S** for Save. You will see a dialog box like the one in Figure 1-27. If you want to access the menu system with your mouse, point to File, press down the left mouse button, and drag the selection bar down to Save on the File menu. When you release the mouse button the Save File dialog box will appear.

At this point, you can type a name for the file into which you want Quattro Pro to store this spreadsheet. The name can be any eight letters or numbers. For this example, type **BOATLOAN**. Note that no spaces are allowed within the name, but you can use underscores for spaces, so that LOAN_101 is acceptable. Although you can use some punctuation in filenames, not all punctuation characters are valid. For this reason, it is best to avoid punctuation when naming files. Do not type the ".WB1" at the end of the filename—Quattro Pro will add these characters for you.

FIGURE 1-27 The Save File dialog box

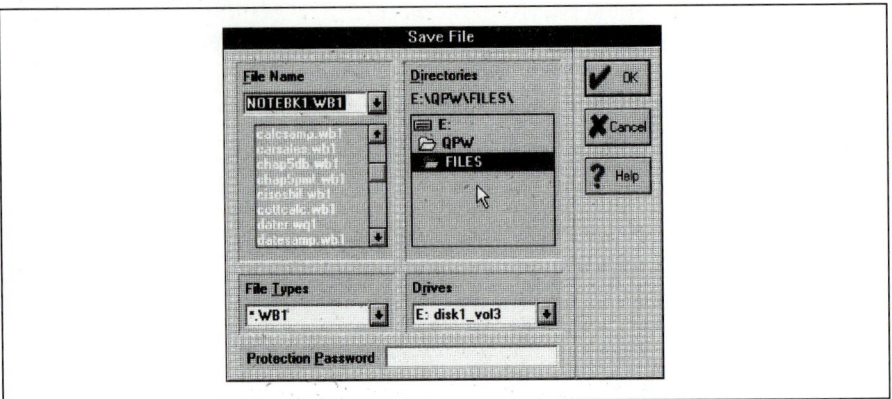

For complete details on file naming, see Chapter 3. When you have typed the name, which will appear in the File Name box, you must click OK or press ENTER.

Now that you have saved your work, the filename appears in the spreadsheet title bar. At this point you are free to close down Quattro Pro. The command for this is File | Exit, which means the Exit command in the File menu, although there are several other ways of exiting Quattro Pro. You can press ALT-F4, which is the shortcut key for the Close command on the program window control button. The same effect is achieved by double-clicking on the Control button, which is located at the left corner of the program title bar. Quattro Pro knows if you have not saved changes to your work and, if this is the case, prompts you to confirm the Exit command. If you do not want to stop working with Quattro Pro, but want to begin a fresh file after saving the last one, you can clear the spreadsheet area by selecting File, and then Close (File | Close). Again, Quattro Pro will prompt for confirmation if you have not saved changes to the current spreadsheet. For more information on file saving, see Chapter 3.

Note that the first time you save a spreadsheet, the program will suggest storing it on the same drive and directory you started the program from, typically C:\QPW. You do not want to store a lot of data files with program files. Doing so can cause overcrowded or confusing directories, so you might want to change the directory before saving the file. You can do this with the Directories section of the Save File dialog box. You can point to a different directory on the tree diagram or double-click the drive letter at the top of the tree to see other directories on that drive. See Chapter 3 for details of how you use the directory tree.

Keystroke Navigation

You have seen that Quattro Pro provides several ways of selecting cells from the keyboard. You can use the arrow or cursor movement keys to move from cell to cell. The PGUP and PGDN keys move the cell selector up and down through the worksheet one screen at a time. You can move the cell selector one screen to the right or left using TAB-SHIFT-TAB or CTRL-RIGHT ARROW and CTRL-LEFT ARROW. HOME places the cell selector in A1.

One key that works a little differently is END. You can test the END key in the loan worksheet you have just made. First select A3. Now press END. You will see the message END appear in the bottom status line. Now press DOWN ARROW. The cell selector moves down to the last consecutively occupied cell in the column, in this case A6. Now press END followed by RIGHT ARROW. The cell selector moves to the last consecutively occupied cell in the row—B6. Now press END followed by UP ARROW, and the cell selector moves to B3, which is the last occupied cell in the direction you pointed.

If you press END and then RIGHT ARROW while the cell selector is in B3, Quattro Pro will move the cell selector to D3, the next unoccupied cell in the direction you pointed. If the current cell is C3, an empty cell, pressing END and then RIGHT ARROW will also select D3. However, if C3 is the current cell and you press END and then DOWN ARROW, Quattro Pro moves the cell selector all the way down to C8192 (you can press HOME to get back to A1). The action of END followed by an arrow key can be summarized as moving the cell selector to either the last or the next occupied cell in the direction indicated by the arrow. END is particularly handy when you are navigating large worksheets.

Another handy key for navigating large worksheets is F5, the Goto key. When you press F5, a dialog box appears, asking you to type the address of the cell you want to select. For example, to select E3, type **E3** (you can also type **e3**—the command is not case sensitive). After you type the cell address, press ENTER, and the cell selector is moved for you.

There are a number of keystrokes that you will find useful when working with dialog boxes in Quattro Pro. You have already learned that CTRL-PGUP and CTRL-PGDN move you between different properties in a compound dialog box. The TAB key moves you from field to field and button to button in a dialog box, making one item after another the current item. When an item is current, you can then change it or select it. For example, when the OK button is the current item, you can press ENTER to select it. When a text field like File Name is current, you can type something in it or edit the existing contents.

Quattro Pro has several different ways of indicating the current item in a dialog box. When you select a text field, a vertical edit cursor appears. When you select a button, the border of the button appears darker. The name of the button is also outlined when the button is selected. When the dialog box contains small checkmark buttons, the name of the button is highlighted when that button is selected. When a list item is selected, a dotted line appears around the first item in the list. Note that you have to press DOWNARROW to activate a list after you have selected it. If you keep pressing TAB in a dialog box, you will eventually come back to the first item in the dialog box. You can move backward through items by pressing SHIFT-TAB.

In the next chapter we will look at further ways of editing spreadsheet entries, and we will build a larger spreadsheet model that uses several notebook pages. We will also experiment with named styles and with the SpeedSum button.

CHAPTER 2

Building Spreadsheet Models

This chapter shows you how to build a basic spreadsheet model, from data entry to numeric formatting and absolute cell referencing. You will learn how to use the requisite menus, keystrokes, and mouse commands. Some of the fundamental concepts of spreadsheet work will be explained, including cell blocks and formula copying. A sample model is used to demonstrate many of the features and commands under discussion.

Making Cell Entries

This section builds on what you learned in Chapter 1 about entering information into spreadsheet cells. You will learn more about data entry techniques, the editing of spreadsheet entries, and how Quattro Pro handles labels.

The Sample Model

By following the numbered steps listed here, you can test for yourself the techniques described in this section. Together with further instructions given later in the chapter, the steps create a model that will illustrate spreadsheet commands in this and several other chapters. The model projects revenue for a regional office of a yacht company. The first stage of the model is shown in Figure 2-1.

As you can see, the model calculates the total projected revenue for the company's Chicago office, based on a particular growth rate. Note that the view in Figure 2-1 has been "zoomed" to enlarge the cell entries and make them easier to see. You can read how to do this at the end of the chapter, under "Zooming Off." To create the model yourself, begin by launching Quattro Pro. When the program has started, you will be presented with a fresh spreadsheet notebook called NOTEBK1.WB1. The cell selector will be in cell A1 of the first page of the notebook, page A. The full name for the current cell is thus A:A1.

After checking that the CAPS LOCK key is off (the message CAP should not appear in the bottom status line) follow these steps:

Chapter 2: Building Spreadsheet Models

1. With cell A1 selected, type **Revenue Projection** and press DOWN ARROW. This enters the label and moves the cell selector to A2.

2. Enter four more labels in the same way—**Office:** in A2, **Period:** in A3, **Total:** in A4, and **Rate:** in A5.

3. Move the cell selector to B2, type **Chicago**, and press ENTER. The results can be seen in Figure 2-2, which also shows the Active Page dialog box that will be described next.

Note Don't worry if you make a mistake while carrying out these instructions. You can refer to the section on undoing mistakes for help in correcting them.

Properties, Defaults, and the Active Page

In a program as flexible as Quattro Pro, you can change many aspects of the way the program works. For example, the columns can be up to

FIGURE 2-1 Model spreadsheet that will be built in this chapter

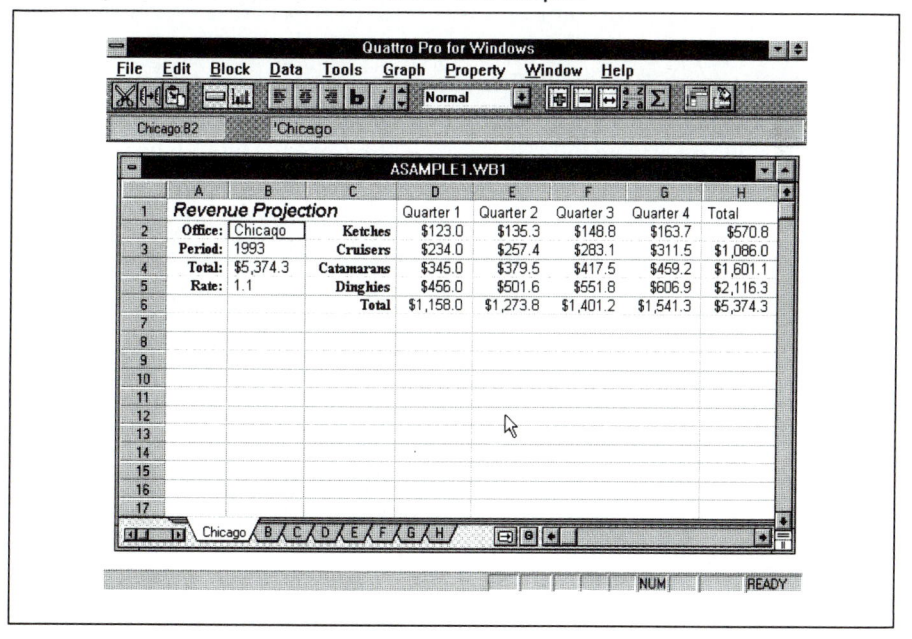

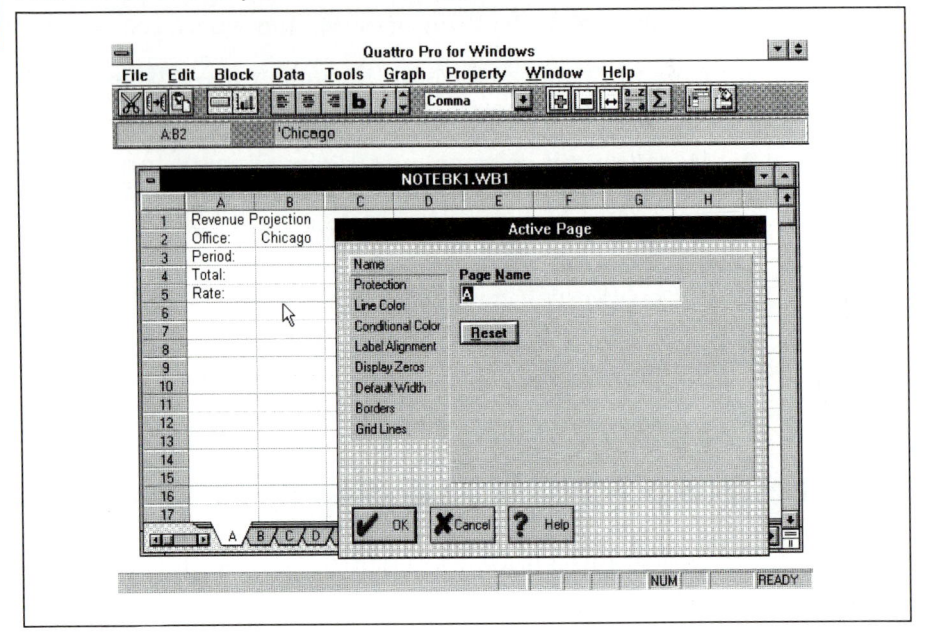

FIGURE 2-2 First entries in the spreadsheet model, and the Active Page dialog box

several hundred characters wide. However, the program gives each new notebook the same standard settings known as the *defaults*. In computer terms, a default is what the program does, or assumes, unless you tell it differently. As you can see from your entries so far, labels are normally aligned on the left. By default, the spreadsheet columns are wide enough to accommodate 9 characters in the default font. To change the default settings for the current page of a Quattro Pro notebook, you use the Object Inspector technique described in Chapter 1. The technique will now be used to alter the default column width, as well as the name of the page.

1. If you are using a mouse, point to the page tab for the current page at the bottom of the screen, in this case, tab A. Now click the right mouse button. If you are using the keyboard press ALT-P to select the Property menu and press P to select the last item on that menu, which is Active Page. Quattro Pro displays the Active Page compound dialog box, as shown in Figure 2-2. (A compound dialog box has several layers within the box, the names of which appear on the left.)

Chapter 2: Building Spreadsheet Models

2. The first item in the property list is Name. Type **Chicago**, and the word will replace the letter A in the Page Name field.

3. Do not press ENTER or click OK yet, as this will simultaneously confirm the name change and close the dialog box. You want to change one other property before you close the Active Page dialog box, so click on Default Width or press CTRL-PGDN until the Default Width property is selected, as shown in Figure 2-3.

Note When you select a new item in the property list, the first item, Name, is displayed in a different color to show that a change has been made to the Name setting.

4. There are two Default Width settings you can adjust. The first is the Column Width and the second is Unit, which can be Characters, Inches, or Centimeters. To change the Column Width, press ALT-W and then a number to replace 9.00. You can also click in the Column Width box and edit the number. To change the Unit setting, press ALT plus the key letter of the option you prefer, or click the setting.

5. For this example, change the Unit setting from Characters to Inches (press ALT-I or click on Inches). Notice that the Column Width setting

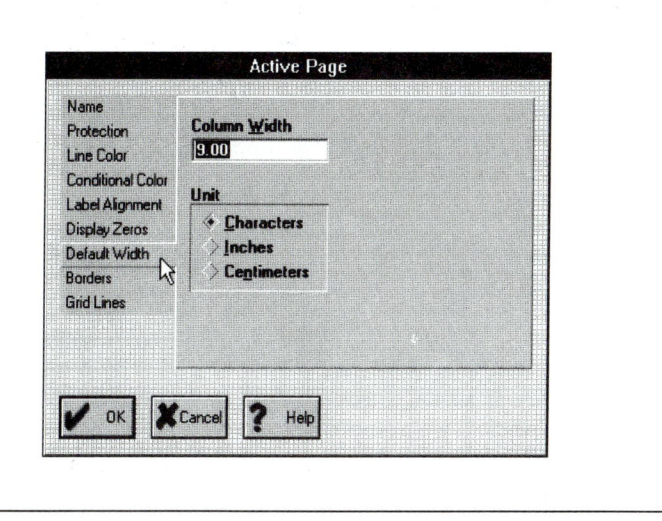

FIGURE 2-3 Adjusting the default column width in the Active Page dialog box

changes from 9.00 to .66, a feature that will be discussed in a moment.

6. Select Column Width again (press ALT-W or click on the box). Replace .66 with .75 to make the columns wider (3/4 inch wide).

7. Press ENTER or click OK to confirm your changes to the Active Page defaults.

When you close the Active Page dialog box and are returned to the notebook, any changes you have made will take effect, as shown in Figure 2-4. In this case, you can see that the name at the bottom of the page is now Chicago instead of A. The current cell is identified as Chicago:B2 instead of A:B2. You can also see that the columns are now wider. You will recall that the Column Width is initially set at 9.00 with Characters as the Unit setting. The Unit setting determines how Quattro Pro measures the width of the column. The Inches and Centimeters options are self-explanatory. In the above example you set the column width to

FIGURE 2-4 Wider columns and a named notebook page

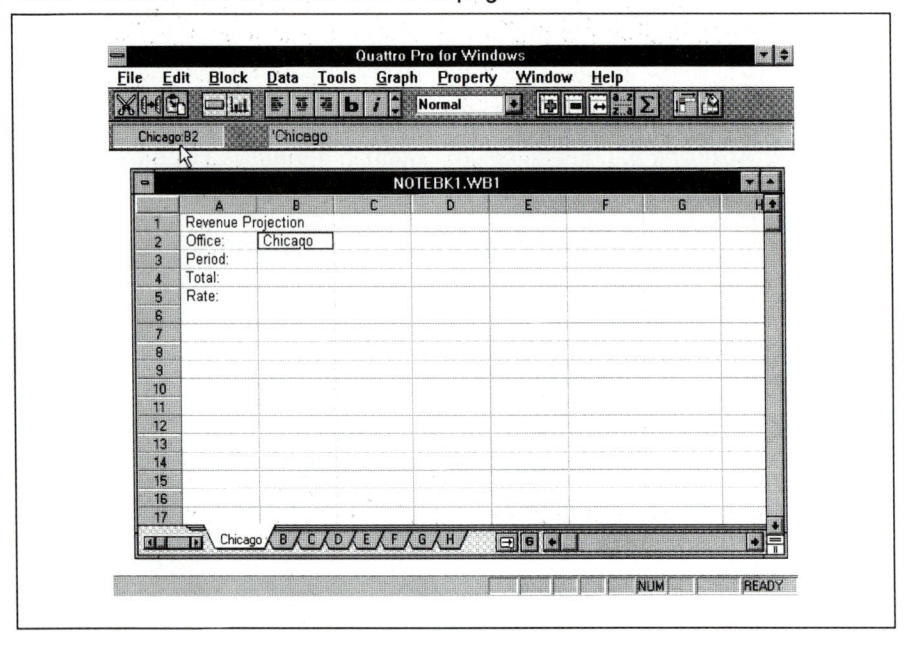

3/4 inch (.75). However, the Characters option needs to have further clarification.

The Characters option is left over from the days before Windows when one of the hardest things for a spreadsheet program to do was print out columns and rows of data in such a way that they matched the screen display. Before Windows, this problem was solved by assuming that your printer could place ten characters per inch across the page, known as 10 pitch, and print six lines per inch down the page. Prior to the advent of laser printers this was a safe assumption, since most printing was done with *fixed pitch* printers that worked within these parameters. The fonts used by these printers were *monospaced,* meaning that all characters and numbers were allocated the same amount of horizontal space. This was convenient because most non-Windows programs used a monospaced font to display information on the screen, which was treated as a grid of characters some 80 columns by 25 rows.

The Courier font that comes with Windows is an example of a monospaced font, but most Windows fonts are *proportional,* meaning that different characters, such as m and i, are allocated space in proportion to their size, just as in the text you are reading now. Furthermore, Windows allows you to print with the same fonts as you see on your screen and to scale fonts up or down in size to fit text onto a page. In practice, this means that you no longer need to think in terms of how many characters you can fit onto a line. Proportional fonts are measured in points instead of pitch, and point sizes refer to the height of the letters, not their width (there are 72 points to the inch). Rather than use Characters, you will probably find it easier to work with a measurement that directly relates to the printed pages, such as Inches.

When the Default Width Unit setting is Characters, Quattro Pro determines the actual width based on the average width of characters in the default font. If the font is 10 points, Quattro Pro uses a scale of 14.5 characters to the inch to convert between inches and characters. When you select Inches as the Unit setting the default character measurement of 9.00 is converted to .66. If you enter a measurement in inches, as in the above example, Quattro Pro will convert it to characters. The commands for adjusting individual column widths will be discussed in the next section.

Labels, Columns, and the Active Block

As you saw in Chapter 1, there are two types of data in a spreadsheet: values and labels. The information you have entered so far in the sample model consists of labels. These are automatically aligned at the left of the cell. Although spreadsheets are thought of as number-crunching tools, the role that labels play is very important. Labels tell you and anyone else using the worksheets what the numbers mean. You should avoid entering numbers without first placing labels to tell what the numbers represent. Quattro Pro automatically creates a label whenever a new cell entry begins with one of the following *label indicators*:

A through Z ! % ^ & *) \ [< > : ; ~ ?] _ | ' "

Note   In addition to these characters, a space at the beginning of an entry also tells Quattro Pro that you are typing a label.

Entries and Alignment

Normally, Quattro Pro aligns labels on the left and puts an apostrophe in front of the text to remind you that this is a label. You can tell Quattro Pro to center a label in the column by starting the label with the caret (^). A label is aligned flush right by preceding it with the double quotation mark ("), sometimes called a double prime. You can try this in the sample model. With the cell selector in B2, type "Chicago and press ENTER. The label moves to the right, as seen in Figure 2-5.

The label alignment characters can be activated in several ways. The Active Page dialog box shown earlier in Figure 2-2 has a Label Alignment setting that can be used to tell Quattro Pro to make all new labels on the current spreadsheet page align left, right, or centered. This setting affects the current page only. It does not affect other pages or files or the labels you have already entered in the current spreadsheet.

Active Block Properties

When you want to vary individual labels from the default label alignment setting, you can simply type the appropriate prefix ahead of

Chapter 2: Building Spreadsheet Models 59

FIGURE 2-5 A single right-aligned label

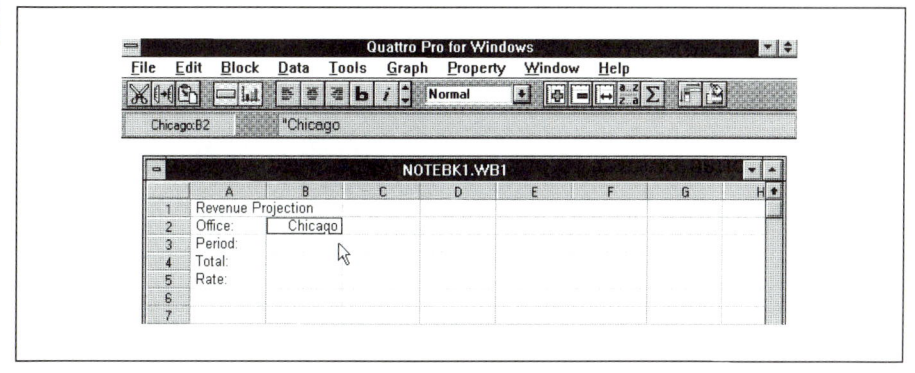

the text of the label, as in **"Chicago** in Figure 2-5. To change the alignment of a group of cells or otherwise adjust the way they are displayed, use the Object Inspector. First, you select the block of cells to adjust. For example, to realign the labels in A2 through A5 and display them in bold:

1. Select cells A2 through A5. (With your mouse, point at A2 and then hold down the left mouse button while dragging the pointer to A5 before releasing the button. From the keyboard, select A2; hold down SHIFT; press END, followed by DOWN ARROW; and release the SHIFT key.)

2. While pointing at the selected cells, press the right mouse button to call up the Active Block dialog box, or press F12, which is the Current Object key.

3. In the Active Block dialog box, select Alignment.

4. Select Right for the Cell Alignment setting (click on it or press ALT-R). Note that the word "Office:" moves to the right of the preview box in the lower right of the dialog box, as shown in Figure 2-6.

5. Select Font from the property list. There is no need to change the typeface at this point. To display the contents of the active block in bold, click the button next to Bold in the Options list or press ALT-B. The preview box shows the effect of the new setting.

6. Click OK or press ENTER to confirm the new settings. The results appear as in Figure 2-7.

FIGURE 2-6 Selecting right-alignment

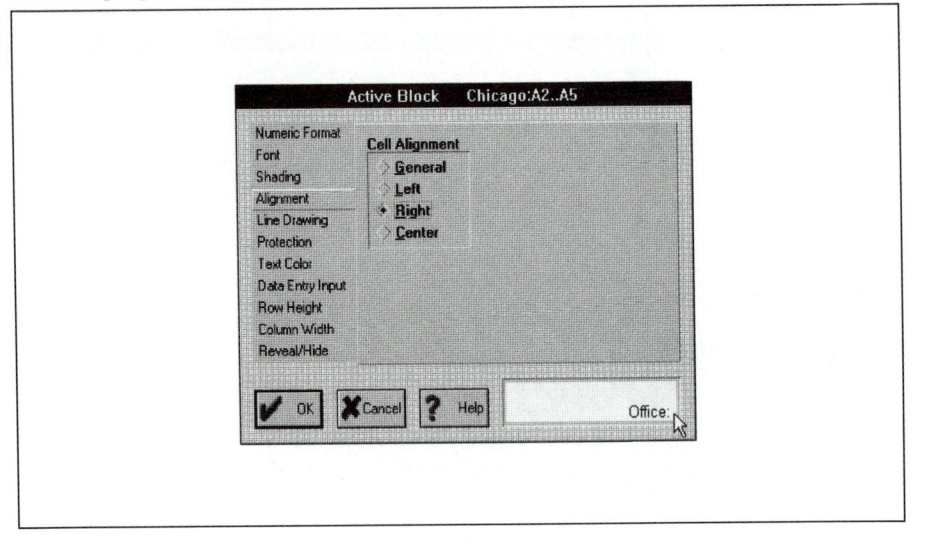

FIGURE 2-7 The effect of new property settings

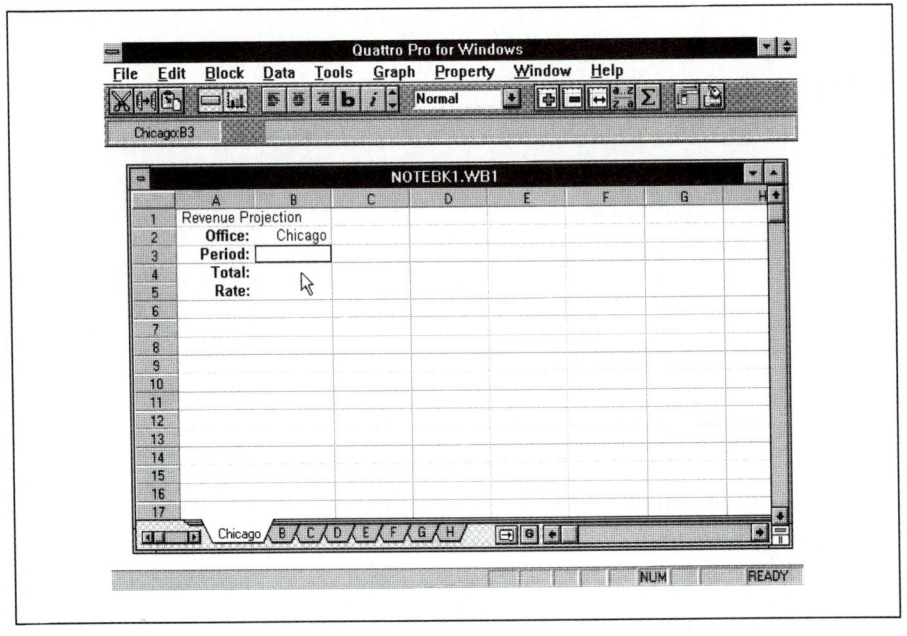

When you confirm the Active Block settings, Quattro Pro returns you to the spreadsheet, but the selected cells remain selected. This allows you to perform other commands on the same cells without reselecting them. As soon as you click on another cell or use the arrow keys the cells are deselected. In Figure 2-7, cell B3 has been selected in preparation for the next entry in the sample spreadsheet.

There are four important points to bear in mind when aligning cell entries:

- The Alignment setting in the Active Block dialog box changes the label prefix of any labels in the block to match the left, right, or center setting. However, any new labels you enter in the block will revert to the default alignment setting made for the spreadsheet with the Label Alignment property in the Active Page dialog box.

- The Alignment setting in the Active Block dialog box not only changes the alignment of labels, it also affects numbers. As you may recall from the last chapter, Quattro Pro normally right-aligns numeric entries. The Active Block Alignment setting can be used to move numbers to the center or left of the column.

- If you change the alignment of a cell with the Active Block Alignment setting, future numeric entries in that cell will continue to correspond with that setting, while future label entries will revert to the default label alignment for the page.

- The General option for the Alignment setting within the Active Block menu tells Quattro Pro to align numbers on the right and align labels according to the current Label Alignment setting for the page. This allows you to return a block of labels to the normal alignment arrangement.

Note Remember that Active Block settings override Active Page defaults only within the selected block.

So far, you have seen that the Active Block dialog box can be used with single cells or simple blocks of cells. It is also possible to use the Active Block dialog box to adjust a collection of unconnected cells, referred to as a *compound block*. For more about blocks and how they are defined, see the section on "Formulas and Blocks" later in this chapter.

Wide Labels and Column Widths

In cell Chicago:B3, type **January to March**. You may notice that the label is wider than the column. As you learned in Chapter 1, a label wider than the cell it occupies is not really a problem unless you need to enter data in the cell immediately to the right. If you were to make an entry in cell C3, the part of the label in B3 that extends beyond the cell border would be truncated. You can see this if you enter the product category labels in column C. Follow these steps:

1. In C2, type **Ketches** and press DOWN ARROW.
2. Enter **Cruisers** in C3 and **Catamarans** in C4 in the same way.
3. In C5, type **Dinghies** and press HOME.
4. Now select B3. The results will appear as shown in Figure 2-8.

You have created four left-aligned labels. You have seen that pressing a cursor movement key, including HOME, during the typing of a new cell entry enters what you have typed so far and moves the cell selector. Note that it is the *display* of the long label in B3 that is affected by the entry in C3, not the actual contents of the cell (which are still fully visible on the input line when you select that cell).

Labels in Quattro Pro spreadsheets can contain up to several hundred characters. In Chapter 10, you will see that Quattro Pro can wrap long labels into a rectangular area on the spreadsheet to let you compose text for letters, memos, and notations on spreadsheet models. For now,

FIGURE 2-8 Additional labels truncate a long label

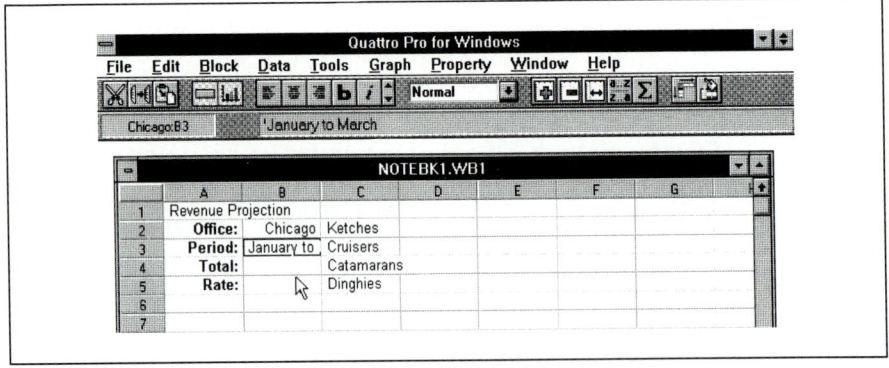

Chapter 2: Building Spreadsheet Models 63

consider the label in B3 of the sample model. Long labels simply borrow space from adjacent cells to display their contents until an entry is made in the adjoining cell. There are several solutions to this problem. You can abbreviate the long label, move the adjacent entry, or widen the column. Later in this chapter you will read how to move cells. At this point, you can try editing the entry in B3 and adjusting the column widths:

1. Select B3 if you have not already done so, type **First Quarter**, and press ENTER.

2. The new entry replaces the old, but it may still be too long. Furthermore, the label Catamarans in C4 is also too long. You are now going to use the Object Inspector to make several adjustments to columns B and C.

3. Select cells B2 through C5 and then, while pointing at the selected cells, click the right mouse button (if you are using the keyboard, select the cells and then press F12, the Current Object key, or press ALT-P followed by ENTER to select Current Object from the Property menu).

4. When the Active Block dialog box appears, select Column Width.

Note A keyboard shortcut for quickly selecting this item is to press CTRL-PGUP twice, since the highlighting in the property list moves "up" from the top of the list and wraps around to the bottom.

5. At the Column Width property menu, select Auto Width (press ALT-A). Doing this will ensure that the columns within the active block are made wide enough to accommodate the longest entries in the active block.

6. Change the Extra Characters setting to 2, as shown in Figure 2-9. This will force Quattro Pro to put additional space between the columns when they are adjusted (use ALT-E to select the Extra Characters box).

7. Leave the Unit setting as Characters, since Quattro Pro will calculate two characters' worth of space for you, basing its calculation on the current font size.

8. Do not click OK or press ENTER yet. Select the Alignment setting, which will allow you to make sure all of the labels in the active block

FIGURE 2-9 Altering the Column Width setting

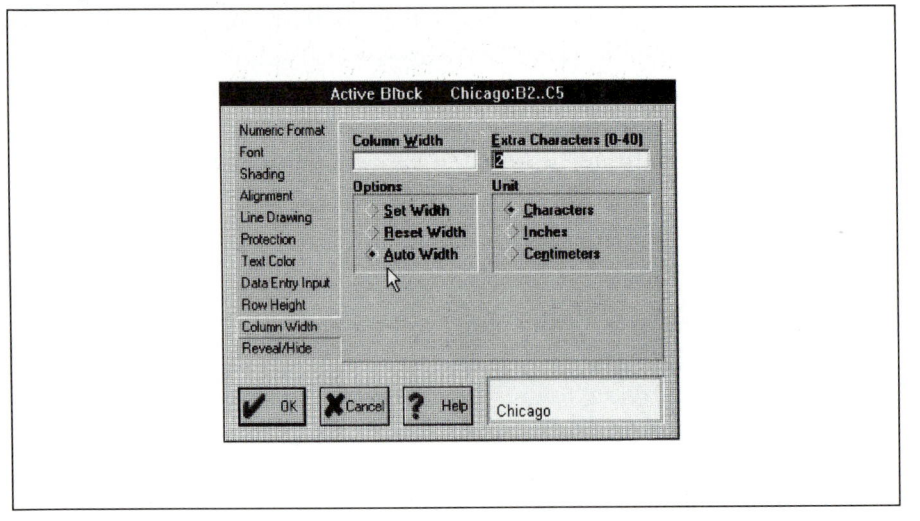

are left-aligned. At the Alignment menu click on the <u>L</u>eft option or press ALT-L to select it.

9. Press ENTER or click OK to confirm the property changes you have made. Figure 2-10 shows the results.

The columns in the active block have been widened to make room for the widest entries in the block plus two additional characters' worth of space. Note that the label in B2, which was right-aligned, is now left-aligned. Also note that there are other ways to adjust column widths and access the Auto Width feature. These are described in a moment, under "The SpeedBar and Column Shortcuts."

Repeating Labels

In addition to the left, right, and center label prefixes, you can also use the backslash (\). This is known as the *cell fill* character and is handy when you want one or more characters to be repeated to fill up a cell. For example, if you enter * Quattro Pro fills the cells with as many asterisks as the cell can hold. If you widen the column, Quattro Pro automatically

Chapter 2: Building Spareadsheet Models

FIGURE 2-10 New settings in effect

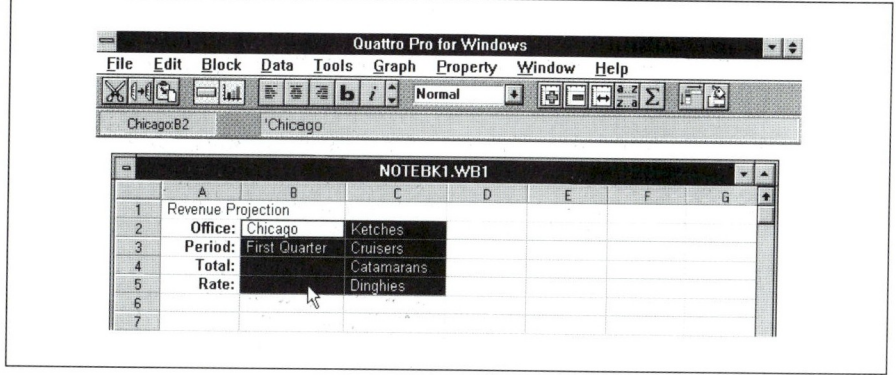

adds more asterisks. The number of asterisks is reduced if the column is narrowed.

The main reason for cell fill is that early spreadsheet programs could not underline text within cells the way that Quattro Pro can, nor could they draw lines for borders. As an alternative, an extra row was added, and cells were filled with hyphens (\-) or equal signs (\=), creating the impression of a line beneath a label or across a spreadsheet as a visual divider. Cell fill is a lot quicker than manually entering a series of symbols and has the added advantage that when columns are altered in width, the cell remains filled. Alternatives to repeating characters for underlining and dressing up your spreadsheet include using an underlined font, drawing a line above or below a cell, and shading cells. These features are described in Chapter 4.

The SpeedBar and Column Shortcuts

The SpeedBar above the input line gives you instant access to commonly used commands. You have already performed several operations using the Object Inspector technique that can also be carried out by means of the SpeedBar. In this section we look at how you use the SpeedBar and reveal several shortcuts that you will find useful when working with columns in spreadsheet models.

Anatomy of a SpeedBar

When you first install and load Quattro Pro you are presented with the default SpeedBar, which looks like this:

As you might imagine, the SpeedBar can be altered to fit your needs, and many different SpeedBars can be created. You have already seen that the default SpeedBar changes automatically when you go from READY mode to EDIT mode. Details of how to make your own SpeedBar can be found in Chapter 6. The suggested SpeedBar can be divided into six sections as follows:

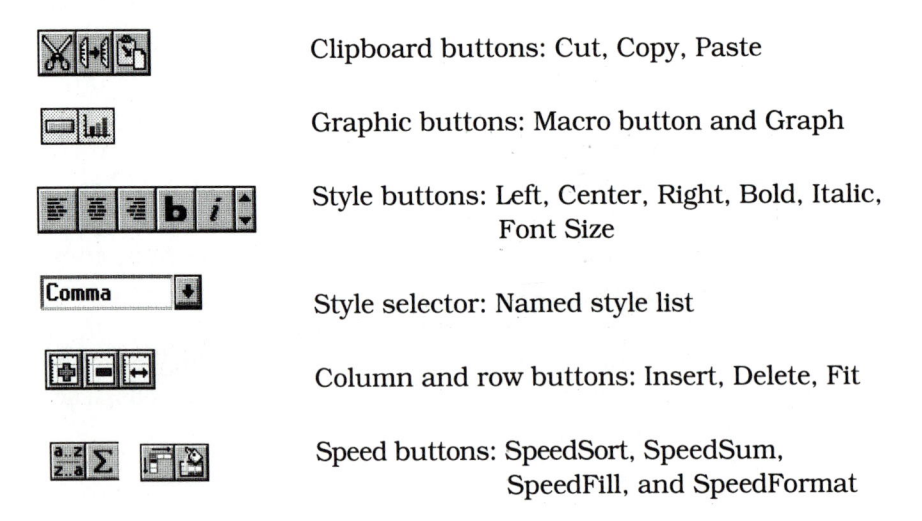

Clipboard buttons: Cut, Copy, Paste

Graphic buttons: Macro button and Graph

Style buttons: Left, Center, Right, Bold, Italic, Font Size

Style selector: Named style list

Column and row buttons: Insert, Delete, Fit

Speed buttons: SpeedSort, SpeedSum, SpeedFill, and SpeedFormat

The Style buttons are described in this section. The Cut, Copy, and Paste buttons are dealt with later in this chapter under "Spreadsheet Editing." Macro buttons are described in Chapter 14, while graphs are covered in Chapter 9. The Style Selector is discussed in the section on named styles. The use of the Column and Row buttons is discussed in the next chapter. Toward the end of this chapter, you find an example of the SpeedSum button in action, while SpeedSort is dealt with in Chapter 6. The SpeedFill and SpeedFormat buttons are described in Chapter 3.

The Style Buttons

The Style buttons are used to alter the appearance of cell entries in the spreadsheet. Suppose that you want to center a group of labels. You simply select them and click the Center button. This is an alternative to using the Object Inspector and making changes to the Alignment settings in the Active Block dialog box. The Left and Right buttons work the same way.

Suppose that you want those same labels to be bold. You simply click on the Bold button. Since cells remain selected in Quattro Pro, you can execute a series of commands on the same cells without having to keep selecting them. There is also an Italic button.

The last part of the Style buttons is a pair of arrows. If you click on the up arrow, the font size is increased for entries in the selected cells. Click the down arrow to reduce the size. To see the Style buttons in action, follow these steps.

1. In the sample spreadsheet, select cells C2 through C5 and click on the Italic button.
2. Select cell A1 and click on the Italic button.
3. Click once on the up arrow just to the right of the Italic button. This will increase the size of the font in A1.
4. With cell A1 still selected, click the Bold button. The results can be seen in Figure 2-11.

Note that the height of row 1 has been increased slightly to accommodate the larger font. Also note that the Italic and Bold buttons are shown as selected when the current cell contains these attributes.

The Fit Button

One other button should be discussed at this point: Fit. This is located toward the right of the SpeedBar and is used to issue the Auto Width command. The Fit button is thus an alternative to the Column Width setting in the Active Block dialog box. When you click the Fit button, the

FIGURE 2-11 Additional format changes using the SpeedBar

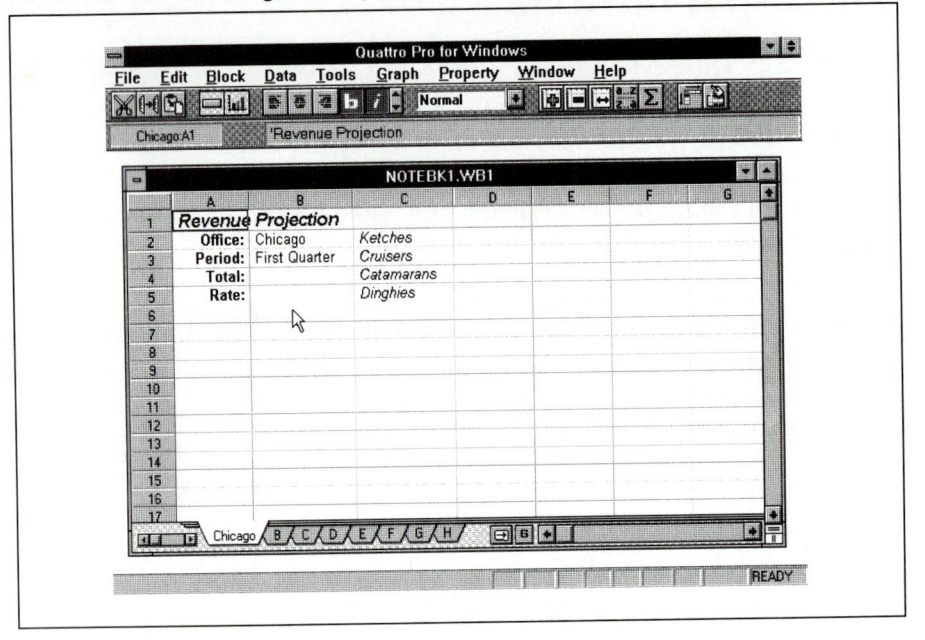

currently selected columns are adjusted. They are widened or narrowed in order to accommodate the longest entry plus one more character (the equivalent to using 1 for the Extra Characters setting). Both the Fit button and the Auto Width setting in the Active Block dialog box follow these rules to determine the longest entry:

- If the current selection is just one cell, the new width depends upon the entry in that cell and all the cells below it.

- If the current selection is a block of cells that is only one row deep, for example A2 through C2, the new widths depend upon the entries in those cells and all cells below them.

- If the current selection is a group of cells more than one row deep, for example A2 through C4, the new widths depend upon the entries in those cells alone.

- If the current selection is an entire column or several entire columns, the new width(s) depend upon all entries in that column or columns.

The Auto Width command and the Fit button are very helpful, but you need to bear the above rules in mind. Selecting a single cell and clicking the Fit button will tell Quattro Pro to check all entries below the current cell, as well as the current cell itself. In a large spreadsheet, you might have entries many rows down whose width setting you do not want to affect. For this reason, it is usually safest to select just those cells that you want Quattro Pro to consider when setting the width. If you have column headings or titles that you want Quattro Pro to ignore when automatically adjusting the column width, leave those out of the selection when using the Fit command. For example, you would want to leave cell A1 out of the selection if you were using the Fit button to adjust columns in the example shown in Figure 2-11.

Columns and Mice

You might wonder how you select "entire columns." This is an option open to mouse users. If you click on the column letter in the top border of the spreadsheet, the entire column will be selected and highlighted accordingly. The same applies to rows. Click on the row number and the entire row is selected.

To select a group of entire columns that are adjacent to each other, click on the letter of the first column of the group and hold down the SHIFT key while you click on the letter of the last column in the group. Quattro Pro will select the first and last columns as well as all of the columns in between. For example, to select columns D through G in the sample model, you first select D by clicking on D in the upper spreadsheet border. Then you hold down SHIFT and click on G. The results can be seen in Figure 2-12, which also shows the special mouse pointer described in the next paragraph.

Note To select several columns that are noncontiguous, or not adjacent to each other, click on the letter of the first column and hold down the CTRL key while selecting additional columns. Quattro Pro will not select intervening columns.

Mouse users also have another way of adjusting column width, using the special double-headed arrow pointer that appears when you point to the line separating column headings, as shown in Figure 2-12. When the

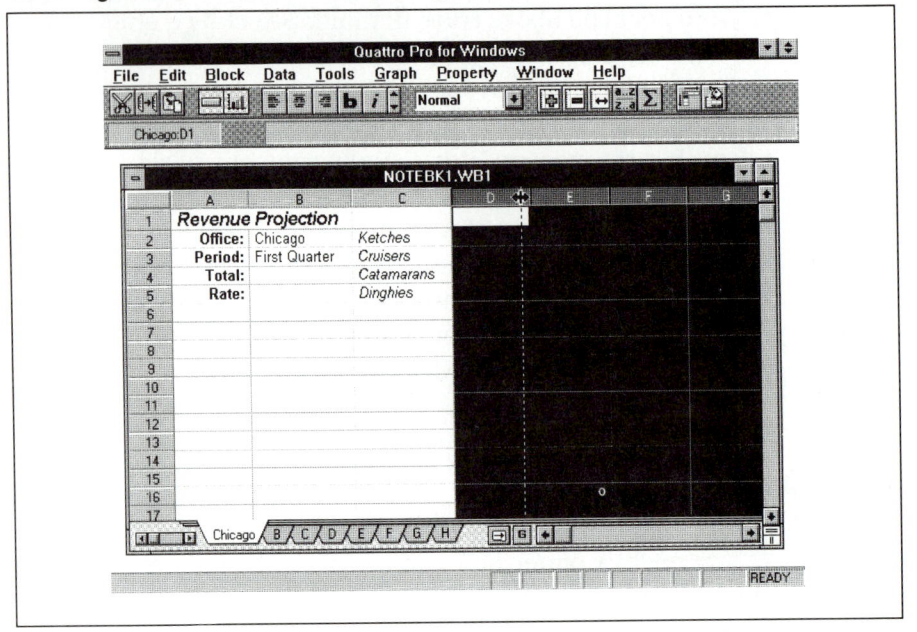

FIGURE 2-12 Selecting entire columns and adjusting widths

pointer changes to the double-headed arrow, you can press down the left mouse button and drag the line dividing the two columns. The new location of the dividing line will be shown as a dotted line. Move the pointer to the right, and you will widen the column to the left of the line. Move the pointer to the left, and you will narrow the column to the left of the line. When the line is in the desired location, release the mouse button to complete the sizing operation.

To adjust the width of a single column, there is no need to select the entire column; simply move the mouse pointer to the line between column letters. To adjust the width of several columns at once using the mouse, you first select the columns, as shown in Figure 2-12, then move the mouse pointer to one of the dividing lines within the column headings. When the pointer changes to the double-headed arrow, you can drag it left or right to narrow or widen all of the selected columns. The same principle applies to row heights, which can be adjusted by moving the mouse to the line between a pair of row numbers. However, care should be exercised when altering row heights (see Chapter 4 for more on row heights and font sizes).

Dragging, Dropping, and Undoing Entries

Sometimes you will need to change data as you type it or after it has been entered. You may find that you have entered the correct data in the wrong location. This section describes how to handle these situations and reverse commands that you have issued in error.

Entry Errors

Suppose you start typing a new piece of data and realize that your cell selector is occupying the wrong cell. In the example above, you might have started typing **Ketches** with the cell selector in B2 instead of C2. Data that you type appears first on the edit or input line, just above the work area. If you start typing a new entry and press ENTER or an arrow key, or click on the check button, Quattro Pro puts the data from the input line into the current cell. If there is already data in the cell, the new data will replace the old.

Suppose you had entered **Ketches** in B2, over the top of Chicago. To correct this error, you would have to reenter **Chicago** and then reenter **Ketches** in cell C2. If you had entered **Ketches** in C3, an empty cell but nevertheless the wrong cell for the new data, then you would have to move the incorrect entry. In a moment, you will learn how to move entries from one location to another by dragging them with the mouse.

Fortunately, Quattro Pro lets you change your mind even before you enter what is on the input line. If you press ESC or click the cross (X) button, whatever you had begun to type is removed from the input line, and you are back in READY mode. READY mode enables you to move the cell selector to the correct location.

Drag-and-Drop Feature

You may enter correct data but in the wrong cells. If you are using a mouse, the easiest way to remedy this situation is to use the *drag-and-drop* feature. This allows you to *drag* cell entries from one location and *drop* them into another. Suppose that you decide the labels occupying cells C2 through C5 would look better in B7 through B10. Follow these steps to move the labels:

1. Select cells C2 through C5.

2. With the mouse pointer somewhere over the selected cells press and hold down the left mouse button. The arrow pointer will change to a hand, as shown in step 1 of Figure 2-13.

3. Move the mouse down, and you will see that the hand drags a frame that matches the size of the selected cells, as shown in step 2 of Figure 2-13.

4. Drag the frame to the new location at B7 through B10 and release the mouse button to drop the labels into the new location, as shown in step 3 of Figure 2-13.

5. After seeing the labels in the new location, you decide they looked better in C2 through C5. Use the drag-and-drop technique to move the labels back where they came from.

FIGURE 2-13 The three steps to the drag-and-drop movement of cell entries

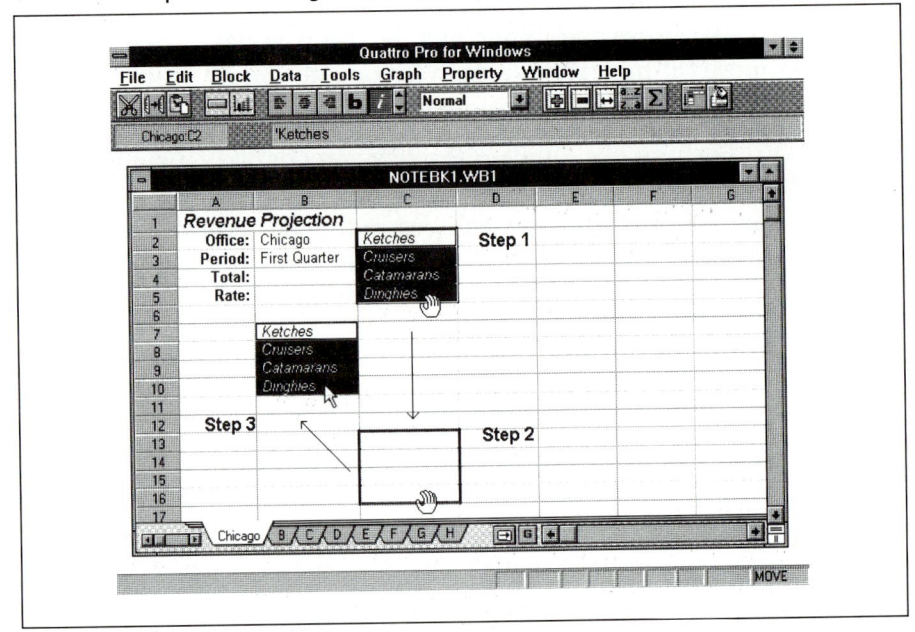

You can see that drag-and-drop is very quick and easy to use, since no menus or keystrokes are involved. If you drag cells by mistake, it is helpful to undo the operation. This is possible with the Undo feature in Quattro Pro, described next. You can use a variation of the above technique to copy cells, as described later in this chapter under "Numbers, Formulas, and Formats." If you want to move cell entries without using a mouse, see the section on cut-and-paste later in this chapter. Drag-and-drop only works on blocks of two or more cells.

The Undo Feature

One way of changing what you have entered or a command you have executed is the Undo feature. Undo is the first item on the Edit menu. In most cases, this command reverses the last action you performed. For example, move the cell selector to B4, which is currently empty. Now type **50** and press ENTER. Select Edit from the menu bar. You will see that the first item is Undo Entry. Select this item, and you will see that the entry is removed and the cell is once again empty.

At this point, the first item on the Edit menu will be changed to Redo Entry. This means that after you have undone an action, you can reverse the undo. The Undo command reverses the last "undoable" operation you performed. Operations that can be undone are

- Cell entries and cell edits, including cell delete, cut, copy, and paste
- Spreadsheet edits, including moves, inserts, and deletions
- File retrievals, spreadsheet erasures, and deletion of named graphs and named blocks

Operations that you *cannot* undo are

- Changes to program settings such as Print Block, Sort Block, and Options
- Saving of files to disk

Note that there is a possibility that when you use the Edit menu the Undo option will be disabled—the menu text is displayed in gray. This means you need to enable the Undo feature. From the menu bar select Property and then Application, or click the right mouse button while pointing to the program title bar directly above the menu bar. The Application property dialog box will appear. Now select Startup, as shown in Figure 2-14 (keyboard users can press CTRL-PGDN to get to the Startup section). In the Options box, select Undo enabled. Now click OK or press ENTER to confirm the new setting.

Note Do not press LEFT ARROW to go back and correct mistakes while typing a new entry, as this simply enters the data into the cell. If you start typing a new piece of data in the right place but make an error or a spelling mistake, use BACKSPACE to back the cursor over the data in the input line until you have erased the error and then resume typing.

Cell Editing

You can change the contents of a cell in several ways. The method you use depends on the type of change you need to make. The following paragraphs explain the different ways of editing using the sample model.

FIGURE 2-14 The Application property dialog box

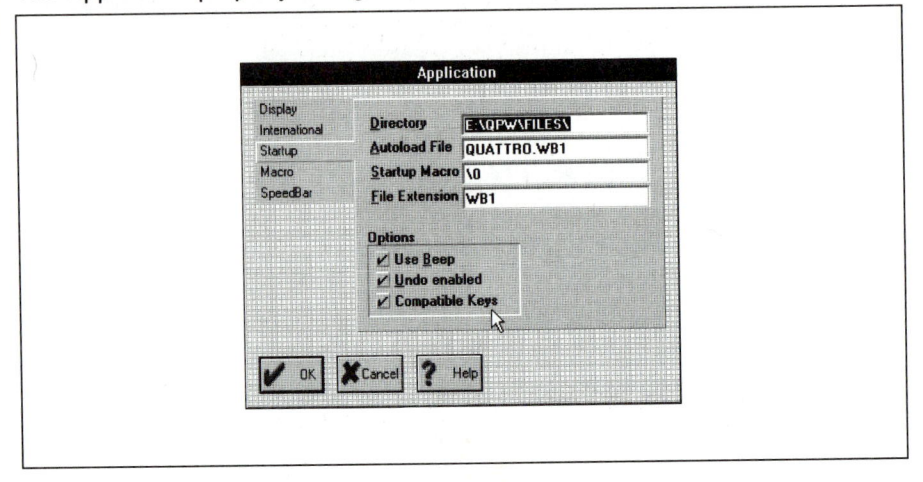

Reentry

When you reenter data into a cell, the contents of the cell are changed. The simplest method of reentry is to type the new data over the old, completely replacing it. For example, if you place the cell selector on B2, which contains the word "Chicago," type **Miami**, and press ENTER, the entire word "Chicago" will disappear, not just the first five letters. Select Edit | Undo Entry to change "Miami" back to "Chicago."

The Edit Key

If you want to change "Chicago" to "Chicago South," you can avoid retyping the entire entry by using EDIT mode. This is activated by pressing F2, the Edit key, or clicking on the input line below the SpeedBar. The input line is then activated and acts as the edit line, with the edit cursor appearing at the end of the current entry. The mode indicator changes to EDIT, and at the bottom left of the screen, Quattro Pro displays the contents of the cell before editing. You can now make changes or additions to the entry and place the revised entry back in the worksheet by pressing ENTER or clicking on the check button.

When you are using EDIT mode, several keys perform differently than in READY mode. Pressing HOME moves the cursor to the left side of the entry. Pressing END places the cursor back on the right side. You can also move around the contents of the cell with LEFT ARROW and RIGHT ARROW. Suppose that you have mistakenly entered **Chidago Soth** in B2. There are several ways to correct this error. You can press F2 to edit the cell and press LEFT ARROW until your cursor is before the erroneous d and press DEL to remove it. Now you can type **c**, which will be inserted automatically into the text, to the left of the cursor. You can then move to the right with the RIGHT ARROW key to put the cursor before the t and type **u** to complete the editing. As soon as editing is completed, you can press ENTER or click the check button, regardless of where your cursor is within the data. The revised information on the edit line will be placed back in the cell.

Mouse users can click anywhere on the edit line to activate EDIT mode. This also changes the SpeedBar, which now adds a pair of buttons that are useful in cell editing, particularly when you are working with formulas. Mouse users can also use the standard Windows mouse editing techniques. You can position the edit cursor within the cell entry by pointing and clicking. You can select a section of text by dragging the edit cursor through it. You can then type fresh text, which will automatically replace the selected text. For example, if you wanted to change "First Quarter" to "Second Quarter," you could select **First** and then type **Second** (do not make this change at the moment).

Insert/Overstrike and Compatible

While you are using EDIT mode, you are also using what is called INS or *insert mode*, where what you type is inserted beside the existing text instead of replacing what was there before. However, there is another method of typing, referred to as *overstrike mode*. You activate overstrike mode by pressing the INS key during editing. The message OVR appears in the status area at the bottom of the screen.

If you go into OVR mode when editing "Chidago Soth," placing the cursor on d and typing **c** replaces the d, without the need to press DEL. However, OVR mode is not always helpful. Typing **u** when the cursor is on the t in "Soth" will replace the t with u. You can press INS a second time to get out of OVR mode. Note that Quattro Pro automatically cancels OVR mode when you leave EDIT mode. In Table 2-1, you can see a list of other keys that are useful in EDIT mode, as well as all of the function keys used by Quattro Pro. See Chapter 7 for alternative edit keys using the Compatible Keys setting.

Clear and Cut

Sometimes you will want to erase the entire contents of a cell. If it is too late to use Edit | Undo, you can clear out a cell with Edit | Clear. Select the cell whose contents you want to erase and issue the command. This removes the entire contents of the cell, not just a single character. If you have enabled the Undo feature, you can reverse this action with Edit | Undo Clear.

If you want to erase a group of cells, simply select them before issuing the Edit | Clear command. Note that Edit | Clear not only removes the contents of cells, it also changes the formatting of the cell back to the normal style for the spreadsheet. If you want to remove the contents of a cell or cells without affecting the style of the cells, use the Edit | Clear

TABLE 2-1 Function Keys and Keys Useful in Edit Mode

Key	Description
F1	Activates the Help system.
F2	Activates EDIT mode so you can change a cell entry.
SHIFT-F2	Activates DEBUG mode so you can execute a macro step by step.
ALT-F2	Displays the Tools	Macro	Execute dialog box.
F3	Displays a list of block names (when prompted for a block or in EDIT mode with the insertion point positioned after an operator). To expand the list of block names to show coordinates, press the Expand key (+); press the Contract key (–) to remove coordinates. Press F3 again to zoom the names list to full screen or to shrink it back down.
SHIFT-F3	Displays a list of available macro commands by category.
ALT-F3	Displays a list of functions in VALUE or EDIT mode.
CTRL-F3	Lets you create a named block (keyboard equivalent of Block | Names | Create).
F4	Makes the cell address to the left of cursor absolute in EDIT, VALUE, or POINT mode. Press again to cycle through the absolute combinations. Use when editing or building a formula in POINT mode.
ALT-F4	Exits Quattro Pro.
SHIFT-F4	Closes a window (dialog box, graph window, notebook, or dialog window).
F5	Moves the selector to a specified cell address.
SHIFT-F5	Works like the SpeedTab button; displays the Graphs page, then returns to a spreadsheet page.
ALT-F5	Toggles Group mode on and off.
F6	If the window is split into two panes, enters POINT mode and jumps to the other pane.
CTRL-F6	Displays the next open window.
F7	Repeats the previous Query command.
SHIFT-F7	Press, then use arrow keys to select a block of text in EXT mode.
ALT-F7	Lets you find and replace text strings.

TABLE 2-1 Cont. Function Keys and Keys Useful in Edit Mode

Key	Description
F8	Repeats the last Data	What-If command.
F9	In READY mode, recalculates the notebook. In EDIT mode, calculates and then displays result of formulas on the input line.
F10	An alternative to pressing / or ALT—moves the selector to the menu bar.
F11	Displays the current graph (press ESC to return to the notebook).
F12	Displays an Object Inspector for the selected object.
SHIFT-F12	Displays an Object Inspector for the active window.
ALT-F12	Displays an Object Inspector for the application.
EDIT Mode Keys	
Key	**Description**
ESC	Erases the contents of the input line. Pressing ESC again exits EDIT mode.
ENTER	Enters the data and exits EDIT mode.
CTRL-ENTER	In Group mode, acts like ENTER, but "drills" data through all grouped pages at once.
UP ARROW	Enters the data, exits EDIT mode, and moves up one cell. When the insertion point follows an operator in a formula, enters POINT mode.
DOWN ARROW	Enters the data, exits EDIT mode, and moves down one cell. When the insertion point follows an operator in a formula, enters POINT mode.
PGDN	Enters the data, exits EDIT mode, and moves down one screen. When the insertion point follows an operator in a formula, enters POINT mode.
PGUP	Enters the data, exits EDIT mode, and moves up one screen. When the insertion point follows an operator in a formula, enters POINT mode.
INS	Toggles between INS and OVR (overstrike) modes. (Insert mode is the default.)
BACKSPACE	Deletes characters to the left of the insertion point.
DEL	Deletes characters to the right of the insertion point, or the selected cell block or graph object.

TABLE 2-1 Cont. Function Keys and Keys Useful in Edit Mode

EDIT Mode Keys	
Key	**Description**
CTRL-\	Deletes all characters from the insertion point to the end of the entry.
CTRL-BACKSPACE	Erases the contents of the input line.
TAB or CTRL-RIGHT ARROW	Moves insertion point five spaces to the right.
SHIFT-TAB or CTRL-LEFT ARROW	Moves insertion point five spaces to the left.
CTRL-SHIFT-RIGHT ARROW	Highlights data to the right of the insertion point.
CTRL-SHIFT-LEFT ARROW	Highlights data to the left of the insertion point.
CTRL-SHIFT-D	Used before entering a date, such as 12/25/92, as a serial number.
F2	Toggles to display an indicator on the status line that tells you what type of data you're editing—either a value or label.
F3	With the insertion point positioned after an operator, displays a list of block names.
SHIFT-F3	Displays a list of macro commands.

Contents command. (For more on the normal style of a spreadsheet see the section on named styles, later in this chapter.)

If you are using a mouse, you can remove the contents of one or more cells by selecting them and clicking the Cut button, which is at the left end of the SpeedBar. This is equivalent to Edit | Cut and actually places the contents of the cell on the Windows Clipboard, allowing you to paste them back into the spreadsheet at a different location or into another Windows application. For more on using the Clipboard see "Edit | Copy and Edit | Paste" later in this chapter.

You may have learned another method of erasing a cell, used in spreadsheet programs that do not have a Clear command. This involves placing the cell selector on the cell you want to delete and pressing the SPACEBAR, and then ENTER. For example, with the cell selector in B4 type 50 and press ENTER. Now press the SPACEBAR and then ENTER. With this method, it appears that the cell has been emptied. But if you look in the cell identifier, you will see an apostrophe, which begins a left-aligned label. You have replaced what was in the cell with a blank label. Now press DEL, and the apostrophe is removed.

Note The SPACEBAR method of cell "deleting" is a bad habit to get into because the cell is not really emptied. Such blank-labeled cells can affect some worksheet calculations, such as @AVG and @COUNT. Unless you place the cell selector on the "empty" cell and observe the cell identifier, there is nothing to see. (You can use the Search-and-Replace feature, described in the next chapter, to find cells that have been erased like this.)

Error Messages

If you enter data that Quattro Pro cannot read, pressing ENTER or clicking the check button to place the data in a cell causes your computer to beep and possibly displays a message box on the screen. For example, Quattro Pro does not accept numbers that contain commas. Try to enter 8,000 in cell B4 of the sample model. The "Syntax error" message is displayed. You can press ENTER or ESC to remove the message.

At this point, Quattro Pro automatically switches to EDIT mode so that you can alter the data. The corrected data could then be placed into the cell with ENTER. For now, you don't want any data in B4. Press ESC during cell editing to completely cancel the erroneous entry (if you did enter something into B4, you can now select the cell and press DEL to erase the contents of the cell).

Quattro Pro gives you different error messages, depending on the type of error. To use the example in Chapter 1, if you were trying to calculate a loan payment but misspelled the @PMT function, the result would be an "Unknown function" message. Many errors in entry give rise to the "Invalid reference" message, which indicates that Quattro Pro is attempting to read what you have typed as a formula.

Mixed Entries

The "Invalid reference" error arises when you want to enter a piece of text that begins with a number, such as **101 Main Street**. When you begin this entry Quattro Pro assumes that you are entering a value, and the mode indicator changes from READY to VALUE. However, except in special circumstances, value entries cannot contain text. The result is that "101 Main Street" is rejected. A related problem arises when you enter something like a phone number. Say that you enter **555-1212**. You get –657 instead of a label that reads 555-1212. The problem here is that Quattro Pro interprets the entry as a numerical expression, reads the hyphen as a minus sign, and subtracts 1212 from 555.

The simplest way to avoid confusion between values and labels when you are working with entries that mix text and numbers is to begin label entries containing numbers by typing an apostrophe or other label prefix. This forces Quattro Pro to accept the entry as a label. (You can also start phone numbers with a square bracket, as in **[415] 555-1212**, because a square bracket is a label indicator.)

A similar problem with a different solution is cell entries that represent dates, such as 12/25/93. Here Quattro Pro reads the slashes as division signs and returns 0.0051613. The problem is not avoided if you type **25-Dec-93** and press ENTER. Quattro Pro objects to the mixture of text and numbers. The solution with dates is to use the Date key, described later in this chapter. If you have a lot of data to enter in your worksheet, you can use the Data Entry Input setting in the Active Block dialog box to force Quattro Pro to accept entries as either labels or dates. This command is described in Chapter 6. The distinctions among values, labels, and dates will be discussed in greater depth in a moment, but first you need to consider storing the sample model on disk.

Storing Information

Further changes and additions to the sample model will be made as the chapter progresses, but at this point, it is a good idea to store the notebook on disk. Although there appears to be little connection between file saving and cell editing, it is important to remember that so far, your cell entries only exist in RAM, the computer's random access memory. This means that the entries will disappear if the computer is turned off or suffers a power failure. A notebook saved on disk will still be there after you turn the computer off. You have only made a few entries in the spreadsheet so far, but it is a good idea to issue the File | Save command fairly early in a session. This enables you to assign a name to the file, simplifying future save operations. Figure 2-15 shows the dialog box that appears the first time you save a notebook.

Remember that you can choose the first eight characters of the name, and Quattro Pro assigns the last three, known as the file extension. The file extension, which is normally WB1 for Quattro Pro notebooks, is separated from the first eight characters of the name by a period. To save the sample file follow these steps

1. Select the File menu and select Save. Because the worksheet does not yet have a name, Quattro Pro presents the dialog box shown in Figure 2-15.

2. Quattro Pro has highlighted the default name NOTEBK1.WB1, so that whatever you type next will replace this default filename. To the right of the name is the location that Quattro Pro will use to store the file, in this case, the directory called E:\QPW\FILES (your

FIGURE 2-15 Saving a notebook for the first time

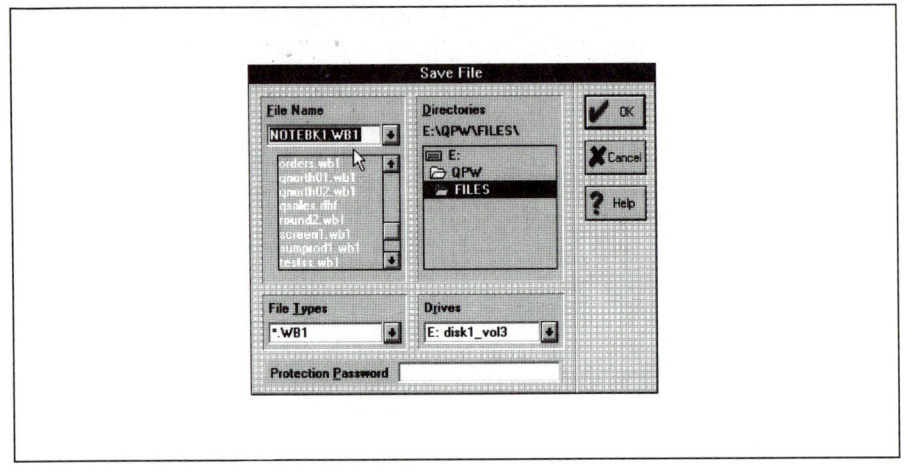

Chapter 2: Building Spreadsheet Models   83

directory may well be different). Below the directory name is a diagram of the disk and directory being used.

3. Type **ASAMPLE** and press ENTER. The worksheet will be stored in a file called ASAMPLE.WB1, and you are returned to READY mode.

Note that the notebook title bar now says ASAMPLE.WB1 instead of NOTEBK1.WB1. Also note that the first time you save a notebook, Quattro Pro checks to see if a file of the same name already exists and asks whether you want to replace it, as shown in Figure 2-16. Choose Replace if you want to replace the contents of the file on disk with the current spreadsheet. Choose Cancel if you do not want to change the file already stored on disk. Choose Backup if you want to replace the contents of the file on disk with the current worksheet but, at the same time, create a copy of the existing file with a new name (the backup file's new name will be assigned automatically by changing the extension from WB1 to BAK, as in ASAMPLE.BAK). Quattro Pro returns you to READY mode after any of these three commands.

FIGURE 2-16 The save confirmation dialog box

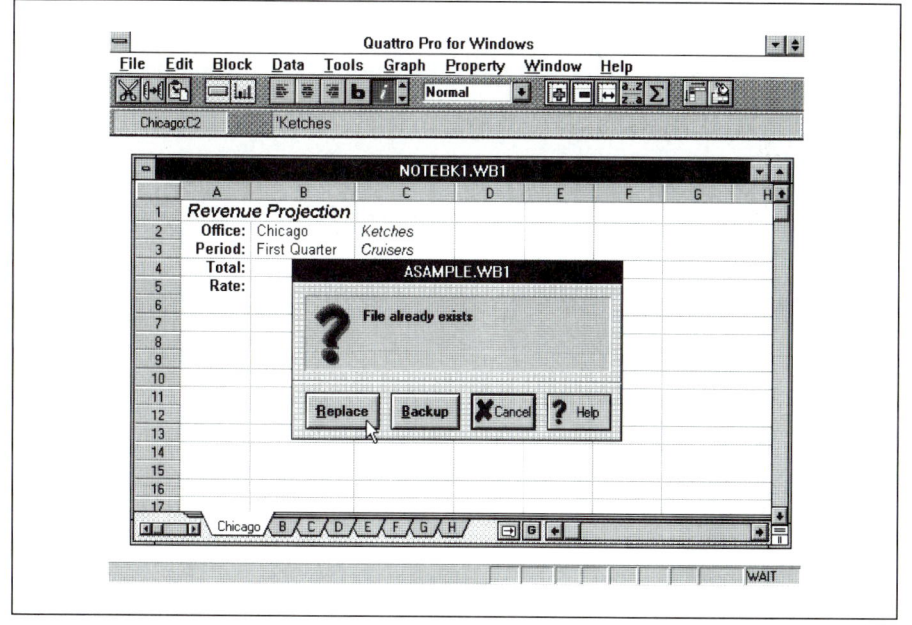

Numbers, Numeric Formats, and Named Styles

This section discusses entering values in a spreadsheet and changing their appearance and introduces the named style feature, giving examples of its application.

Value Indicators

You have seen that Quattro Pro distinguishes between value and label entries by the first character of a new entry. Anything that begins with one of the following characters is treated as a value:

0 through 9 . + − (@ # $

These items are called *value indicators.* If you do not begin an entry with one of these characters, Quattro Pro treats the entry as a label. Try entering some numbers into the sample model:

1. Select cell D2, type **123**, and press DOWN ARROW.
2. Use the same technique to enter **234** in cell D3, **345** in cell D4, and **456** in cell D5.
3. Select cell B3, type **1993**, and press ENTER. The number will replace the label First Quarter.
4. Select cell B5, type **1.1**, and press ENTER. The results will appear as in Figure 2-17.

Note that Quattro Pro normally aligns numbers on the right of the cell, as in cells D2 through D5. However, the numbers in B3 and B5 are aligned on the left. This is because earlier you set the Alignment property for these cells to left alignment.

Chapter 2: Building Spreadsheet Models 85

> **FIGURE 2-17** Numbers entered in the sample spreadsheet

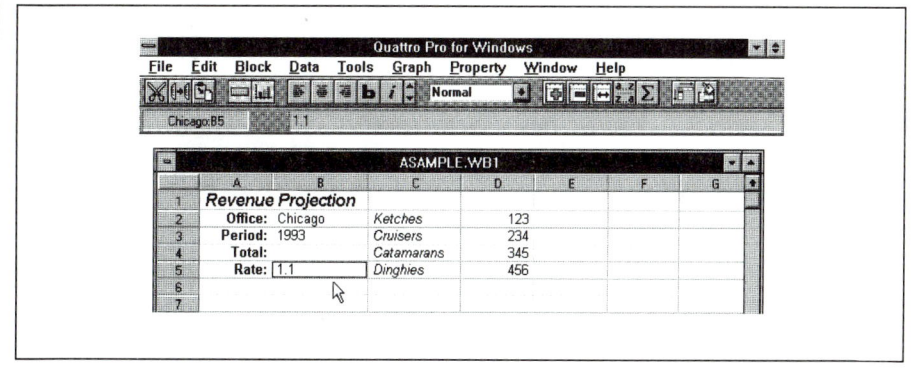

Long Numbers

You will occasionally need to enter a large number into a Quattro Pro worksheet. With the cell selector in B4, type **1234567890123** and press ENTER. This entry causes something like 1.23457E+12 to be displayed in the spreadsheet. The input line lets you know that the number 1234567890123 is still stored by Quattro Pro. What you are seeing is the scientific notation 1.23457×10 to the power of 12. The reason that Quattro Pro alters the appearance of long numbers is that the column can only accommodate a limited number of digits, particularly since there needs to be some space between the last digit on the right and the right edge of the cell. If Quattro Pro did not maintain this space, currently equivalent to one character, long numbers in adjoining cells would appear to run together. Widening the column restores the number to its normal appearance, but if you regularly work with numbers in the millions and billions, you might want to use the Scientific setting for the Numeric Format property using the commands described next. Before you continue, press DEL to clear cell B4.

Numbers, Formulas, and Formats

The appearance of numbers in the worksheet is controlled by something called *numeric format.* You saw earlier that if you put commas in a number you are entering, Quattro Pro will reject it. Quattro Pro assumes that you will enter plain numbers and then dress them up with a suitable numeric format. When you create a fresh worksheet, Quattro Pro uses the General format to begin with. As you can see from cells B3 and B5 of the sample model, this format does not show decimal places unless you enter them. If you enter **1993**, you get 1993 with no decimal digits. If you enter **1.1**, you get 1.1.

The same is true when you enter formulas. If a formula results in a value with decimal places, the General format displays the decimal digits. However, the General format may not be able to show all of the digits to the right of the decimal point. If you enter **100/3** you will see 33 followed by a decimal point and as many 3s as will fit in the cell. To see how numeric formats affect your work, you can now make further entries in the sample spreadsheet. These entries show the first two quarters of projected revenue. Following the steps below will produce the results shown in Figure 2-18:

1. Select cell D1, type **Quarter 1**, and press RIGHT ARROW.

FIGURE 2-18 Formulas entered in the sample spreadsheet

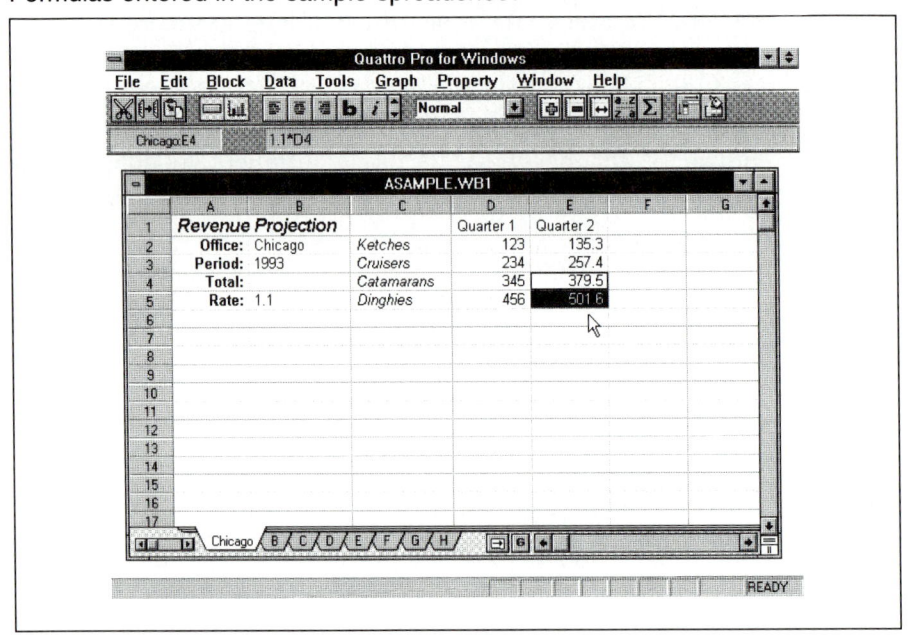

Chapter 2: Building Spreadsheet Models   87

2. In cell E1, type **Quarter 2** and press DOWN ARROW.

3. In cell E2, type a formula for the second quarter revenue that will make it ten percent larger than the first quarter revenue in D2—type **1.1*D2**.

4. When you have entered the formula, select E3 and enter **1.1*D3**.

5. Now you need two more formulas to complete the entries in column E. You can do this by copying the formulas you have already created.

6. If you are using a mouse, select cells E2 and E3 and copy them using the drag-and-drop technique. Point to the selected cells and hold down the CTRL key while you press down the left mouse button. The mouse pointer turns into a hand. Drag the hand down so that the frame outlines cells E4 and E5. Now release the mouse button, and then the CTRL key. The results appear as in Figure 2-18.

Note Holding down the CTRL key while "dragging and dropping" will copy the contents of the original cells, rather than moving them.

If you are not using a mouse you can perform the operation in step 6 by following these steps:

1. Select E2 and E3 (select E2 then hold down SHIFT and press DOWN ARROW).

2. Issue the Edit | Copy command (keyboard shortcut: CTRL-INS). A copy of the cells has been placed in the Windows Clipboard. The Edit | Copy command will be discussed in greater detail later in this chapter where you will learn more about how Quattro Pro is able to replicate formulas.

3. Select E4 and issue the Edit | Paste command (keyboard shortcut: SHIFT-INS). The cells are copied from the Clipboard to the spreadsheet.

To test the new formulas, enter a different value in D2, such as 101. You will see that E2 changes. The value in E2 is 1.1 times whatever you enter in D2.

If you look at Figure 2-18, you can see that when the number of decimal places produced by the formulas varies, the decimal point appears at varying positions in the cell. This looks somewhat unprofessional, and you will learn how to improve the appearance of numbers in a moment. The numeric format can be changed for a part of the notebook page or for all of it. For example, if most of the numeric entries in a spreadsheet represent currency, you might want to make Currency the normal or default numeric format. To do this efficiently, you first need to learn about named styles.

Named Styles

Every cell in a Quattro Pro notebook has a *named style* setting. A named style is a collection of attributes such as font, alignment, and numeric format that have been given a name, such as Heading, Total, or Normal. The named style setting for a cell is visible in the Style Selector in the SpeedBar when that cell is selected. So far, all of the cells in the sample model have had the Normal style. This is because whenever you create a new notebook, all of the cells in all of the pages start out with the Normal style. You have seen that it is possible to change one or more attributes of a cell without changing the named style setting for that cell. For example, earlier you changed cell A1 to a larger font in bold and italic. However, if you look closely at Figure 2-16 where the current cell is A1, the Style Selector still reads Normal. This is because the named style setting is merely the starting point for a cell's appearance.

Although you can alter various attributes of the cell without using a different style name, there are several advantages to using named styles. For example, suppose that you like the appearance of the labels in A2 through A5 and you would like to make other cells look like that. You can create a new named style from cells A2 through A5 and then apply it to other cells. Follows these steps to see how this works:

1. Select A2 through A5.

2. Choose Edit from the menu bar and then select Define Style. The Define/Modify Style dialog box appears, as in Figure 2-19.

3. At the moment, the named style for the current block is Normal, but the name is highlighted so that whatever you type next will replace

Chapter 2: Building Spreadsheet Models

FIGURE 2-19 The Define/Modify Style dialog box

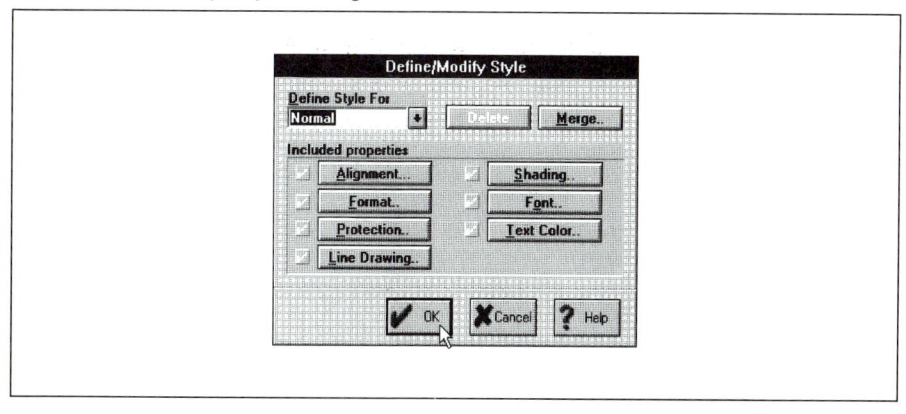

[Define/Modify Style dialog box shown]

it. Type **Category** and then select Merge. The following dialog box pops up:

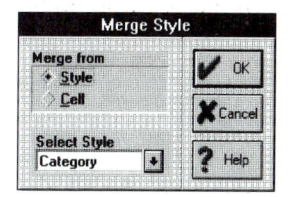

[Merge Style dialog box shown]

4. If the Merge from setting is Style, Quattro Pro will add the attributes of the currently selected cells to the named style that appears in the Select Style field (this is currently Comma because Comma is the first style in the named style list). If the Merge from setting is Cell, Quattro Pro will copy the attributes of the current cell to the new style you are defining.

5. Select Cell, and the Select Style box will change to Select Cell. The current entry is Chicago:A2, because this is the current cell.

6. Press ENTER or click on OK, and you will return to the Define/Modify Style dialog box. Choose OK again. Keyboard users press TAB to select OK and then press ENTER.

7. Now select cells A2 through A5. You will format these cells with the new Category style (at this point, their style is still Normal).

Quattro Pro for Windows Inside & Out

8. Click on the arrow to the right of Normal in the SpeedBar. This will pop up an alphabetical list of available named styles, as shown in Figure 2-20. Note that Category is now in the list.

9. Select Category, and the selected cells will be reformatted to match the Category style. Repeat this for cells C2 through C5.

The advantage of using a named style for cell formatting is that you can edit the style at a later date, and all cells formatted with that style will be altered in the same way. For example, suppose that you would like the Category style to use a different font. Follow these steps, and you will see that changing the font for the Category style will alter the appearance of all cells that have been assigned the Category style.

1. Select Edit | Define Style (it does not matter which cell you select before issuing the command).

2. A Define/Modify Style dialog box appears like the one in Figure 2-19. The Define Style For field contains the name of the style used in the

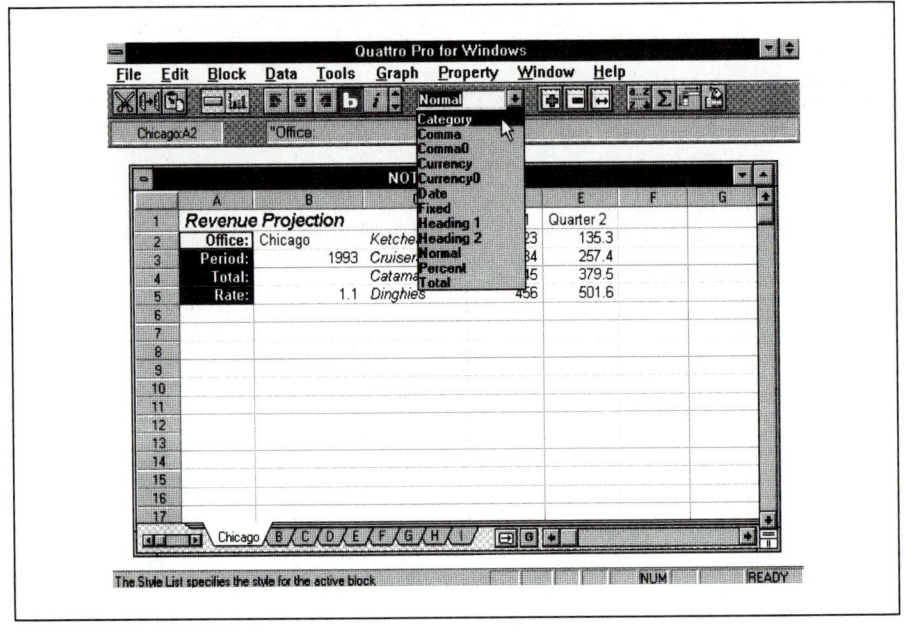

FIGURE 2-20 The list of named styles presented by the Style Selector

current cell (if this is not Category, use the list arrow to pop up a list of named styles and select Category from the list).

3. Note the included properties section of the dialog box, seven buttons that show which properties of the cell's appearance are affected by the style (not all properties have to be affected).

4. Click on the Font button and select Roman or Times/Roman from the Typeface list.

5. Click OK once and then click it again, or press ENTER twice. This will confirm your modification of the Category style. You will immediately see a change of typeface in the cells formatted with the Category style, as shown in Figure 2-21.

You can see that using a named style gives you tremendous power over the appearance of your spreadsheet entries. If you take the time to apply the same style to all cells that need to share the same attributes, you can then adjust the appearance of all of those cells at the same time. Bear in mind that a named style does not have to alter all of the properties of a cell, as will be demonstrated in the next section. Quattro Pro provides you with several named styles to get started. These are described in Table 2-2. As you can see, many of the styles only affect the numeric format property of cells. This makes them useful for quickly altering the appearance of numbers, as described next. In Chapter 7, we will return to named styles and user-defined numeric formats.

FIGURE 2-21 The revised Category style applied

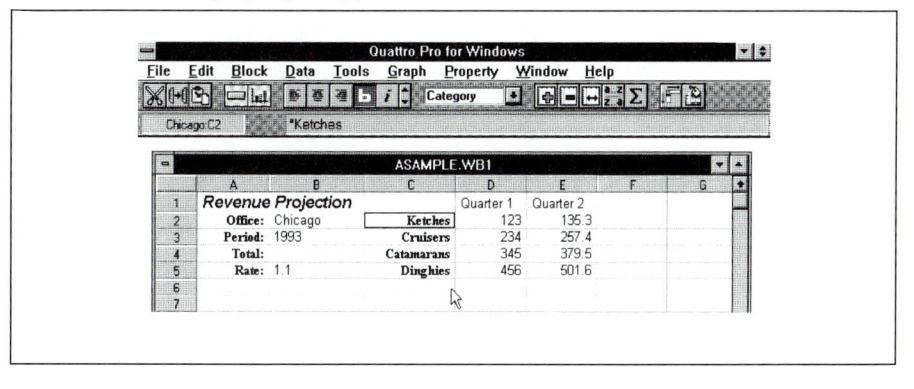

TABLE 2-2 The Default Named Styles

Style	Action
Comma	Only changes numeric format—to Comma, 2 decimal places (also Comma0)
Currency	Only changes numeric format—to Currency, 2 decimal places (also Currency0)
Date	Only changes numeric format—to Date, MMMM DD, YYYY style
Fixed	Only changes numeric format—to Fixed, 2 decimal places
Heading 1	No change to numeric format—changes font to default typeface, 18 points bold
Heading 2	No change to numeric format—changes font to default typeface, 12 points bold
Normal	Changes numeric format to General—changes font to default typeface, 10 points plain
Percent	Only changes numeric format—to Percent, 2 decimal places
Total	No change to numeric format or font—adds double line at top of selected cell or block

Styles and Numeric Formats

The numbers in columns D and E of Figure 2-21 represent revenue dollars—you would like them all to be displayed with dollar signs and two decimal places. You can do this by using the style named Currency. Select D2 through E5 and pull down the list of named styles from the SpeedBar. Select Currency, and the results will appear as in Figure 2-22.

In addition to using named styles to alter the numeric format for part of a spreadsheet, you can also use the Active Block dialog box. Select the cells to be formatted and click the right mouse button or press F12, the Current Object key. The Active Block dialog box will appear. The first item on the list of properties is Numeric Format, as shown in Figure 2-23.

FIGURE 2-22 Applying the Currency style

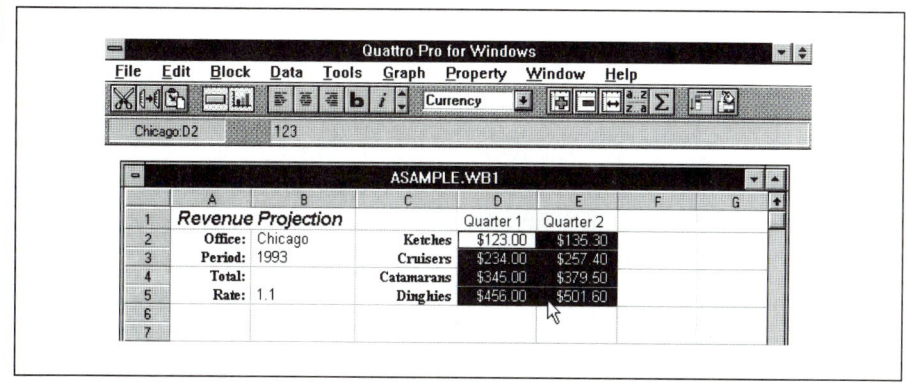

This dialog box allows you to set the number of decimal places from 0 to 15, giving you a wider range of options than those provided by the basic collection of named styles. Using the Active Block dialog box to set a different numeric format from the one currently used in the selected cells will override the named style setting.

Of course, you can always put a specific numeric format into a new named style. Suppose that each of the numbers in columns D and E of the sample stands for a thousand dollars. You would like the numbers to be displayed with just one decimal place, not two. There is no

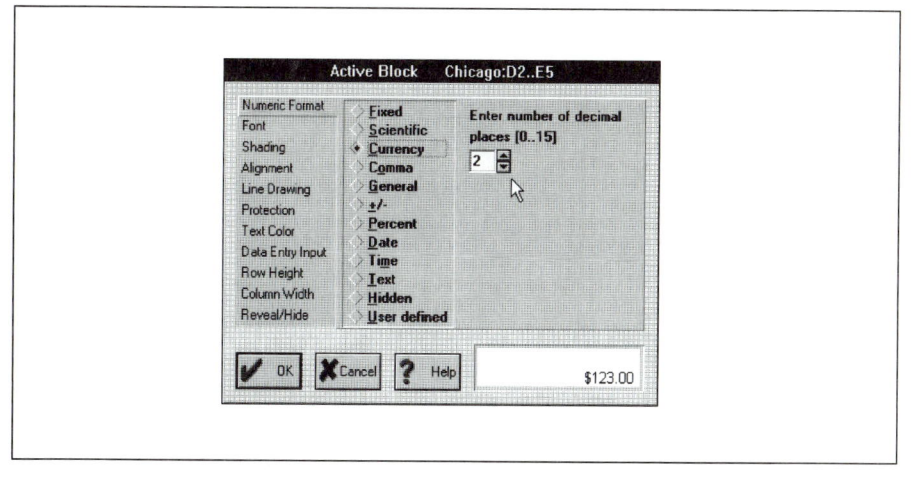

FIGURE 2-23 The Numeric Format setting in the Active Block dialog box

predefined named style that matches this format, so you will create one and call it Revenue.

1. Select cells D2 through E5 and issue the Edit | Define Style command.

2. The Define/Modify Style dialog box appears, as in Figure 2-24. Because the current named style for the selected cells is Currency, the settings for the Currency style are indicated. You can see that the only property that is activated is Format. This means that using the Currency style does not affect other aspects such as Alignment or Shading.

3. Type **Revenue**, and it will replace Currency in the Define Style For field. Click on the Format button (or press ALT-F.)

4. The Numeric Format dialog box appears, and each format has its own key letter. You do not need to change the format from Currency.

5. You do need to alter the decimal place setting. Type 1 over the two in the decimal place field or click the down arrow to the right of it (press TAB to activate the decimal place field).

6. Click on OK or press TAB to select the OK button and press ENTER. This returns you to the Define/Modify Style dialog box. Click OK or press TAB to select the OK button and press ENTER to confirm the definition of the Revenue format.

FIGURE 2-24

The Define/Modify Style dialog box

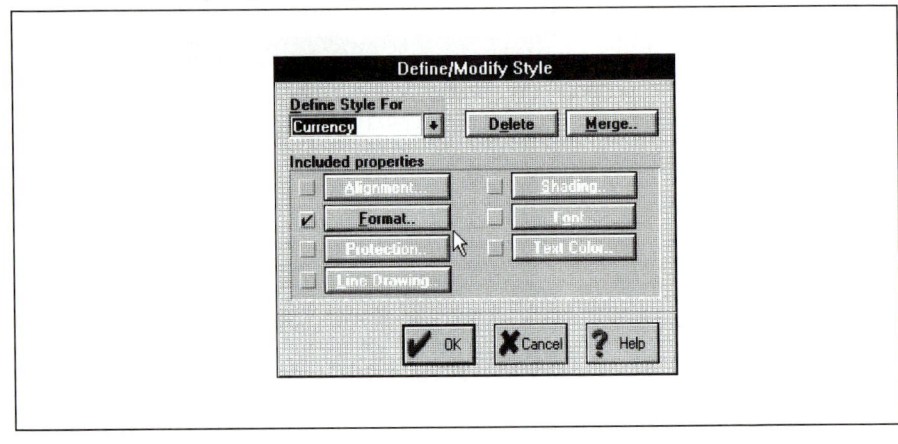

7. The format is not immediately applied to the selected cells, although cells D2 through E5 remain selected. Use the Style Selector in the SpeedBar to select Revenue. The results will appear as shown in Figure 2-25.

The new style, Revenue, can be used whenever you want this particular appearance for numbers. The style does not affect any aspects of cells other than their numeric format. The Revenue style and the Category style created earlier are now available to all pages of the current notebook. If you create a new notebook and want to use a style from a previous notebook, all you have to do is copy one cell formatted with that style from the old notebook to the new one. The style is then added to those available in the new notebook.

Dates and Date Formats

You have already seen that Quattro Pro has a problem with labels that begin with numbers and numbers that contain text. If you take a moment

FIGURE 2-25 The Revenue style applied

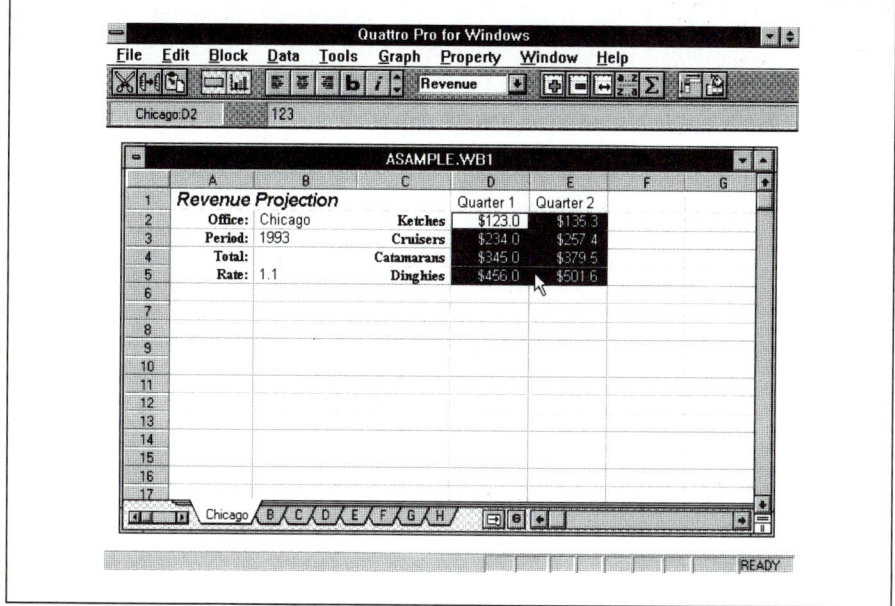

to think about dates you will see that they form a special category of problem entries. For example, if you enter **1/1/93**, Quattro Pro thinks that you want to divide 1 by 1 and then by 93. However, if you enter **1/1/93**, the apostrophe will force Quattro Pro to see what follows as a label. The problem with this approach is that labels have no value. You may want to calculate the number of days between two dates, and you cannot do this if they are both labels. In this section, we look at how you enter dates in Quattro Pro so that the program can treat them as date values rather than labels.

As far as spreadsheet programs are concerned, dates are a special type of number. Quattro Pro is designed to perform math with dates and times. For a computer program to read a date, such as 1/1/93, as something that has value, the date must be converted to a single number. Quattro Pro performs this conversion by calculating the number of days between the date involved and the end of the last century. This is the date's *serial number*. Thus, January 1, 1900, is date number 1. Move ahead 1000 days, and you have September 27, 1902. The date 1/1/93, New Year's Day, 1993, is day number 33,970.

To make Quattro Pro accept 1/1/93 (for example) as a date, press CTRL-SHIFT-D and then type the date. When you press CTRL-SHIFT-D, DATE appears in the lower right of the screen. When you have typed the date, you can press ENTER or click the check mark. Quattro Pro then converts the date to its serial number, but displays it as a date. You can use CTRL-SHIFT-D to enter a date in any of the formats shown in Figure 2-26. If you use the *DD-MMM* format, Quattro Pro calculates the serial number based on the current year. The *MMM-YY* format assumes you mean the first day of the indicated month.

As you can see from Figure 2-26, the formats that are listed in the spreadsheet are the same as the ones presented by Quattro Pro when you choose Date in the Numeric Format property settings dialog box. After you have entered a date with CTRL-SHIFT-D, you can change its appearance by applying any of the Date formats. Bear in mind that the first and fourth formats may produce a date that is too wide for the default column width. Also note that dates entered with CTRL-SHIFT-D are automatically aligned at the right of the cell. The dates shown in Figure 2-26 were centered for purposes of illustration. For more information about dates and times and the ways they can be used in calculations, see Chapter 5.

FIGURE 2-26 The date entry formats

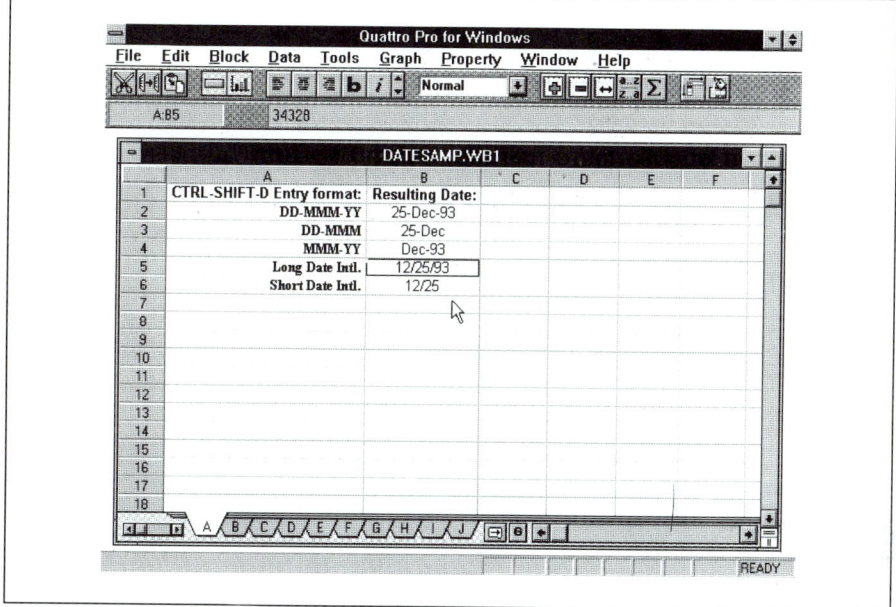

Spreadsheet Editing

One of the great advantages an electronic spreadsheet holds over pencil and paper is the ability to copy and rearrange cells. In this section, you will begin to learn how to copy and move cells when building a spreadsheet model.

Copy and Paste

Earlier it was pointed out that the formula in E2, 1.1*D2, actually means 1.1 times the cell to the left. You saw that if that formula is copied from E2 to E3, Quattro Pro changes the cell reference so that the formula in E3 means the same thing, 1.1 times the cell to the left. Copy the formula from E3 to E4 and Quattro Pro changes it, *relative* to its new location, and the copy reads 1.1*D4. To test this feature, copy the formula from E2 to F2 to begin calculating the third quarter revenue:

1. Select E2 and do one of the following: select Copy from the Edit menu (Edit | Copy); press CTRL-INS, which is the copy shortcut key; or click on the Copy button in the SpeedBar (the second button from the left). This places a copy of cell E2 in the Windows Clipboard.

2. Select F2 and do one of the following: select Paste from the Edit menu; press SHIFT-INS, which is the paste shortcut key; or click on the Paste button in the SpeedBar (the third button from the left). This places a copy of the Windows Clipboard in cell F2.

Observe the formula in F2, which is 1.1*E2. In other words, cell F2 is 1.1 times the cell to the left, preserving the meaning of the original formula and replicating it relative to the new location. This ability to work with *relative cell references* and copy formulas is a great help in building spreadsheet models. Also note that the display format of the copied cell was reproduced in F2, including the style setting.

Now you can complete the four quarters' worth of revenue figures with a single command. Select cells E2 through G5 and issue the Paste command using one of the three techniques described in step 2 above. The result is eight copies of the cell E2, as shown in Figure 2-27. As you can see, the Paste command gives you one or more copies of the last item that was copied to the Windows Clipboard. Note that Figure 2-27 also shows two new column headings, which you can create like this:

1. Select E1 and issue the Copy command.

2. Select F1 and G1 and issue the Paste command.

3. Edit F1 to read **Quarter 3**.

4. Edit G1 to read **Quarter 4**.

5. Since the new entries may be wider than the notebook window, select C2 through G5 and click the Fit button on the SpeedBar (the one next to the arrow in Figure 2-27). This adjusts the columns to fit the contents of the selected cells. Now select A2 through B5 and click on the Fit button again. Your model should now look like the one shown in Figure 2-27.

Note that the Paste command remembers the last items you copied and also makes an interesting assumption. It gives you as many copies

FIGURE 2-27 The effects of Copy and Paste

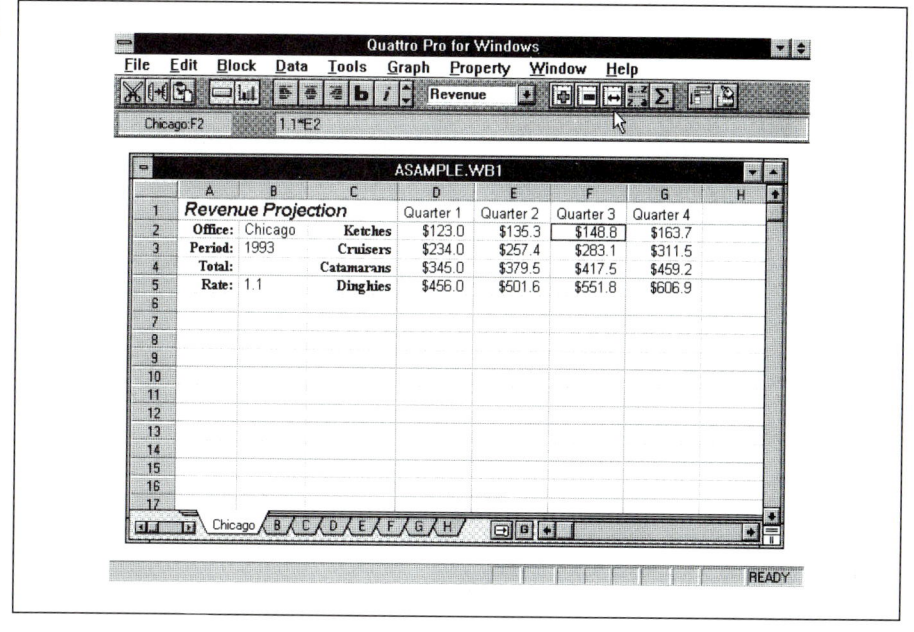

of the cell being copied as will fit in the group of cells you selected before issuing the Paste command. This is only true if the item being copied is a single cell. If you want to copy several cells, the Paste command makes another interesting assumption. For example, suppose you want to copy the entire model, from A1 through G5, to page B of the notebook (the copied cells will form the basis for a model of projected revenue in the Miami office). Follow these steps to perform the copy:

1. Select A1 through G5 and issue the Copy command.

2. Now click on the page tab marked B or press CTRL-PGDN to make B the active page. Cell B:A1 will be the current cell.

3. Issue the Paste command. The result is a complete copy of cells A1 through G5. It pasted in the whole block of copied cells even though you only selected a single cell in the target location.

4. Now select cell B2 on page B and enter **Miami** to replace Chicago, as shown in the background of Figure 2-28.

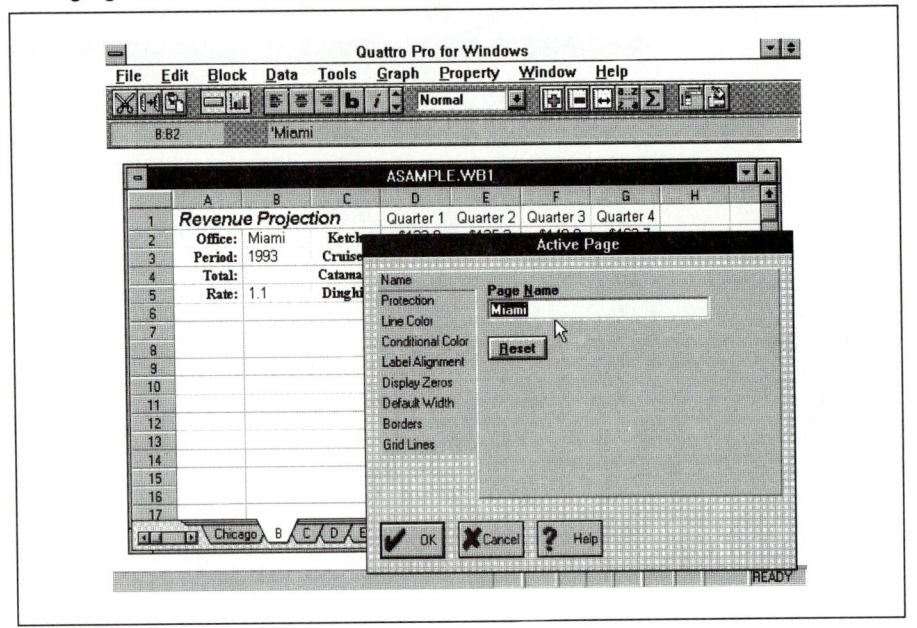

FIGURE 2-28 Changing the name of the second page of the notebook

5. Finally, right click on the page B tab and change the Page Name setting to Miami, as is being done in Figure 2-28 (if you are using the keyboard issue the Property | Active Page command). Click OK or press ENTER to complete the change.

You have very quickly created a second page in the sample spreadsheet notebook using a single copy/paste operation. The only difference between the two copies is that the column widths are not duplicated on page B (this will be dealt with later). You have just seen what happens when the source of your copy is more than one cell (such as A1 through G5) and you select a single cell as the destination for the Paste command (A1). In effect, Quattro Pro assumes that the destination cell is the top left cell in a block of cells equal in size and shape to the source.

In most cases, this is a helpful assumption as it saves you having to select a destination that exactly matches the source. However, you should be aware that Paste does not check that the cells to the right and below the destination cells are empty. This means that your paste operation can wipe out existing cell entries with the copied data. For example, if there had been previous entries in cells B2 or G5 of page B, they would have been replaced by the copied cells. Also bear in mind that if you have copied more than one cell, the destination for the paste must either be a single cell, as in the above example, or a group of cells that exactly matches the source in size and shape.

Paste Special

So far, you have seen Quattro Pro copy both the contents of a cell and its format. At times you may need to copy one or the other. For example, suppose you want to copy the formatting of the title in A1 to another cell. After selecting A1, you issue the Copy command. Then you select the cell to which you want to apply the formatting and issue the Edit | Paste Special command. This produces a dialog box like the one shown in Figure 2-29. To paste the formatting, check Properties and uncheck Contents. If you want to copy the cell contents without the formatting, then you would check Contents and uncheck Properties.

If you check Contents, you have a choice between Formulas or Values only. If you select Formulas, any formulas that you are copying will be preserved. The Values only option converts any formulas being copied to their results. Suppose you had finalized the revenue projections in the sample model and wanted to replace the calculations with simple numeric values. You would select cells E2 through G5, copy them, select E2, and use Edit | Paste Special with the Values only option. This would replace the formulas in E2 through G5 with values. Note that formulas take up more space in memory than values, so you can conserve memory

FIGURE 2-29 The Edit | Paste Special dialog box

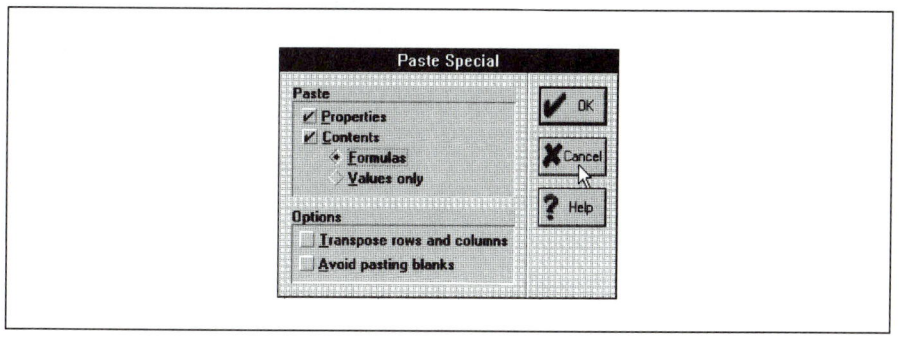

by converting formulas to values. Do not convert the formulas in the sample model, however, as they are not yet complete.

Clear Contents

Earlier you saw that the Edit | Clear command removes the contents of the currently selected cell or cells. It is important to remember that Clear also removes formatting from cells and returns the style setting to Normal. This can be inconvenient at times, so Quattro Pro offers the Edit | Clear Contents command. As the name suggests, this command removes the contents of the currently selected cell or cells, but does not alter their style or formatting. Use the DEL key as a shortcut for the Edit | Clear Contents command.

Cut and Paste

There are times when you want to rearrange spreadsheet entries. One way to do this is use the cut-and-paste technique. Just like the Edit | Copy command, the Edit | Cut command places a copy of the currently selected cell or cells in the Windows Clipboard. However, Cut also removes the contents *and* formatting of the selected cell(s), just as though you had used the Edit | Clear command. This means that you can take out a section of the spreadsheet with Cut and then, if you want to, place it back in a different location. Suppose that you want to see what the table on the Chicago page of the notebook would look like moved down the page. Here is how you would handle the job with Cut and Paste.

1. Select the Chicago page and select cells C1 through G5.
2. Issue the Edit | Cut command (shortcut keystroke: SHIFT-DEL).
3. Select B8 and issue the Edit | Paste command (shortcut keystroke: SHIFT-INS). The table is relocated in B8 through F12.

Note that the formulas in the table are all translated relative to their new location. The formula in E2 that read 1.1*D2 is now located in D9 and reads 1.1*C9. At this point, you decide that the table looked better where it was, so you issue the Edit | Undo command, or use the drag-and-drop technique to move the table back to its original location. Drag-and-drop is basically a visual way to cut and paste.

Both drag-and-drop and the Edit commands work with rectangular blocks of cells. These are referred to as "simple blocks." It is also possible to group noncontiguous cells together as "compound blocks." However, to copy or move such blocks you need the Copy and Move commands on the Block menu, described in the next chapter. You cannot use drag-and-drop or the Edit commands with compound blocks. For more on the distinction between simple and compound blocks, see the next section.

Using Formulas

It is not hard to see that formulas are where much of the power of a spreadsheet lies. Whether you are simply adding cells together or calculating internal rate of return on an investment, the ability to establish a relationship between cells gives you tremendous number-crunching ability. The built-in formulas (functions, or @functions), such as the one used to calculate a loan payment in Chapter 1, are discussed in depth in Chapter 4. In this section, you will create column and row totals and try out the SpeedSum button.

Formulas and Blocks

In the sample model, you want to total up the revenue for the first quarter and place the answer in D6. You might be tempted to enter the formula D2+D3+D4+D5. This is a good effort, but Quattro Pro would reject it as a formula because it begins with D. Because this is a letter, Quattro Pro reads the entry as a label. A better effort is **+D2+D3+D4+D5**. This is accepted as a formula because it begins with a plus sign (+), which is a value indicator. The plus sign is very handy when you have to enter a formula that consists solely of cell references. When you entered the growth formula **1.1*E2**, you did not need to precede it with a plus sign because the first character was 1, a value indicator. However, to start with the cell reference, you would have had to enter **+E2*1.1** as the formula.

Although the formula +D2+D3+D4+D5 gives the correct total for the revenue in the first quarter, there is another method of adding these items. If you consider these cells to be part of a group, or block, you can apply a function that sums the contents of the block. The function that does this is @SUM. Like the other Quattro Pro functions, the @SUM function consists of the @ sign followed by the function name, SUM, followed by parentheses that contain the function *argument.* These functions are also called *@functions*. The argument used by @SUM is the block of cells to which the function is applied. Since all of the Quattro Pro functions begin with @, they can be referred to by their name, for example, SUM.

Quattro Pro defines a *block* of cells as a rectangular group of cells on which you perform the same operation or command. You can refer to a block of cells by stating two diagonal coordinates. If you write this down, it is normal to separate the two cells with a pair of dots. Thus, you would refer to the block of cells from A1 through G5 as A1..G5. The diagram in Figure 2-30 shows what is considered to be a block, and what is not. The block of cells D2 through D5 is written as D2..D5. The correct formula for cell D6 of the sample model is thus @SUM(D2..D5).

Note that in some situations, Quattro Pro allows you to work with compound blocks. These are also referred to as *noncontiguous blocks*. For example, the L-shaped group of cells in Figure 2-30 is a compound block—it can be selected and formatted as a single group or used as the argument in a SUM function. However, for compound blocks to be described in formulas they are broken down into a series of simple blocks that are rectangular. These simple blocks are connected in a function argument with commas. Thus, the L-shaped block in Figure 2-30 could be stated as G10..G21,H20..I21. To sum the contents of the L-shaped block, you could use this formula:

@SUM(G10..G21,H20..I21)

The L-shaped block might also be stated as G10..G19,G20..I21. The exact choice of coordinates depends on the sequence in which the parts of the compound block were selected. You select a compound block by highlighting a series of simple blocks with your mouse while holding down the CTRL key. For example, to select the L-shaped block in Figure 2-30, you would follow this procedure:

1. Select the top left cell of the first simple block, in this case G10.

2. Press CTRL and the left mouse button while you drag the mouse pointer to the bottom right cell, in this case G21, and release CTRL. You have now selected G10..G21.

3. Press CTRL again and hold it down while you point to the top left cell of the second part of the block, H20, and drag to the bottom right cell, I21.

4. Release CTRL and the left mouse button, and you have added H20..I21 to the compound block.

When the second block is selected, you can repeat steps 3 and 4 to add other groups of cells if you want. The important point to note is that you hold down CTRL before you do the cell selecting. This is to avoid confusion with drag-and-drop copying, in which you select a group of cells and *then* hold down CTRL as you point to the selection and drag a

FIGURE 2-30 Examples of valid blocks (note that noncontiguous blocks are possible)

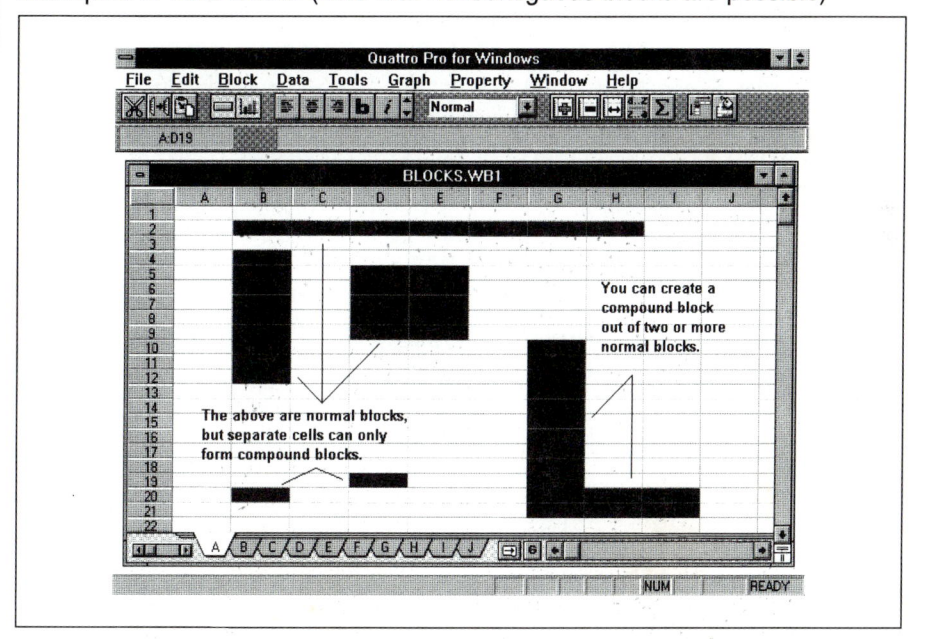

copy to another part of the spreadsheet. You cannot use drag-and-drop to copy or move a compound block. Instead, you use the Block | Copy and Block | Move commands, described in the next chapter.

There are several ways of creating formulas in Quattro Pro. The most direct method is to type the formula:

1. Move the cell selector to D6.
2. Type **@SUM(D2.D5)**, noting that you only need to type one period.
3. Press ENTER and notice from the input line that Quattro Pro records this as @SUM(D2..D5), adding an extra period to make the block easier to see. The correct answer displayed in the spreadsheet is 1158. You will format this in a moment.

Instead of typing formulas, you can use the pointing method. This works either with keystrokes or with the mouse. First, here's the keystroke method:

1. Select the cell that is to contain the formula, in this case E6.
2. Type **@SUM(** to begin the formula.
3. Press UP ARROW to select E2. Type a period (.) to anchor the block as E2..E2.
4. Press END and then DOWN ARROW to extend the block so that it is E2..E5.
5. Type a closing parenthesis and press ENTER to finish the formula.

Instead of typing the beginning of the formula as just described in step 2, you can use these two steps:

1. Press ALT-F3 to display a list of functions. Press F2 to search for the SUM function. Quattro Pro will prompt you by saying at the bottom of the screen:

   Search for: *

2. Type **S**. Quattro Pro highlights the first function that begins with S. Now type **U**; the highlight moves to SUM. Press ENTER and Quattro Pro displays @SUM(on the edit line.

Instead of typing formulas, you also can use the mouse. Here is how to create the total in F6 using the mouse method:

1. Select the cell that is to contain the formula, F6.

2. Click on the edit line to activate EDIT mode and click on the @ button on the SpeedBar. Click on the vertical scroll bar to bring the SUM function into view. Highlight SUM and click OK or double-click on SUM. Quattro Pro puts @SUM(on the edit line.

3. Point to cell F2, press the left mouse button and hold it down while you drag down to cell F5, and then release.

4. Type a closing parenthesis and click on the check mark.

Using SpeedSum

If you have tried all of the above techniques, you will have created formulas in cells D6 through F6. If not, create the formulas now. You can create the formula in G6 by copying the formula in F6. Select F6, issue the Copy command (CTRL-INS), then select G6 and issue the Paste command (SHIFT-INS). Alternatively, select F6 and F7, hold down CTRL and the left mouse button and drag a copy to G6. In Figure 2-31, you can see all of the column formulas in place. Note that the zoom factor has been altered, as described in a moment, in order to show more of the spreadsheet. Also note that the block D2..H6 has been selected. This is in preparation for the next step.

So far you have seen several different ways of creating a SUM formula. However, none are as quick as the SpeedSum feature. You can use SpeedSum to create formulas in column H that sum the rows of the table.

1. Select all of the cells to be summed, plus a column of adjacent blank cells, in this case D2..H6, as shown in Figure 2-31.

2. Click on the SpeedSum button, as indicated by the mouse pointer in Figure 2-31.

The results can be seen in Figure 2-32. A set of SUM formulas was automatically created in the blank cells of the selected block. You can use the SpeedSum button with single rows or columns as well as larger blocks. In fact, you could have generated all of the SUM formulas in Figure 2-32 at a single stroke. If you had selected D2..H6 before any SUM formulas had been created in cells D6 through G6, a single click of the SpeedSum button would have produced the result seen in Figure 2-32. You only have to remember to include a blank cell at the bottom of each column and at the right of each row. The blank cells give SpeedSum a place to create the formula.

If you move to the Miami page, last seen in Figure 2-28, you can use SpeedSum to create a full set of column and row totals (click on the Miami page tab or press CTRL-PGDN to move there from the Chicago page). Select D2..H6, as shown in Figure 2-33, and click the SpeedSum button.

FIGURE 2-31 Completed column formulas and cells selected for SpeedSum

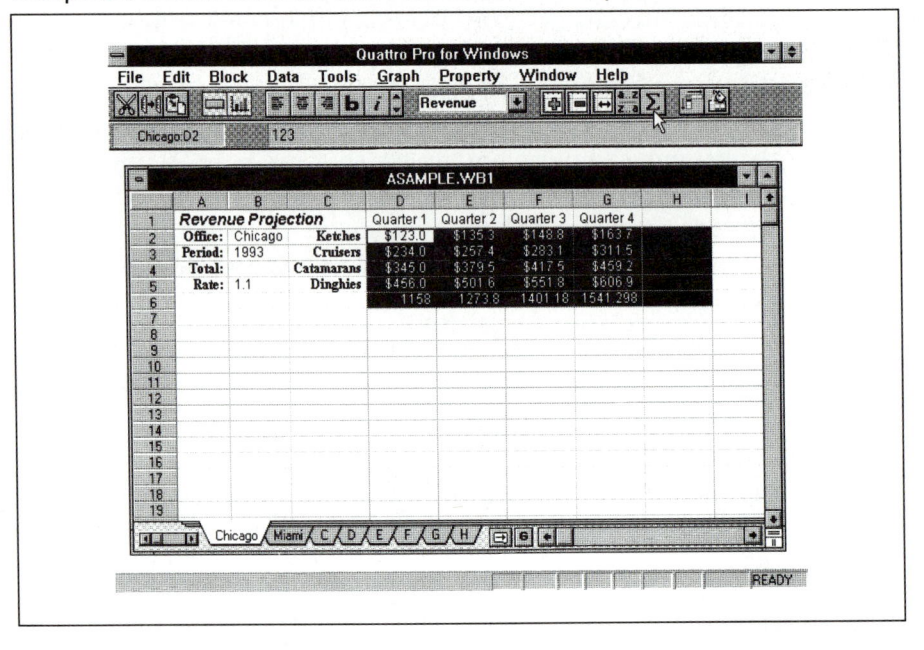

Chapter 2: Building Spreadsheet Models

FIGURE 2-32 Using SpeedSum

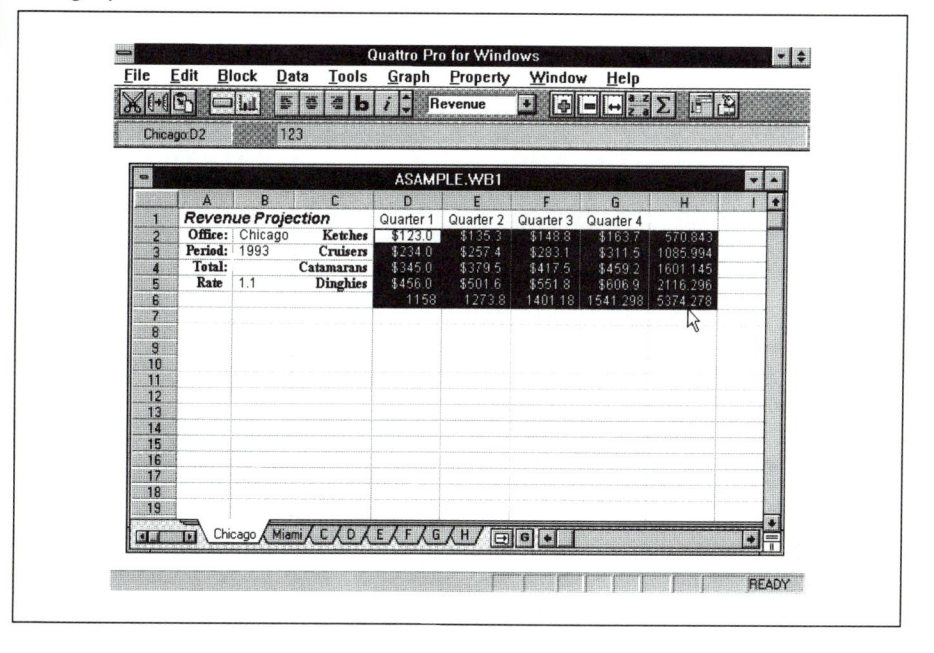

FIGURE 2-33 Preparing to SpeedSum columns and rows on the Miami page

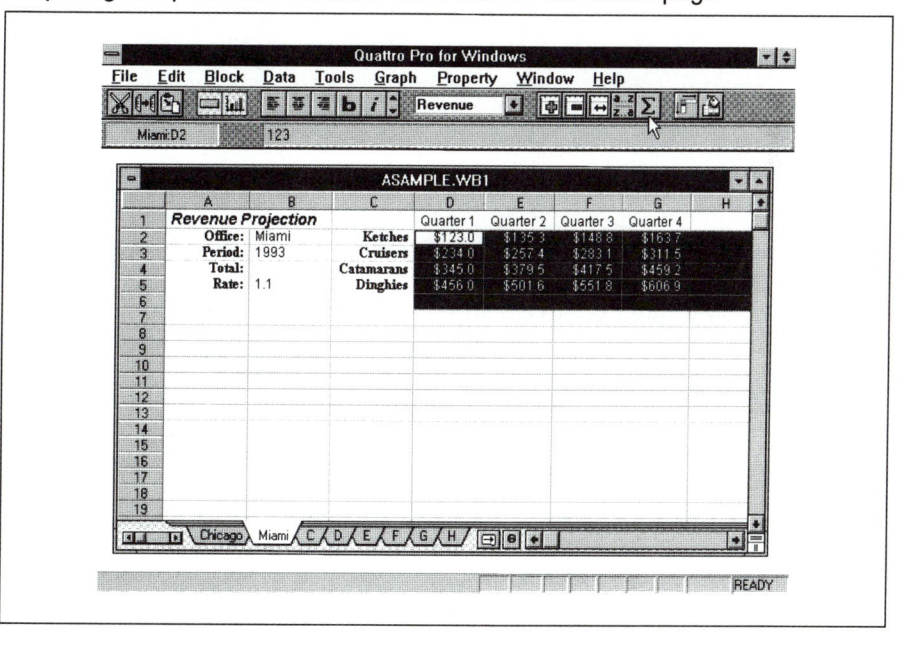

The result is a complete set of sum formulas. As you will see in the next section, the SpeedSum button can do even more impressive calculations when you are consolidating multiple spreadsheets in a Quattro Pro notebook. However, amazing though the SpeedSum feature is, it does not affect the formatting of cells. The SUM results in both the Chicago and Miami pages of the model still need to be styled to match the rest of the table. Also, as you can see from Figure 2-33, the column widths need to be adjusted on the Miami page. Using the Group mode, described next, Quattro Pro allows you to format several pages of a notebook at once. You can even perform math and make entries across several pages at the same time.

Group Work

The example in this chapter has shown you how a spreadsheet simplifies the task of duplicating repetitious calculations from one column to another and from one row to another. You have also seen that a spreadsheet notebook makes it easy to duplicate similar models. For example, if you are projecting revenue for several sales offices that all sell the same products, projections for all of the offices can be created very quickly. Each office can have its own page, but all of the information is stored in the same file. In a moment you will see how easy it is to format several pages at the same time, but first we will look at how you consolidate information from a group of pages.

Temporary Groupings

The yacht company that is the subject of the sample model has another office, in Seattle. You can use Edit commands to create a page for the Seattle office and a fourth page that will be used to consolidate figures from the three offices. Begin by selecting the Miami page of the sample notebook. You can do this by clicking on its tab at the bottom of the page. If you are currently viewing the Chicago page, you can move to the Miami page by pressing CTRL-PGDN. Having selected the Miami page, follow these instructions to create the page for the Seattle office:

Chapter 2: Building Spreadsheet Models 111

1. Select all of the cells being used on the Miami page, A1 through H6.

> **Note** Here is a quick way to select all of the active cells in a spreadsheet: press HOME, then hold down SHIFT and press END followed by HOME.

2. Issue the <u>E</u>dit | <u>C</u>opy command (keyboard shortcut: CTRL-INS). This places a copy of the selected cells in the Windows Clipboard.

3. You will now create a temporary group of pages on pages C and D. Select cell A1 on page C. Then hold down the SHIFT key while selecting page D (you can use CTRL-PGDN to do this). Note the line that appears under the two page letters' tabs.

4. When two or more pages are grouped like this and you paste the contents of the Clipboard, they are duplicated on all of the pages. Issue the <u>P</u>aste command (keyboard shortcut: SHIFT-INS). The immediate results can be seen in Figure 2-34.

5. Now press CTRL-PGUP to view page C. Change Miami in B2 so that it reads **Seattle**. Change the rate in B6 to read **1.2** Enter new first quarter values. Cell D2 is **89**, D3 is **78**, D4 is **67**, and D5 is **56**.

FIGURE 2-34 The model pasted into the temporary grouping of pages C and D

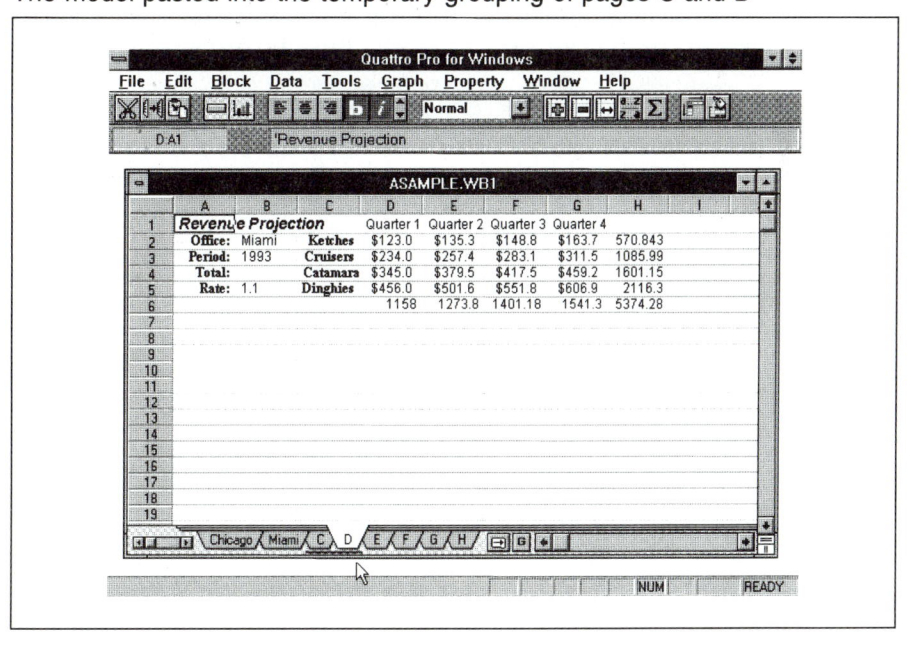

6. Change the page name to **Seattle** using the Page Name field on the Property | Active Page dialog box (you can right-click on the page tab to access the Active Page dialog box). The effects of this and the other changes are shown in Figure 2-35.

At this point, you have three offices set up, each with its own page. Now you need to turn page D into the Total page that will consolidate the figures from the three other pages. You can follow these steps, which include a powerful use of the SpeedSum button:

1. Use CTRL-PGDN to move back to page D. Change the page name to **Total** using the Active Page dialog box.

2. Change cell B2 to read **All**. Select cells A5..B5 and press DEL to clear their contents (you can also use the Edit | Clear Contents command).

3. Now select cells D2..H6 of the Total page and press DEL. This clears the cells ready for the consolidated totals that you are about to create with the SpeedSum button.

FIGURE 2-35 Three office pages set up

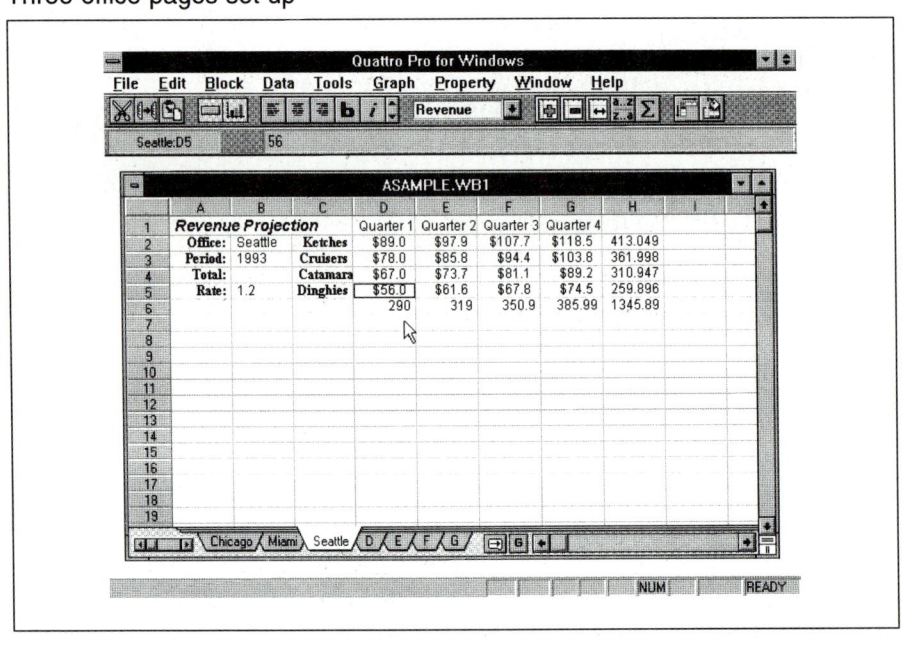

Chapter 2: Building Spreadsheet Models

Note You can use the compound block feature to delete both A5..B5 and D2..H6 in one step. Select A5..B5, and hold down CTRL while you select D2..H6. You can now press DEL to clear the contents of both groups of cells.

4. Move to the Chicago page and select cells D2..H6. This constitutes all of the numeric data that you want summed on the Totals page.

5. Hold down SHIFT and select the Totals page (you can press CTRL-PGDN three times). Your screen should appear as in Figure 2-36. Note the black line beneath the tabs connecting the pages in a temporary group. Now click the SpeedSum button.

The results can be seen in Figure 2-37. Do not worry about the asterisks that are displayed in some cells. This simply indicates that the contents are too wide for the current column width, which will be adjusted in a moment. The important thing to notice is the formula in D2, which reads

@SUM(Chicago..Seattle:D2)

FIGURE 2-36 Preparing the Totals page

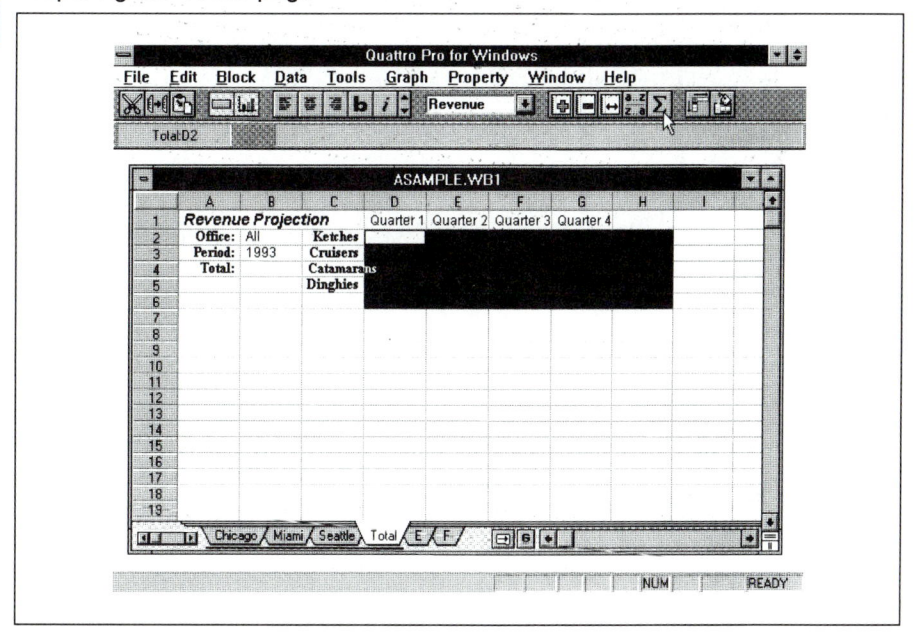

FIGURE 2-37 Totals pasted into the Totals page

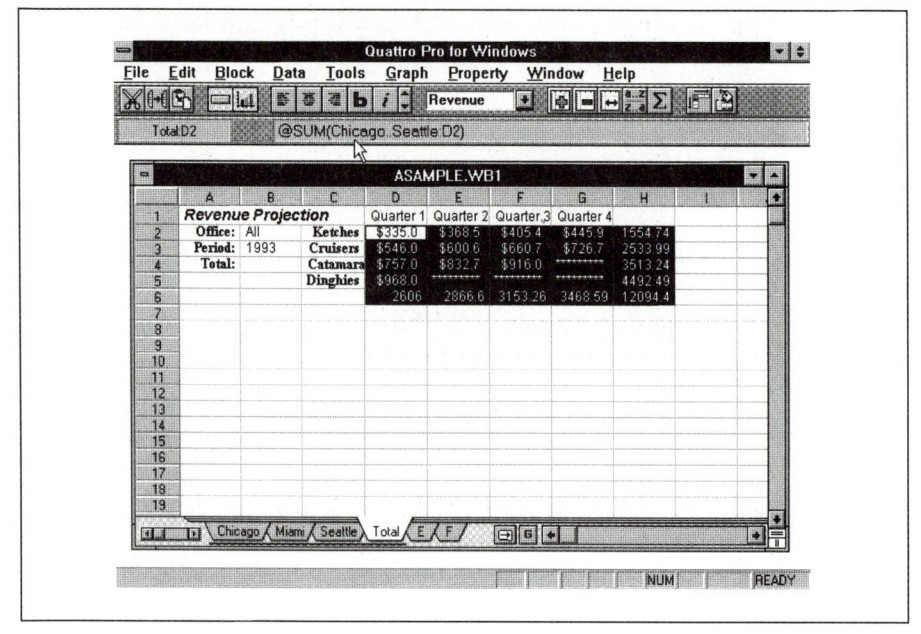

You can see that SpeedSum is intelligent enough to know that you want D2 of the Totals page to sum the contents of D2 in each of the three other pages in the group. Each of the values in D2 through H6 is a similar formula, summing across multiple pages.

Of course, you can create SUM formulas of this type yourself, using the first and last page names followed by a colon and then the cell or cells you want summed. For example, an alternative formula in H6 of the Total page would be

@SUM(Chicago..Seattle:D2..G6)

This formula sums D2..G6 on all three pages from Chicago to Seattle. There is no limit on the number of pages you can include in a multipage block, but the pages must be contiguous within a single block. You would sum cell D2 in pages F through H and K through M like this:

@SUM(F..H:D2,K..M:D2.

Named Groups

In the above steps, you saw the way that the SHIFT key is used to create a temporary group of pages. After you have created a temporary group, any movement to another page causes Quattro Pro to abandon the group. There are times when you want a group to be more permanent. For example, if you define a group and give it a name you can use the *Group mode*, which allows simultaneous formatting of all pages in the group. To see how this works, you can place the four revenue projection pages in a group. Begin by selecting all of the pages as a temporary group (select Chicago, then hold down SHIFT while you select Total). Now issue the Tools | Define Group command. You will see a dialog box like the one shown in Figure 2-38. You can now type the **Company** in the Group Name field.

Note that a *named group* is defined by the first and last pages in the group. In this case, the first and last pages are already entered for you—they were selected when you issued the command. However, you can issue the command from any page and create a group by entering

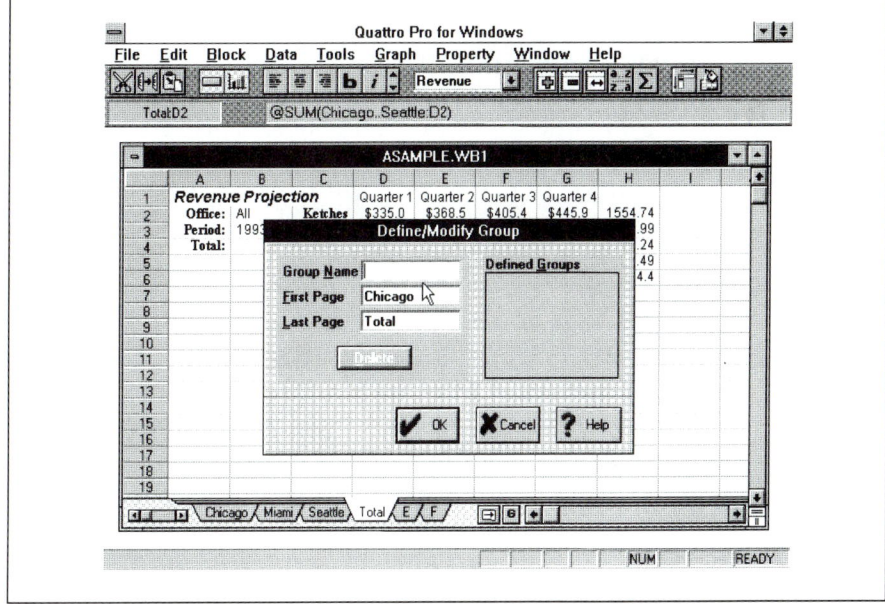

FIGURE 2-38 Giving a new permanent group of pages a name

the page names in the First Page and Last Page fields. The same dialog box also allows you to delete group names that are no longer required.

Having typed a name for the group, you can use the OK button to confirm it and return to the spreadsheet. The advantage of naming the group is that you can activate the Group mode (click on the Group Mode icon, which features a letter G and is located to the right of the notebook page tabs). When you activate Group mode, the G is underlined. At the same time, a line is drawn to connect the pages of the group. This looks like the line that appears when you create a temporary group, but it is displayed in a different color. When Group mode is activated, many changes that you make in one page of the group will be duplicated in the other pages of the group, saving a lot of time and effort.

To see Group mode in action, follow these steps after selecting the Total page and turning on the Group mode by clicking on the G icon:

1. Select D1..H6 and apply the Revenue style from the Style Selector in the SpeedBar. This will format the column and row totals.

2. With D2..H6 still selected, click the Fit button to adjust the column widths (you also can use the Active Block property settings, choosing Column Width, and then Auto Width).

3. Now select A2..C5 and use the Fit button again.

You can now move to the Chicago page using the CTRL-PGUP key and admire your work. Note that the style changes have been made throughout the group (the sum totals were not formatted before and the columns were not adjusted properly).

Group Entries

When you are operating in Group mode, you can enter data on one page of the group and have the same data simultaneously entered in the same cell of all the other pages of the group. If you select H1 of the current spreadsheet page, type **Year**, and press ENTER, you only make a difference to cell H1 of the current page, regardless of whether Group mode is activated. However, if Group mode is on and you select H1, type **Year**, and then press CTRL-ENTER, it will be entered in cell H1 of all pages of the group. This ability to make the same entry across multiple pages can save you a lot of time and effort, as you will see in these steps to update the model:

1. Make sure that Group mode is on, select H1, and type **Year**. Now press CTRL-ENTER. Click on the Center button in the SpeedBar to center this entry.

2. Select C6, type **All Models**, and press CTRL-ENTER.

3. Select the Category style from the style list in the SpeedBar.

4. In B4, type **+H6** and press CTRL-ENTER. This pulls the total figure from the table into B4.

5. Select the Revenue style for B4. You might see asterisks in the cell after you do this; if so, click on the Fit button to adjust the column width.

If you use CTRL-PGDN to move to the Total page, you will see that the above entries have been made on each page. The results for the Total page will appear as in Figure 2-39.

FIGURE 2-39 Completed Total page

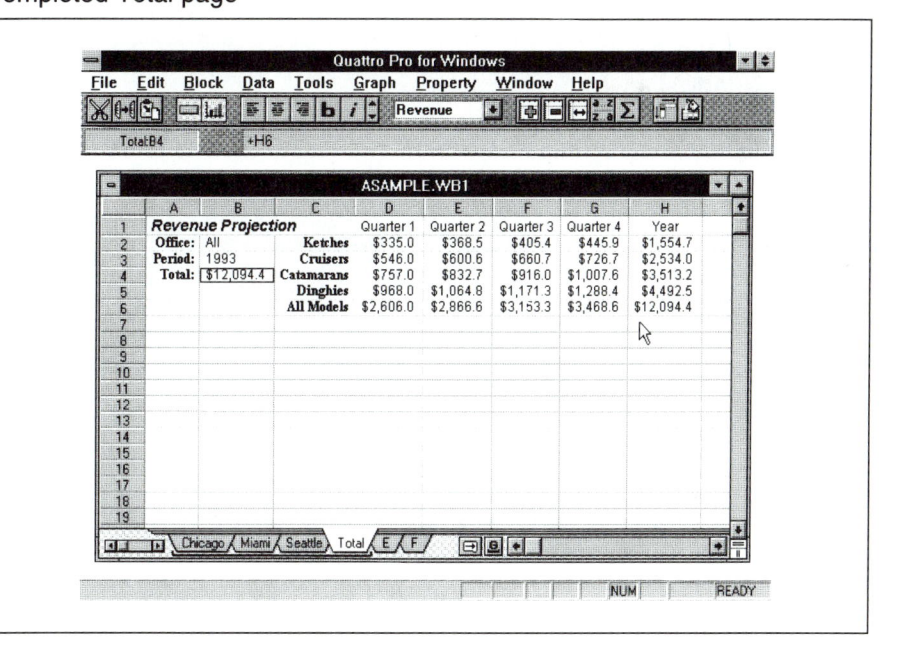

You can now save the updated file using the File | Save command. Alternatively, you can save the latest version of the model in a new file by using the File | Save As command. This command gives you a chance to enter a new name for the file whereas the Save command simply overwrites the previous version of the current file with the new data. For more on file saving, see Chapter 4.

Zooming Off

Finally, you may want to shrink or enlarge your view of the notebook in order to see more of your worksheet or to look more closely at something. The setting that determines the scale of your notebook view is the *Zoom Factor*, a part of the Active Notebook settings. Right-click on the notebook title or issue the Property | Active Notebook command to call up the Active Notebook dialog box. As you can see from Figure 2-40, the Zoom Factor is the second setting.

The default Zoom Factor is 100 percent. Settings above 100 enlarge the cells, useful for detail work, and settings below 100 shrink them, helpful when you want to get "the big picture." You can type in a percentage or select one of the predefined values from the pop-up list

FIGURE 2-40 Adjusting the Zoom Factor

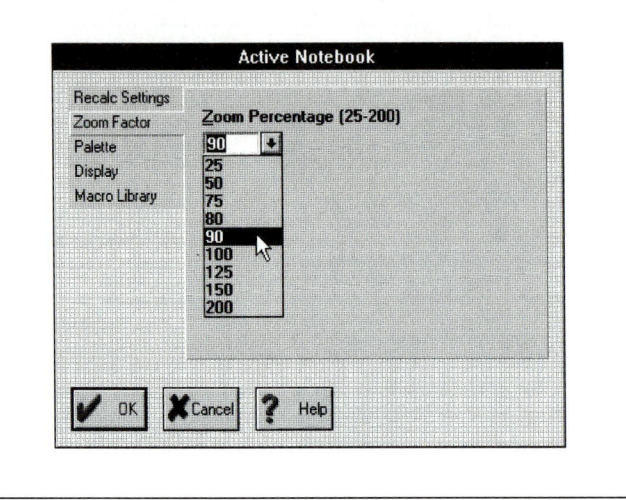

shown in Figure 2-40. The Zoom Factor is a notebook setting. It affects all pages of the current notebook but does not affect other notebooks.

There are other ways of adjusting the Quattro Pro display, which will be dealt with in the next chapter. Also in the next chapter we will look at ways of improving and expanding the sample model using commands from the Block menu, as well as the Search and Replace command from the Edit menu. To learn how to print reports from your spreadsheets, you can turn to Chapter 4.

CHAPTER 3

Blocks and Names

122 Quattro Pro for Windows Inside & Out

This chapter covers a variety of subjects that could be called "intermediate spreadsheet topics," because they build on the basic knowledge about spreadsheet making that you have acquired in Chapters 1 and 2. Now that you have seen how a spreadsheet model is developed and how to work with several pages of a spreadsheet notebook, you are ready to use the block commands and more advanced editing commands, such as Search and Replace and also SpeedFill. We will also look at how naming cell blocks can make them easier to work with. We begin by looking at two problem areas in spreadsheet modeling: absolute cell references and rounding formula results.

Absolutely Accurate

In the last chapter, you saw that the cell references in the copies are altered, relative to the new location, when Quattro Pro copies formulas. The formula in cell E2 of the model in Figure 3-1 is 1.1*D2, which Quattro Pro reads as "1.1 times the cell to the left." When you copy that formula to F2, the copy becomes 1.1*E2 so that it still means the same thing: "1.1

FIGURE 3-1 Formula in E2 of spreadsheet model

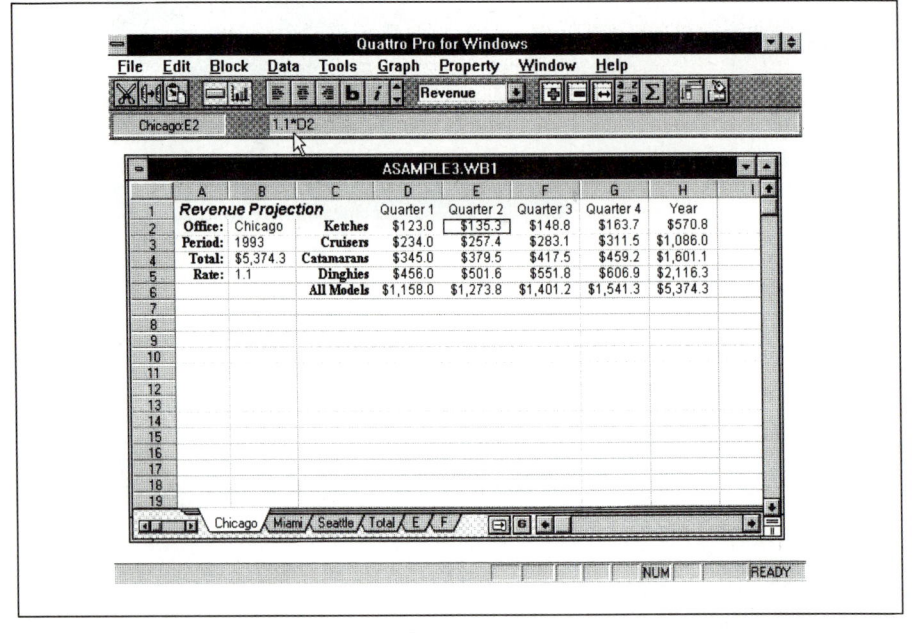

times the cell to the left." Most of the time this method of handling formulas in copies is very useful, allowing you to build extensive models very quickly. However, in this section we look at problems that can arise when Quattro Pro makes relative adjustments to formulas. We also examine the problem of rounding spreadsheet values and problems this can create.

Problems with Relatives

The model in Figure 3-1 shows revenue growing at a rate of 10 percent per quarter. Because the growth rate is stated in B5, you might be tempted to change the formula in E2 from 1.1*D2 to +B5*D2. You could then copy the new formula to all the calculated cells. That way you could simply change the growth factor in B5, and it would be reflected throughout the model.

This sounds good in principle, but remember that the formula +B5*D2, entered in E2, means "multiply the cell to the left by the amount in the cell three down and three to the left." If you copy this formula from E2 to E3, you get +B6*D3, which also means "multiply the cell to the left by the amount in the cell three down and three to the left." However, that cell, B6, is empty, so the result is incorrect. You can see this in Figure 3-2, which shows the result of copying the formula +B5*D2 from cell E2 to E2..G5.

The first lesson to be learned here is that whenever you copy a formula, you should always check the results. If the answers look wrong, move the cell selector to the first cell with a suspicious result and check the contents in the input line. When you think about the formula in Figure 3-2, you can understand why it is wrong. The second lesson is how to prevent this problem. The solution lies in the difference between the *relative* cell references you have used so far and a different type of reference, discussed next.

Absolute Solutions

The solution to the problem of copying relative cell references is to decide which references should not be relative and change them before

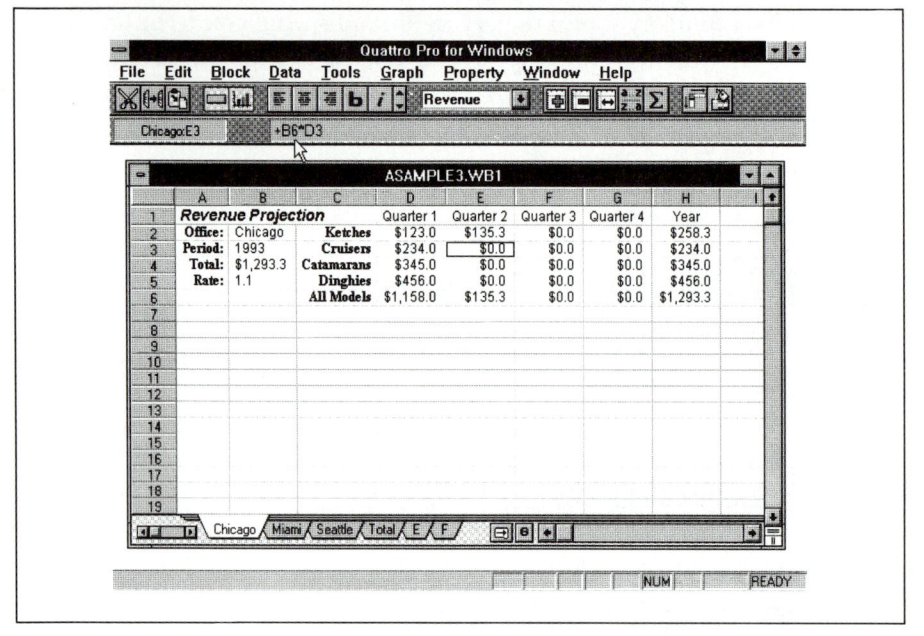

FIGURE 3-2 Relative formula incorrectly placed references the wrong cell

they are copied. In the above example, the formula +B5*D2 refers to two cells. The first cell must not change, regardless of where the formula is copied or moved to. To fix a cell reference so that it does not change during move or copy operations, you make the reference *absolute.* All that is required to make a cell reference absolute is a dollar sign in front of the column letter and the row number. For example, $B$5 fixes the reference so that no matter where it is placed, the formula refers to cell B5. A better formula for E2 of the sample model is thus +$B$5*D2. Wherever you copy this formula, it will read +$B$5 times "the cell to the left."

In the last chapter, you saw that Quattro Pro allows you to create formulas in one page of a notebook that refer to cells in other pages of the same notebook. Strictly speaking, the cell containing the growth rate is not just B5 but Chicago:B5. Bearing this in mind, Quattro Pro allows you to make formulas that are relative to the page as well as to the column and row. If you copy +$B$5*D2 from the Chicago page to the Miami page, the formula will refer to B5 of the Miami page. You might want a formula

Chapter 3: Blocks and Names

to always refer to a specific page, so Quattro Pro allows you to create an *absolute page reference*, for example, +$Chicago:$B$5.

There are two ways to edit a cell reference to make it absolute. You can type in the dollar signs yourself, or you can use the Absolute (Abs) key, which is F4. When you press F4 in EDIT mode, Quattro Pro adds dollar signs to the cell reference, as long as the edit cursor is somewhere within the cell reference. If you keep pressing F4, Quattro Pro will show you all of the possible cell references, as listed in Table 3-1.

In the sample model, you would like the reference to B5 to be absolute with respect to the column and row, but relative as far as the page is concerned. This is how you would go about correcting the problem shown in Figure 3-2:

1. Select cell E2 and press F2, the Edit key, or click on the input line to edit the formula +B5*D2.

2. Place the edit cursor between B and 5 and press F4, the Absolute key. Note that Quattro Pro changes the reference from B5 to $Chicago:$B$5.

TABLE 3-1 Cell References and Their Meanings for Pages, Columns, and Rows

Reference	Page	Column	Row
$Chicago:$B$5	Absolutely Chicago	Column B	Row 5
$Chicago:B$5	Absolutely Chicago	Any column	Row 5
$Chicago:$B5	Absolutely Chicago	Column B	Any row
$Chicago:B5	Absolutely Chicago	Any column	Any row
$B$5	Any page	Column B	Row 5
B$5	Any page	Any column	Row 5
$B5	Any page	Column B	Any row
B5	Any page	Any column	Any row

3. Keep pressing F4 until the formula reads **$B$5*D2**.

4. Press ENTER or click the check button to confirm the new formula. Note that the value in E2 does not change.

5. Issue the Edit | Copy command while E2 is still selected.

6. Select the block E2..G5 and issue the Edit | Paste command.

7. The existing formulas are replaced with the new formula, which has an absolute reference to B5. The results are more reasonable.

You can test the formula by entering a new growth rate of **1.2** in B5. The results can be seen in Figure 3-3, where the cell E3 is selected to show how the corrected formula looks when copied. Note that all of the cells from E2 through H6 (that depend on B5) change when the value in B5 is altered.

You can see that there are advantages to building models in this way, with the growth factor or other assumptions placed in separate cells. You can now adjust the growth factor by altering one cell rather than copying a new formula each time you want to see the effect of a different rate. An

FIGURE 3-3 Improved results with an absolute reference

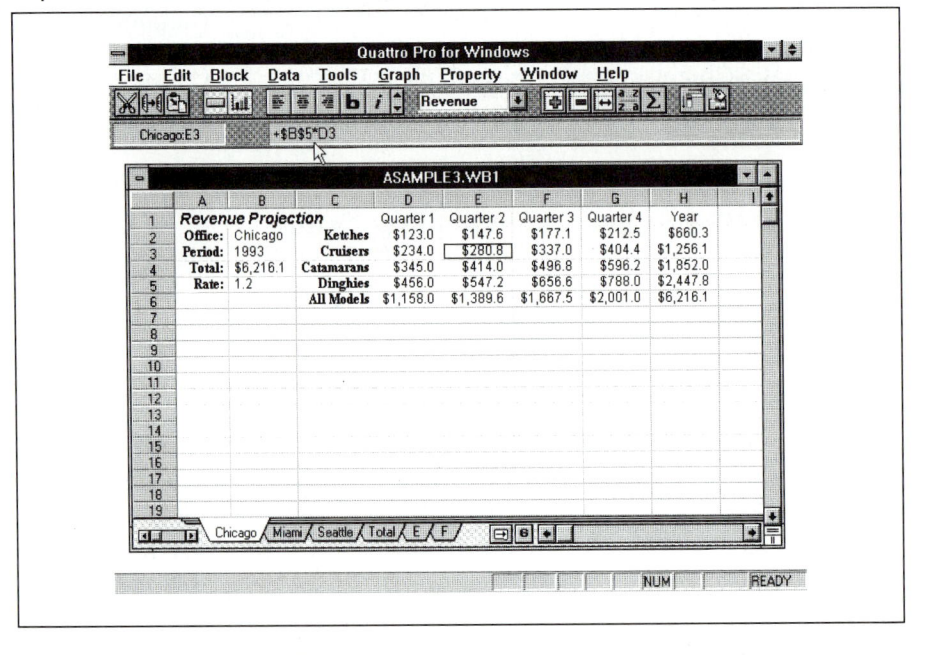

absolute reference is useful whenever you are writing formulas that are going to be copied but still need to refer to the same specific cell or block of cells from their new locations.

Unlike many other spreadsheet programs, however, Quattro Pro also provides a method of copying formulas without adjusting cell references relative to the new location. This involves the Block | Copy command, described later in this chapter, after we have examined another problem with Quattro Pro formulas.

Note The Abs key, F4, can be used when you are building formulas by the pointing method as well as when you are editing a formula.

Rounding Out

If you take a close look at the model in Figure 3-3, you can see that the totals in cells G6 and H6 do not seem to add up. Once again there is a lesson to be learned—always check your spreadsheet work! Presenting this particular spreadsheet to the boss could be embarrassing, especially if you can't explain why the totals are "off."

The reason for the anomaly in Figure 3-3 is the rounding operation that Quattro Pro performs in order to display values in a numeric format that has only one decimal place. A numeric format setting rounds numbers for the purpose of display, but Quattro Pro actually retains the full value of each calculation to 15 decimal places. You can see this very clearly if you change the numeric format back to General (select D2 through H6, press F12 or right-click on the cells to access the Active Block settings, and then change Numeric Format to General). The results are shown in Figure 3-4. The numbers now visible do add up correctly, even though they are rather difficult to read due to the varying number of decimal places displayed by the General format (you can use Edit | Undo Property Set to return the cells to the Revenue style and its single decimal place Currency format).

The solution to the apparent error introduced by the formatting is to use the ROUND function. This will round the results of a calculation to the number of decimal places you specify, thus preventing the accumulation of minor fractions like those that cause the apparent inaccuracies in Figure 3-3. When the results of a formula need to be rounded, make

FIGURE 3-4 General format reveals decimal places

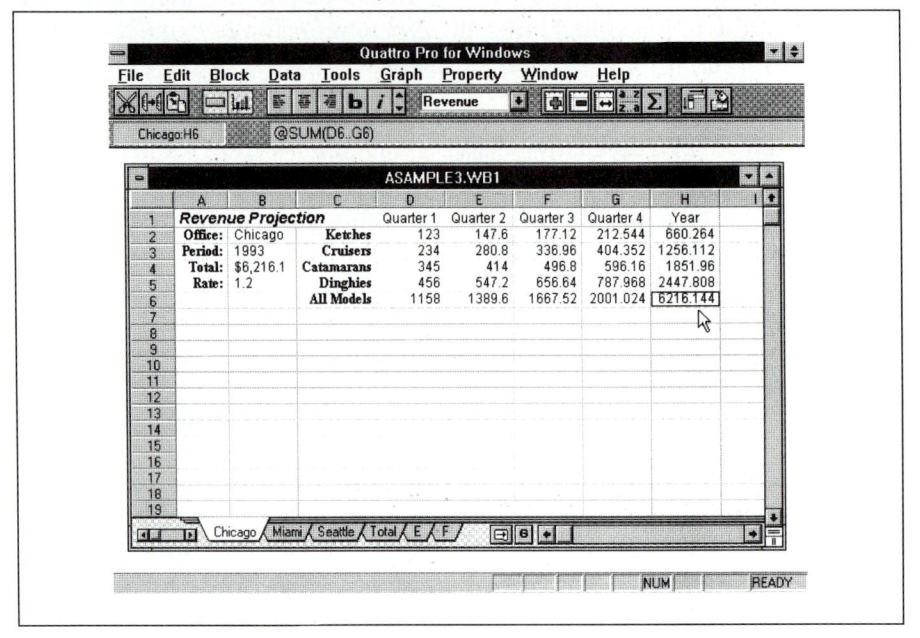

the formula the first argument of the ROUND function. The second argument is the number of decimal places. Thus, the formula in E2 of the sample model, rounded to one decimal place, would look like this:

@ROUND($B$5*D2,1)

You can apply the ROUND function to the sample model by following these steps:

1. Select cell E2 and either press F2 or click on the input line to enter EDIT mode.

2. Press HOME to move the edit cursor to the beginning of the formula. Type **@ROUND(** and press END to move the edit cursor to the end of the formula.

3. Type **,1)** to complete the formula and press ENTER.

4. Issue the Copy command from the Edit menu with the cell selector still in E2.

| FIGURE 3-5 | Applying the ROUND function to get correct results |

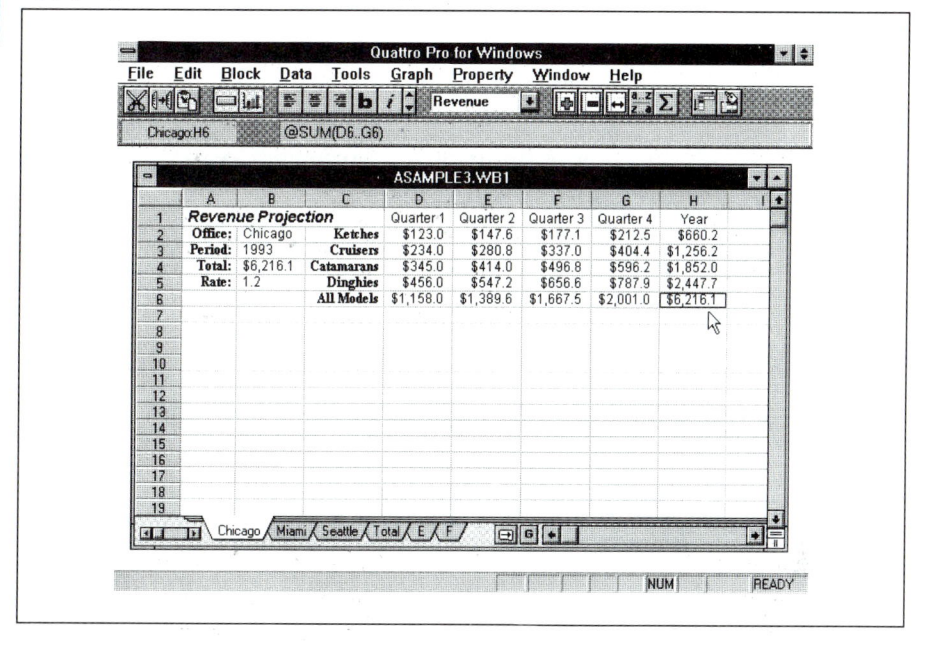

![Figure 3-5: Quattro Pro for Windows screenshot showing ASAMPLE3.WB1 spreadsheet with Revenue Projection data including Chicago office, 1993 period, totals for Ketches, Cruisers, Catamarans, Dinghies, and All Models across Quarter 1 through Quarter 4 and Year columns]

5. Select E2..G5 and issue the Edit | Paste command.

The results can be seen in Figure 3-5, where the Revenue style has been restored. The columns now add up correctly. The ROUND function is very valuable when you are working with a fixed number of decimal places and your spreadsheet has to be accurate. Unless you use ROUND, Quattro Pro will retain up to 15 decimal places for each formula result. Remember that if you apply ROUND to the first level of calculation, further levels, such as the SUM formulas in Figure 3-5, will take care of themselves.

Block Editing

Quattro Pro provides numerous tools to help you edit your spreadsheets. Chapter 2 concentrated on the Edit menu commands: Cut, Copy, Paste, Clear, and so on. This section shows how to use the Block menu, which offers additional tools and some alternatives to the Edit menu commands. The first command on the Block menu is Move, and many of the techniques described for this command also apply to the other commands on the same menu.

Note At this point in the book, the step-by-step approach to examples gives way to a more descriptive approach. Commands are discussed in more general terms, with hypothetical examples. There will still be sufficient detail for you to try out the commands, but instructions will be less explicit so that you can start to substitute your own data for that used in the text.

Block Operations and Block | Move

When it comes to moving cells, Quattro Pro offers a variety of techniques. You can move a block of cells from one place in a spreadsheet to another by using Cut and Paste from the Edit menu. This technique has several advantages. You do not have to paste the cells immediately after you cut them, since they are stored in the Windows Clipboard. Also, you can cut cells from one spreadsheet and paste them into another. You have also seen that the drag-and-drop feature offers an alternative to the cut-and-paste movement of cells. You simply select the cells to be moved and then place the mouse pointer over them, hold down the left mouse button, and drag. An empty frame representing the block of cells moves wherever you point, and Quattro Pro moves the contents of the selected cells into the frame whenever you release the mouse button.

If you move a block of cells with drag-and-drop and then pull down the Edit menu, you will see that the first item is Undo Block Move. You can deduce from this that drag-and-drop is a mouse-driven version of the Move command on the Block menu. However, there are several advantages to using Block | Move instead of drag-and-drop, including the ability to move blocks between pages. To see how Move works, select a block of cells, preferably one containing formulas (do not select a compound block because Move, like drag-and-drop, does not work with compound blocks).

Having selected the block of cells to be moved, issue the Block | Move command, and you will see a dialog box like the one in Figure 3-6. This features two fields: From and To. Users of non-Windows spreadsheets, such as 1-2-3 Release 3, will notice that the dialog box in Figure 3-6

FIGURE 3-6 Block Move dialog box

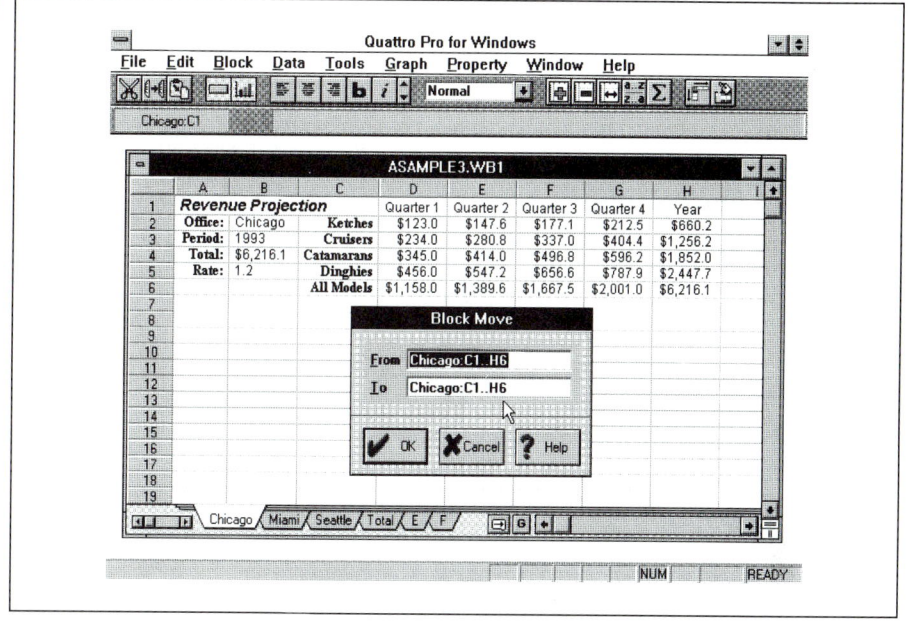

duplicates the Move command in such programs. When you use Move in 1-2-3, the program requests the coordinates of the block or range to be moved "From" and the coordinates it is being moved "To."

In Quattro Pro for Windows, a block of cells can be selected prior to the Block | Move command (in this case, C1..H6 of the Chicago page). Quattro Pro then assumes that the cells selected before you issue the command are the ones you want to move. This is fairly logical and, as you can see from Figure 3-6, the coordinates of the block are recorded in the From field. However, the From coordinates are highlighted so that you can change them if you want to. This means that you can issue the Move command from anywhere in the spreadsheet without preselecting the cells to be moved.

Block Coordinates and POINT Mode

Suppose that after you select C1..H6 and select Block | Move, you decide that you only want to move cells C6..H6. There are several ways to change the From setting. Since the entry in the From field is already highlighted, whatever you type next will replace the current coordinates. This means that you can type **C6..H6**, and it will replace Chicago:C1..H6. In fact, you do not have to type both dots between the cell numbers; you can type **C6.H6**, and Quattro Pro will add the second dot for you when you complete the operation. You do not have to include the page name unless you want to move cells from a different page.

Note Whenever you omit a page reference from a pair of cell coordinates, Quattro Pro assumes you mean the current page.

You should not press ENTER after you have typed new coordinates in the From field, since the OK button is the default button for the Block Move dialog box and pressing ENTER will tell Quattro Pro to proceed with the move operation. If you prefer not to type cell coordinates, you can point to the cells you want for the From block. To do this with the mouse, double-click on the From field. The result can be seen in Figure 3-7. Quattro Pro puts the Block Move dialog box away and shows you the current block selection.

Note that the input line now states the block coordinates, and a title bar labeled "Block Move" has appeared above the input line. In the lower right of the screen, the MODE indicator has changed to POINT. Now you can make your new From selection. For example, if you point to C6 and drag through to H6, the input line will show C6..H6. You can then click on the arrow button to the right of the Block Move title bar (or press ESC). This restores the Block Move dialog box with the new coordinates entered in the From field.

Note You can also supply block coordinates by using block names, which are described later in this chapter.

If you prefer to use the keyboard to point out new From block coordinates, you can press F2 while viewing the Block Move dialog box. This produces the same result as in Figure 3-7. If you now press any cursor movement key, the current block (C1..H6) will be abandoned, and you are free to point out a new block. The coordinates of the block will be shown on the input line.

Chapter 3: Blocks and Names 133

FIGURE 3-7   Double-clicking the From field highlights the selected block without moving it

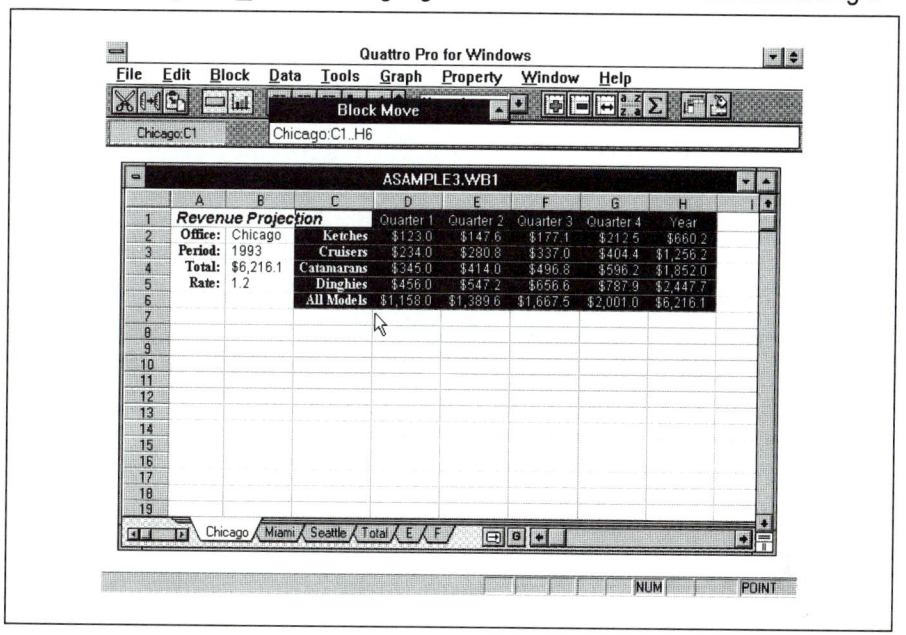

There are two ways to point out a block with the keyboard. You can point to the first cell of the block and then hold down the SHIFT key while using the cursor movement keys to extend the highlighting to the last cell. Note that as soon as you point with the SHIFT key held down, the cell coordinates are shown connected with dots, as in C6..D6. You can also type a period after pointing to the first cell. This "anchors" the first cell, as indicated by the double dots, as in C6..C6. Now you can move the cell pointer to the last cell in the block without holding down the SHIFT key. When you have pointed out the block you want to move, you can press ESC to return to the Block Move dialog box.

Note   A shortcut for changing block coordinates in any dialog box is to highlight the current entry, like the From coordinates in Figure 3-6, point at the block's first cell on the notebook page, and hold down the left mouse button. This automatically puts you into POINT mode. Drag through to the last cell and release the mouse button. The Block Move dialog box will reappear with the new block coordinates entered.

The Move Destination

You have seen in this chapter that if you select a block of cells before issuing the Block | Move command, Quattro Pro automatically enters the coordinates of this block in the From field. It might help to think of the From block as the source for the move, while the To field describes the destination. What may be slightly confusing is the fact that, as you can see from Figure 3-6, the entry in the To field starts out the same as the one in the From field. As you might expect, choosing OK (or pressing ENTER) when the From and To coordinates are the same has no effect on the spreadsheet. To move the cells shown in the From field, you need to indicate the new location in the To field. If you are using a mouse, you can double-click on the To field to enter POINT mode, as described above. Keyboard users can press ALT-T to activate the To field and then press F2 to enter POINT mode.

The new location for the cells you are moving does not need to be stated in full. For example, to move C6..H6 of the example spreadsheet to C7..H7 you only need to indicate C7 as the To setting. Quattro Pro only needs the top-left cell of a block in order to figure out the location. When you have pointed out the To location and returned to the Block Move dialog box, you can choose OK to complete the command. The block is moved, and any formulas in the block are updated as required. For example, if you were to move C1..H6 to C2..H7, the formula that was in E2 would now be in E3 and would change from

@ROUND($B$5*D2,1)

to

@ROUND($B$5*D3,1)

Further, the SUM formulas at the bottom of the columns would now sum rows 3 through 6 instead of 2 through 5.

The ability to move blocks like this is very handy when you are designing a spreadsheet model. You will find that the Block | Move command is slightly faster than cut and paste. However, you need to be clear about the assumptions that Quattro Pro makes during a move. If you tell the program to move a row of six cells to C7 it will assume that you mean C7 plus the five cells immediately to the right of C7. This assumption can be very useful. Indicating a single cell as the To setting saves time. Even if you do indicate a block as the To setting, Quattro Pro will make the same assumption, using the top-left cell of the block as the starting point of the new location. Quattro Pro will not complain if the To block is too small for the block being moved.

There is a downside to the assumptions made by Quattro Pro—a block of cells being moved or copied to a new location will automatically overwrite existing entries in the new location. For this reason, it is a good idea to enable the Undo feature before using Move or any of the other Block commands. Another powerful but dangerous assumption is made by Quattro Pro when you have activated the Group mode, described in the last chapter. If Group mode is on, indicated by a line connecting page tabs and a line under the letter G icon, a move or copy operation will be carried out across all pages in the group. On the one hand, this can save a tremendous amount of time, but on the other, copying or moving can have a disruptive effect if you are not aware of the consequences of Group mode operation.

Block | Copy

In the previous chapter, you saw that holding down the CTRL key while using drop-and-drag changed it from block moving to block copying. You also saw that the Edit | Copy command, together with Edit | Paste, can be used to duplicate one or more cells. The Copy command on the Block menu represents another approach to copying spreadsheet entries. Suppose that you want to add expense projections to the spreadsheet illustrated in Figure 3-7. You could do this by copying the revenue projection entries from A1..H6 and then editing them into expenses.

Note If you perform this operation in Group mode, you can create copies in all of the pages in the group (in the previous chapter a group called Company was defined that included the Chicago, Miami, Seattle, and Total pages). To activate Group mode, click on the G icon to the right of the page tabs.

To copy A1..H6 to A8..H13 with the Block | Copy command, select A1..H6 and issue the Copy command from the Block menu. A dialog box like the one in Figure 3-8 appears. This is identical to the Block Move dialog box, except for the addition of the Model copy option, which will be described in a moment. Note that in Figure 3-8, as well as Figure 3-6,

FIGURE 3-8 Block Copy dialog box

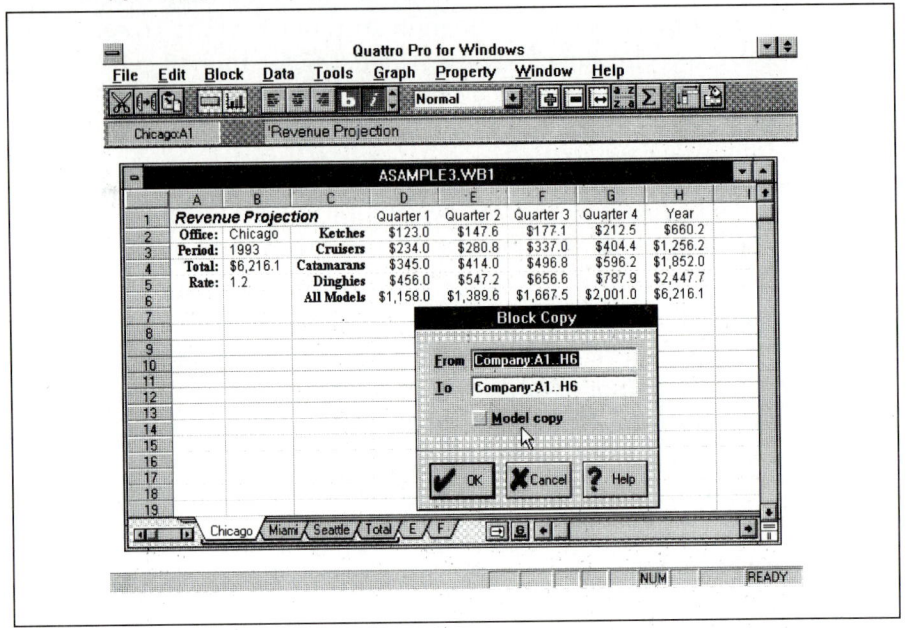

the dialog box has been moved slightly from its default location in the middle of the screen. Like other Quattro Pro dialog boxes, the Block Copy and Block Move dialog boxes can be moved around the screen in order to give you a clearer view of the underlying spreadsheet. To move a dialog box with your mouse, simply click on the title bar and drag the box to a new location. To move a dialog box using the keyboard, first press ALT-SPACEBAR to open the window Control menu and press ALT-M to select the Move command. An arrow icon then appears, and you can use the arrow keys to move the box to a new location and press ENTER.

In the From field of the Block Copy dialog box, you can see the coordinates of the cells that were selected when the command was issued. To complete the operation, you need to indicate the To coordinates using the pointing techniques described earlier in this chapter. A simple approach is to press ALT-T to activate the To field and type **A8**, the top-left cell of the area into which you want to copy the selected block of cells. When you have indicated the To cell, you can choose OK, and the block is copied. You can see the results in Figure 3-9.

FIGURE 3-9 The results of a block copy

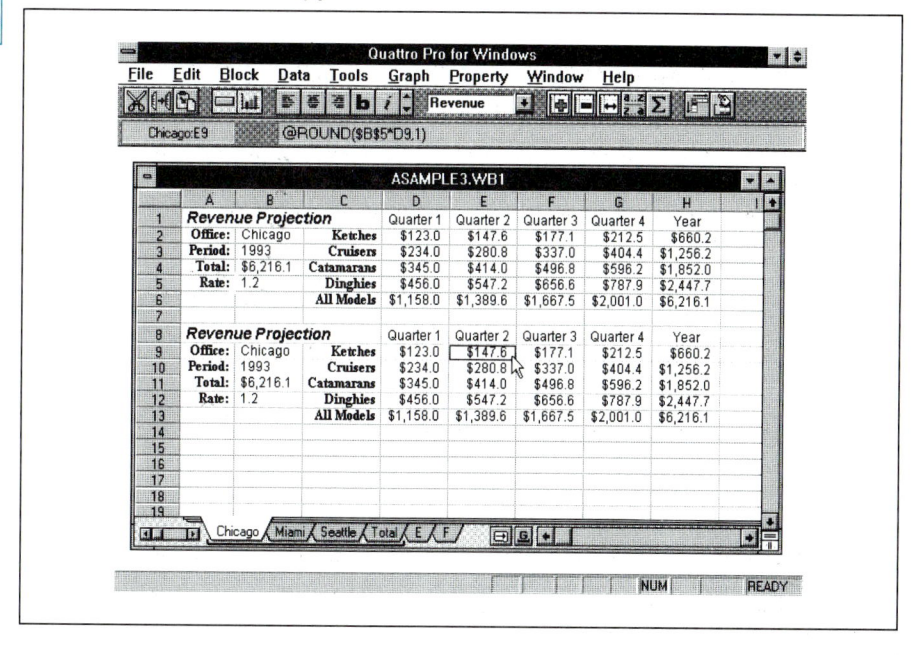

[Screenshot of Quattro Pro for Windows showing spreadsheet ASAMPLE3.WB1 with cell Chicago:E9 selected containing @ROUND($B$5*D9.1). The spreadsheet shows a Revenue Projection table in rows 1-6 and a copy in rows 8-13 with identical values.]

Model Copying

In Figure 3-9, you can see that cell E9 has been selected to show how the copy operation treats formulas. You will notice that because the reference to B5 is absolute, it does not change in the copy. If you are going to create an expense projection model out of the cells in A8..H13, you might well prefer the formula in E9 to refer to B12 rather than B5.

What you are seeing is a negative consequence of the otherwise helpful assumptions that Quattro Pro makes about absolute and relative cell references. What you wanted in this case was a copy of the *model* in A1..H6, including the relationship between the growth rate in B5 and the rest of the model. This is why the Block Copy dialog box includes the Model copy option. If you undo the copy shown in Figure 3-9 and redo it with the Model copy option checked, the results form the basis for the model shown in Figure 3-10.

The label in A8 has been edited from Revenue Projection to Expense Projection, and the categories in C9..C13 have been edited, as have the starting values in D9..D13. The growth rate in B12 was changed from

FIGURE 3-10 Using the Model copy option

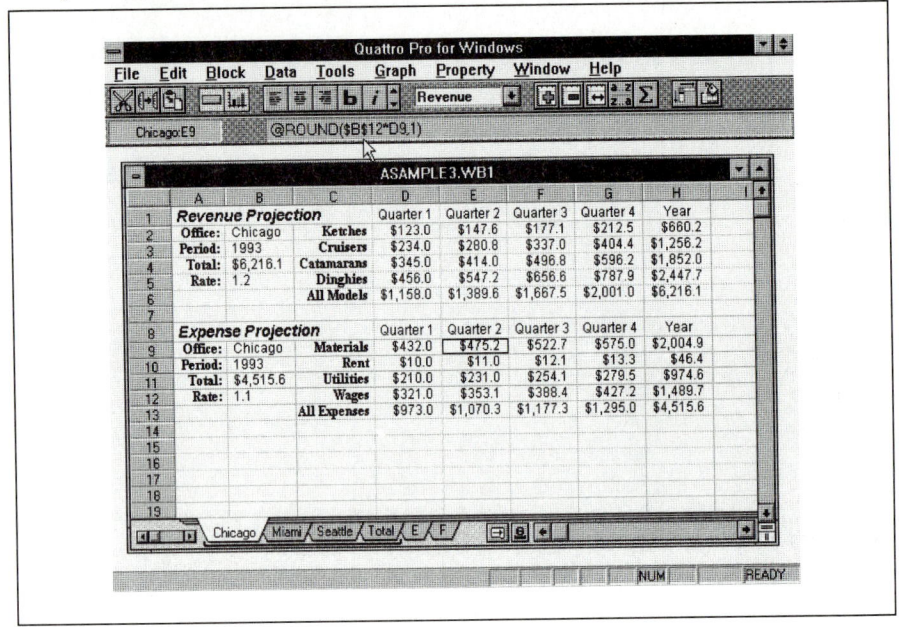

1.2 to 1.1. However, the important thing to note is the formula in E9. This now refers to the rate in B12, *not* the one in B5. This allows you to use a growth rate for expenses that is different from the one for revenue. This also illustrates the difference between a regular Block | Copy or copy-and-paste and a model copy. The model copy duplicates the block and translates any absolute references within the block, relative to the block's new location. This saves a lot of editing when you are duplicating models like the one in the example.

Note When you are editing cells and want the results to be duplicated in all pages of the group, use CTRL-ENTER instead of ENTER. If you forget to press CTRL-ENTER, you can go back to the cell, press F2 to edit it, and then press CTRL-ENTER to force the result into all pages.

Bear in mind that Block | Copy not only allows you to perform a model copy, but also allows you to copy blocks that are not on the current page of the spreadsheet. You can copy compound blocks and perform reverse copying, as described next. Like the Block | Move command, Block | Copy works with block names, which are described later in this chapter.

Reverse Copying

The normal procedure for copying is to select the cells you want to copy and then indicate where the copy is to be placed. There may be times when you are viewing the location into which you want cells copied and would like to perform the copy operation right away. You can do this by using the Block | Copy command and a technique referred to as *reverse copying*.

Suppose that you want to create a new notebook that uses the same basic information as the revenue projection for the Chicago office. In Figure 3-11, you can see that the File | New command has been used to open a new notebook called NOTEBK5. The Block | Copy command has been issued, and the dialog box indicates the basic Quattro Pro assumption that the block selected when the command is issued is the block you want to copy from and to.

FIGURE 3-11 Opening a new notebook

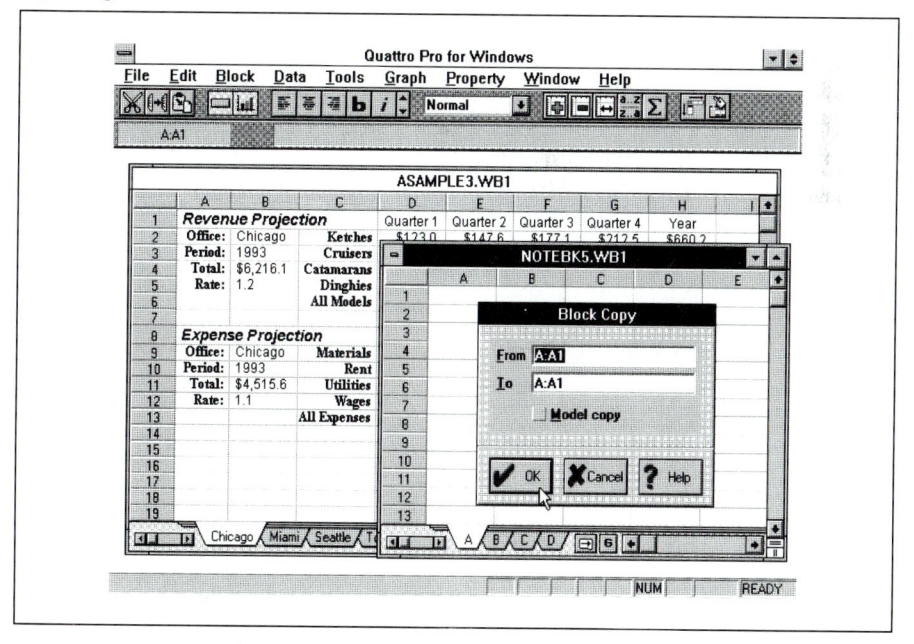

In a normal block copy operation, you have to change the To setting. In a reverse copy, you change the From setting, in this case, clicking on cell A1 of the Chicago page of the sample model and dragging through to cell H6. When you release the mouse button, the coordinates are entered in the From field, and you can leave the To field as cell A:A1 of the new notebook. Choose OK, and Quattro Pro pulls a copy from the sample notebook into the new notebook.

Note If you copy a block of cells from a page that is part of a group and Group mode in the source notebook is on, the copy will contain cells from all pages of the source group.

Block | Insert

There will be times when you want to add columns or rows to a spreadsheet to improve the appearance of a model. This has the effect of moving entries you have already made. Suppose that you want an additional blank line between the revenue and expense sections of the sample spreadsheet. One way to do this is to select cell A8, which contains the label "Expense Projection", and issue the Block | Insert command. You will notice that the Insert command is one of several on the Block menu that have an arrow to the right of them. This indicates that a further menu will appear when the item is selected. You can see this in Figure 3-12 where the Block | Insert submenu is displayed.

If you normally use your mouse to select menu items, you will find that you can drag the highlight down the Block menu to Insert, and then across to the right to pop up the Insert menu. If you use the arrow keys to select menu items, you will find that secondary menus can be displayed by selecting the main menu item, in this case Insert, and then pressing the RIGHT ARROW key. This highlights the first item on the secondary menu, which can be selected by pressing ENTER. You can use UP ARROW and DOWN ARROW to highlight other items that are in the secondary menu.

Inserting Rows

As you can see from Figure 3-12, there are four items that you can insert. These include notebook pages, as well as rows and columns. You can also use the Block | Insert menu to insert a spreadsheet file as a new page in the notebook, as described in Chapter 7. If you select Rows from the Block | Insert menu, you will get a dialog box like the one in Figure 3-13. Once you know how to use the Insert Rows dialog box, you will see that it tells you how many rows will be inserted, where they will be placed, and how they will affect the spreadsheet.

As Figure 3-13 shows, the Block setting initially contains the cell or cells that were selected when the command was issued, in this case, cell A8 of the Chicago page. Note that this is referred to as Company:A8 because the page is part of the group named Company, and Group mode is active. This reminds you that the action you are about to perform will affect all pages of the group.

FIGURE 3-12 Block | Insert menu

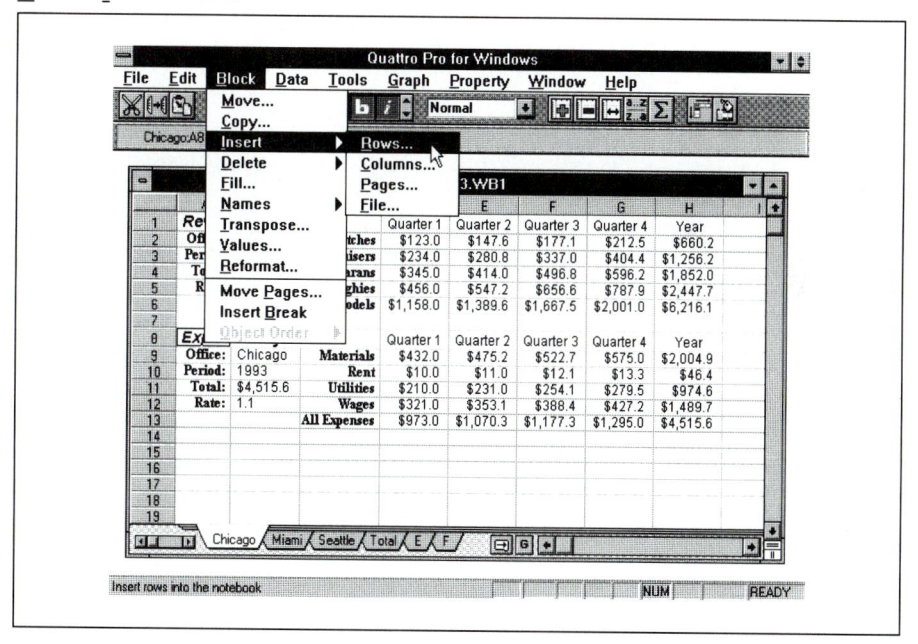

FIGURE 3-13 Insert Rows dialog box

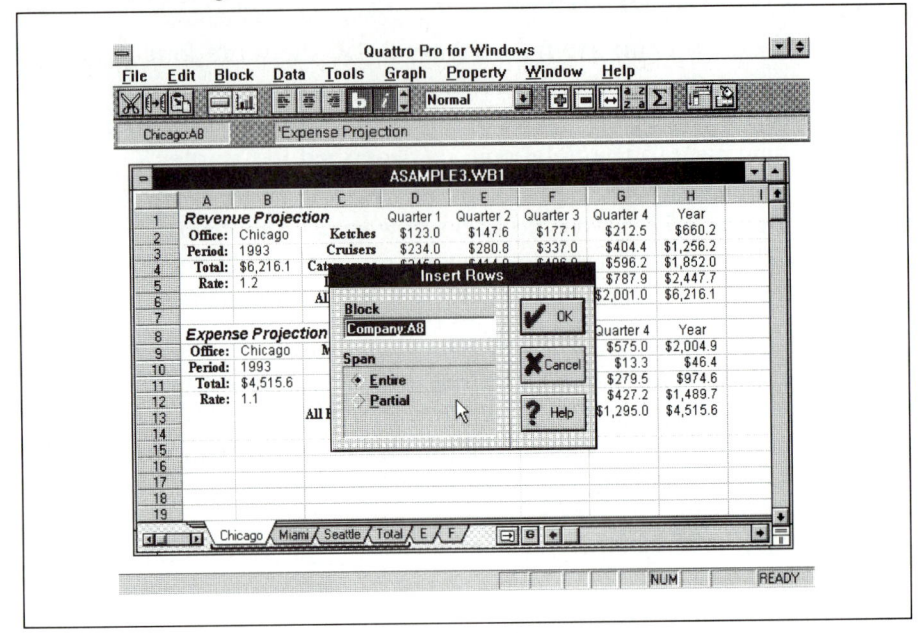

When you get to the Insert Rows dialog box, you can either choose OK to complete the command or change the settings. You can change the Block setting using the same mouse and keyboard techniques described earlier for the From and To settings of the Block | Move and Block | Copy commands.

Rows are always inserted above the selected block. In this example, choosing OK creates a new row 8. The previous contents of row 8 are pushed down to row 9, as shown in Figure 3-14. If the block only contains one row, as in this case, only one row will be inserted into the spreadsheet. If the block contains several rows, the number of rows inserted will equal the number of rows in the block (for example, if the block were A8..A10, three rows would be inserted). The number of columns in the block has no effect on how many rows are inserted. You can reverse the effect of inserting rows by using the Edit | Undo command.

The Span setting in the Insert Rows dialog box determines how much of the spreadsheet is affected by the command. The default setting is Entire, which means that the inserted row(s) will extend all the way across the spreadsheet page. The Partial setting means that the inserted

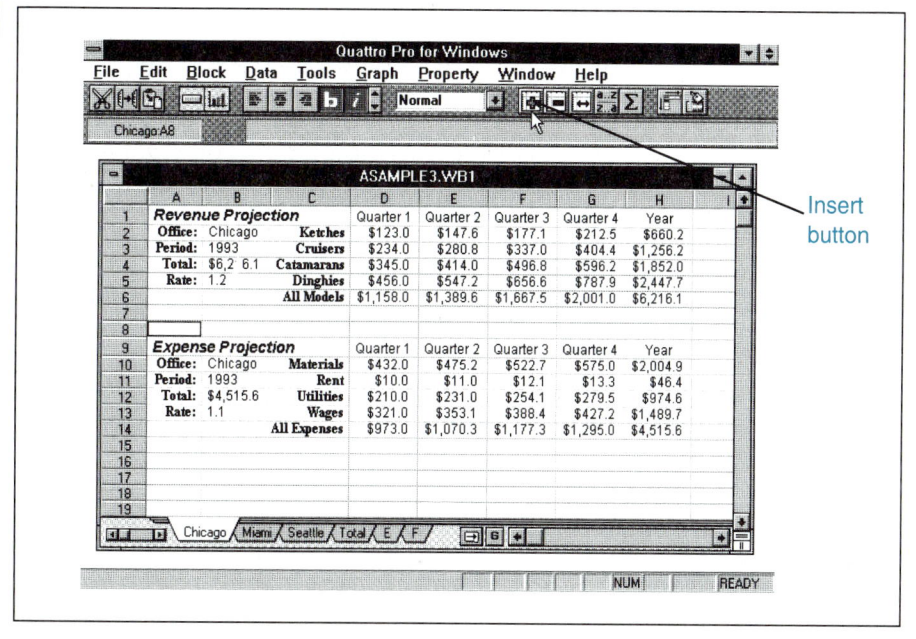

FIGURE 3-14 Spreadsheet after a row has been inserted

Insert button

rows will only be as wide as the block of cells in the Block setting. For example, if the Block setting were A8..H8, the new row would be inserted in columns A through H, and the effect would be a downward move of the contents of A8..H8 and all the other cells below them. If you performed a partial row insert with just A8 selected, the effect would be to move the labels in A8..A12 to A9..A13. Furthermore, if there were any entries further down column A, they would also be moved down one cell. However, columns B through H would be unaffected.

Inserting Columns

Columns are inserted in the same manner as rows. When you select Columns from the Block | Insert menu, you get an Insert Columns dialog box with the same fields as the Insert Rows dialog box in Figure 3-13. The Block setting initially contains the cell or cells that were selected when the command was issued. You can either choose OK to complete the command or change the settings. You can change the Block setting using the same mouse and keyboard techniques described earlier for the From and To settings of the Block | Move and Block | Copy commands.

Columns are always inserted to the left of the selected block. For example, if you select C8 and complete the column insert command with the default settings, you create a new column C. The previous contents of C are moved to column D. If the block only contains one column, only one column will be inserted into the spreadsheet. If the block contains several columns, the number of columns inserted will equal the number of columns in the block (for example, if the block were C8..E10, three columns would be inserted). The number of rows in the block has no effect on how many columns are inserted.

The Span setting determines how much of the spreadsheet is affected by the column insert operation. The default setting is Entire, which means that the inserted column(s) will extend all the way down the spreadsheet page. The Partial setting means that the inserted columns will only be as long as the block of cells in the Block setting. For example, if the Block setting was C1..C6, the effect of a partial column insert would be to move the contents of C1..H6 one column to the right without affecting any of the entries below row 6. Bear in mind that any entries in rows 1 through 6 of columns beyond H would also be shifted one column to the right.

Tips on Inserting

As you might expect and can see from Figure 3-14, inserting rows does not adversely affect spreadsheet formulas. The same is true of inserting columns. The cell coordinates in those formulas that move are adjusted relative to the new location. Adjustments are also made to formulas in cells that do not move but refer to moved cells.

If you are working with macros, bear in mind that inserting rows can have a disruptive effect on macro code stored in the spreadsheet. Otherwise, inserted columns and rows have few negative side effects, and all block insert operations can be reversed with the Edit | Undo command. In fact, if you insert a column or row within a block that is referenced by a formula, the block coordinates will be expanded automatically to accommodate the new cells. Examples of how this works can be found in Chapter 5.

There are several shortcuts you can use when inserting columns and rows. The Insert button on the SpeedBar, indicated by the mouse pointer in Figure 3-14, performs an insert based on the state of the spreadsheet when you click it. If there is only one cell selected when the Insert button

Chapter 3: Blocks and Names

is clicked, the Insert dialog box is presented, as shown in Figure 3-15. Note that the appearance of the Insert button changes to indicate that it has been clicked. Also note that the row added in Figure 3-14 has since been removed.

The operation of the Insert dialog box is much the same as that of the Insert Rows and Insert Columns boxes described earlier, except that there is an additional item, Dimension. This determines whether the insert operation adds Columns, Rows, or Pages (note that the key letter for Partial under the Span setting changes from P to a). The reason for the Dimension setting is that the program cannot guess which of the three items you want to insert. The default selection is Rows. Just select the dimension you want before choosing OK. Use the Span setting to determine whether the insertion is throughout the entire spreadsheet or just partial. Use the Block setting if you want to choose cells other than those that were selected when you clicked the Insert button.

The main advantage to using the Insert button comes when you want to insert entire rows, columns, or pages. If you select one or more rows, columns, or pages in their entirety before clicking the Insert button, the command is executed without any further input. Remember that you

FIGURE 3-15 Insert dialog box

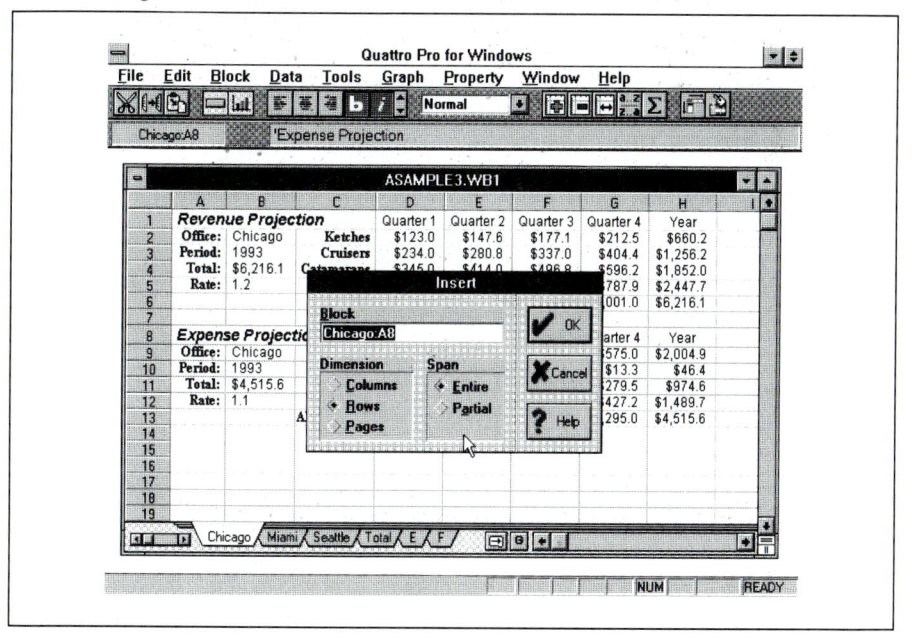

select an entire row or column by clicking the number or letter in the spreadsheet border. In Figure 3-16, you can see that rows 7 and 8 have been selected in this manner. If you were to click the Insert button at this point, two rows would be inserted automatically without a dialog box. This technique only works on multiple columns or rows if they are adjacent (selected with SHIFT and click, rather than CTRL and click). The operation of the Insert button is summarized in Table 3-2.

Note The Block | Insert command is also sensitive to what you select before issuing the command. If you select an entire row, column, or page before issuing the command, the command completes automatically without displaying the dialog box for confirmation.

As you might expect, the effects of inserting are considerably altered if you are in Group mode. Inserting columns and rows in Group mode affects all pages in the group. If you select one page of a group and click Insert while Group mode is active, you insert as many new pages as there are pages in the group.

Remember that you select an entire notebook page by clicking on the spreadsheet border above the row number and to the left of the column letters, as indicated by the mouse pointer in Figure 3-17. All cells on the page are then shaded. Clicking the Insert button with one page selected inserts one new page in front of the selected page (unless you are in Group mode). If you were to select the Miami page, as in Figure 3-17, and click Insert, you would create a new page B in front of Miami.

Inserting and Moving Pages

You have seen that the Block | Insert menu includes an option to add pages to a notebook. This is very useful if you need to expand a model.

TABLE 3-2 Insert Button Options

Items Selected	Operation
One or more cells	Prompts for parameters
One or more entire rows	Inserts row(s) immediately
One or more entire columns	Inserts column(s) immediately
The entire page	Inserts a new page immediately

Chapter 3: Blocks and Names 147

FIGURE 3-16 Using the Insert button to insert two entire rows

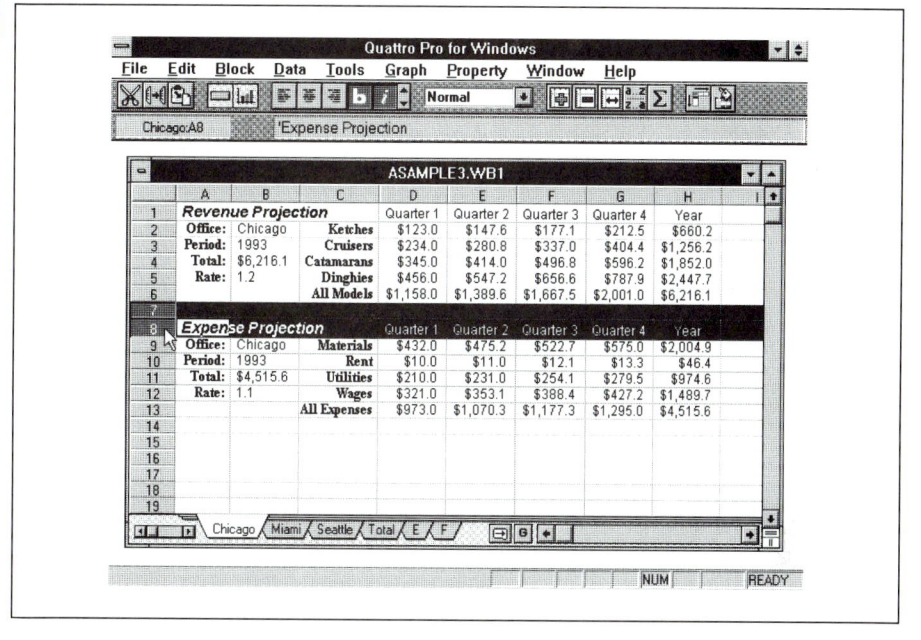

FIGURE 3-17 Selecting an entire page

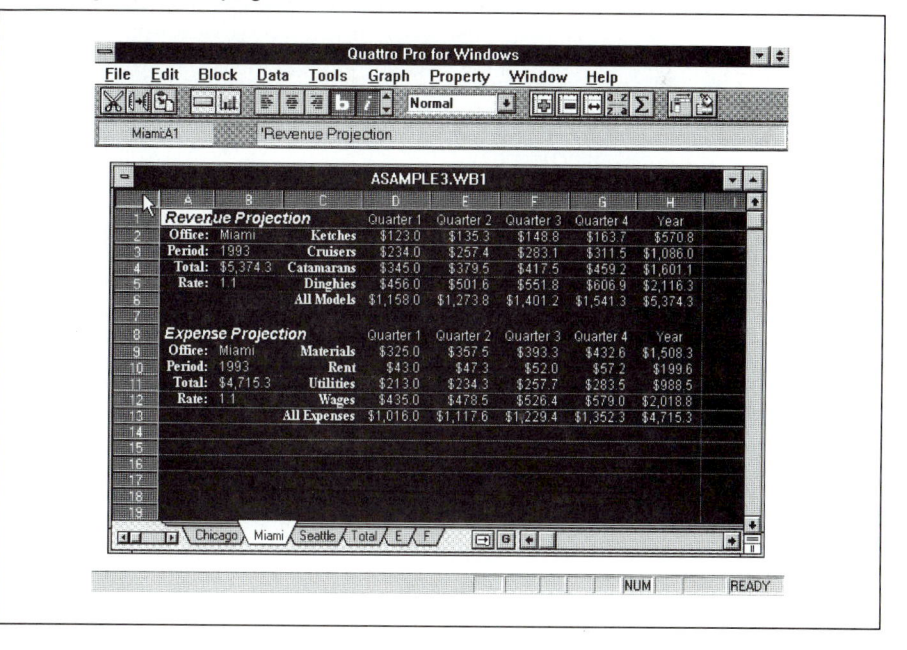

You have also seen that the Insert button can be used to insert pages. If you select an entire page and click the Insert button, a fresh page is added in front of the selected page. You can insert more than one page by selecting a temporary group of pages. You do this by selecting the first page and clicking on the page tab for the last page while holding down the SHIFT key. A temporary group line appears under the selected pages and, when you click Insert, as many pages are inserted as you have included in the group.

Just as columns and rows inserted within blocks referenced by formulas are included in those formulas, so too are pages. Suppose that you need to add another page to the sample model for the new Portland office. You could select the Miami page, as shown in Figure 3-17, and click the Insert button or issue the Block | Insert command. This inserts a fresh page called B, as shown in Figure 3-18. The Active Page dialog box can then be used to change the name of the new page from B to Portland. Note that the new page starts out as B because it is inserted as the second page in the notebook. Also note that the new page uses the default column width for all of its columns.

FIGURE 3-18 A fresh page inserted

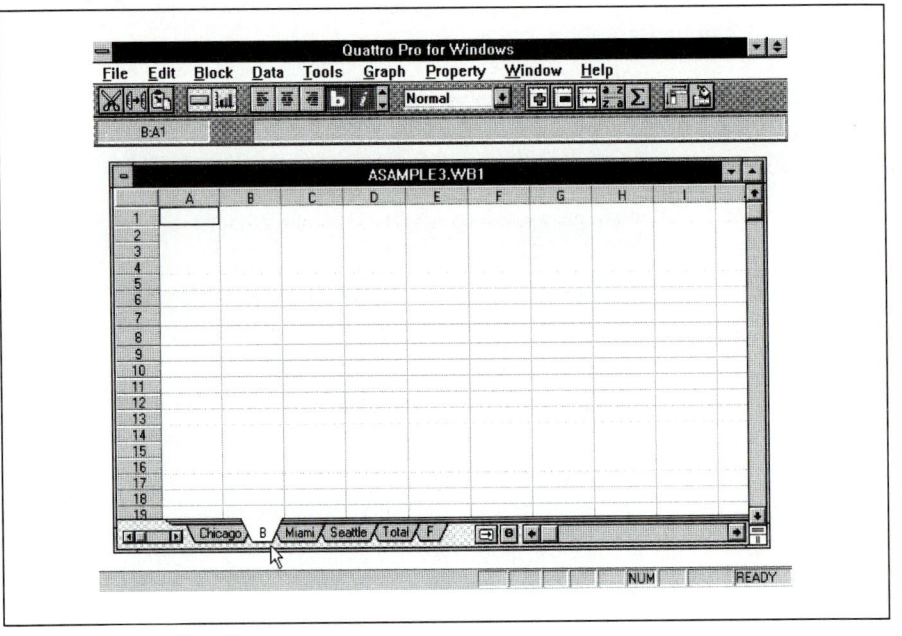

You can now copy the projection model from Miami or Chicago to the new page and edit it to reflect the figures for the Portland office. Note that when you do this, using either copy-and-paste or a block copy, the column widths are not transferred to the new page. Column widths are one aspect of formatting that is not copied. The result in this case is that some of the columns in the new page will be too narrow for their contents. One solution to this problem is to select affected cells on the new page and click the Fit button. This will widen the columns so that the contents are clearly visible. Another approach is to turn on Group mode, move to the Miami or Chicago page, and confirm the width of each column.

You can quickly confirm a column's width by moving the mouse over the line to the right of the column letter in the spreadsheet border. When the mouse pointer turns into the double arrow, position it directly over the line and click once. This confirms the current width and, when you are in Group mode, makes sure all other pages in the group have the same width for that column.

When you insert a new page between pages that are referenced in a multipage formula, the new page is automatically added to the formula. Thus, by simply adding the Portland page before Miami and after Chicago, the entries on that page will be included in the sum formulas on the Total page. You will recall that cells on the Total page sum all cells from Chicago through Miami to Seattle, using formulas like this one in Total:D13:

@SUM(Chicago..Seattle:D13)

If you insert a page between Chicago and Seattle, cell D13 of that page will be summed in D13 of the Total page.

Note that the new page would not have been included in the formula if you had used the Insert command while the Chicago page was selected. In that case, the new page would have preceded Chicago and fallen outside of the summed block of pages. Likewise, if you had issued the Insert command with the Total page selected, the new page would be after the summed block of pages and not included in the formula.

Once you have inserted a page, you might want to move it. There are two ways of doing this. You can use the Block | Move Pages command, which produces the following dialog box:

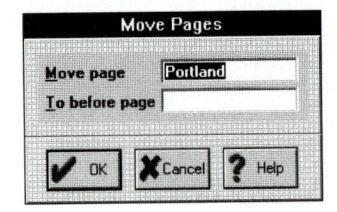

The first field contains the name of the page or pages you want to move, while the second indicates the new location. This is stated as "before page," so that to move the Portland page to be after Miami but in front of Seattle, the second field should be Seattle. To move two or more pages, the first field of the Move Pages dialog box should contain the first and last names of the group of pages, separated by a pair of dots. Thus, to move both Chicago and Portland, you would enter **Chicago..Portland** (you only need to type in one period). You can also use the pointing method to select the pages for the Move Pages dialog box, indicating a single page by clicking on its tab. Two or more pages are selected by clicking on the tab of the first page and then SHIFT-clicking on the tab of the second page.

You can also use the mouse to move pages by dragging their tabs. In Figure 3-19, you can see the Portland page being moved. To move a page with the mouse, you first point to the page tab and then drag it down until the mouse pointer turns to a hand. Then you can move the page left or right. As you do so, the other page tabs are highlighted in turn. The highlighted tab indicates the page in front of which the moved page will be located when you release the mouse button. You can move two or more pages in this manner by selecting them with SHIFT-click before dragging.

When you move pages that have letters instead of names, the letters change according to the new location of the page. Thus, moving page C so that it is in front of page F actually changes the page letter from C to E. The program does this to keep the page lettering consistent. You will recall that when you insert a new page, it gets a letter based on its new location.

Note Be careful—when you move a page outside of a group that is referenced in a formula, it may affect the accuracy of the formula.

Chapter 3: Blocks and Names 151

FIGURE 3-19 Moving the Portland page

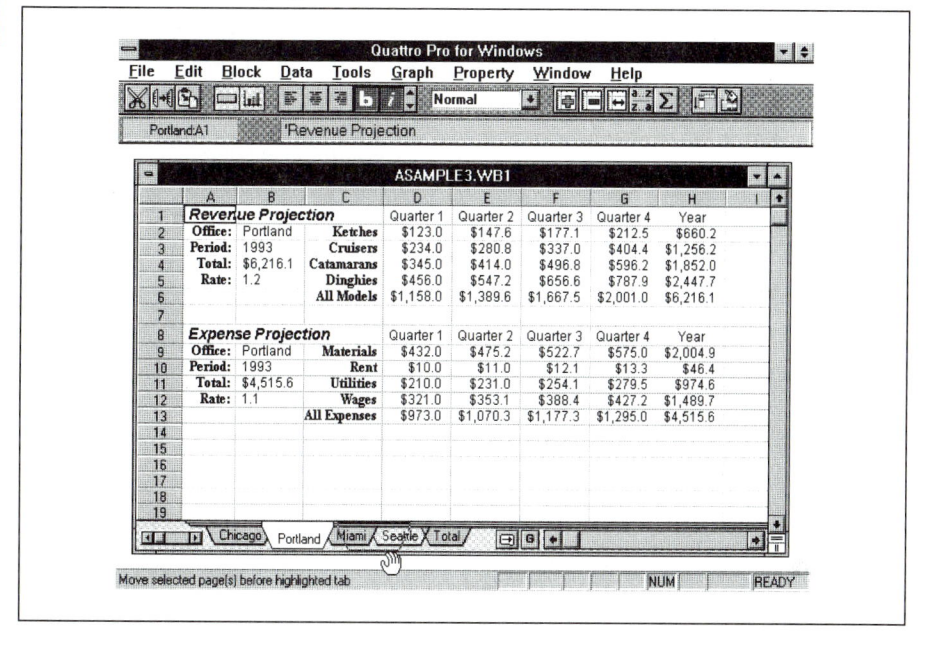

Block | Delete

Just as you sometimes need to add columns or rows to a spreadsheet to create the arrangement of data you want, you will occasionally need to delete columns and rows. This can be done with the Block | Delete menu or the Delete button, which is to the right of the Insert button on the SpeedBar. The Block | Delete menu has three options: Rows, Columns, and Pages. The dialog box presented by the Insert button has the same three Dimension options. If you select an entire column, row, or page and click the Delete button, that item will be deleted without confirmation. This makes the Delete button very convenient but also rather dangerous. Make sure that the Undo feature is enabled before using the Delete button.

You can delete rows and columns across the entire spreadsheet or partially. A partial row delete has the effect of moving up only cells below the selected cells. A partial column delete has the effect of moving to the left only cells to the right of the selected block. Bear in mind that deleting a column, row, or page that is the reference point for a block formula will adversely affect that formula. For example, if a spreadsheet uses the formula @SUM(D2..D5), deleting row 2 or row 5 will cause the formula to return the ERR result (this is true regardless of where in the spreadsheet the formula is located). The problem is that removing a referenced cell confuses Quattro Pro, which cannot figure out what to use as a replacement. In this case close examination of the formula will show that it has been changed to read @SUM(ERR).

Note The ERR result in one cell may affect other cells. A formula that uses the result of a cell that returns ERR will itself return ERR.

Do not confuse a block delete with the Edit | Clear command, which removes the formatting and contents of the currently selected block of cells, or the Edit | Clear Contents command, which uses the DEL key as its shortcut.

Block | Fill and SpeedFill

Many spreadsheets contain entries that are sequential, such as, in Figure 3-19, the headings, Quarter 1, Quarter 2, and so on. In Figure 3-20, you can see a similar series, Q1, Q2, and so on. Figure 3-20 also contains several series of numbers, such as 5.00 through 10.00 in cells H11..H16. Other models require months of the year, days of the week, and numeric sequences. Quattro Pro includes several tools that help you create such sequences. Among these are the Block | Fill command and the SpeedFill button.

The SpeedFill Button

Activated by the second button from the right on the SpeedBar, the SpeedFill feature is designed to make it as easy and quick as possible to create sequences of data. Consider the model in Figure 3-20, which was created almost entirely through the use of SpeedFill. The user typed less than a dozen cell entries. The rest of the work was done by seven SpeedFill operations, one click of SpeedSum, and a couple of formatting choices.

Chapter 3: Blocks and Names

FIGURE 3-20 Growth predictions spreadsheet created with SpeedFill

[Screenshot of Quattro Pro for Windows showing FILLER.WB1 spreadsheet with Growth Predictions for XL Range, with SpeedFill button indicated]

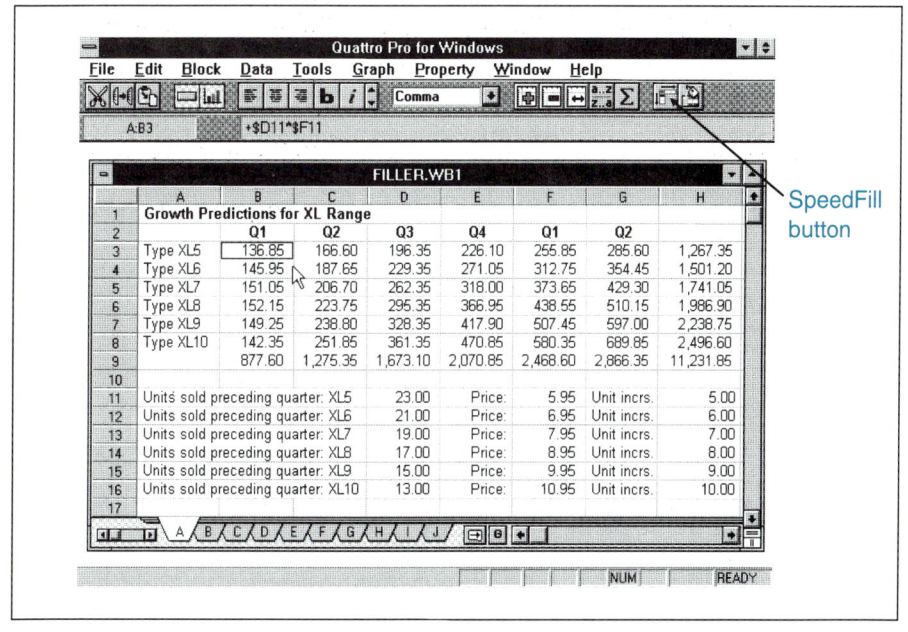

As you can see, the model in Figure 3-20 contains numbers, labels, and formulas. All of these can be replicated by SpeedFill because it is an "intelligent" command, performing different operations according to the contents of the block of cells selected when the command is issued. SpeedFill can fill a block with numbers, labels, or formulas, depending upon the first entry in the block that you select. If you want to see how this works, open a new notebook or move to a blank page in the current notebook. Enter **Type XL5** in A3 and select A3 through A8. Now click SpeedFill. The result is the series of labels shown in A3..A8 of Figure 3-20. To accomplish this, SpeedFill did the following:

- Examined the first entry in the selected cell block
- Located the serial component, in this case the number 5
- Filled up the block with copies of the first entry
- Incremented the numeric component by 1

If you want to increment the numeric component in a series by something other than 1 you must create the first two entries to show SpeedFill what the increment should be. If you enter **Type XL5** in A3 and **Type XL7** in A4, select A3..A8, and click SpeedFill, the entries created in A5 through A8 will be Type XL9, Type XL11, Type XL13, and Type XL15. When you select a block that has entries in the first two cells, SpeedFill creates a series based on the difference between the two entries.

Note SpeedFill will not overwrite existing cell entries. You must have empty cells in the fill block for SpeedFill to work.

If there is no sequential component in an entry, such as the label "Price:" used in Figure 3-20, SpeedFill works like a copy command. Thus, if you enter **Price:** in E11, select E11..E16, and click SpeedFill, the label is copied down the column (the cells E12 through E16 must be empty for this to work). If the first entry in the fill block is a formula, SpeedFill copies the formula. In Figure 3-21, you can see a diagram of the fill operations used to create the model shown in Figure 3-20.

FIGURE 3-21 The SpeedFill operations that filled the previous figure

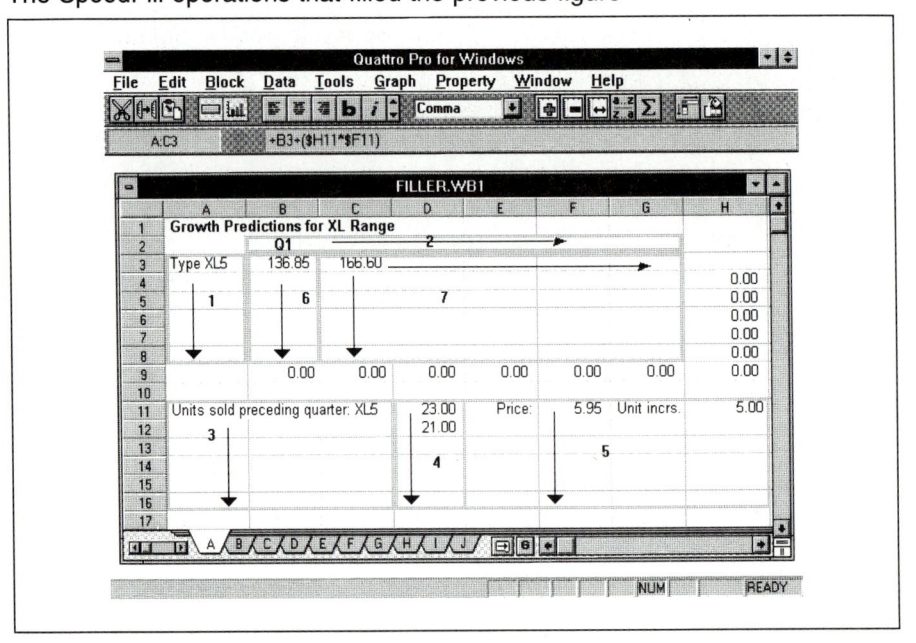

Chapter 3: Blocks and Names   155

Note the use of a partially relative cell reference in B3 and C3. When the formula **+$D11*$F11** is copied from B3 to B4, it changes to **+$D12*$F12**. In other words, the row reference is adjusted relatively, but the column reference remains absolute. The formula in C3 is

+B3+($H11*$F11)

When you copy this formula to C4, it becomes

+B4*($H12*$F12)

When you copy C3 to D3, the formula becomes

+C3+($H11*$F11)

Careful use of absolute references means that formulas can be copied without altering their meaning.

When it comes to deciding what constitutes a "sequential component" in a cell entry, SpeedFill uses a wide range of parameters. For example, if you include a number at the end of a label, the number will be incremented. If the number is not at the end of the label, the label is copied rather than incremented, unless the label represents a date. For example, if you use the label "1 March" in the first cell of a fill block, Speed will create "2 March," "3 March," and so on.

Labels without a number in them are not incremented unless they are parts of a date, such as Mon, Monday, Mar, March, and so on. The incrementing of entries is normally sequential, but if the label is Quarter 1, Qtr 1, or Q 1, SpeedFill assumes you are referring to quarter of a year and only numbers up to 4, starting over at 1 if there are more than 4 cells in the fill block. As you can see from Figure 3-21, SpeedFill can fill blocks that contain multiple columns and rows. When filling such blocks with numbers, the results follow the pattern shown here:

1	2	3
2	3	4
3	4	5
4	5	6

For greater control over the way numeric sequences are created you can use the Block Fill command described next. You will find a summary of SpeedFill operations in Table 3-3. Note that you can create several different series at once, as in operation number 5 in Figure 3-21. In this

TABLE 3-3 SpeedFill Button Options and Actions

Category	Example	Action
Text Label	Price:	Copies label to selected cells
Date Text Label	Mon, July	Increments to next day or month
Quarter Label	Qtr 1, Q 1	Increments number up to 4 only, then repeats from 1
1 label ending with number	Book 1	Increments number in both directions by 1
2 labels ending with numbers	XL2 XL4	Increments number by interval between numbers (XL6 next)
1 number	1	Increments number by 1
2 numbers	2	4	Increments by interval between numbers (6 next)
Formula	+A$1+1	Absolute references and constants unchanged; relative references adjusted

case, SpeedFill filled several columns at once because there was an entry in the first cell of each column.

Block | Fill

The Block | Fill command enables you to fill a group of cells with consecutive numbers. You choose the starting number, the interval between numbers, and the ending number. For example, suppose that you have created the employee listing in Figure 3-22 and you want to fill A3..A16 with a series of numbers, one for each employee. You begin by selecting the block A3..A16 and issue the Block | Fill command. The cells can be empty. You do not need to create the first entry as required by SpeedFill. Unlike SpeedFill, the Block | Fill command overwrites existing data, so you do not need to clear a block before filling it.

Note Be careful when using Block | Fill that you do not fill a block of cells that contains data you wish to keep!

Chapter 3: Blocks and Names

FIGURE 3-22 Using the Block | Fill command

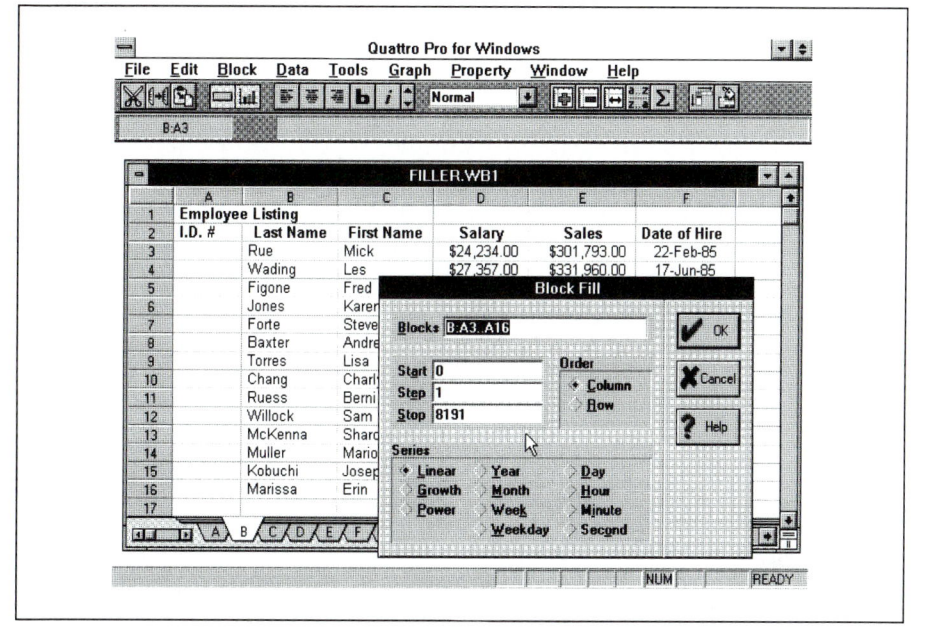

When you issue the Block | Fill command, you get the dialog box shown in Figure 3-22. The Order and Series options will be described in a moment. As you can see, the Blocks field already contains the selected cells (Blocks is plural because the fill command works on compound blocks as well as normal blocks). Notice that there are default values for the Start, Step, and Stop settings. These are 0, 1, and 8191, respectively. Suppose that you want your employee numbers to start at 1001 and increment or step by 1. You would change the Start setting to 1001. However, there is no need to change the Step or Stop settings.

In this example, the Step is correct, and you do not need to be concerned that the Stop setting is a larger number than you want in your series. Quattro Pro creates entries in the selected block of cells only as far as either the Stop value or the size of the block permits. In this case, the largest number in the series that will fit within the block is 1014. Bear in mind that the Stop value will have to be changed if you are working with a series that needs to go beyond 8191. You may also need to change the Stop value if you are working with a negative Step value (this creates a diminishing series of values, so the S‍top value must be less than the St‍art value).

In other circumstances, you might want to select a block of cells larger than you actually need and change the S‍top value to limit the number of entries created. For example, if you wanted to create numbers for a total of 200 employees, you could select A3..A210, enter **1001** as the St‍art value, leave 1 as the Ste‍p value, and enter **1200** as the S‍top value. This would create a series from 1001 to 1200, and it would not matter that the block you selected was slightly larger than the number of cells required.

When you have used the B‍lock | F‍ill command, Quattro Pro remembers the B‍locks, St‍art, Ste‍p, and S‍top settings. If you issue the command again and have not preselected a block of cells, the settings will be exactly as before, including the page reference. This allows you to quickly repeat the B‍lock | F‍ill command. Suppose you have a table of loan payments like the one in Figure 3-23. The payments are based on a range of rates, currently from 12% to 17%. These values were entered into C3..H3 with the B‍lock | F‍ill command. If you want to change the range of values you can simply repeat the B‍lock | F‍ill command and alter the St‍art value (for

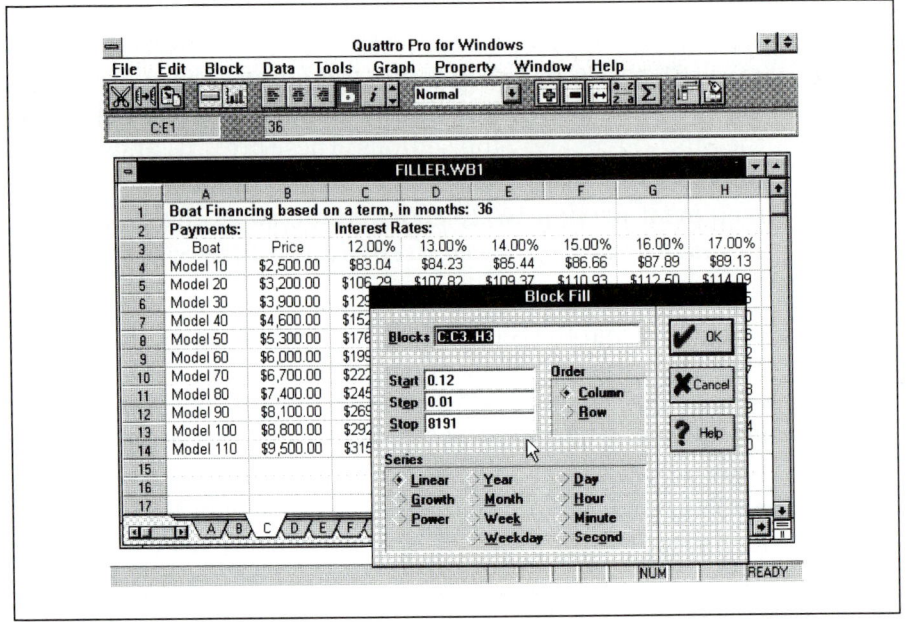

FIGURE 3-23 When used again, B‍lock | F‍ill remembers settings

example, a start value of 0.10 will create rates from 10% to 15%). Note that you do not have to reselect the filled block in order to do this. The block is remembered from the last time, as shown in Figure 3-23, where the current cell is in fact E1.

This ability to repeat the fill operation compensates for the command's major shortcoming—*the answers it creates are not dynamic.* That means the numbers in the series do not automatically change when you alter the first number in the series. For that you need to use a series based on formulas, as described in a moment. You can enter formulas or cell references for the values used by Block | Fill. For example, if you wanted a series of numbers that grew by a quarter, you could enter **1/4** instead of **.25** as the Step value. If you want to grow a series of numbers by the value in B4, starting with the value that is in D6, you can enter **D6** as the Start value and **B4** as the Step value. If you decide to use cell references or formulas for Block Fill values, you will find that they are converted to values the next time you use the command (for example, if you use 1/4 as the Step value, it will appear as .25 the next time you use Block | Fill).

Further Series Settings

You can use Block | Fill to create a series of dates using date serial numbers, which were discussed in the previous chapter, or the DATE function, described at the end of Chapter 5. For example, to create a series of dates representing successive Fridays, you would begin by finding out the date serial number for the first day in the series. Do this by entering the date with the CTRL-SHIFT-D key. If you press CTRL-SHIFT-D and then enter **1/1/93**, which happens to be the first Friday in 1993, Quattro Pro will display 01/01/93 in the current cell. From the cell identifier you can read that the date serial number in this case is 33970. You can now create the date series by using 33970 as the Start value and 7 as the Step value.

Block | Fill does not supply the date format to cells. You have to use the Numeric Format settings in the Active Block dialog box to format the date serial numbers as dates. To create a date series with the DATE function, refer to the section on date functions at the end of Chapter 5.

The three columns of Series settings in the Block Fill dialog box can be used to alter the way Quattro Pro treats a fill operation. The normal setting in the first column is Linear. This results in a normal sequence of values, where the Step value is added to the Start value. The Growth setting means that the Start value is multiplied by the Step value. Starting with 3 and stepping by 2 a growth series would create 3, 6, 12, and so on. The Power setting uses the Step value as the exponent of the Start value. Thus, starting with 3 and stepping by 2 would yield a power series of 3, 9, 81, and so on.

The settings in the second and third columns of the series section allow you to increment time and date values in units of time (selecting one of these items automatically selects Linear in the first column). Suppose you want to create a series of loan payment dates, set for the 15th of each month, starting on March 15th of 1993. After selecting the cells and issuing the Block | Insert command, you enter the first date as the Start value (press CTRL-SHIFT-D and type **3/15/93**). Make sure that the Step value is 1 and that the Stop value is greater than the last date serial number in the series. Then select Month in the Series field and choose OK to complete the operation (you may want to format the values to show the date in the style you prefer).

The result is a series of dates, each of which is the 15th of the month. This is quite different from incrementing the dates by 30 days, owing to the differing number of days in a month, a factor that the Month setting takes into account. The Step setting does not have to be 1. If it is 2, the monthly series is every other month. If the step is 3, you get quarterly dates. The Year setting increments dates by the number of years specified in the Step setting, taking into account leap years. The Week setting simply uses seven days as an increment, so that a Step of 4 means every four weeks.

Note The default Stop value, 8191, is the date serial number for June 4, 1922, so modern date series require that you change the default Stop value. You can quickly enter a huge number by typing **99999** (as a date serial number, this takes you well into the twenty-second century).

Another way of numbering consecutively is to use formulas. For example, to create the employee number entries for the spreadsheet in Figure 3-22, you could start by entering **1001** in A3 and entering the formula **1+A3** in A4. Copying the formula from A4 to A5 through A16 will produce a series that looks just like the one created by Block | Fill (you can actually use SpeedFill to copy the formula down the column). The formula approach has several advantages. You can create new numbers very easily. If you had to add a new item in row 17 at the bottom of the list, you could copy the formula from A16 to A17 and get 1015. Another advantage of a formula series is that you can change the whole series by altering the first number. By changing A3 from 1001 to 3001, you would change the numbers below accordingly to 3002, 3003, and so on.

The advantages of a formula series are also its weaknesses. The numbers are not fixed, so copying a row from the employee inventory table to another part of the spreadsheet alters the number, rendering it incorrect. Fortunately, with Quattro Pro you can create a series of numbers with formulas and then convert the formulas to their results, essentially "fixing" the values. This is done with the Block | Values command described later in this chapter.

Block | Names

If you make frequent use of a particular block of cells it is worthwhile to attach a name to them for easier reference, much the same way that pages of the notebook have been named. *Block names* have many uses. When you are creating formulas, you can refer to blocks by name instead of by their coordinates. When you want to move to a location in the spreadsheet that has been given a block name, you can do so very quickly. When you begin to write macros, you will find that they rely very heavily on block names.

Naming Blocks

Consider the salary figures in column D of the spreadsheet in Figure 3-22. The figures need to be totaled, and the total may be used in several different places. If you attach a suitable name to the cells in the block D3..D16, such as SALARY, you could then use the following formula:

@SUM(SALARY)

Of course, you cannot use a block name in a formula until you have created the name. To name a block of cells, you select the block and issue the Block | Names command. This produces the following submenu:

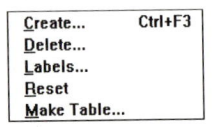

```
Create...      Ctrl+F3
Delete...
Labels...
Reset
Make Table...
```

Use the Create command to assign a name. When you select Create, the Create Name dialog box appears, as shown in Figure 3-24. Type the name for the block in the Name field, for example, **SALARY**. Then choose OK to complete the command.

Note that there is a shortcut to the Create Name dialog box, CTRL-F3. Also note that if you select the wrong block before issuing the Block | Name | Create command, you can use the Block(s) setting to point out the cells, just as you do with other block commands described earlier in this chapter. You can assign names to compound blocks.

FIGURE 3-24 Create Name dialog box

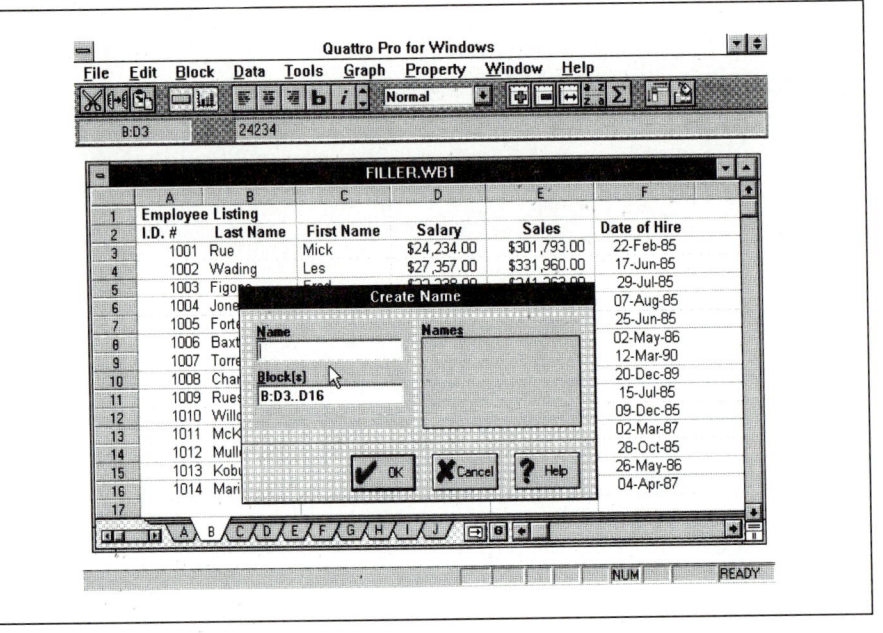

Block Name Rules

As you might imagine, the names you use for blocks must follow certain rules. They can contain as many as 15 characters. You can use the letters A through Z and numbers 0 through 9, as well as punctuation characters (avoid characters used as math operators such as + and –, as well as parentheses). The names should, ideally, bear some meaningful relationship to the contents of the cells, but at the same time not be too long. Long names would negate the convenience of using the blocks.

Block names should not be the same as any valid cell reference. For example, do not name a block Q4, because there is a cell called Q4 on row 4 in column Q. Using Q_4, or 4Q, or even FOURTH_Q would be better. Avoid using spaces in block names, as this can make them confusing to use in formulas. You can use any number of block names, and the blocks can overlap. For example, in Figure 3-23, you could name E3..G6 as both CHICAGOQ1 and QUARTER1.

If you use the Block | Names | Create command, and named blocks already exist, you will see the names listed alphabetically in the Create Name dialog box, as shown here:

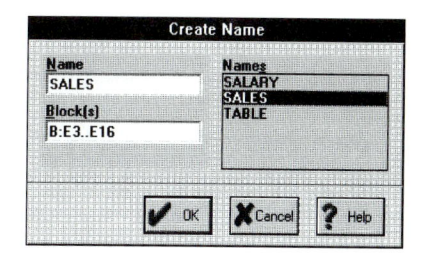

You can see that there is a block called SALES as well as one called TABLE. If you select a block in the Names list, the coordinates will appear in the Block(s) field.

Deleting and Tracking Block Names

If you name a cell or block of cells and later decide that the name is no longer necessary, you can remove it by using the Delete command on the Block | Names menu. Quattro Pro presents a list of names, and you can highlight the one you want to delete and press ENTER. Note that this deletes the block name but does not affect the contents of the named cells. If you have used a block name in a formula, Quattro Pro will automatically replace the block name with the block coordinates. However, if you have referred to the block in a macro, you might need to edit the macro after deleting the block name. There is no confirmation of this command, but you can reverse it with Edit | Undo.

The Block | Names | Delete command cannot delete more than one block name at a time. This is the task of the Reset command that is on the Block | Names menu, which deletes all block names at once. Because this step can accidentally erase names settings, Quattro Pro requires you to confirm this action with a Yes/No response.

The Make Table command on the Block | Names menu is used to create a two-column alphabetical list of the block names, together with their cell coordinates, in an area of the spreadsheet that you designate. This task is best done in an area set aside for worksheet housekeeping. Such a table is useful in larger worksheets for keeping track of block names you have used and their locations. However, the table is not automatically updated when block name assignments change, and you have to reissue the command to get a current table.

When you want to use a block name in a formula, you can press the F3 key to list named blocks. For example, to sum the block called SALARY you could type **@SUM(** and then press F3. The Block Names list appears, and you can select a name from the list. This is one of the advantages of assigning block names. Whenever you type information for Quattro Pro, you run the risk of making an error, plus it is often easier to remember a name, such as SALARY, than a set of coordinates, such as D3..D16. Consider what happens if you enter **D3..D6** by mistake, Quattro Pro does not know you missed several rows of numbers. But if you enter **SALARI** by mistake, Quattro Pro beeps and tells you that the name is not correct.

At first, the Block Names list only shows the names of the blocks, but if you press the Expand key (the plus key on the numeric keypad), you get the cell coordinates for the blocks as well:

Chapter 3: Blocks and Names   165

```
         Block Names
  SALARY     B:D3..D16
  SALES      B:E3..E16
  TABLE      B:A2..F16




      ✓ OK    ✗ Cancel
```

If there are a lot of block names, you can press F3 to make the list box longer. Press F3 again to switch back to a shorter list. Use the Contract key to switch back to the less detailed list format (the Contract key is the minus sign on the numeric keypad). Note that page references are included with cell coordinates. If you change the name of the page from B to Employees, the expanded block name list will reflect this:

SALARY   Employees:D3..D16

You can also use block names for navigation. When you press the Goto key (F5) you can type the name of the block and press ENTER. If you have named A2..H16 as TABLE, you can press F5 and enter **TABLE**. This will select cell A2 because using F5 with a named block that is more than one cell in size has the effect of selecting the top-left cell of the block. When you press F5 and are prompted for an address, you can supply a block name either by typing it or selecting it from the list, as shown here:

```
              Go To
  Reference [List:F16           ]

  Block Names
  SALARY
  SALES
  TABLE




   ✓ OK    ✗ Cancel    ? Help
```

Creating Names from Labels

The Labels command on the Block | Names menu enables you to assign names from labels in the spreadsheet. For example, in the spreadsheet in Figure 3-25, you could use the Labels command to name cells C2 through C5 with their labels (which appear in the cell to the left), like this:

Cell	Will Be Named
C2	KETCHES
C3	CRUISERS
C4	CATAMARANS
C5	DINGHIES

You can see the Create Names From Labels dialog box in Figure 3-25. The cells containing the labels, B2..B5, were selected before the Block | Names | Labels command was issued. At this point, you need only select

FIGURE 3-25

Create Names From Labels dialog box

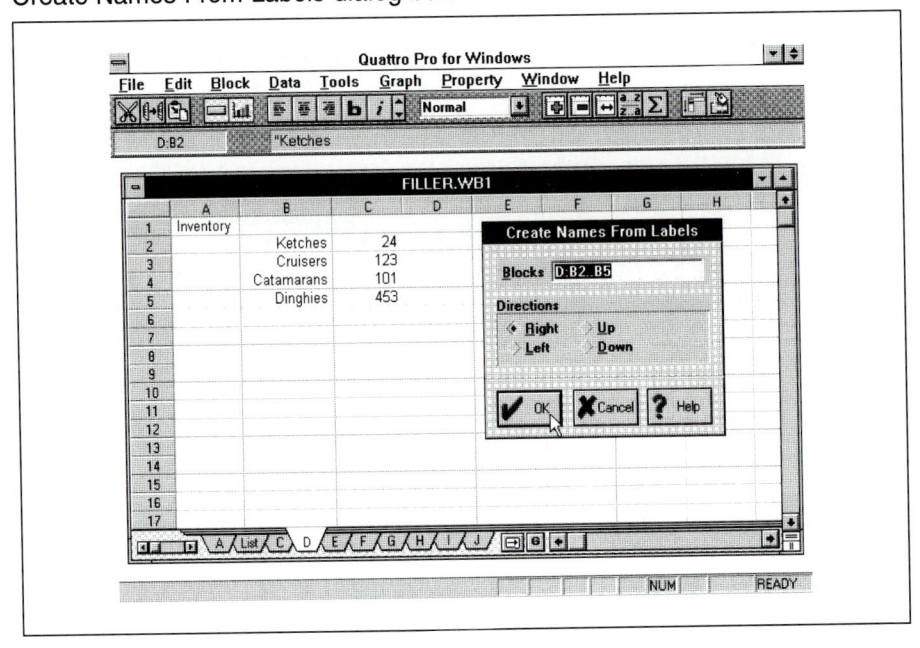

from among the Directions choices: Right, Left, Up, and Down. In this scenario, the cells being named are to the right of the labels, so you would select Right. When you choose OK, Quattro Pro uses the labels in B2..B5 to name the cells in C2..C5.

If one or more of the cells in the block of labels is empty, it does not affect the command. For example, if the labels in the entries in columns B and C of Figure 3-25 were double-spaced, as in Figure 3-26, you could still select the block shown to label the cells to the right. This technique is particularly useful when you are working with macros and databases, as you will discover in later chapters.

Block Shapes and Values

There are two more Block commands that will be dealt with in this chapter: Transpose and Values (the Reformat command will be dealt with in Chapter 12, since it relates to text handling, and the Insert Break command will be discussed in the next chapter, since it relates to printing).

FIGURE 3-26 Creating labels from block with blank cells

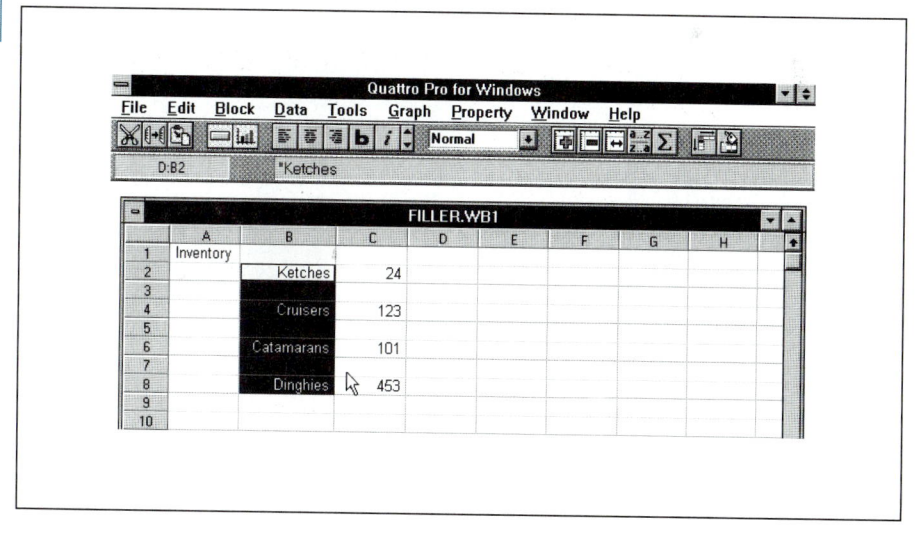

Block | Transpose

At times you may want to change the arrangement of information in a worksheet. For example, the table of inventory in the top of Figure 3-27 could be rearranged, as in the lower half. To alter entries in this fashion, use the Block | Transpose command. The table in the lower part of Figure 3-27 was created by selecting B2..C7 and issuing the Block | Transpose command. This produces the Block Transpose dialog box, shown in Figure 3-27. At first, the To setting is the same as the From setting. In this case, the To setting was changed to B10. The effect of choosing OK is the table displayed with its upper-left cell in B10.

Because the Transpose command copies cells and does not actually move them, you will want to use a To setting that does not overlap the From setting. This avoids confusing, duplicated cells in the results. You can always delete the original copy if you are satisfied with the transposed entries. The cell entries that you transpose will retain their cell formatting and alignment. However, formulas that are transposed may not work properly. You can see this in Figure 3-27, where the value of 0 for the

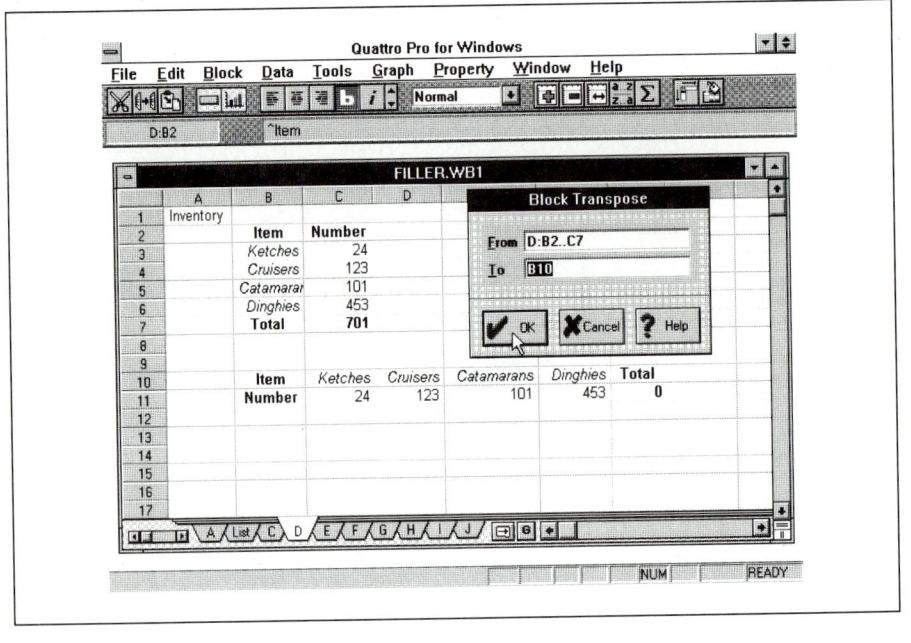

FIGURE 3-27 Block Transpose dialog box

Chapter 3: Blocks and Names   169

Total indicates a problem. One solution is to convert formulas to values before transposing. You can do this with the Block | Values command.

Values on the Block

There will be times when you use formulas to generate numbers but no longer need the formulas. In other words, you want to "fix" the resulting values. You do this with the Block | Values command. Consider the worksheet in Figure 3-28, which is being used to calculate increased salaries. The formulas in column F create the new salary based on the percentage increase in F1. At this point, a change to the percentage in F1 will alter all of the entries in F4..F16. When the rate of increase has been finalized, there will be no need to make further changes to the New Salary figures.

To replace the formulas in F4..F16 with permanent values, select F4..F16 and issue the Block | Values command. The selected cells form the From block. You can see that they also form the To block, which means that when you choose OK, Quattro Pro will copy the values over

FIGURE 3-28 Formulas that calculate new salaries

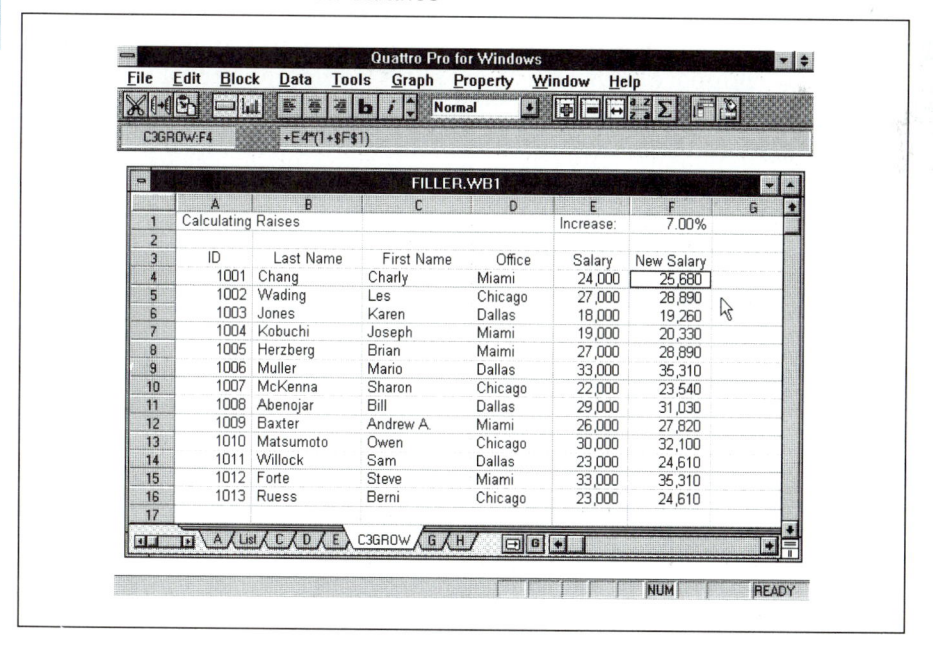

the top of the formulas, directly replacing formulas with results. You can also select a cell for the To setting that is outside the From block. This has the effect of copying the values to a different part of the worksheet.

You can convert a single formula to its result by selecting the cell and pressing F2 followed by F9. This sequence of the Edit key followed by the Calc key is handy because it shows you the formula result on the input line. This means you can press the ENTER key or click the check button to write the result over the formula. Alternatively, you can press ESC twice or click the X button, which leaves the formula unchanged.

Search and Replace

There is one Edit command that we have so far ignored, but which comes in handy when editing worksheets. This is the Edit | Search and Replace command. Typically associated with word processing programs, *search and replace* refers to a program's ability to search for every instance of one string of characters and replace it with another.

Basic Search and Replace

Suppose that the yacht sales company used in previous examples decides that the term "Office" is no longer appropriate to describe its operations in various cities. The new term is "Marina," and all references to "Office" in the revenue and expense projections need to be changed. The sample notebook would need considerable editing to meet this requirement. This is a job for Search and Replace.

When you select Search and Replace from the Edit menu, you get the dialog box shown in Figure 3-29. The first setting to establish is Block(s). Typically, you will select the block to be searched before issuing the command, so the Block(s) setting will already be made. You should include all cells that you need to change. In this case, the block is Company:A2..A13. You might expect the block to be Chicago:A2..A13. However, you will note that Group mode is in effect and the current group is called Company. This means that the operation will include A2..A13 in all pages of the group.

Chapter 3: Blocks and Names 171

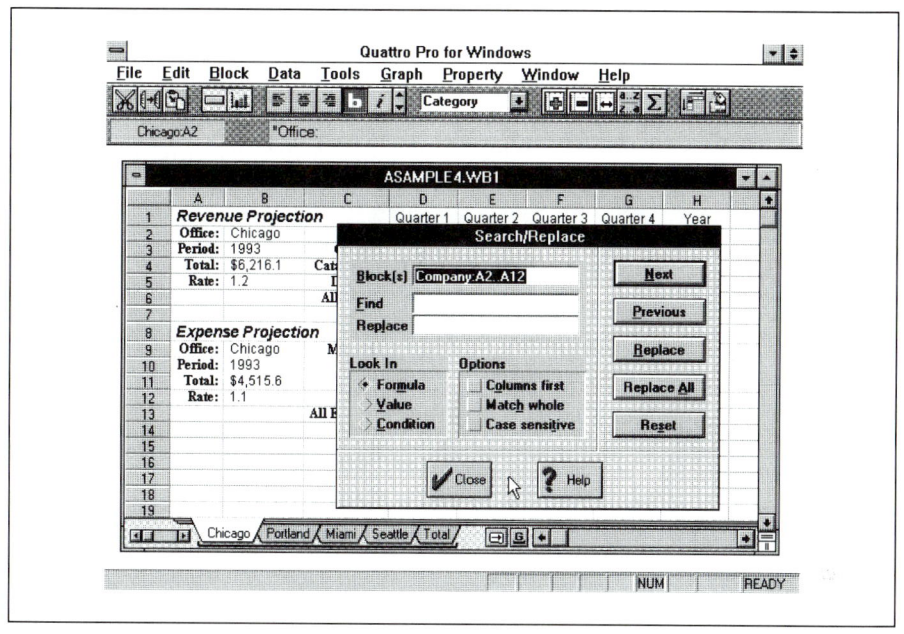

The Search/Replace dialog box

Note To select all cells on a page for a search and replace or any other operation, you can use the following shortcut: Press HOME to select A1 and then hold down SHIFT and press END followed by HOME. This extends the block from A1 to the last column and row of the spreadsheet, that is, the ones farthest from column A and row 1 that contain any data.

After selecting the block of cells to be searched, select the Find field and type the characters you want Quattro Pro to search for. These can be letters, numbers, math signs within formulas, or any character or string of characters you have entered into the cells. In this case, you would type **Office**. Now select Replace and enter the characters to replace the ones you are searching for, in this case, **Marina**. If you do not wish to replace the item you are searching for but rather want to delete it, leave the Replace setting blank. The Look In settings, which are listed in Table 3-4, enable you to fine-tune the operation. In this case, the default settings will work nicely.

To proceed with the operation, choose Next, and Quattro Pro will highlight the first cell it finds that contains the characters you are

TABLE 3-4 Search and Replace Options

Type Option	Action
Look In:	
Formula	Looks for search string within formulas, cell references, block names, and so on. A search for 2 finds 2*2, B2, B52s, and so on, but does not find 6*7
Value	Values the formula in each cell and looks for the search string in the result. Converts formula to value if result contains a search string. Thus, a search for 2 with 5 as a replace string will find 6*7 and convert it to 45
Condition	Enables you to set a condition in the search string, such as +B2>12, where B2 is the first cell in the search block, and you want to find all cells with a value greater than 12.
Options:	
Column first	Searches the block from the current cell on, proceeding column by column; otherwise, proceeds row by row.
Match whole	Requires that the match be the entire cell contents, except for the label indicator, so that a search string of **mar** would not locate a cell containing **mars**; otherwise, searches for partial cell entries, so that a search string of **mar** would find **martian** and **market**.
Case sensitive	Requires that the match be exact as far as case is concerned. A search string of **ERIN** would not find **Erin**; otherwise, does not require a match in cases, so that a search string of **erin** would find **Erin** and **ERIN**.

Note: A search initiated with Next moves forward through the block from the current cell, whereas a search initiated with Previous moves backward. Both choices search the entire block.

searching for (you may need to move the dialog box to see the cell). You can then pick Replace to change this instance of "Office" to "Marina" and move to the next. Choosing Next leaves this instance as it is. Selecting Replace All tells Quattro Pro to proceed with an automatic search and replace from this point on. Do not pick Replace All unless you are certain about what will happen. If you are not careful, you could change instances of the search characters you did not anticipate.

The Close button tells Quattro Pro to stop the process before all instances have been changed. In this case, the last cell found becomes the current cell. After the last instance of the searched characters has been reached and your decision has been entered, Quattro Pro returns to READY mode. The next time you use the Search and Replace command for this spreadsheet in this session, it will remember the Find and Replace settings that you entered. In fact, the Search and Replace command will remember the settings, even if you move to a different notebook, enabling you to repeat the same operation on similar spreadsheets, one after another. If you need to change the settings, pick the Reset option from the dialog box.

CHAPTER 4

Filing, Printing, and Styling

In this chapter we take a closer look at commands that open, save, and close notebooks and the commands that print reports from them and make the reports look good. Most of the commands discussed in this chapter are on the File menu, although we will also discuss how to embellish notebook reports using a variety of design elements such as fonts and shading.

Working with Files

When you need to create a new notebook, store a notebook, or load a notebook you made earlier, you use the File menu, shown in Figure 4-1. The File menu is a standard feature in Windows programs. If you have used other Windows applications you are probably familiar with the New, Open, Close, Save, and Save As commands. In this section we review how these commands are used in Quattro Pro. We also look at some of the mechanics behind disk files so that you have a better understanding of how these commands work.

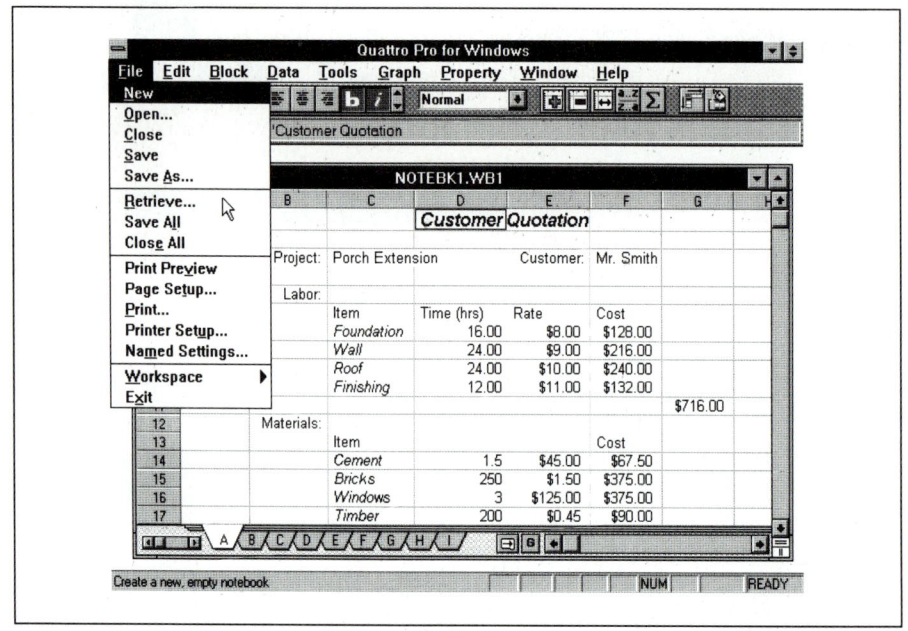

FIGURE 4-1 The File menu

Of Files, Disks, and Directories

As you start to create your own notebooks and begin working with several notebooks at once, it is important to fully understand the File menu commands. You have seen that the data you enter into a notebook is not immediately stored in a worksheet file on disk. Instead it is temporarily retained in the computer's random access memory (RAM). Think of RAM as an electronic desktop. Because it is electronic, the work that you do on this desktop, such as entering and calculating, is performed very quickly. By retaining most of your notebook in memory while you manipulate it, Quattro Pro 4 can provide fast responses and rapid calculations.

Unfortunately, an electronic desktop has its disadvantages. The problem with RAM is that everything you have entered into it is erased when the power to your PC is turned off or interrupted. That is why, as we pointed out in Chapter 1, it is very important to use the File | Save command on a regular basis to copy the notebook from memory to disk. Just as Quattro Pro for Windows comes to you on disks, data created with the help of programs is also stored on disks.

Information is stored on disks in *files*. As you work with your computer you quickly create many files. To keep these files manageable, most large-capacity disks, particularly hard disks, are divided into sections called *directories*. Directories are an important part of organizing files on your hard disk. You can divide directories further into *subdirectories*.

To understand subdirectories, consider a collection of company records in a three-drawer filing cabinet. The first drawer of the cabinet is labeled ACCOUNTS, the second ORDERS, and the third PERSONNEL. Within the ACCOUNTS drawer are file folders marked ASSETS, BUDGET, INVENTORY, and so on. Within the BUDGET folder are two folders, one marked INCOME and the other marked EXPENSE. Within the latter you will find documents pertaining to EXPENSEs, which is BUDGET-related ACCOUNTS information.

What you have here is a *hierarchical* file structure, with folders inside folders inside drawers. In computer terms, each disk drive is like a filing cabinet drawer. In a simple computer, you might have a floppy disk drive (drive A) and a hard disk drive (C). Larger systems might have two floppy disk drives (A and B) and more than one hard disk (C, D, E, and so on).

If your computer is part of a network, you might store files on another computer that presents itself as an additional drive letter.

Dividing each disk are directories, which are like the folders in a drawer. A directory might be further divided into subdirectories, which are like folders within folders. Files are the documents, and can be stored in directories or subdirectories. If you run the Windows File Manager, you can see a pictorial representation of your computer's file structure. In Figure 4-2, you can see drive E of a computer that is running Quattro Pro. There are six directories, one of which is called QPW. This contains the Quattro Pro program files. There are three subdirectories of QPW: FILES, DATA, and QUOTES. The rectangle on the left half of the window indicates that the QPW directory has been selected. The right side of the window shows a list of the files and directories in it.

Note To see both files and directories listed in a File Manager window, use File Manager's View menu to select Tree and Directory. Use the View | Split command to adjust the relative size of the two sides.

FIGURE 4-2 Using the File Manager to view files and directories

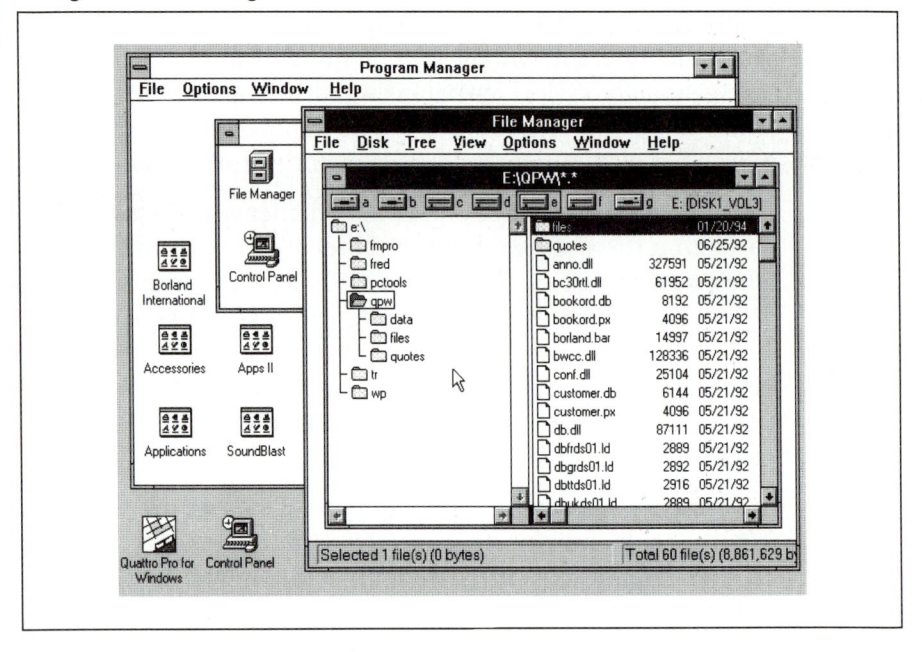

Chapter 4: Filing, Printing, and Styling 179

While the File Manager uses file folders to represent directories, the term "tree" is sometimes used to describe a directory structure. According to this analogy, subdirectories are seen as limbs on a tree. In the diagram on the left of the File Manager window, the tree is actually upside down, like a family tree. In fact, the main directory of a disk is usually called the *root directory*, from which all others spring. This is where the first level of directories are created. In the DOS file syntax, the disk drive letter is followed by a colon (:), and "directory" is represented by a backslash (\). The root directory on drive E is referred to as E:\ (the root directory needs no other name), and a directory called QPW on the same disk is described as E:\QPW. A subdirectory of QPW called FILES is thus called E:\QPW\FILES.

You will sometimes hear the terms "parent" and "child" used in reference to directories. You can say that the FILES directory is a child of the QPW directory. The QPW directory is the parent directory of FILES directory. The parent directory of QPW is E:\, the root directory of the drive. You will find that some programs use a pair of dots (..) as a symbol for the parent directory of a subdirectory.

Note In the examples in this chapter, hard disks are referred to using the letters C and E, but your hard disk might well have a different letter.

When Quattro Pro for Windows was installed on your computer, a subdirectory called QPW was created to hold the main program files. It is a good idea to store your Quattro Pro for Windows data files in a separate subdirectory, such as \QPW\DATA. You can create such a directory using the Create Directory option in the Windows File Manager. The QUOTES directory in Figure 4-2 was created in this way. After opening File Manager and selecting the correct drive from the row of drive icons below the title bar, the QPW directory folder was selected. Then the File menu was activated and the Create Directory option selected. This produced the dialog box in Figure 4-3, into which the name of the directory was typed. Choosing OK places a new folder into the directory structure, within the folder/directory that was current when the Create Directory command was issued.

Once a directory has been created, you can move files to it. If you are using Windows 3.1, you can move files by simply dragging the picture of

FIGURE 4-3 Creating a new directory with the File Manager

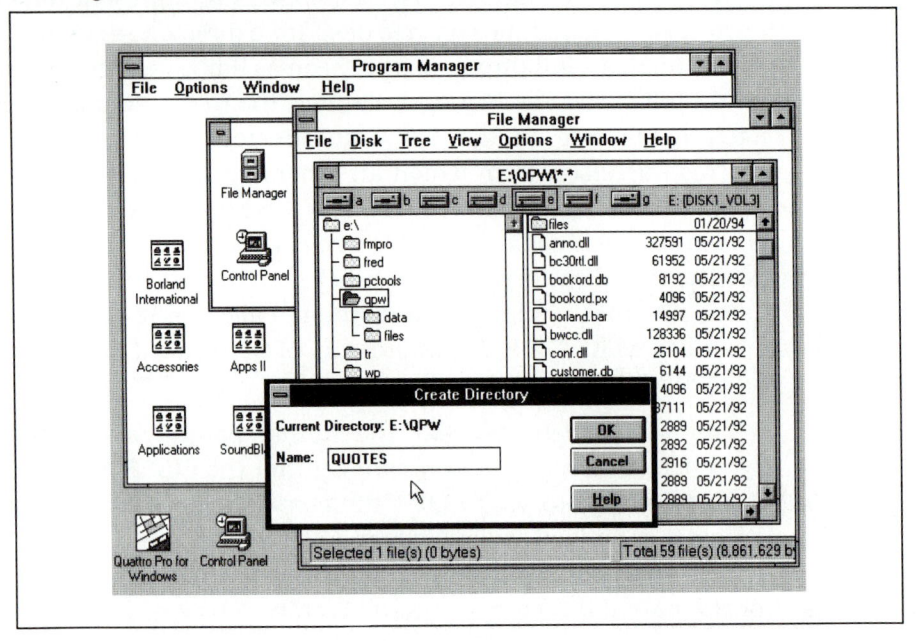

the file to the picture of the destination folder (or drive) and releasing the mouse button. This is known as the *drag-and-drop* technique. For example, to move notebook files from the QPW directory to a data directory, double-click on the QPW directory so that its contents are listed on the right of the window. Then select files on the right by pointing and clicking. Drag the selected file to the new location by clicking on the file, holding the button down, and moving the mouse (an icon of the file moves along with the pointer). A box will appear around the folder to show that it has been selected as the destination for the file. Release the mouse button, and Windows asks you to confirm the move.

Note To select several files, select the first file, point to the next one you want, and CTRL-click. You can do this for as many files as you like. The files become highlighted, and can all be moved at the same time. To select a group of files that are next to each other in the file list, click on the first file and SHIFT-click on the last file. All the files between the first and last file are selected.

Paths and Names

In order to use a file stored on disk, a program needs directions on where to find it. This information is the file's *path*. If you have a file called QSMITH.WB1 stored in a directory called \QPW\QUOTES on drive E, the path to that file is E:\QPW\QUOTES.

When you first install Quattro Pro, it assumes that you want to save notebooks in the same directory that holds the program files (typically \QPW). As you can see, the QPW directory already has lots of files in it, which makes it hard to locate your saved notebooks. To change this assumption—for example, to tell Quattro Pro to store notebooks in the \QPW\DATA directory—you change the startup directory using the Properties | Application command (right-click on the Quattro Pro application title bar). The Application Startup dialog box appears, as in Figure 4-4. Once you edit the Directory field and choose OK, Quattro Pro will automatically remember it for this and future sessions.

Every file in the same directory of a disk must have a unique name. This name is composed of three parts: a filename, a period, and an optional extension as follows:

FILENAME.EXT

The filename consists of up to eight letters (upper- or lowercase—DOS file syntax is not case sensitive) or numbers without spaces.

FIGURE 4-4 Recording the default data directory in the Application settings

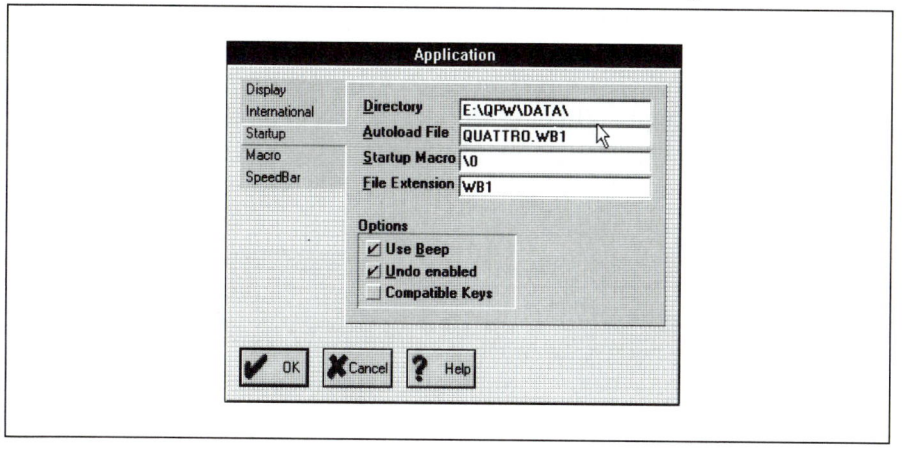

You can use some punctuation marks in a filename, but it is usually easier to use numbers and letters rather than to try to remember which punctuation marks are acceptable. Valid punctuation characters in a filename are

( ) ! @ # $ % & − _ ' { } ~ | ^

One punctuation mark has a special role in filenames: the period. It connects the filename with its extension. The extension is up to three characters long and follows the same rules as those for filenames.

Extensions are generally used to distinguish between types of files. For example, Quattro Pro notebooks have the extension WB1. Earlier versions of Quattro used the extension WQ1. 1-2-3 files use WK1 and WK3, depending on the version of the program (version 2 uses WK1; version 3 uses WK3).

When you save a notebook, Quattro Pro will assign the default extension of WB1. If you want Quattro Pro to save to a format that can be read by another program such as 1-2-3, you can enter the filename and the appropriate extension. For example, if you name the file BUDGET.WK1, Quattro Pro will save the notebook as a 1-2-3 file. If you want Quattro Pro to use a particular extension all the time, you can enter that extension as part of the program defaults using the File Extension field of the Startup setting in the Application dialog box. For more on setting defaults, see Chapter 7. For more on working with file types other than WB1, see Chapter 8.

When you create a directory (as opposed to a file), you can use up to 11 letters for the name, but any more than 8 have to be added as an extension, after a period. It is a good idea to avoid directory names that are more than 8 letters long. Note that Quattro Pro and Windows might sometimes list directory names and filenames in lowercase and at other times display them in uppercase. We consistently use uppercase in this text, but bear in mind that none of the DOS filename commands are case sensitive.

File Saves and File Lists

As you saw in Chapter 1, the File | Save command is fundamental to your work with Quattro Pro. This command stores the current notebook

Chapter 4: Filing, Printing, and Styling 183

on disk so that it can be used at a later date. The act of storing data on disk is often referred to as "writing to disk." Loading data from the disk into memory is referred to as "reading from disk." If the current notebook has already been stored on disk, the File | Save command requires no further input—it simply writes the latest version of the notebook to disk, overwriting the last version. The progress bar on the bottom left of the screen will indicate when the action has been completed.

The first time you issue the Save command in a fresh (untitled) notebook, you are prompted to supply a name for the notebook, as shown in Figure 4-5. Let's take a moment to examine this dialog box, as it is similar to the one used by two other important commands: File | Open and File | Retrieve. (We won't address the Protection Password at this point. Password protection and other advanced file-handling issues are covered in Chapter 8.)

The first field in the Save File dialog box, File Name, shows the name that will be given to the file you are about to write to disk (when you are using the Open or Retrieve command, this field shows the name of the file that you are going to read from disk). As you can see in Figure 4-5, a provisional name of the notebook is in this field but highlighted, so that whatever you type next will replace it.

Typically, you will select Save, type the first eight characters of the desired filename, and click on the OK button, the default button for this

FIGURE 4-5 The Save File dialog box

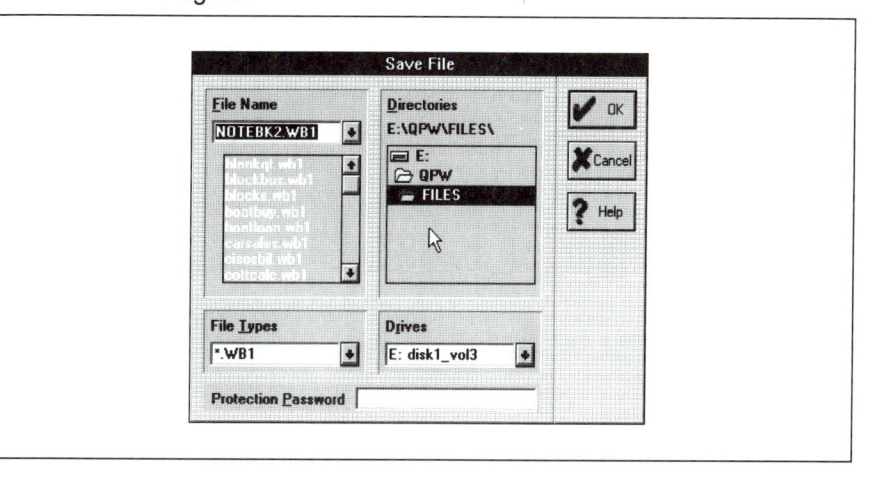

dialog box (its outline is bolder than the others), or press ENTER, which selects the default button. Quattro Pro then saves the file to disk using the name you have typed and the default extension, WB1. Below the File Name field is a list showing files that already exist in the current directory. It is possible to pick a file from this list and save the current notebook into it, but doing so will overwrite the contents of the other file.

To pick a name from the list of existing files using the keyboard, first press the TAB key. This puts a dotted line around the first name in the list. If you now press DOWN ARROW, you will find the first filename highlighted in the list and also entered in the File Name field. Keep pressing DOWN ARROW or RIGHT ARROW to highlight each name in turn. Move back up the list with UP ARROW or LEFT ARROW. If there are more than eight files in the list, the list scrolls as you continue to press the arrow keys. The PGUP and PGDN keys work to move you up and down the list one group of files at a time, END takes you to the last file, and HOME takes you to the first.

Note If you know the first name of the file you are looking for you can press the Edit key, F2, and type the letter. This selects the first file that begins with that letter.

Mouse users can select a name from the list by pointing to it and clicking the left mouse button. You can scroll the list by either clicking on the up or down arrowheads on the scroll bar to the right of the box or dragging the elevator box (scroll button) down the scroll bar.

When you select the filename you want, you can press ENTER to use the filename that is highlighted. Mouse users can double-click the name instead of clicking once and pressing ENTER (pressing ENTER chooses the default button for the Save File dialog box, which is OK). Because choosing OK in the Save File dialog box tells Quattro Pro to write the current notebook into the file you have selected and thus overwrite existing data with that name (an error here could be disastrous), Quattro Pro asks you to confirm the action, as shown here:

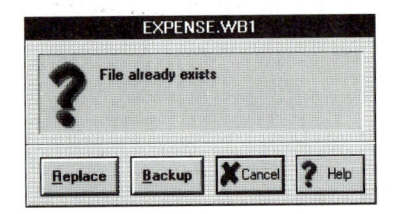

Chapter 4: Filing, Printing, and Styling

The dialog box shows you the name of the file you are attempting to overwrite. Your choices are

- **Replace** This writes the current notebook into the file named in the dialog box title, completely replacing the contents of that file.

- **Backup** This saves the current notebook using the name in the dialog box title but also creates a copy of the previous version of the file using the same name with the extension BAK instead of WB1 (thus the former EXPENSE.WB1 would be backed up as EXPENSE.BAK). You can retrieve the BAK file later by entering its full name in the File Name field of the Open File dialog box.

- **Cancel** Selecting this button terminates the Save File operation and returns you to the notebook (you can press ESC to select Cancel).

- **Help** If you're not certain what to do, get Help. Because you are involved in a save operation, the help screens will display information on saving files. When you finish reading the help screens, you can proceed with the save or cancel the operation.

You will see this dialog box the first time you try to save a file using File | Save with a name that already exists in the current directory. This is true whether you deliberately select the name from the file list or accidentally type a name that is already in use. The same dialog box also appears every time you use File | Save with a name that already exists.

Changing Directories and Drives

Whenever you are using a file dialog box like the one in Figure 4-5, you can use the Directories section to change the current directory. The directory diagram displays the current directory as an open file folder that is highlighted. If the directory has a parent (a directory above it in the tree structure), the parent is also shown as an open file folder. Thus in Figure 4-5, the current directory is FILES, which is a subdirectory of QPW, which is in turn a subdirectory of drive E, all of which are open. Any subdirectories of E:\QPW\FILES would be shown in the diagram as closed folders.

You can open the parent of the current directory by double-clicking its folder or highlighting the folder and pressing ENTER. To highlight a folder with the keyboard, press ALT-D or use the TAB key to select the Directories field (a dotted line will appear around the highlight bar in the diagram). Then you can use the UP ARROW, DOWN ARROW, END, and HOME keys to navigate the list of directories. These keys select, respectively, one folder up, one folder down, the last folder, and the first folder. In Figure 4-6, you can see that the user has highlighted the QPW directory. Next, press ENTER to open it.

In this case, there are three subdirectories of QPW. Each one is shown as a closed folder. If you want to change the current directory to DATA, highlight DATA and press ENTER. To reveal all of the first-level directories on the drive, double-click the drive icon at the top of the diagram, or highlight the drive letter and press ENTER. Using these techniques, you can navigate your way around the drive. When you change the current directory, the file list will change to show files in that directory. If you are using the File | Save command, your file will be saved into whichever directory is current when you choose OK.

Each time you use a File menu command dialog box, Quattro Pro shows you the directory that was used last. Suppose you issue the Save command, and the E:\QPW\FILES directory is listed. You change the directory to E:\QPW\DATA and complete the command. The DATA directory will then be displayed the next time you use a file dialog box.

FIGURE 4-6 Viewing the parent directory of E:\QPW\FILES

Chapter 4: Filing, Printing, and Styling

However, if you issue the Save command, change the directory from FILES to DATA, but cancel the command, the FILES directory will be displayed the next time you use a file dialog box. The drive and directory that Quattro Pro displays the first time you use a file dialog box during a session is determined by the Application property settings, shown earlier in Figure 4-4.

If you have several drives on your computer, you can use the Drives field in the file dialog box to change the drive that is displayed. When you select this field, you can use the DOWN ARROW key or click on the DOWN ARROW button to display a list of available drives, as shown in Figure 4-7. The drives are listed alphabetically by drive letter. If drives have volume labels, these are also listed. You can scroll down the list to see any additional drives. When you have highlighted the drive you want to view you press ENTER. Mouse users can drag the highlight down the list. When you release the mouse button, Quattro Pro will switch to the drive that is highlighted.

File Types and Wildcards

The Save File dialog box, shown in Figure 4-7, always presents a name in the File Name field above a list of existing files. The name presented is the default or provisional name for the current notebook. Thus, when

FIGURE 4-7 Viewing the list of available drives

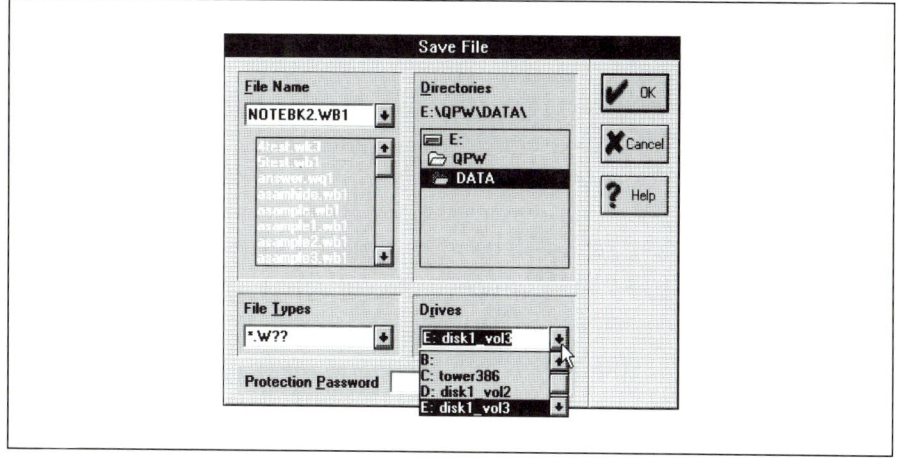

you save NOTEBK1.WB1, that is the name presented. If you retrieve a file called SALES.WB1 and then save it, SALES.WB1 is the name filled in. If you don't want to use the name Quattro Pro suggests, you can edit the suggestion or select a different name from the list of files.

You can control which files are included in the list by adjusting the File Types setting. This uses a *file specification* to filter out unwanted files from the list. A file specification consists of one or more letters, numbers, and *wildcard characters*. A wildcard is a special character that stands for one or more other characters. There are two wildcards: the asterisk (*), and the question mark (?). The asterisk stands for "any number of characters." Thus the file specification SALES* means all files that have names starting with SALES, such as SALES.WB1 or SALESMAN.WK1. The file specification *.WB1 means all files that have .WB1 as their extension.

The question mark is used to represent any single character, so that Q???.WB1 stands for all .WB1 files with four-letter filenames that begin with Q. One particularly handy file specification that uses the ? is *.W??, which means all files with a three-letter extension that begins with W. This includes many of the spreadsheet file formats that Quattro Pro can read, such as .WKS, .WQ1, and .WB1. To change the entry in the File Types field, click the arrow to the right of it. A list of file specifications that Quattro Pro knows about and supports appears, as shown here:

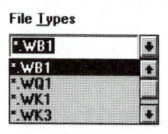

File Types
```
*.WB1
*.WB1
*.WQ1
*.WK1
*.WK3
```

You can drag the highlight down the list and release it when you have highlighted the specification that you want. You can also use the scroll bar to view more of the list and click on the specification you want. The selected specification is displayed in the File Types field, and the list displays only files that match the selected type. If you are not using a mouse, you can press TAB or ALT-T to select the File Types field and then press DOWN ARROW to display the list. Continue pressing DOWN ARROW to see more of the list. Press ENTER to select the highlighted specification.

Besides being able to select from a list of file types that Quattro Pro supports, you can also view a list of files based on any specification you want. To do this, you ignore the File Types field and enter your own specification in the File Name field. For example, you might want to view all notebooks that relate to quotes. You have consistently given these notebooks names that begin with the letter Q. If you enter **Q*.WB1** in the File Name field, the file list will be limited to notebooks beginning with Q. You can then select the exact name of the file you want from the list presented. Note that the * wildcard replaces everything to its right, either up to the period or the end of the extension—using *Q.WB1 is the same as using *.WB1.

Note   Quattro Pro will not complete a file save or open operation if the entry in the File Name field refers to more than one file.

Further File Menu Commands

You use the techniques described in the preceding section for listing files, browsing directories, and changing drives. This section discusses the other File menu commands, such as Open and New that are found in many Windows programs, and several File commands in Quattro Pro that you may not have encountered in other programs, which are designed to help you when you are working with multiple notebooks.

File | New

When you launch Quattro Pro, the program loads into memory and presents you with a blank notebook provisionally called NOTEBK1.WB1. At this point, you can start entering data. As soon as you have entered data that you want to keep, you should Save the notebook in a file that has a suitable name. Suppose you have entered the first few items in a customer quotation like the one shown earlier in Figure 4-1. You issue the Save command and call the file QSMITH.WB1 because the quote is for Mr. Smith. Now you want to start a quote for Mr. Jones. At this point, you might need the New command.

All that New does is open up a fresh notebook. There are no options or dialog boxes. When the command is issued, a new notebook automatically appears, positioned above any other notebooks that you have open. The provisional name for the new notebook depends on how many new notebooks you have created during the current session. If you have started Quattro Pro, entered data in NOTEBK1.WB1, and issued the New command, the new notebook will be NOTEBK2.WB1, the third notebook you open will be NOTEBK3.WB1, and so on.

If your reason for opening a new notebook is to create a file similar to one that already exists, you may want to consider one of several different strategies. Suppose that you are creating a series of customer quotations similar to the one shown earlier in Figure 4-1. The first quotation, for a Mr. Smith, was saved as QSMITH.WB1. You have further quotes to prepare for other customers, starting with Mr. Jones. There are several ways of proceeding:

- Use New to open a fresh notebook and copy the contents of QSMITH.WB1 to the new notebook. Edit the new notebook so that it becomes a quote for Mr. Jones, and then use Save to store the notebook as QJONES.WB1.

- Change the current quotation's labels so that they read "Jones" instead of "Smith" and use the File | Save As command to store the edited notebook as QJONES.WB1. You will then have two separate but similar files, and if you want to work on them both at the same time, you can use File | Open to load QSMITH.WB1 as well as QJONES.WB1.

- Instead of opening a new notebook for Mr. Jones, use a new page of the same notebook and name it Jones. With 256 pages each, notebooks are a good way of keeping related spreadsheets together. You can create a group of pages for quotations and use Group mode to format them all in the same way. Remember that if you use Block | Insert | Pages you can add a new page that is automatically included in a group.

File | Open and File | Retrieve

When you launch Quattro Pro and the program presents you with a blank notebook, you may not want to use it, but rather use one you created and saved earlier. There are two ways to do this. You can use File | Open or File | Retrieve. Both use a dialog box like the one shown in Figure 4-8. You can see that a file called BLOCKS.WB1 has been selected

FIGURE 4-8 The Open File dialog box

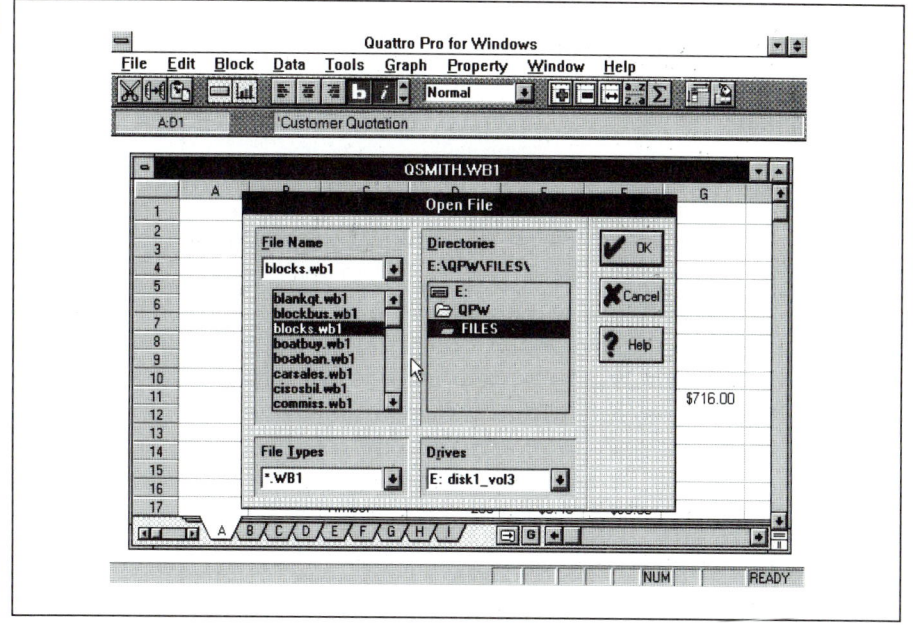

from the list. The Open File dialog box is similar in operation to the one used when saving a file and you can change the filename and directory using the techniques described earlier.

While they use similar dialog boxes, it is important to be clear about the difference between the Open and Retrieve commands. Open loads the selected file into memory, leaving any other currently open notebooks open. After you select a file from the list of names presented and choose OK, the file is opened with no further questions or dialog boxes.

Unlike the Open command, the Retrieve command *replaces* the current notebook with the file you select from the list. Using Retrieve in Figure 4-8 instead of Open would mean that BLOCKS.WB1 would replace QSMITH.WB1. The size of the notebook window that is occupied by QSMITH.WB1 would not be changed. However, the entire contents of the file QSMITH.WB1 would be erased from memory and replaced by those of BLOCK.WB1. Performing a Retrieve is like doing a Close followed immediately by an Open.

If you have finished working on one file and want to put it away and work on a different file, Retrieve saves time over the Close-then-Open alternative. However, if you want to preserve the changes you have made to the current notebook, you must save it before performing a Retrieve. If you issue the Retrieve command before you have saved the current notebook, you will get this warning:

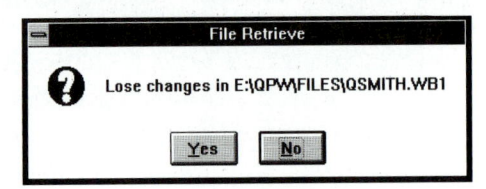

```
┌─────── File Retrieve ───────┐
│  ?  Lose changes in E:\QPW\FILES\QSMITH.WB1  │
│                                              │
│           [ Yes ]    [ No ]                  │
└──────────────────────────────┘
```

Selecting Yes means that Quattro Pro will discard any changes you have made to the current notebook since the last time it was saved. Choosing No will cancel the operation. Choose No if you want to save the changes you have made. You can then issue the Save command before trying the Retrieve again.

File | *Close*

Continually loading notebooks into memory with Open or New can lead to congestion, and you might run out of memory. When you no longer need a notebook, you can put it away with the File | Close command. This command shuts down the current notebook (removes it from the computer's RAM) and, if all of the changes to the notebook have been saved, requires no further input. However, the command is smart enough to check that changes have been saved and, if not, you are presented with the following dialog box:

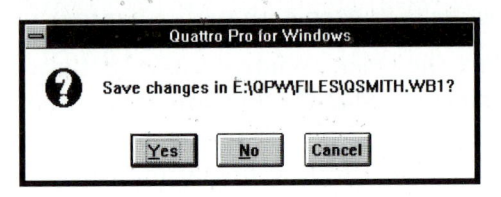

```
┌─────── Quattro Pro for Windows ───────┐
│  ?  Save changes in E:\QPW\FILES\QSMITH.WB1?  │
│                                               │
│         [ Yes ]  [ No ]  [ Cancel ]           │
└───────────────────────────────────────┘
```

The default button is Yes, which saves the latest changes before closing the notebook. Choosing the No option means that Quattro Pro will put the notebook away *without* saving any changes to the notebook since the last time it was stored on disk. The Cancel option, which can be selected by pressing ESC, means that the attempt to close the notebook is abandoned.

File | Save As

Instead of using the Save command to replace the original version of a notebook with the current one, you can use the File | Save As command to save a notebook under a different filename (or location). For example, if you regularly create quotation notebooks, you might have a blank quotation notebook called BLANKQT.WB1 that you use as a starting point or *template* for creating new quotes. When you need to create a new quote, you open or retrieve BLANKQT.WB1 and enter the new data. At this point, you do not want to use the Save command because this will replace the blank notebook with one that has been filled in. You use the Save As command. This presents the same Save File dialog box you saw earlier in Figure 4-7. The name of the current notebook, in this case BLANKQT.WB1 as opposed to NOTEBK1.WB1, has been placed in the File Name field and selected so that you can change it.

When you have typed a new name (or selected one from the list of existing files), you can choose OK to save the notebook. In this fashion you can quickly create a whole series of notebooks. Note that instead of simply typing a new name in the File Name prompt, you can edit the existing name. This is useful for situations in which the new name is similar to the existing name—for example, to save a file called SALES92.WB1 to SALES93.WB1. To edit the name, just press the RIGHT ARROW or LEFT ARROW key. This will remove the highlighting from the name and activate the edit cursor. You can then move the edit cursor through the filename and make changes in the same way that you edit entries in spreadsheet cells.

Unlike the Save command, Save As always checks to see if the filename you have chosen already exists in the current directory. If it does you will get the "File already exists" message and a chance to replace the existing file, create a backup, or cancel the command.

File | Save All

Suppose you are working on several different notebooks at the same time, and you get a call saying that the electricity could be turned off at any minute. You want to save your work before you abandon your desk, but you don't want to move from notebook to notebook issuing the Save command. The File | Save All command does this for you. Each file is saved in turn, according to the window number (see the section on managing windows in Chapter 7 for more about window numbers).

The Save A_ll command operates like Save A_s, giving you the R_eplace/Cancel/B_ackup choices described earlier *if* you specify a name for a notebook that has previously been used. Note that the notebooks are saved, but not closed. To close all of the open notebooks you need the Clos_e All command, discussed next.

File | Close All

If you want to close all of the open notebooks, perhaps to move on to a different project, you can accomplish this with the F_ile | Clos_e All command. This command closes each notebook in turn, based on the window number. If a notebook has been changed since the last time it was saved, you are prompted to save the file. Your choices are Y_es/N_o/Cancel. Select Y_es to save the latest version of the notebook. Select N_o to abandon changes made since the last time the notebook was saved. Choose Cancel to terminate the command without closing the notebook (you can press ESC to choose Cancel).

When you have closed all notebooks, the Quattro Pro work area is empty, and no style name appears in the SpeedBar. If you use the F_ile menu when there are no notebooks open, you will find all menu items disabled, except for N_ew, O_pen, W_orkspace, and E_xit. Note that there is no need to issue the Close A_ll command to close your notebooks prior to closing down Quattro Pro. When you issue the F_ile | E_xit command, Quattro Pro automatically closes notebooks and prompts you to save your work.

File | Workspace

If you regularly open the same several notebooks at the same time, perhaps because they relate to the same project, you might want to create a *workspace*. This is a special file, with the extension WBS, that stores the current arrangement of windows and files. In other words, not only does a workspace file remember which notebooks you want to work with, but it also remembers how they should be arranged on the screen.

To create a workspace file, you open just those files you want the workspace to remember, arrange them the way you like, and give the File | Workspace command. This presents a submenu with two choices: Save or Restore. Select Save, and a dialog box appears, much like the Save File dialog box described earlier in the chapter (the only difference, besides the name, is that there is no password protection field in a Save Workspace dialog box, and the box lists only *.WBS files). Type a name for the workspace and choose OK.

The notebooks are not affected by the Workspace | Save command, nor are their contents saved. What you have done is record the current arrangement of the work area. The next time you want to work with the same arrangement of notebooks, you issue the File | Workspace | Restore command and choose the workspace you want from the list of WBS files presented.

Note As soon as you restore a workspace, Quattro Pro forgets what you called it. This means that whenever you issue the File | Workspace | Save command, you have to supply the correct name, as Quattro Pro will not enter the name for you.

File | Exit

When you want to close down Quattro Pro, you can choose Exit from the File menu. Before returning you to the Program Manager, the Exit command closes all notebooks, prompting you to save notebooks that contain changes made since the last time they were saved. There are several ways to exit Quattro Pro apart from the Exit command:

- Press ALT-F4.
- Double-click on the application Control button that is on the left of the title bar.
- Press ALT-SPACEBAR and then ALT-C to select Close from the application control panel.
- Press CTRL-ESC to pop up the Windows Task List and select End Task.

Note You don't have to close Quattro Pro when you want to work on another application.

One of the great advantages to working under Windows is that you can load several applications at once and switch between them. You can use the Task List to switch between the Program Manager and any applications you have loaded. Press CTRL-ESC to pop up the Task List or, if any part of the Windows desktop is exposed, double-click on it to display the Task List. You can also switch between applications by holding down ALT and tapping TAB. This presents one application after another, as long as you keep the ALT key held down. Each time you press TAB, a different application is presented. Release the ALT key when you see the application you want to use.

If you are going to use a different application and return to Quattro Pro, you can "put away" the program without closing it or your notebooks. Simply click the minimize button on the right of the title bar or press ALT-SPACEBAR followed by ALT-N to select Mi_n_imize from the application control menu. The application shrinks to a small icon, which you can double-click to reuse.

Printing

Quattro Pro enables you to print professional reports from your notebooks, complete with headers, footers, and other embellishments. To print a report, you must turn to the File menu. There are five items on this menu that pertain to printing. All five are described here, along with tips on printing spreadsheet reports. If you are looking for ways of dressing up your reports, we will be discussing fonts, styles, and other graphic elements later in this chapter.

The Print Block

The printing process begins with selection of the cells that you want to print. These are then referred to as the *print block*. Cells can be selected in the usual fashion, either with the mouse or SHIFT-ARROW keys. You can select several groups of cells by holding down the CTRL key while pointing with the mouse to create a compound block. For example, if you were working with the spreadsheet shown in Figure 4-9, you might want to

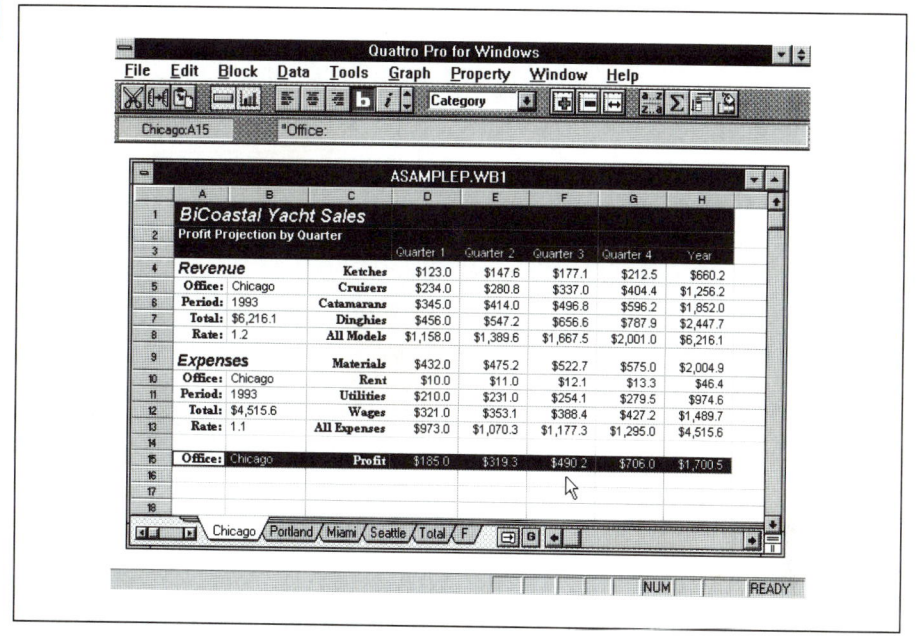

FIGURE 4-9 Selecting a pair of blocks to be printed

print a summary comprised of two blocks: A1..H3 and A15..H15. You would select A1..H3, hold down CTRL, and select A15..H15.

You can also select blocks that include more than one page of a notebook. This can be a 3-D block, such as A1..H15 in pages A through D, or just a number of blocks selected from different pages. You may want to print all pages of a named group, such as the Company group used in the sample notebook shown in Chapters 2 and 3 and seen in the background of Figure 4-10.

If you turn on Group mode and select a block of cells in one page of the group, the same block will be selected in all the other pages of the group. For example, in Figure 4-10 you can see the result of issuing the File | Print command after Group mode was turned on in the sample notebook and cells A1..H13 of the Chicago page were selected. The Print blocks(s) field lists Company:A1..H13, which means cells A1..H13 in all pages of the Company group.

If you issue the Print command and then decide you want to change the Print block(s) setting, you can use the block techniques described in

FIGURE 4-10 The Spreadsheet Print dialog box

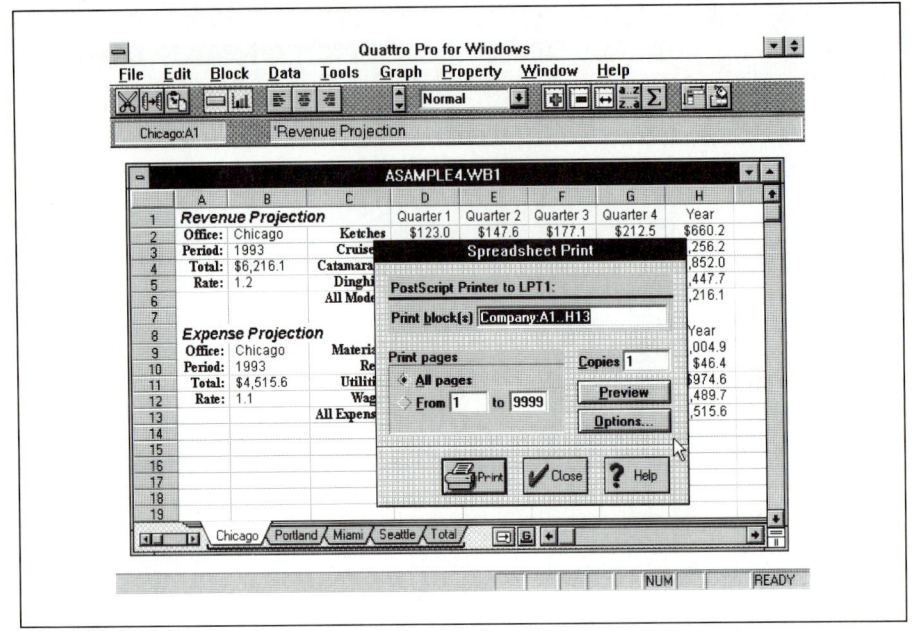

Chapter 3 to alter the selection. Remember that you can select additional blocks by typing a comma after the coordinates of the preceding block. Quattro Pro prints multiple blocks in the order they are selected. You can adjust the spacing between blocks by using the Options button, described later under "Print Settings and Print Preview."

In fact, you do not *have* to select a block at all. If you open a new notebook, make some entries, and issue the Print command, Quattro Pro will assume that you want to print all of the entries you have made. In other words, Quattro Pro automatically selects a print block that extends from the first cell you have used to the last. (If you assume that there are no other entries in the spreadsheet in Figure 4-9 except the ones shown on the screen, the last cell is H15.)

If a block of cells in the spreadsheet is selected and you select Print, Quattro Pro will assume that you want to print that block of cells, as opposed to any other block you might have previously selected as a print block. In other words, the coordinates of the print block are constantly being updated. If you have previously selected a print block and do not want Quattro Pro to change the print block coordinates, make sure that

Chapter 4: Filing, Printing, and Styling 199

only one cell is selected when you select Print (the same warning applies to the File | Preview command described in a moment).

Note To store print settings, including the print block coordinates, so that they are available at a later date, use the File | Named Settings command, described later in this chapter.

The Print Process

Once you are accomplished in the art of spreadsheet printing and know how to set the print parameters, you will be able to select the blocks you want to print, issue the Print command, and immediately choose Print. This sends the report to the printer, and no further input is required although a dialog box does appear, as shown in Figure 4-11 (this allows you to cancel printing if you want). However, there are many parameters involved in printing, some of which are established by the Spreadsheet Print dialog box shown in Figure 4-10. You may need to change settings in this dialog box or in one of the other print dialog boxes, as discussed in a moment.

FIGURE 4-11 The Printing dialog box (you can press ESC at this point to cancel printing)

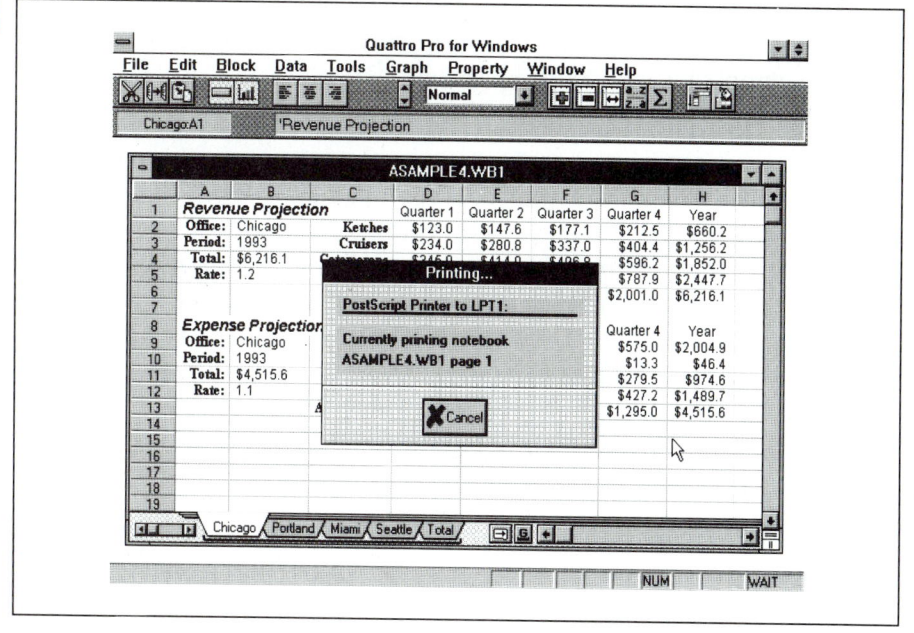

Note The first line of the Spreadsheet Print dialog box tells you which printer is currently selected. To change the printer use the File | Printer Setup command, described later in this chapter.

When working with the Spreadsheet Print dialog box, you should bear in mind that the Print button is the default button, so careless use of the ENTER key can send the report to the printer prematurely. If this happens you can click on Cancel or press ESC when the Printing dialog box appears, as shown in Figure 4-11. This aborts the print operation and returns you to the notebook. If you act quickly, you can stop the printing process before any data has reached the printer. This is because, under normal circumstances, reports are handled by a Windows program called Print Manager.

The Print Manager intercepts print commands from applications such as Quattro Pro. Because some printers can take several minutes to print a page, the Print Manager stores the information to be printed on disk and feeds it to the printer while you continue to work with your application. This is known as *background printing*. Writing data to disk is much quicker than printing it, so a considerable amount of time is saved by using the Print Manager. If you do not use the Print Manager, you must wait for the printer to finish processing the report before you can continue working with Quattro Pro. Furthermore, if you have several different printing tasks, or print jobs, to perform, the Print Manager organizes them in a line or *queue*. You can then use the Print Manager window to control the print queue.

In Figure 4-12, you can see the Print Manager window with three print jobs in a queue for the HP LaserJet. If you send a report to the printer by choosing Print from the Spreadsheet Print dialog box command, you can use the Windows task switcher to open the Print Manager window and monitor the progress of the print operation. As you can see, the window lists all of the printers installed on this particular computer, with a printer icon identifying the one currently in use. A second printer icon shows you which print job is being processed. The name of the document is listed with the percentage of the file that has been processed (in this case 0% of a 2K file). The time and date are also listed.

Using the Delete button at the top of the screen, you can terminate the highlighted print job (the Pause and Resume buttons are used to pause and resume printing of documents). The Options command on the

FIGURE 4-12 The Print Manager window

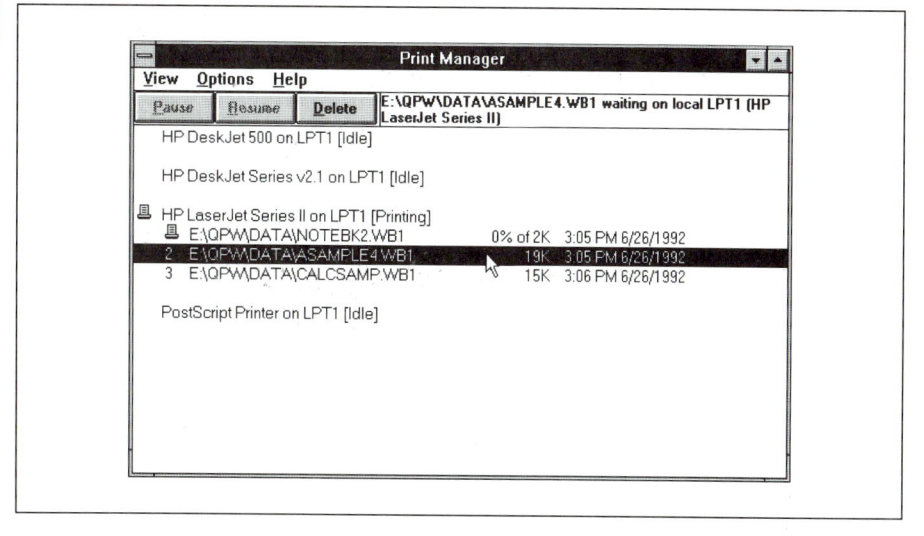

Print Manager menu bar allows you to change the priority given to a particular print job. You will find clear explanations of this and the other menu items under the Help command on the Print Manager menu bar. During normal printing with Quattro Pro, you will not need to access the Print Manager window, as its background operation is automatic. However, it is helpful to know what happens to your report after you send the Print command.

Note To make sure that the Print Manager is turned on (enabling you to continue working while your document prints in the background), open the Windows Control Panel and use the Printers icon to open the Printers dialog box. Select the Use Print Manager box in the lower left of the screen if it isn't already checked.

Print Settings and Print Preview

As you saw in Figure 4-10, there are three settings you can change in the Spreadsheet Print dialog box: Print block(s), Print pages, and Copies. We have already discussed setting the print block. The Copies setting allows you to specify in the box the number of copies of the report to print. The default setting is 1. The Print Pages setting is only relevant when the report extends beyond one page. The default setting is All pages, meaning that all of the pages are printed, regardless of how long the report is. If you only want to print certain pages, use the From and to settings. In the From box you type the number of the first page you want to print. In the second (to) box, which can be reached with the TAB key or mouse, enter the number of the last page you want printed.

Of course, choosing which pages to print is rather difficult unless you know how many pages are in the report. This depends upon many factors, including the size of the print block, the size of the paper, and the size of fonts you have used. Several factors are determined by the Page Setup command in the File menu. Several other factors are determined by Options, one of two special buttons in the Spreadsheet Print dialog box. The other special button is Preview, which, as you can see in Figure 4-13, uses the screen to show you what your report will look like when it is printed, based upon the settings you have chosen.

Note The top-left corner of the print preview screen shows you how many pages there will be in a report, regardless of the Print pages setting; however, you must choose the All setting if you want to view all pages of the report.

The page being previewed in Figure 4-13 is the first page of a report from the sample spreadsheet using the settings shown earlier in Figure 4-10, that is, printing cells A1..H13 of the five notebook pages that make up the Company group. The figure has been annotated to explain some of the commands. Print preview is a very environment-friendly feature, since it saves paper that would otherwise be wasted on trial-and-error print runs.

Even to the untrained eye, there are problems with the report as it appears in Figure 4-13. The margins are uneven, there are no page numbers or titles, and the bottom of the page appears to split one of the tables rather awkwardly. This is quite a normal state of affairs. Selecting the block of cells to be printed is only the start of the report-making process. After your initial look at the report in Print Preview, you will want to make adjustments.

Bear in mind that Quattro Pro has to break up any print block that will not fit on a single page. Page breaks are inserted to avoid data running off the bottom and right side of the paper. The way Quattro Pro breaks a report into pages for printing is as follows:

Chapter 4: Filing, Printing, and Styling

☐ Fit as many columns as possible across the page and print all rows in those columns, using as many pages as needed.

☐ Return to the first row and start over at the first column that has not yet been printed.

To see where the breaks will appear, use the File | Print Preview command. You do not have to go through the Print command to select your print block. You can simply select the block of cells and then select Print Preview. Alternatively, you can select Print and then choose the Preview button.

When you get to the Print Preview screen, you have direct access to both the Page Setup and Print Options settings. The SpeedBar in Print Preview tells you which page you are viewing and the total number of pages in the report. The left and right arrow buttons allow you to browse

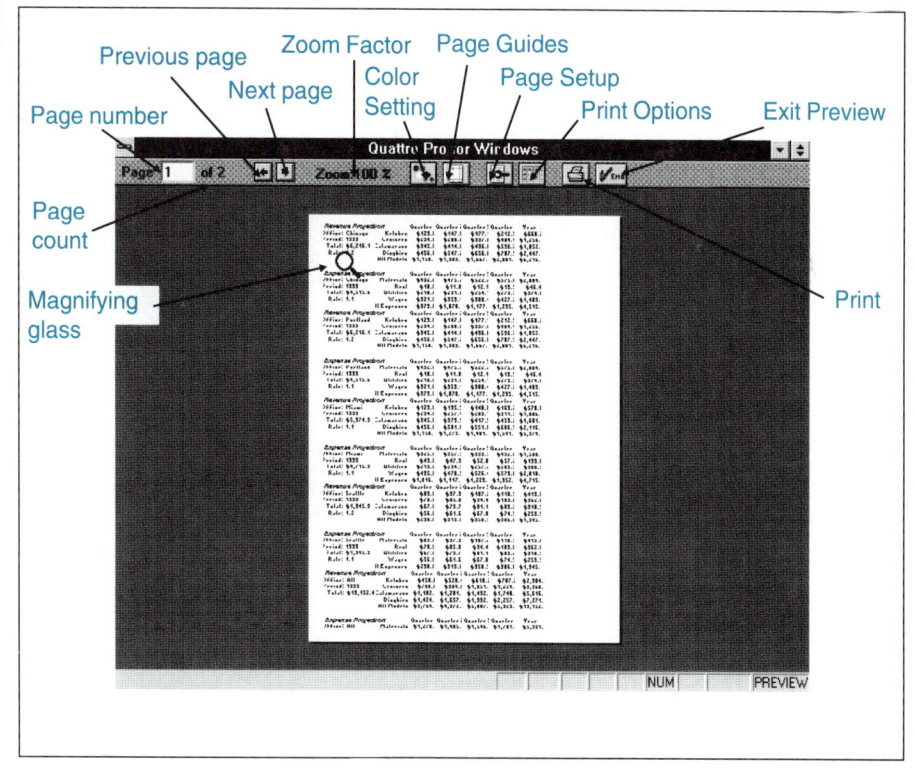

FIGURE 4-13 Using Print Preview to view the effect of print settings

through reports (each time you click one of the buttons, you move to the next page in the direction of the arrow). The rest of the buttons are as follows:

- **Color Setting** This button changes the use of color from full-color to gray-scale to black and white. Unless you have used color in the worksheet, you will not see any change when clicking this button. If you keep clicking the button, you will repeatedly cycle through the three options.

- **Page Guides** This button displays the print area on the page as a series of dotted lines. The print area depends upon Page Setup and Print Options. Margins can be adjusted in page preview by dragging lines with the mouse.

- **Page Setup** This button displays the same Spreadsheet Page Setup menu you get when you issue the File|Page Setup command. Settings in this dialog box are discussed in a moment.

- **Print Options** This button displays the same Spreadsheet Print Options dialog box you get when you issue the File|Print command and then select Options from the Spreadsheet Print dialog box.

- **Print** This button sends the report to the printer. This is the same as choosing Print from the Spreadsheet Print dialog box.

- **Exit Preview** This button closes the print preview. If you entered the preview from the Print Preview command, this returns you to the notebook. If you entered the preview by selecting Preview in the Spreadsheet Print dialog box, this button takes you back to that dialog box.

In addition to these buttons, the preview area offers you a zoom command. You can see on the SpeedBar that when you first enter the print preview, the zoom factor is 100%. This is quite separate from the zoom factor in the Active Notebook settings. A print preview zoom setting of 100% means that a full page is displayed. To zoom in for a closer look, you simply move the mouse pointer onto the page so that the pointer changes to a magnifying glass. When you click the left mouse button, the view is zoomed up to the next level, 200%. Click again and the view is zoomed to 400%, as shown in Figure 4-14.

FIGURE 4-14 An enlarged view of the document using 400% zoom in print preview

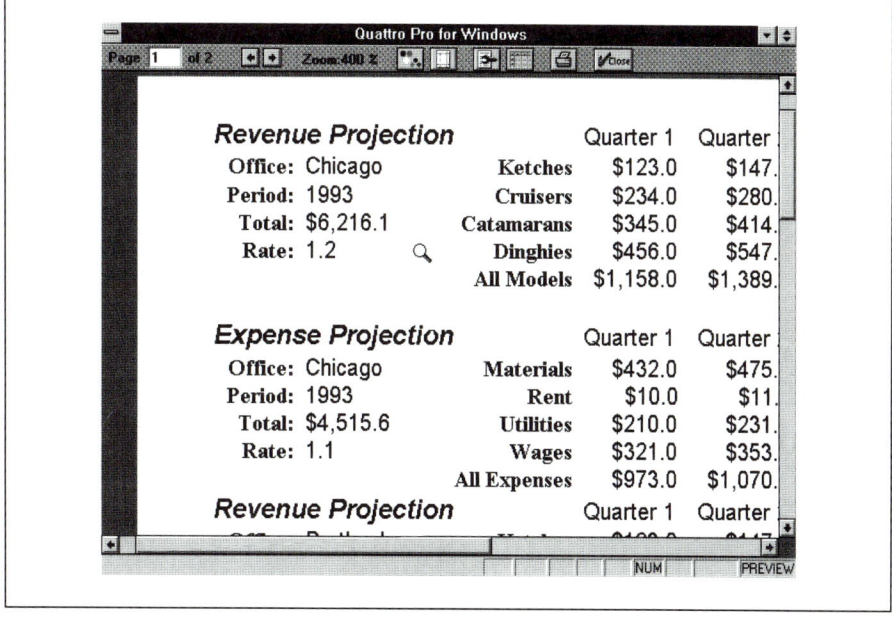

Note that scroll bars now appear on the right and below the page. This allows you to scroll different parts of the page into view. If you keep clicking the left mouse button you can increase the zoom factor up to 1600%. To reduce the zoom factor you click the right mouse button. Repeatedly clicking the right mouse button eventually returns the zoom factor to 100%. The close-up in Figure 4-14 reveals one of the problems with the report: there is no space between the sections of the report that come from different pages of the notebook. Thus, the Portland entries follow those for Chicago with no gap. Spacing between sections of a report is controlled by Print Options.

Print Options

There are several ways to get to the Spreadsheet Print Options dialog box shown in Figure 4-15. You can select Print and then select Options, which presents the dialog box in front of the normal spreadsheet view, as shown in Figure 4-15, or you can click the Page Options button on

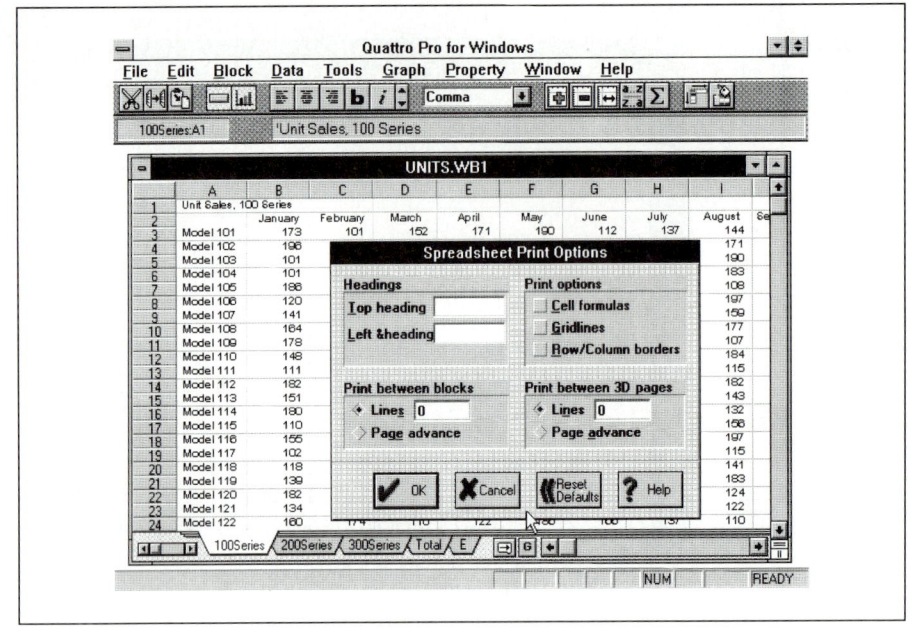

FIGURE 4-15 The Spreadsheet Print Options dialog box

the Print Preview SpeedBar, shown in Figure 4-13. This presents the same dialog box in front of the page preview. The advantage to the second approach is that changes you make to the option settings are reflected in the preview as soon as you select OK.

Headings

In the Spreadsheet Print Options dialog box there are two Headings fields, one for the Top and one for the Left. These are sections of the notebook that are repeated on each page of a printed report to act as headings for the data you are reporting. Headings are useful when printing large spreadsheet models because they allow you to carry column and row titles over to the next page when the data will not fit on a single page. Consider the boring but very typical spreadsheet in the background of Figure 4-15. This lists twelve months' worth of sales figures for a series of products.

The whole table is 57 rows long and 14 columns wide (there are 55 products plus a row of month names and a row of column totals; there

Chapter 4: Filing, Printing, and Styling

is one column for each of the 12 months plus one column for the model names and one for the row totals). If you exclude the title in A1, the table occupies A2..N58. When you print it, you find that it does not fit on a single page. Unless you shrink the letters to a very small size, you cannot fit 14 columns across a regular piece of paper. The table still does not fit, even if you can change the orientation of the paper. By default the orientation is Portrait (the paper is taller than it is wide), which is what you see in Figure 4-13. You can change the orientation to Landscape, shown in Figure 4-16 (the print orientation is a Page Setup option, discussed in a moment).

Close examination of Figure 4-16 reveals that all 14 columns fit on the page. However, while all of the columns fit in Landscape orientation, some of the rows are pushed onto a second page, as you can see in Figure 4-17, where the view of the second page has been zoomed to 200%. This reveals the problem that the Headings setting is designed to correct—the columns on the second page have no month labels. The solution is to print the row of month labels as a Top heading.

The month labels occupy cells B2..N2. You can enter this block in the Top heading field of the Spreadsheet Print Options dialog box, either by

FIGURE 4-16 Previewing a document set to print in Landscape orientation

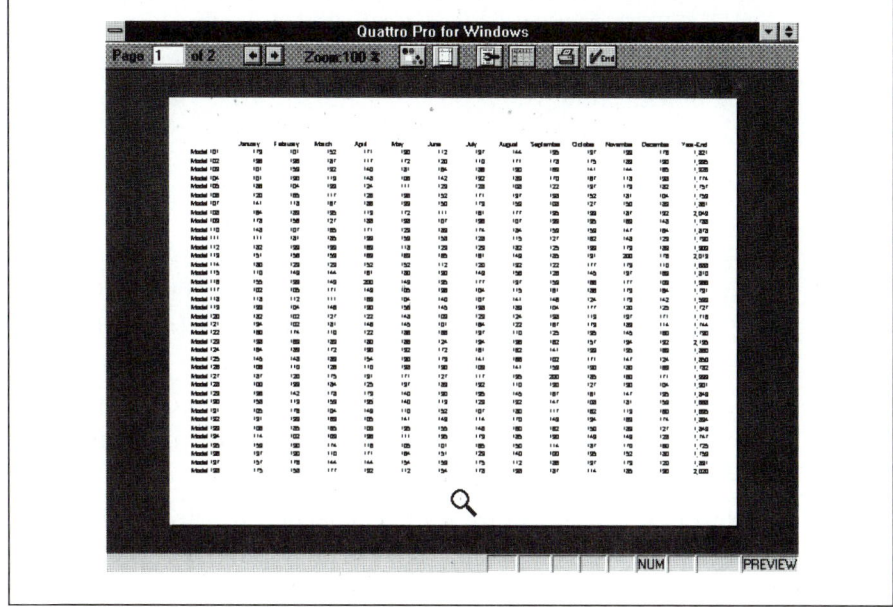

FIGURE 4-17 A zoomed view of the second page of a document (note lack of headings)

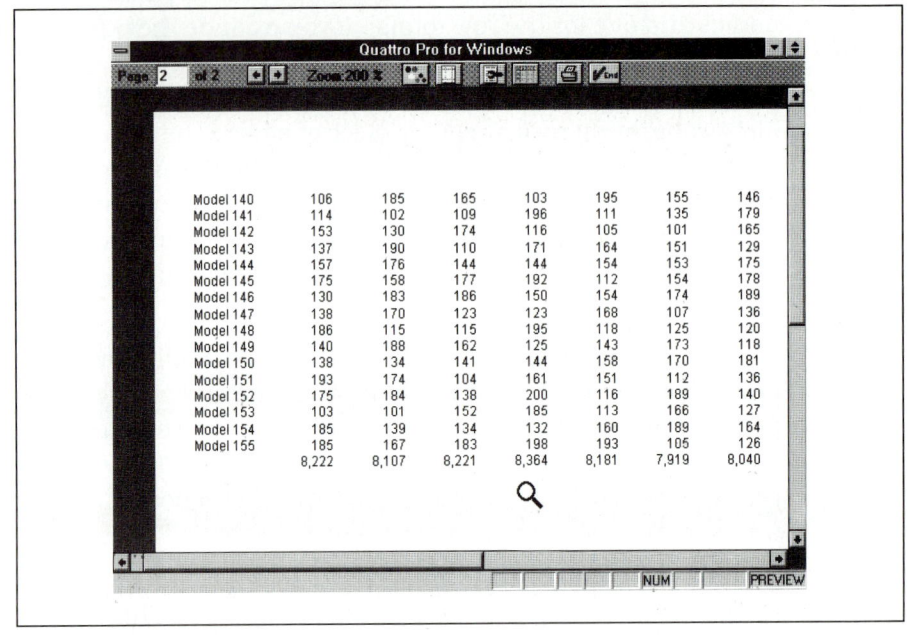

typing the coordinates or by using the pointing techniques described in Chapter 3. In Figure 4-18 you can see that this has been done, and you can see the results in the background. The second page of the report now has column headings to match the first page. Bear in mind, though, that if you use either a top or left heading, you must omit those cells from the print block. Thus, the report in Figure 4-18 is based on a print block of A3..N58, not A2..N58.

If there are both too many columns and too many rows for a page, you can use the Left heading setting as well. This would be a column of labels on the left side of the print block that you want repeated on successive pages. Again, you must remember to exclude heading cells from the print block; otherwise, you will get two sets of headings on the first page of the report.

Spacing

You can see in Figure 4-13 that when a print block extends across several notebook pages in Group mode, Quattro Pro does not automati-

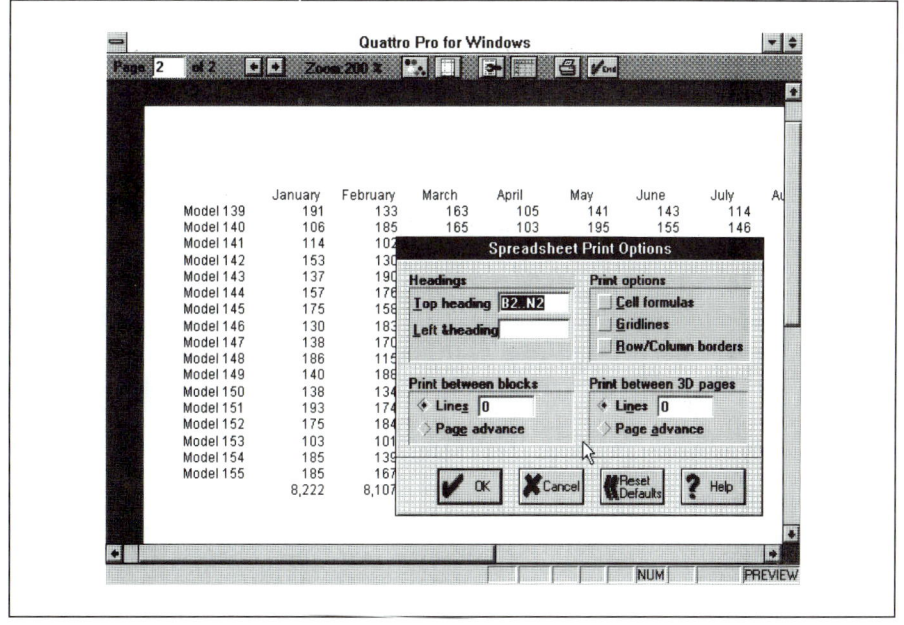

FIGURE 4-18 Setting a Top heading in the Spreadsheet Print Options dialog box

cally insert space between the pages. The same is true of multiple blocks selected for printing as a compound block. The Spreadsheet Print Options dialog box lets you adjust spacing between multiple blocks (Print between blocks) and between pages in a group (Print between 3-D pages). Both settings can either be Lines or Page advance. The Page advance setting means that after printing the last cell of one block or notebook page, Quattro Pro will move to the top of the next sheet of paper before printing the first cell of the next block or notebook page. The Lines setting allows you to specify a number of blank lines to be inserted between blocks or notebook pages. The default Lines setting for Print between blocks is 0, meaning no gap at all.

Miscellaneous Options

As you can see from Figure 4-18, you can choose any of the following Print options (the default is not to include any of them):

☐ **Cell formulas** Checking this option tells Quattro Pro to print the contents of cells as they appear on the input line, not in the spreadsheet. This means that formulas are printed as formulas and not their results, as shown in Figure 4-19, a report generated from the model seen in Figure 4-18. Note that the cells are listed one per line down the left of the page. Cell coordinates are stated in full, starting with the name of the notebook page. This type of report is sometimes used to document a spreadsheet, so that it can be audited or reconstructed.

- **Gridlines** Checking this option means that grid lines are printed around cells. The effect, shown in Figure 4-20, is useful in some situations such as documenting a spreadsheet. Selecting Gridlines as a print option is different than drawing lines around cells with the Line Drawing property described later in this chapter.

- **Row/Column borders** Checking this option prints the relevant sections of the row and column borders of the spreadsheet along with the cell contents. The effect, also shown in Figure 4-20, is useful for documenting spreadsheets when you need to show where entries are located. The notebook page is printed in the upper-left corner of the borders.

FIGURE 4-19 Previewing the effect of the Cell formulas option

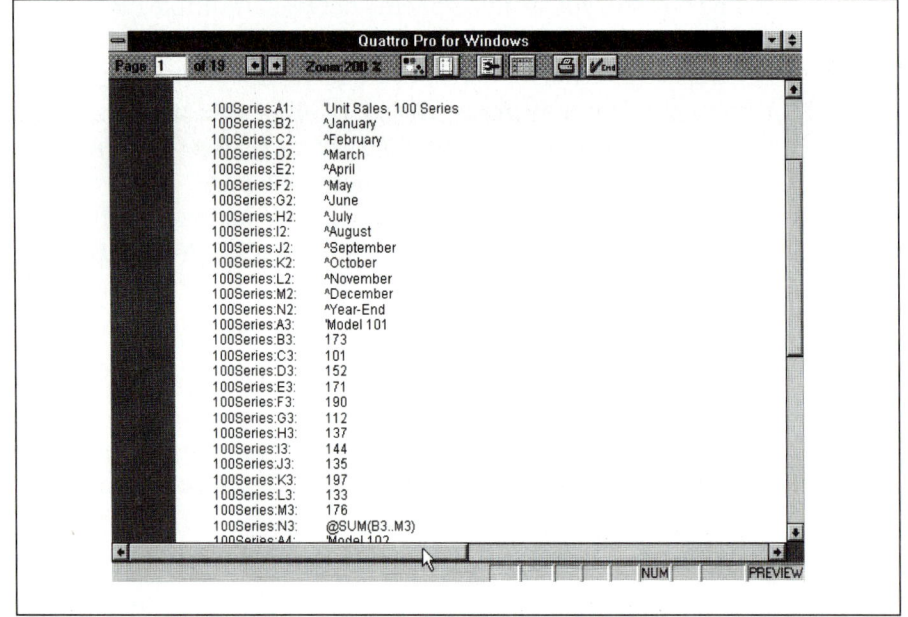

Chapter 4: Filing, Printing, and Styling 211

FIGURE 4-20 Previewing the effect of the Gridlines and Row/Column borders options

File | Page Setup

There are several ways to get to the Spreadsheet Page Setup dialog box, shown in Figure 4-21. These settings control some of the most important print parameters, including margins and paper size. You can select File | Page Setup, which presents the dialog box on top of the normal spreadsheet view, or you can click the Page Setup button on the Print Preview SpeedBar. This presents the same dialog box on top of the Page Preview, as shown in Figure 4-21. The advantage to the latter approach is that you can see the changes you make to the option settings in the preview as soon as you select OK.

The Spreadsheet Page Setup dialog box in Figure 4-21 contains the default settings except for the addition of header and footer text. In the background you can see the first page of a report created from the sample spreadsheet using these settings. Note the dotted lines on either side of the page. These represent the page margins, which are displayed when you click the Page Guides button on the print preview SpeedBar.

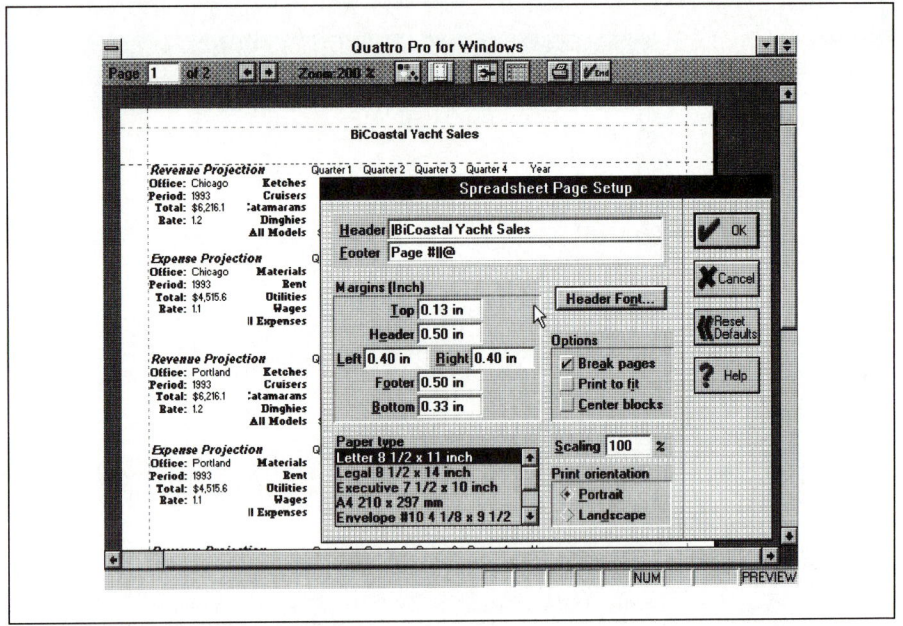

FIGURE 4-21 The Spreadsheet Page Setup dialog box (note centered header)

Headers and Footers

Headers and *footers* are pieces of text that are repeated at the top and bottom, respectively, of each page of a report. Quattro Pro allows you one line for each. In the background of Figure 4-21 you can see the text "BiCoastal Yacht Sales" displayed as a header. You will notice that in the Header field, the text is preceded by the vertical bar character (|). This tells Quattro Pro to center the text; two vertical bars (| |) tells Quattro Pro to align text flush right; otherwise, text is aligned flush left. There are several codes that you can use in headers and footers to control the way the text is printed. These codes are described in Table 4-1 and in the onscreen help text for the Page Setup dialog box. The footer in Figure 4-21 uses several codes. The word "Page " is followed by the page number code and is printed at the left margin. The code | |@ causes the current date to print, flush with the right margin.

You can also adjust appearance of the header and footer text by changing the font. Normally this is printed in the default font. When you

TABLE 4-1 Header/Footer Codes and Their Meanings

Code	Instruction or Display
|	Center what follows (flush left is default)
||	Right-align what follows
#n	Print what follows on a new line (maximum of two lines)
#d	Display date, short International format per Control Panel
#D	Date, long International format per Windows Control Panel
#ds	Date, Quattro Pro short date format
#Ds	Date, Quattro Pro long date format
@	Date, DOS system format—Quattro Pro for DOS-compatible code
#t	Time, short International format per Control Panel
#T	Time, long International format per Control Panel
#ts	Time, Quattro Pro short time format
#Ts	Time, Quattro Pro long time format
#p	Spreadsheet page number
#p+*n*	Adds number *n* to page number (on page 1, #p+3 would show 4)
#	Spreadsheet page number—Quattro Pro for DOS-compatible code
#P	Printout page number
#P+*n*	Adds number *n* to printout page number
#f	Name of notebook without path or drive (e.g., NOTEBK1.WB1)
#F	Notebook name, with full path (e.g., C:\QPW\NOTEBK1.WB1)

click the Header Fo<u>n</u>t button, you get a standard font selection dialog box in which to make changes. For more about fonts, see the section called "Fonts" later in this chapter.

Margins

Quattro Pro allows you to adjust all four margins of the printed page individually. The Left and Right margin settings in the Spreadsheet Page Setup dialog box are measured from the edge of the page, as are the Top and Bottom margins. The Header and Footer measurements control the distance between the top and bottom margin and the header and footer text. Mouse users can also adjust the margins in page preview without the Spreadsheet Page Setup dialog box. By clicking the appropriate button on the SpeedBar, you can turn on the page guides, which appear as dotted lines, as shown in Figure 4-21. To adjust a margin, move the mouse pointer over it, at which point the mouse pointer turns into a double-headed arrow. You can then drag the arrow to increase or decrease the margin. You cannot use this technique while the Page Setup dialog box is displayed; however, the next time you use the Page Setup dialog box, the margin settings will display the new measurements.

The measurements shown in Figure 4-21 are the defaults and, as you can see, they are measured in inches (in). You can specify margins in centimeters if you wish. There are two ways to specify centimeters for margin measurements. You can type a value followed by the abbreviation for centimeters (as in **.5 cm** for 1/2 centimeter), or you can use the International module in the Windows Control Panel and select Metric in the Measurement field. This will automatically convert Quattro Pro's measurements to centimeters.

Paper Type

The Paper type section of the Spreadsheet Page Setup dialog box lists the paper sizes supported by your printer. The default paper size is shown highlighted in the list. Remember that the Print command assumes you want to use the printer specified in the Windows Control Panel, or the printer selection you have made with the File | Printer Setup command, described in a moment. The name of the current printer appears in the Spreadsheet Print dialog box.

If you want to format the report for a paper size other than the one already highlighted, click on the size you want or, if you are not using a mouse, press ALT-Y to activate the list and then use the arrow keys to move the highlighting to the size you want. Note that the Paper type setting is separate from the page orientation, described next.

Print Orientation

Your reports can be printed in one of two orientations. The page shown in Figure 4-21 is in Portrait orientation, while the report shown earlier in Figure 4-16 is in Landscape orientation. You will find that wider reports, such as yearly figures broken down by month, lend themselves to Landscape printing. Formal financial reports, such as assets and liabilities, often have to be presented in Portrait mode. When you change the Print orientation setting, the same margin settings are applied. In other words, the Top setting still controls the margin at the top of the page, even though this is the long side of the paper and not the short.

Soft and Hard Page Breaks

You have already seen that Quattro Pro breaks up the print block and places it on separate pages to avoid data running off the bottom right side of the printed page. The page breaks inserted by Quattro Pro are called *soft page breaks* because when you alter print settings such as the margins, these soft page breaks move in relation to the data being printed. For example, if you decrease the size of the Top margin setting, soft page breaks will move to allow more rows to be printed on each page.

At times you will want to make sure that a page break occurs at a specific location, no matter which page setup, by inserting a *hard page break*. One way to do this is with the Page advance setting in the Print Options dialog box, shown in Figure 4-15. This allows you to make sure that a page break occurs between blocks or separate pages of a group. To insert a page break elsewhere, for example, after a block that forms the title page of a report, use the Block | Insert Break command in the normal spreadsheet view. Before issuing the command, you should select the cell on the left edge of the row at which you want to insert the break. When you issue the Block | Insert Break command a new row is added to the spreadsheet page and the special code for a hard page break is entered. This code is a vertical bar followed by two colons (|::).

The vertical bar is a special label prefix that tells Quattro Pro not to print the characters that follow in the same cell or any cells to the right. That is why a fresh row is inserted by the Block | Insert Break command. You can enter the page break label yourself, but be careful not to enter it on a row that contains data you want to print.

If you uncheck the Bre__a__k pages setting in the Spreadsheet Page Setup dialog box, Quattro Pro removes soft page breaks and ignores hard page breaks. It also ignores headers and footers and their margin spaces. The entire print block is considered to be a single page. The result is one long stream of data, which is only broken into separate pages by the printer itself. You might use this option when printing to disk, as discussed in Chapter 12, or when printing continuous-feed mailing labels.

When you check the Print to f__i__t option, Quattro Pro scales down the data you are printing so that it fits onto as few pages as possible. In Figure 4-22 you can see the effects of this in the sample report. All of the pages of the notebook are included on a single page, and the top left of the screen shows that there is only one page in the report. The Print to f__i__t option does not affect the size of the print margins, except for the space allowed for header and footer, which are shrunk in proportion to the rest of the report. The Print to f__i__t option will not shrink your text beyond the point of legibility, and if shrinking to fit a single page is not feasible, the report will be shrunk to two pages, and so on.

FIGURE 4-22 Previewing a report with centered blocks, a footer, margin lines, and Print to f__i__t

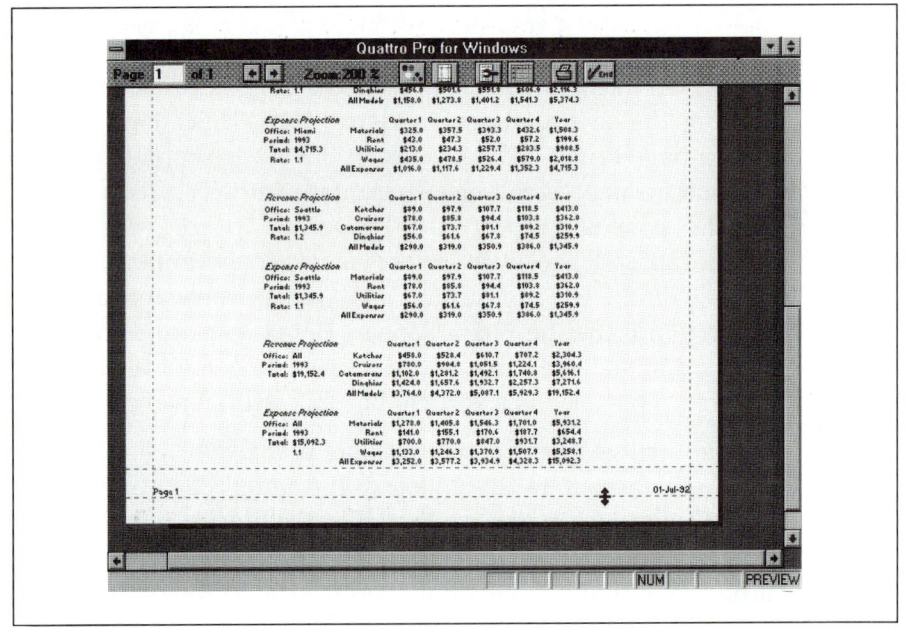

Figure 4-22 shows several other features besides Print to fit. You can see the footer created by the settings shown earlier in Figure 4-21. The page guides are turned on, and the mouse pointer is being used to adjust a margin. Also, the report is centered between the left and right margins. The positioning of data between the left and right margins is controlled by the Center blocks setting in the Page Setup dialog box. Turning this on makes sure that the columns of data are centered, which often makes for a more attractive report and avoids having to widen the left margin to achieve the same effect.

Scaling

Normally your reports will print at 100% scaling. This means that columns set to one inch wide in the notebook will print one inch wide on the page. However, there may be times when you want to adjust the scale of the report. The Scaling setting in the Page Setup dialog box is one way to do this. Suppose that you have a fairly small table of figures to print. You might want to increase the print scaling so that the table takes up more room on the page. On the other hand, you might want to shrink a report so that more of it will fit on each page.

Scaling a report to fit the page can also be done with the Print to fit option. However, this uses its own rules to decide how much adjustment to make in the scale of the report and only scales downward, that is, shrinks the report to less than 100% scaling. For example, checking the Print to fit option in the sample notebook results in a shrinking of the two-page report so that it fits on one page. However, this makes the print fairly small. Another approach is to use 120 as the Scaling % setting, so that the report fills up page 1 and lets a substantial portion flow to page 2, making the report better looking than if only a few lines were printed on page 2.

File | Printer Setup

The choice of printer for your report is made through the File | Printer Setup command, which produces the dialog box shown in Figure 4-23. This displays a list of printers that have been installed in Windows on your computer. Normally, you highlight the printer you want to use and

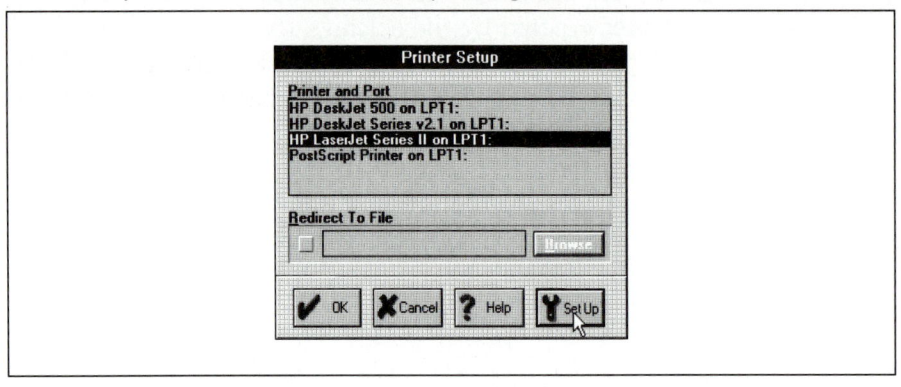

FIGURE 4-23 The Set Up button in the Printer Setup dialog box

choose OK. This puts the dialog box away, and the printer you chose will be used the next time you issue the Print command. To alter or add to the selection of printers in the Printer Setup dialog box, use the Windows Control Panel, as described in Chapter 7.

The Set Up button in the Printer Setup dialog box allows you to fine-tune the printer settings, using a dialog box like the one shown in Figure 4-24. This allows you to select the default paper size for the printer and inform Quattro Pro about the printer's features. For more on how to use this dialog box and the similar one that appears when you install a printer using the Windows Control Panel, see Chapter 7.

Named Settings

When you have refined the various print settings to create a good-looking report, you should save the settings. This is done with the File | Named Settings command. If you use these print settings frequently, it is much easier to call up a single name than to choose each setting manually, one at a time. Pick a meaningful name, and you'll save yourself a lot of time. When you choose Named Settings from the File menu, the Named Print Settings dialog box appears. To create a named setting based on the current settings, choose Create and enter a new name. To use existing settings, highlight the name and choose OK. To record changes to a named setting, choose Update. Named print settings are stored in the notebook file.

FIGURE 4-24 Setting up a printer using the Set Up button's dialog box

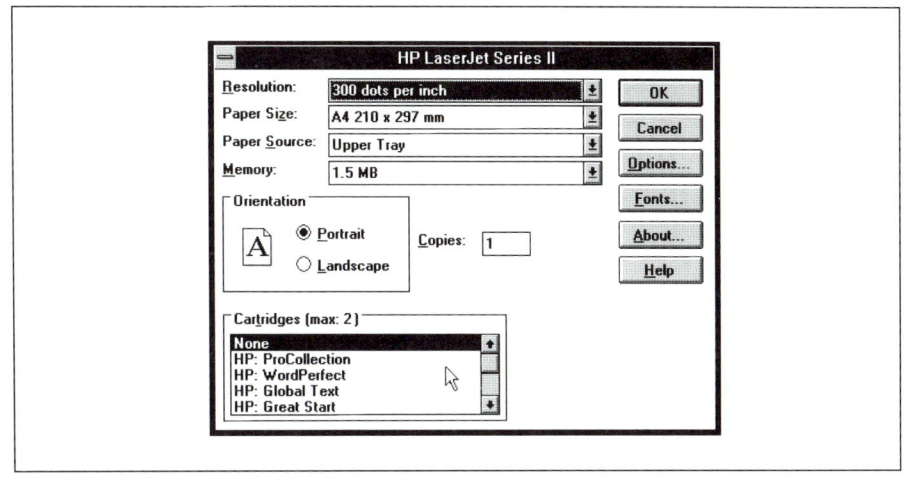

Adding Style to Reports

Now that you have seen how the print process works, you may want to experiment with designing and printing reports. This involves more than just arranging numbers and labels on the notebook page. There are graphic elements you can use to enhance the appearance of reports. These include fonts, lines, and shading.

Fonts

In every notebook there is a default font, one that is used for all entries in the notebook, unless you select a different font for a particular cell or block of cells. For example, in the background of Figure 4-25, the default font is Arial 10 point, but you can see that some cells have been changed. There are fonts of different sizes, italic and bold fonts, and a mixture of typefaces.

Strictly speaking, a font is a collection of characters all bearing the same characteristics, such as shape, size, and style. For example, Times New Roman 18-point bold italic, as used in cell C1 of Figure 4-25, is a *font*. A collection of fonts that have the same basic appearance is a

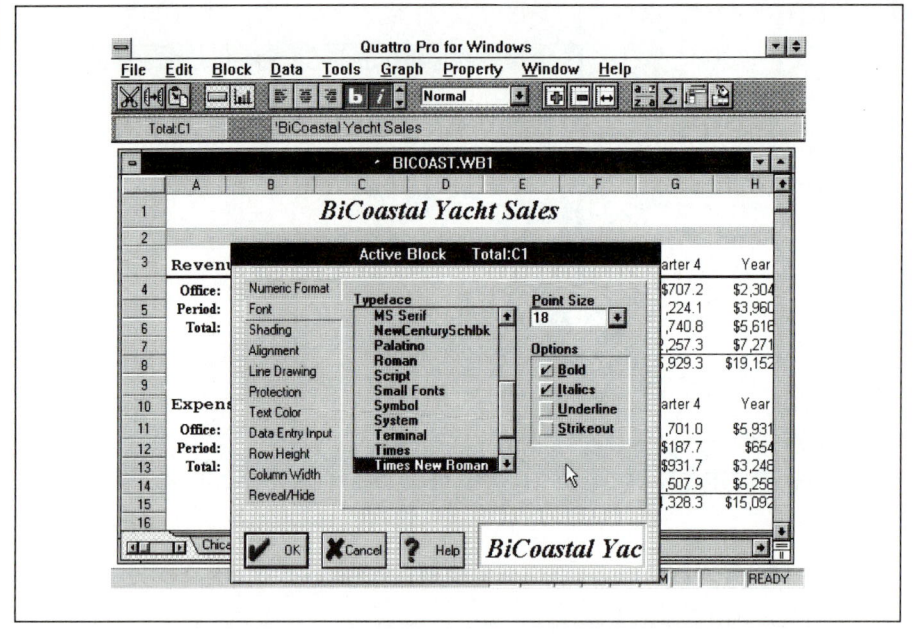

FIGURE 4-25 The Font property in the Active Block dialog box

typeface or type style, so Times New Roman would be a *typeface*. There are several ways of changing the font for a block of cells. You can select the cells and then click the bold, italic, and size buttons on the SpeedBar. The size buttons are the up and down arrows to the right of the italic *i*—click the up arrow to increase the size of the font, the down arrow to reduce it.

Alternatively, you can alter the font of a block of cells with the Fonts section of the Active Block dialog box, shown in Figure 4-25. This shows you the current settings and the aspects of the font that you can change. As you make changes, they are reflected in the preview window at the bottom right of the dialog box. Only when you choose OK are the changes put into effect.

The list of typefaces in the Font settings includes all of those that have been installed in Windows and are available on the currently selected printer. Simply make your choice from the list. The Point Size option works the same way, enabling you to choose from a list of available sizes. The Options (Bold, Italic, Underline, and Strikeout) can be turned on or off. Note that Underline creates lines under labels that extend only as far as the label, not across the whole cell occupied by the label. When your font and other property settings are complete, choose OK; Quattro Pro returns you to READY mode.

Selecting Text Color from the list of properties on the left of the dialog box in Figure 4-25 presents a palette of colors. You can choose the color you want, and it will be used to display text in the active block. Remember, you can't print the text in color unless you have a color printer. If you apply color in a spreadsheet and then use Print Pre*v*iew, your colors will appear in the preview, but you can click on the Color Setting button in the preview SpeedBar to change the colors to either gray or black and white, depending upon the capabilities of your printer. This allows you to see the report as it will print.

When using color and fonts, it is wise to exercise some restraint. Using too many different typefaces can be confusing, and light colors for text can be difficult to read. You can use the Shading setting, described in a moment, to give a dark background to light text; but even so, a dark text on a light background is easier to print and read in most cases.

Lines

Another way of improving the look of a report is to use lines. The Line Drawing property in the Active Block dialog box allows you to control where lines are drawn in relation to the selected cells. You can see this dialog box in Figure 4-26 and lines used on the spreadsheet in the background to separate certain areas.

To draw a line, first choose a line type from the Line *T*ypes list on the right. Then select where you want to place lines by clicking in the corresponding area of the sample block under *L*ine Segments. This tells Quattro Pro visually where to place a line of the type you have selected. You can also choose a preset pattern of lines by clicking one of the three pattern boxes. These are

- **A*ll*** This option draws lines along all cell edges within the block and around the block.

- **O*utline*** This option draws lines around the outside of the block only.

- **I*nside*** This option draws lines inside the block only.

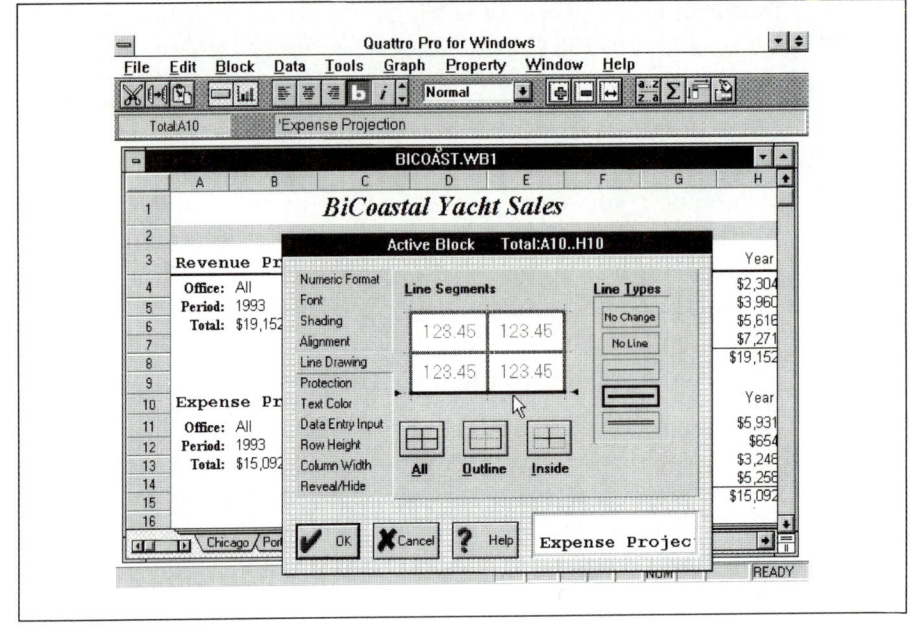

FIGURE 4-26 The Line Drawing property in the Active Block dialog box

The lines drawn in the sample box indicate where lines will be drawn in the selected block when you choose OK. Thus, clicking the outer edges of the sample box draws lines only on the outside of the selected block; clicking the inner lines in the sample box draws lines between every row or column in the selected block. You can combine line-drawing options in the same block. For example, you can draw a thick line as a border around a block and then use single vertical lines between the columns in the block.

Keyboard users can assign lines by first pressing ALT-T to choose a line type (use the arrow keys to move between the five choices). When you have highlighted the line you want to use, press ALT-L to activate the Line Segments section and use the arrow keys to point to the desired line (LEFT ARROW and RIGHT ARROW move you between the three vertical locations while UP ARROW and DOWN ARROW move you between the horizontal locations). When you have selected the desired location for a line, press the SPACEBAR to draw the line.

To draw a line underneath a row of titles like the one on row 10 of Figure 4-27, select the cells (A10..H10) and issue the Active Block command (F12 or right-click) and select Line Drawing (press CTRL-PGDN

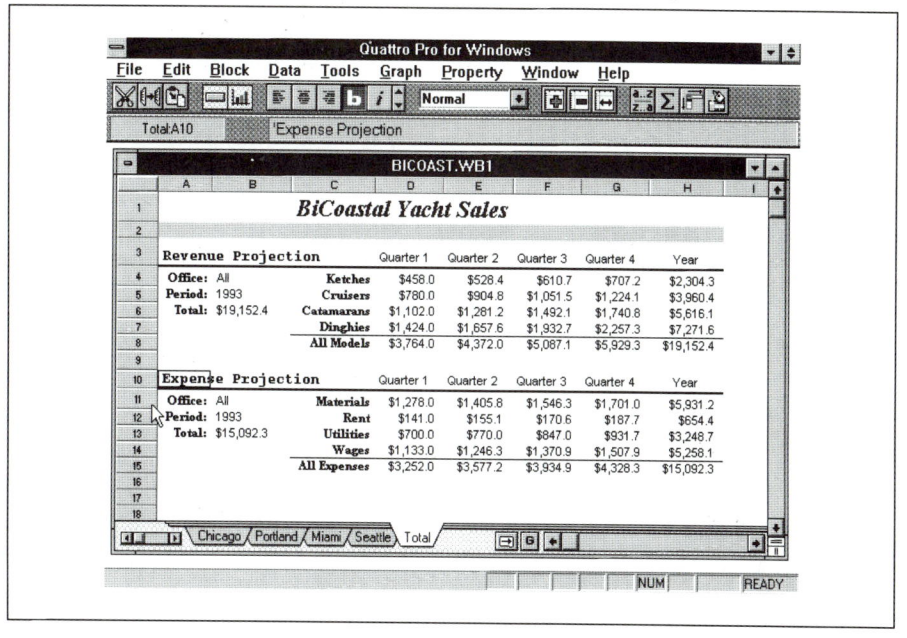

FIGURE 4-27 Model formatted with lines, shading, and adjusted row heights

to move between properties). Then select the line type and click the bottom line of the sample box. If you use the double or thick line types along the bottom of a row, you might want to adjust the Row Height setting of the row immediately below it, to prevent the line from obscuring the tops of characters in this row. Row 11 in Figure 4-27 is set to 15 points, while the default row height is 12 points.

To remove lines, choose the No Line type and click the lines you want to remove in the Line Segments sample block. If you change your mind while specifying lines, click the No Change line type and click the line you just changed. This returns the line to the type in effect before you used the Active Block dialog box. To change the screen color of lines, change the Line Color property in the Active Page dialog box (Active Page settings are reviewed in Chapter 7).

Shading

The Active Block Shading property controls the color of cells. In Figure 4-27, you can see that row 2 has been shaded gray. This is an effective design feature, useful for breaking a report into sections. You can always increase or decrease the Row Height setting to make the shading row thicker or thinner, and the same principle applies to shaded columns and column width.

Note You can achieve useful design effects by altering the Row Height setting. To add space between rows you can increase the height of a row instead of adding a new row to the spreadsheet. To create narrow bands of shading, shade a row and decrease its height.

As you can see from the dialog box in Figure 4-28, where shading is again used to segment the spreadsheet, the color used for the shading color is a mixture of two colors.

When you have chosen Color 1 and Color 2 (these can be black and white), the Blend squares offer you seven different mixture proportions of the two colors. In Figure 4-28, the mixture is made up of white and black, and the second of the Blend squares has been selected. To change the colors available in this dialog box, use the Palette property in the Notebook property menu (Notebook properties are reviewed in Chapter 7).

Note With some color choices, you need to deselect the block to see the new shading. This is because selected cells are shown in reverse color.

Hiding and Sizing Columns and Rows

You might not always want all the data you see on the screen to be printed in a report. You may want to temporarily remove rows or columns of data from view and from printouts, but still be able to use the data in calculations. You can do this with the Reveal/Hide property. For example, in Figure 4-28 the first three months of a 12-month model are displayed, along with the year-end totals (note that the column letters go E, F, P, Q), but the last nine months have been hidden. The expense figures for each office have also been hidden (rows 9-15 and 23-29 are not visible). This feature allows you to prepare several different reports from the same basic data.

The Reveal/Hide property conceals rows and/or columns without losing the data they contain. You can later redisplay the rows or columns by changing the Reveal/Hide property setting. To hide rows or columns

Chapter 4: Filing, Printing, and Styling

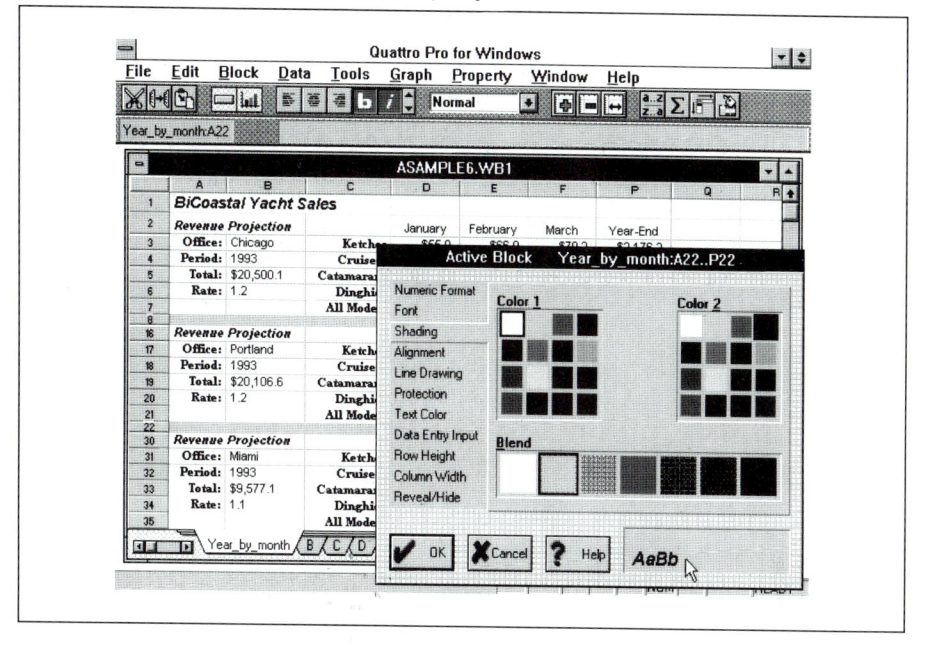

FIGURE 4-28 Selecting colors for the Shading property

from view, select a cell in the row or column you want to hide. If you want to hide multiple rows or columns, select a block that encompasses them (do not select entire columns or rows by clicking on the column and row headings). When you right-click the selected cell or block, choose the Reveal/Hide setting and select the Dimension (either Rows or Columns) and then the Operation (Hide).

When you choose OK, columns to the right of the hidden columns move left to fill in the masked space, and the rows below the hidden rows move up. However, the identifying row numbers and column letters in the borders do not change. In other words, if you hide column B, the columns on screen are labeled A, C, D, and so on. To return one or more hidden rows or columns to the screen, right-click a block containing cells on both sides of the hidden area and choose Reveal/Hide. Then choose Rows or Columns and choose Reveal.

Column width, row height, and cell formatting remain unaffected by the hide-and-reveal process. When you use block-pointing techniques to indicate cell references, Quattro Pro temporarily reveals hidden columns, marked by asterisks, so that they can be considered in the command. For example, if you use the Block | Move or Block | Copy command and point out the block you want to use, the hidden columns and rows will be temporarily revealed so that you can correctly complete the operation. If you use <u>T</u>ools | <u>E</u>xtract to save part of a notebook that includes hidden rows or columns, Quattro Pro saves the hidden rows or columns in the new file, although they will still be hidden from view when you load the new file.

Instant Formatting

With the many ways to embellish and adjust the appearance of your spreadsheets you can easily spend a lot of time formatting reports. One shortcut is to use a predefined format available from the SpeedFormat button. This is the last button on the right of the SpeedBar, indicated by the mouse pointer in Figure 4-29.

In fact, Figure 4-29 is an early version of the sample model with no special formatting of any kind. The Revenue section has been selected, and the user is about to click the SpeedFormat button, which reveals a selection of predefined formats, the first of which is called Bach. There

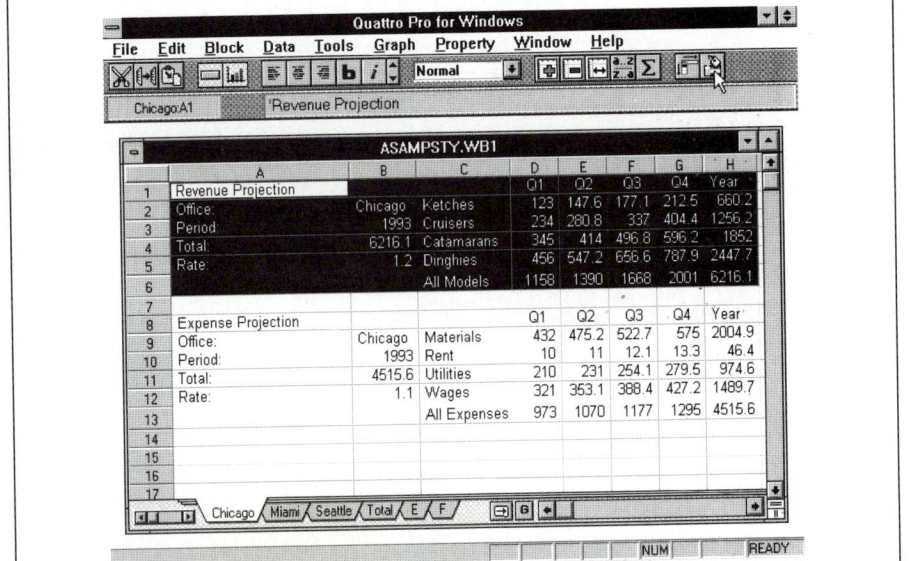

FIGURE 4-29 Cells selected, ready to use SpeedFormat

Chapter 4: Filing, Printing, and Styling 227

FIGURE 4-30 The SpeedFormat dialog box

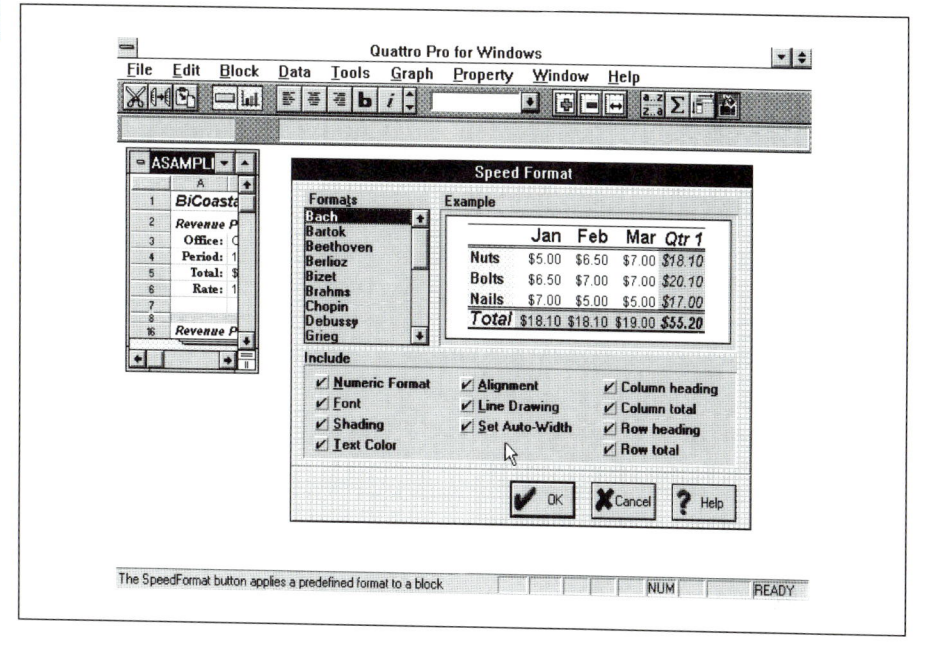

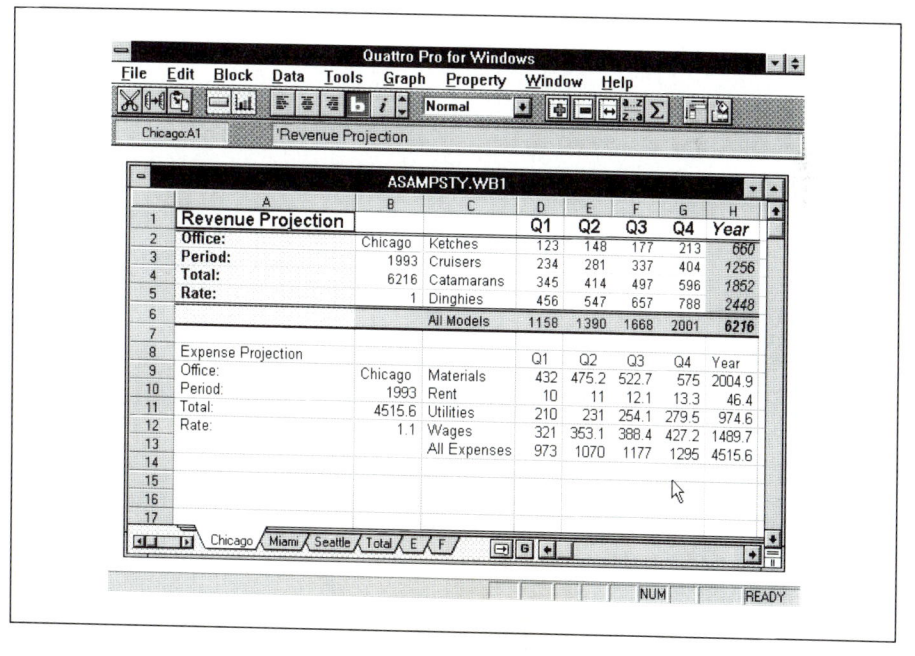

FIGURE 4-31 The effect of selecting the first of the SpeedFormat choices, with all properties included

are over 20 formats to choose from. As you can see in Figure 4-30, the dialog box gives you an example of what the current format looks like. You can browse through the formats until you find the one you like. When you choose OK, the format you are currently viewing is applied to the selected block. If none of the predefined formats is exactly what you want, you can use the Include section to exclude features or properties in the format, such as Numeric Format and Font. Turning a property off means that the rest of the properties in the format will still be applied.

Clearly, the SpeedFormat feature has to make some assumptions about the arrangement of data in the selected block. However, the assumptions match many typical spreadsheet layouts. In Figure 4-31, you can see the effect of choosing the first of the available formats, Bach. Note that the selected block was deselected before a "snapshot" of this screen was captured. This is because, as noted previously, colors and shading are not always accurately displayed (they're reversed) when a block is selected.

CHAPTER 5

Mastering Functions

In previous chapters, you have seen that Quattro Pro understands a wide range of formulas, from simple addition to loan payment calculations. You have learned how to build these formulas using the mouse or the keyboard. You have seen how block names and absolute cell references affect formulas and how it is possible for formulas to refer to different notebook pages and files. This chapter reviews many of the functions that Quattro Pro provides to enhance your formulas.

Formulas as Instructions

Although the word "formula" may remind you of algebra and science classes, in the context of Quattro Pro, the term means an *instruction* written in a form that the program can understand. The way you give Quattro Pro instructions can be as straightforward as "add cell A1 and cell A2." In fact, even complex instructions follow a consistent arrangement, or *syntax*. Quattro Pro offers more than a hundred functions and they all use the same basic syntax.

The Format of Formulas

Simple Quattro Pro formulas combine *values*—like numbers or cells containing numbers—with *operators*, such as the division sign or the plus sign. For example, the formula in cell B5 of Figure 5-1 can be diagramed as follows:

```
B5 = 0.1      *      B3
     ↑        ↑       ↑
    Value  Operator  Value
```

Figure 5-1 includes the yacht purchase and loan payment formulas from Chapter 1, plus an alternative version of the same calculations and a formula for calculating the yacht's sail area. Notes have been added in columns C and F to explain the calculations. These boldface entries are merely labels and are not used by Quattro Pro in any of the calculations.

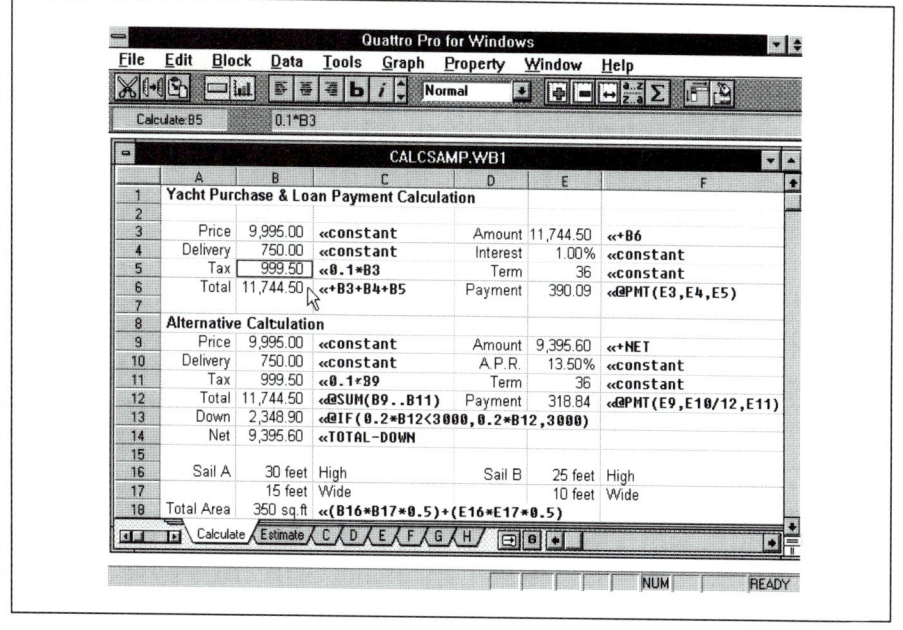

Chapter 5: Mastering Functions   231

FIGURE 5-1 Loan payment calculations use formulas

```
                    Quattro Pro for Windows
File  Edit  Block  Data  Tools  Graph  Property  Window  Help
Calculate: B5      0.1*B3
                        CALCSAMP.WB1
         A          B          C              D          E         F
1    Yacht Purchase & Loan Payment Calculation
2
3        Price     9,995.00   «constant      Amount   11,744.50  «+B6
4        Delivery    750.00   «constant      Interest     1.00%  «constant
5        Tax         999.50   «0.1*B3        Term           36   «constant
6        Total    11,744.50   «+B3+B4+B5     Payment     390.09  «@PMT(E3,E4,E5)
7
8    Alternative Calculation
9        Price     9,995.00   «constant      Amount    9,395.60  «+NET
10       Delivery    750.00   «constant      A.P.R.      13.50%  «constant
11       Tax         999.50   «0.1*B9        Term           36   «constant
12       Total    11,744.50   «@SUM(B9..B11) Payment     318.84  «@PMT(E9,E10/12,E11)
13       Down      2,348.90   «@IF(0.2*B12<3000,0.2*B12,3000)
14       Net       9,395.60   «TOTAL-DOWN
15
16       Sail A    30 feet    High           Sail B    25 feet   High
17                 15 feet    Wide                     10 feet   Wide
18       Total Area 350 sq.ft «(B16*B17*0.5)+(E16*E17*0.5)
```

Quattro Pro formulas are algebraic in format. Thus you can include, within a formula, other formulas separated, or *delimited*, by pairs of parentheses, as in the following:

B18 = (B16*B17+E16*E17)/2

This formula means "multiply B16 by B17, add that to the product of E16 multiplied by E17, then divide the answer by 2." This formula is used in B18 to calculate the total area of sail for the yacht, given the height and width of the two sails and the fact that they are both right-angle triangles (in other words, half of a rectangle). Note that the values in rows 16 and 17 are formatted with a custom numeric format that supplies "feet" as the unit of measurement. Another user-defined numeric format can be seen in cell B18. This supplies "sq. ft" as the unit of measurement as part of the format.

You can ask Quattro Pro to make decisions about the data to be calculated, as in the following formula, which uses the IF function to tell Quattro Pro that the down payment in B13 should be 20 percent of the purchase price in B12, unless the product of those two values comes to more than 3000, in which case B13 should be 3000:

B13 = @IF(0.2*B12<3000,0.2*B12,3000)

The formula not only calculates the down payment but also reflects the buyer's desire to put down 20 percent of the purchase price but no more than $3000. An expense report that breaks down expenses for each week by type might use a similar construction.

G13=@IF(@SUM(WEEK)=@SUM(TYPE),@SUM(TYPE),@ERR)

This formula says that G13 will have one of two possible answers, depending on a decision made by the IF function. If the sum of the block of cells called WEEK is equal to the sum of the block of cells called TYPE, the program should insert that sum; otherwise, it should give an error message (created by the ERR function). By the end of this chapter, you will be able to read such formulas and compose them with Quattro Pro's formula syntax and functions.

Note Do not include spaces in formulas. Enter formulas in upper- or lowercase letters. The program will capitalize all cell references, block names, and function names.

Acceptable Values

The values in a Quattro Pro formula can be cells containing values, as in +B3+B4+B5. They can be a block of cells containing values, either stated as coordinates, as in B9..B11, or described by block names. They can also be functions like PMT, which is used in Figure 5-1 to calculate a loan payment in cell E6 and again in E12. Note that the alternative calculation in E12 states the interest as an annual percentage rate and then divides it by 12 to get the monthly rate.

Values in Quattro Pro formulas can also be *constants*. A constant is a number, date, or piece of text that you enter directly, such as the value 12 used in the formula in E12 to divide a monthly interest rate out of an annual one. Constants are used in many situations, for example, the formula to find the circumference of a circle is 2*@PI**Radius*.

Operators and Priorities

Formulas can use a variety of operators. First, there are the standard arithmetic operators: add (+), subtract (−), multiply (*), and divide (/). Another operator, the exponent (^), produces powers of a number. The formula +B2^3 returns 27 if the value in B2 is 3 (3*3*3 = 27). There is another class of operators known as *logical operators*. These include greater-than (>) and other comparison operators (in Chapter 6 you will learn how to create database search conditions using logical operators). Table 5-1 lists all of the operators recognized by Quattro Pro with their levels of priority in a formula.

If all the operators in a formula are of the same level, as in 2*3*4 (=24), then the calculation is performed from left to right. You can affect the order of calculation by using parentheses, as shown here:

2*3+4=10
2*(3+4)=14

TABLE 5-1 Operators and Order of Precedence (7=highest)

Operator	Used For	Priority
&	Placing text in string formulas	1
#AND#	Logical AND formulas	1
#OR#	Logical OR formulas	1
#NOT#	Logical NOT formulas	2
=	Equal in conditional statements	3
<>	Not equal in conditional statements	3
<=	Less than or equal to	3
>=	Greater than or equal to	3
−	Subtraction	4
+	Addition	4
*	Multiplication	5
/	Division	5
−	Negation (preceding a formula)	6
+	Positive (preceding a formula)	6
^	Exponentiation (to the power of)	7

This means that the formula in cell B20 of Figure 5-1 could be stated in several different ways. You could use

(B16*B17*0.5)+(E16*E17*0.5)

as well as

(B16*B17+E16*E17)/2

In fact, the formula rules and order of precedence in Quattro Pro mean that no parentheses are required, as in

+B16*B17*0.5+E16*E17*0.5

which returns the correct answer. There may be times when parentheses are useful in making a formula clear to read, even though they are not required. What Quattro Pro formulas *do* require is close attention to the results. You should always check the result that Quattro Pro gives you to make sure that the formula has been correctly stated. Never assume that the result of a formula is correct just because it has been calculated by a computer!

Note A good way to verify the accuracy of a formula is to try several different input values and check the consistency of the results. For example, if you increase the rate of interest used in a loan payment calculation, the size of the payment should increase accordingly.

Formulas and Blocks

Some formulas and functions use blocks of cells. As you saw in Chapter 3, Quattro Pro allows both simple and compound blocks. A simple block can be described by typing the diagonal coordinates of the block as you create the formula. You can also use the SHIFT key with the arrow keys to highlight the block during formula editing. Keyboard users can also employ the point-and-anchor method. You move the cell selector to the upper-left corner and anchor the coordinate by typing a period. Then you use the DOWN ARROW and/or RIGHT ARROW as necessary to point out the lower-right corner of the block. To enter a compound block, you create a series of simple blocks, typing a comma after each set of block coordinates, as in B11..B12,B13..D14.

Blocks can be selected with the mouse. For example, after typing **@SUM(** you can point to the top-left cell in the block, press the left mouse button, and hold it down as you drag the mouse pointer to the bottom-right cell of the block. You then release the mouse button and type the closing parenthesis. If the block is very large, you can click on the top-left cell and use the scroll bars to bring the lower-right cell into view. Then you can select the lower-right cell by SHIFT-clicking (holding SHIFT while clicking) the left mouse button. This selects the entire block from the top-left cell to the lower-right.

Mouse users can employ the CTRL key to select noncontiguous blocks. If you hold down CTRL while pointing out a block of cells, those cells will not be deselected if you select a second set of cells. In fact, the second set will be added to the first set in the formula, separated by a comma.

Editing and Calculating Formulas

In previous chapters, you have learned how to use cut-and-paste techniques to edit a spreadsheet. You can apply similar techniques to the editing of formulas and other spreadsheet entries. Suppose you need to enter a formula that includes instructions you have already entered in another cell. For example, in B5 you have entered the following:

@PMT(B2,B3/12,B4)

You now want to enter **+B3/12** in D5. If you select B5 and use drag-and-drop or Edit | Copy to copy the contents of B5 to D5, the cell references in the formula will be altered relative to the location of the copy. Instead, you could select B5, point to the input line, and drag the edit cursor with the mouse pointer to select the piece of formula that you want.

If you are using the keyboard:

1. Press F2 to activate EDIT mode and move the edit cursor so that it is just to the right of the number 12.

2. Press SHIFT-LEFT ARROW five times to select B3/12.

3. With B3/12 selected, issue the Copy command from the Edit menu and press ESC twice or click the cross button to exit from EDIT mode and leave the contents of B5 unchanged.

Now you can create the formula (+B3/12) you want.

1. Select D5 and type the plus sign. This ensures that anything entered into the cell will be treated as a value, not a label.
2. Issue the Paste command from the Edit menu. The text that you copied while editing B5 will be inserted on the input line, and you can press ENTER or click the check mark to confirm the new entry.

Once you are familiar with this technique, you will find it can save a lot of time and typing, particularly when working with long formulas.

After you have entered a formula, the spreadsheet cell displays the *result* of the formula, not the formula itself. However, the input line still displays the formula, not the value, whenever you highlight a cell that contains a formula.

You might not, however, want the value generated by the formula to be *dynamic* (change when the spreadsheet is recalculated). To *fix* a value, you can convert the formula to the value it produces. This can be done in several ways. If there is just one cell involved, press F2 while you highlight the cell containing the formula. This prepares the formula for editing. Now press the Calc key (F9), and the formula is turned into its result. You can then place this result into the cell by pressing the ENTER key.

To convert a simple block of formulas to values you can copy them with Edit | Copy and then use the Edit | Paste Special command, described in Chapter 2, to convert the cells with the Values only setting. You can also use the Block | Values command, described in Chapter 3, to convert a compound block of formulas to their resulting values.

Named Blocks and Pages

Naming blocks with the Block | Names command, as described in Chapter 3, is very useful when you are developing formulas. You can use block names instead of cell coordinates. Even attaching a name to a single cell can be productive. It is often easier to type +TOTAL–DOWN than +B12–B13, particularly if you are composing the formula in another area of the spreadsheet, such as AB99. You do not need to check where these elements are and do not need to take the time to point them out. Furthermore, if you type +B112–B31 by mistake, Quattro Pro will not tell you that this is an error; but if you try to enter an invalid block name, you will get an error message. Quattro Pro will switch to EDIT mode so that you can correct the mistake.

Many people find that block names are easier to use than cell coordinates, particularly because you can press the Choices key (F3) to pop up a list of block names from which to choose while you are composing a formula, as shown in Figure 5-2. If you press the plus key (+) on the numeric keypad, you get a more detailed version of the Block Names list, showing the coordinates of each block, as seen in Figure 5-3. Note that the list includes blocks that are in other pages of the notebook and precedes their coordinates with the page name. At this point you can select the name you want to insert in the formula and click OK or press ENTER. The list is put away and the name is typed for you on the input line. You can also double-click on a name to select it and put the list away. Press ESC or click Cancel to put the list away without selecting from it.

The same basic principle applies to naming notebook pages. If you name a page, it is much easier to refer to in a formula. Remembering and entering CHICAGO:TOTAL is easier than using A:G9, particularly as the detailed version of the Block Names list includes page names with block coordinates. If you have a lot of block names, you can press F3 a second time while viewing the Block Names list to get a larger list box.

Common Formula Errors

If there is a mistake in a formula that you are creating—such as a misspelled block or function name, an invalid cell reference, or an unrecognized symbol—Quattro Pro will not accept the formula when you try to enter it. Instead, the program will beep and display a message. When you press ENTER or ESC to acknowledge the message, the program changes to EDIT mode and attempts to position the edit cursor near the error you have made. The exact error message you get depends on the error. For example, entering **@SUM(B2..TC12)** earns the response "In-

FIGURE 5-2 Block Names menu

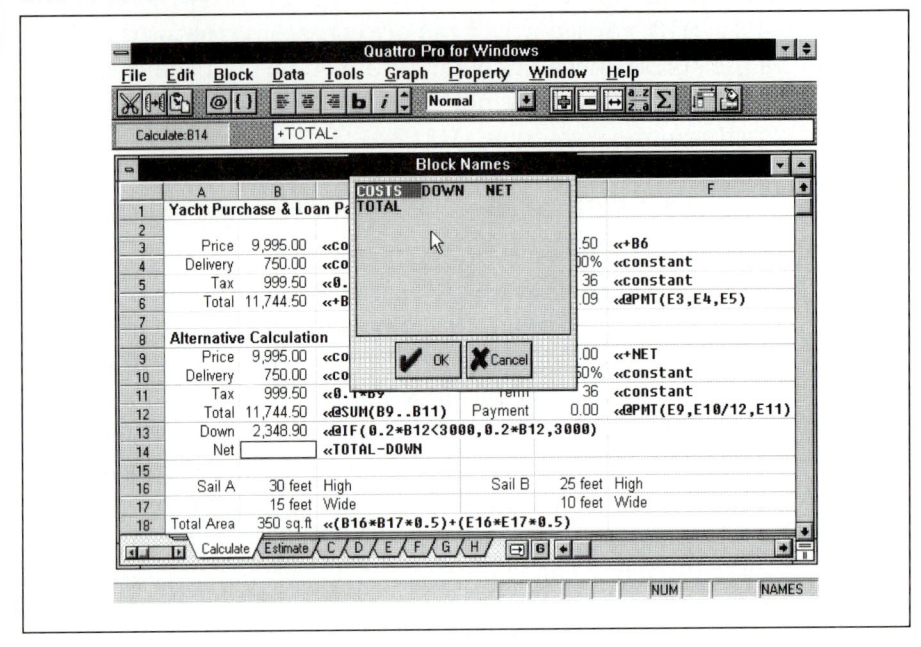

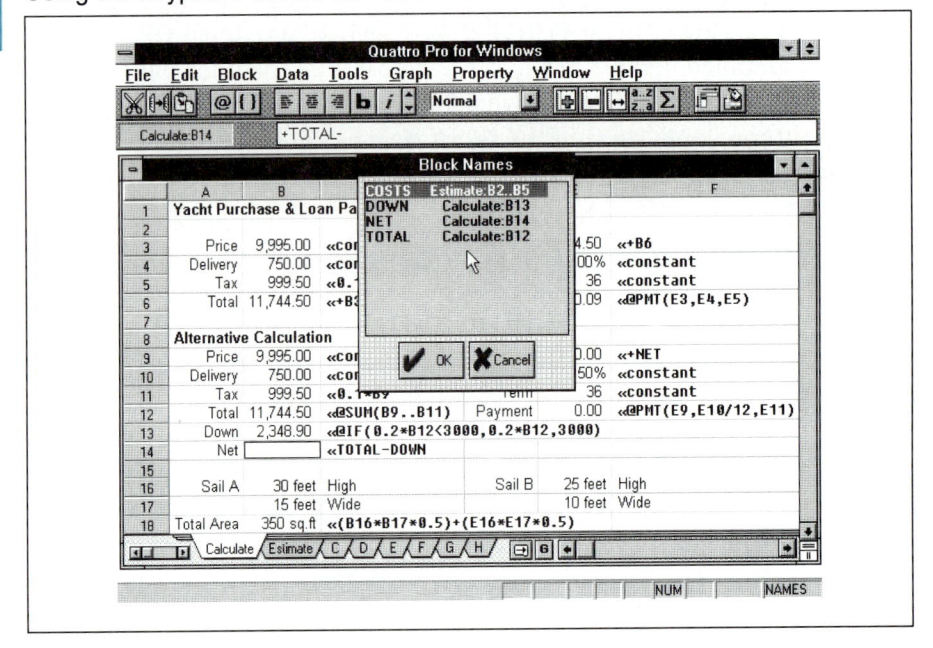

FIGURE 5-3 Using the keypad + shows the Block Names list in more detail

valid Reference," because there cannot be a cell TC12. When you see a message of this type, check the formula to find the error. You may have neglected to close a pair of parentheses or quotations, or you may have omitted the @ sign before a function name. Table 5-2 lists possible error messages.

TABLE 5-2 Common Entry Error Messages

Message	Problem/Solution
Formula too long	You exceeded the limit of 254 characters in a formula; break formula into several subformulas.
Incomplete formula	You left something out; check for operators not followed by arguments.
Invalid argument	You have tried to use an argument that does not fit the @function you are using; check the syntax of the argument.
Invalid cell or block address	You entered something that is being read as a nonexistent cell reference or block name; check that you have typed the formula correctly and defined all block names used in the formula.
Invalid character	You used a character that does not fit the syntax; check for trailing commas or other punctuation that is out of place.
Missing arguments	You forgot to supply an argument where one is expected; check your entry.
Missing operator	You forgot to separate values or functions with an operator; check your entry.
Missing right parenthesis	You opened one or more sets of parentheses than you closed; check for missing right parenthesis or extra left parenthesis.
Syntax error	You have made an error that does not fall into the other categories; check spelling of your entry and syntax requirements of the functions you are using.
Too many arguments	You have supplied more arguments than the function can accept; check syntax and punctuation of what you entered.
Unknown @function	You used a function name that is not recognized; check spelling and try using Functions (ALT-F3) to list functions.

Note To edit an existing formula, highlight the cell and press F2 to enter EDIT mode. The formula can then be altered on the input line. To initiate editing with a mouse simply select the cell and then click on the input line.

A common mistake is to enter spaces between the elements of a formula. Although the documentation occasionally appears to show spaces, they are generally not allowed in formulas. Unlike Lotus 1-2-3, Quattro Pro does sometimes allow spaces in formulas, although you do not need to type any. To be on the safe side, however, you should avoid spaces completely. You may succeed in entering a formula only to see CIRC appear among the status indicators. This message tells you there is a *circular reference* in your formula, meaning that the formula refers to itself. You cannot ask Quattro Pro to sum a block that includes B11 and put the answer in B11. This kind of problem, which usually becomes apparent as soon as you see what you have attempted to do, is solved by retyping the formula.

If you see the CIRC message and cannot determine which cell is producing it, you can use the Active Notebook dialog box to find the cell. As you can see from Figure 5-4, the Recalc Settings screen shows the location of the circular reference. You can then edit the cell in question.

FIGURE 5-4 Active Notebook dialog box

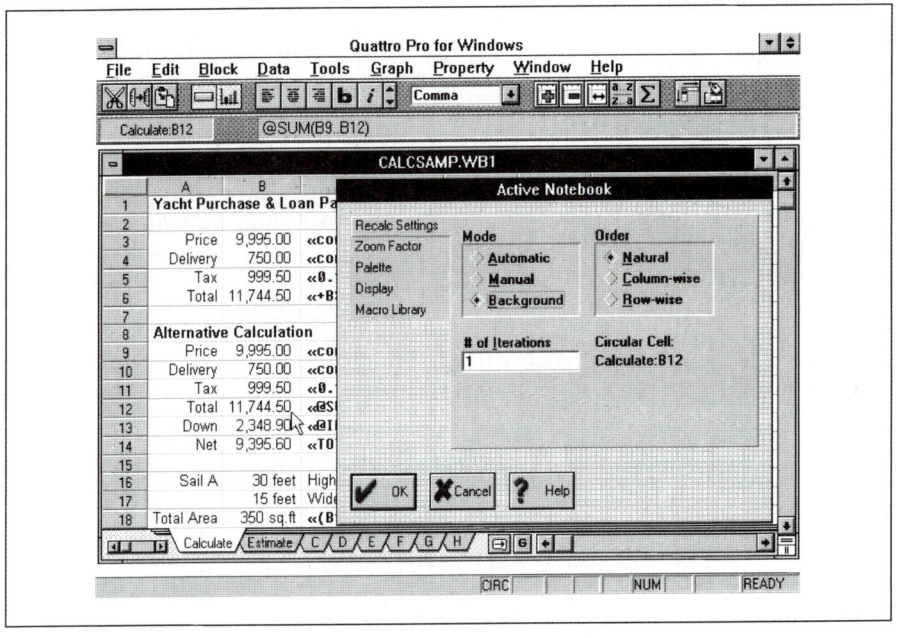

One way to save the typing you have already done on a rejected formula is to press HOME when Quattro Pro switches to EDIT mode. Then you type an apostrophe or other label prefix character. This enables you to temporarily enter the formula as a label and review it. When you have figured out the problem, you can edit the formula and press HOME followed by DEL to remove the apostrophe before pressing ENTER.

Functions as Built-in Formulas

Quattro Pro provides you with the basic building blocks of complex formulas in the form of *functions*. These built-in formulas are specially coded commands that facilitate typical calculations. Using functions, you do not have to enter lengthy instructions. Quattro Pro recognizes these built-in functions because they are preceded by the @ character, and thus they are also known as *@functions*.

Function Arguments

Some functions simply generate values by themselves. For example, PI (entered as **@PI)** gives the value of pi. The date function NOW tells you what your PC thinks the current date and time is (the results of NOW must be formatted as a date before they can be read properly).

Most functions, however, require additional information, called *arguments*. For example, the principal, interest, and term required by the PMT function are said to be the arguments of PMT. A function combined with any arguments is a *function statement*. Some functions, such as PMT, require several specific arguments. Others, like SUM, only need one argument, in this case the block of cells you want to sum. However, you can include additional arguments for SUM, as in

@SUM(B1..B3,D1..C3,F1)

which totals the first three rows of columns B and D, plus the first cell in column F.

The arguments required by functions can be broken down into three types: *numeric,* such as cells containing numbers, as in @PMT(E1,E2,E3);

block, such as a block of cells being summed with @SUM(B1..B3), or a named block, such as @SUM(COSTS); and *string*, a label or piece of text entered into a cell, entered into a function in quotes, or produced by another function. Strings are discussed in Chapter 12.

Numeric functions can reference a mixture of cell coordinates and block names, as in @PMT(E1,INTEREST,TERM). Functions are often combined with operators and values in formulas, just like any other formula element.

Function Syntax

There are more than a hundred functions and several ways of classifying them. In addition to the distinction between numeric and string functions, which is much like that between values and labels, functions can be grouped by the type of work they apply to: financial, date, logical, and so on.

All Quattro Pro functions are always entered in the same basic format, using a standard arrangement of parts, or *syntax*:

- Functions begin with the leading @ sign.
- Next is the name of the function, typed in upper- or lowercase or a combination and spelled accurately.
- There should be no spaces between the @ and the function name.
- The arguments, when required, follow the function name enclosed in parentheses.
- With more than one argument, you must separate one argument from the next with a comma; the arguments must be in proper order.

The Functions Key, ALT-F3

One way to prevent errors like misspelled function names is to use the Functions key, ALT-F3. Pressing ALT-F3 when you are using either VALUE mode or EDIT mode pops up a list of the functions, as shown in Figure 5-5. The same list appears when you click the @ button on the SpeedBar.

Chapter 5: Mastering Functions

FIGURE 5-5 Functions pop-up list

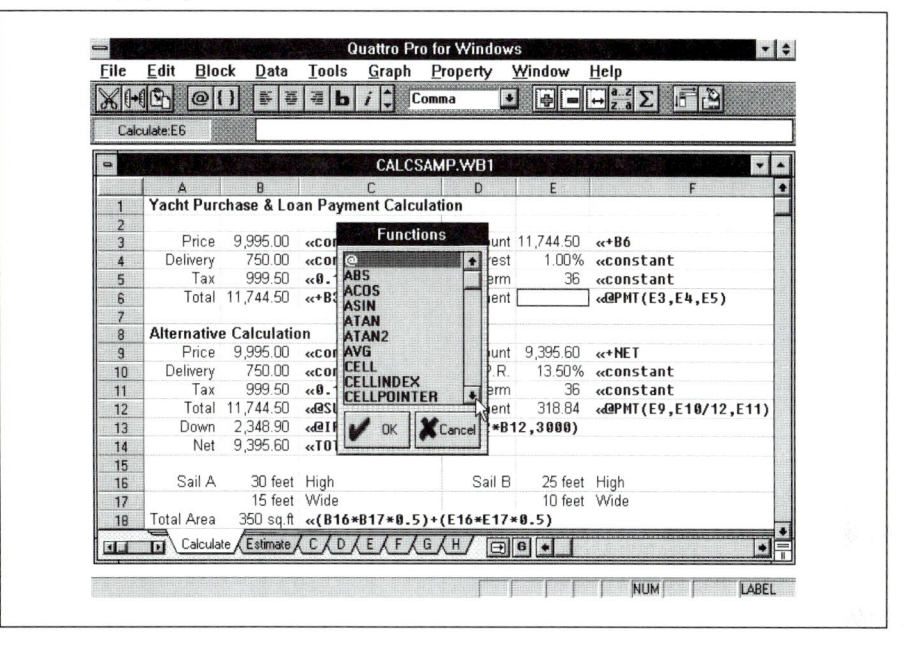

If you press ALT-F3 in READY mode, Quattro Pro pops up the list of functions.

You can browse through the Functions list with the arrow keys, moving a page at a time with PGUP or PGDN. You can use your mouse to browse the list by means of the scroll bar.

When you see the function that you need, highlight it and press ENTER or click OK to place it onto the edit line. You can also double-click on a function name to select it. Note that Quattro Pro also types the @ sign for you and an opening parenthesis if one is required. In addition, the arguments required by the function are listed at the bottom of the screen to help you construct the function statement correctly. For example, when you select PMT, the message at the bottom of the screen says

@PMT(PRINCIPAL,rate,term)

The argument required next is given in capitals. When you supply the first argument and comma separator, Quattro Pro puts it into lowercase and capitalizes the second argument, leading you through the process of creating the function statement.

When you use the Functions list, you can look up a function by spelling part of the name. When the Functions list appears, press the Edit key (F2), and you will see the message "Search: *" appear in the status line at the bottom of the screen. Just start typing what you can remember of the name and the list box will move to the closest match. For example, if you type **P**, then you will be taken to the first function beginning with P, which is PAYMT. Type **M** and you will get to PMT. To back up a step, press BACKSPACE, and you will move back to PAYMT. Press ENTER to confirm your selection.

Mastering Functions

It would be hard to memorize all of Quattro Pro's functions. By using a few simple techniques, however, you can make full use of them.

- **Always assume there is an appropriate function.** Chances are that the calculation you want to perform is one that many other spreadsheet users need to perform, so it is probably provided by Quattro Pro. You may need to combine several functions in one formula to do the job, sometimes using an intermediate cell to produce part of the answer before completing the calculation in another cell. Remember that columns can be hidden from the display and printed reports so that extra columns required purely for calculations need not affect the way the spreadsheet looks.

- **Use the Functions button on the SpeedBar or the Functions key (ALT-F3) to look up and enter functions.** This prevents typos and reminds you of the wide range of functions that can be used and the arguments that your chosen function requires. When you are constructing formulas containing block names, use the Choices list (F3) to make sure you use correctly defined block names.

- **Save useful function statements.** When you come up with a good formula that you are likely to use often, you might consider saving the spreadsheet under a different name to keep a copy of the formula for reference. Chapter 7 discusses how to save portions of a spreadsheet to separate files and how to combine several files into one. This technique allows you to build a library of useful functions.

If you follow these guidelines and are prepared to spend some time experimenting with functions, you will find that they offer tremendous power. A complete examination of each function is beyond the scope of this book, since at three pages per function, this chapter alone would grow to 300 pages. What you will find in the rest of this chapter is a series of discussions on different sets of functions grouped according to their practical roles. Examples are given in most cases together with references to other parts of the book where functions are described.

You will find several commands for performing complex calculations on the Tools menu. These commands are described in Chapter 11 and include Solve For, which enables you to work backward from a desired answer to the values required to produce it. For example, in the revenue projection spreadsheet given as an example in Chapter 2, you calculated the total revenue based on a given rate of growth. Using Solve For, you can determine the exact rate of growth required to create a specific target figure for total revenue. The Optimizer command, also found on the Tools menu, performs a complex analysis of problems with more than one variable.

Aggregate Functions

Aggregate functions perform some of the most commonly used calculations in spreadsheet work. In addition to SUM, this group includes functions that count the contents of a block, average the block, find the largest and smallest numbers in the block, and determine the degree of variance. These functions also work with several different blocks at once or with numerous individual cells.

SUM

The SUM function is one of the most frequently used functions. In Figure 5-6, SUM is used to add the values in a block of cells—the earnings of a group of commodity brokers. You can use SUM to total columns, rows, and blocks that include columns and rows. All that SUM needs to know is the coordinates or name of the block to be summed. Its syntax is

@SUM(*Block*)

The block does not need to contain values in every cell; the empty cells will be ignored. The SUM function works well with block names. For example, @SUM(TOTAL) totals the values in the block of cells named TOTAL. You can sum several different blocks at once if you separate each from the next with a comma, as in @SUM(TA,TD), which sums two blocks, one named TA, the other TD. There are several advantages to using SUM to add up cells, rather than a "cell+cell+cell" formula. Rows or columns inserted within a summed block are automatically included in the block. For example, consider these two approaches to adding up values.

B2:	100		B2:	100
B3:	200		B3:	200
B4:	300	or	B4:	300
B5:	============		B5:	============
B6:	@SUM(B2..B4)		B6:	+B2+B3+B4

FIGURE 5-6 Adding values with SUM

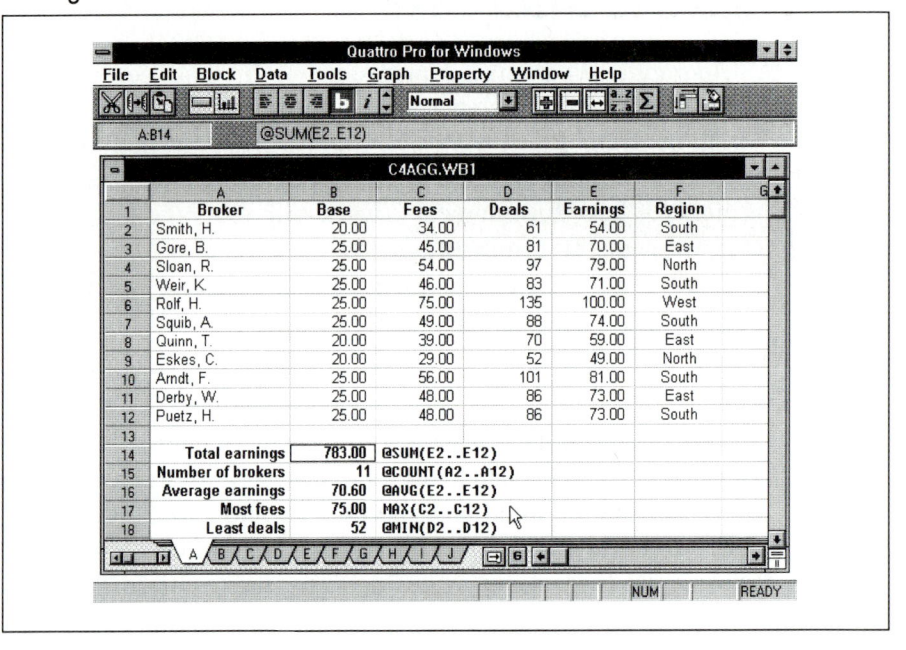

	A	B	C	D	E	F
1	Broker	Base	Fees	Deals	Earnings	Region
2	Smith, H.	20.00	34.00	61	54.00	South
3	Gore, B.	25.00	45.00	81	70.00	East
4	Sloan, R.	25.00	54.00	97	79.00	North
5	Weir, K.	25.00	46.00	83	71.00	South
6	Rolf, H.	25.00	75.00	135	100.00	West
7	Squib, A.	25.00	49.00	88	74.00	South
8	Quinn, T.	20.00	39.00	70	59.00	East
9	Eskes, C.	20.00	29.00	52	49.00	North
10	Arndt, F.	25.00	56.00	101	81.00	South
11	Derby, W.	25.00	48.00	86	73.00	East
12	Puetz, H.	25.00	48.00	86	73.00	South
13						
14	Total earnings	783.00	@SUM(E2..E12)			
15	Number of brokers	11	@COUNT(A2..A12)			
16	Average earnings	70.60	@AVG(E2..E12)			
17	Most fees	75.00	MAX(C2..C12)			
18	Least deals	52	@MIN(D2..D12)			

Chapter 5: Mastering Functions

In the formula on the left, it will not matter if you need to insert an extra row into the spreadsheet to include another value in the calculation. For example, if you place the cell selector on row 4 and issue the Block | Insert | Rows command to include one more row, cells B4, B5, and B6 become cells B5, B6, and B7. The formula that was in B6 but is now in B7 becomes @SUM(B2..B5). If you enter a new value in B4, it will be included in the SUM calculation.

The same is not true if you have used the cell+cell method of adding. Here you can see the results for both of the examples above, after a row and a new value of 250 was inserted at B4:

B2:	100		B2:	100
B3:	200		B3:	200
B4:	250	or	B4:	250
B5:	300		B5:	300
B6:	============		B6:	============
B7:	@SUM(B2..B5)		B7:	+B2+B3+B5

Inserting new rows within the summed block increases the block coordinates to include the new cells. Individually referenced cells are not automatically added to + formulas.

The integrity of the SUM formula is preserved if you insert a row at B2, because the whole set of numbers is moved down. However, because Quattro Pro inserts new rows above the current cell, the new B2 would not be included in the SUM formula. If you were to enter a value into B2 at that point, it would not be included in the sum. If you insert a row into the original example at B5, the accuracy of the formula is preserved, but again, the new cell is not included. As a rule, then, you add a cell to a summed column if you insert the row while selecting the second cell of the block, the last cell, or any cell in between.

Because it is quite natural to add numbers to the bottom of a list, you might want to include the row below the last number when you create a SUM formula. For instance, you could include cell B6 in the SUM argument in the last example. Then you could place the cell selector on row 6 below the last number, insert a new row, and have that row be included in the summed block. When Quattro Pro finishes calculating, the labels in the block would have a value of 0, and thus would not affect the answer.

SUMPRODUCT: *Sum of the Products*

Unlike SUM, SUMPRODUCT is a function that you will not find in all spreadsheet programs. This function is used to sum the results of multiplication between blocks of cells—in other words, add up a series of products. For example, at the top of Figure 5-7, you have two sets of numbers in two columns, and you want to know what you get if the pairs of numbers that are on the same row are multiplied together, and the results added up.

When you multiply 10 by 30 you get 300. When you multiply 20 by 40 you get 800. Add together 300 and 800 and you get 1100, which is the answer returned by SUMPRODUCT. For its arguments, the SUMPRODUCT function requires two blocks of equal size, separated by a comma. This function does not work if any of the cells in the blocks are empty. As you can see from the lower half of Figure 5-7, the blocks used by SUMPRODUCT can be either columns or rows, as long as their dimensions are equal.

FIGURE 5-7

SUMPRODUCT adds up a series of products

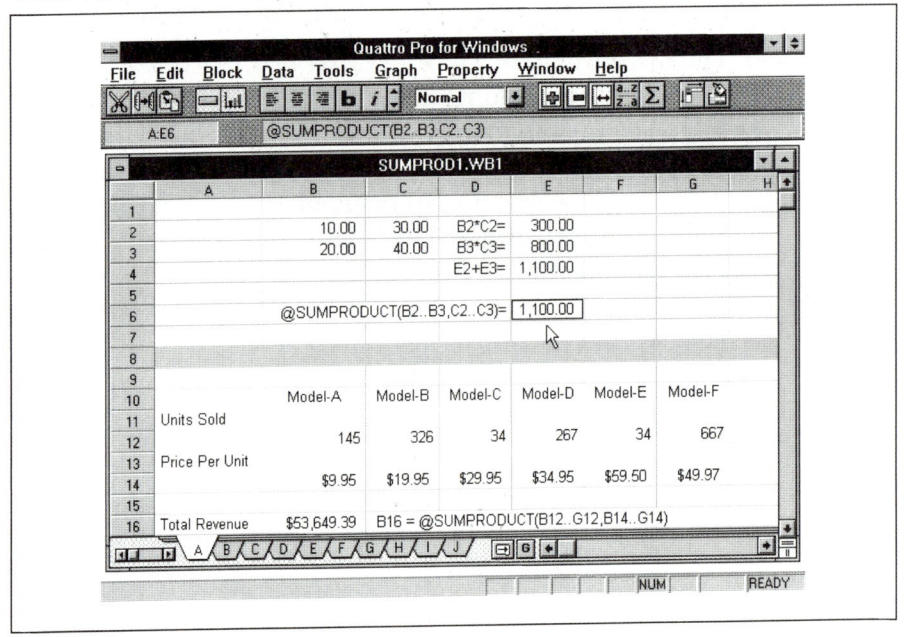

COUNT

The COUNT function counts the number of items or nonempty cells in a block of cells. This function is useful for such projects as inventory tracking, because COUNT can tell you how many entries there are in a column, and thus how many inventory items there are in a list. You simply need to tell the function the location of the cells to be counted. The syntax is

@COUNT(*Block*)

Quattro Pro includes labels when calculating COUNT. Thus, the count for a summed range that includes a line of labels might be greater than you expect. For example, the following arrangement results in an answer of 6 when summed, an answer of 4 when counted (only if cell B4 were empty would the count be 3).

B1:	2	B1:	2
B2:	2	B2:	2
B3:	2	B3:	2
B4:	============	B4:	==============
B5:	@SUM(B1..B4)	B5:	@COUNT(B1..B4)

AVG: Average Value

The AVG function gives the average of values in a block of cells. You can see the usefulness of this function in Figure 5-6, where it was used to calculate the average earnings of the brokers. The function is simply

@AVG(*Block*)

Like SUM, the AVG function works well with columns, rows, and larger blocks, particularly if you use a block name. However, label cells are used in calculating the average. Essentially, the AVG function combines SUM with COUNT; you could say that @AVG = @SUM / @COUNT. Because COUNT gives a value of 1 to a label, the arrangement seen here would produce 6 when summed, but 1.5 when averaged (only if cell B4 were empty would the average of the values, 2, be correctly determined by AVG).

B1:	2	B1:	2
B2:	2	B2:	2
B3:	2	B3:	2
B4:	=============	B4:	=============
B5:	@SUM(B1..B4)	B5:	@AVG(B1..B4)

MAX: Maximum Value

Shown earlier in Figure 5-6, this function finds the largest value in a specified block:

@MAX(*Block*)

You can also use MAX with a series of single cells if you separate each from the next with a comma. Thus, @MAX(B5,G3,K7) tells you the largest amount in those three cells. This is handy when you want to perform a tax-form calculation and need to enter the larger of the numbers on two rows. You can also use MAX to compare a cell to a number. Thus, @MAX(G5,10) will return the value in G5 if it is greater than 10; otherwise, you will get the value 10. This is also useful for tax calculations, when a subtraction results in a negative number but you must enter 0 instead of the negative number. The formula @MAX(G5,0) will return either the value in G5 or 0, whichever is greater. If G5 is negative, the result is 0.

MIN: Minimum Value

Corollary to the MAX function, the MIN function returns the smallest value in a block of cells:

@MIN(*Block*)

This function can be used to identify low levels in projections and inventory lists. You can also use MIN and MAX to determine the highest and lowest balances for a customer's credit or checking account.

STD: Standard Deviation

This function returns the standard deviation for a given block of cells that represent a population of data:

@STD(*Block*)

The *standard deviation* of a set of values is a measure of how much variation there is from the average of the values. The standard deviation is the square root of the variance. If you want to compute sample standard deviation, use the STDS function.

VAR: Variance

The VAR function returns a measure of variance for a block of cells, that is, the amount of variation between individual values and the mean of the population.

@VAR(*Block*)

The result of this function is the square of the standard deviation of the same set of values. To calculate variance for a sample rather than a population, use VARS.

Arithmetic Functions

These functions affect the way numbers are calculated. They are often used when the outcome of a formula needs to be modified; for example, the outcome should be rounded, or a negative number should be turned into a positive number.

ABS: Absolute Value

The absolute value of a number is its value without a sign. To arrive at the absolute value of a number, you use the ABS function. The syntax is

@ABS(*Value*)

For example, the formula @ABS(B5) returns the absolute value of the contents of B5. The absolute value of a number is its positive equivalent; so if B5 is –1.5, @ABS(B5) equals 1.5.

INT: Number as an Integer

At times you need to drop the decimal places from a number, rather than round them up or down. This can be done with the INT function. Its syntax is

@INT(*Value*)

Thus, when cell B5 contains 2.75, the formula @INT(B5) returns 2. The value is stripped of digits following the decimal place, rather than rounded up to 3.

MOD: Modulus, the Remainder

You use the MOD function when you need the number that is left after two other numbers are divided. This returns the remainder of *x* divided by *y*, as in

@MOD(*x*,*y*)

Thus, the formula @MOD(B5,5) returns 1 when B5 contains the value 36 (5 goes into 36 7 times, with a remainder of 1). This function is very useful when you need to figure shipping factors. You could use, for example,

@MOD(*CasesInOrder,CasesPerTruck*)

to determine how many cases will be left after a large order has been put on the trucks. Note that using 0 as the value for *y* is not valid, because you cannot divide by 0. Doing so produces an ERR message in the formula cell.

RND: Random Number

When you need a random number in a cell you can use RAND. This function takes no argument:

@RAND

The RAND function produces a uniformly distributed random number greater than or equal to 0 and less than 1. You normally want to combine it with a formula to produce a random number within a certain range. You do this by putting the high end and the low end of the range, separated by a minus sign, in a pair of parentheses and then multiplying that by the RAND function added to the low-end number. Thus, a random number from 3 to 12 would be produced by

(12–3)*@RAND+3

Note If you need to get a whole number from the RAND function, you will need to use INT or ROUND.

Although random numbers might not seem to be very useful in a program that is designed to help you organize and accurately analyze information, they can be useful when you want to fill cells with numbers to test a spreadsheet design. Several of the models in this book were created from random numbers.

The RAND function returns a new random number every time the spreadsheet recalculates. This can cause problems if you are trying to use the function to create values used elsewhere in the spreadsheet. Data generated by RAND can be fixed by using the Block | Values command to change the formula to a value. This also enables you to hide the fact that the numbers you have created with RAND are just random numbers.

ROUND

In some models, you may need to round the numbers that are displayed and printed. Quattro Pro retains up to 15 decimal places in calculations that result in fractions. When you use a display format that sets the number of decimal places to less than 1, these fractions are not displayed but are still active. This produces a visual problem when numbers containing fractions are summed but formatted for a small fixed number of decimal places. As the fractions accumulate, the total appears to be incorrect.

To solve this problem, the numbers being totaled can be rounded with ROUND. The format of the function is as follows:

@ROUND(x,y)

The function rounds off the value of x using y as the number of digits to round to. The value of y should be between –15 and +15 and should be an integer (whole number). Quattro Pro will round y to an integer.

The effect of ROUND was seen in Chapter 3, where the rounding of numbers for display purposes produced an apparent discrepancy in column totals. In Figure 5-8, you can see three versions of the same set of sales projections. The first version uses the Comma format with two decimal places and uses no ROUND function in the growth formulas that increase February and March figures by 9 percent. The figures in column H of the first example do not add up properly.

In the second version of the same calculations, the figures are shown in the General format. Now you can see the accumulated fractions created by the growth formula. The third version of the figures uses the ROUND function as part of the growth formula, as seen in cell F16. The General format is used to show that there are no further fractions beyond the two decimal places specified in the ROUND function. This leads to a correct total in column H.

You can combine ROUND with RAND to produce a whole number within a specified range, as in the following formula, which produces a number from 18 to 48 with no decimal places:

@ROUND(((48–18)*@RAND+18),0)

Chapter 5: Mastering Functions 255

FIGURE 5-8 Columns of figures, with and without the ROUND function

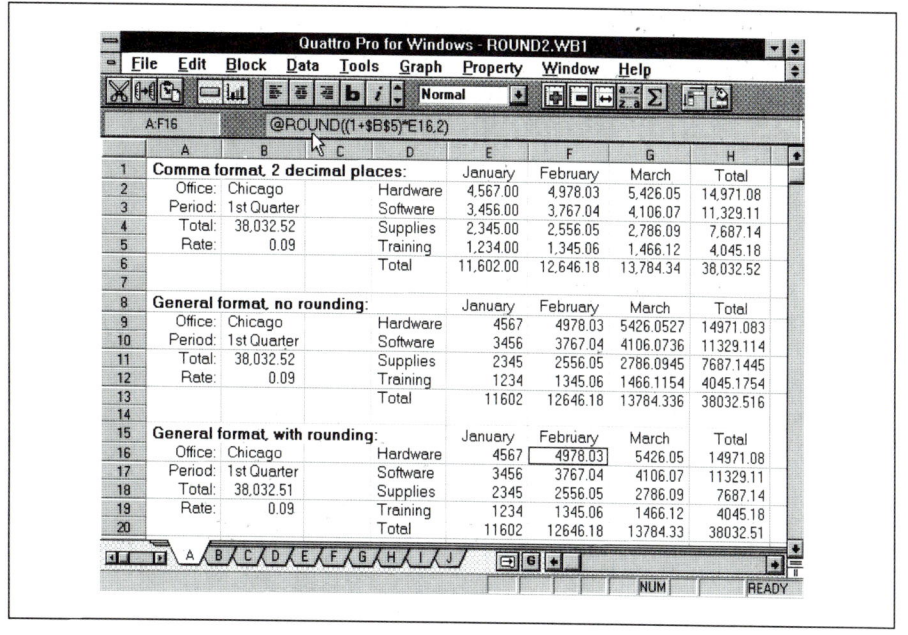

EXP: Exponent

The EXP function returns the value of *e* (a constant, approximately 2.7182818) raised to the power of the function's argument, as in

@EXP(*x*)

where *x* is a numeric value less than or equal to 709. Thus, if *x* is 2, then *e* will be squared. This function is the inverse of a natural logarithm, LN. If the value of *x* is greater than 709.85, then the @EXP function will return ERR.

SQRT: Square Root

You can find the square root of a number or formula in Quattro Pro with the SQRT function. This function uses the syntax

@SQRT(*Value*)

For example, @SQRT(B5) returns the square root of the value in B5. Square roots of negative numbers produce the response ERR. Use the negation operator or the ABS function to make the value a positive number. One typical application of SQRT is in the calculation of the hypotenuse, or slope, of a right triangle:

@SQRT(*Base*Base+Height*Height*)

LN and LOG: Logarithms

The LN(*x*) and LOG(*x*) functions return the log base *e* of *x* and the log base 10 of *x*, respectively. Thus, @LN(100) equals 4.60517 and @LOG(100) equals 2. If the value of *x* is less than or equal to 0, these functions return the ERR message in the cell in which they were applied.

Database Functions

When you want to find the total of a column, you normally use the aggregate function SUM. Likewise, to calculate the average of a column of numbers, you use the AVG function. If you want to sum selected values, however, such as the fees for all brokers in the South, you would turn to the database functions shown in Figure 5-9. These appear similar to the aggregate functions, but they begin (after the @, of course) with a D. In the lower half of the figure, you can see the seven database functions typed out in formulas, to the right of the answers that those formulas produce. In the upper half of the screen are the records referred to in the formulas as well as a small criteria table. The database functions use several of the concepts to be discussed in Chapter 6, such as query block and criteria.

The basic operation of a database function is to tell Quattro Pro which block of cells is involved, which column of the block you want the function applied to, and which records to include based on the criteria table. For example, in cell B16 in Figure 5-9, DAVG averages the earnings from only the records specified by the criteria table, in this case where Region =

FIGURE 5-9 The seven database functions and a criteria table

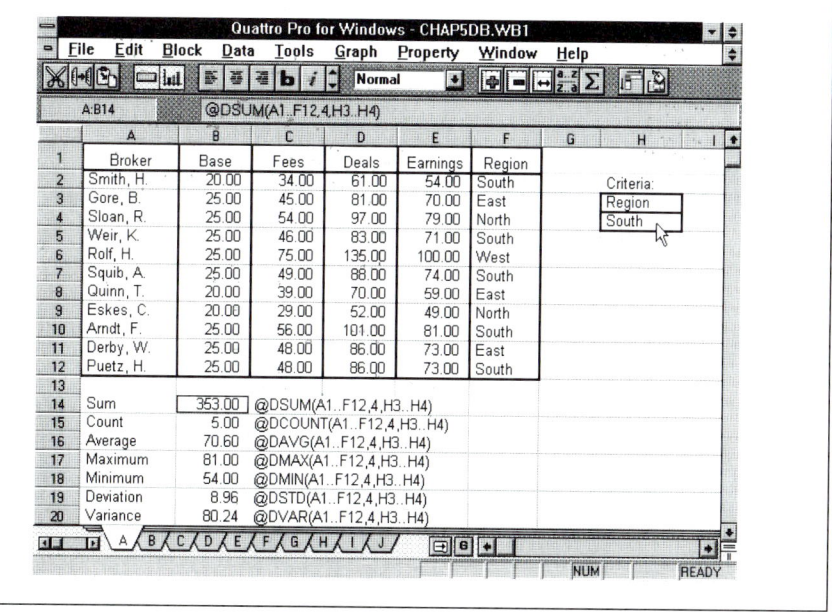

South. All database functions have the same syntax. In the case of DAVG, it is

@DAVG(*Block,Column,Criteria*)

Block is the cell block containing the database, the rectangular group of consecutive rows and named columns that constitute a database, including the field names at the top. *Column* is the number of the column containing the field you want to average, with the first column as 0, the second as 1, and so on. *Criteria* is a cell block containing search criteria.

The DAVG function averages selected field entries in a database. It includes only those entries in the column number specified whose records meet the chosen criteria. "Criteria" refers to the coordinates of a block containing a criteria table that specifies search information, as in H3..H4. This is the criteria table for all the formulas in the lower half of Figure 5-9, which analyze the earnings for all brokers in the South region. Criteria tables are described in detail in Chapter 6.

The field specified in the criteria and the field being averaged need not be the same; you can average earnings for all brokers in the South Region or average fees for all brokers earning over $45.00. The field averaged is that contained within the column you specify with the column number. You can specify all or part of a database as the block, but field names must be included for each field you include in the block. All of the other database functions use the same three arguments: *Block*, *Column*, and *Criteria*.

DMAX: *Maximum Value*

The DMAX function finds the maximum value of selected field entries in a database. The function includes only those entries in the specified column whose records meet the criteria in the criteria table. The DMAX function syntax is

@DMAX(*Block,Column,Criteria*)

DMAX is a very useful function when you are analyzing a large group of numbers, such as the broker earnings reports for each of four regions. The DMAX function eliminates the need to sort through the records and manually choose ones to compare to find the largest earnings number for brokers in one region. You might also find DMAX useful for determining the largest figure in the earnings column for all brokers who had earnings greater than a certain level. This would give you some basis with which to compare the higher-earning brokers.

DMIN: *Minimum Value*

The DMIN function finds the minimum value of selected field entries in a database. It includes only those entries in the specified column whose records meet the criteria in a criteria table. Its syntax is

@DMIN(*Block,Column,Criteria*)

You can use this function for such applications as inventory tracking. If one column in your inventory database is called Quantity On Hand

and another is called Required Delivery Time, you can have DMIN show the smallest current quantity on hand for all inventory items that need less than ten days' delivery time. By watching this number as inventory is added or deleted from the database, you know when you must order more items.

DSTD: Standard Deviation Measure

The DSTD function finds the population standard deviation value of selected field entries in a database. It includes only those entries in the specified column whose records meet the criteria in a criteria table. Its syntax is

@DSTD(*Block,Column,Criteria*)

If you want to compute sample standard deviation, use the DSTDS function, but be aware that this function may not be compatible with earlier spreadsheet programs.

DSUM: Sum Value

The DSUM function totals selected field entries in a database. It includes only those entries in the specified column whose records meet the criteria in the criteria table. Its syntax is

@DSUM(*Block,Column,Criteria*)

This function quickly returns such useful answers as the total earnings paid to brokers in one region.

DVAR: Variance Measure

The DVAR function calculates variance for selected field entries in a database. It includes only those entries in the column specified whose records meet the criteria in the criteria table. Its syntax is

@DVAR(*Block,Column,Criteria*)

To calculate variance for a sample rather than a population, use DVARS, but bear in mind that this function may not be compatible with earlier spreadsheet programs.

Financial Functions

The functions provided for financial calculations in Quattro Pro are extensive. You can calculate annuities, mortgage payments, present values, and numerous other figures that would otherwise require you to create a lengthy formula. Some basic terms and conditions are common to all Quattro Pro financial functions. Table 5-3 lists the arguments that Quattro Pro financial functions require and the abbreviations used for them. These abbreviations are used in the following descriptions.

Quattro Pro stipulates that when interest rates are required in financial function arguments, they must be stated as a percentage per period. For example, when you are figuring monthly loan payments with the PMT or PAYMT functions, you state the interest argument as percentage per month.

TABLE 5-3 Financial Function Arguments

Argument	Definition
Rate	Interest rate per period, as defined in *Nper*, should be greater than –1.
Nper	Number of periods—for example, 12 months or 1 year; an integer greater than 0.
Pv	Present value, an amount valued today.
Pmt	A payment, a negative cash flow amount.
Fv	Future value, an amount to be accumulated.
Type	Either 0 or 1. *Type* indicates the difference between ordinary annuity (0) and annuity due (1). Argument of 0 means payments are made at the end of each period; 1 means that they are made at the beginning. The default assumption is that *Type* = 0.

A connoisseur of spreadsheet programs might describe the financial functions in Quattro Pro as a subtle blend of the best from 1-2-3 and Excel. While retaining "backward" compatibility with 1-2-3 Release 2 and earlier versions of Quattro Pro, the newer functions allow more sophisticated financial calculations, using optional arguments for the timing of payments. In Table 5-4, you can see the older functions and the newer alternatives. Unless you are creating spreadsheets that need to be compatible with older programs, you will probably want to employ the newer Quattro Pro functions.

Payment Functions

Several financial functions relate to loan payments. They are PMT, PAYMT, IPAYMT, and PPAYMT. These are considered as a group here because they serve as a good example of the power and flexibility provided by Quattro Pro's financial functions. For example, the PAYMT function can be used to perform several different calculations, depending on the number of arguments provided.

PMT: Basic Loan Payment Function

As you have seen in several examples so far, the PMT function calculates the amount required to pay back a loan in equal payments

TABLE 5-4 Older Functions and New Alternatives*

Old-Style Function	New-Style Function
@CTERM(*Rate,Fv,Pv*)	@NPER(*Rate*,0,–*Pv*,0)
@FV(*Pmt,Rate,Nper*)	@FVAL(*Rate,Nper,–Pmt*,0,0)
@PMT(*Pv,Rate,Nper*)	@PAYMT(*Rate,Nper,–Pv*,0,0)
@PV(*Pv,Rate,Nper*)	@PVAL(*Rate,Nper,–Pmt*,0,0)
@Rate(*Fv,Pv,Nper*)	@IRATE(*Nper*,0,–*Pv,Fv*,0)
@TERM(*Pv,Rate,Fv*)	@NPER(*Rate,–Pmt*,0,*Fv*,0)

*Negative arguments indicate cash flows assumed to be negative.

based on a given principal or amount borrowed, a rate of interest, and a loan term. The format of the function is

@PMT(*Pv*,*Rate*,*Nper*)

Present value (*Pv*) is the principal, the amount being borrowed. *Rate* is the interest being charged, and number of payments (*Nper*) is the life of the loan. The values for *Pv*, *Rate*, and *Nper* can be numeric constants, numeric fields, or formulas that result in a number. Note that *Rate* must be greater than –1 and *Nper* cannot be 0.

Figure 5-10 shows a loan calculation spreadsheet, which demonstrates the argument requirements of the PMT function. Because the rate is requested in percentage per period but is normally quoted as an annual percentage rate (as in cell K3), the middle argument divides the contents of cell K3 by 12. Likewise, the term of the loan (*Nper*) is stated in years in K2 for convenience and then multiplied by the payments per year (12) in the formula. This value could be adjusted for quarterly (4), semiannual

FIGURE 5-10 Loan calculation spreadsheet using the PMT function

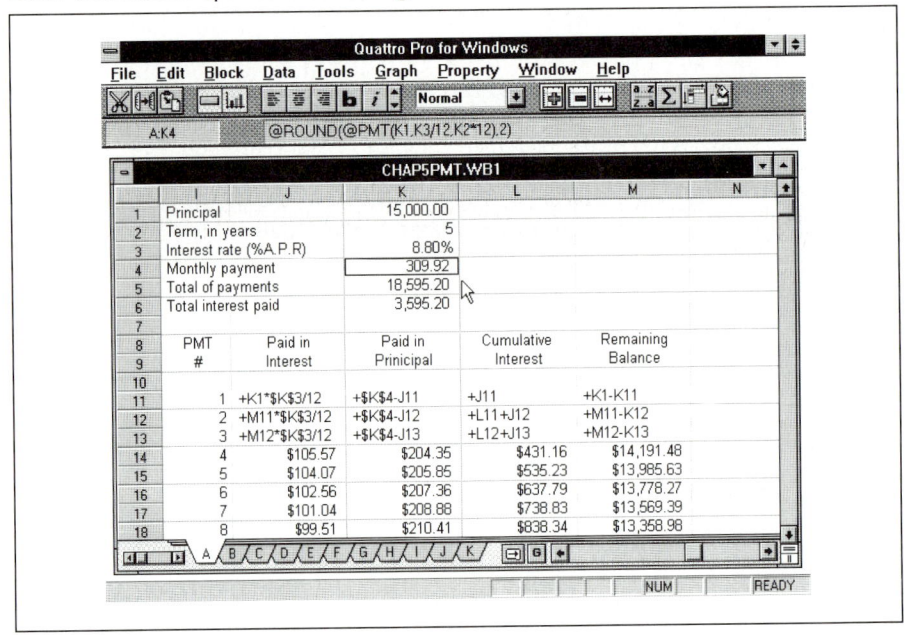

(2), or annual (1) payments. Note that Figure 5-10 includes a loan table, showing the progress of the loan. The first few rows have been formatted with the Text format to show the formulas used.

PAYMT: Sophisticated Loan Payment Function

A more sophisticated function for calculating loan payments and other values is PAYMT. In its simplest form, the PAYMT function works like PMT to return the size of payment required to amortize a loan across a given number of periods, assuming equal payments at a constant rate of interest. However, the first difference between the two functions is apparent in the order and number of arguments they use. The format of the PAYMT function is

@PAYMT(*Rate,Nper,Pv,Fv,Type*)

The function's purpose can be defined as determination of the fully amortized mortgage payment for borrowing a present value amount at rate percent of interest per period over a specified number of periods.

You can use a numeric constant, a numeric field, or a formula that results in a number for the principal (*Pv*), *Rate*, and term (*Nper*) arguments. Note that the interest rate must be greater than –1, and that the term cannot equal 0. The last two arguments, future value (*Fv*) and *Type*, are optional and are discussed in a moment. Figure 5-11 shows an example of the PAYMT function being used to calculate the payment required to repay $26,000 over 36 months when borrowed at 12.00% A.P.R. Here is where you can see the second major difference between PMT and PAYMT; the latter produces a negative value. The reason for this is the financial assumption that a payment is a negative item from a cash flow point of view.

In the example in Figure 5-11, the labels in column B are used to name and identify the figures in column C, using the Block I Names I Create command, described in Chapter 3. Note that the interest rate is stated as 12.00% in cell C7, meaning 12% per year. It is then divided by 12 when used as the *Rate* argument in the PAYMT function statement in cell C8. This is to comply with the Quattro Pro requirement that *Rate* be stated as interest per period.

FIGURE 5-11 Home loan using the PAYMT function

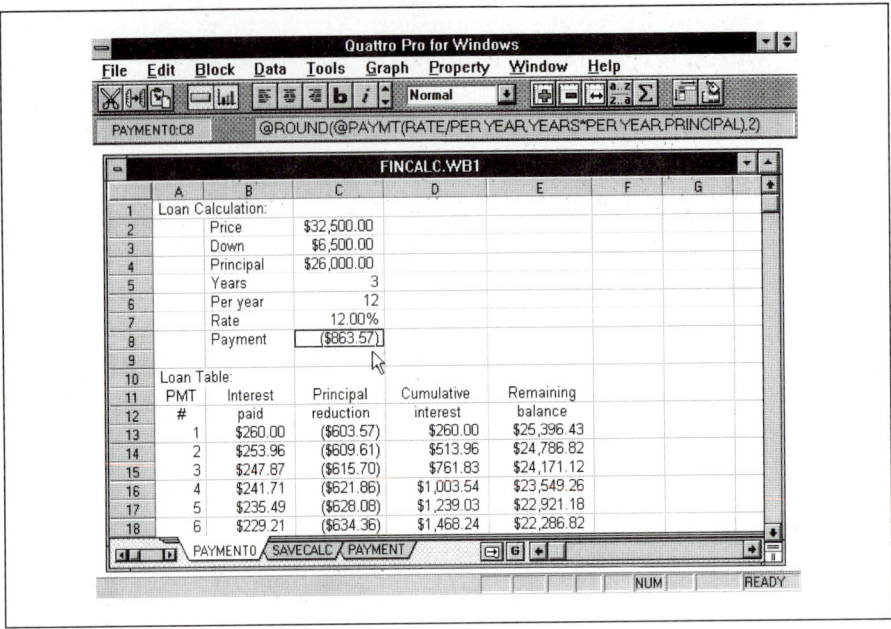

Future Value and PAYMT The optional future value (*Fv*) argument in a PAYMT function statement is used when you use PAYMT to calculate the size of payments you need to make each month to accumulate a specific sum of money in the future. For example, suppose you want to accumulate $26,000 to purchase a new car. You are going to put away an amount of money every month for two years. That money will earn 8.00 percent interest. How large does the monthly payment have to be? You can see the answer in Figure 5-12, which shows two versions of the calculation. Note that when you use the future value argument, you cannot just omit the present value argument. A zero is commonly used as a placeholder for the present value argument, as in

@PAYMT(*Rate*/12,*Nper*,0,*Fv*,*Type*)

You might also note in Figure 5-12 the calculation of principal paid into the account and the amount of interest earned. These calculations are not automatically carried out by Quattro Pro but provide a useful perspective on the PAYMT function.

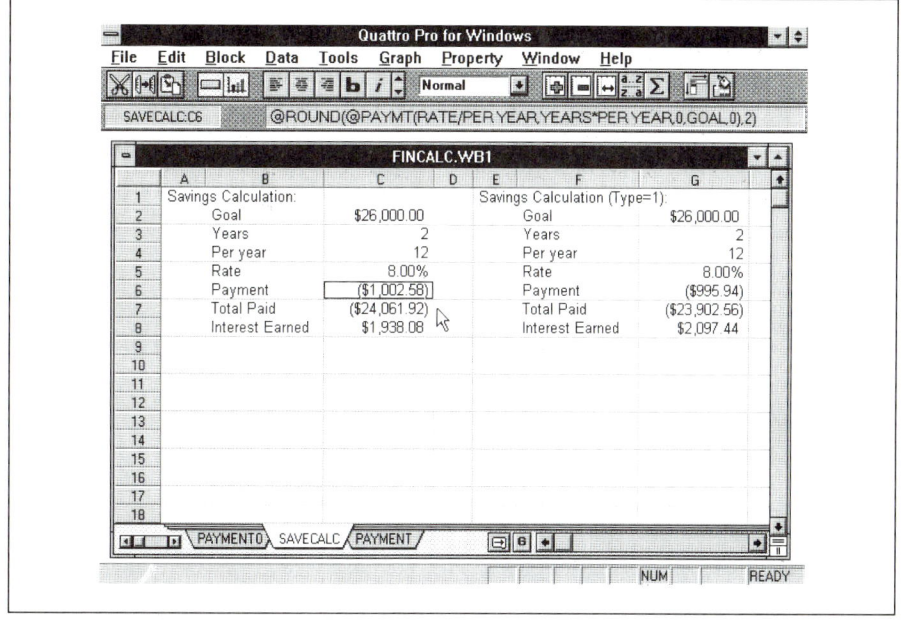

FIGURE 5-12 Calculating the size of payments needed to save a certain amount of money

```
SAVECALC:C6    @ROUND(@PAYMT(RATE/PER YEAR,YEARS*PER YEAR,0,GOAL,0),2)
```

FINCALC.WB1

	A	B	C	D	E	F	G
1	Savings Calculation:				Savings Calculation (Type=1):		
2		Goal	$26,000.00			Goal	$26,000.00
3		Years	2			Years	2
4		Per year	12			Per year	12
5		Rate	8.00%			Rate	8.00%
6		Payment	($1,002.58)			Payment	($995.94)
7		Total Paid	($24,061.92)			Total Paid	($23,902.56)
8		Interest Earned	$1,938.08			Interest Earned	$2,097.44

The Type Argument The calculation on the right in Figure 5-12 uses the other optional argument for the PAYMT function: *Type*. Quattro Pro can calculate interest based on two types of payment arrangements. In Figure 5-12, you can see the effect of going to type 1 on a future value savings plan calculation. The effect is positive, because it assumes that you begin the savings plan by making the first deposit. On the left in Figure 5-12, the assumption was that the payment on the plan was at the end of the period, thus requiring larger payments to achieve the same goal. The *Type* argument is likely to be 0 for such calculations as loans, but 1 for such items as annuities and savings plans.

When you use PAYMT, the program assumes, as do many consumer loans, that payment is due at the end of the period. In other words, the first payment is due one month from when you receive the principal of the loan, and at the end of each one-month period after that. This assumption is type 0. If you omit a *Type* argument, Quattro Pro will assume type 0, as in Figure 5-11.

The alternative type, based on having the payment due at the beginning of each loan period, is type 1. You can force this assumption by including 1 as the *Type* argument, as shown in the revised loan payment plan in Figure 5-13. You can see that the amount of each payment is less under a type 1 loan. Of course, the practical effect of going to a type 1 loan is to reduce the term of the loan by one period and pay the first payment from the proceeds of the loan, a practice that was once followed by some banks.

Loan Tables

You may want to see a table of payments for a loan, showing the split between interest and principal and the amount of principal left unpaid. A table of payments can be laid out below the loan calculations, as shown earlier in Figure 5-10 and again in Figure 5-14. Note that the ROUND function is used to round the payment to the nearest cent (two decimal places). This is necessary when you are performing real-world loan calculations rather than just estimates.

The loan payment table consists of five columns, starting with the payment number, which runs from 1 to 60 (5 years × 12 payments each).

FIGURE 5-13 The home loan, using the Type1 argument, with payments at the beginning of the period

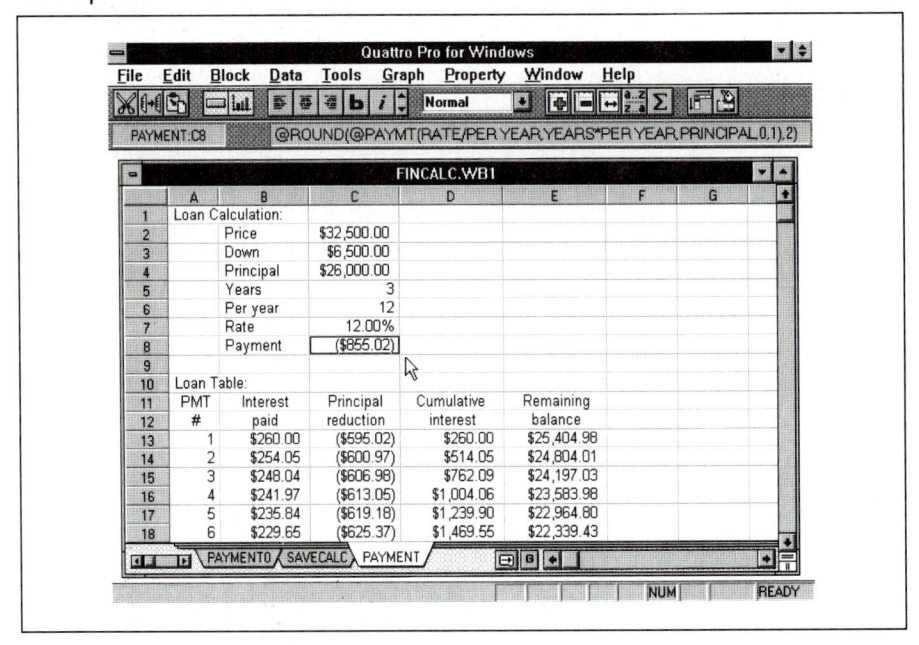

Chapter 5: Mastering Functions 267

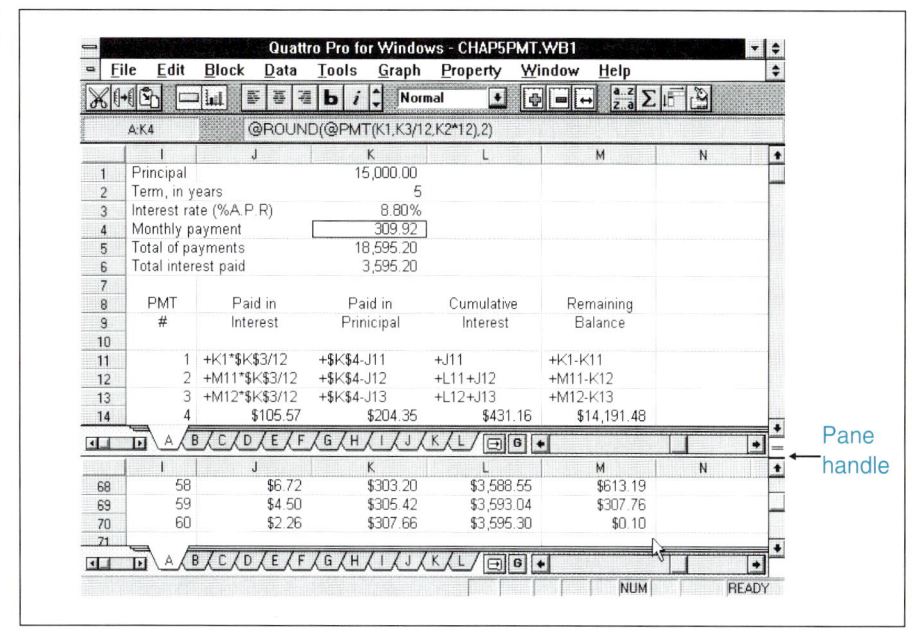

FIGURE 5-14 Loan calculations and a table of payments

	I	J	K	L	M	N
1	Principal		15,000.00			
2	Term, in years		5			
3	Interest rate (%A.P.R)		8.80%			
4	Monthly payment		309.92			
5	Total of payments		18,595.20			
6	Total interest paid		3,595.20			
7						
8	PMT	Paid in	Paid in	Cumulative	Remaining	
9	#	Interest	Prinicipal	Interest	Balance	
10						
11	1	+K1*$K$3/12	+$K$4-J11	+J11	+K1-K11	
12	2	+M11*$K$3/12	+$K$4-J12	+L11+J12	+M11-K12	
13	3	+M12*$K$3/12	+$K$4-J13	+L12+J13	+M12-K13	
14	4	$105.57	$204.35	$431.16	$14,191.48	

	I	J	K	L	M	N
68	58	$6.72	$303.20	$3,588.55	$613.19	
69	59	$4.50	$305.42	$3,593.04	$307.76	
70	60	$2.26	$307.66	$3,595.30	$0.10	

Cell A:K4 contains `@ROUND(@PMT(K1,K3/12,K2*12),2)`

← Pane handle

In Figure 5-14, the Window | Pane | Pane Options | Horizontal command has been used to show the bottom of the table, as well as the top. (You could also drag the horizontal pane handle, the icon in the lower-right corner with the two horizontal lines.) Column J calculates the amount of each payment that is interest, while column K shows the amount paid to reduce the principal. In column L, a running total of interest paid is maintained, while the declining principal is tracked in column M. You can see the formulas that make up the loan payment table in Figure 5-14.

The total figures in K6 and K5 show the total interest and total payments, respectively. You might notice that the total principal reduction is actually 10¢ less than the amount of the loan. This is a result of the need to accept payments in dollars and whole cents. As any banker knows, there are several ways of dealing with this kind of minor imbalance in a loan amortization. (You might want to experiment with these using Quattro Pro; for example, the actual payment required to retire the sample loan in exactly 60 payments is $309.92135307589.)

Finally, it should be noted that the method of calculating the remaining balance on the loan shown in Figure 5-14 is simple interest, the method commonly used by banks for mortgages and personal loans. Some lending institutions use the rule of 78 to determine the amount left unpaid. This method uses a system like sum-of-the-years'-digits, shown later in the discussion of the SYD function, to determine interest.

IPAYMT and PPAYMT: Interest and Principal

There may be times when you want to figure out how much of a loan payment is going toward interest and how much toward principal. Quattro Pro has functions for both of these calculations. The interest portion of a payment is calculated with IPAYMT, whereas the principal portion is calculated with PPAYMT. Of course, if you already know the size of the payment, you can easily calculate these amounts from a loan table, or you can subtract the result of IPAYMT from the amount of the payment to get the result of PPAYMT. However, both IPAYMT and PPAYMT can be used without first figuring the payment amount. They return the portion of the total payment for a specific payment, for example, for the 30th payment of 36. The form of both functions is the same:

@IPAYMT(*Rate,Period,Nper,Pv,Fv,Type*)

and

@PPAYMT(*Rate,Period,Nper,Pv,Fv,Type*)

where *Rate* is the interest rate, *Period* is the period of the loan you are calculating interest for, *Nper* is the total number of periods in the loan, and *Pv* is the principal of the loan. Quattro Pro will assume the *Fv* argument to be 0 if not supplied, and that *Type* is 0 unless otherwise specified. The *Fv* argument is used when you are calculating an accumulated future amount.

To apply the IPAYMT argument to the loan in Figure 5-14 and get the interest portion of the 59th payment you would use the formula:

@IPAYMT(K3/12,59,K2*12,K1)

The result would be –4.49599 to five decimal places, only slightly different from the result in the loan table, due to the rounding of the payment in the table. The PPAYMT and IPAYMT functions are handy for a number of lending related calculations.

NPER: Number of Payments

A great function for window shoppers is the NPER function, which calculates the number of payments required to pay off a loan at a given payment amount. Suppose you want to buy a $10,000 car and can afford $200.00 per month. If the going rate of interest on car loans is 13 percent, you would use the formula

@NPER(0.13/12,–200,10000)

to calculate that just over 72 payments are required to pay off the loan. Note that the payment argument is entered as a negative value, because it is a negative cash flow item. The NPER function uses the form

@NPER(*Rate,Payment,Pv,Fv,Type*)

and returns ERR if the *Payment* amount is not enough to amortize the loan. (As you might expect, the *Payment* amount must at least equal the interest rate per period times the principal.) The *Type* argument is used to indicate whether the payments are being made at the beginning or end of the period. The default, assumed if you omit the final argument, is 0—at the end of the period.

The optional *Fv* argument is used when you want to calculate the payments required to create a future sum of money. For example, to calculate how many payments of $200 per month are required to reach a lump sum of $50,000 when you are earning 10 percent interest per year and have $2000 already invested, you would use the following:

@NPER(0.1/12,–200,–2000,50000,0)

The answer is roughly 132 payments. Note that this changes to 131 if you change the final argument from 0 to 1 to indicate that the payments are made at the beginning of the period. Also note that the current balance is a negative amount, as are the payments.

TERM: The Older Function

An alternative function to use if you have a target figure or goal in mind for your investments is TERM. Like NPER, this function calculates how long it will take a series of equal, evenly spaced investments to accumulate to a target amount based on a steady rate of interest. The syntax of the TERM function is

@TERM(*Payment,Rate,Fv*)

This function does not offer a present value or type argument and is provided in Quattro Pro, essentially, for backward compatibility.

CTERM: Number of Periods

The CTERM function calculates the number of periods it takes for a single investment to grow to some future amount. The CTERM function has the following format:

@CTERM(*Rate,Fv,Pv*)

Rate is a numeric value representing the fixed interest rate per compounding period. *Fv* is a numeric value representing the future value that an investment will reach at some point. *Pv* is a numeric value representing the present value of the investment.

In Figure 5-15, you can see that the goal of reaching $1 million from an initial investment of $10,000 earning 12 percent per year will take 41 years to achieve.

Investment Functions

Quattro Pro offers several financial functions, discussed next, that assist in the task of evaluating investments. These are PV, PVAL, NPV, FV, FVAL, RATE, IRATE, and IRR.

Figure 5-15 Calculating future payments with CTERM

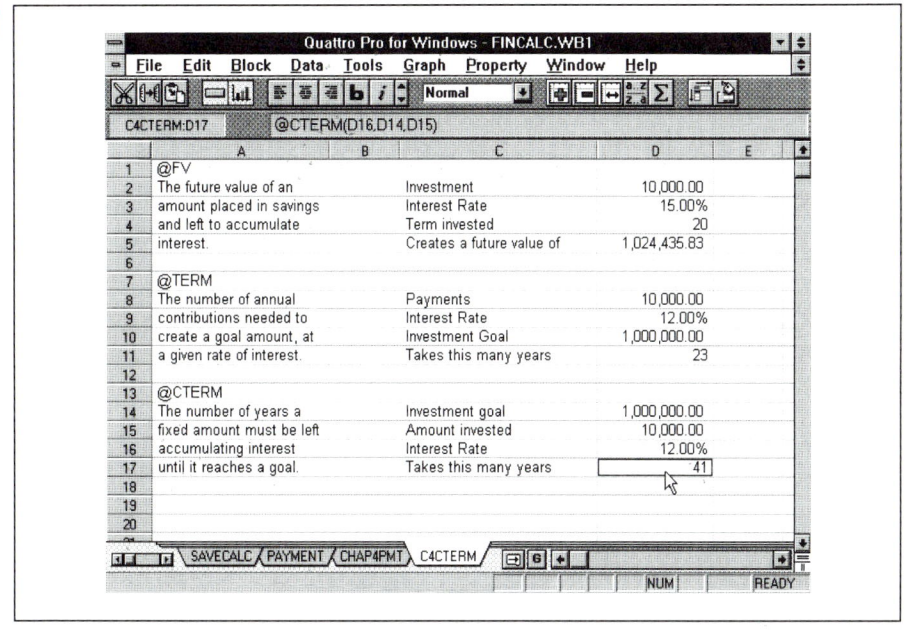

The Importance of Present Value

When you are evaluating a potential investment, it helps to know the present value of the investment. Suppose you have been offered an investment opportunity that promises to pay you $1050 after one year if you invest $1000 now. You know that simply putting the $1000 in a good savings account will turn that $1000 into $1060, so the investment does not seem worthwhile. To put it another way, the investment promises a 5 percent yield, whereas you can get 6 percent elsewhere. Another way of comparing the promised yield of an investment with your estimate of realistic alternative yields is to *discount* the payment from the investment. If the discounted value is greater than the amount you are considering investing, the investment is a good one. Another term for the discounted value is *present value*.

Consider the present or discounted value of a venture offering a 12-month return of $1050 on an initial investment of $1000. You would take the $1050 and divide it by the number of payments plus the rate of return on the alternative investment, in this case 6 percent. The formula is thus 1050/(1+.06) and the answer, the present value of $1050 received a year from now discounted at a rate of 6 percent, is $991. Because the present value of the promised return is less than the price of the investment, $1000, the investment is not a good one. To use Quattro Pro for this kind of analysis, you use the PV and PVAL functions, which can handle investments promising more than one annual payback amount.

PVAL: Present Value

PVAL returns the present value of an investment based on periodic and constant payments and a constant interest rate. The function has the following format:

@PVAL(*Rate,Nper,Pmt,Fv,Type*)

Payments (*Pmt*), interest *Rate*, and term (*Nper*) can be numeric constants, numeric fields, or formulas that result in a number. *Rate* must be greater than or equal to –1. The future value (*Fv*) and *Type* arguments are optional.

An example of a PVAL calculation is shown in Figure 5-16. The promised return on an investment of $150,000 is five annual payments of $25,000. Entering the payments, the discount rate, and the term into the PVAL function in B6 you get the result $158,821.18, the most you should consider investing to get the promised return. Note that PVAL treats payments as negative values. The entry of –B4 in the PVAL statement causes the function to return a positive value for the present value rather than a negative value.

Because the present value of the promised return is shown to be greater than the proposed investment amount, you might want to approve the investment. However, while the PVAL function enables you to take the time value of money into account when comparing investment opportunities, you must still bear in mind less readily quantifiable factors such as risk. Typically, the discount rate represents a zero-risk alternative such as CDs or Treasury notes.

Chapter 5: Mastering Functions

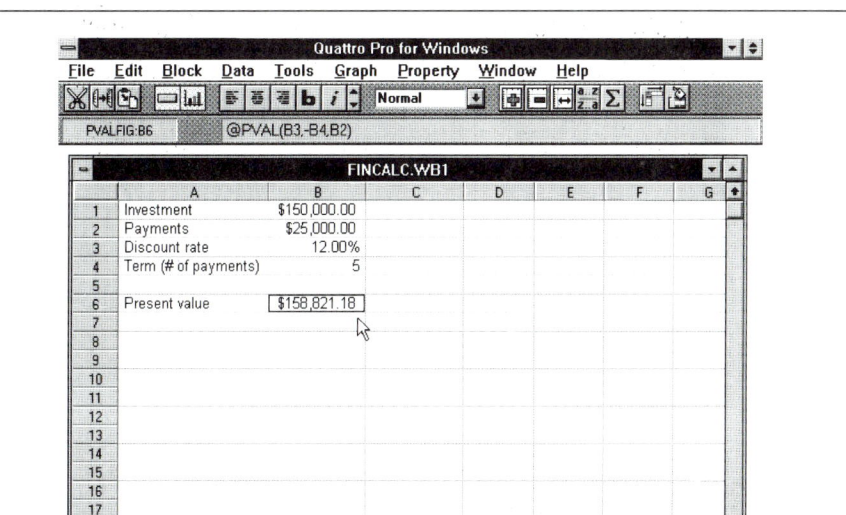

> **FIGURE 5-16** A PVAL calculation shows the present value of a proposed investment

```
                    Quattro Pro for Windows
File  Edit  Block  Data  Tools  Graph  Property  Window  Help

PVALFIG:B6        @PVAL(B3,-B4,B2)

                        FINCALC.WB1
        A              B           C      D      E      F      G
  1  Investment     $150,000.00
  2  Payments        $25,000.00
  3  Discount rate       12.00%
  4  Term (# of payments)     5
  5
  6  Present value  $158,821.18
  7
  ...

  PAYMENT / CHAP4PMT / C4CTERM / PVALFIG
                                                NUM    READY
```

Suppose that an investment of $100,000 was going to pay a lump sum of $150,000 at the end of the five years, rather than installments of $30,000. This can be calculated using the optional future value argument of the PVAL function, as in

@PVAL(0.12,5,0,−150000)

The result is $85,114.03, considerably less than the amount of the proposed investment, indicating that the investment is not a good one. This makes sense, because you are deprived of the use of the money until the end of the investment period. You would have to get over $190,000 at the end of five years for the use of your $100,000 to exceed the return from the 12 percent discount rate. Note that the 0 in the PVAL statement represents the missing future value argument.

Although the future value option makes the PVAL function more versatile, most PVAL calculations do not use the other optional argument, *Type*. Quattro Pro assumes that the payments from the investment will be made at the end of the periods, not at the beginning. To change the assumption to the beginning, include the argument 1 for *Type*, as in

@PVAL(0.12,5,–30000,0,1)

The result of this formula is $121,120.48, indicating that the investment is more attractive if the return is paid at the beginning of the periods.

PV: The Older Function

Another way to calculate the present value of a simple annuity—that is, a regular series of equal payments—is to use the PV function, which takes the form

@PV(*Payment,Rate,Nper*)

The arguments can be numeric constants, numeric cells, or a formula that results in a number. Interest must be greater than –1. An example of this calculation is shown in Figure 5-17. The promised return is five annual payments of $30,000, or $150,000. Entering the payments, the discount rate, and the term into the PV function gives you the result of $108,143.29, the most you should consider investing to get the promised return. The PV function enables you to take the time value of money into account when comparing investment opportunities. However, the PV function is mainly included for backward compatibility with programs like 1-2-3.

NPV: Net Present Value

A function closely related to PVAL is NPV, which calculates the *net present value* of returns on an investment, based on a discount rate. The net present value of an investment should be greater than 0; otherwise, it offers no better return than investing at the discount rate. Whereas PVAL assumes equal amounts of cash flow from the investment or a single lump sum, the NPV function handles unequal amounts returned from the investment, using the format

@NPV(*Rate,Block,Type*)

Chapter 5: Mastering Functions

FIGURE 5-17 Using the PV function

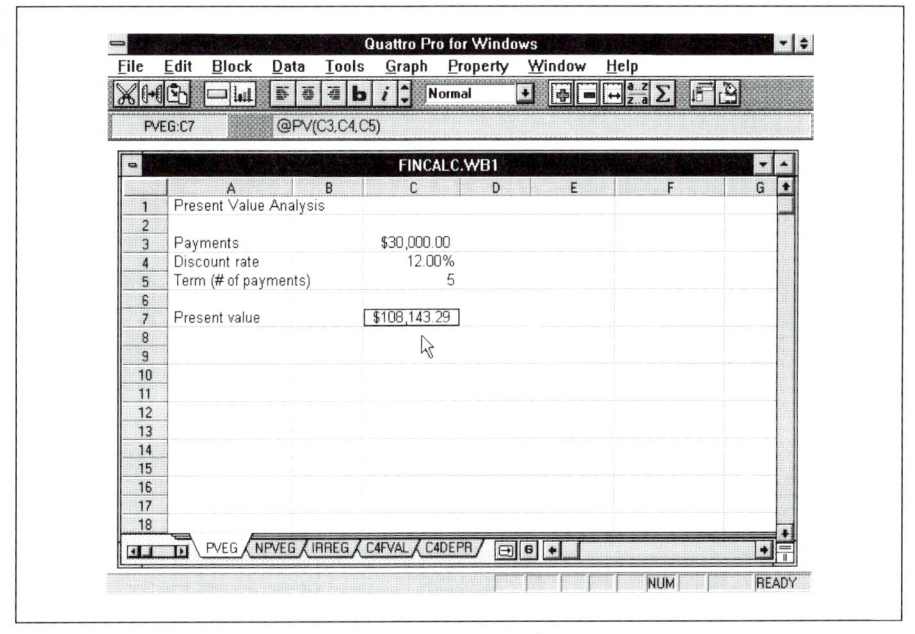

[Screenshot of Quattro Pro for Windows showing FINCALC.WB1 worksheet with Present Value Analysis: Payments $30,000.00, Discount rate 12.00%, Term (# of payments) 5, Present value $108,143.29. Formula bar shows @PV(C3,C4,C5)]

where *Rate* is the discount rate of interest and *Block* is a block of cells containing the cash outlay and flows from the investment. Typically, the first value in the block is the amount invested, and further amounts are returns on the investment. The stream of cash is assumed to be constant, that is, at regular intervals, but the amounts can vary. For example, suppose you are promised three annual payments of $30,000, $40,000, and $50,000 in return for your investment of $100,000. The net present value of this proposition is calculated with the formula

@NPV(0.12,B1..B4)

The first argument is the discount rate of 12 percent. The second argument is the block of cells containing the values –100,000, 30,000, 40,000, and 50,000. The result is less than zero (–5,122.78 in fact), which suggests that this is not a good investment.

Suppose you are still interested in the investment and counter with an investment of $98,000 with returns of $35,000, $40,000, and $50,000. The result is positive ($648.90), suggesting that the investment is now much more profitable. In Figure 5-18, you can see two calculations used to evaluate a further proposal that offers payments over a period of four years in return for an initial investment of $110,000. Note that you state the NPV value arguments as a block, rather than as separate cells. In this case, E3..E7 has been named CASH and is referenced by its name. The two different calculations show the effects of timing on financial transactions.

With all financial functions, including NPV, you need to pay attention to Quattro Pro's assumptions about timing. When you use NPV, Quattro Pro permits you to specify a *Type* argument, which can be either 0 or 1, depending on whether the cash flows are at the beginning or end of the period. If you do not specify a type argument, Quattro Pro assumes payment at the end of the period in NPV calculations. This means that the formula in B7 in Figure 5-18 actually represents putting out $110,000 one year from the beginning of the project and receiving the first payment of $27,500 at the end of the second year. It is more likely that you will want to base calculations on paying out the funds for the investment at the beginning of the first period and receiving the first payment in return at the beginning of the second period. To accommodate

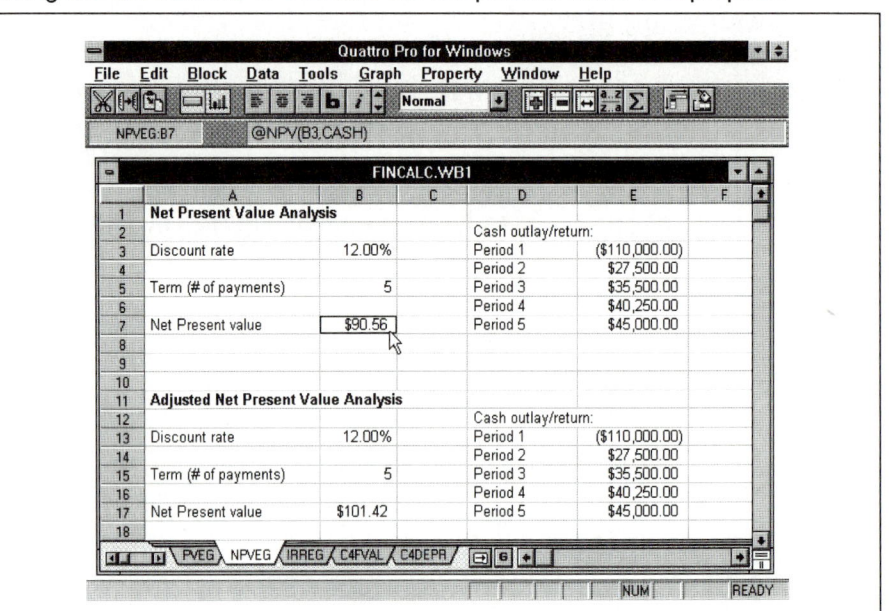

FIGURE 5-18 Using two calculations to evaluate the net present value of a proposal

this assumption, you can specify a *Type* of 1, as in B17 in Figure 5-18, where the formula is @NPV(B13,E13..E17,1). The result shows that the investment is slightly better under the new assumptions.

IRATE: Compound Growth Rate

Suppose you are considering two investments. One offers to pay you four annual payments of $1000 in return for your investment of $3000. The other offers 48 monthly payments of $80 for the same $3000. You might want to calculate a rate of return for both of these investments in order to see which is the better deal. The rate at which your $1000 is expected to grow is the *compound growth rate*, calculated by the IRATE function using this format:

@IRATE(*Nper,Pmt,Pv,Fv,Type*)

The last two arguments are optional. In the case of the first investment the formula would be

@IRATE(4,1000,–3000)

The result is an annual rate of return percentage, because the *Nper* argument is entered as years. In this case the result is .125898325, or 12.59 percent when expressed with just two decimal places. The rate of return of the second investment is expressed as

@IRATE(48,80,–3000)

The result is .010562829, or 1.06 percent, which is a monthly rate of interest, because the *Nper* argument is expressed in months. To calculate an annual rate of return for the second investment you would use

@IRATE(48,80,–3000)*12

The result is 12.68 percent, which is marginally better than the first investment, despite the fact that it pays less cash (48 * $80 = $3840, as opposed to $4000).

The IRATE function arrives at its answer by performing a net present value calculation. Quattro Pro guesses at the rate of return on the investment and figures the net present value of the investment at the guess rate. If the resulting net present value is greater than 0, the program guesses a higher rate and recomputes the net present value. If the guess rate results in a net present value lower than 0, a lower rate is used. In fact, the rate of return on an investment is the percentage that most closely results in a net present value of 0. Quattro Pro repeats, or iterates, the calculation until it arrives at the correct rate or has completed 20 iterations. If it does the 20 iterations without getting the right rate, you see an error message.

RATE: The Older Function

An alternative to the IRATE function is the RATE function, which takes the following form:

@RATE(*Fv,Pv,Nper*)

The RATE function returns the rate of interest required to grow a present value sum into a specified target value over a stated term. This function is mainly provided for backward compatibility with earlier programs.

IRR: Internal Rate of Return

When you want to compare the payback you will receive from different investments, you can use the IRR function to calculate the internal rate of return. This function uses the format

@IRR(*Guess,Block*)

where *Guess* is your estimate of what the answer will be and *Block* is a reference to a range of cells containing amounts of cash flow. Typically, the first number in the range will be a negative one, indicating the initial payment or investment. The IRR function assumes that the payments occur at the end of the period. This function works much like the IRATE function except that, like the NPV function, it can handle a range of unequal cash flows.

Generally, an investment is attractive if it shows an internal rate of return greater than the rate you can obtain elsewhere, the rate known as *comparison* or *hurdle rate*. The IRR function can be seen at work in Figure 5-19, where three different investments are compared. The third one offers the best return, because it results in the highest IRR. Notice that the formula in I12 does not include a *Guess* argument. The *Guess* argument is optional and only required if Quattro Pro has difficulty reaching an IRR result. If you enter an IRR formula and get an error in return, try altering or adding the *Guess* argument, using a percentage close to what you would estimate the return to be.

FVAL: Future Value

To see what a series of payments will be worth over time, given that they earn interest, you use the FVAL function. This is shown in Figure 5-20, where the FVAL function returns the future value of the annual retirement fund contribution of $10,000, which earns 15 percent per year. FVAL has the following format:

@FVAL(*Rate,Nper,Payment,Pv,Type*)

FIGURE 5-19 Comparing investments with the IRR function

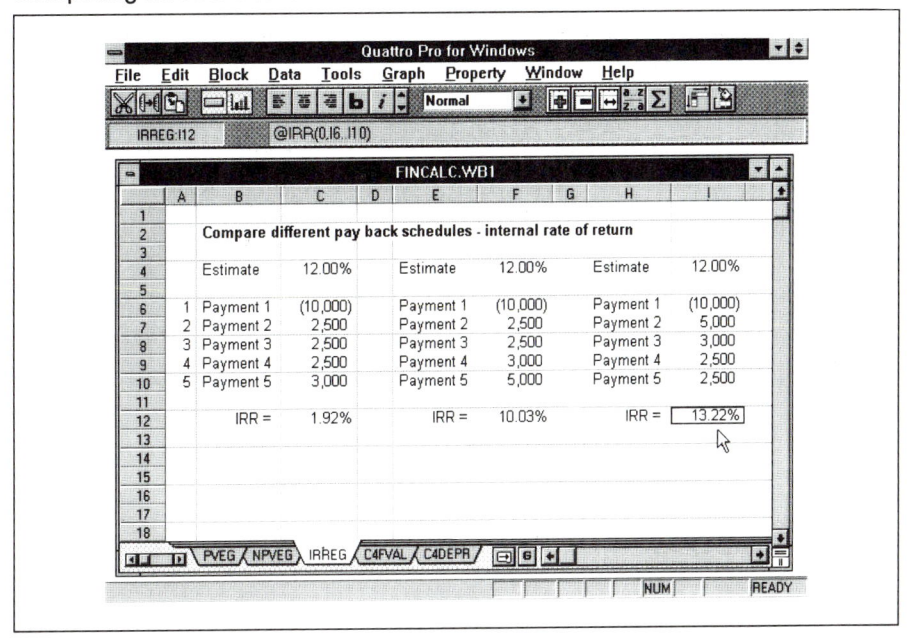

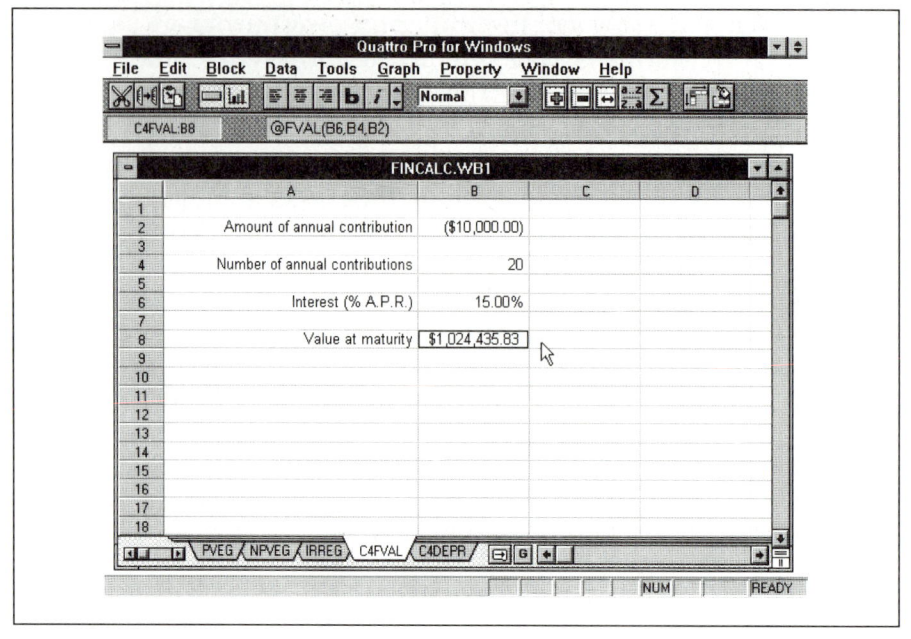

FIGURE 5-20 Calculating the future value of an investment with FVAL

	A	B
2	Amount of annual contribution	($10,000.00)
4	Number of annual contributions	20
6	Interest (% A.P.R.)	15.00%
8	Value at maturity	$1,024,435.83

Cell: C4FVAL:B8 — @FVAL(B6,B4,B2)

Rate is a numeric value greater than 0, representing the periodic interest rate. *Nper* is a numeric value, representing the number of periods of the investment. *Payment* is a numeric value, representing the amount of equal payments to be made.

The FVAL function calculates the future value of an investment where the payment is invested for a number of periods at the specified rate of interest per period. You can use FVAL to see the effects of regular savings plans and evaluate such investments against alternative uses of funds. You can use the *Pv* argument to indicate an existing value in the program and the *Type* argument to indicate whether the payment is made at the beginning or end of the period. For example, you might want to put $1000 into a savings account at the beginning of each of seven years, and you would like to know what the account would be worth at the end of the seven years. The account earns 8.5 percent per year, so the formula would be

@FVAL(.085,7,–1000,0,1)

which returns the answer of $9830.64. If the account already had $2500 in it when the plan began, the formula would be

@FVAL(.085,7,–1000,–2500,1)

which returns the answer of $14,255.99. If you decided to make the payments at the end of each period the formula would be

@FVAL(.085,7,–1000,–2500,0)

which yields $13,485.85.

FV: The Older Function

Another function for calculating future value is FV. This function is shown in Figure 5-21, where it returns the future value of an annual

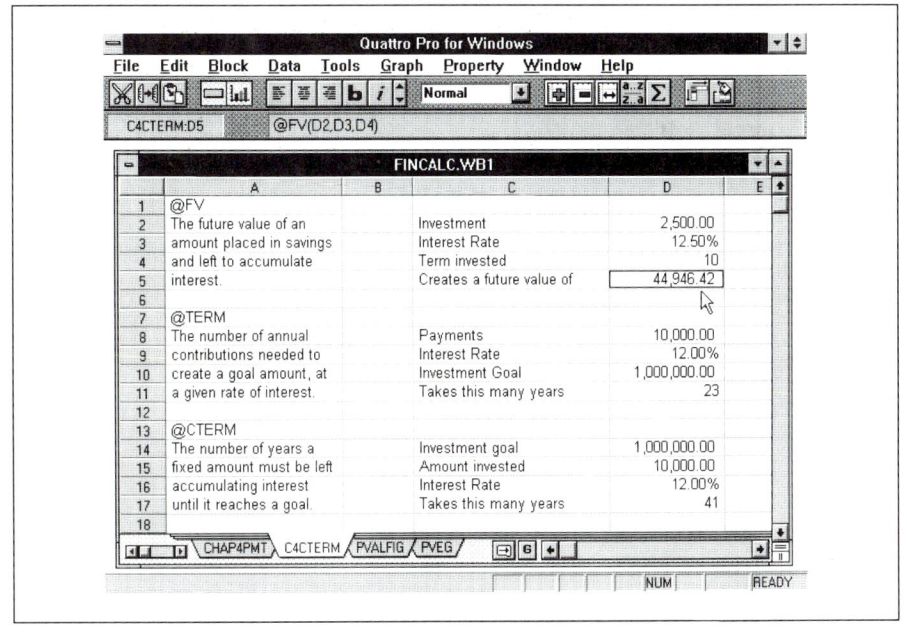

FIGURE 5-21 Using FV to determine the future value of an annual retirement fund investment

retirement fund investment of $2500, earning 12.5 percent per year over a ten-year term. The FV function has the following format:

@FV(*Payment,Rate,Nper*)

Payment is a numeric value representing the amount of equal payments to be made. *Rate* is a numeric value greater than 0 representing the periodic interest rate. *Nper* is a numeric value representing the number of periods of the investment.

Although you can use FV to see the effects of regular savings plans and evaluate such investments against alternative uses of funds, it is mainly provided in Quattro Pro for backward compatibility. The assumption in FV is that the payments are made at the beginning of the period.

Depreciation Functions

Quattro Pro offers three different methods for calculating depreciation, all of which are shown in Figure 5-22. These methods are used because

FIGURE 5-22 Calculating depreciation three ways

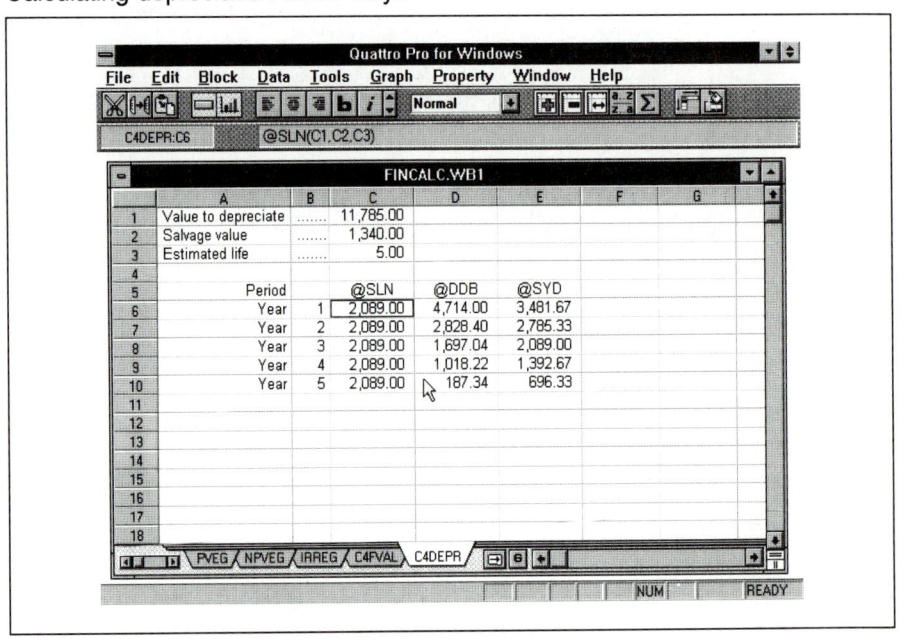

Chapter 5: Mastering Functions

most goods lose value over time, and most state and federal tax laws allow businesses to deduct some of this lost value from taxable income, which in turn encourages new investment.

SLN: Straight-Line Depreciation

The straight-line method results in an equal amount of depreciation per period:

@SLN(*Cost,Salvage,Life*)

This is the simplest form of depreciation. As in all of the depreciation functions, *Cost* is a numeric value representing the amount paid for an asset; *Salvage* is a numeric value representing the worth of an asset at the end of its useful life; and *Life* is a numeric value representing the expected useful life of an asset.

SYD: Sum-of-Years' Depreciation

The SYD function uses a method called the sum-of-years'-digits to vary the rate at which depreciation is taken. This function requires knowing the year for each calculation and takes the form:

@SYD(*Cost,Salvage,Life,Period*)

Period is a numeric value representing the time period for which you want to determine the depreciation expense.

An interesting application of the SYD function is in the computation of a loan payout based on the "rule of 78," which results in a slower payoff for loans than the simple interest calculation shown earlier in Figure 5-14. The rule of 78 payout table is shown in Figure 5-23, with the SYD formula highlighted in B11.

DDB: Double-Declining-Balance Depreciation

The DDB function calculates depreciation based on the double-declining-balance method using the following elements:

@DDB(*Cost,Salvage,Life,Period*)

Period is a numeric value representing the time period for which you want to determine the depreciation expense.

The DDB function determines accelerated depreciation values for an asset, given the initial cost, end value, life expectancy, and depreciation period.

Accelerated Cost Recovery

Some tax calculations no longer use the three methods of depreciation just described, but rather a method known as the modified accelerated cost recovery system (MACRS). The rate of depreciation allowed by MACRS varies each year of the asset's life and depends on when the asset was placed in service. There is no MACRS function in Quattro Pro, but you can use the INDEX function to create IRS tables of depreciation rates,

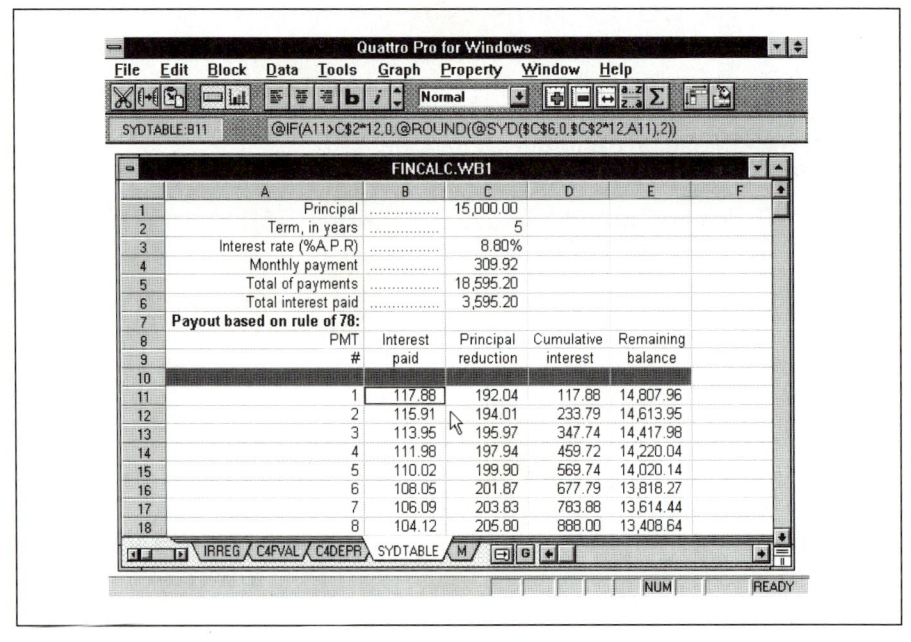

FIGURE 5-23 Figuring a "rule of 78" payout table with the SYD formula

based on the month placed in service and the year of the asset's life. INDEX is one of the logical functions, described next.

Logical Functions

Quattro Pro provides a variety of functions that can be very useful in situations where logical arguments need to be entered into fields.

IF

The IF function instructs Quattro Pro to choose between two actions based on a condition being either true or false. Suppose that you are budgeting quarterly revenue and expenditures for a computer store, using a spreadsheet like that shown in Figure 5-24. You have gotten good results from spending 5 percent of all sales revenue on advertising. Thus,

FIGURE 5-24 Using the IF function to decide how much money to spend on advertising

advertising is normally Sales × 0.05. However, you know that money spent on advertising beyond a certain dollar amount is not effective (say, $110,000, expressed as 110.00 in the model).

What you want to do is to budget your advertising expenditures with a ceiling of 110. You can do this by adding the IF function to the advertising expense formula to tell Quattro Pro that if Sales × 0.05 is less than 110, Advertising = Sales × 0.05; otherwise, Advertising = 110. In the spreadsheet this is written as

@IF(0.05*B10<110,0.05*B10,110)

The format of the IF function is as follows:

@IF(*Condition,True,False*)

This syntax means that if the condition is true, then the response is that stated in the *True* argument. Otherwise, the result is that stated in the *False* argument. True and false results can be constants, value or label cells, or other formulas, and they can be any type of data.

The IF function is extremely versatile because it allows the spreadsheet to become intelligent, that is, to do one of two things based on a condition that you establish. This conditional result can be used in numerous situations in a typical spreadsheet.

For example, you can use IF to test the integrity of a spreadsheet, as in the expense report spreadsheet shown in Figure 5-25. Anyone who has filled out expense reports knows that the sum of the rows should equal the sum of the columns. When you lay out this kind of report in Quattro Pro, the calculation is done for you. However, you should never assume that just because the work is done electronically, it is always done correctly. The IF formula in cell G17 says that if the sum of the columns equals the sum of the rows, the cell should contain the sum of the columns; otherwise, it should contain an error message (produced by the ERR function) to show that a mistake has been made. When a mistake has been detected, the ERR message will appear as a label in cell G17.

Suppose Quattro Pro detects an error. You review the spreadsheet. Close examination reveals that someone typed a number over a formula in column G. This caused the sum of the columns to be incorrect. When

Chapter 5: Mastering Functions

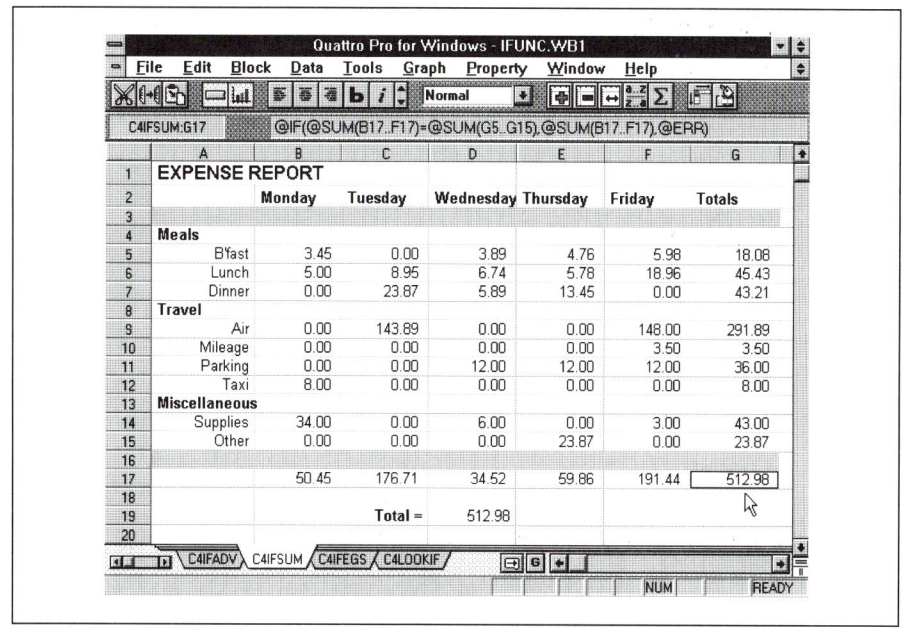

FIGURE 5-25 Testing a spreadsheet's integrity with IF

[Screenshot of Quattro Pro for Windows - IFUNC.WB1 showing the expense report spreadsheet with formula @IF(@SUM(B17..F17)=@SUM(G5..G15),@SUM(B17..F17),@ERR) in cell G17]

	A	B	C	D	E	F	G
1	EXPENSE REPORT						
2		Monday	Tuesday	Wednesday	Thursday	Friday	Totals
3							
4	Meals						
5	B'fast	3.45	0.00	3.89	4.76	5.98	18.08
6	Lunch	5.00	8.95	6.74	5.78	18.96	45.43
7	Dinner	0.00	23.87	5.89	13.45	0.00	43.21
8	Travel						
9	Air	0.00	143.89	0.00	0.00	148.00	291.89
10	Mileage	0.00	0.00	0.00	0.00	3.50	3.50
11	Parking	0.00	0.00	12.00	12.00	12.00	36.00
12	Taxi	8.00	0.00	0.00	0.00	0.00	8.00
13	Miscellaneous						
14	Supplies	34.00	0.00	6.00	0.00	3.00	43.00
15	Other	0.00	0.00	0.00	23.87	0.00	23.87
16							
17		50.45	176.71	34.52	59.86	191.44	512.98
18							
19			Total =	512.98			
20							

the erroneous value is replaced by the correct formula, the ERR message disappears, and the expense report is correct.

When you want to apply several conditions to a calculation, you can *nest* IF statements—place one within another. For example, you may, in a large report, want to allow a small margin of error in the figures. In the case of Figure 5-25, this would not exactly be appropriate, but you could amend the statement in G17 to read as follows:

@IF(@SUM(B17..F17)>@SUM(G5..G15)*1.01,@ERR,
@IF(@SUM(G5..G15)>@SUM(B17..F17)*1.01,@ERR,
@SUM(B17..F17,G5..G15)/2))

This tells Quattro Pro that if the total down exceeds 101 percent of the total across, there is an error. Likewise, if the total across exceeds 101 percent of the total down, there is an error. Otherwise, the answer should be the average of the total down and the total across. If the figures are entirely accurate, the answer will be accurate. Otherwise, the answer will be within 1 percent of the correct total.

Another example of nesting IF statements is shown in the formula used in Figure 5-26 to calculate commissions based on a percentage (4 percent to 6 percent) of sales. The statement in D5 reads

@IF(C5<40000,0.04*C5,@IF(C5<50000,0.05*C5,0.06*C5))

This formula says that if the sales in C5 are less than $40,000, the commission will be 4 percent (0.04) of sales; otherwise, if sales are greater than or equal to $40,000 but less than $50,000, the commission will be 5 percent. If sales are greater than or equal to $50,000, the commission will be 6 percent. The nesting of IF statements takes a little planning, but if you write out the statement first, you can usually frame the actual formula to fit most conditional situations.

The IF function can return labels as well as values. For example, in the broker transaction record shown in Figure 5-27, the word "Yes" in cell K9 is the result of an IF formula. The record needs to show if special handling is required. This is based on the amount of the transaction, shown in H11. The formula in K9 states @IF(H11>20000,"Yes","No").

FIGURE 5-26 Nesting IF statements

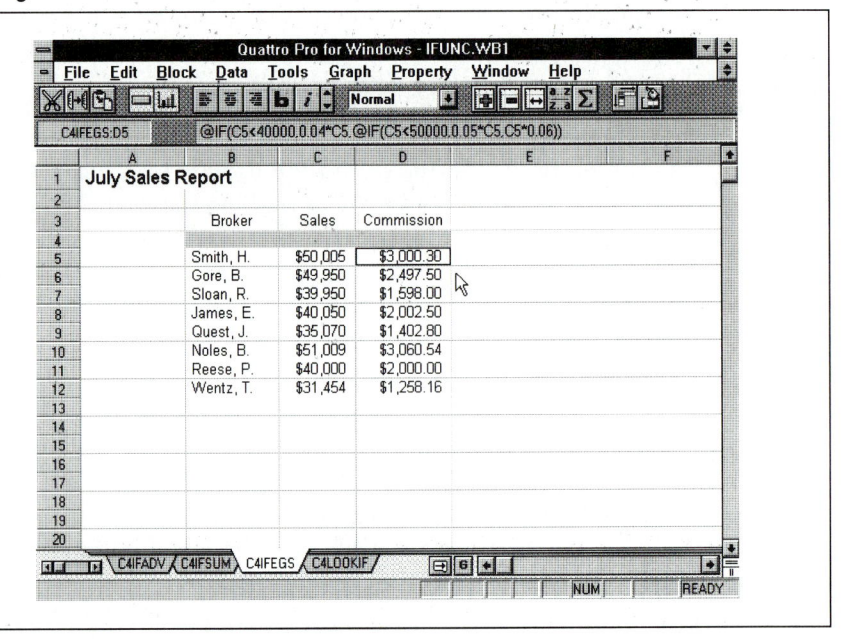

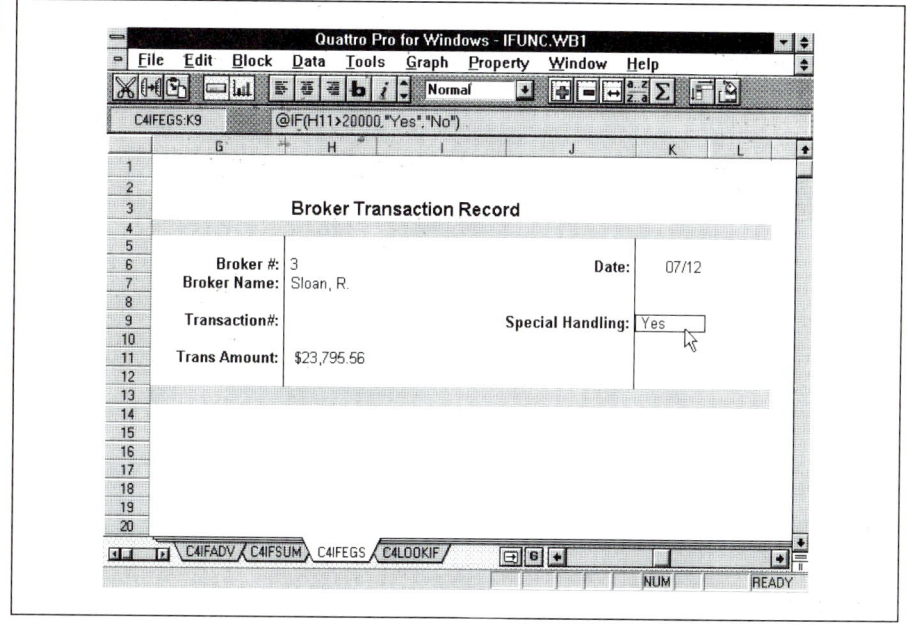

FIGURE 5-27 Returning labels with the IF function

Thus, Yes is returned in this case, because the amount in H11 is greater than 20,000. Note the use of quotes to indicate text.

The name of the broker could also be entered with an IF formula that looks for the broker number entered in H6 and responds with one of three names, like this:

@IF(H6=3,"Sloan, R.",@IF(H6=2,"Doe, J.",
@IF(H6=1,"James, E.",@ERR)))

This formula will result in the ERR message if the broker number is not 1, 2, or 3.

Lookup Tables, VLOOKUP, and HLOOKUP

When you want to make a formula dependent on a range of conditions, you have an alternative to nesting IF functions. You can have Quattro Pro refer to a table of conditions, called a *lookup table*. This is a vertical or horizontal list of numbers or labels that you can use to look up related numbers or labels.

Figure 5-28 shows a commission table that offers a simple way to determine the rate based on a broader range of sales levels. The vertical list of sales levels in column E and related commission rates in column F show the rate applicable to any given level of sales. Any sales amount below $35,000 earns a commission of 3.50 percent. Sales from $35,000 to $35,999 earn 3.75 percent, and so on. This table of numbers, consisting of cells E3 through F19, has been named TABLE with the Block | Names | Create command. In cell D3, the formula reads

@VLOOKUP(C3,$TABLE,1)*C3

This means that the vertical lookup function is invoked to look up the value of cell C3 in the block of cells named TABLE in column 1. The value that is found in the table, in this case the commission rate of 8 percent, is then multiplied by cell C3 to calculate the commission amount. The syntax of the vertical lookup function is thus

@VLOOKUP(*Index, Table, Column*)

The *Index* is the cell containing the value you are looking up in the table. The *Table* should be consecutive columns of values. The *Column* is the column in the table that the formula should look to for its result. The column numbering is 0 for the first column, 1 for the next column to the right, and so on. In the example, the contents of C3 and column 0 of the lookup table must both be values. The table's column 0 values must be an incremental range of values. However, the contents of column 1 and any additional columns in the table can be labels.

The lookup table can be laid out horizontally, as shown in Figure 5-29. The formula in H5 uses the HLOOKUP function. This example supposes that each broker has a number and writes that number on sales transaction slips. A clerk then records the slips in the format shown in Figure 5-29. As the clerk enters the broker number, Quattro Pro looks up that number in the horizontal table of names. (The table is shown on screen in Figure 5-29 for the purposes of illustration.) The first row of a horizontal table is row 0; successive rows are numbered 1, 2, 3, and so on. The syntax of the HLOOKUP function is

@HLOOKUP(*Index, Table, Row Number*)

Chapter 5: Mastering Functions

FIGURE 5-28 Using a vertical lookup table for sales commissions

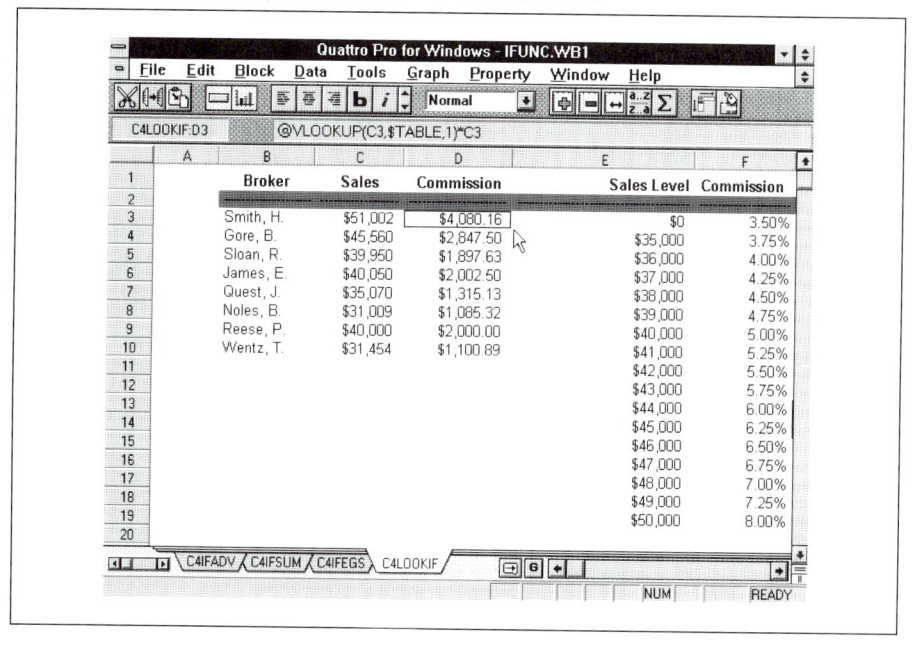

*[Screenshot of Quattro Pro for Windows showing VLOOKUP formula @VLOOKUP(C3,$TABLE,1)*C3 in cell C4LOOKIF:D3]*

	Broker	Sales	Commission		Sales Level	Commission
3	Smith, H.	$51,002	$4,080.16		$0	3.50%
4	Gore, B.	$45,560	$2,847.50		$35,000	3.75%
5	Sloan, R.	$39,950	$1,897.63		$36,000	4.00%
6	James, E.	$40,050	$2,002.50		$37,000	4.25%
7	Quest, J.	$35,070	$1,315.13		$38,000	4.50%
8	Noles, B.	$31,009	$1,085.32		$39,000	4.75%
9	Reese, P.	$40,000	$2,000.00		$40,000	5.00%
10	Wentz, T.	$31,454	$1,100.89		$41,000	5.25%
11					$42,000	5.50%
12					$43,000	5.75%
13					$44,000	6.00%
14					$45,000	6.25%
15					$46,000	6.50%
16					$47,000	6.75%
17					$48,000	7.00%
18					$49,000	7.25%
19					$50,000	8.00%

FIGURE 5-29 The HLOOKUP function uses a horizontal lookup table

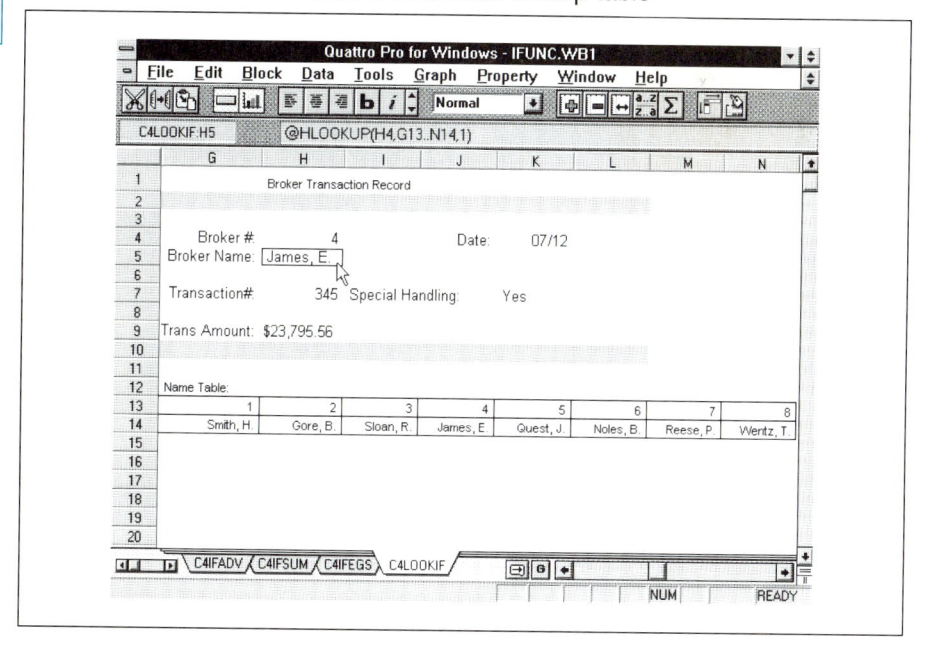

[Screenshot of Quattro Pro for Windows showing HLOOKUP formula @HLOOKUP(H4,G13..N14,1) in cell C4LOOKIF:H5]

Broker Transaction Record

Broker #: 4 Date: 07/12
Broker Name: James, E.

Transaction#: 345 Special Handling: Yes

Trans Amount: $23,795.56

Name Table:

	1	2	3	4	5	6	7	8
	Smith, H.	Gore, B.	Sloan, R.	James, E.	Quest, J.	Noles, B.	Reese, P.	Wentz, T.

Row 0 must be a series of values or an alphabetical list of labels. Successive rows can be values or labels. Row 1, which the formula references in this case, is a set of labels. Note that you do not have to use a block name for the lookup table reference in the formula. None was used in Figure 5-29. However, a block name makes it easier to refer to the cells of the table than typing G13..N14, particularly if you want to copy the formula containing the reference to the table and thus need to make the cell references absolute, as in $G$13..$N$14. A reference to a block name can be made absolute simply by preceding it with a dollar sign, as in $TABLE.

Given the multiple page structure of Quattro Pro notebooks, it often makes sense to position a lookup table on a separate page from the formula in which the table is used. You can see an example of this in Figure 5-30, where a commission schedule is located separately from the commission calculations. Note that the lookup formula must reference the table by page name as well as cell coordinates.

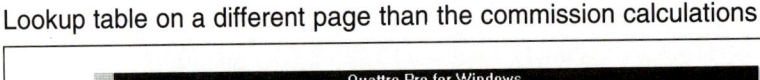

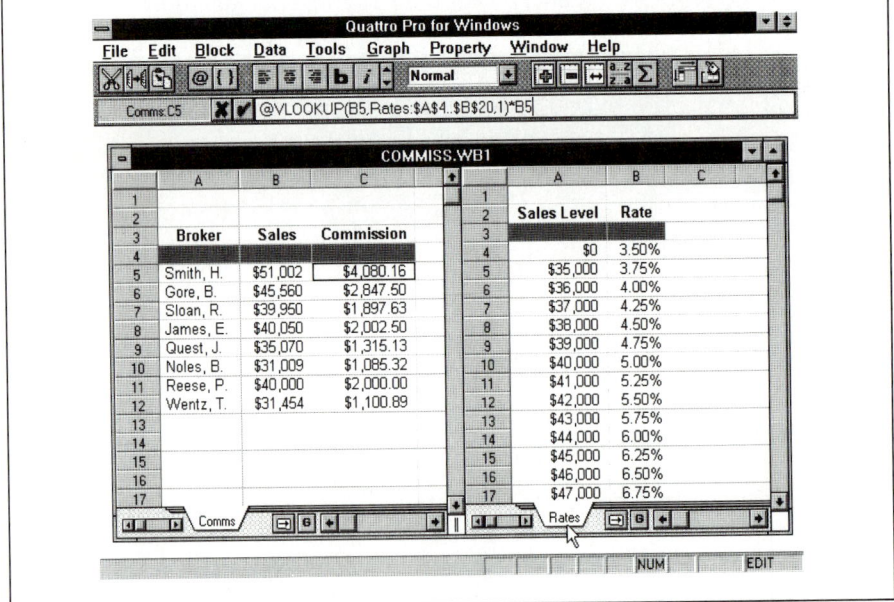

FIGURE 5-30 Lookup table on a different page than the commission calculations

CHOOSE

A function directly comparable to a lookup table is CHOOSE, which selects its responses based on a number. For example, if there were just a few brokers, you could use the CHOOSE function in place of HLOOKUP in cell H5 of Figure 5-29. If there were just four brokers, the formula in H5 could read

@CHOOSE(H4,"Smith, H.","Gore, B.","Sloan, R.","James, E.")

The number entered in cell H4 would thus determine the name placed into H5. The syntax of the CHOOSE function is

@CHOOSE(X, $Case0$, $Case1$,...,$CaseX$)

If x equals 1, $Case0$ is used. If x equals 2, $Case1$ is used, and so on. The value of x must be an integer greater than or equal to 0 and less than the total number of results in the argument. Values of x outside that range will cause an error. If x includes a decimal, Quattro Pro rounds off the value. The x value can be a numeric constant, a cell, or a formula, as in the previous example, where this function is a compact way of handling small lists of results. The results can be constants or formulas of any data type.

INDEX: More Complex Lookup Tables

The INDEX function is a hybrid of the vertical and horizontal lookup tables. For this function, you state the column number and row number for a value set in a table of values. The function has the syntax

@INDEX($Block, Column, Row$)

There are a number of interesting applications for this function, including the accelerated depreciation schedule shown in Figure 5-31. This is a table of the allowed rates of depreciation for real property placed in service before March 15, 1984. The months are numbered across the top and the years of asset life are listed down the side. By answering the questions in rows 2 through 5 in column E, you provide the index data

FIGURE 5-31 An accelerated depreciation schedule

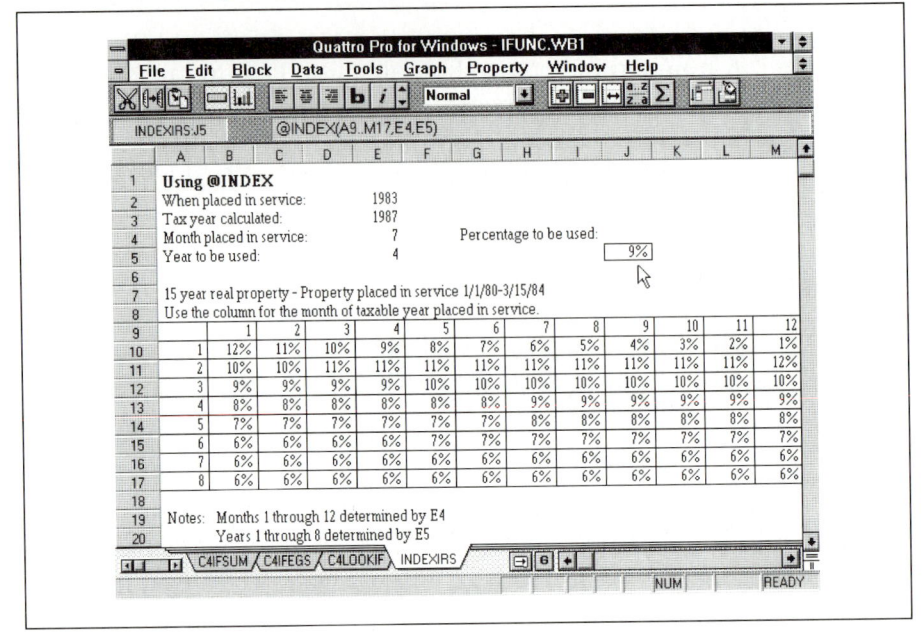

needed for the formula used in J5: @INDEX(A9..M17,E4,E5). The number 7 in E4 is the column coordinate; the number 4 in E5 is the row coordinate. The cell at which they intersect, H13, contains the value 9 percent returned by the INDEX formula. Note that the number of the indexed block corresponds to the numbers you assign to the header column and row, not the 0, 1, 2, 3 numbering used in the VLOOKUP function.

Trigonometric Functions

If you work with geometry and trigonometry, Quattro Pro offers many useful functions. Although these functions are mainly used in engineering and scientific applications, they can be very handy in many other situations.

PI

The PI function provides the value of pi to 11 decimal places. For calculations that require the value of pi, you can type **@PI**. The PI function takes no argument; it simply returns the value 3.14159265359. The formula to calculate the circumference of a circle (in Quattro Pro syntax) is thus 2*@PI*Radius. The area of a circle can be calculated by combining PI and the exponent function, @PI*(Radius^2), which calculates pi times the square of the radius.

Degrees and Radians

Another application of PI is to convert radians to degrees. In Quattro Pro, the trigonometric functions like SIN and COS produce answers in radians. You can use pi to express angles measured in radians as degrees, and to convert degrees to radians, using the following formulas:

$$1 \text{ Radian} = \frac{360}{pi \times 2} \quad \text{or } 180/pi$$

$$1 \text{ Degree} = \frac{pi \times 2 \times radian}{360} \quad \text{or } pi/180$$

For trigonometric functions in 1-2-3, you must use 180/@PI and @PI/180 to make the necessary conversions from radians to degrees and vice versa. However, Quattro Pro has two functions called DEGREES and RADIANS that simplify this conversion.

DEGREES

Used to convert radians to degrees, the DEGREES function is an alternative to using *180/@PI when you need to calculate an angle measurement. The syntax is

@DEGREES(*x*)

where *x* is a measurement in radians. You can see an example of this in Case 3 of Figure 5-32, where an angle is calculated by the ASIN function from the measurements of two sides of a right-angle triangle.

RADIANS

Used to convert degrees to radians, this function is an alternative to multiplying by @PI/180. The syntax is @RADIANS(*x*), where *x* is a measurement in degrees. You can see an example of this in Case 1 of Figure 5-32, where the TAN function is being used to calculate the length of one side of a triangle.

FIGURE 5-32 Degrees and radians used in trigonometric functions

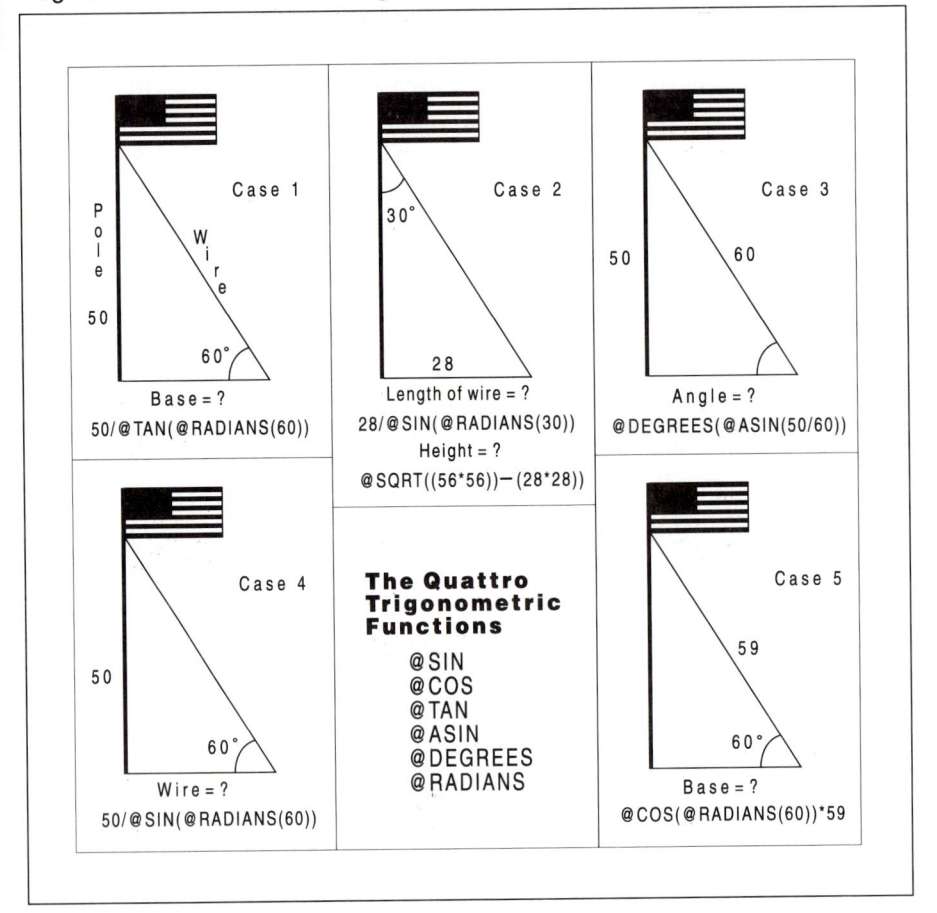

Case 1
Pole = 50, angle 60°, Wire
Base = ?
50/@TAN(@RADIANS(60))

Case 2
30°, 28
Length of wire = ?
28/@SIN(@RADIANS(30))
Height = ?
@SQRT((56*56))−(28*28))

Case 3
50, 60
Angle = ?
@DEGREES(@ASIN(50/60))

Case 4
50, 60°
Wire = ?
50/@SIN(@RADIANS(60))

The Quattro Trigonometric Functions
@SIN
@COS
@TAN
@ASIN
@DEGREES
@RADIANS

Case 5
59, 60°
Base = ?
@COS(@RADIANS(60))*59

SIN, COS, and TAN: Sine, Cosine, and Tangent

The SIN(x), COS(x), and TAN(x) functions return the trigonometric sine, cosine, and tangent, respectively, of x, an angle measured in radians. You can convert an angle measured in degrees to one expressed in radians by using the RADIANS function. Thus, @SIN(@RADIANS(60)) returns the sine of a 60-degree angle. A result in radians can be converted to degrees with the DEGREES function, so that the formula @DEGREES(@ACOS(a/b)) returns the angle between a and b expressed in degrees. These functions are shown in the problems in Figure 5-32.

ASIN, ACOS, ATAN, and ATAN2: Inverse Trigonometric Functions

The inverse trigonometric functions—expressed as ASIN(x), ACOS(x), ATAN(x)—save you from having to create them from the COS, SIN, and TAN functions. They return an angle measured in radians, given its sine, cosine, or tangent. The @ATAN2(x,y) function calculates a four-quadrant arctangent from the x and y coordinates of a point.

Trigonometric Applications

There are a wide variety of ways in which the trigonometric functions can be used. You can use them to generate curves that show one set of values plotted against another. An example of this is a biorhythm chart, which is used to plot levels of physical, emotional, and mental energy on a time scale. The SIN function is used to generate the curve shown in Figure 5-33, a simple biorhythm chart. The spreadsheet from which this was calculated is shown in Figure 5-34. The current date and the subject's birthdate are recorded and then extrapolated for the three different cycles: 22 days for the physical level, 28 for the emotional level, and 32 for the mental level.

Quattro Pro for Windows Inside & Out

FIGURE 5-33 A biorhythm chart

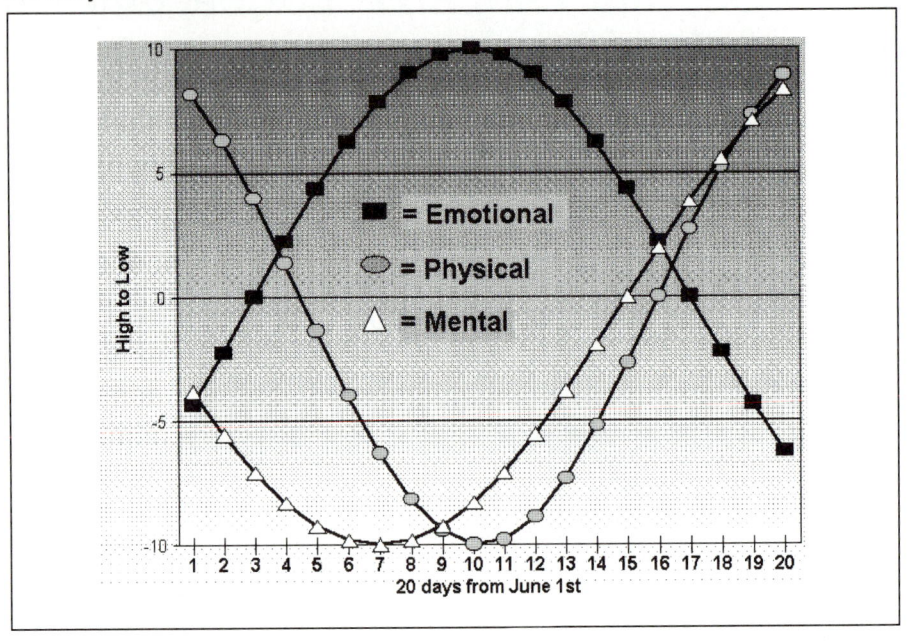

FIGURE 5-34 Data for the biorhythm chart

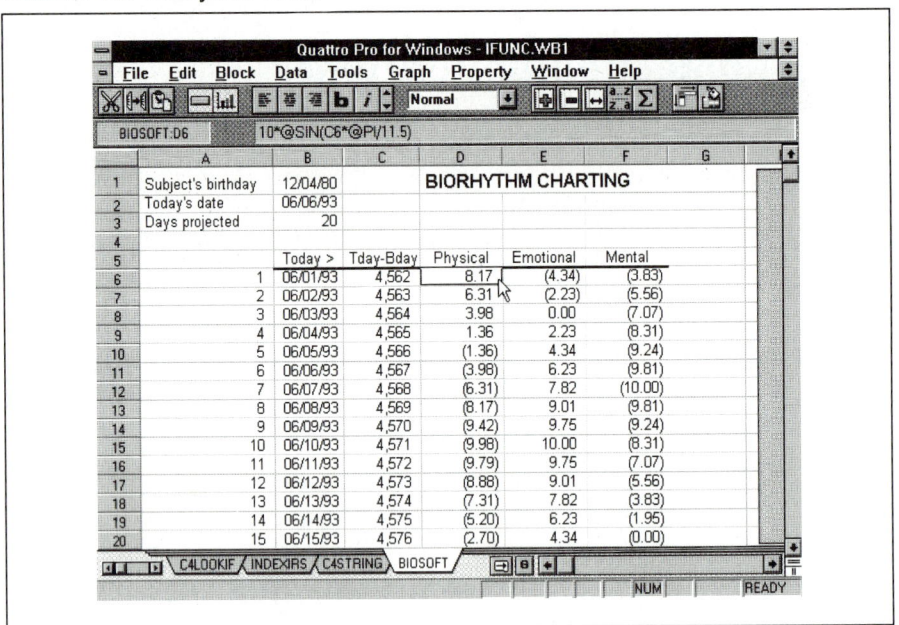

Date and Time Math

Date and time information constitutes a special area of math. Quattro Pro understands dates as serial numbers, based on day 1 being December 31, 1899. The first day of 1991 was serial number 33239. You can enter a date by pressing CTRL-SHIFT-D, typing the date in a recognized format, such as 1/1/91, and then pressing ENTER. However, there are other ways of creating dates, and plenty of ways of manipulating dates with Quattro Pro's functions.

Entering Dates with DATE

In addition to the CTRL-SHIFT-D method of entering dates, you can create a date with the DATE function. This function has the syntax

@DATE(*YY,MM,DD*)

where *YY* is a numeric value between 0 and 199, *MM* is a numeric value between 1 and 12, and *DD* is a numeric value between 1 and 31.

The DATE function returns the serial number of the date specified with year, month, and day arguments. Thus, @DATE(90,12,25) returns the value 33232, or 25-Dec-90. Since Quattro Pro can handle dates well into the next century, the year 2000 is referred to as 100, 2001 is 101, and so on. The highest date available is December 31, 2099, referred to as @DATE(199,12,31).

The number created by DATE can be a whole number of days plus a fraction of a day expressed as a decimal. The whole number (to the left of the decimal point) in a date serial number is the number of days from January 1, 1900, to the date referenced in the formula. The fractional portion of a date serial number is used for the time functions, which are discussed later in this chapter.

To display a date's serial number so that it looks like a date, use the Numeric Format setting and select one of the five Date formats. This suppresses the numeric display, showing instead the date in its more common form (for example, 1-Jan-87 instead of 31778). Any illegal dates, such as @DATE(87,2,29), return ERR as their value. This date corresponds to February 29, 1987, which is an invalid date, since 1987 was not a leap year.

DATEVALUE: Converting a Date Label to a Value

Another method you can use to enter dates in Quattro Pro is the DATEVALUE function. There may be times when you will be working with spreadsheets that contain dates entered as labels. This often happens when data is transferred to Quattro Pro from another program, and the date values are converted to text in the process. The DATEVALUE function produces a serial date value from a string of text or labels. This function has the syntax

@DATEVALUE(*DateString*)

where *DateString* is a string value in any valid date format. An example would be the label '25-Dec-92. If the value in DateString is not in the correct format, an ERR value is returned. There are five valid formats for labels to be read as values with the DATEVALUE function:

- DD-MMM-YY (25-Dec-92)
- DD-MMM (25-Dec) (assumes the current year)
- MMM-YY (Dec-92) (assumes the first day of the month)
- The Long International Date format, the format specified as the system default: MM/DD/YY (12/25/92)
- The Short International Date format: MM/DD (12/25)

Provided they are written in these formats, dates entered as labels can be converted to values. You can display the resulting date values in standard date formats with the Numeric Format Date setting. If you want to include the string in the function statement directly, you must enclose it in quotes. Thus, @DATEVALUE("25-Dec-90") returns the value 33232, which can be formatted to 12/25/90 using the D4 Date format. The statement @DATEVALUE(A1) returns the same value if A1 contains the label 25-Dec-90. For further discussion of strings and their conversion to values, see Chapter 12.

Date Deduction

When dates are stored as values, you can perform math with them. A typical application of this is tracking accounts receivable. If a payment is due on a date that has passed, you can calculate how many days between then and now. Take the due date away from the current date, since the serial value of dates increases the farther away they are from the turn of the century. Use the TODAY function to find out the current date from your computer's clock. The practical value of knowing exactly how many days a payment is late comes when calculating interest on the amount due. A late fee can be calculated by multiplying the number of days past due by 1/365th of the annual percentage rate.

The NOW and TODAY functions read your computer system's date from DOS and, if you have the system clock set correctly, will always show the current date. The TODAY function returns a day serial number, whereas NOW returns the date and time, with the time being a decimal fractional of one day.

Note Use one of the time numeric formats to view the result of the NOW function in conventional time notation.

Dynamic Date Series

With Quattro Pro, you can perform math with dates in order to create a series of dates. Instead of typing labels for January, February, and so on, months can be entered as date values. If you enter a starting date and then create the second date in the series with a formula that adds days to the start date, you can change the entire series simply by altering the start date. This is different from filling a block of cells with dates using the Block | Fill command described in Chapter 3. A Block | Fill operation creates a static series, whereas date math allows you to create a series of formulas that are easily updated.

To create a series of months with date values, enter the start date as the first day of the first month of the series. Since you can format dates with the MMM-YY format, entering **1/1/90** and changing the format to MMM-YY produces Jan-90. You can then add 31 days to this date to produce the first of the next month, Feb-90, and so on. While the actual dates created by repeatedly adding 31 to the first of January are not the first of every month, because of the differing number of days in a month, the third date format (MM-YY) ignores the day of the month to give the date series just created an acceptable appearance. The technique of repeatedly adding 31 days to a beginning date of January 1 will produce acceptable consecutive MMM-YY dates for about 54 months.

Creating a date series by adding a fixed number of days to the previous date (either by copying formulas or filling a block) works in situations where the interval between dates is fixed. Thus, in the previous example, you assume that the payment schedule works on a fixed cycle of 30 days. When the cycle is based on calendar months, the calculations become more complex because of the differing number of days per month.

YEAR, MONTH, and DAY: Date Part Functions

In addition to simple addition and subtraction, there are a number of other ways to manipulate dates. You have already seen how the TODAY, DATE, and DATEVALUE functions are used to create dates and convert labels to dates. There are also date functions that allow you to extract parts of a date value for specialized calculations. Several Quattro Pro functions are designed to extract part of a date from a date value. The DAY function extracts the day of the month from a date value. It has the syntax

@DAY(*DateNumber*)

where *DateNumber* is a number under 73050.9999999, which is the highest date possible, December 31, 2099. The DAY function converts the date serial number you supply as *DateNumber* into the number (1-31) associated with that day. Thus, the formula @DAY(A1) would return the answer 25 if A1 contained the number 33232 or the formula @DATE(90,12,25).

The MONTH function, which has the syntax

@MONTH(*DateNumber*)

returns the number (1 through 12) corresponding to the month of the year represented by the *DateNumber*. Thus, @MONTH(A1) returns 12 if the number in A1 is 33232 or A1 contains @DATE(90,12,25).

The YEAR function returns the year of a date value and has the syntax

@YEAR(*DateNumber*)

The formula @YEAR(A1) would produce the answer 95 if A1 was any serial number or date within 1995. Likewise, the formula @YEAR(A1)+1900 would result in 1995.

The date part functions can be used with cell references or in combination with other date functions. Therefore, using the formula @MONTH(@DATE(90,12,25)) returns 12. You can combine date functions with other functions for useful formulas, such as

@CHOOSE(@MONTH(B2)–1,"January","February","March","April", "May","June","July","August","September","October", "November","December")

This formula lets you create the full name of the month represented by the date serial number in cell B2. None of the built-in date formats produce the full name of the month. This formula uses the CHOOSE function to pick a name from the list of names that are typed as labels in the formula. Remember that the syntax of the CHOOSE function is

@CHOOSE(*X,Case0,Case1,Case2,CaseX*)

where *X* is the number of the case to be selected from the list of cases, *Case0*, *Case1*, and so on. The cases are either numbers or labels. Thus, the formula has the 12 months entered as the cases. Because they are labels, they are entered in quotes. The @MONTH(B2)–1 formula returns a number from 0 through 11 for the case number, which the CHOOSE function then reads into the cell.

A similar formula is seen in the following, where the name of the day of the week for the date number in A1 is returned by dividing the number by 7 and looking up the remainder (0-6) in a list of seven cases.

@CHOOSE(@MOD(@DATE(B2),7),"Sat","Sun","Mon","Tue","Wed", "Thu","Fri")

Bear in mind that you can create custom numeric formats that show the names of days and months, as described in Chapter 7.

Another use of the date part functions is when you need to create a date series representing the first day of every month. This series cannot use the +30 method used earlier, because of the varying number of days in a month. The formula you see here uses the CHOOSE function to pick the appropriate number of days of the month from a list of days:

@CHOOSE(@MONTH(B2)–1,31,@IF(@MOD(@YEAR(B2),4)=0,29,28), 31,30,31,30,31,31,30,31,30,31)

An IF function statement is used for the second month number to determine if the year in question is a leap year and adjusts the number of days for February accordingly.

Time Functions

In addition to measuring calendar time, Quattro Pro can calculate hours, minutes, and seconds. You can calculate clock time with the NOW function, a more precise version of the TODAY function. Suppose you enter NOW into a fresh spreadsheet cell a little after 8:30 on the morning of December 10, 1993. The immediate result will be a number like this one:

34313.35449

This represents the day of the year (34313) and the part of the day taken up by eight and a half hours (.35449, the number of digits visible depending on the format used and the cell width). This figure will be updated every time you change the spreadsheet or use the Calc key (F9). To fix the number so that it is no longer updated but recorded as a static time value, press F2 followed by F9 and ENTER.

If you apply the first of the four time formats to the above number, the results look like this:

Chapter 5: Mastering Functions

08:30:28 AM

In other words, 28 seconds past 8:30 in the morning.

There are four Time formats listed under the Numeric Format settings. The first Time format, shown above, produces a display that may be too wide for the default column width of 9 because it displays not only hours, minutes, and seconds, but also the A.M. or P.M. indicator. The second Time format is quite a bit shorter. There are two International formats, long and short, which correspond to your Time Format selection on the International settings for the Application properties.

You can record static time values in a spreadsheet with the TIME function. The syntax of this function is

@TIME(*HH,MM,SS*)

where *HH* is the hours from 0 to 24, *MM* is the minutes from 0 to 59, and *SS* is the seconds from 0 to 59.99999. Because the TIME function works on a 24-hour clock, 11:35:00 P.M. is expressed as @TIME(23,35,00). However, if you want to use the shorter time format, you need to add 30 seconds to the time as it is being entered. Otherwise, Quattro Pro will round down the display to the previous minute.

Time values and math are useful when you need to calculate elapsed time between events, such as between hospital admission and discharge. Bear in mind that the basic unit is a day, and 1 day equals 24 hours. Thus, 12 hours is represented by 0.5 and 1 hour by 0.04166, recurring decimal. If you have times that are entered as labels, you can convert them to time values with the TIMEVALUE function. Like the DATEVALUE function, this process converts a string to a value if the string conforms to the standard Time formats. Thus, the syntax of the function is

@TIMEVALUE(*TimeString*)

where *TimeString* is a label in one of the following formats:

HH:MM:SS
HH:MM
Long International
Short International

The string must be enclosed in quotes if it is included in the function statement directly. Thus, @TIMEVALUE("21:39:52") returns the value 0.902685, which is 9:39 P.M. when formatted with the second time format. The statement @TIMEVALUE(A1) returns the same value if A1 contains the label 21:39:52.

HOUR, MINUTE, and SECOND: Time Part Functions

Just as Quattro Pro can extract parts of the date from a date value, so it can extract the elements of a time value. The time part functions are these:

@HOUR
@MINUTE
@SECOND

Thus, @HOUR(@TIME(10,30,00)) produces 10, and @MINUTE(A1) produces 30 if A1 contains the value @TIME(10,30,00) or the number 0.4375, which is the serial number of 10:30 A.M.

Miscellaneous Functions

There are numerous functions that do not fit into any of the categories so far reviewed in this chapter. Some are described here, while others are presented later in the book where they can be explained in context.

Special Functions

There are several functions referred to as special functions. Typically these are used in advanced spreadsheets and are explained in Chapter 14, where they are shown applied to practical situations. These functions are @@, CELL, CELLINDEX, CELLPOINTER, COLS, ROWS, CURVALUE,

FILEXISTS, MEMAVAIL, MEMMEMSAVAIL, NUMTOHEX, and HEXTONUM.

ERR: Error

When you want a cell to reflect an error you can use the ERR function. This function takes no arguments; it is simply entered as **@ERR**.

ERR returns the value ERR in the current cell and, in most cases, also creates the ERR message in any other cells that reference the cell in which you created the ERR condition. The exceptions to this are COUNT, ISERR, ISNA, ISNUMBER, ISSTRING, CELL, and CELLPOINTER formulas. These formulas do not result in ERR if they reference a cell that contains ERR. The ERR value resulting from this function is the same as the ERR value produced by Quattro Pro when it encounters an error.

NA

The NA function works the same as ERR, except that it returns the value NA, which distinguishes it from the ERR message that Quattro Pro uses when a formula is typed incorrectly.

TRUE and FALSE

If you want to give a value to a conditional statement, you can use the TRUE and FALSE functions to provide a 1 and a 0, respectively. These functions require no arguments and are discussed in Chapter 14.

The IS Functions

You will notice a series of functions in the Functions list (ALT-F3) beginning with IS. They are ISERR, ISNA, ISNUMBER, and ISSTRING. Used in a variety of situations, for example to find out if the value in a

FIGURE 5-35 String functions can convert cell entries into strings

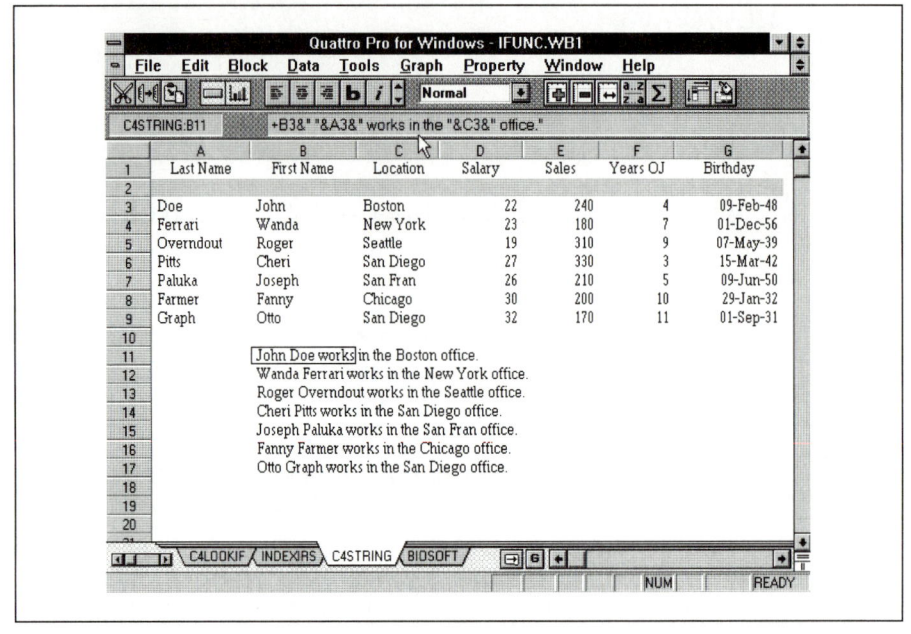

certain cell is a string, these functions relate to errors and nonvalues for numbers and dates. They are described in detail in Chapter 14.

String Functions

A particularly powerful group of Quattro Pro functions are those that help you manipulate strings. This is not an electronic version of marionettes, but rather a sophisticated way of handling sequences of characters or text. To Quattro Pro, a *string* is a sequence of characters with no numerical value. This can be words, like "Quattro Pro", or a group of characters, like '123, because they are preceded by a label prefix. The words "John" and "Doe" entered into separate cells can be pulled together, or *concatenated,* by string formulas. As you can see in Figure 5-35, you can use string functions to create text from spreadsheet entries. The string functions can convert numbers to strings and vice versa. Because string functions relate directly to the way in which Quattro Pro handles text, they are included in Chapter 12.

CHAPTER 6

Database Commands

You have seen that Quattro Pro has a wide range of commands to help you enter and organize tables of information in spreadsheet notebooks. This chapter looks at two further aspects of managing information in a spreadsheet: sorting and querying. We begin with sorting, which is made fast and relatively easy by the SpeedSort button. We then go on to examine the commands used to query a collection of information assembled as a database.

Sorting and SpeedSort

In spreadsheet terms, *sorting* is the process of rearranging rows of information according to alphabetical or numerical order. There are two ways to sort in Quattro Pro. You can use the Data | Sort command or the SpeedSort button (the SpeedSort button is the one indicated by the mouse pointer in Figure 6-1).

Using SpeedSort

In Figure 6-1 you can see three versions of the sample model of projected revenue used in earlier chapters (the block C2..H5 is highlighted to illustrate a point that will be raised in a moment). In the first version the table of revenue appears as it was entered in earlier examples. In the second version the table is sorted alphabetically by category of boat, that is, column C determines how the table is sorted. The third version of the table is sorted according to total revenue for the year, in other words, sorted according to column H.

You can see that sorting the table does not affect the results of the formulas in the table, either in the Year column or on the All Models row. To sort a table like this Quattro Pro needs to know two things:

- **Which data to sort?** This is the block of cells that contain the rows you want to rearrange. For example, to sort the first table in Figure 6-1 you would select C2.H5.

Chapter 6: Database Commands 311

FIGURE 6-1 Three versions of revenue projection showing the effects of sorting

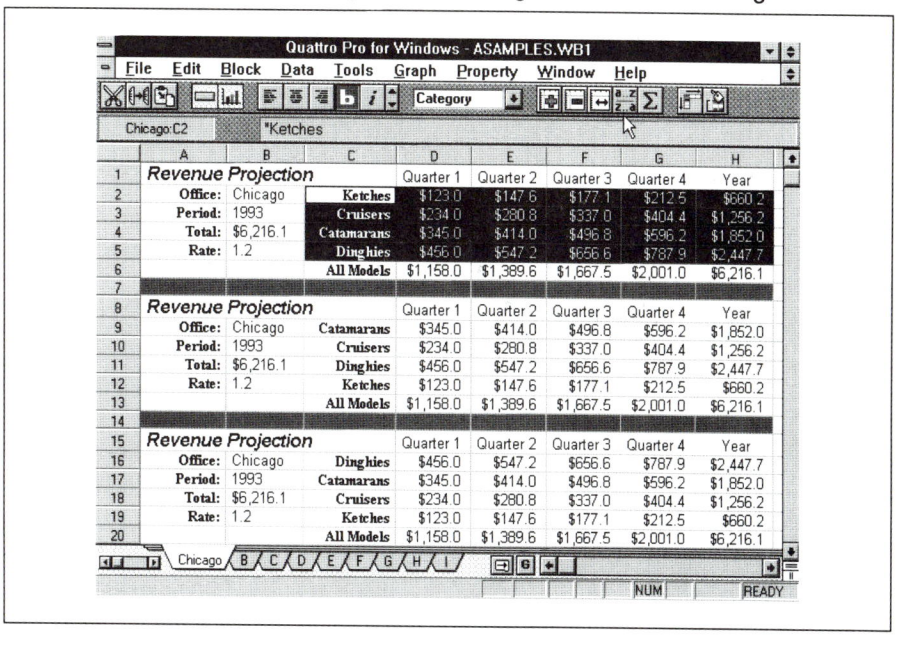

☐ **Which columns to sort by?** The column or columns that are the key to the sorting. For example, to sort the first table in Figure 6-1 by category you would select column C.

To sort a block of cells using SpeedSort you first select the block, as shown in the first table in Figure 6-1. Then you select the key column. There are several ways of doing this. If you highlight the block by selecting the top-left cell and dragging through to the bottom right, then the top-left cell remains the current cell. Clicking on SpeedSort at this point means that the leftmost column in the block is used as the key column. For example, in Figure 6-1 the user only needs to click on the SpeedSort button to sort the first table by the first column, that is, to sort by category of boat.

Note that there are two parts to the SpeedSort button. You click on the top half to sort in ascending order, from A up to Z in the case of labels, from smaller values to larger values in the case of numeric data. If the key column contains dates in ascending order it means they are ordered from earliest to latest, according to the date serial number (in other words, yesterday is listed above today). To sort in descending order you click the lower half of the SpeedSort button, which orders labels from Z down to A, and numbers from largest to smallest. If you want greater control over the order in which data is sorted then you can use the Data|Sort command instead of the SpeedSort button.

If you highlight the sort block by dragging from the top-right cell down to the bottom left, clicking on SpeedSort will sort the block by the last column on the right. For example, in Figure 6-2 you can see a list of boats for sale. The block of cells to be sorted was selected by dragging from I3 through A17. This leaves I3 selected and so clicking the top half of the SpeedSort button at this point will sort the block in ascending order according to the entries in column I. You can see the results of this sort in Figure 6-3.

Note The sort block should not include labels used as headings at the tops of list columns, such as those in A2 through I2 in Figure 6-2 (including such labels in a sort means they get mixed in with the rest of the rows in the block).

FIGURE 6-2 Selecting a block of cells to be sorted (note column headings are excluded)

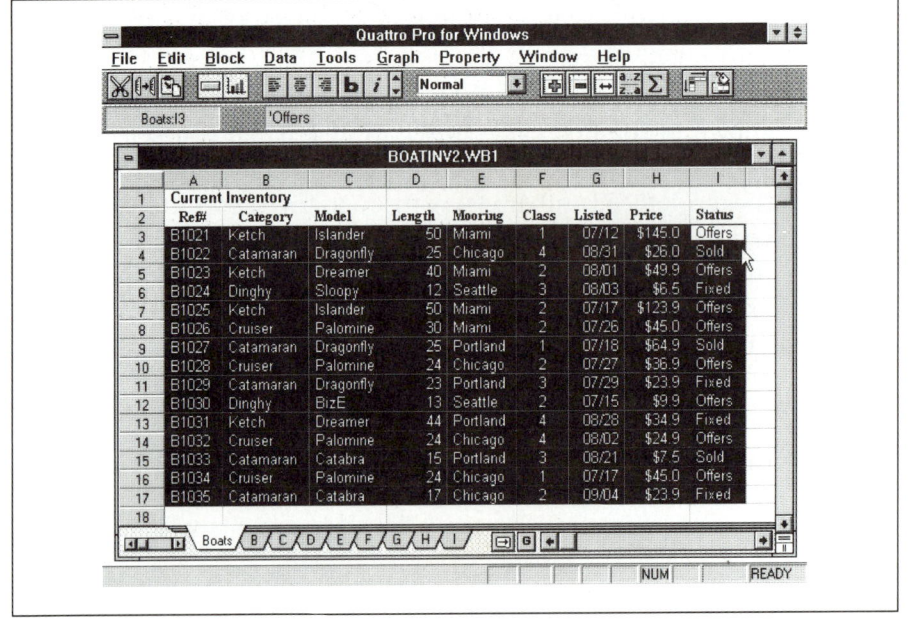

Chapter 6: Database Commands

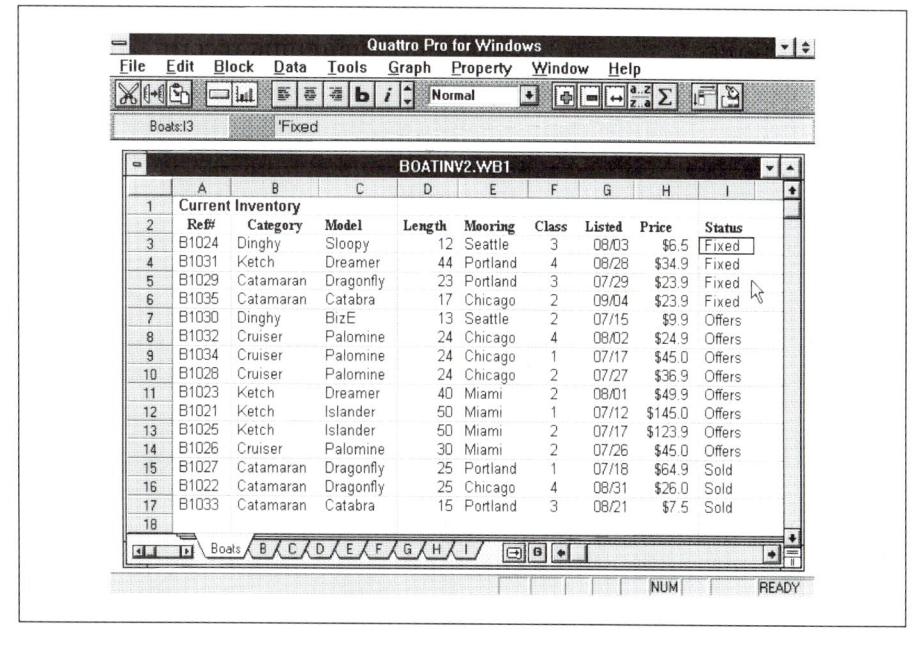

FIGURE 6-3 The effects of sorting by the Status column

	A	B	C	D	E	F	G	H	I
1	Current Inventory								
2	Ref#	Category	Model	Length	Mooring	Class	Listed	Price	Status
3	B1024	Dinghy	Sloopy	12	Seattle	3	08/03	$6.5	Fixed
4	B1031	Ketch	Dreamer	44	Portland	4	08/28	$34.9	Fixed
5	B1029	Catamaran	Dragonfly	23	Portland	3	07/29	$23.9	Fixed
6	B1035	Catamaran	Catabra	17	Chicago	2	09/04	$23.9	Fixed
7	B1030	Dinghy	BizE	13	Seattle	2	07/15	$9.9	Offers
8	B1032	Cruiser	Palomine	24	Chicago	4	08/02	$24.9	Offers
9	B1034	Cruiser	Palomine	24	Chicago	1	07/17	$45.0	Offers
10	B1028	Cruiser	Palomine	24	Chicago	2	07/27	$36.9	Offers
11	B1023	Ketch	Dreamer	40	Miami	2	08/01	$49.9	Offers
12	B1021	Ketch	Islander	50	Miami	1	07/12	$145.0	Offers
13	B1025	Ketch	Islander	50	Miami	2	07/17	$123.9	Offers
14	B1026	Cruiser	Palomine	30	Miami	2	07/26	$45.0	Offers
15	B1027	Catamaran	Dragonfly	25	Portland	1	07/18	$64.9	Sold
16	B1022	Catamaran	Dragonfly	25	Chicago	4	08/31	$26.0	Sold
17	B1033	Catamaran	Catabra	15	Portland	3	08/21	$7.5	Sold

If you want the key to the sort to be something other than the first or last column, select the sort block, and then CTRL-click on any cell in the desired column that is outside of the sort block. You can use CTRL-click to select a second key column if you want SpeedSort to perform a "multi-level" sort. The second key column acts as a "tie-breaker." In other words, if two or more rows contain the same entry in the first key column the second key column determines the order they are placed in.

In Figure 6-3 you can see that the sorting in column I had the effect of arranging the table into three groups: Fixed, Offers, Sold. You might want each of these three groups to be sorted further, so that, for example, all boats with a "Fixed" price are listed in alphabetical order by city. This would be particularly helpful if the list were much larger than the example used here (note that sorting is by no means limited to blocks that fit in the spreadsheet window; Quattro Pro will happily sort much larger blocks than this).

To perform this two-level sort keyed on columns I and E you first select the sort block, then CTRL-click in column I, and then CTRL-click in column E. Note that whenever you use two key columns you must select each one with CTRL-click. You can sort by up to five key columns. For example, when sorting a list of people that has separate columns for first name, last name, and middle initial, the last name column would be used as the first key. The first name column would be used as the second key, and the middle initial column would be the third key.

Note Always check the results after clicking SpeedSort. If they are not what you expect you may have made a mistake when selecting the sort block and/or key column(s). You can use Undo to reverse a sort.

The Data | Sort Command

You can execute a sort using the Data | Sort command, which presents the dialog box shown in Figure 6-4. If you have already used the SpeedSort button in a notebook, the dialog box will contain the settings used in the last SpeedSort. That is why the Block field in Figure 6-4 already contains the coordinates Boats:A3..I17. Also note that cell I3 is already entered in the 1st field in the Column section.

FIGURE 6-4 The Data Sort dialog box

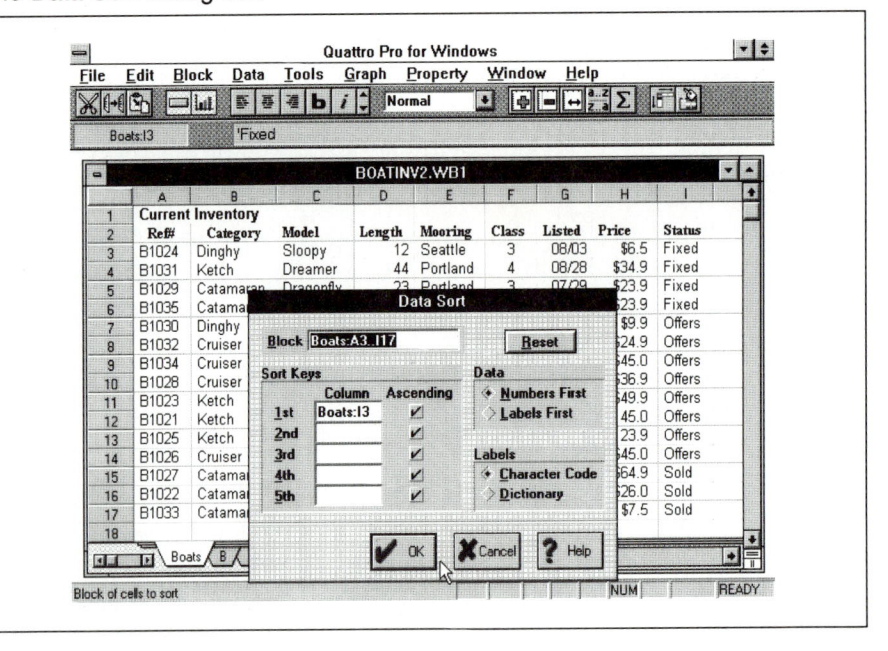

You can either preselect a block of cells before issuing the Data | Sort command or select the block using the Block field and the block techniques described in Chapter 3. In the Column fields, enter the coordinate of a single cell in each of the columns you want to use as keys in the sort. When you have provided this information, you can select OK to activate the sort. However, there are several optional settings you might want to adjust, notably Ascending. This refers to the order of the sort. This setting can either be ascending (when the box is checked) or descending (the box is un-checked) for *each* key column. The default sort order used by Quattro Pro in an ascending sort is listed in Table 6-1. The table shows how Quattro Pro deals with key columns that contain a variety of data such as labels and numbers.

TABLE 6-1 Ascending Sort Order

Item	Description
1. Blank cells	These appear at the top of the list, even before cells that contain only blank spaces.
2. Labels beginning with space	These are arranged according to the number of spaces preceding the first character, with more spaces preceding fewer; then alphabetically from A to Z, according to characters after an equal number of spaces.
3. Labels beginning with numbers	These come before labels that begin with words and are arranged numerically.
4. Regular labels	These are arranged according to the alphabet, from A to Z, according to the rules in the following description.
5. Labels beginning with special characters	Such characters as @ and $ come after Z. When two labels begin with the same special character, they are arranged according to the second character, so that $NEW comes before $old. There is a consistent order among special characters, which is, lowest to highest: !"#$%&()*+-./:;<=>?@[\]^'{¦}~
6. Numbers from lowest to highest	This applies to the value of the number, not its formatted appearance. Thus 10 and 1.00E+01 are equal, as are 0.1 and 10.00%.

Sort Rules

The Ascending setting is not the only way of altering the order in which data is sorted. The Data and Labels options also affect the way Quattro Pro handles entries in the key column. The Data option is either Numbers First or Labels First, with Numbers First being the default. When the setting is changed to Labels First, the effect is to change the order of items in Table 6-1 to 6, 1, 2, 3, 4, 5.

The Labels option can either be Character Code or Dictionary. The Dictionary setting means that Quattro Pro sorts labels alphabetically, with those that begin with special characters coming after those that begin with ordinary letters. In ascending order, the Dictionary sort will place words with uppercase letters before identical words with lowercase letters, as in FRED, FREd, FRed, Fred, fred.

The default Labels setting is Character Code, which uses the ASCII code of the first character of the label as the basis of the sort. *ASCII* stands for American Standard Code for Information Interchange, a system of codes in which each character has a numeric value, from 0 to 255 (for example, the letters A through Z are assigned codes 65-90, and a through z are assigned 97-122). The effect of selecting ASCII order in sorting a list based on a column of labels is likely to be surprising if you are not familiar with ASCII. For example, all labels beginning with capital letters will come before all those beginning with lowercase letters, and some special characters will also come before lowercase letters. Also, in ascending sorts using Character Code, labels beginning with numbers will precede any labels beginning with letters.

Sorting Tips

From one sort to the next, Quattro Pro will remember the sort settings. This allows you to quickly resort a list after editing the contents. You can choose Reset in the Data | Sort dialog box to move from sorting one area of a spreadsheet to another. Reset clears all five key columns, as well as the sort block. It also returns all of the sort order settings to their defaults.

When you add data to the *bottom* of a list, Quattro Pro does not automatically include the added data in the sort block, nor does the program automatically place new data in the correct alphabetical order.

Chapter 6: Database Commands 317

For example, suppose you are adding a new salesperson to the bottom of the list in Figure 6-5. After adding the information, you need to redefine the sort block and use Data | Sort or SpeedSort to sort the new records into the list.

Quattro Pro will automatically extend the sort block to cover new additions to a list *if* you insert a row *before* the end of the list. Remember that rows inserted into the spreadsheet within any named or recorded block of cells become part of that block. The coordinates of the block expand to accommodate the new cells.

Inserted rows will be added to the sort block if you use the Insert button or the Block | Insert | Rows command with your cell selector on any row in the sort block except the first one. Thus, if you want to add new staff to Figure 6-5 in the correct alphabetical location within the list, you can do so by first inserting space. In Figure 6-6 you can see a new person being added to the list. Because row 13 was inserted into the block, the sort block will automatically be expanded to A3..I18.

To insert a row into the list without affecting the arrangement of cells outside the list, use Partial for the Span setting in the Insert Rows dialog box. This tells Quattro Pro not to insert the row all the way across the

FIGURE 6-5 Adding a new item at the bottom of the list

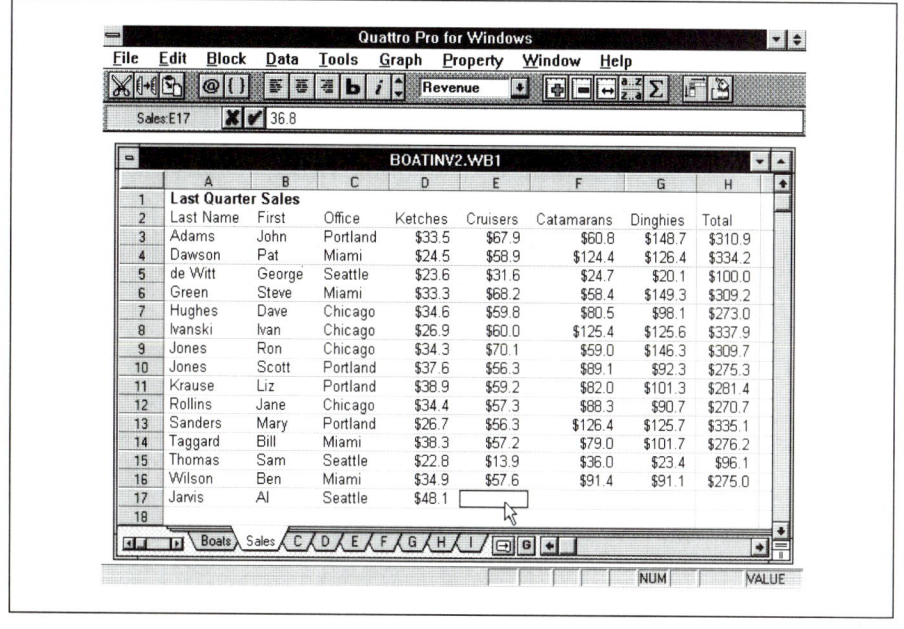

	A	B	C	D	E	F	G	H
1	Last Quarter Sales							
2	Last Name	First	Office	Ketches	Cruisers	Catamarans	Dinghies	Total
3	Adams	John	Portland	$33.5	$67.9	$60.8	$148.7	$310.9
4	Dawson	Pat	Miami	$24.5	$58.9	$124.4	$126.4	$334.2
5	de Witt	George	Seattle	$23.6	$31.6	$24.7	$20.1	$100.0
6	Green	Steve	Miami	$33.3	$68.2	$58.4	$149.3	$309.2
7	Hughes	Dave	Chicago	$34.6	$59.8	$80.5	$98.1	$273.0
8	Ivanski	Ivan	Chicago	$26.9	$60.0	$125.4	$125.6	$337.9
9	Jones	Ron	Chicago	$34.3	$70.1	$59.0	$146.3	$309.7
10	Jones	Scott	Portland	$37.6	$56.3	$89.1	$92.3	$275.3
11	Krause	Liz	Portland	$38.9	$59.2	$82.0	$101.3	$281.4
12	Rollins	Jane	Chicago	$34.4	$57.3	$88.3	$90.7	$270.7
13	Sanders	Mary	Portland	$26.7	$56.3	$126.4	$125.7	$335.1
14	Taggard	Bill	Miami	$38.3	$57.2	$79.0	$101.7	$276.2
15	Thomas	Sam	Seattle	$22.8	$13.9	$36.0	$23.4	$96.1
16	Wilson	Ben	Miami	$34.9	$57.6	$91.4	$91.1	$275.0
17	Jarvis	Al	Seattle	$48.1				
18								

spreadsheet. For example, the new row in Figure 6-6 was created by selecting cells A13..H13 and then clicking the Insert button. The following dialog box appeared to confirm that a partial row was to be inserted:

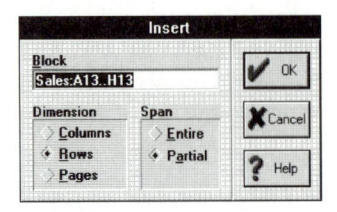

Choosing OK at this point created the cells being used for information about Jim Morris in Figure 6-6.

Placing data in order can be useful when you are attempting to analyze or report it. Consider the list of sales statistics in Figures 6-5 and 6-6. Instead of having them arranged alphabetically by salesperson, you may want to sort the numbers according to the Total column. This will show you which people are turning in the best overall performance. To see who is selling more of a particular product, you could sort by the product column. Later in this chapter you will learn how to find specific items

FIGURE 6-6

Adding a new item in the middle of the list

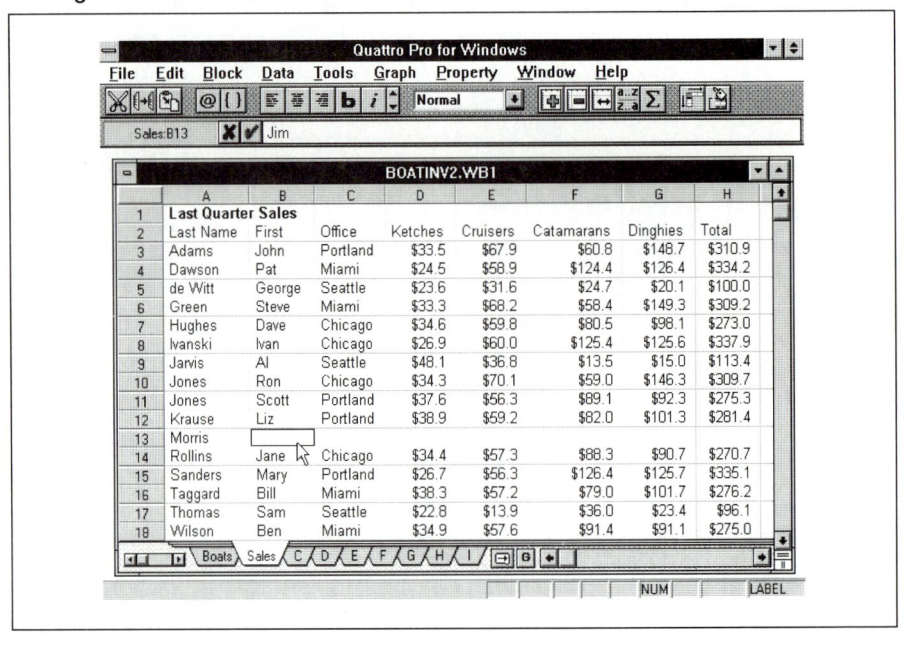

within a list using the Data | Query command, but it is important to bear in mind that simply sorting data makes it easy to find your way around a list and to draw conclusions from it.

In addition to analyzing data, sorting is useful when you are creating reports from a spreadsheet. A budget report will look better if the items are placed in some meaningful order rather than arranged haphazardly. If you were a manager using the list in Figure 6-6, you might need to produce a list of all sales staff who produced sales totals above a certain amount for the quarter. Placing the list in alphabetical order makes it easier to read, as well as more professional looking.

A related use of sorting is to tidy up data entry errors. For example, it is quite possible to accidentally enter the same data into a list several times. Duplication can be quickly identified when the list is sorted.

All About Databases

Quattro Pro not only has the ability to sort lists and tables of information, it can locate specific data and copy it to a separate list. Consider the table in Figure 6-6, which lists how much each person sold in four product categories (the numbers represent thousands of dollars, so that $1 equals $1000). Quattro Pro can locate all salespersons whose total sales in column H were more than $300,000. Furthermore, information about those salespersons can be copied to a separate list, in the same notebook or even a different notebook. In order to do this your data must be arranged as a *database*. In simple terms, this means a table with headings for each column. Thus the tables in 6-4 and 6-6 constitute databases, whereas the ones in Figure 6-1 do not because there are no headings for the labels in column C.

Defining a Database

In general terms a database can be defined as a collection of information arranged in a meaningful way. Any collection of information—from a phone book, to medical records, to an inventory list—can be considered a database. The information can be laid out in a table of columns and rows with headings (a *tabular database*). It can also be organized as a collection of separate pages or forms (a *form-oriented database*). In Figure 6-7 you can see a diagram of the two styles of organization applied to the same data. Clearly, a spreadsheet lends itself to the tabular style of database organization.

Dedicated Programs

Programs dedicated to handling large collections of information are called *database-management software.* The database-management capabilities of Quattro Pro enable you to enter, store, and then manipulate collections of data. Quattro Pro has two database functions: sorting and selecting data. The sort capability, described earlier, enables you to reorder data according to your specifications. Sorting does not require or make reference to column headings. The query commands allow you to search for and locate selected data, as long as you have headings for each column in the table.

Database management software can be divided into two groups: relational and flat-file. A *relational database manager* is one that can relate the data in several different files based on common elements. These programs can handle large amounts of data. Examples are dBASE and Paradox from Borland International. Quattro Pro is not a relational database. However, it can keep a sizable amount of related information in one spreadsheet page: up to 8191 records with as many as 256 fields. Because the database commands in Quattro Pro follow the same pattern

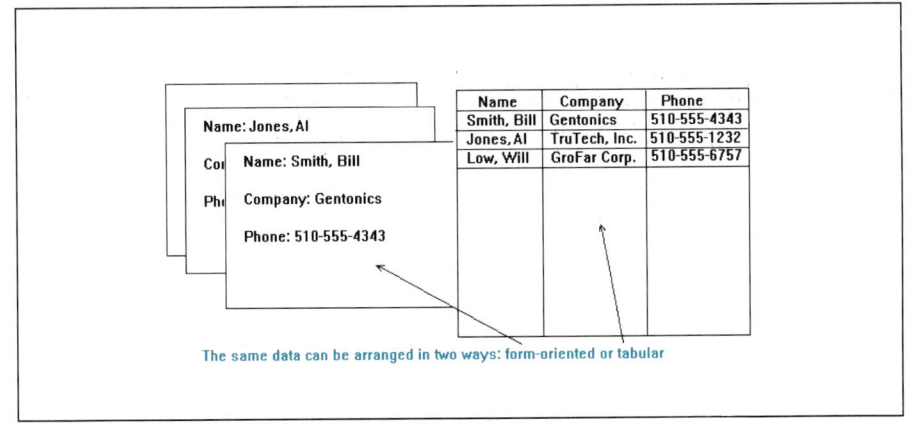

FIGURE 6-7 Form-oriented and tabular database structures

as the spreadsheet commands, you can perform database management tasks without learning a new program. In addition, you have all the power of Quattro Pro's built-in functions and graphics on hand to help analyze your data. Quattro Pro can read data from dBASE, Paradox, and other relational databases and export files to them as well. Furthermore, the adaptable user interface and macro command language of Quattro Pro make customized menu-driven applications a powerful possibility.

A *flat-file database manager* is the personal-computer equivalent of a rolodex or a box of filing cards. The Cardfile program that comes with Windows is a simple example of a flat-file database. More sophisticated are FileMaker from Claris and Reflex from Borland. However, most flat-file programs lack the graphics and math capabilities found in Quattro Pro. For this reason, if you are learning Quattro Pro for spreadsheet work anyway, you will probably want to use it for simple database applications as well. In this way, you can easily add database-management capabilities to your repertoire of computer skills without needing to learn another program and still keep all of your data in the same format.

Fields and Records

Information in a database is categorized by fields. *Fields* are the categories into which each set of facts, called a *record*, is broken down. In Quattro Pro, each field is a separate column, and each field has a name, which is placed at the top of the column. In other words, a Quattro Pro database, such as the one shown in Figure 6-8, consists of a series of consecutive labeled columns. The fields in Figure 6-8 are Last Name, First, Office, Ketches, Cruisers, Catamarans, Dinghies, and Total. As you can see, each field typically contains consistent types of data. For example, a field might contain labels only or dates only. Each column must be given a unique title.

A set of facts about each item in a database is called a record. A record corresponds to each line on a list or to each card in a card file. In a Quattro Pro database, each complete set of facts occupies one row. Thus in Figure 6-8, the block A3..H3 represents one record, the details about Ivan Ivanski. The rows of records are placed one after another with no empty rows between them. There should not be a blank row between the column headings and the first record. (Note that the table in Figure 6-8 is

FIGURE 6-8 An inventory database sorted by the result of a SUM formula

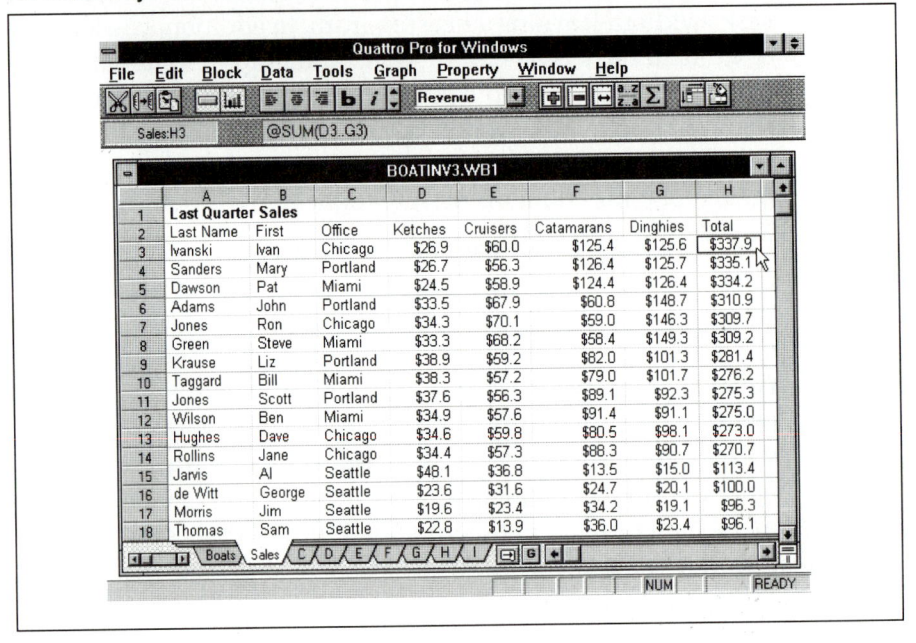

	A	B	C	D	E	F	G	H
1	Last Quarter Sales							
2	Last Name	First	Office	Ketches	Cruisers	Catamarans	Dinghies	Total
3	Ivanski	Ivan	Chicago	$26.9	$60.0	$125.4	$125.6	$337.9
4	Sanders	Mary	Portland	$26.7	$56.3	$126.4	$125.7	$335.1
5	Dawson	Pat	Miami	$24.5	$58.9	$124.4	$126.4	$334.2
6	Adams	John	Portland	$33.5	$67.9	$60.8	$148.7	$310.9
7	Jones	Ron	Chicago	$34.3	$70.1	$59.0	$146.3	$309.7
8	Green	Steve	Miami	$33.3	$68.2	$58.4	$149.3	$309.2
9	Krause	Liz	Portland	$38.9	$59.2	$82.0	$101.3	$281.4
10	Taggard	Bill	Miami	$38.3	$57.2	$79.0	$101.7	$276.2
11	Jones	Scott	Portland	$37.6	$56.3	$89.1	$92.3	$275.3
12	Wilson	Ben	Miami	$34.9	$57.6	$91.4	$91.1	$275.0
13	Hughes	Dave	Chicago	$34.6	$59.8	$80.5	$98.1	$273.0
14	Rollins	Jane	Chicago	$34.4	$57.3	$88.3	$90.7	$270.7
15	Jarvis	Al	Seattle	$48.1	$36.8	$13.5	$15.0	$113.4
16	de Witt	George	Seattle	$23.6	$31.6	$24.7	$20.1	$100.0
17	Morris	Jim	Seattle	$19.6	$23.4	$34.2	$19.1	$96.3
18	Thomas	Sam	Seattle	$22.8	$13.9	$36.0	$23.4	$96.1

basically the same as the one shown earlier in Figure 6-6 except that the details about Morris are complete and the records have been sorted according to column H.)

Limits

Since a Quattro Pro database consists of a block of consecutive rows and named columns, there are limits to the database dimensions. The maximum number of fields is 256, the total number of columns. The maximum number of records is the total number of rows minus one row for the field names: 8191. The maximum field size is approximately 320 characters (the maximum column width is actually 20 inches, which translates to about 320 characters in a 10-point font).

Creating a Database

The Quattro Pro database is not a special area of the program. As far as Quattro Pro is concerned, any data entered into a spreadsheet and falling within the definition of consecutive rows and named columns is a database. You may already have created a database while you were working on a spreadsheet. For example, the data in Figure 6-8 might have been entered simply to total the sales of each salesperson. However, because the columns are labeled and each person's data occupies a single row, the table already constitutes a database. As you can see from Figure 6-8, entries in a database may be labels or values. The alignment of labels does not affect the operation of the database commands. The values can be numbers, formulas, or dates.

Column Widths

The requirements of Quattro Pro database design allow only one row for each record. This means that fields containing lengthy information may require extensive widening of their columns. Remember that you do not have to make each column wide enough to show all the data that it contains in order for Quattro Pro to store long entries. However, if you want all of the data to print, you will need to expand columns prior to printing.

One solution to this dilemma is to use the Auto Width setting for the Column Width. This can be applied to any block of cells by selecting them and clicking the Fit button on the SpeedBar, as described in Chapter 2. This enables you to set the width of a group of columns all at once, making each column wide enough to display its longest entry, plus a fixed number of blank spaces. A typical use of the Fit button would be after entering data into the database but before you print out reports.

Note The Reveal/Hide property in the Active Block dialog box, described in Chapter 4, will let you temporarily hide selected columns from view without deleting them. This enables you to print selected columns of the database.

Problem Data

Many databases contain nonnumeric numbers, that is, numbers that are entered as labels. A typical example is ZIP codes in addresses. If you enter **01234** as a value, it will appear as 1234 in the cell because a leading 0 in a number does not register. You get around this problem and the ones created by nine-digit ZIP codes, telephone numbers, and part numbers that contain letters as well as digits by entering these numbers preceded by label prefixes. If you do not do so, the ZIP code **94109-4109** entered as a value would result in 9000, because Quattro Pro will read the dash as a minus sign. Note that when you enter telephone numbers with area codes, beginning the entry with a square bracket will make it a label, as in **[800] 555-1212**. Quattro Pro can still sort and search for numbers even if they are entered as labels.

The distinction between values and labels gives rise to another data entry problem, one that is immediately apparent when you try to enter a typical street address, such as 10 Downing Street. Quattro Pro takes its cue from the first character of the entry, in this case the number 1. This is a value, and it leads Quattro Pro to assume that what follows is also a value, an assumption that proves erroneous when you type the rest of the address and attempt to enter it, only to get an error message. As with ZIP codes, the answer is to place a label prefix at the beginning of any alphanumeric entry that is not a formula. One feature in Quattro Pro that helps solve some of these problems is the Data Entry Input setting, which is part of the Active Block settings. This feature is described toward the end of this chapter.

Formulas in Databases

Be careful when working with formulas in a database. If the formulas refer to cells in their own row within the table, they do not pose a problem. For example, each value in the Total column in Figure 6-8 is the result of a SUM formula that refers to cells on the same row as the formula. You have already seen that sorting does not corrupt formulas that follow this convention.

If formulas in a database block refer to cells outside the database block, such as a single cell containing a constant rate of growth, you must make those cell references *absolute*. For example, in Figure 6-9, cell F3 uses the following formula (look on the input line) to calculate commission:

+E3*$Raises:$H$3*1000

Placing the dollar sign in front of the page, column, and row references prevents the coordinates from changing when the formula is sorted to another row. If you sort A3..F18, the commission formula for each record will remain correct. (Absolute referencing of cells was described in Chapter 3.)

Quattro Pro's numeric dates, described in Chapter 2, are particularly important in databases. Collections of information often include dates. Records may need to be sorted or selected according to dates, such as the date of hire in column D of the table in Figure 6-9.

Making Inquiries

To locate specific records or groups of records within a database, you use the Data | Query command to *query* the database. Having located records, you can browse through and edit them. You can even copy matching records to a separate list. (The Data | Query command is quite different from the Edit | Search and Replace command described in Chapter 3.)

FIGURE 6-9 A database using an absolute cell reference

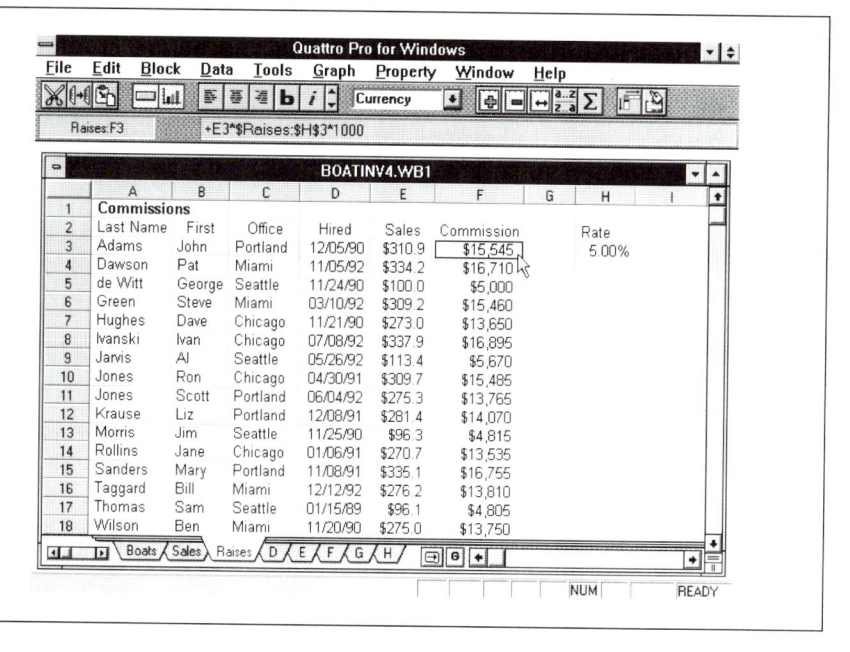

Lines of Questioning

Suppose that, as sales manager in charge of the people listed in Figure 6-9, you need to review the records of all persons in the Miami office. Of course, one way to do this would be to sort the database using column C as the first key column (you could use A as the second key and B as third if you wanted the records to be in alphabetical order by name within each office). However, if your database is large or if you want to leave it in the current sort order, the Data | Query command may be preferable. As you will see in a moment, this command allows you to perform quite sophisticated searches. When you select Query from the Data menu, the Data Query dialog box, shown in Figure 6-10, appears.

In order to find data that matches your search conditions, which Quattro Pro refers to as *criteria*, the Data | Query command needs to know two things:

- **Where the data is located** This is the Database Block, which contains the entire database including the field names.

- **Which data to find** This is the Criteria Table, which is used to specify the conditions of your search.

After you have provided these two pieces of information in the Data Query dialog box, you can choose Locate, which highlights matching records, or Extract, which copies matching records to a separate area of the notebook (you have to provide a third piece of information, the Output Block, in order to use Extract).

The easiest way to define the Database Block is to select it before selecting Query. When you issue the command, it assumes the pre-selected cells to be the Database Block, and the coordinates are filled in for you. Remember that the Database Block includes the field names, as well as the records that are in the database. You can use the block pointing techniques to change the coordinates from inside the dialog box if you wish.

The second piece of information you need to supply is the location of the Criteria Table. In this example, the Criteria Table must tell Quattro Pro that you want to find "all records that have Miami in the Office column." In Figure 6-10, you can see that the Criteria Table setting is

FIGURE 6-10 The Data Query dialog box

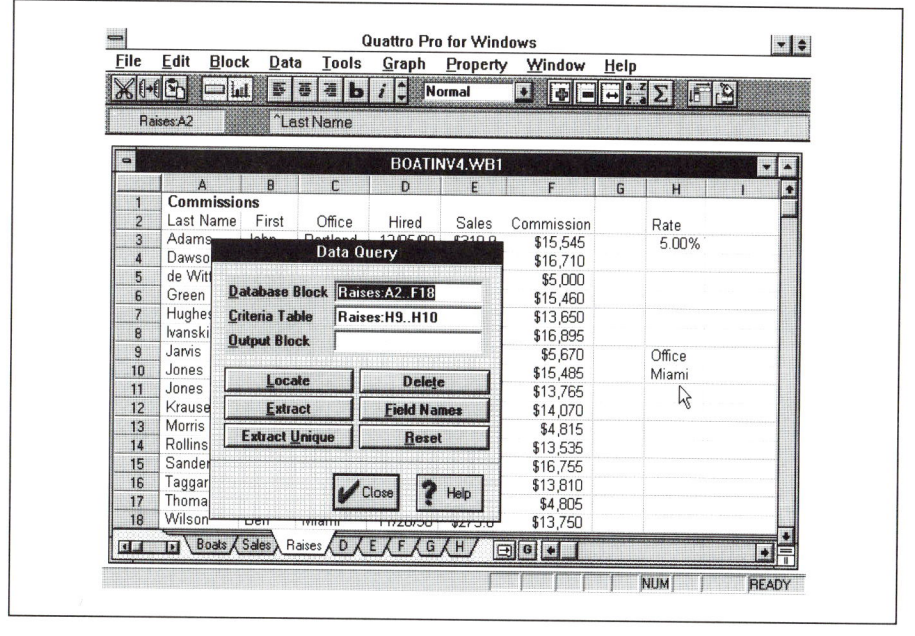

cells H9..H10. If you look in the underlying spreadsheet, you can see the entries in these two cells. This is the simplest form of criteria table—it consists of a field name above a piece of data. To find all personnel in the sample database who are based in the Miami office, you enter the name of the field (Office) and below it, the label or value in that field that you want to match (Miami).

These criteria entries are made into cells of your spreadsheet that are separate from the database block. When you ask Quattro Pro to locate the records, it tries to match what you have specified in the criteria table to each row of the appropriate column in the Database Block. In this example, the program looks in the field or column that is headed by "Office." The program checks each record for "Miami." When a match is found, the record that contains the matching text is selected.

You define a criteria table by selecting the Criteria Table field in the Data Query dialog box. You can then point out the appropriate cell block with your mouse or the cursor keys. The quickest way is to point to the top-left cell of the block (in this example, H9) and drag to the bottom-right corner (H10). While you do this the dialog box temporarily disappears, reappearing when you release the mouse button, at which point the block coordinates are entered for you. Keyboard users can select the Criteria Table field and press any arrow key to get into block pointing mode. Point to the first cell and then hold down SHIFT while you point to the last cell. Press ENTER to confirm the block. Be careful not to include any blank lines below the Criteria Table, because this causes Quattro Pro to select everything in the database.

Locating Data

When you have defined the Database Block and the Criteria Table, you can choose Locate. This tells Quattro Pro to highlight the block of cells that make up the first record that meets your criteria, as shown in Figure 6-11. In the lower right of the screen, the mode indicator changes to FIND. At this point, normal mouse and keyboard operations are suspended. The only actions you can perform are listed in Table 6-2. These allow you to browse through records that match the criteria and edit any of the information in those records. You can exit from FIND mode back to the Data Query menu by pressing ESC. To go from FIND mode directly to READY mode, you can press CTRL-BREAK.

Note If no records meet your criteria, you get an alert dialog box telling you so. Choose OK or press ESC at this point to get back to the Data Query dialog box. You can then check to see that you have specified the criteria correctly.

TABLE 6-2 Keys You Can Use in FIND Mode

LEFT ARROW	Moves cell selector one field to the left
RIGHT ARROW	Moves cell selector one field to the right
END	Selects last matching record
HOME	Selects first matching record
F2	Edits current cell
F7	Exits FIND mode to menu or READY mode
ESC	Exits FIND mode to menu or READY mode
CTRL-BREAK	Exits FIND mode to READY mode

The Locate feature is very useful for quick searches when you do not want to print out a separate list, for example, to perform a quick check of a specific item in stock or an employee record. If you want to copy the located data to another part of the spreadsheet or to another spreadsheet, you need the Extract command, described later in this chapter.

The criteria table should be set apart from the database block in an unused portion of the spreadsheet. Do not worry too much about the positioning of a criteria table on the spreadsheet, as it is not critical to performance of the Data | Query command; however, there are some practical factors regarding location that you should consider:

☐   Do not place the criteria table directly to the right or left of the database if you plan to later add or delete database records by inserting or deleting entire rows (deleting records with the Delete button will be described in a moment).

☐   Use the Partial setting in the Insert and Delete dialog boxes if you are using them to add or delete rows in the database block.

FIGURE 6-11 The first matching record located in the database

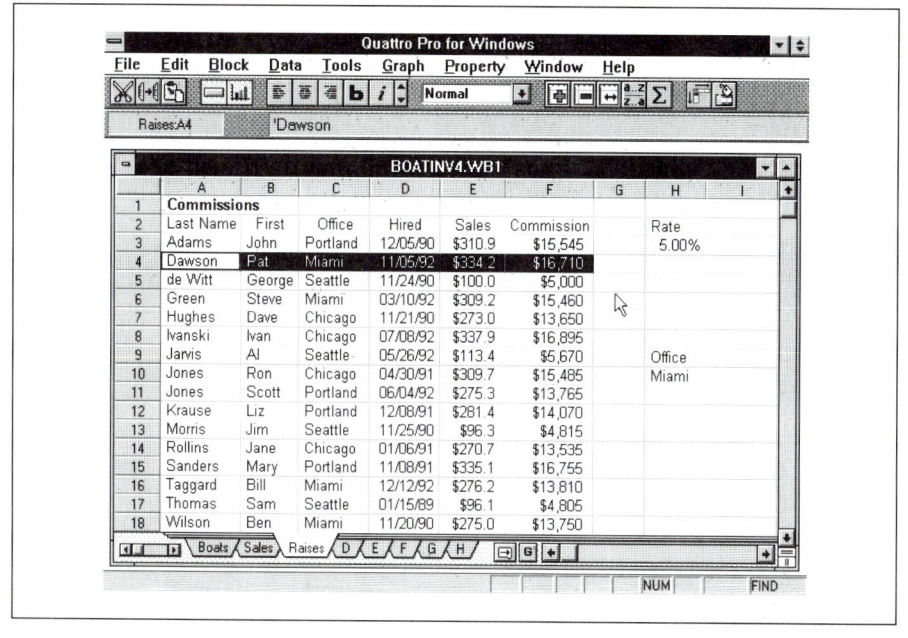

☐ Do not move the criteria table too far from the database because this needlessly consumes memory.

Repeating a Query

The F7 key repeats the last query you performed. Suppose that in the sample database, you finish looking at the Miami records and want to find the Seattle records. After quitting from FIND mode and the Data Query menu, you simply type **Seattle** in cell H10 and then press F7. A Locate is performed immediately, using the same Database Block and Criteria Table as the last one, but with the new entry in cell H10 of the Criteria Table.

The F7 key is very helpful when you are performing a series of queries—it repeats the last query command. If, on the last occasion that you used the Data | Query command query, you chose Extract instead of Locate, an Extract is performed the next time you press F7 (the Extract feature will be discussed in a moment). When you press ESC to exit FIND mode, you are returned to the Data Query dialog box, unless you entered FIND by pressing F7, in which case ESC takes you directly to READY mode.

Additional Criteria

So far you have seen that a criteria table offers a simple but effective way of telling Quattro Pro what you want to find. You can take the criteria table further by adding fields to it and by using formulas and block names to create detailed search specifications.

Multiple Criteria

Suppose that you have a much larger version of the database in Figure 6-11 and need to locate one person. You can set up a criteria table with two headings, Last Name and First, and then enter the name of the employee beneath the headings, as shown in the background of Figure 6-12. After redefining the Criteria Table to include all four cells, you can

Chapter 6: Database Commands

select Locate. The next time you need to look up somebody in the list, you simply type the name in the criteria table and press F7. The same Criteria Table and Database Block are used, but with the new entry in the criteria table. In this way you can find a succession of people with relatively few keystrokes.

When you use two criteria in this way the effect is to narrow down the search conditions. In other words, the criteria in Figure 6-12 mean "select all records that have Jones in the Last Name column, *as well as* Ron in the First column." A quite different effect is obtained by placing a second criteria one line below the first criteria, as shown here:

Last Name	First
Jones	
	Ron

If you select these six cells as the Criteria Table the effect is "select all records with Jones in the Last Column *plus* all records with Ron in the First column." Clearly this is a much broader search criteria than the previous example. The rule is that multiple search conditions on the same

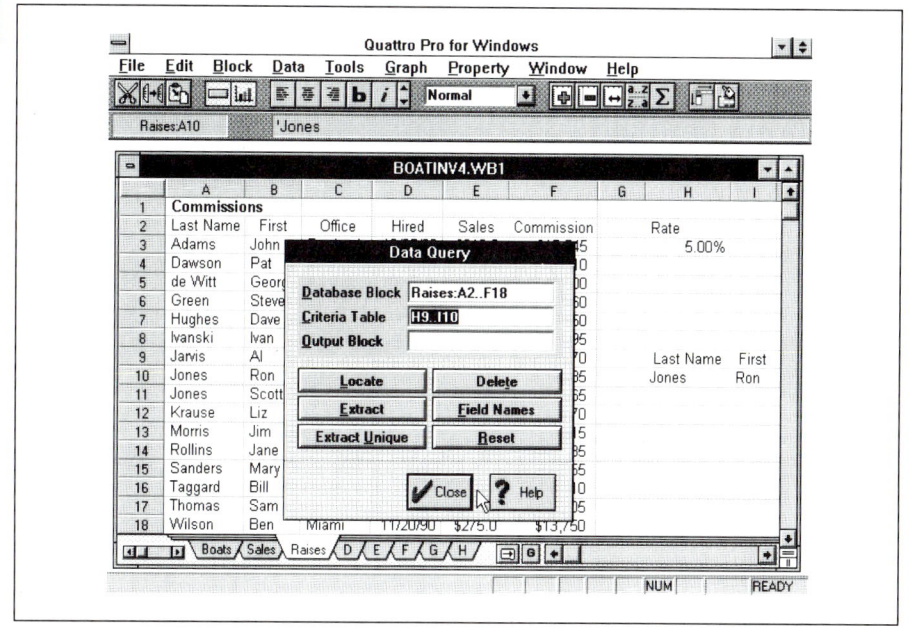

FIGURE 6-12 Using two columns in the Criteria Table to narrow down the search

line are combined with AND while conditions on separate lines are combined with OR.

Criteria Techniques

A quick way to create and use a criteria table is to copy the entire set of field name labels to a new location and then define those names and the row beneath them as the Criteria Table. You then enter the data you want to match under the appropriate field name prior to a search. For example, in Figure 6-13, you can see an example of the full set of field names used for a criteria table. The entire block A21..F22 has just been selected as the Criteria Table (the current criteria are entered in A22 and C22 and mean "all records that have Jones in the Last Name column AND Seattle in the Office column."

One advantage of copying the field names to the criteria table is that you avoid problems that can arise from typing. For example, if you typed

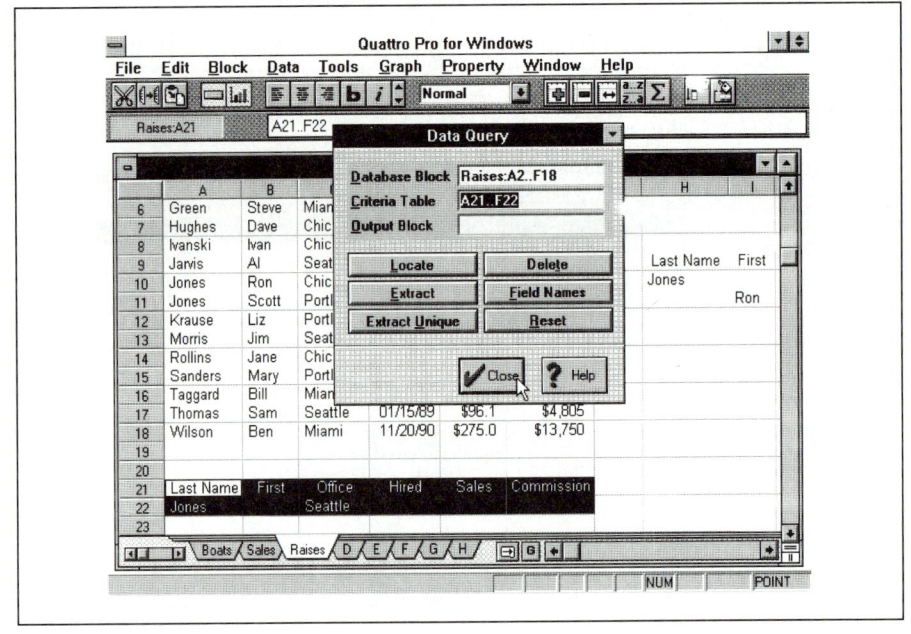

FIGURE 6-13 Using a Criteria Table with all the fields included

the criteria table in Figure 6-13 manually and spelled "Office" as "Officer", the query would not work correctly. Note that you don't have to have an entry in every column of the criteria table for it to work. However, there must be an entry in the final row of the criteria table; otherwise the query will find every record.

As you can see from Figure 6-13, it is possible to set up more than one set of cells in a spreadsheet as a criteria table and choose the block you want to use as your criteria. Although only one block at a time can be the *current* criteria table, you can quickly switch tables by using block names. For example, you could create three different sets of criteria located in blocks called CRIT1, CRIT2, and CRIT3, respectively. Suppose you have just performed a Locate operation with CRIT1 as the Criteria Table, and now you want to use CRIT2. When you issue the Data | Query command, select Criteria Table and press F3 for a list of block names. Highlight CRIT2 and press ENTER to confirm. You can now choose Locate to perform the search based on the contents of CRIT2.

Naming Fields

The Data Query dialog box, shown in Figure 6-13, has an option called Field Names. This gives block names to each cell in the second row of the current Database Block, using the field names in the first row. Why would you want to do this? You have already seen that you can query your database without carrying out this operation. The value of the Field Names option appears when you start to develop more sophisticated search criteria. So far, you have seen how to search for something that is an exact match, telling Quattro Pro to match such things as Seattle and Jones. You have also seen that placing criteria on separate rows creates an OR match. When you come to search for a range of values, such as "Sales greater than 330", block names come in very handy.

The Field Names option is very easy to use. After you have defined the Database Block, just select Field Names. You will not see anything happen. However, when you exit the Data Query dialog box and use the Block | Names | Create command, you will see a list of the block names you have just created. If you press the plus key (+) on the numeric keypad, you will see the cell coordinates listed next to the names, as shown here:

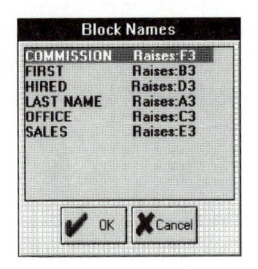

These names can be used in search formulas. Note that block names are stored in capital letters. In fact, Quattro Pro is not at all case-sensitive when it comes to queries. A query based on "YES" also finds "yes" and "Yes". When you put together criteria tables and formulated criteria, it will not matter if you refer to field names in upper- or lowercase letters.

Formulated Criteria

To make queries more versatile, you can use formulas instead of labels and values. For example, if your criteria table consists of the field name Sales and the value 330, your query will identify only those records that have exactly 330 in the Sales column. Criteria formulas use *comparison operators,* together with the block name assigned to the first cell in each column by the Field Names option, to locate a range of values. Thus, you can enter **+SALES>330** as a condition and locate all persons with a sales greater than 330, as shown in Figure 6-14.

Note that the entry in H10 is +SALES>330, even though it appears to be 0. The reason for this is that Quattro Pro reads the formula as asking "is the value in E3 greater than 330?" The cell E3 is the one that was named SALES by the Field Names option. The response is 0 because the answer is "no" or "false." If the value in E3 had been larger than 330, the answer in the spreadsheet would be 1, meaning "yes" or "true." When you issue the Locate command, Quattro Pro asks the same question of all cells in column E, starting with E3 and ending at the last row of the database block. When the answer is true or 1, Quattro Pro will select that row as a match.

Each criteria formula includes three elements: *field, comparison operator,* and *value.* These tell Quattro Pro which field contains the value you

Chapter 6: Database Commands

FIGURE 6-14 The first result of using +SALES>330 as a criteria formula

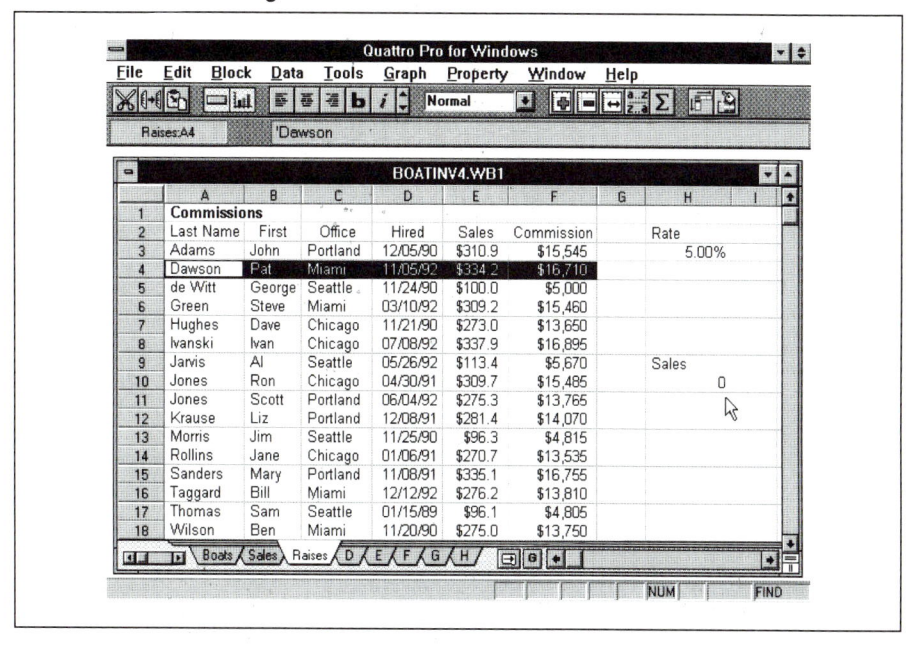

are attempting to match, whether you want to match an exact value or a range of values, and the value itself. The comparison operators you can use are as follows:

Sign	Meaning	Example	Finds
>	Greater than	+Sales>330	331, 332, etc.
<	Less than	+Sales<330	329, 328, etc.
>=	Greater than or equal to	+Sales>=330	330, 331, 332, etc.
<=	Less than or equal to	+Sales<=330	330, 329, 328, etc.
<>	Not equal to	+Sales<>330	anything but 330
=	Equal to	+Sales=330	only 330

Note You generally will not use an expression like +Sales=330 unless it is part of a larger formula, because there is no need to use a formula if the criterion is a single case. Simply use 330 as the criterion.

When you create criteria formulas using block names, you can use F3 to supply the name. For example, to create the formula +SALES>330, type + and press F3. Select SALES from the list of names by highlighting it and pressing ENTER. Now you can type **>5** and press ENTER again to complete the formula. This avoids typing errors such as incorrect spelling of block names.

To place additional qualifications on the criteria you use for querying items, you can add *logical operators,* which set up more categories to match. The logical operators shown here set up two or three criteria for the sales staff list:

#AND#	Office="Miami"#AND#Sales>300
#OR#	Office="Miami"#OR#"Seattle"
#NOT#	Office="Miami"#AND#Sales>300#NOT#First="Joe"

The logical operator must be placed in the formula within # signs, as shown in the examples. Label *values* (not field names) must be placed in double quotes.

You create multiple conditions with logical operators to make your search more specific. For example, to locate all staff based in Miami with sales greater than 300, you would type **+OFFICE="Miami"#AND#SALES>300** as shown on the input line of Figure 6-15 (this criteria table will find Pat Dawson). Notice that the field name in the criteria table in Figure 6-15 is Sales, but the Sales field is not the only one referred to in the formula. In fact, when you are using formula criteria that reference named cells in the database, you can use any field name in the database as a heading. For example, you can use a formula referencing the fields called Sales and Hired, entered under the field name Office.

Note When you work with formula criteria, it is helpful to format cells with the Numeric Format called Text. This will display the *text* of the formula inside the cell, rather than the result. In Figure 6-15, you can see that this was used on cell H10.

Matching Text

If what you want to match in a criterion is a piece of text—that is, something that has been entered as a label—and you want to incorporate it into a formula, you must place it in double quotes. For example, miami will find Miami and MIAMI, as well as miami. When you use the comparison operators with labels, Quattro Pro interprets > as meaning

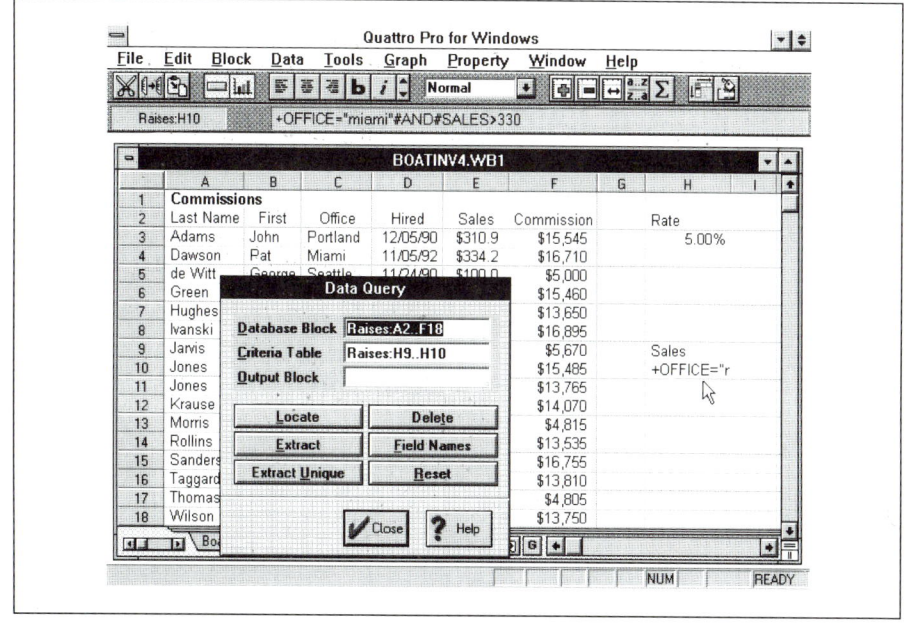

FIGURE 6-15 Preparing a query—note the text format of the criteria formula

further in the alphabet. This means that you can use these operators with nonnumeric fields like ZIP codes to specify codes equal to or greater than, say, 94100, which would be written as +ZIP>="94100".

To add scope to your searches for a text match, you can use *wildcards*. These are the question mark (?), the asterisk (*), and the tilde (~). The question mark stands for any character in that position in a string, as in V?LE, which would find VALE, VOLE, VILE, and so on. The asterisk means anything from this character to the end of the label, as in VERN*, which would find anything beginning with VERN, like VERNAL, VERNON, and so on. Tilde means "not," as in ~Miami, which would find everything but Miami.

Query Extract

So far you have seen that Quattro Pro is adept at locating records in a database. At some point you will probably want a list of items matching your criteria. You create a list of data selected from a Quattro Pro database by choosing Extract in the Data Query dialog box, rather than choosing Locate.

Setting Up an Extract

When you use Extract, any data meeting your criteria is copied into a separate area of the spreadsheet. In addition to the Database Block and the Criteria Table settings, an Extract operation needs two more pieces of information:

- **Where to output** The spreadsheet cells into which you want the matching data copied

- **What data to output** The names of the fields to be included in the new list

This information is supplied in the form of a series of field names, which are then defined as the Output Block in the Data Query dialog box. For example, in Figure 6-16, you can see the result of an Extract as well as the settings that created it. The list in E25..H28 is the result of using Extract, with the labels in E25..H25 defined as the Output Block. The Criteria Table is A21..F22, which contains the formula +SALES>330.

Note that the output only lists those items for which you supplied field names in the Output Block cells E25..H25. There is no limit to the number of fields you can include in the Output Block, and you do not need to include fields that were part of the criteria. The order of fields in the output does not have to match that used in the database. When you define the Output Block, you can select just the field name row, as in E25..H25. However, you may want to extend the block beyond the row of field names for as many rows as you think it will take to accommodate the expected output. If you only select the field name row as the Output Block, you are telling Quattro Pro that it can use any number of rows below the field names for the output. This could result in output overwriting cells that already contain data.

When you have performed the extract, the data can be printed, copied, or further manipulated. As with the Locate command, you can repeat the last query with F7. Thus, you can change the level of sales you are looking for and press F7 to get a new list in the output block. Note that when

Chapter 6: Database Commands 339

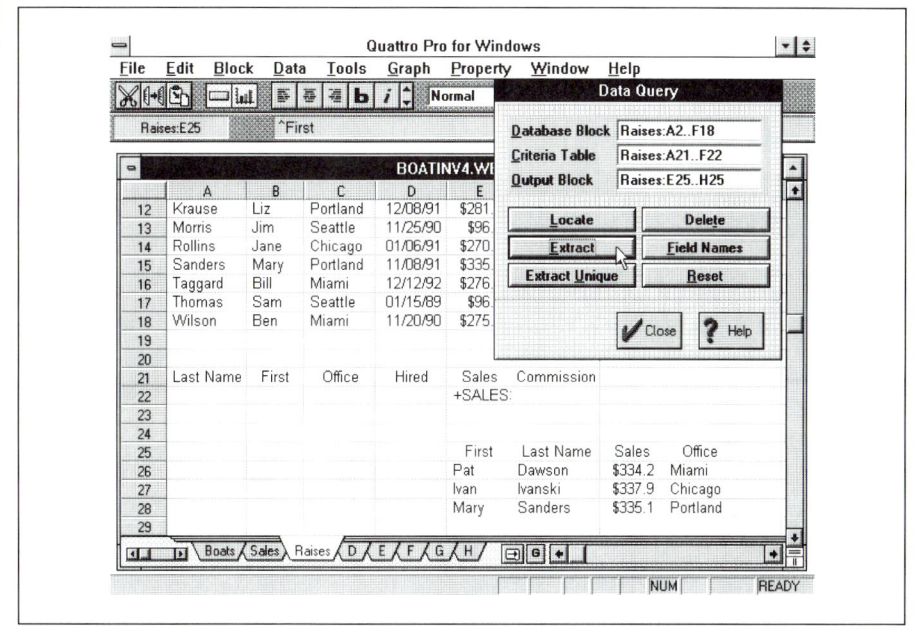

FIGURE 6-16 The result of an Extract showing the Output Block setting

Quattro Pro extracts numbers from the database to an output range, they are only numbers. Formulas in the database block are converted to their numeric value upon extraction. Also note that Quattro Pro erases the output block's previous contents before creating new output. This means that extracting a short list after a long list does not leave previous output in the list.

Unique Records

There may be situations in which you want to extract only the unique values in one or more fields. For example, suppose you have a database of wines classified according to Country, Region, and Year. You want a list of all regions of France represented in the database. You can use a criterion of Country="France" and an output field with the heading Region. When you use Extract, however, the resulting list will contain one region name entry for every record that has France in the Country field, meaning there will be many duplicates in the list. In a situation like this, when you want each region name listed only once, use Extract Unique rather than Extract.

The Extract Unique button, located in the Data Query dialog box, lists any item that is identical to another item in the output block, only. In other words, Extract Unique lists unique values, whereas the Extract option lists all values.

Working with Extracted Data

Extracted data appears as a series of consecutive columns and rows; in fact, by extracting data you have created a new database. This database can now be sorted. If you were asked to provide a list of all the staff in Miami, you would want the list alphabetized or put in some other order. You can do this by defining the Block in the Data Sort dialog box as the output data block, excluding the row of field names. Remember that Quattro Pro remembers the last data sort block and sort keys you used, so it is wise to select the Reset command from the Data Sort dialog box before performing a sort on a new block.

To print a database, you simply need to define the database block as the block of cells to be printed. Quattro Pro arranges the data on pages according to the quantity of information and the size of the page, as described in Chapter 4. Using field names as a top heading that will appear on each page is very useful when the report covers several pages. Multiple-page listings will also benefit from headers that number the pages. You can also use the Line Drawing option in the Active Block dialog box to create a line under the field names.

Deleting Records

When you are cleaning up or maintaining a database, you may need to get rid of records. One way of doing this is to find the record and then delete it with the Block | Delete | Rows command. However, unless you use the Partial setting you will remove any data that is on the same row as the deleted record, all the way across the spreadsheet. Quattro Pro has an automated alternative, which is the Delete button in the Data Query dialog box.

To use the Delete button, you set the criteria for the records you want deleted and select Delete instead of Locate or Extract. You will be prompted to confirm this action because Delete can be dangerous. Test your criteria with a Locate operation before using Delete and perform a File | Save before proceeding. Another safeguard is to make sure that the Undo feature is enabled. This will allow you to reverse the effect of Delete by using Edit | Undo.

Foreign Databases and Multiple Spreadsheets

You can see that managing a database requires several elements in addition to the data itself. Querying the database requires a Criteria Table. An Output Block is required for an Extract to be performed. One way to manage these elements is to divide them between different notebooks or between different pages of the same notebook. In this section, we discuss how you can do this and offer directions for using data from sources other than Quattro Pro.

Splitting Up Your Work

You can keep your database in one spreadsheet and the criteria table and output block in a separate spreadsheet. This can either be a completely different notebook or a different page of the same notebook. You can see this arrangement in Figure 6-17 where two spreadsheet pages, DATABASE and REPORT, are shown side by side. The REPORT spreadsheet is where the user is specifying the criteria and extracting the data (this arrangement of spreadsheet views is achieved by means of the Window | New View command, described in the next chapter).

With the REPORT spreadsheet active, you set the Database Block by defining the cells occupied by data in the DATABASE spreadsheet. Staying with the REPORT spreadsheet you define the Criteria Table and Output Block using cells in the REPORT spreadsheet. You can see that this has been done in Figure 6-17, which also shows the results of the Extract operation based on these settings.

To extract data from the DATABASE spreadsheet into REPORT, you make REPORT the active spreadsheet and then issue the Extract com-

FIGURE 6-17 Performing a query using two different spreadsheets

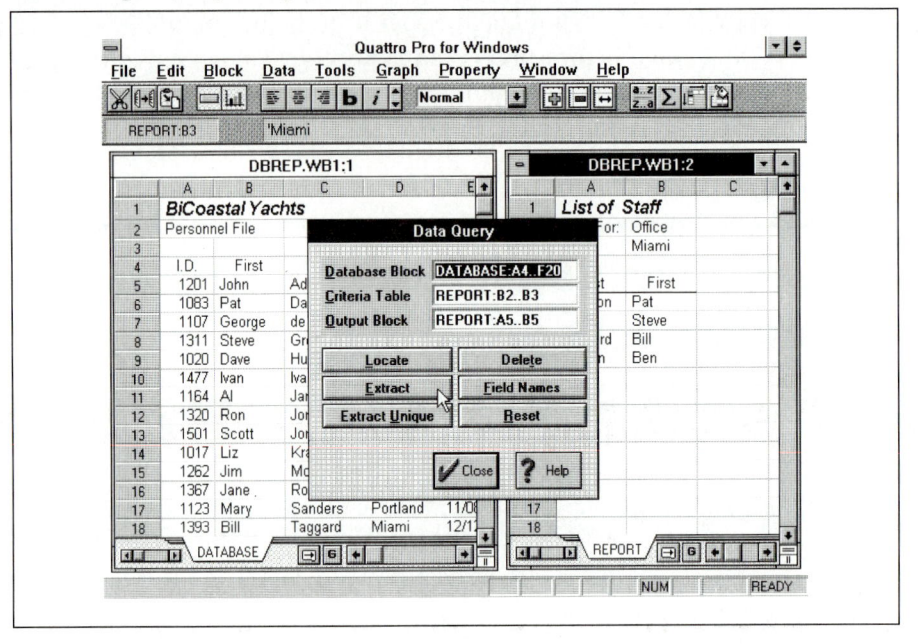

mand. Records from DATABASE that meet the criteria in REPORT will be copied into REPORT. You can also use the Locate command from REPORT. In this case, Quattro Pro takes you to the DATABASE spreadsheet and shows you the selected records there. When you leave FIND mode, you are returned to the REPORT spreadsheet.

An extension of the multiple-spreadsheet approach would be to have several different "report" pages in the same notebook, each one containing different criteria tables and output blocks. You could then switch criteria simply by making a different spreadsheet window active before executing the query.

Working with Foreign Databases

Although many users find that a Quattro Pro spreadsheet is the ideal place to keep track of their data, no one expects all of the world's databases to be available in Quattro Pro format. Because there is so much useful data stored in databases created by other programs, Borland gave Quattro Pro the ability to read files created by other popular database programs such as dBASE and Paradox. This means that you can load these files as part of a notebook. Techniques for doing this, and for using the Database Desktop and Table Query commands on the Data menu, are described in Chapter 8.

A few database programs store data in files that Quattro Pro cannot read. However, just about any program can create ASCII files, which can then be imported into a Quattro Pro notebook using the Tools | Import command, described in Chapter 12.

Data Entry Techniques

Database entries in spreadsheets take far more keystrokes than regular spreadsheets, in which the bulk of the entries are created by formulas that are copied. In addition, databases often need extensive editing to be kept current. If you are maintaining a sizable database, you may wish to employ a typist to edit or input the data. Some steps you can take to make the work easier for someone unfamiliar with Quattro Pro appear here.

Input Form

If you are having spreadsheet novices perform data entry for you, you can make an input form to assist them. The first step is to protect the spreadsheet. To do this, issue the Property | Active Page command and select the Protection option, where you select Enable. This prevents any formulas or important data on that page from being altered. Then you can use the Protection setting on the Active Block dialog box to Unprotect cells, in which the data will be entered or edited.

When you are ready to have someone work on the database, you can issue the Restrict Input command from the Data menu. You then select a block of the spreadsheet that includes the unprotected cells. When you choose OK, this area becomes the *input block*. User access is now limited to any unprotected cells in the input block. The diagram in Figure 6-18 shows how the input block and unprotected cells work together to create a *mask* over the spreadsheet.

The effect of the Data | Restrict Input command is considerable. The message INPUT appears in the mode indicator. The cursor keys will not take you outside of the defined input block of cells and will only move to those cells within the input block that are unprotected. You can type data and press ENTER, or you can edit data with F2 and reenter it. The program menus are not available, so typing / begins a new label instead of activating the menu.

To break out of the INPUT mode, you press ESC or ENTER while the INPUT message is displayed. This means that it is very easy to override the Data | Restrict Input command. In fact, the command is most effective when used in macros that further control the user's access to commands, as described in Chapter 14.

Data Control

Earlier in this chapter, we mentioned the need to type a label prefix when you enter nonnumeric numbers such as ZIP codes. Another chore for data entry workers is making sure that dates are entered as dates. To

FIGURE 6-18 A diagram of the restricted input feature

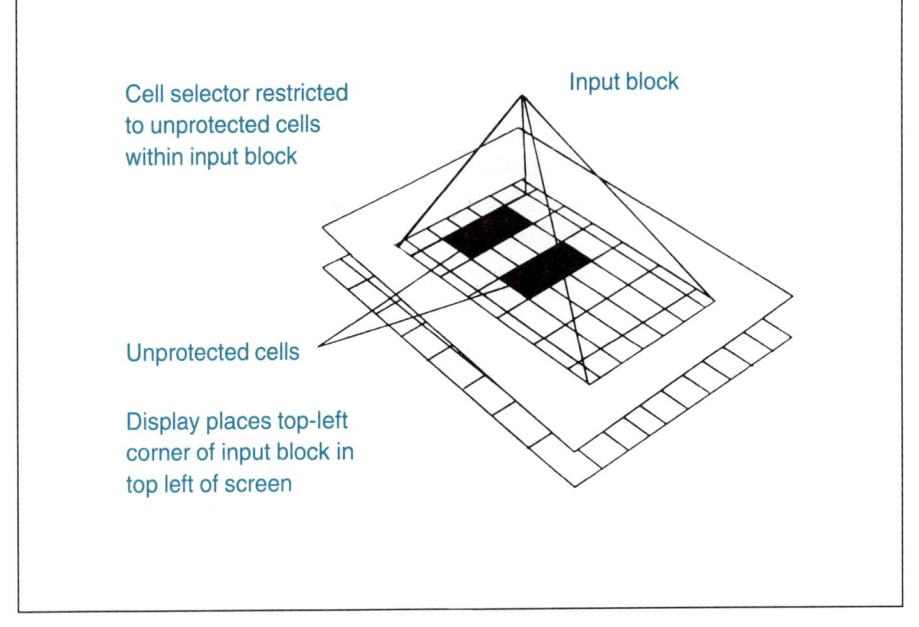

overcome this problem, Quattro Pro enables you to designate certain cells in a spreadsheet as Labels Only. To do this, you use the Data Entry Input option on the Active Block dialog box. This gives you a choice between General, Labels Only, and Dates Only. Setting Data Entry Input to Labels Only for a block of cells means that anything entered into those cells will be automatically preceded by a label prefix. If the cells to which you applied the Labels Only setting already contain numbers or formulas entered as values, these contents retain their status. However, if you edit and then reenter one of these entries, it will be converted to a label.

The Dates Only setting helps avoid errors when entering date fields. Cells affected by the Dates Only setting accept dates typed in any of the standard date formats, which were described in Chapter 2. You do not have to press CTRL-SHIFT-D before entering a date in a Dates Only cell. The General setting is provided so that you can return cells to normal operation.

Data Functions and Data Tables

In the previous chapter, you saw how the Quattro Pro database functions help you analyze a collection of data organized as a database. In this section we review these functions in light of the database commands and look at how they can be used in combination with the Data | What-If command.

Data Function Basics

The basic operation of a database function is to tell Quattro Pro which block of cells to act upon, which column of the block you want the function applied to, and which records to include in the calculation, based on the criteria table. For example, in cell H13 of Figure 6-19 the DSUM function adds up the sales for just those records specified by the criteria table, in this case where the entry in the Office column is Miami. All database functions have the same syntax. In the case of DSUM, it is

@DSUM(*Block,Column,Criteria*)

where *Block* is the cell block containing the database, including the field names at the top. *Column* is the number of the column containing the field you want to sum, with the first column of the database block as 0, the second as 1, and so on (in Figure 6-19 the column for Sales is 4). *Criteria* is a cell block containing search criteria.

Data Table Basics

The Data | What-If command allows you to create tables of results from a spreadsheet formula, based on a range of input values. You can see an example of this in Figures 6-20 and 6-21. In Figure 6-20 you can see the What-If dialog box with the necessary settings in place. In Figure 6-21 you can see the results created when the Generate button is pushed.

Cell F5 of the underlying spreadsheet in these figures contains the formula +C3*$F$3*1000. This is the formula that calculates commission, based on the sales value in C3 and the commission rate in F3 (together with the fact that sales are stated in thousands). The purpose of the table being created in cells F5..I14 is to show what commissions will be, based on a range of rates and a sample of sales levels. The row of cells in G5..I5

FIGURE 6-19 Using the DSUM function to sum a select group of records

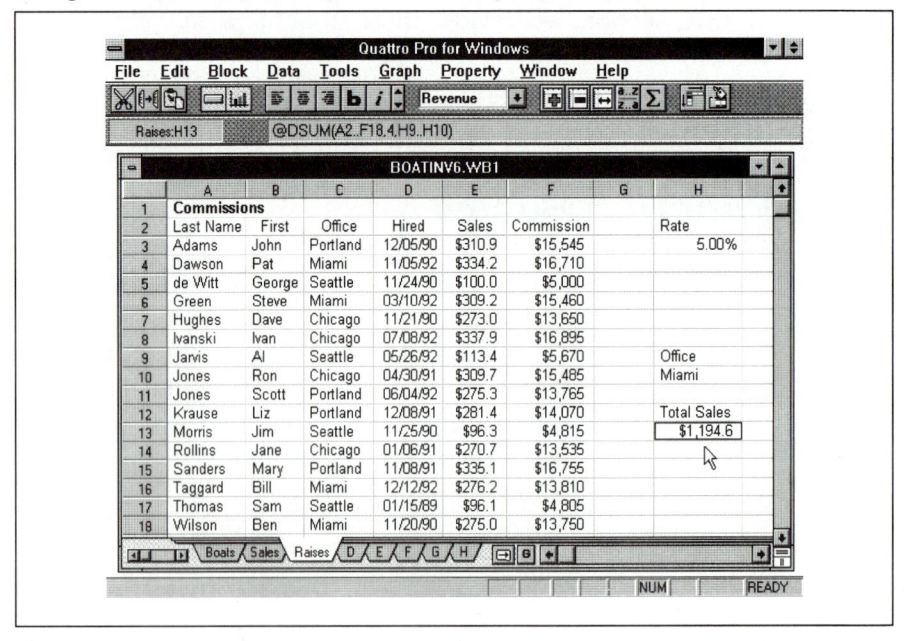

Chapter 6: Database Commands

FIGURE 6-20 A spreadsheet set up to tabulate possible commissions

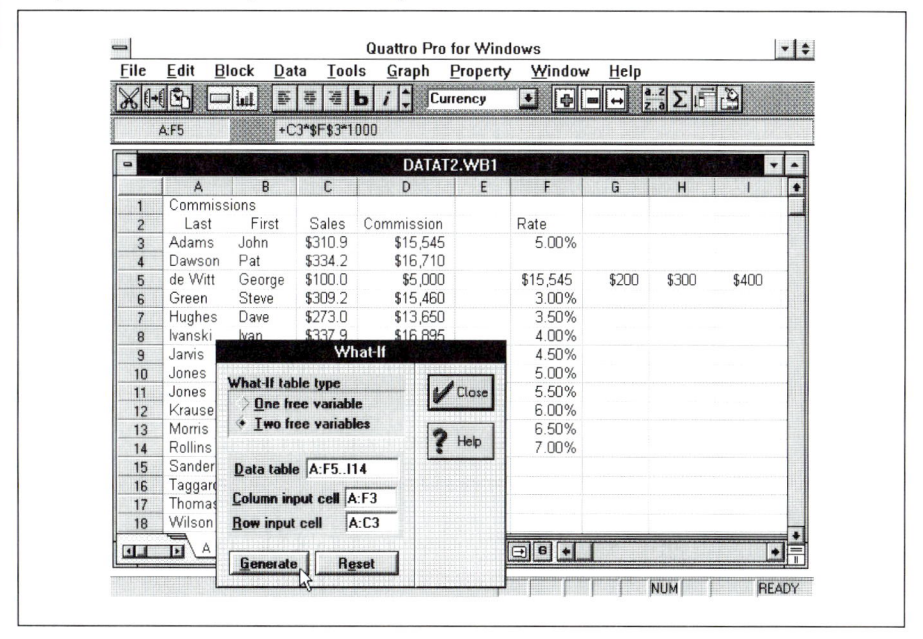

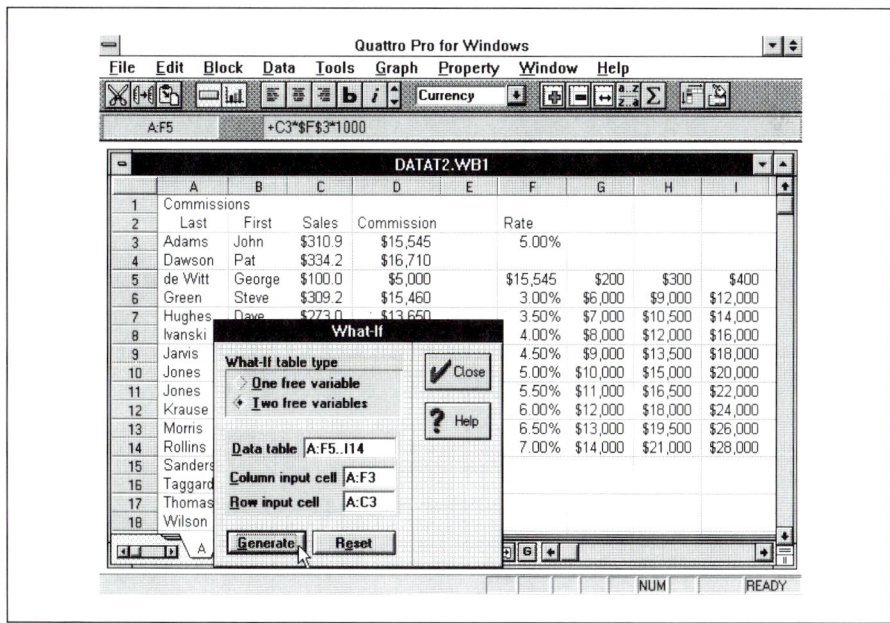

FIGURE 6-21 A table generated to show commissions based on a range of rates and sales values

contains sample values for sales, from $200 to $400. The column of cells in F6..F14 contains a range of numbers that can be used for a commission rate.

In the What-If dialog box, the block F5..I14 is defined as the Data table. The Two free variables option is selected so that there are two input cells. The Column input cell is F3, which means that when the Generate button is pushed, the rates in the left column of the table will be fed into cell F3. At the same time, the row of sales values will be fed into C3, the Row input cell. The resulting calculations are placed in the appropriate cell of the table. This shows you that, for example, sales of $300 (thousand) earn a commission of $15,000 if the rate is 5.00%.

Data Cross-Tabulation

You can combine the What-If feature with database functions to perform cross–tabulations of database information. For example, given the database shown on the left of Figure 6-22, you might want to know the total sales broken down by office. To do this, you first create a list of the categories by which you want the results broken down, in this case, the four offices. You can see that these have already been entered in G8..G11 in Figure 6-22, in alphabetical order.

This list of office names will be the column input for the What-If command. Above the column that will contain the results of the What-If command, you enter the formula that you want to calculate. In this case the formula is located in H7 and reads

@DSUM(A2..E18,2,G2..G3)

The first block is the database. The number 2 represents the column in the database to which you want the DSUM function applied, in this case the Sales column. The block G2..G3 is the criteria table that will be used to determine the results.

You will note that G2 contains the heading Office. This means that Quattro Pro will feed each of the column of values from the data table (G8..G11) into G3, one after another, and the @DSUM function will look each one up under the Office heading in the database. When a match is found the corresponding value from column 2 is added to the sum. The

Chapter 6: Database Commands 349

FIGURE 6-22 Preparing to cross-tabulate sales by office

```
                    Quattro Pro for Windows
File  Edit  Block  Data  Tools  Graph  Property  Window  Help

A:H7              @DSUM(A2..E18,2,G2..G3)

                        DATAT2.WB1
      A        B       C       D        E         F      G          H
1   Commissions
2   Last     First   Sales   Office   Hired            Office
3   Adams    John    $310.9  Portland 12/05/90
4   Dawson   Pat     $334.2  Miami    11/05/92
5   de Witt  George  $100.0  Seattle  11/24/90
6   Green    Steve   $309.2  Miami    03/10/92                 Total Sales
7   Hughes   Dave    $273.0  Chicago  11/21/90                    $3,994
8   Ivanski  Ivan    $337.9  Chicago  07/08/92         Chicago
9   Jarvis   Al      $113.4  Seattle  05/26/92         Miami
10  Jones    Ron     $309.7  Chicago  04/30/91         Portland
11  Jones    Scott   $275.3  Portland 06/04/92         Seattle
12  Krause   Liz     $281.4  Portland 12/08/91
13  Morris   Jim     $96.3   Seattle  11/25/90
14  Rollins  Jane    $270.7  Chicago  01/06/91
15  Sanders  Mary    $335.1  Portland 11/08/91
16  Taggard  Bill    $276.2  Miami    12/12/92
17  Thomas   Sam     $96.1   Seattle  01/15/89
18  Wilson   Ben     $275.0  Miami    11/20/90
```

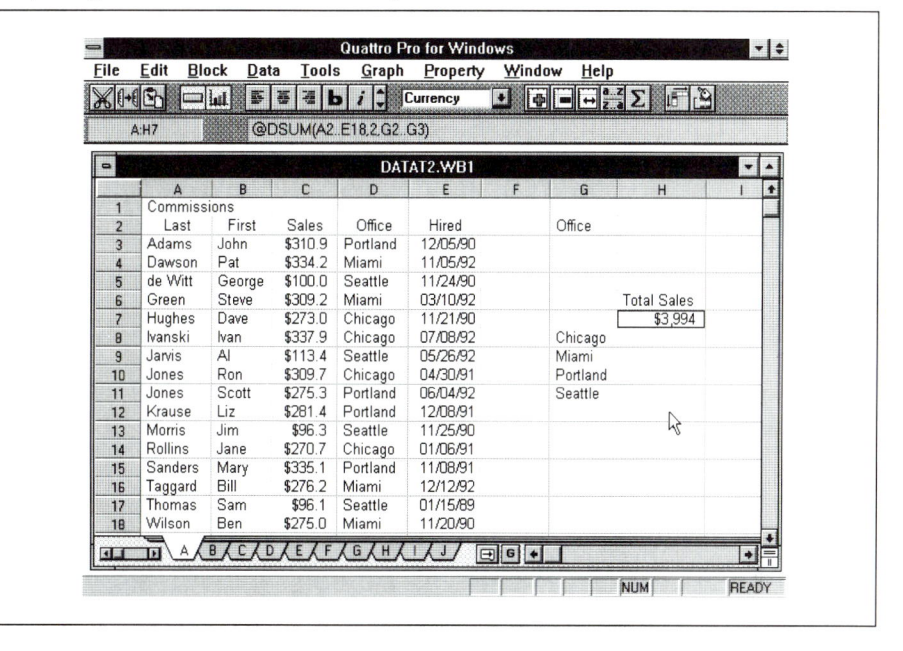

result that you see in H7 in Figure 6-22 reflects the total sales for all offices, since there is no entry in G3 (an empty criteria tells Quattro Pro to select all items).

The label in H6 is merely cosmetic, describing the items below it (there is no need for this label and no need for it to match the heading used in the database and criteria table). When the What-If dialog box is completed, as shown in Figure 6-23, and the Generate command is issued, the results appear as shown in Figure 6-23.

You can expand this type of operation to include a second variable. For example, earlier in this chapter you saw an inventory database listing yachts for sale. You can cross-tabulate this list to show the value of yachts for sale, categorized by type of boat and location. In Figure 6-24 you can see the inventory listing and, below it, the results of just such a cross-tabulation.

To perform this cross-tabulation, there are two columns in the criteria table (Mooring and Category). The criteria table is referred to by the formula at the top left of the table, in cell A20. The formula is located above the column input values and to the right of the row input values.

350   Quattro Pro for Windows Inside & Out

FIGURE 6-23   The completed What-If settings and resulting cross-tabulation

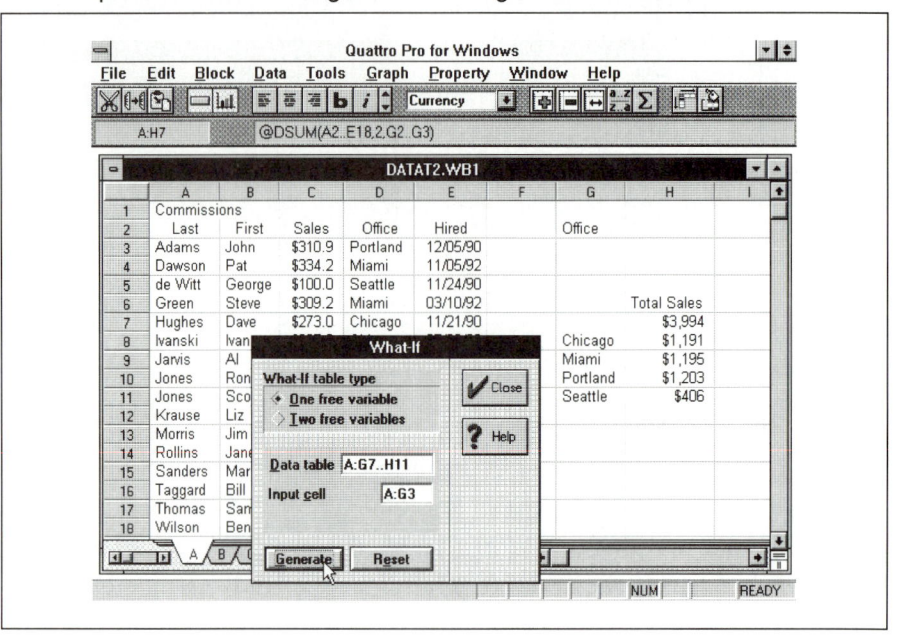

FIGURE 6-24   Cross-tabulating an inventory list by category and mooring

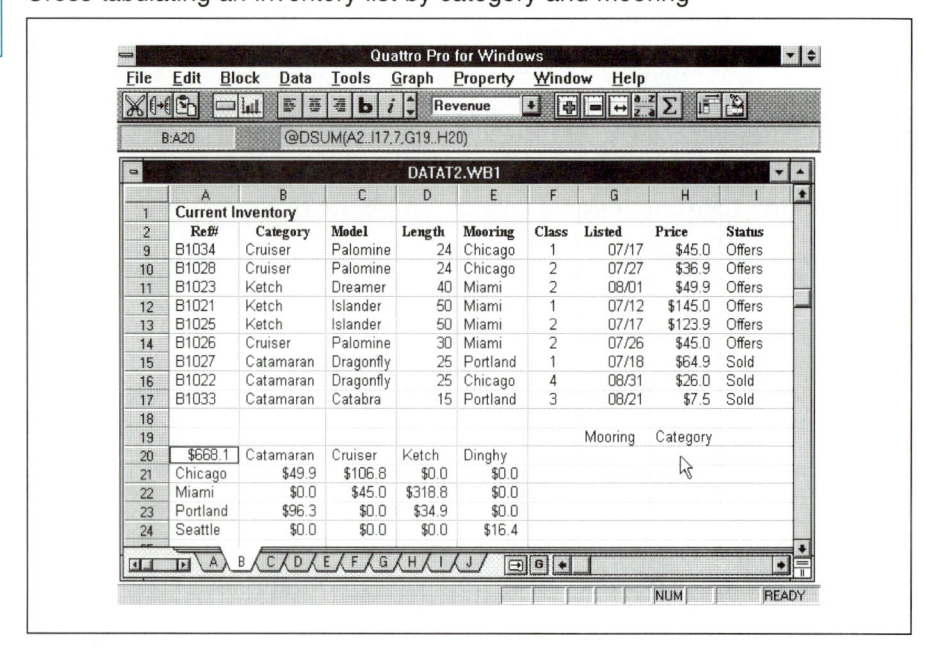

When the Data | What-If command is issued, the table and input cells are identified as shown here:

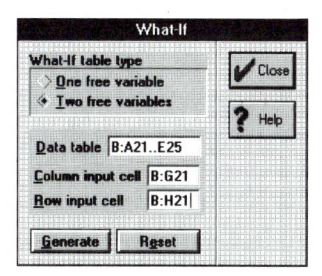

The names of the four different moorings are passed through cell G21, while the four categories are passed through H21. The resulting table is a very useful breakdown of the values in the database.

When you use the What-If command for database cross-tabulation, you have to format the results yourself, since they do not automatically use the same format as the corresponding values in the database. Furthermore, the spelling of field names and labels used as input values must be accurate. Also note that in Figure 6-24, part of the inventory list (rows 3-7) has been scrolled off the top of the screen, but the field names are still visible. This effect is achieved by use of the Window | Locked Titles command, described in the next chapter.

CHAPTER 7

Views, Titles, and Defaults

By now you can see that Quattro Pro makes numerous assumptions about how you want the program to look and behave. In this chapter we review these assumptions, known as *default settings*, and tell you how to change them. We also look at how to create custom numeric formats that can save a lot of time when you need to work with unusual units of measure, such as foreign currency or bits and bytes. However, we begin by looking at some of the commands and strategies you can use to improve your view of notebooks.

Viewing Options

In the course of using larger models, like the one in Figure 7-1, you will want to use some of the viewing options that Quattro Pro provides. The model in Figure 7-1 records monthly revenue and expenses for four different offices for a one-year period, totaled by year and month. The model extends from A1 to P71, so only a portion of the page can be seen at one time.

You have already seen that the Zoom Factor, described at the end of Chapter 2, allows you to shrink the spreadsheet in order to fit more columns and rows in the notebook window (the notebook in Figure 7-1 is being viewed with a Zoom Factor of 90%). Quattro Pro also provides several commands that allow simultaneous viewing of two parts of the same spreadsheet. In addition, you can lock parts of a model so that they do not move and thus will act as column and row headings. By turning on or off various window attributes you can adjust the display for different uses.

In Chapter 3 you saw that the Open and New commands (on the File menu) create additional notebook windows without replacing notebooks that are already open. This allows you to have several different notebooks available in the work area. Quattro Pro has several commands that help you manage multiple notebooks and organize the work area.

Chapter 7: Views, Titles, and Defaults 355

FIGURE 7-1 The Window menu displayed over a large notebook

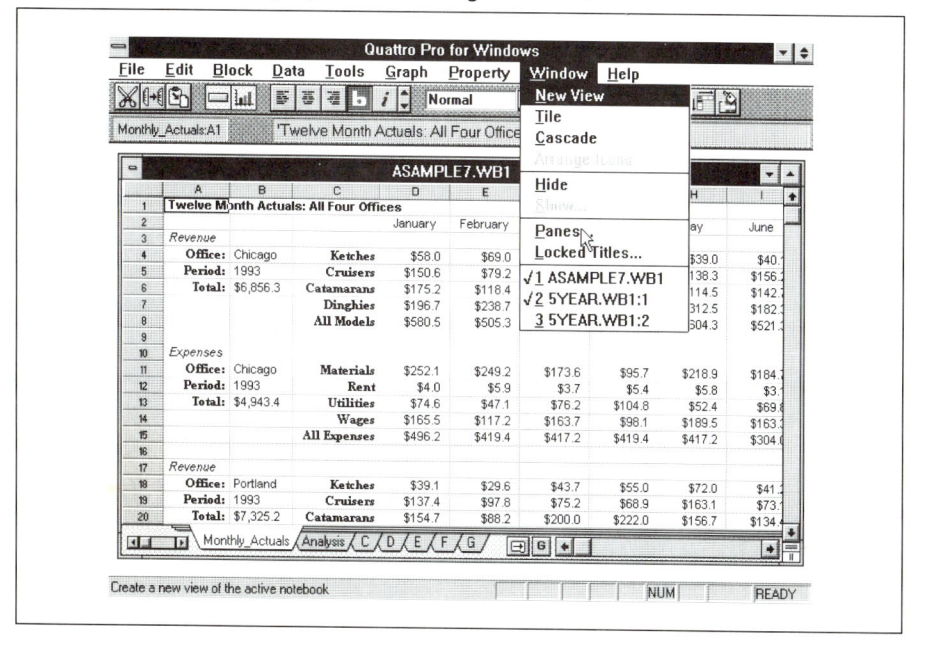

The Window Menu

In Figure 7-1 you can see the Window menu dropped down. At the bottom of the menu is a list of open windows. There is one entry for each notebook unless you have created more than one view or window for the same notebook, in which case each one is listed (more on multiple views in a moment). In Figure 7-1 there are two windows listed for the notebook called 5YEAR.WB1. The currently active window is indicated in the list by a check mark.

When you want to make a different window active, you can select the window from the Window menu. The window is then displayed above the other windows. The windows are numbered in the Window menu according to the order in which they were opened. The number is underlined so you can use it to select the window (for example, in Figure 7-1 pressing ALT-2 will select 5YEAR.WB1:1). You can also move between windows by pressing CTRL-F6. If you keep pressing this key, you will cycle through all available windows.

Hide and Show

The term "all available windows" is used because you can open a window and then hide it. For example, you might have macros or special formulas stored in a notebook that you need to access but do not want to display. You open the notebook and then issue the Window | Hide command. This removes the notebook from view and from the list of windows in the Window menu. You cannot even get to the notebook with the CTRL-F6 key. However, you can use values from hidden notebooks in formulas and you can use macros stored in hidden notebooks.

If you want to view or edit a hidden notebook, you must first use the Window | Show command to reveal it. You will note that this command is unavailable (the letters are gray) in the Window menu in Figure 7-1. This is because there were no hidden windows at the time the menu was displayed. When you issue the Show command, you are presented with the dialog box shown in Figure 7-2. Select the window that you want to reveal from the list provided and choose OK. The window is revealed and becomes the current window. Note that you can only select one window at a time from the Hidden Windows list.

Minimize and Maximize

In Figure 7-2 you can see that the ASAMPLE.WB1 window has been reduced in size. This reveals two notebook icons in the work area. These represent minimized notebook windows. Minimizing or turning a notebook window into an icon is one way of tidying up the work area without closing notebooks. You use the down arrow Minimize button on the right of the window title bar to turn a window into an icon. Keyboard users can press ALT-- to activate the window control menu and select Minimize, as shown here:

Chapter 7: Views, Titles, and Defaults 357

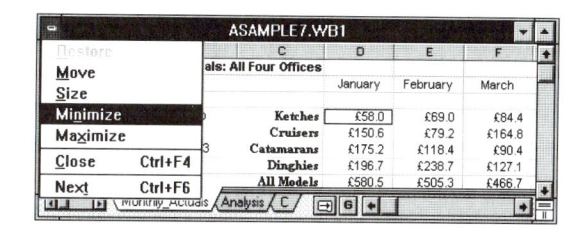

You double-click on a minimized notebook icon to restore it to a window or select Restore from the window control menu (this item is shaded in the menu above to show it is only active when the window has been minimized). Note that you can use the Next command on the same menu to activate the next window instead of pressing CTRL-F6. You can also move to minimized windows via the Windows menu. You can still use values and macros stored in "iconized" notebooks but the notebooks take up less work space.

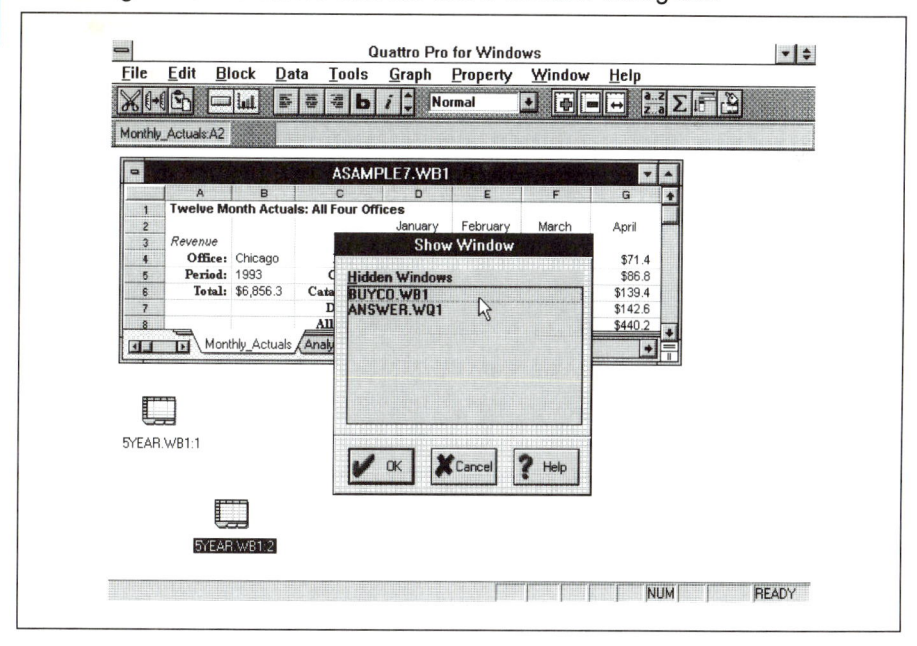

FIGURE 7-2 Revealing hidden windows with the Show Window dialog box

Window Arrangements

The Move and Size commands on the window Control menu are used to alter the shape and position of windows within the work area. The Move command can be used to move a notebook icon within the work area or it can be dragged with the mouse. Of course, you can also move an open notebook window by dragging its title bar. You can size a notebook window by dragging the window borders or the window corners. You can click on the Maximize button on the far right of a notebook window title bar to expand the window so that it fills the work area (several notebooks were displayed this way in Chapter 5). When a notebook window is maximized, a Restore button appears on the right of the menu bar. Click it to return the window to its "pre-maximized" dimensions.

When you have a number of notebook icons in the work area, you can use the Window | Arrange Icons command to put them in orderly rows (this command works just like the Window | Arrange Icons command in the Windows Program Manager). Two other commands that appear on the Window menu in both Quattro Pro and Program Manager are Cascade and Tile. In Quattro Pro, these commands are used to arrange windows within the work area. In Figure 7-3 you can see the result of using the Window | Cascade command. Two notebooks are stacked one in front of the other starting in the top left of the work area. Note that there are also two notebook icons at the bottom of the work area. Neither the Cascade nor the Tile command affects windows that are minimized. Hidden windows are not affected either.

Note that the window on top of the stack is the one that was active when the Cascade command was issued. A similar rule applies when you use the Tile command, the effects of which can be seen in Figure 7-4. The ASAMPLE7.WB1 window was active when the Tile command was issued, so it gets the top-left position within the tile arrangement and remains the active window. The Tile command is useful when you want to get a quick look at a lot of different windows, but it works better if you have a large monitor and run Windows at higher resolution (the view in Figure 7-4 is from a 640 × 480 display).

Remember that you can use the File | Workspace | Save command to store an arrangement of notebook windows. Workspace files use the WBS extension and contain the names of the open notebooks and their

Chapter 7: Views, Titles, and Defaults

FIGURE 7-3 The arrangement of open notebook windows created with <u>C</u>ascade

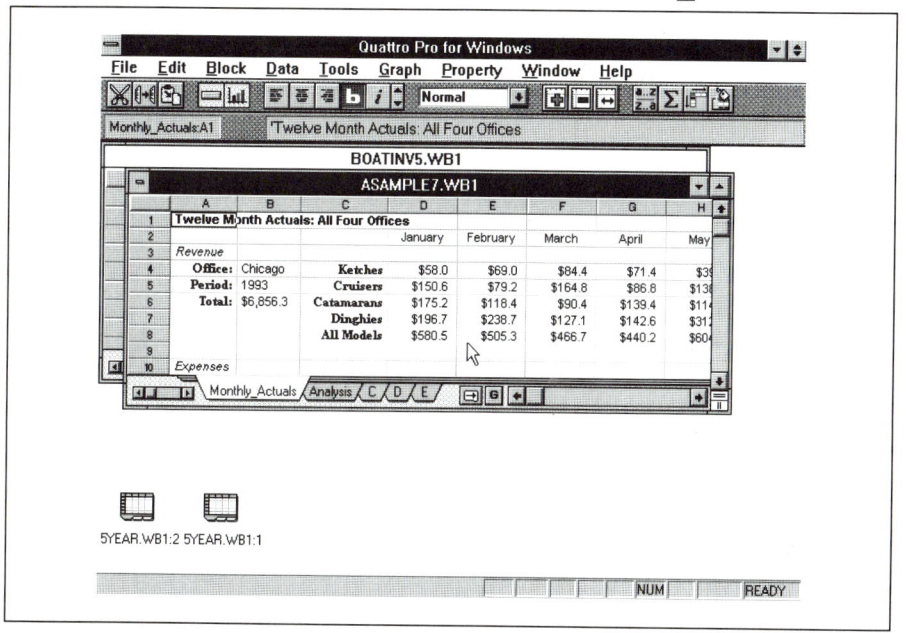

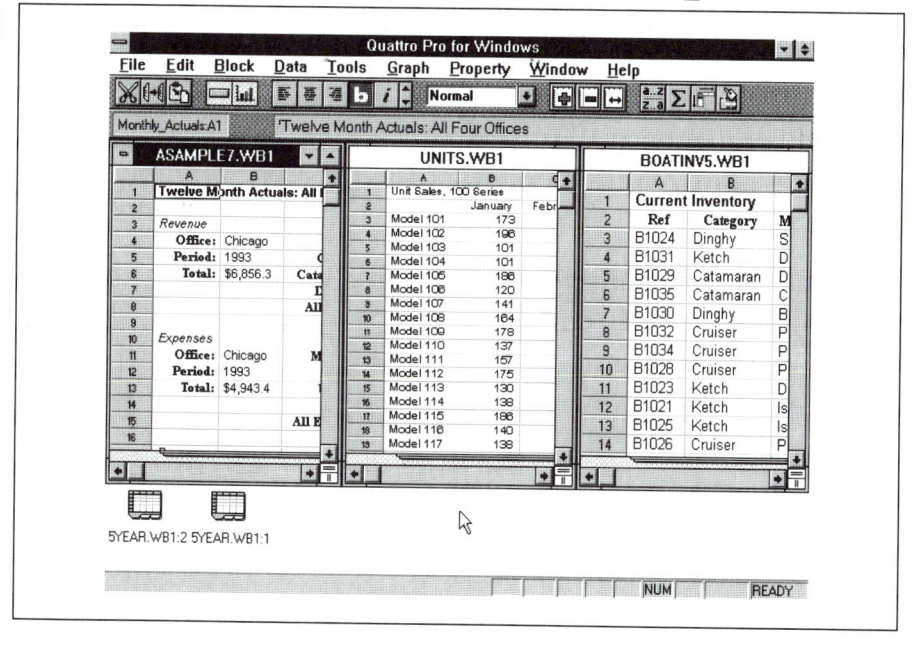

FIGURE 7-4 The arrangement of open notebook windows created with <u>T</u>ile

window sizes and locations. When you issue the File | Workspace | Restore command and select a workspace file, the requisite notebooks are opened with their window arrangements as they were when the workspace file was saved. Note that workspace files will not restore notebooks as icons. Notebooks that were icons when the workspace was saved will be restored as open windows.

New Views

The first item on the Window menu is New View. When you select New View, Quattro Pro opens a fresh window on the current notebook. Initially this window appears on top of what was the current window. The new window is numbered in the title bar, so that, for example, the first new view of the notebook called ASAMPLE7.WB1 is called ASAMPLE7.WB1:2 while the original view has ":1" added to its title. In previous figures you have seen two windows for the 5YEAR.WB1 notebook.

After opening a new view, you can use the normal Windows control techniques to position the new window according to your needs. For example, in Figure 7-5 the second window is being used to view the revenue for all offices at the bottom of the model, while the first window shows the revenue for the Chicago office at the top of the model. Note that selecting a different area of the notebook in one view does not affect the view in the other window.

You can see from Figure 7-5 that the Zoom Factor in the new window differs from the original window. The Zoom Factor is set separately for each new view of the same notebook (window 1 is 90%, while window 2 is 100%; new views always start out at 100%). However, you can make changes to data or active block properties from any view of the notebook and the notebook will be updated in all other views.

To close a view of a notebook you simply double-click the Control button at the left of its window title bar or press CTRL-F4. Quattro Pro will not ask you to save changes to the notebook unless the view you are closing is the only view of the notebook. In that case, CTRL-F4 is the same as File | Close. However, if you use Close when there are several views of the same notebook in the work area, all views are closed at once.

FIGURE 7-5 A second view opened on the same notebook

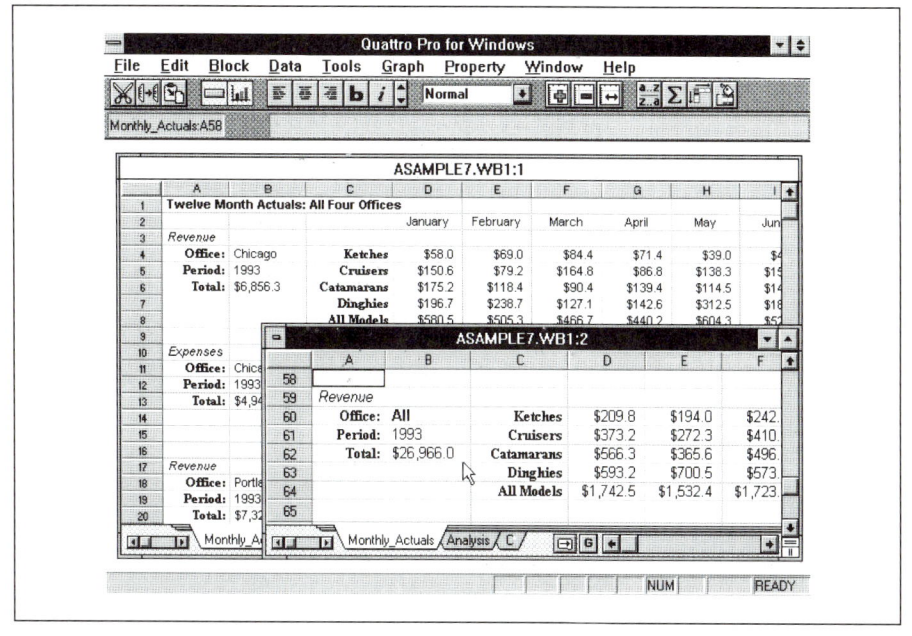

Window Panes

An alternative to opening a new view of a notebook is to split a single view, either horizontally or vertically, into two parts, called *panes*. In each pane you can view a different part of the spreadsheet. You can synchronize the panes so that moving the cell selector in one pane scrolls the view in the other one. Alternatively, you can remove this synchronization to adjust each pane independently of the other.

There are two ways to access the pane feature. You can use the pane handles or menu commands. The pane handles are located in the bottom-right corner of the notebook window frame. The vertical pane handle is a pair of vertical lines, while the horizontal pane handle is a pair of horizontal lines. If you grab one of these handles with the mouse and drag it onto the notebook, you will see a dotted line appear and the mouse pointer change to a double-headed arrow, as shown in Figure 7-6.

In this case it is the vertical pane handle that has been dragged onto the notebook. The dotted line indicates where the split between panes

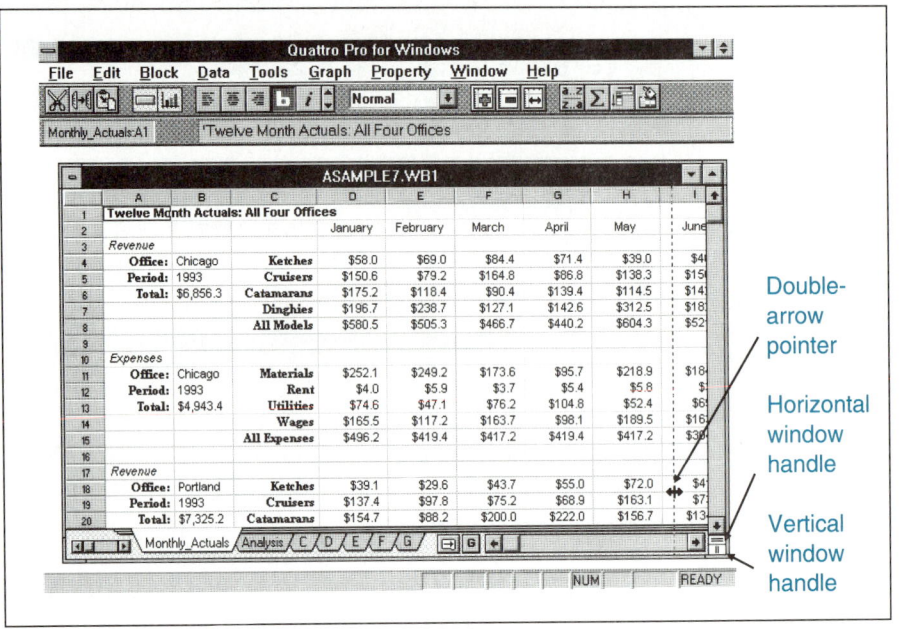

FIGURE 7-6 Dragging the vertical pane handle to create a split window

will be placed. If the line is placed beneath the W of the notebook name in the window title bar, the split will appear as in Figure 7-7. Now you have two sets of column and row headings and two sets of scroll bars. Also note that there is now a vertical pane handle in the bottom-right corner of the left pane. This allows you to make further adjustments to the position of the pane or to remove it. You remove a pane by dragging the pane handle back to the bottom-right corner of the window. Note that you cannot split the window into more than two panes—you cannot add a horizontal split while you have a vertical split in place.

Before looking at how you use window panes, we will describe how you create them using an alternative to the pane handles: the Window | Panes command. Before you issue this command, you must select the cell at which you want the split to appear. Vertical splits are created to the right of the current cell and horizontal splits are created above the current cell. When you issue the Panes command, you are presented with the following dialog box, the first two options on which are Horizontal and Vertical:

Chapter 7: Views, Titles, and Defaults

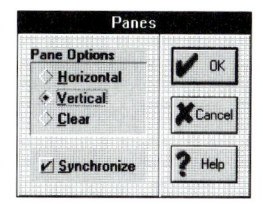

These options correspond to the horizontal and vertical pane handles. First select the type of split you want and then choose OK. You select the third option, Clear, when you want to remove panes from the window.

The Synchronize option allows you to switch between the default of synchronized panes and the alternative, unsynchronized panes. Unsynchronizing the panes has an effect on how the two sides of the panes react when you are navigating the notebook. With a vertical split and the panes synchronized, pressing UP ARROW or DOWN ARROW eventually moves the spreadsheet up and down *on both sides of the split*. You will see that the row numbers of the right-hand pane match those of the left-hand pane. With a horizontal split, synchronization means that RIGHT ARROW

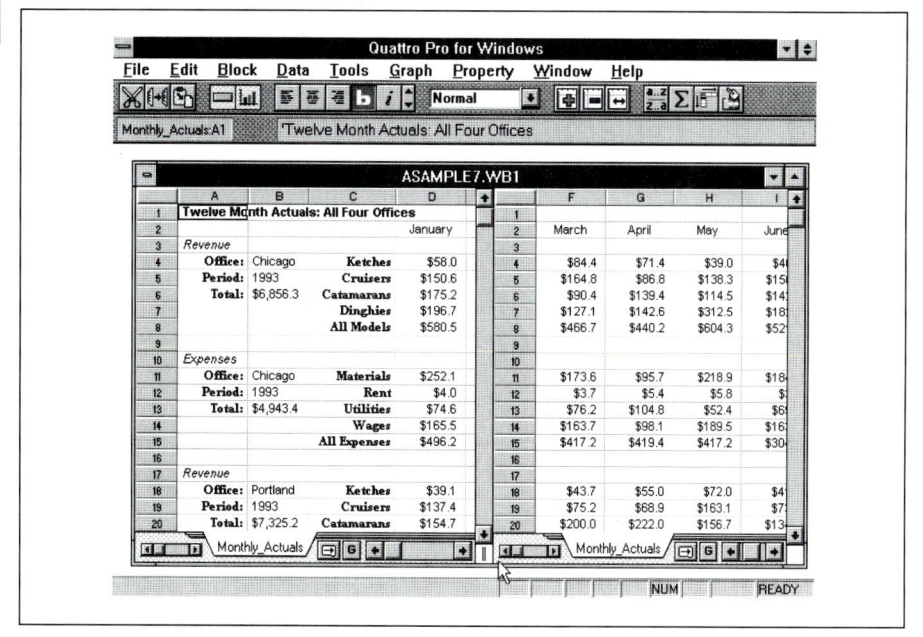

FIGURE 7-7 A vertical split producing two panes within the same window

or LEFT ARROW move the top and bottom panes in unison, with the column letters below the dividing line matching those in the top border.

If you uncheck Synchronize before you choose OK in the Panes dialog box, the effect is to allow the views within the two panes to be adjusted independently. For example, in Figure 7-8 you can see that the right-hand pane contains the bottom-left corner of the model, while the left-hand pane contains the top of the model. This allows you to change values at the beginning of the model and see the effects in the grand total.

Note that you have to use Window | Panes if you want to alter the synchronization of panes. However, if panes are already in place when the command is issued, using the Panes dialog box to adjust synchronization will not alter the location of the split. You can move the cell selector between the two sides of a split window by pressing the Windows key, F6, or clicking in the pane you want to activate.

Also note that establishing a synchronized split does not stop you from moving between notebook pages. Moving to another page in one pane does not move you to the same page in the other pane. However, if vertically split panes are synchronized and are displaying different pages,

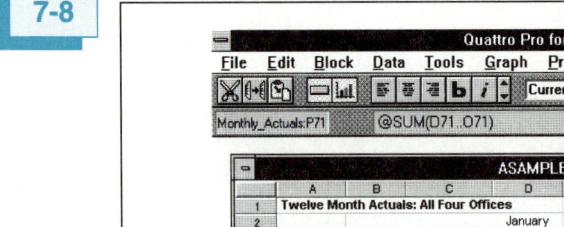

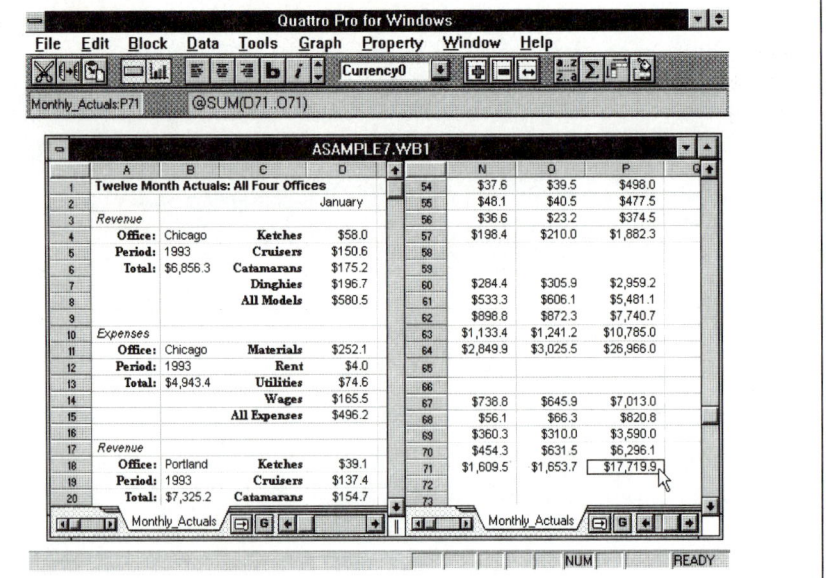

FIGURE 7-8

When panes are not synchronized, you can scroll one side and not the other moving up and down the rows of one page will move you up and down on the other page as well. Similarly, if the window is split horizontally, movement across columns will be synchronized.

Titles

Unfortunately, as you can see from Figure 7-8, the column headings disappear when the right side of the notebook is moved down. This makes it hard to tell what the numbers represent. In fact, you may have found this to be a problem when working without panes. As you move away from A1, in a large model, the column and row labels disappear. This is particularly critical when you have to update cells in the middle of a large spreadsheet. The Quattro Pro solution is to *freeze* certain rows and columns as titles that will not disappear.

To freeze titles, place the cell selector in the first cell that is below and to the right of the area that you want to use as titles. When you use the Window | Locked Titles command, you get the dialog box shown in Figure 7-9. You can choose Horizontal, which freezes the area above the cell selector; Vertical, which freezes the area to the left of the cell selector; or Both, which locks areas above and to the left of the cell selector. Select Clear when you want to unlock titles.

When you make your choice and choose OK, you are returned to the spreadsheet. Now you can move around the model, and the locked column and/or row headings remain visible on screen, as shown in Figure 7-10, where the lower right of the model is being examined while the top-left section has been locked to remain visible. After you lock titles, pressing HOME takes you to the cell in which you performed the title lock (in Figures 7-9 and 7-10, that would be cell D3). Note that the mouse pointer in Figure 7-10 has been changed to a "no entry" sign. This happens whenever the mouse pointer is placed over the frozen title area, in this case all columns to the left of D and all rows above 3.

With the titles now in a "no go" area, you might wonder how you can make changes to the cells within the title area. You can do this by unlocking titles (Window | Locked Titles | Clear), or you can use the Goto key, F5. When you press F5, type the address of the title cell you want to edit, and press ENTER, the cell is brought out from the title area. Press F2 to edit the cell and press ENTER to place the cell contents back in the cell.

FIGURE 7-9 The Locked Titles dialog box

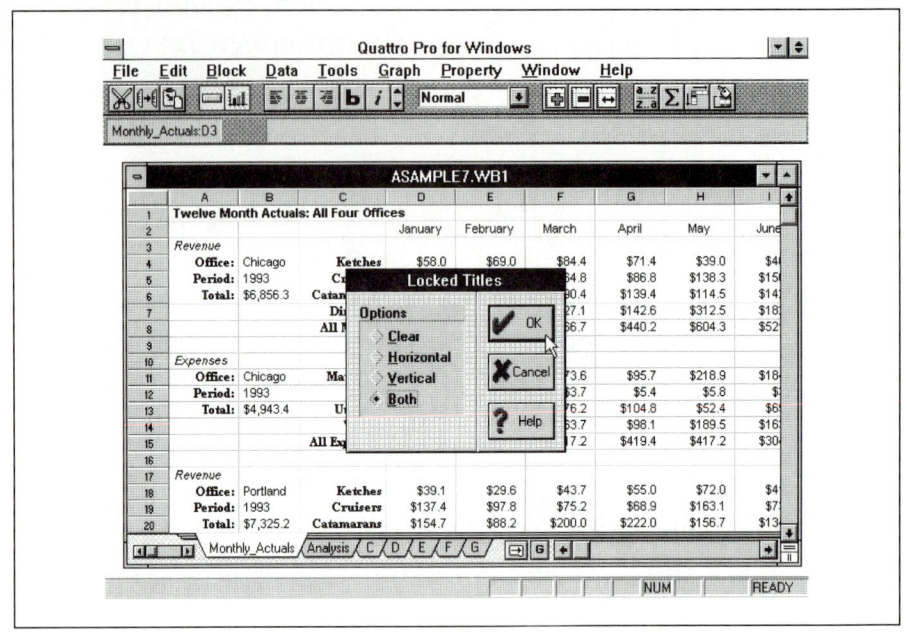

FIGURE 7-10 The effect of locking titles (note mouse pointer as "no entry" sign in title area)

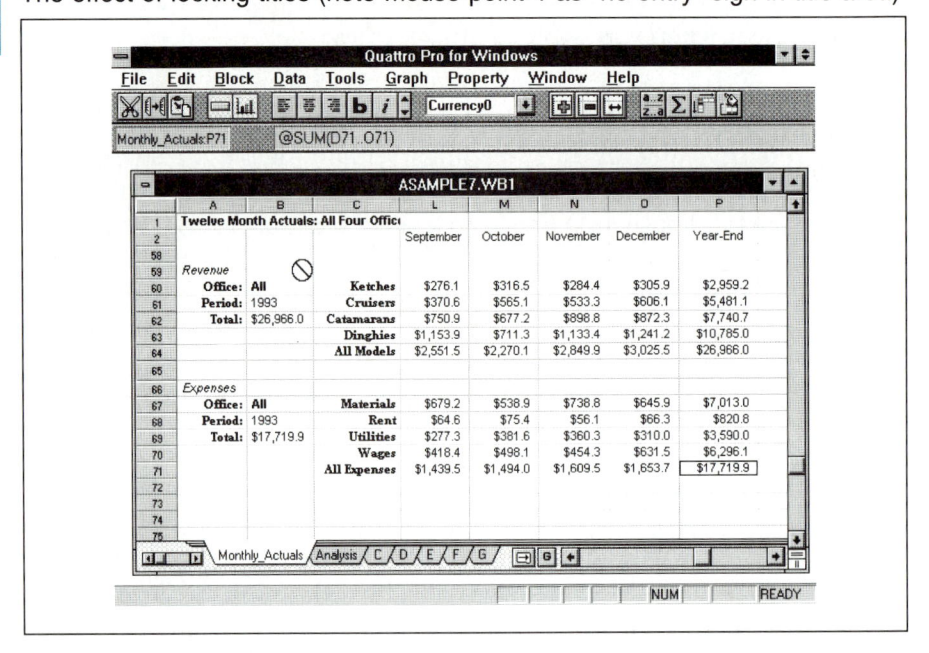

To put the updated title back into place on the screen, scroll the window by pressing PGDN and then TAB, and then press HOME.

Borders and Lines

In Figure 7-11 you can see a different view of a Quattro Pro notebook. First of all, the notebook was maximized to fill the work area. Then the column lettering and row numbering were removed with the Borders setting in the Active Page dialog box. This allows you to see more cells displayed on your screen, an attractive option when you want to emphasize the content of a spreadsheet rather than the mechanics of its operation—for example, when you are using Quattro Pro to give computer-based presentations.

Further adjustments were made to create the special view in Figure 7-11. The Grid Lines setting in the Active Page dialog box was used to turn off the column and row grid lines. When you do this the current cell,

FIGURE 7-11 A substantially altered view of a notebook

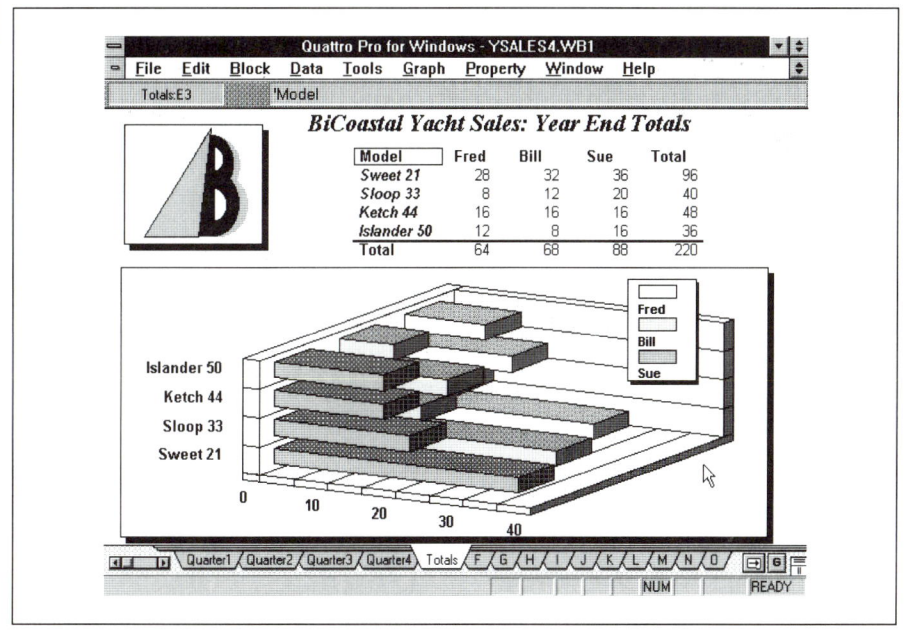

in this case, Totals:E3, is marked with a simple box, and you can use the cell identifier to confirm location. Note that the vertical scroll bars were turned off with the Display settings in the Active Notebook and the Display section of the Application settings was used to hide the SpeedBar. In the following sections you can read how the page, notebook, and application settings are used to customize Quattro Pro.

Levels of Defaults

A computer program's defaults are what the program does unless you tell it to do something differently. Most programs have defaults of one kind or another because the program has to make some basic assumptions about how you will be using it. For example, most word processing programs arrange text between margins and tabs, and so they begin with default margin and tab settings. In the same way, Quattro Pro has default column and format settings that determine how wide the columns will be and how numbers will be displayed.

The default settings in Quattro Pro are controlled at several levels. At the top level are Application settings such as whether Undo is enabled and how the outer area of the screen should look. Changing these settings affects all work with the program, regardless of the settings in the individual notebook files you load. Changes to these settings are automatically stored in the Quattro Pro program files so that they remain in effect from one session to the next.

Below Application settings are Notebook settings. These control such things as the calculation and appearance of a single notebook. These settings are stored in the notebook file. Changes to these settings do not affect other notebooks. The next level down is the Active Page, where the settings control details such as page name and default column width. These settings affect the currently selected page or pages.

At the lowest default level, settings are determined by the Active Block dialog box, which has been described extensively in earlier chapters. These settings affect specific cells and are used to vary them from the Active Page settings. In the next three sections we will review the Application, Notebook, and Active Page settings. This will give you a clearer picture of how the different levels work together to give you the working conditions and notebook appearance you want.

Application Settings

To adjust the Application settings you issue the Property | Application command or right-click on the program title bar. You can also press the shortcut key ALT-F12. All three actions present the compound dialog box shown in Figure 7-12. The first page of settings pertains to Display. Remember that you can use CTRL-PGDN to move down through the pages of a compound dialog box and CTRL-PGUP to move up through the pages.

> **Note** You can also get to the Application dialog box by right-clicking on the blank work area behind notebooks

FIGURE 7-12 The first page of the Application dialog box

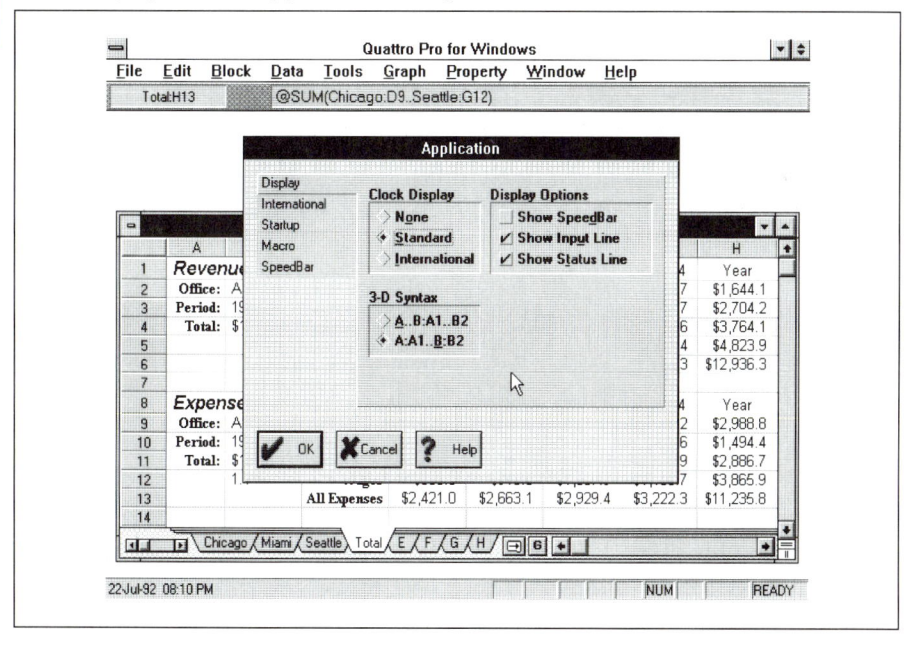

Display Settings

The Display settings allow you to adjust three areas of program operation: Clock Display, Display Options, and 3-D Syntax. When you first install Quattro Pro, the Clock Display setting is None, but if you select Standard or International, you get the current date and time displayed on the left of the status line at the bottom of the screen. You can see the Standard setting in Figure 7-12. The appearance of the date and time when you select International depends upon your choices in the Date Format and Time Format fields of the International page of the Application dialog box.

The Display options allow you to hide three different parts of the normal Quattro Pro screen. You can hide the SpeedBar, as in Figure 7-12, and also the input line and status line. Turning off these parts of the display gives you a larger work area, but can make normal operations rather difficult. For example, with no input line it is hard to edit cell entries. Typically, you will only want to hide the input line when running macros that offer alternative commands and methods of data input.

The 3-D Syntax setting controls how Quattro Pro displays the coordinates of blocks that extend across two or more pages. The normal setting is the first one, which states the range of pages followed by the range of cells. The alternative is to state cells with their pages, as in the second setting. To see how this works in practice, take a look at cell H13, which sums a 3-D block in the Total page in Figure 7-12 . The block is described using the second 3-D Syntax setting, as in

@SUM(Chicago:D9..Seattle:G12)

If you use the first 3-D Syntax setting, the formula will state the block like this:

@SUM(Chicago..Seattle:D9..D12)

You can type 3-D references using either syntax, regardless of the 3-D Syntax setting. However, the setting determines how the references are displayed on the input line. Typically, the first setting takes up less room, particularly when it is referring to a 3-D compound block. For example, to sum B5..G9 on pages A, C, and E, the syntax under the first setting would be

@SUM(A,C,E:B5..G9)

Using the second setting the syntax for the same calculation would be

@SUM(A:B5..G9,C:B5..G9,E:B5..G9)

International Settings

The International page of the Application settings, shown in Figure 7-13, contains numerous options that allow Quattro Pro to match more closely the conventions used in countries other than the U.S.A. For example, the notebook in the background of Figure 7-13 is displaying values in British pounds sterling (£) instead of dollars.

In fact, Currency is just one of five areas in the list headed Selection, each of which can be adjusted to meet the needs of international users. In each of these five areas you can choose between Windows Default and a range of other settings. The Windows Default option is a great help for

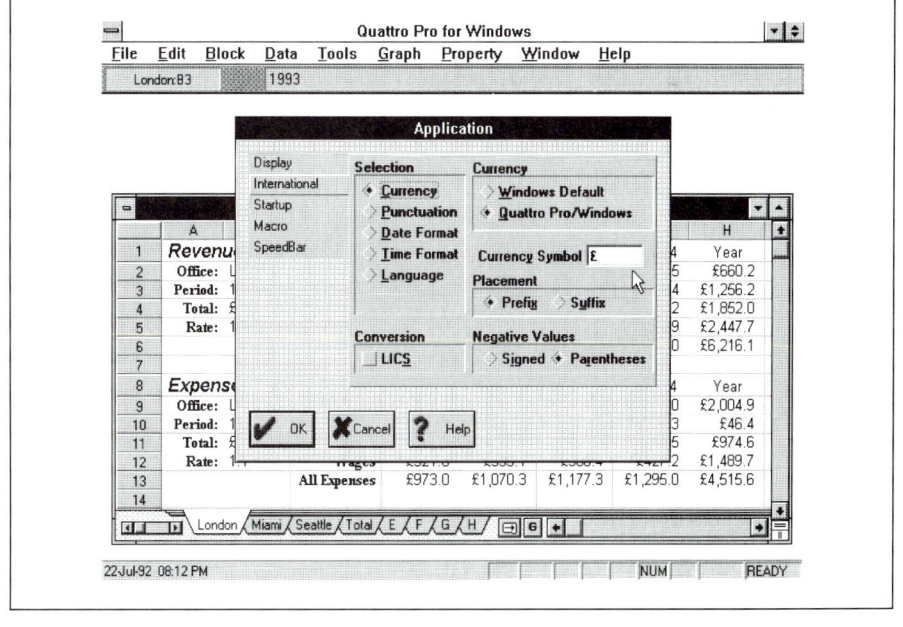

FIGURE 7-13 The International page of the Application dialog box

users who have already customized Windows using the International icon in the Control Panel. This allows you to specify your preferences for the following aspects of programs running under Windows: Country, Language, Keyboard Layout, Measurement, List, Date, Time, Currency, and Number.

If you have already made satisfactory changes using the Windows International icon you will probably want to choose Windows Default for all of the items in the Selection list on the International page of Quattro Pro's Application settings. However, there may be times when you want to vary a notebook from the normal settings, for example if you are an American user but need to present a bid for work in a foreign currency. There are two ways of coping with this scenario. You can either change the settings on Quattro Pro's International page or create a user-defined numeric format. The latter option, described at the end of this chapter, is often preferable because changing the International settings in the Application dialog box affects all notebooks that you open.

To understand this situation, suppose that you are an American user and you change the Currency Symbol from $ to £, as in Figure 7-13. Any notebook that you open that uses a standard currency format will display £ instead of $. However, if you create a user-defined format for pounds, you can display values with the £ sign in selected cells without affecting any other cells or notebooks (there are tips for typing foreign characters at the end of this chapter).

Listed below are all of the options, other than Windows Default, that are available under the five different Selection areas of Quattro Pro's International settings.

Punctuation

The Punctuation setting specifies the characters used to

- Separate thousands in numbers (for display only, usually a comma in North America)

- Designate a decimal separator in numbers (usually a period in North America)

- Separate arguments in @function statements and macro commands (usually a comma or semicolon)

Semicolons are always accepted as argument separators regardless of the Punctuation setting. Default Punctuation setting is to match the International Number Format settings in the Windows Control Panel. You can replace this with one of the alternatives:

1,234.56 (a1,a2)   1.234,56 (a1.a2)
1,234.56 (a1;a2)   1.234,56 (a1;a2)
1 234.56 (a1,a2)   1 234,56 (a1.a2)
1 234.56 (a1;a2)   1 234,56 (a1;a2)

where a1 represents the first argument and a2 represents the second argument in a macro command or @function.

Date Format

This setting specifies the international date formats given as options for date display. Default setting is to match the International Date Format settings in the Windows Control Panel. Choose one of the four formats, listed in long and short versions (the latter in parentheses). The format you choose appears (in both long and short form) as a choice in the Numeric Format property in the Active Block dialog box. The long version is used as the international clock setting:

MM/DD/YY (MM/DD) as in 12/25/93 and 12/25
DD/MM/YY (DD/MM) as in 25/12/93 and 25/12
DD.MM.YY (DD.MM) as in 25.12.93 and 25.12
YY-MM-DD (MM-DD) as in 93-12-25 and 12-25

Time Format

This setting specifies the international time formats given as options for time display. Default setting is to match the International Time Format settings in the Windows Control Panel. Choose one of the four formats, listed in long and short versions (the latter in parentheses). The format you choose appears (in both long and short form) as a choice in the Numeric Format property in the Active Block dialog box. The long version is used as the international clock setting (all international time settings use 24-hour formats (000 to 2359):

HH:MM:SS (HH:MM) as in 13:30:05 and 13:30
HH.MM.SS (HH.MM) as in 13.30.05 and 13.30
HH,MM,SS (HH,MM) as in 13,30,05 and 13,30
HHhMMmSSs (HHhMMm) as in 13h30m05s and 13h30m

Language

This setting changes the sort order to meet language requirements. By default, sorting is based on ANSI sort order, which places uppercase letters before lowercase and accented letters after the z's (A to Z; then a to z). Quattro Pro sort rules are compatible with those used in Borland SOR files and are compatible with other Borland products, such as Paradox. To change the sort order select the appropriate language from the list:

Danish	Icelandic
Dutch	Italian
English (American)	Norwegian
English (International)	Portugese
Finnish	Spanish
French	Spanish (Modern)
French Canadian	Swedish
German	

LICS Conversion: This setting determines whether Quattro Pro translates Lotus International Character Set (LICS) characters used in 1-2-3 WK1 spreadsheets into standard ANSI characters. If you check LICS Conversion and save the file, Quattro Pro writes these characters back to the LICS equivalents.

Startup Settings

The Startup page of the Application dialog box, shown in Figure 7-14, controls several important areas of program operation. You can set a default data directory, enable the Undo feature, and control actions that Quattro Pro performs when it is loaded.

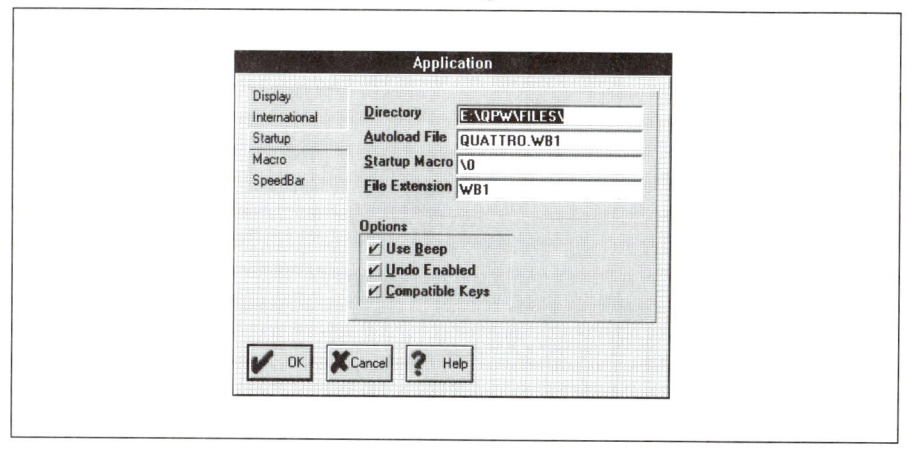

FIGURE 7-14 The Startup page of the Application dialog box

*D*irectory

As was mentioned in Chapter 4, the Directory setting on the Startup page of the Application dialog box tells Quattro Pro where to look for files you want to open and to save. In other words, this field provides a default working directory for Quattro Pro. You can still always use the Directories setting in the File dialog boxes to switch to a different directory.

If you do not make an entry in the Directory field but leave it blank, Quattro Pro will use the program directory (typically C:\QPW). Mixing data files and program files is not good data management practice, so you are well advised to create and use a separate directory for notebooks. If you have a lot of data files you should split them into a number of directories with suitable names.

If you are using Windows 3.1 or later, you might want to leave the Directory setting on the Startup page blank. This allows you to use the Program Item Properties setting in Windows to specify a working directory for Quattro Pro. In Figure 7-15 you can see three different icons set up for Quattro Pro. Each one starts the program with a different working directory. To set a working directory for a Windows program, select the program icon and press ALT-ENTER. This produces the Program Item Properties dialog box shown in Figure 7-15.

FIGURE 7-15 The Program Item Properties dialog box in Program Manager

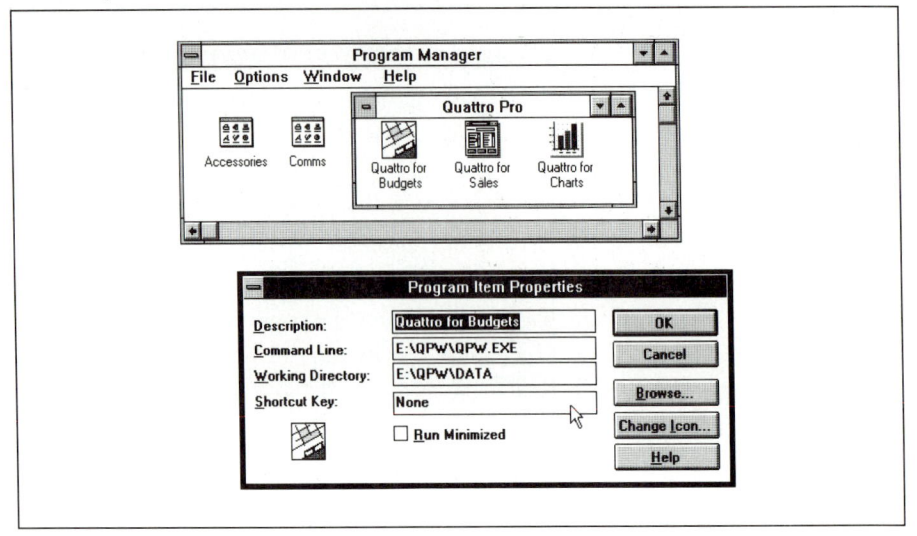

The title that appears under the icon is entered in the Description field. The program path and name are entered in the Command Line field. Most importantly, the Working Directory field is where you put the name of the directory that you want Quattro Pro to use as the default directory when this icon is used to load the program. Note that if you later enter a directory in the Directory field on Quattro Pro's Startup page, it will override the Working Directory setting in the Program Manager's icon settings.

Note To create a new icon for Quattro Pro using Windows 3.1's Program Manager, open the program group in which you want the icon to appear and then use the File | New command on the Program Manager menu. See that Program Item is checked and then choose OK. A blank Program Item Properties dialog box will appear. When you have entered the program name in the Command Line field, you can then select Change Icon to choose one of the many icons that are stored in the QPW.EXE program file.

Autoload File

If there is a notebook that you use every time you work with Quattro Pro, you can have the file loaded automatically when Quattro Pro is launched. Simply enter the name of the file in the Autoload File field of the Startup page or store the notebook using the default name, QUATTRO.WB1. If the autoload file is stored in the working data directory set on the Startup page, you need only enter the name of the file. If the file you want autoloaded is not in the working directory, you must include the full path to the file.

You can also get a file autoloaded by including it in the Command Line field of the Program Item Properties dialog box, described in the previous section and shown in Figure 7-15. For example, to load BUDGET.WB1, stored in E:\QPW\DATA\BUDGET.WB1, the entry in the Command Line field would be

E:\QPW\QPW.EXE E:\QPW\DATA\BUDGET.WB1

This approach requires that the full path to the file be stated.

Startup Macro

When you are working with macros you may want a macro to be run as soon as a notebook is opened. To do this, name the macro \0 (backslash zero) or name it something else, such as FIRST, and enter that name in the Startup Macro field. Any number of notebooks can contain a macro that has the same startup name. If you include a macro with the startup name in the autoload file you can set a whole series of events in motion simply by launching Quattro Pro.

File Extension

Normally, Quattro Pro stores files with the WB1 extension. However, as you will read in Chapter 8, it is possible to save files with different extensions in order to export data to other programs. If you want Quattro Pro to use a different extension all the time, change the WB1 entry in the File Extension field to the desired extension.

Use Beep

There are times when Quattro Pro beeps to warn you of an error. This is generally helpful, but if you want to do away with the beep, uncheck the Use Beep option. This option is handy when using Quattro Pro on a portable computer in a meeting or public place.

Undo Enabled

To make use of the very handy ability to undo commands you execute by mistake, you should make sure that the Undo Enabled setting is checked. This requires slightly more memory than operating without the ability to undo, but the feature is invaluable—unless you never make mistakes.

Compatible Keys

The Compatible Keys setting on the Startup page of the Application dialog box controls the use of certain keys when editing cells. When you first install Quattro Pro for Windows, the keystrokes used for editing are the same as those in the DOS version of the program and in other non-Windows spreadsheets, such as versions 2.*xx* and 3.*xx* of Lotus 1-2-3. For example, pressing DOWN ARROW when in EDIT mode returns you to READY mode and moves the cell selector down one cell, while simultaneously entering what you have been editing.

Obviously, some users will appreciate being able to use this "traditional" set of editing keys. For example, if both versions of Quattro Pro are used in the same office this degree of compatibility between them may well be helpful. However, if everyone in the office uses Windows-based programs, you might want to use the other set of editing keys provided by the Windows version of Quattro Pro. These keys more closely adhere to the editing conventions in Windows. They are listed in Table 7-1, which shows both sets of editing keys. Note that when the Compatible Keys option is checked, you get the DOS-style keys. When the option is unchecked you get Windows-style keys.

TABLE 7-1 Compatible Keys and the EDIT Mode

Key	Function
ESC	Exits EDIT mode, but if Compatible Keys is unchecked, it also erases the contents of the input line.
ENTER	Enters the data and exits EDIT mode regardless of Compatible Keys setting.
UP ARROW	Enters the data, exits EDIT mode, and moves up one cell. When the insertion point follows an operator in a formula, enters POINT mode. If Compatible Keys is unchecked, moves the insertion point up a line (with data wrapped on more than one line).
DOWN ARROW	Enters the data, exits EDIT mode, and moves down one cell. When the insertion point follows an operator in a formula, enters POINT mode. If Compatible Keys is unchecked, moves the insertion point down a line (with data wrapped on more than one line).
PGDN	Enters the data, exits EDIT mode, and moves down one screenful. When the insertion point follows an operator in a formula, enters POINT mode, regardless of Compatible Keys setting.
PGUP	Enters the data, exits EDIT mode, and moves up one screen. When the insertion point follows an operator in a formula, enters POINT mode, regardless of Compatible Keys setting.
BACKSPACE	Deletes characters to the left of the insertion point, regardless of Compatible Keys setting.
DEL	Deletes characters to the right of the insertion point, or the selected cell block or graph object, regardless of Compatible Keys setting.
CTRL-BACKSPACE	Erases the contents of the input line, regardless of Compatible Keys setting.
TAB/CTRL-RIGHT	Moves insertion point five spaces to the right, or, if Compatible Keys is unchecked, to the next word.
SHIFT-TAB or CTRL-LEFT	Moves five spaces to the left, or, if Compatible Keys is unchecked, to the previous word.

Macro Settings

The Macro page of the Application dialog box, shown in Figure 7-16, controls how macros work in Quattro Pro. These settings will be important if you do a lot of work with macros, which are described extensively later in this book. In their simplest form, macros are collections of keystrokes and commands that are executed by the user with a single keystroke.

The Macro Suppress-Redraw settings allow you to control what Quattro Pro does with the screen while a macro is executing. The default setting is Both, which means that the screen is not updated until the macro is completed. For example, if the setting is Both and you execute a macro that copies a label into a cell with the Block | Copy command, you will not see any of the steps involved, just the result. Because the program does not have to redraw the screen until the macro is over, the Both setting helps macros to run faster.

The Panel setting suppresses the redrawing of menus, dialog boxes, status line, and the input line, but allows the screen to redraw within the notebook window so that you can see changes to cells. This is helpful when you are designing macros and debugging them to correct mistakes. The Window setting suppresses redrawing within notebook windows but shows changes in menus and dialog boxes. The None setting means that all redrawing during macro execution is displayed—the slowest option.

FIGURE 7-16 The Macro page of the Application dialog box

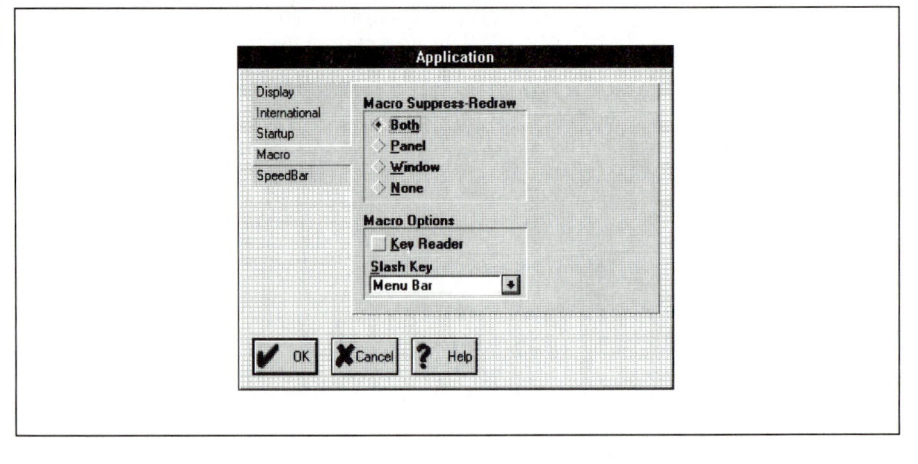

SpeedBar Settings

You have already seen that the Quattro Pro SpeedBar changes during certain operations. For example, new buttons are added when you are in EDIT mode. In the next chapter, you will see that a whole new SpeedBar is displayed when you are working with graphs. You can actually create your own SpeedBars, as described later in the book. You can display a secondary SpeedBar of your own design beneath the primary SpeedBar, as shown in Figure 7-17. Note that the primary SpeedBar in this figure looks different from the usual SpeedBar. This will be explained in a moment. The secondary SpeedBar in Figure 7-17 has several buttons on the left for file operations and some on the right for printing. A secondary SpeedBar like this gives you mouse access to a wider range of commands. Through the use of macro command language, the buttons on the SpeedBar can perform a wide range of functions.

To create a SpeedBar, you have to go to the Graphs page of a notebook (to get to the Graphs page, which comes after page IV, click the SpeedTab button, just to the right of the Group button on the bottom of the

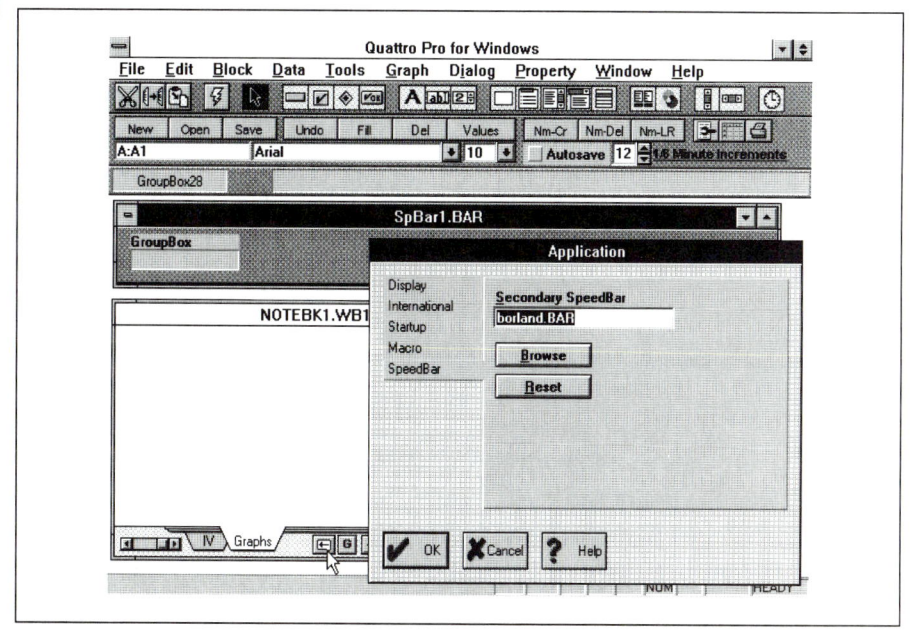

FIGURE 7-17 The SpeedBar page of the Application dialog box with sample SpeedBar added

notebook window). When you get to the Graphs page the selection of buttons on the primary SpeedBar changes to help you work on graphic objects. In Figure 7-17 you can see the Graphs page and a new SpeedBar being built. SpeedBars are stored separately from notebooks, in files with the BAR extension.

As you can see from Figure 7-17, the SpeedBar page of the Application dialog box allows you to name the Secondary SpeedBar that you want Quattro Pro to display. The Browse button allows you to search drives and directories for files with the BAR extension. The Reset button clears any name from the Secondary SpeedBar field so that when you choose OK, the secondary SpeedBar is removed. If you also use the Display page of the Application settings described earlier, you can hide the primary SpeedBar and just use the custom SpeedBar.

Active Notebook Settings

There are various aspects of Quattro Pro operations that can be varied by notebook. In other words, when you save a notebook, certain parameters are saved with it. These are independent of changes made to the Application settings. To adjust the Active Notebook settings, you issue the Property | Active Notebook command or right-click on the notebook title bar. You can also press the shortcut key SHIFT-F12. All three actions present the compound dialog box shown in Figure 7-18. The first page of settings is Recalc.

Note You must resave a notebook in order to record changes you make in the Active Notebook dialog box.

Recalc Settings

One of the great features of a spreadsheet is that you can enter numbers and formulas and immediately see the effect of changes. This feature is known as *automatic recalculation,* the constant rechecking of all cells affected by each new entry into the spreadsheet. However, such a powerful feature has its drawbacks: As your spreadsheet grows, the time taken for each new item to be checked against the other cells

FIGURE 7-18 The first page of the Active Notebook dialog box

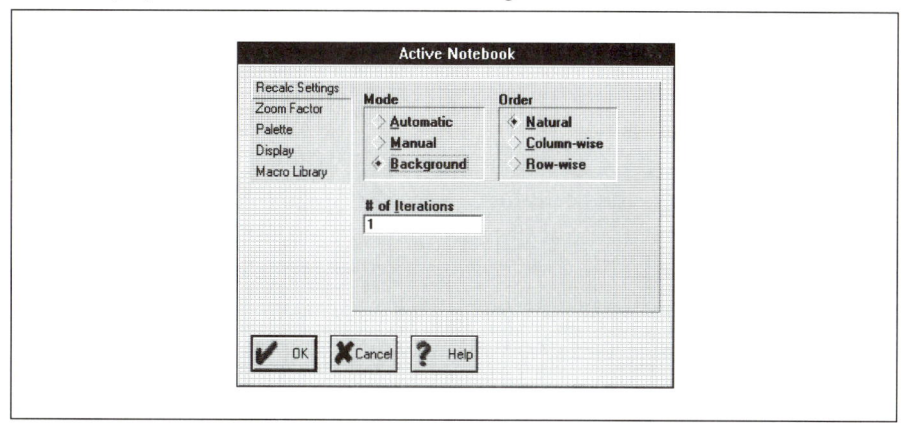

increases. This recalculation time can take so long that it slows down the entry of new data. To avoid this problem, Quattro Pro has an added feature called *background recalculation*. This enables you to carry on working while the program is recalculating in the background.

As you can see from Figure 7-18, you have three Mode options for the Recalc Settings in Quattro Pro: Automatic, Manual, and Background. Since Background mode does your math automatically while you work on other things, you may wonder what is the point of the other two choices. You use the Manual option when you do not want new spreadsheet entries or changes to old ones to affect other cells. This is valuable when you have a lot of data to enter into a large spreadsheet that is beginning to slow down Quattro Pro's response time. Time is saved because in Manual mode, the program does not check whether a newly entered formula affects other results on the spreadsheet.

Although Manual mode means that your spreadsheet is not always up to date, Quattro Pro has safeguards to prevent errors. Even when you are using Manual mode, the program will calculate a formula as it is entered. It will also recalculate formulas that are edited or copied. Although Quattro Pro will not update other cells when in Manual mode, it does know when you make changes to the spreadsheet. It reminds you that you have made changes that may affect the contents of other cells by displaying the CALC message on the status line. Whenever it is convenient, for example, after entering a new set of data, you can press the Calc key (F9), and Quattro Pro will perform a complete recalculation of the spreadsheet. The CALC message is then removed to let you know all changes have been accounted for.

If you use Manual mode, you should make sure that before you print, save, or make decisions based on the spreadsheet figures, you press the Calc key (F9). Otherwise, you may be working with inaccurate data. The Automatic recalculation setting is primarily used as an alternative to Background, the difference being that automatic mode will not let you proceed with further data entry until recalculation is complete.

The way in which Quattro Pro calculates your spreadsheet is based on the natural mathematical relationship between cells in formulas. This is referred to as *natural recalculation*. The least dependent cells are calculated first, on through to the most dependent. Earlier spreadsheet programs could only calculate row by row down the spreadsheet or column by column across. These methods were called row-wise and column-wise, respectively, but they were not always that "wise." For example, row-wise calculations can produce errors if row 5 is based on the outcome of a calculation in row 10. Users of these programs usually worked around this problem and produced spreadsheet models that worked correctly if they were calculated in the correct order, either by column or by row. As you can see from Figure 7-11, the Order options in the Recalc settings enable you to emulate these earlier programs, and so can accommodate spreadsheets designed to use these methods of calculation. Unless you know a specific reason why the spreadsheets you are working on will not be accurate unless calculated in a specific order, you will not need to change Order setting from the default of Natural.

Many of the problems of row-wise and column-wise calculations can be solved by repeating the calculation process a number of times. The repetition of calculation is called *iteration*. You can use the # of Iterations field on the Recalc settings page to repeat the recalculation process as many as 255 times each time you press F9. If you have selected Row-wise or Column-wise as the Order setting, you should set # of Iteration to at least 2 to avoid errors. If you are constructing complex financial formulas containing circular cell references that require a specific number of iterations to produce a correct answer, you can enter this number in the # of Iterations field.

If you are using natural recalculation, Quattro Pro refers to the iteration number only if you have circular references in the spreadsheet.

As you can see from Figure 7-19, the Recalc page of the Active Notebook dialog box tells you the location of a circular cell reference in the spreadsheet if you have the CIRC message in the status line at the bottom of the screen. The CIRC message means you have entered a formula into a cell that uses the result of the cell to solve the formula. For example, in Figure 7-19 the formula @SUM(B4..B8) entered into B8 creates a circular reference. The formula should read @SUM(B4..B7).

The calculation preferences you select are specific to the notebook, and the setting is stored with the notebook file. This helps to prevent errors and inconvenience. Whenever you retrieve that large notebook in which you set recalculation to Manual, the mode is already set. However, when you switch to a small notebook where the recalculation is Background, the correct mode will be in operation.

Zoom Factor

The Zoom Factor was described at the end of Chapter 2 as a way of displaying more columns and rows in a notebook window. If you set a

FIGURE 7-19 The Recalc Settings showing a circular reference

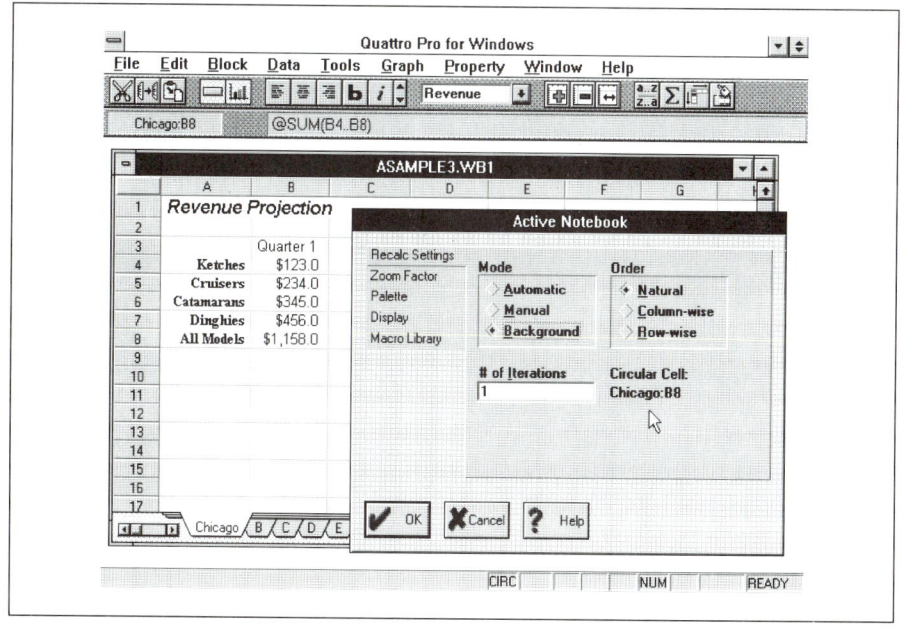

Zoom Factor of less than 100, the notebook display is scaled down to reveal more of the notebook but in smaller type. A Zoom Factor of more than 100 enlarges the type but displays fewer cells. Note that the Zoom Factor does not affect the size of printed reports from a notebook.

Palette Settings

The Palette page in the Active Notebook dialog box, shown in Figure 7-20, determines which colors are available to you in the palettes provided by those Quattro Pro commands that allow you to select colors. For example, both the Shading and Text Color pages of the Active Block dialog box allow you to pick colors from palettes.

When you first install Quattro Pro, the Shading and Text Color pages of the Active Block dialog box present a standard set of colors. However, you can substitute your own set of colors for the standard colors. To create your own set of colors, select Notebook Palette on the Active Notebook Palette page and then highlight the first color you want to alter. Next, choose Edit Color and select the color you want to substitute, using the Edit Palette Color dialog box shown here:

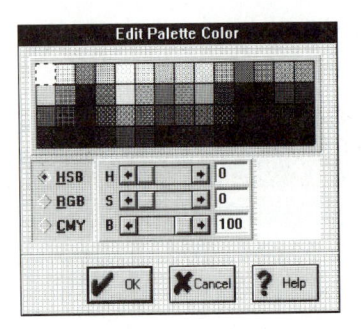

You can choose a color from the squares provided or you can create the color by adjusting the three slide controls. These slide controls set values from 0 to 255 in three categories, defined by the setting to the left of the sliders, which determines the model or method used to create the color. The three choices are

- **HSB** Hue, Saturation, Brightness

☐ **RGB** Red, Green, Blue

☐ **CMY** Cyan, Magenta, Yellow

For example, when you select RGB, the three sliders control red, green, and blue. After you have chosen the model you want to use for the color, you can adjust the sliders to create just the right shade, with the results appearing in the sample box to the right of the sliders. Keyboard users can press TAB to select each of the sliders in turn and use the arrow keys to increase or decrease the values. You can also press TAB to select the value field for each of the three categories and thus enter a value directly. When the color is just right, select OK, and you will be returned to the dialog box shown in Figure 7-20, where the new color will have replaced the one that was selected when you chose Edit Color. Repeat the process for any other colors you want to alter.

Palette changes will only affect the current notebook; however, any existing use of color in the current notebook will be altered to reflect the new palette. Thus, if you have used yellow for cell shading and then substitute purple for yellow in the Palette setting, the areas that were shaded yellow will become purple. To restore the original palette, choose Reset Defaults.

FIGURE 7-20 The Palette page of the Active Notebook dialog box

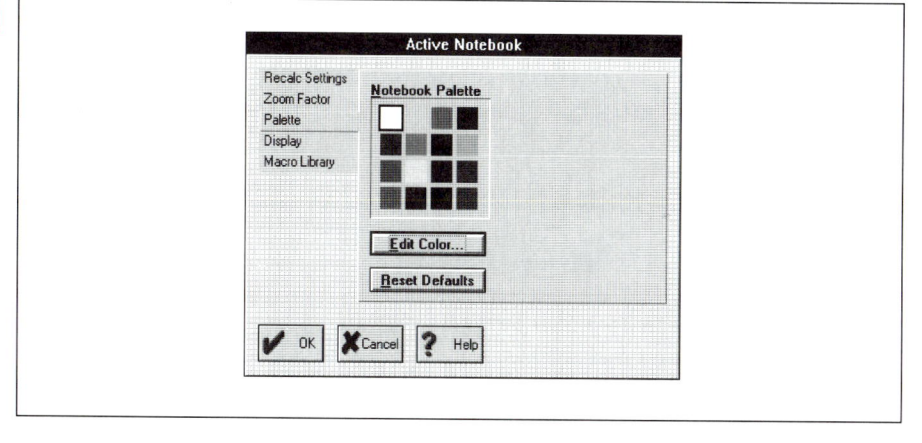

Notebook Display Settings

The Display page of the Active Notebook dialog box allows you to turn off or restore three areas of the notebook window:

- **Vertical Scroll Bar** On the right of the window, moves you up and down the notebook page
- **Horizontal Scroll Bar** On the bottom right of the window, moves you across the notebook page
- **Page Tabs** On the bottom left of the window, allows you to select pages and move from page to page

You will probably want to leave these three items turned on unless you have a special reason for disabling them, for example, when creating applications with macros to control movement.

Macro Library

The Macro Library setting for any notebook can either be Yes or No. The Yes setting means that the notebook can be used as a macro library to store macros that are used in other notebooks. When you execute a macro Quattro Pro looks for it first in the current notebook. If the macro you have requested is not in the current notebook, Quattro Pro checks to see if there are any notebooks that are open and have Yes for the Macro Library setting. If such a notebook is open, then Quattro Pro searches it for the macro you have requested. Macros in a notebook that has No for the Macro Library setting can only be run from within that notebook.

Active Page Settings

To adjust the Active Page settings for the current page, you issue the Properties | Active Page command or right-click on the page tab. Both actions present the compound dialog box shown in Figure 7-21. To

FIGURE 7-21 The first page of the Active Page dialog box

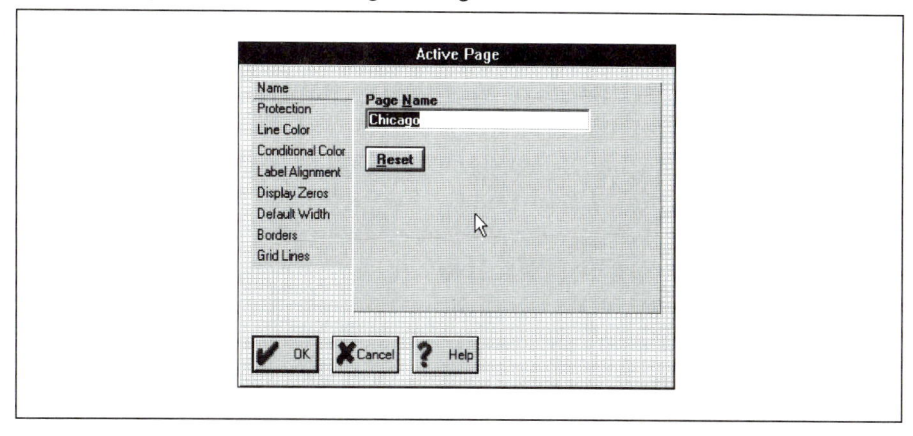

change the settings for several pages at once, select all of the pages you want to affect before you call up the Active Page dialog box.

Note To select several pages at once, click the page tab of the first page and then hold down SHIFT and click the tab of the last page. This creates a temporary group. To create a more permanent group select the pages as just described, issue the Tools | Define Group command, and give the group a name. Now you can click on the Group icon to activate Group mode. This means that changes to the current page will be carried over to all other pages in the same group.

Name

The first setting is Name, used several times in previous chapters to change the name of the page. Notebooks in which you have used more than one page are much easier to work with if the pages have names rather than letters of the alphabet. To add or change a name, you simply select the Page Name field and edit it to the name you want. You can use the Reset button to remove a page name and restore sequential page lettering (A, B, C, and so on).

Protection

The Protection setting in the Active Page dialog box allows you to safeguard the hours of work that go into making a good spreadsheet and makes it possible for less proficient users to enter data into a spreadsheet page without undue risk of damaging its underlying formulas. To turn on protection, select Enable. To turn it off you select Disable. Selecting Enable is like placing a sheet of glass over the page. You will be able to see the data but you will not be able to change it. New data cannot be placed into the cells and they cannot can be edited. Selecting Disable turns off this protection, allowing you to edit and alter the spreadsheet.

Saving a notebook with protection enabled on all pages containing data means that anyone who retrieves the notebook will have to turn off the protection before changing data. Remember that you can select several pages at once before changing the Active Page settings. If you want to allow limited changes to cells on a page, for example, for data entry, you can turn on protection and then Unprotect specific cells with the Protection setting in the Active Block dialog box. This means that you can move all over the page, but only change those cells that have been unprotected.

Line Color

The Line Color setting allows you to control the color of any lines drawn on the page with the Line Drawing option in the Active Page dialog box. A palette of colors is present, and you choose the color you want. This setting affects all lines drawn on the current page and does not affect lines drawn on other pages. The choice of colors is determined by the Palette setting in the Active Notebook dialog box.

Conditional Color Settings

The Conditional Color page, shown in Figure 7-22, allows you to use a system of coloring that automatically assigns a range of colors to numbers in cells based on their value. When you check the Enable

Chapter 7: Views, Titles, and Defaults

setting, these four conditions will determine the color of the text used to display values on the page:

- **Below Normal Color** Used for all values less than the value entered in the Smallest Normal Value field (default setting: red)

- **Normal Color** Used for all values greater than the value entered in the Smallest Normal Value field and less than the value entered in the Greatest Normal Value field (default setting: black)

- **Above Normal Color** Used for all values larger than the value entered in the Greatest Normal Value field (default setting: green)

- **ERR Color** Used for all formula results that are ERR (default setting: red)

If the default colors are not to your liking, you can select one of the four categories and then choose the desired color from the palette. Suppose that you have a notebook page that you use for balancing your checkbook. You want all negative values to appear in red. To warn you of errors that result in numbers too large to be true, you want values above one million to appear in blue. You want errors to be yellow. The default entry in the Smallest Normal Value field is already zero and the default setting for Below Normal Color values is red, so the first requirement is already taken care of. You enter **1000000** in the Greatest Normal

FIGURE 7-22 The Conditional Color page of the Active Page dialog box

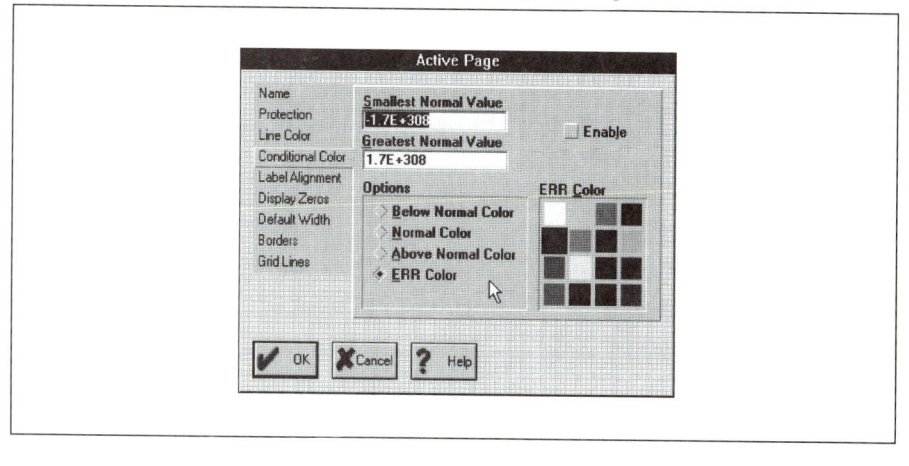

Label Alignment

The Label Alignment setting for the Active Page determines how labels are aligned by default as they are entered. The choices are Left, Right, and Center. Remember that you can override the Label Alignment setting for specific cells by using the Alignment page of the Active Block dialog box. Also, you can use one of the label alignment prefix characters when making a label entry (' for left," for right, and ^ for center).

Display Zeros

If you create a blank spreadsheet model into which someone has to enter values you may have a lot of cells that show only 0 for an entry. If you don't like the way this looks, you can tell Quattro Pro to hide any values that are 0 and any formulas that result in 0. To do this, choose No in the Display Zeros page of the Active Page settings. Note that this is somewhat risky as it can mislead users into thinking there is nothing in a cell when in fact the cell contains a valuable formula that is currently coming up with 0 for an answer. You might want to use Protection to prevent users from overwriting hidden cell entries.

Note that hiding zeros does not solve the problem of errors resulting from division by zero. Suppose cell B3 of a spreadsheet contains the total value of a wheat shipment. Cell C3 contains the number of tons in the shipment. A formula in D3 calculates the value per ton by dividing B3 by C3. The formula is +B3/C3. However, if the value in C3 is not yet available and a zero has been entered until the correct value is known, the result in D3 will be ERR. This is Quattro Pro's way of telling you that you cannot divide by zero (in this formula, a blank cell and a label would also have a value of zero). The solution is to use the ISERR function, as shown here:

@IF(@ISERR(B3/C3),"Not Known",B3/C3)

This formula tells Quattro Pro to display the text "Not Known" if B3/C3 produces an error. Otherwise, if there is no error, the formula simply displays the result of B3/C3.

Default Width Settings

As you saw in Chapter 2, Default Width page in the Active Page dialog box allows you to set the width of all columns in the page that are not individually adjusted. The default entry in the Column Width setting is 9 and the default Unit setting is Characters. If you change the Unit setting to Inches or Centimeters, the characters in the Column Width field are converted to the appropriate measurement (based on the average width of characters in the default font).

Border Settings

The Borders page is used to turn on and off the Row Borders and the Column Borders. These are, respectively, the row numbers and column letters. You might want to turn these off if you are using macros to control user movement on the notebook page.

Grid Line Settings

As you saw earlier in Figure 7-11, you can turn off both the Horizontal and the Vertical grid lines that are normally drawn on the notebook page. Again, this is sometimes desirable when you are working with macros and macro buttons. You might also want to turn off grid lines on the screen when working with graphs pasted onto a notebook page. Bear in mind that the display of grid lines is quite separate from the option to print grid lines.

Formats, Custom and Default

The hierarchy of settings in Quattro Pro goes from Application to Active Notebook to Active Page. The lowest level is Active Block which, as you have seen in previous chapters, allows you to vary the properties of individual cells and groups of cells from those imposed by the higher levels of property setting. In Figure 7-23 you can see the Active Block dialog box and the eleven aspects of cells that it can adjust.

You can use the Active Block dialog box to change such things as the shading or the numeric format for a block of cells so that they differ from the rest of the page. The cells that will be affected are stated in the title bar of the dialog box, along with the page they are on. However, you may have noticed that nowhere in the Application, Active Notebook, or Active Page is there any facility to change the defaults for such settings as numeric format or font. The way to change the default setting for these items is to edit the Normal style. In fact, by modifying the Normal style with the Edit | Define Style command, you can set the default values for each of the first seven items in the Active Block dialog box.

FIGURE 7-23 The Active Block dialog box

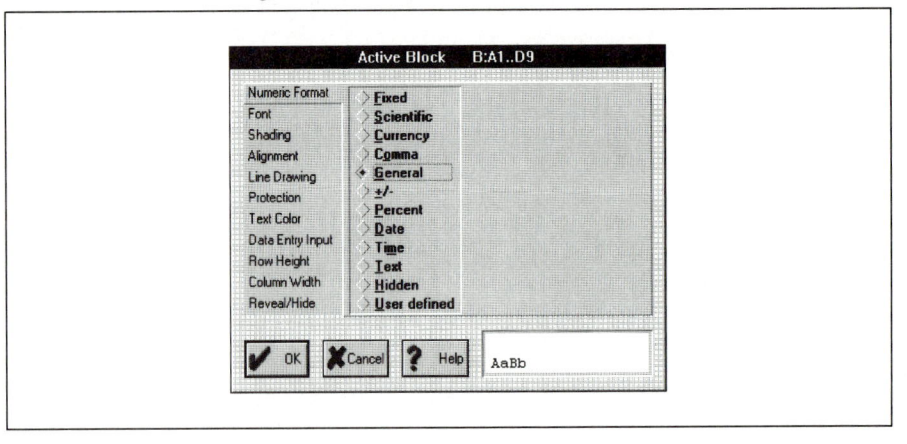

The Normal Style

All cells in a new notebook start out with the Normal style. In Chapter 2 you saw that you can apply different named styles to cells by using the Style Selector on the SpeedBar, and you can define and name your own styles. Define Style can also be used to modify the Normal style. This allows you to change the default value for all of the included properties listed in the Define/Modify Style dialog box shown here:

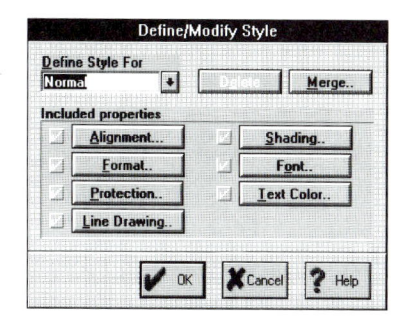

For example, if you want to use a different font as the default font in all cells of a notebook, select Font in this dialog box (after making sure that the entry in Define Style For is Normal). A Font dialog box appears, and you make your selection. Then choose OK to close the Font dialog box and choose OK again to close the Define/Modify Style dialog box. At this point, all cells in the notebook that have the Normal style will be formatted with the font you selected. The only exceptions are cells in which you have previously changed the font with the Active Block dialog box or a named style that includes font attributes.

This ability to edit the Normal style gives you great control over the basic settings in a notebook, including numeric format, text color, and shading. When you save the notebook, the revised Normal style is saved with it. Note that changing the Normal style in one notebook does not affect the styles or settings in any other notebook. If you want to use an edited version of the Normal style in all your new notebooks you can create a "template" notebook, in which you have edited the Normal style to your liking. You can save the notebook with a name like TEMPLATE.WB1 and open it whenever you need a new notebook. Use the File | Save As command to save the notebook under a new name and leave TEMPLATE.WB1 unchanged.

User-Defined Numeric Formats

The appearance of numbers in Quattro Pro cells is determined by their numeric format setting. A wide range of predefined formats is provided, such as currency, comma, and fixed. However, you may want numbers to appear in a format other than those set up by Quattro Pro. For this you use the user-defined format feature. In Figure 7-24 you can see the Numeric Format page of the Active Block dialog box. The User defined option has been selected, and a list of formats has been popped up below the Formats defined field. This list contains formats that have already been defined using the custom format symbols, described in Table 7-2.

Using this extensive collection of symbols, you can define any number of formats, such as the French Franc format seen in Figure 7-24. This is defined as N9,999.0F (which means numeric format, commas as the thousands separator, a period as the decimal point, always followed by one decimal place and the letter F). In the same column of numbers, you can see an Australian dollar format, which is defined as $9,999.0A.

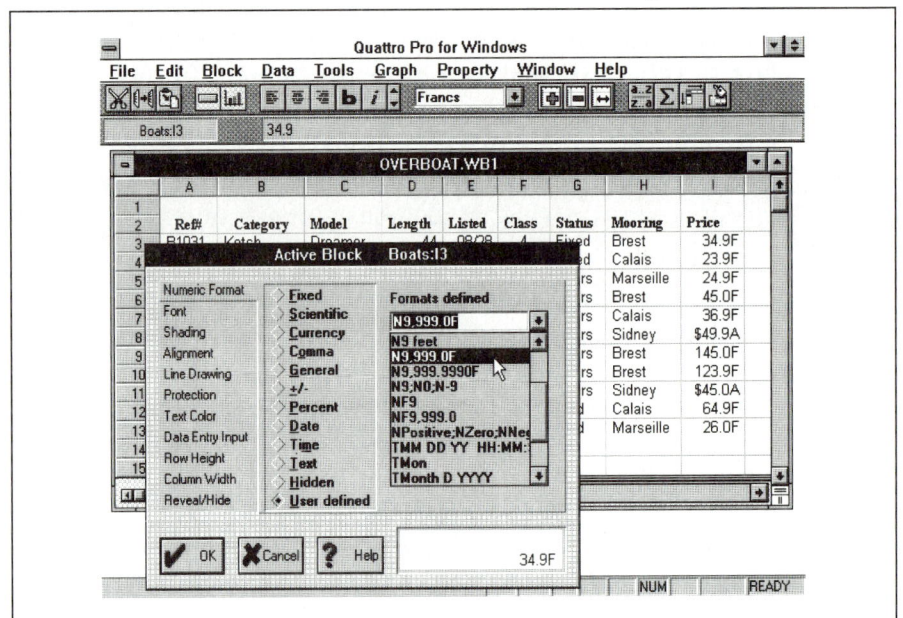

FIGURE 7-24 The list of user-defined formats in the Active Block dialog box

TABLE 7-2 Custom Format Symbols

Code	Description
N or n	Shows that the codes that follow constitute a numeric format, not dates or times
0	Displays a digit whether or not the number includes a digit in this position
9	Displays a digit unless the number lacks a digit in this position
%	Displays the number as a percentage
,	Inserts a thousands separator (a comma unless otherwise specified under Options International Punctuation)
.	Inserts a decimal separator (a period unless otherwise specified under Options International Punctuation)
E– or e–	Displays the number in scientific notation, preceding negative exponents with a minus sign. If the format includes at least one 0 or 9 after this symbol, you get the number in scientific notation, which uses E or e. If the exponent contains more digits than 9s or 0s following this symbol, the extra digits are displayed
E+ or e+	Displays numbers in scientific notation, preceding a negative or positive exponent with a minus or plus sign, respectively. If the format includes at least one 0 or 9 following this symbol, you get the number in scientific notation, which uses E or e. If the exponent contains more digits than 9s or 0s following this symbol, the extra digits are displayed
T or t	Shows that the codes that follow constitute a format for dates and times, not numbers
d or D	Displays the day of the month as a one- or two-digit number (1 through 31)
dd or DD	Displays the day of the month as a two-digit number (01 through 31)

TABLE 7-2 Custom Format Symbols (*continued*)

Code	Description
wday, Wday, WDAY	Displays the day of the week as a three-character WDAY abbreviation, all lowercase, with the first letter capitalized, or all uppercase
weekday, Weekday, WEEKDAY	Displays the day of the week all lowercase, with the first letter capitalized, or all uppercase
m or M	If not preceded by h, H, hh, or HH, displays the month as a one- or two-digit number (1 through 12). Otherwise, displays the minute as a one- or two-digit number (1 through 59)
mm or MM	If not preceded by h, H, hh, or HH, displays the month as a two-digit number (01 through 12). Otherwise, displays the minute as a two-digit number (01 through 59)
Mo	Displays the month as a one- or two-digit number (1 through 12)
MMo	Displays the month as a two-digit number (01 through 12)
mon, Mon, MON	Displays the month as a three-character abbreviation, all lowercase, with the first letter capitalized, or all uppercase
month, Month, MONTH	Displays the name of the month all lowercase, with the first letter capitalized, or all uppercase
yy or YY	Displays the last two digits of the year (00 through 99)
yyyy or YYYY	Displays all four digits of the year (0001 through 9999)
h or H	Displays the hour as a one- or two-digit number. If the format includes ampm or AMPM, the number will be between 1 and 12. If ampm or AMPM is not included, 24-hour format is used (0 through 23)

TABLE 7-2 Custom Format Symbols (*continued*)

Code	Description
hh or HH	Displays the hour as a two-digit number. If the format includes ampm or AMPM, the number will be between 01 and 12. If ampm or AMPM is not included, 24-hour format is used (00 through 23)
Mi	Displays the minute as a one- or two-digit number (1 through 59)
MMi	Displays the minute as a two-digit number (01 through 59)
s or S	Displays the second as a one- or two-digit number (1 through 59)
ss or SS	Displays the second as a two-digit number (01 through 59)
AMPM or ampm	Displays the time in 12-hour format with characters for morning (AM) or afternoon (PM)
\	Displays the next character in the format, so to display a backslash, type \\
*	If the formatted entry is shorter than the column width, this fills the column by repeating the character to the right of the asterisk
" "	Displays the characters inside the quotes as part or all of the cell contents. Used when you want to use text that would be ambiguous otherwise, such as Thh:mm "in the" AMPM. This formats time like this: 10:30 in the AM. Without the quotes, h would be read as the hours code

Virtually any unit of measure can be accommodated in a custom format, and there are symbols for creating custom date formats; for example, TMonth D YYYY, which would display the last day of the century as December 31, 1999.

To create a new custom format, you can edit the entry in the Formats defined field. Type the symbols that you want and when you choose OK, the format you have defined is applied to the cells in the active block. The format is also added to the list that appears under the Formats defined field. The new format will appear in this list, in alphabetical order, from now on, and will be available in other notebooks. You can also use the Edit | Define Style command to create a named style that incorporates the new format, as with the Franc style used in Figure 7-24.

Note The International settings in the Application dialog box allow you to change the appearance of currency formats, but these changes affect all predefined currency formats in all notebooks and do not allow you to mix currencies without resorting to custom formats.

There is a simple way to type a foreign character, such as £, in a format definition, a label, or as the Currency Symbol in International Settings. If you know the ANSI code number of the character, you simply hold down the ALT key, type the number *on the numeric keypad*, and then release the ALT key. When you release the ALT key, the character will appear. The ANSI code for £, for example, is 0163, so you would press ALT and type **0163**; then release ALT. Windows 3.1 users can look up ANSI codes using the Character Map accessory. There is also a table of ANSI codes in the *Building Spreadsheet Applications* manual that comes with Quattro Pro.

CHAPTER 8

Data Sharing and Transfer

*I*n this chapter you will learn how to bring data into Quattro Pro from other programs and export data from Quattro Pro so that other programs can read it. You will also learn how to extract and combine sections of notebooks using the Tools menu. However, we begin by reviewing some tactics that you might want to consider in order to protect your data.

Safeguarding Your Data

These days, a lot of very valuable information is entrusted to personal computers, and a significant proportion of that information is stored in spreadsheet files. Loss of data in those files or unauthorized access to that data could be damaging for you and/or your organization. To combat the threat to your data we recommend a "layered" approach:

- **Access Control** Control access to the site where your computer is, to the computer itself, and to sensitive files.

- **System Support** Safeguard your power supply by using a surge protector, for example. Back up your work, in case of the disaster that can't be avoided. Be vigilant—for example, if you use disks from outside, check to see that they don't have a virus embedded in them.

- **Channel Protection** Do you modem to and from a bulletin board? Verify the identity of anyone who has access to your system through the phone lines. Make use of any support offered by the administrator of your bulletin board. If you're on a network, observe the network rules for password protection, particularly when you log on.

You can see a diagram of this approach to data security in Figure 8-1. Start with controls on site access, followed by controls on computer system access and file access controls. Access control measures should be complemented by support for hardware, regular backups of data files, and controls on communication channels, such as file transfers by telephone line and network connections (for more on how to implement a comprehensive security system for your data see *The Stephen Cobb Complete Guide to Personal Computer and Network Security*, (Tab/McGraw-Hill).

Chapter 8: Data Sharing and Transfer 403

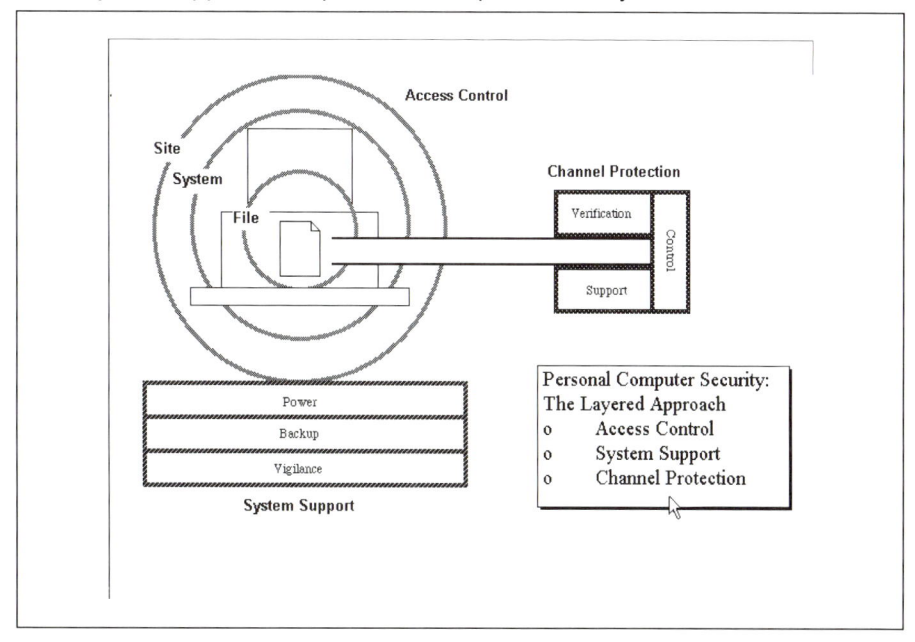

FIGURE 8-1 The "layered" approach to personal computer security

Password Protection

Many security measures cost little or nothing to implement. These days, most PCs have come with a key that locks up the keyboard. Some require a password to be entered when booting up. When your computer is on and you have to leave it unattended, you can use Windows 3.1 to blank your screen and require a password from anyone who tries to use the computer (this feature is available through the Desktop icon in the Control Panel). To prevent unauthorized access to a notebook file stored on disk, Quattro Pro allows you to assign a password to a file while you are saving it. Thereafter the file cannot be opened unless the correct password is supplied.

To assign a password to a notebook in Quattro Pro for Windows, you save it using the File | Save As command. When you have issued the command and checked that the filename and directory settings are correct, you then select the Protection Password field and type the password, as shown in Figure 8-2. As you type the password you will see

FIGURE 8-2 Using the Protection Password option when saving a file

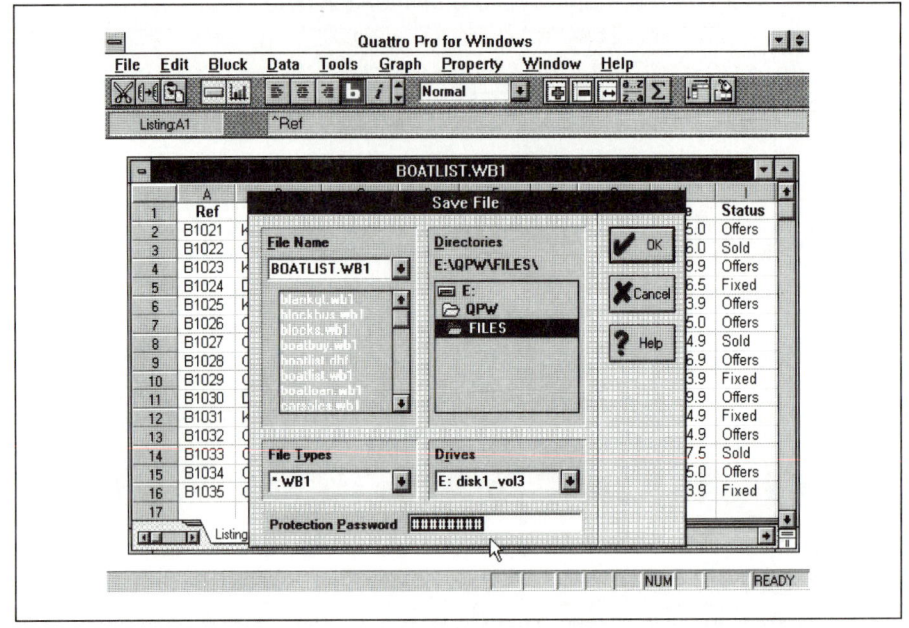

one # sign for every letter you type. This is a precaution against someone reading the password over your shoulder as you type it.

The password can actually be one or more words, numbers, and spaces up to a total length of 15 characters. Be sure to use a password that you can remember. When you use a password to protect a file the information in the file is *encrypted*; that is, the data is scrambled to make it unintelligible, even to a sophisticated, well-trained programmer. Neither Borland nor anyone else can retrieve the data if you forget the password.

When you choose OK to complete the command, you will be prompted to verify the password by typing it again in the dialog box that appears:

The theory is that if you can type the word twice, you know what it is and did not make a mistake the first time you typed it. When you have typed the password a second time and chosen OK the file is saved, unless

Chapter 8: Data Sharing and Transfer

- The second version of the password does not match the first, in which case you are alerted to the mistake and the File | Save As command is canceled

- The second version of the password matches the first but the file already exists, in which case you get the usual Replace, Backup, Cancel dialog box

When you attempt to retrieve or open a password-protected file, you are prompted for the password by the following dialog box:

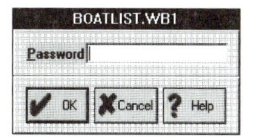

This time you need only type the password once and then choose OK to access the file. If you type an incorrect password, Quattro Pro alerts you to the fact and cancels the file opening command.

Note   The password feature is case sensitive, so if the password is Fred's Key, you cannot open the file with FRED'S KEY or even Fred's key.

When you have successfully opened a password-protected file and made changes to it, no special commands are required to resave the file. The File | Save command immediately saves the file to disk while Save As prompts you before overwriting the previous version of the file. Neither command requests you to enter the password again because you had to know the password to open the file.

When you want to remove password protection from a file, you first open the file, and then use the Save As command. The Protection Password field contains the # characters to show that a password is in place. Simply delete the characters and complete the command, and the password will be permanently removed.

Using passwords can be a nuisance, so you should decide whether the need for security is real. If it is, you should use proper passwords. A password is of little use if it is a common choice such as "password," "pass," your first name, the filename, and so on. Believe it or not, you can buy lists of common passwords in some circles, and the serious data thief is likely to guess most words that do not have two or more of the following features:

- At least six characters
- A mixture of text and numbers
- Some odd characters, like @, spaces, and commas
- A mixture of uppercase and lowercase letters
- No obvious connection with the file contents

Because passwords that meet these criteria can be difficult to remember, you should make proper provision for recording and securing your passwords. A sheet of paper locked in a drawer is a reasonably good measure, as long as it is not plainly labeled "passwords for Quattro Pro notebooks." For occasional passwords you might try acronyms of favorite song titles, such as YLTLF for "You've Lost That Loving Feeling." For a constant supply of passwords consider employing a book, such as the dictionary, and using the last word on the page. You can then keep track of passwords with a list of filenames and corresponding page numbers.

Data Loss and Recovery

The rule of thumb for preventing data loss is the same as the rule for steady monetary accumulation: "Save regularly and often." In practice this means using the Save command once for every 15 minutes of work and once more before you do any of the following:

- Perform a file retrieve
- Exit Quattro Pro
- Leave your PC unattended
- Move or copy a large block
- Sort data or perform an extract or block fill operation
- Combine files

Even if you try to live by these rules, there is always a possibility that something will go wrong. Quattro Pro has a built-in method of helping out: the Undo feature. For more about the Undo feature, see Chapter 2.

Foreign Files

Quattro Pro can read and write not only its own spreadsheets but also data files created by several other popular programs. In Table 8-1 you can see a list of the different file formats that Quattro Pro can read. There are several ways of using data stored in these formats:

- Open the file with File | Open or File | Retrieve.
- Insert the file into a notebook with Block | Insert | File.
- Copy data from the file using Tools | Combine.
- Select data from the file with Data | Query

Opening Foreign Files

You do not have to do anything special to load a foreign file into Quattro Pro. Simply enter the name in the Open File or Retrieve File dialog box, and the file is read and presented as a Quattro Pro notebook. In the background of Figure 8-3 you can see a Lotus 1-2-3 worksheet called BOATS.WK1 that has been opened by Quattro Pro.

When you want to save a foreign file that you have opened, the Save command assumes that you want to store the data in its original format, using the same file extension. The same is true of the Save As command, as you can see from the dialog box in Figure 8-3. If you open a 1-2-3 spreadsheet called BOATS.WK1 and select Save As, the suggested name and extension will be the same, BOATS.WK1. If you use this name, the file will be stored as a 1-2-3 spreadsheet. However, when you use Save As, you can edit the file extension in the File Name field. If you change the extension to WB1 and choose OK, Quattro Pro will store the file as a normal Quattro Pro notebook file. See the next section for more on converting notebook pages to foreign file formats.

FIGURE 8-3 A 1-2-3 file opened in Quattro Pro

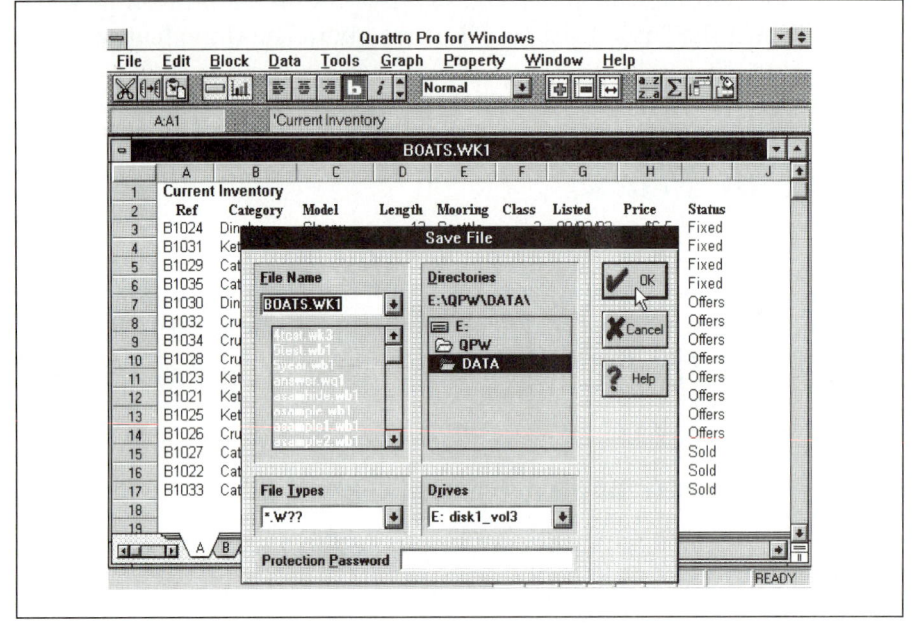

If you are doing a lot of work with foreign files, you might want to take advantage of the File Types option in the Open File dialog box, as shown in Figure 8-4. This allows you to change the file filter used in the File Name field. The default filter *.W?? lists a wide range of spreadsheet file types. However, if you want a more specific filter there are filters for every file type that Quattro Pro supports (the filters are listed in Table 8-1). Thus, if you want to list only the Lotus 1-2-3 Release 2 format files, you should choose the *.WK1 filter.

Note that when you open a 1-2-3 spreadsheet with the WK1 or WK3 extension, Quattro Pro checks to see if there is an accompanying format file created by one of the 1-2-3 add-in programs (these are called Allways and Impress, although the latter is also referred to as Wysiwyg). These format files contain information about advanced formatting, such as fonts and lines, and have the extension FMT or FM3. For example, if you have used Impress/Wysiwyg to format the SALES.WK1 spreadsheet, a file called SALES.FMT will have been created. Quattro Pro can read many, but not all, of the settings in this file and can translate them to the corresponding Quattro Pro settings. Table 8-2 lists the features of FMT

TABLE 8-1 File Formats Quattro Pro Can Read and Write

File Type/Filter	Description
QPW (*.WB1)	Quattro Pro for Windows notebooks
QPro/DOS (*.WQ1)	Quattro Pro for DOS spreadsheet files
1-2-3 v2.x (*.WK1)	1-2-3 Release 2 worksheet files
1-2-3 v3.x (*.WK3)	1-2-3 Release 3 worksheet files
Excel (*.XLS)	Excel spreadsheet files
Paradox (*.DB)	Paradox database files
dBASE (*.DBF)	dBASE database files (version III and later)
dBASE II (*.DB2)	dBASE database files (version II only)*
Reflex v1 (*.RXD)	Reflex version 1 database files
Reflex v2 (*.R2D)	Reflex version 2 database files
Quattro (*.WKQ)	Original Quattro spreadsheet files
Surpass (*.WKP)	Surpass spreadsheet files
1-2-3 v1.0 (*.WKS)	1-2-3 Release 1 worksheet files
1-2-3 Ed (*.WKE)	1-2-3 Educational edition worksheets
Sym v1.2 (*.WRK)	Symphony version 1.2 sheet files
Sym v2.0 (*.WR1)	Symphony version 2 sheet files
Visicalc (*.DIF)	Spreadsheets in the Visicalc DIF format
Multiplan (*.SLK)	Spreadsheets in the Multiplan SYLK format

*Note that dBASE II files normally have the extension DBF, but you should save from Quattro Pro with the DB2 extension if you need to export to dBASE II format; then rename the file to DBF to be read by other applications.

or FM3 files that Quattro Pro does and doesn't recognize. Bear in mind that the FMT or FM3 file must be in the same directory as the WK1 or WK3 file when you retrieve the spreadsheet.

Writing to Foreign Files

You can save notebook data into some foreign file formats simply by changing the file extension. For example, to save a notebook called

FIGURE 8-4 The File Types list in the Open File dialog box

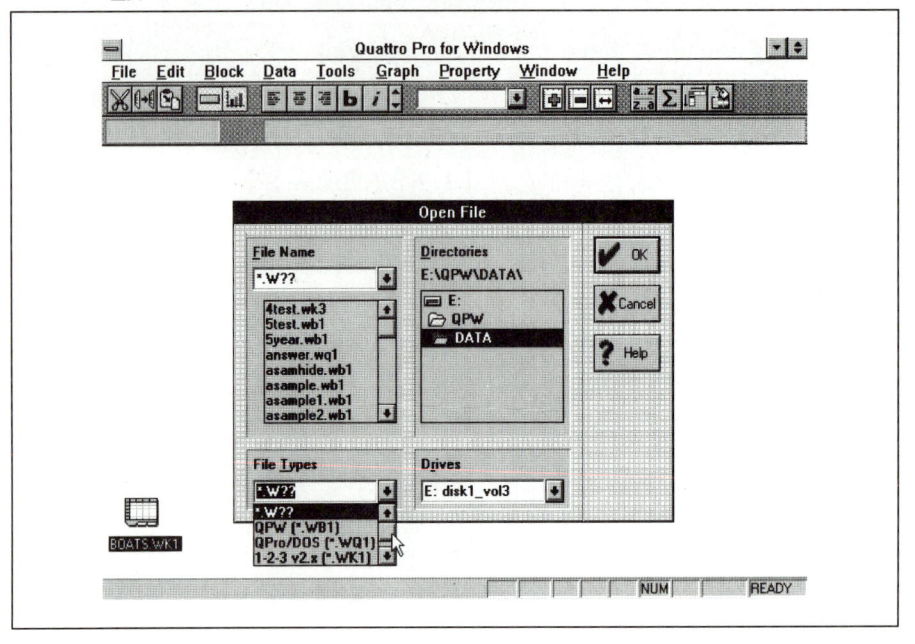

TABLE 8-2 How Wysiwyg/Impress Files Are Handled

Quattro Pro for Windows Recognizes	Quattro Pro for Windows Does Not Recognize
Fonts, including boldface, italic, underline, and colors	Column page breaks and column widths
Inserted graphs	Formatting embedded in text
Named styles	Display options such as colors, mode, and zoom
Text alignment (except left-of-cell overlap)	Line shadow and line colors
Row height page breaks	Inserted Clip art and drawings
Print range, configuration and orientation, and print-to-fit compression	Page size and bottom border breaks
Print layout margins and titles	Grid or frame printing
	Printer type

Chapter 8: Data Sharing and Transfer 411

BOATLIST.WB1 so that it can be read by 1-2-3 Release 3, you would use Save As, change the filename to BOATLIST.WK3, and choose OK to proceed with the save. In addition to creating a file called BOATLIST.WK3, Quattro Pro creates BOATLIST.FM3 to store the format settings of the notebook so that they can be carried over into 1-2-3.

There are several additional steps that can arise in this "export" process. If you use the WK1 format, which only supports single-page spreadsheets, Quattro Pro checks to see how many pages of the notebook have been used. If only one page has been used, Quattro Pro saves it into the 1-2-3 format dictated by the file extension you have used. However, if you have used more than one page of the notebook and are using the WK1 extension, Quattro Pro warns you that only the current page will be saved in the WK1 file:

At this point you can select No to stop the operation or Yes to carry on. If you carry on, Quattro Pro will ask you which type of format file you want to create to accompany the WK1 data file:

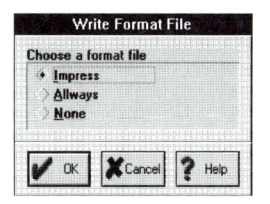

When you have made your choice you can select OK to continue, and the process will be completed. If you are sending the 1-2-3 file on to another user who needs the formatting information, be sure to send both the data file and the format file. If the formatting information is not important, you can choose None in the Write Format File dialog box.

You can save data from a Quattro Pro spreadsheet to a database format such as dBASE or Paradox. For example, in the background of Figure 8-5 you can see a list of boats stored in page A of a notebook called

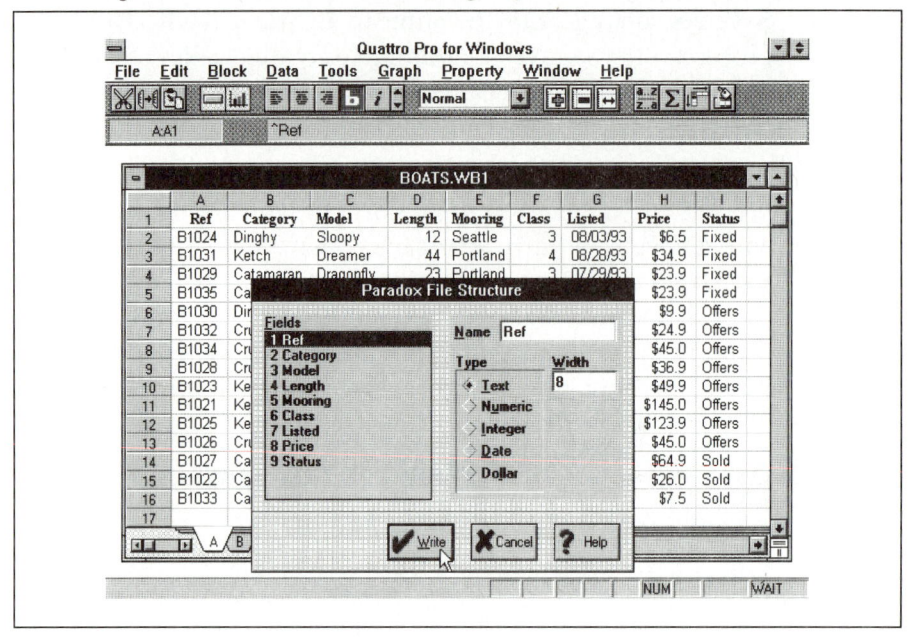

FIGURE 8-5 Reviewing the file structure of data being exported to a database

BOATS.WB1. The Paradox File Structure dialog box is displayed because the user issued the Save As command and entered the filename BOATS.DB in order to store the data in a Paradox database file.

Whenever you try to save a notebook using a database file extension, Quattro Pro analyzes the notebook and attempts to convert the columns and rows of spreadsheet data to the field and record structure of the database. Since this is a rather difficult task, Quattro Pro presents the appropriate file structure dialog box so that you can review the assumptions made as part of the conversion. These include, for each field, the name of the field, the field type, and the width. You can highlight each field in turn and check the settings, changing them if necessary to more accurately match the data.

If any of the fields has a number but no name, it is likely that the name used in the notebook contains "illegal" characters. You can select the field in the file structure dialog box and enter a suitable name in the Name field. For example, if the label in cell A1 of Figure 8-5 had been Ref# instead of Ref, Quattro Pro would have rejected it if you had been saving the file in dBASE format (DBF). Once the structure is acceptable, you can choose Write to create the file.

Note that in order to use Save As to export notebook data to a database file format, the notebook must meet fairly restrictive conditions. The data must already be arranged in the tabular Quattro Pro database format (consecutive rows beneath headed columns, as described in Chapter 6). Furthermore, the table must start at cell A1, as in Figure 8-5. If the table begins further down or across the spreadsheet, you should use the Tools | Extract command, which is described in the next section, in order to export the data.

Extracting, Combining, Inserting, and Linking

If you are familiar with older spreadsheets, you may have encountered a pair of commands known as Extract and Combine. These were used to move data between spreadsheets in the days when you could only open one spreadsheet at a time and could not establish links between spreadsheets. The Extract command copies a portion of a spreadsheet into a separate file on disk. The Combine command reads all or part of a spreadsheet from disk into the current spreadsheet. Quattro Pro has its own version of these commands in the Tools menu, Tools | Extract and Tool | Combine. They are described in this section, along with some of the alternatives to these commands now available in Quattro Pro.

Data Extraction

Suppose that you need to send a colleague a copy of some data that you have entered in a Quattro Pro notebook, and your colleague is a 1-2-3 user. The notebook is the one in the background of Figure 8-6. You need to send details on boats moored in Chicago, which occupies the block B2..J7. To do this you select the block and then issue the Tools | Extract command. This produces the dialog box shown in Figure 8-6. Note that the left side of this dialog box is quite similar to the Save File dialog box, but on the right side there are several additional fields.

414   Quattro Pro for Windows Inside & Out

FIGURE 8-6 The File Extract dialog box

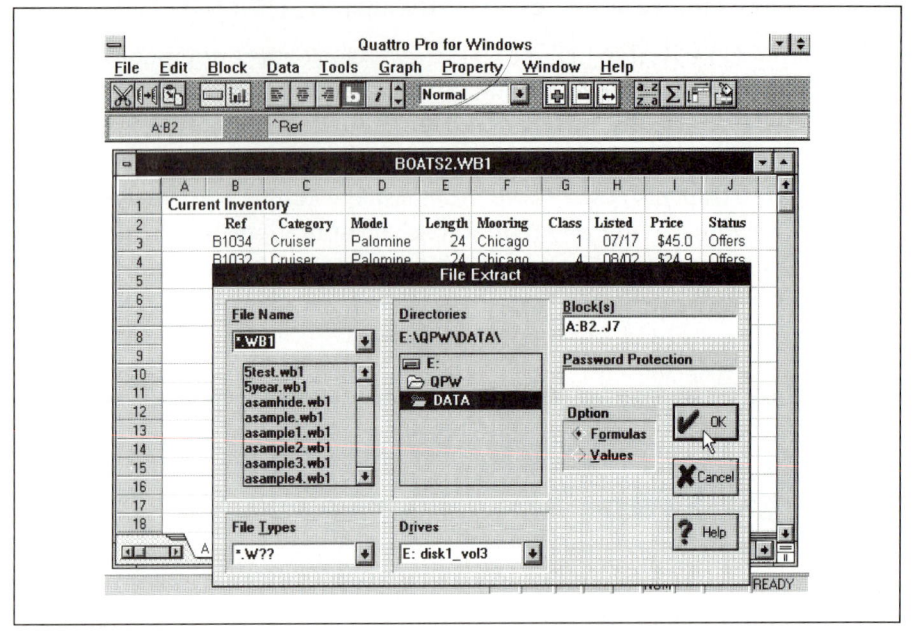

The added fields in the File Extract dialog box allow you to respecify the block of cells that will be copied into the file you are about to save on disk, to assign password protection to the file, and to export either Formulas or Values. The Values option converts any formulas in the extracted block into their results before saving them in the extract file. The Formulas option preserves formulas in the extract file, *if* that file is being saved in a spreadsheet format (database files cannot preserve spreadsheet formulas). Do not use the Formulas option if the block you are copying into the extract file contains formulas that reference cells outside the block. Such formulas will not make sense in the extract file.

When you have selected your options and typed a filename, you can choose OK to complete the command. In this example you would use a filename that has the extension WK1. You can use an existing filename from the file list on the left side of the dialog box, but bear in mind that this will cause the extracted data to overwrite the data already stored in the file. When you choose OK, Quattro Pro writes a file that contains only the data in the block specified in the Block(s) field (you can select compound blocks for this command). If you use a foreign file extension, such as WK1, the extract data is stored in a file of the appropriate format.

You might want to use the Tools | Extract command when you have to export data from a Quattro Pro notebook to a database format such as dBASE or Paradox and the data does not fit the requirements for the File | Save As command discussed earlier. This is the case in Figure 8-6, where the top-left corner of the table of data is not located at A1. In situations like this, you select the block of cells in the spreadsheet that encompasses the database fields and records, issue the Tools | Extract command, and enter a filename that has the required database extension. A file structure dialog box will appear, like the one in Figure 8-5, allowing you to check the structure of the file before selecting Write to complete the operation.

Note When extracting to a database file, you must include the column headings in the selected block, but exclude any cells above or to the left of the column headings.

An alternative to using Tools | Extract to export data from within a notebook to a database is to copy the block of data to a cell A1 of a new notebook and then save the notebook with the database file extension. You can copy the data with either Edit | Copy or Block | Copy.

Combining Data

The Tools | Combine command allows you to read data into a notebook from another file without opening that file. Since Quattro Pro allows you to open several files at once, it would seem that there is little need for this command. If you have data that you want to copy into a notebook from another file, you can simply open that file and use Edit | Copy or Block | Copy to do the job. However, Tools | Combine can be useful when you are automating the process of consolidating data from separate files and do not want to go through the trouble of opening all the files. The command is particularly well suited to situations where data needs to be copied from a number of files that use the same arrangement of data. Furthermore, Combine can perform math on data that is being copied.

In Figure 8-7 you can see two notebooks. The CHICAGO.WB1 file is one of a number of similarly structured files that contain sales data from regional offices (MIAMI.WB1, PORTLAND.WB1, and so on). The ROUNDUP.WB1 file will be used to combine the sales data from these files using Tools | Combine. Note that the CHICAGO.WB1 file is only open in Figure 8-7 for purposes of illustration (you do not have to open files to copy data from them with the Tools | Combine command). Also note that there is no requirement that the receiving or destination file use column labels that match those in the source file. The same labels are used in both files in Figure 8-6 merely for convenience (data that is copied between files with Combine does not even have to be arranged as a database table).

The first step in combining data is to select the top-left cell of the area into which you want the incoming data to be copied. This has been done in Figure 8-7, where cell A3 has been selected. Quattro Pro will assume that the entire area below and to the right of A3 is available for data copied from the other file. Because of this assumption, you should exercise great care when using the Tools | Combine command; otherwise, data coming from the source spreadsheet will overwrite existing data in the destination spreadsheet.

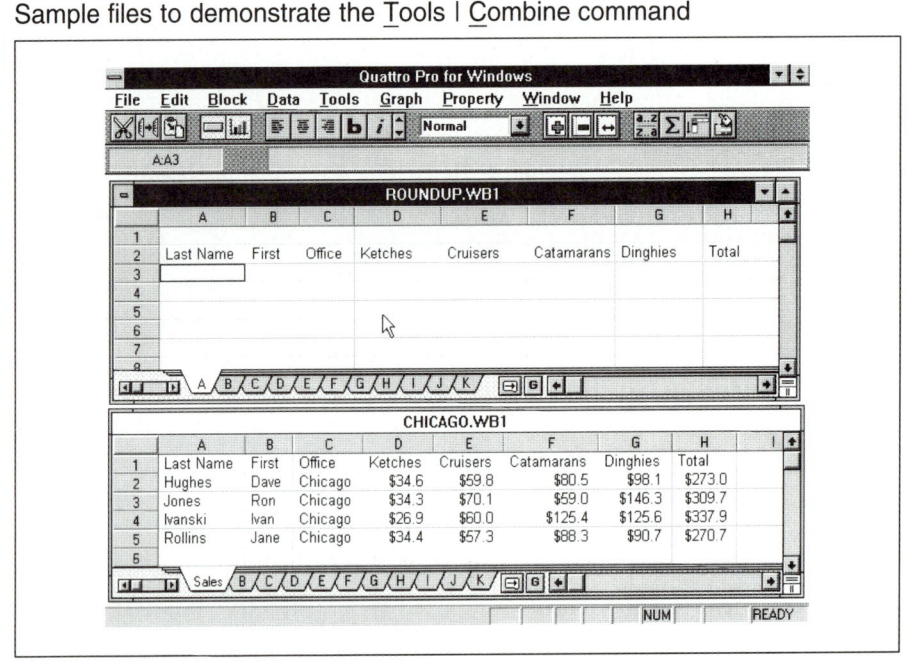

FIGURE 8-7 Sample files to demonstrate the Tools | Combine command

When you select Combine (from the Tools menu), you get the dialog box shown in Figure 8-8. This has been filled in with the name of the source file in the File Name field and the Operation and Source settings desired. Note that you can combine the Entire File or selected Block(s), the latter being specified either by block name or by cell coordinates. In this example the block named DATA will be copied from the file called MIAMI.WB1.

Note that blank cells in the source will not overwrite data in the destination spreadsheet. The Operation setting allows you to perform math between existing values in the destination file and values read from the source file. This is useful in situations such as reading monthly sales figures into a year-to-date file, where the incoming values are added to those already entered in the destination spreadsheet. In addition to Add, you can use Subtract, Multiply, and Divide. For a straight copy with no math you use Copy. You can see the results of the operation in Figure 8-9. Note that incoming data retains its numeric formatting and label alignment. Data combined from other Quattro Pro notebooks retains style settings as well. However column widths are not transferred.

Inserting Files

While Chapter 3 covered most of the commands on the Block menu, it skipped Block | Insert | File, since this is quite different from the other

FIGURE 8-8 The File Combine dialog box completed

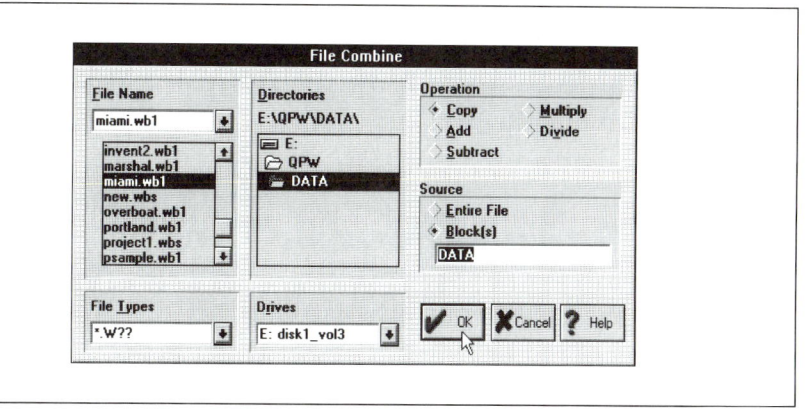

FIGURE 8-9 The results of combining data from the Miami file

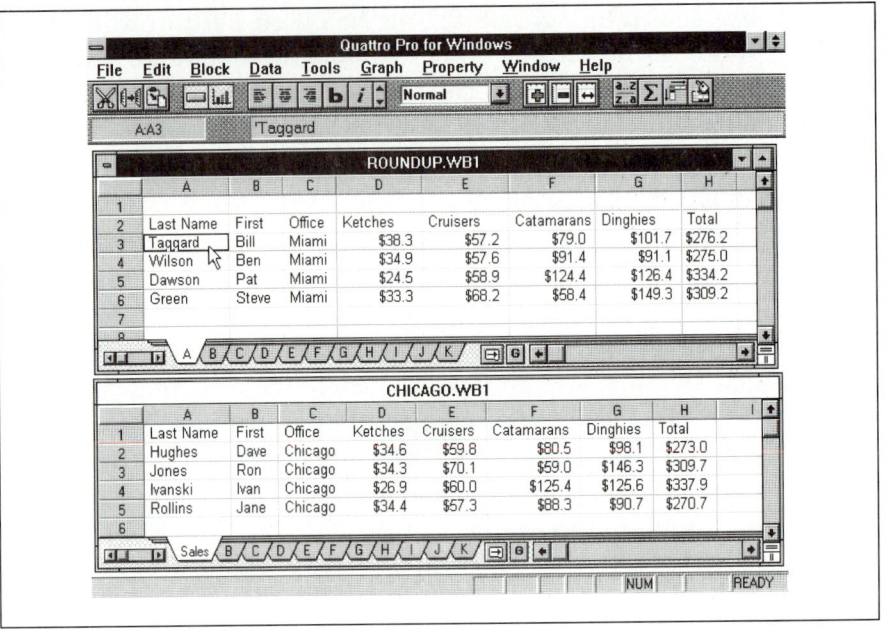

[Screenshot of Quattro Pro for Windows showing two notebook windows: ROUNDUP.WB1 and CHICAGO.WB1]

ROUNDUP.WB1

	A	B	C	D	E	F	G	H
1								
2	Last Name	First	Office	Ketches	Cruisers	Catamarans	Dinghies	Total
3	Taggard	Bill	Miami	$38.3	$57.2	$79.0	$101.7	$276.2
4	Wilson	Ben	Miami	$34.9	$57.6	$91.4	$91.1	$275.0
5	Dawson	Pat	Miami	$24.5	$58.9	$124.4	$126.4	$334.2
6	Green	Steve	Miami	$33.3	$68.2	$58.4	$149.3	$309.2

CHICAGO.WB1

	A	B	C	D	E	F	G	H
1	Last Name	First	Office	Ketches	Cruisers	Catamarans	Dinghies	Total
2	Hughes	Dave	Chicago	$34.6	$59.8	$80.5	$98.1	$273.0
3	Jones	Ron	Chicago	$34.3	$70.1	$59.0	$146.3	$309.7
4	Ivanski	Ivan	Chicago	$26.9	$60.0	$125.4	$125.6	$337.9
5	Rollins	Jane	Chicago	$34.4	$57.3	$88.3	$90.7	$270.7

Block | Insert commands. Inserting files is another means of combining data from different sources. You can use Block | Insert | File to read in a WK1 file. This will appear as a new page in the notebook. The page name will reflect the worksheet filename. If you read in a WK3 file with multiple sheets, each one is added as a new page. You can read in other Quattro Pro notebooks, and all of the pages will be added to the current notebook. As you can see from the Insert File dialog box in Figure 8-10, Quattro Pro assumes you want the inserted file to appear in front of the current page. You can use the Before page field to change where the inserted file is placed.

Extracting from Foreign Files

One way to bring selected data into a Quattro Pro notebook from foreign database files is to use the Data | Query command. You will recall that this command requires three pieces of information: the Database Block, the Criteria Table, and the Output Block. The Database Block is

FIGURE 8-10 The Insert File dialog box

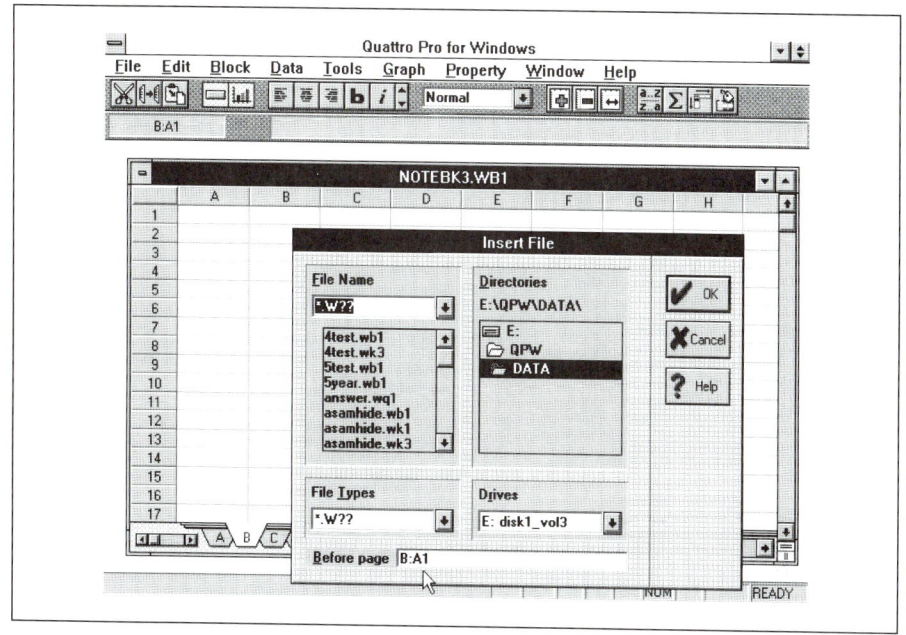

the database, the collection of information you want to query. The Criteria Table is the set of conditions that determine which records are read from the Quattro Pro database. The Output Block is an area of a spreadsheet into which the selected records from the database are written. In Figure 8-11 you can see a notebook set up to extract records from a dBASE file.

The dBASE file is called BOATINV.DBF and is stored in the current data directory. The Criteria Table in G1..H2 tells Quattro Pro to select records with Chicago in the Mooring field and the entry 4 in the Class field. Matching records will be read into the Output Block of NOTEBK3.WB1 identified as A:A4..I12. Note that the Output Block limits the extracted records to nine rows, protection against an unexpectedly large number of extracted records overwriting data further down the notebook page. Also note that the field names entered in the notebook areas defined as your Criteria Table and Output Block must match those in the DBF file.

When you want to extract records from a file other than the current notebook, you refer to the file by name in the Database Block setting. In

FIGURE 8-11 Using Data | Query to extract data from a dBASE file

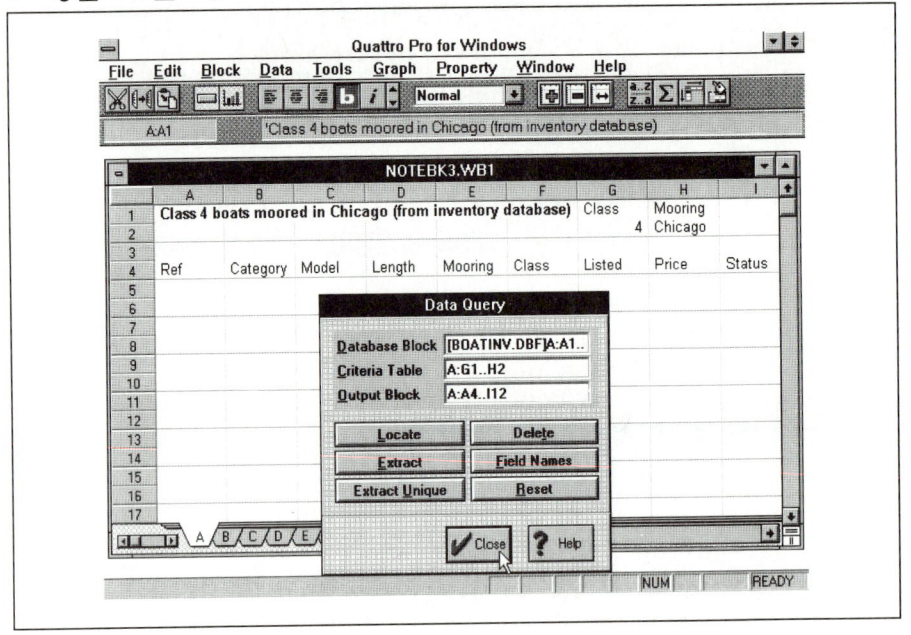

FIGURE 8-12 The result of the data query

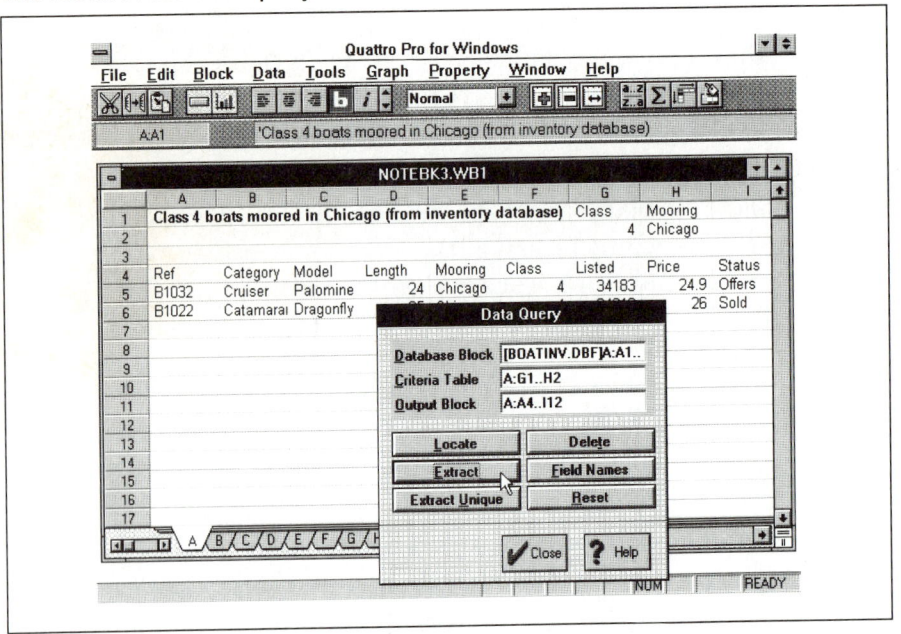

this case the setting is [BOATINV.DBF]A1..A2. The filename requires the full path if it is in a directory other than the current data directory. The cell reference of A1..A2 is used as a reference point in the foreign database file, regardless of the number of fields and records in the file. In Figure 8-12 you can see the results of choosing Extract with the settings in Figure 8-11. Note that the incoming data is not formatted (dates in the "Listed" field appear as serial numbers). The column widths are not adjusted either. The data must be formatted within the notebook. Also note that Data | Query does not create a dynamic link between the notebook and the DBF file. The extracted records will not be updated automatically if the DBF file is altered.

The Database Desktop

One further method of reading data from database files is to use Database Desktop, shown at work in Figure 8-13. This program employs features from another Borland program, Paradox for Windows, in order to complement Quattro Pro.

FIGURE 8-13 Database Desktop at work

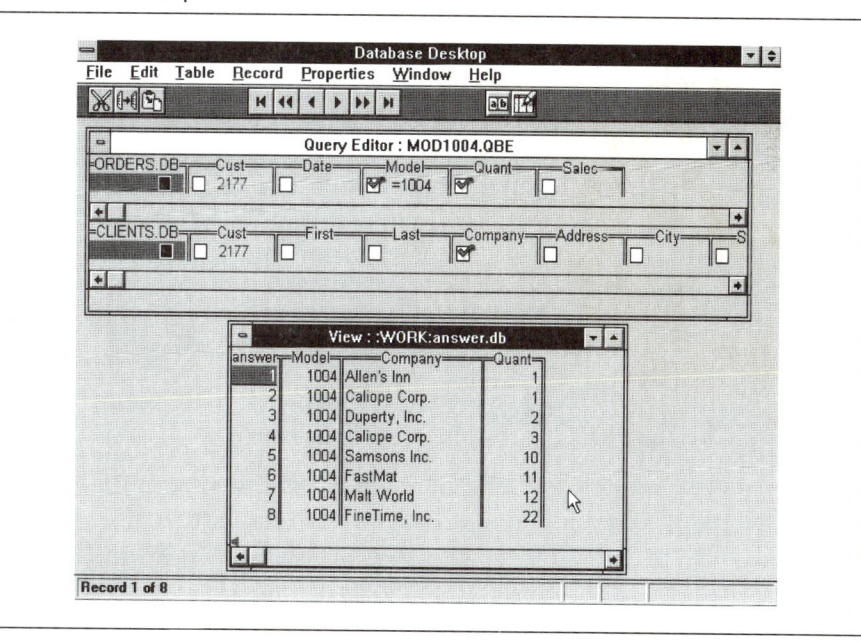

In this section we introduce you to Database Desktop and give a simple example of its operation. For more information about how the feature works use the Help command on the Database Desktop menu. You might also want to consult a good guide to Paradox for Windows, such as *Paradox for Windows Made Easy* by Edward Jones (Osborne McGraw-Hill, 1992).

What Database Desktop Does

You can use Database Desktop to browse through data stored in dBASE and Paradox files. These files are referred to as tables, since they are displayed in table format, like the one called answer.db in the lower half of Figure 8-13. This lists companies that purchased Model 1004 and the quantity they purchased. This information was obtained from two separate database files, one of which records customer orders (ORDERS.DB), while the other lists the customer details such as names and addresses (CLIENTS.DB).

The table called answer.db is the result of a query created and performed by Database Desktop. As you saw in Chapter 6, a query is a question you ask about information in database tables. However, whereas the Data | Query command in Quattro Pro uses a criteria table to define queries, Database Desktop uses a query method called QBE, or Query By Example. To perform a QBE query, you give Database Desktop an example of the result you want. Database Desktop then determines the best way to arrive at the result. A Database Desktop query can be a simple question about the information in a single table or a complex question about information in several tables. Queries are flexible, interactive, and iterative. If a query doesn't quite obtain the results you want, you can easily refine it and perform the query again.

Running Database Desktop

You can run Database Desktop without running Quattro Pro, but loading Database Desktop from within Quattro Pro allows you to copy data straight from a database file into a notebook. To load Database Desktop from within Quattro Pro use the Data | Database Desktop

Chapter 8: Data Sharing and Transfer

command. In Figure 8-14 you can see what happens when you issue this command. The Database Desktop window appears on top of the Quattro Pro window.

If you want, you can use the Maximize button to expand the Database Desktop window to fill the screen, as in Figures 8-13 and 8-15, or you can work within the smaller window. The Database Desktop window is organized the same way as the Quattro Pro window. Below the title bar there is a menu bar and below that a SpeedBar. Below the SpeedBar is a work area where Database Desktop will display queries and query results within separate windows.

When you first load Database Desktop, there are only three menus on the menu bar (File, Window, and Help). There is just one button on the Database Desktop SpeedBar. This button is the New Query button, as indicated by the message in the status area at the bottom of the Database Desktop window. As in Quattro Pro, the status area in Database Desktop explains buttons when you point to them in the SpeedBar.

FIGURE 8-14 Database Desktop loaded from Quattro Pro showing New Query button

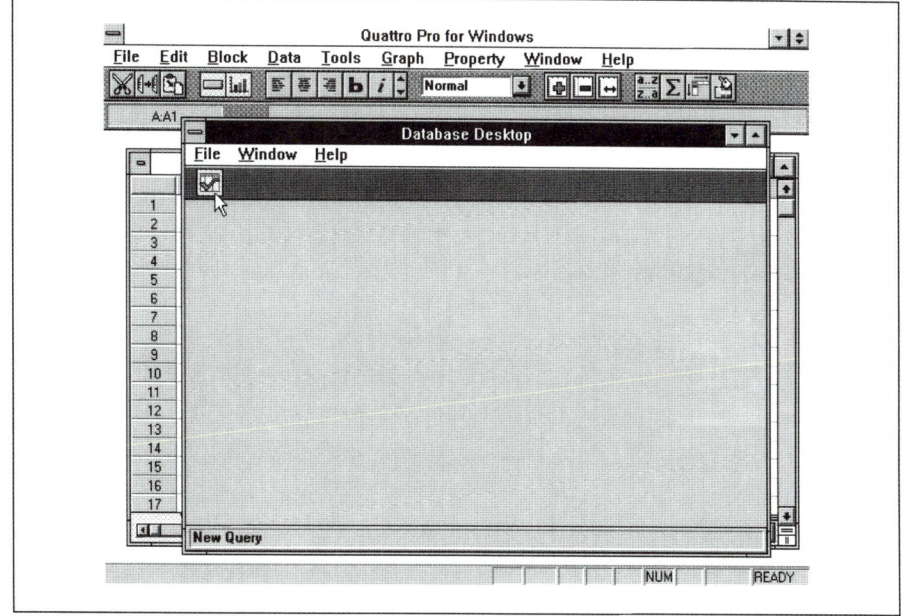

FIGURE 8-15 Selecting a file with Database Desktop in full-screen mode

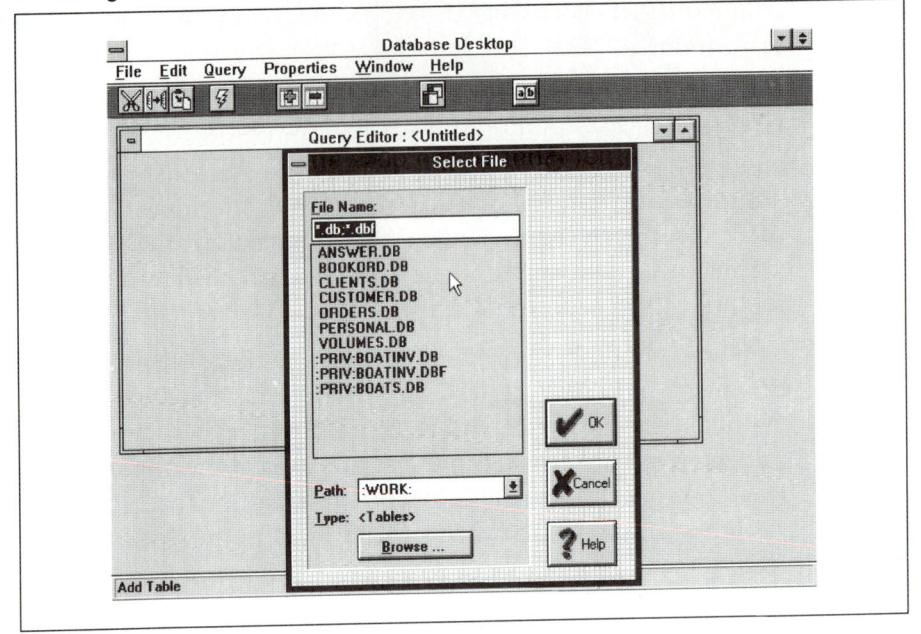

To start using Database Desktop, click on the New Query button. This does several things: new buttons appear on the SpeedBar; a Query Editor window is opened; and a Select File dialog box appears, as shown in Figure 8-15. The list of files includes both dBASE (DBF) and Paradox (DB) files, and you select the file you want to query.

When you have selected a file and clicked the OK button, the field names of the file are displayed in the Query Editor window, as shown in Figure 8-16. If there are more field names than will fit in the window, you can scroll through them with the horizontal scroll bar that is displayed below the field names. You can also adjust the width allotted to each field and the filename. To do this you drag the appropriate line with your mouse, as shown in Figure 8-16, where the space allotted to the filename is being increased. Note that the mouse pointer changes to a double-headed arrow when you perform this operation.

You can see that there is a check box below each field name. This is used to indicate whether or not the field should be included in the query, much the same way as entering a field name in the output block determines the contents of an extract performed with the Data | Query

Chapter 8: Data Sharing and Transfer 425

FIGURE 8-16 The file added to the Query Editor window

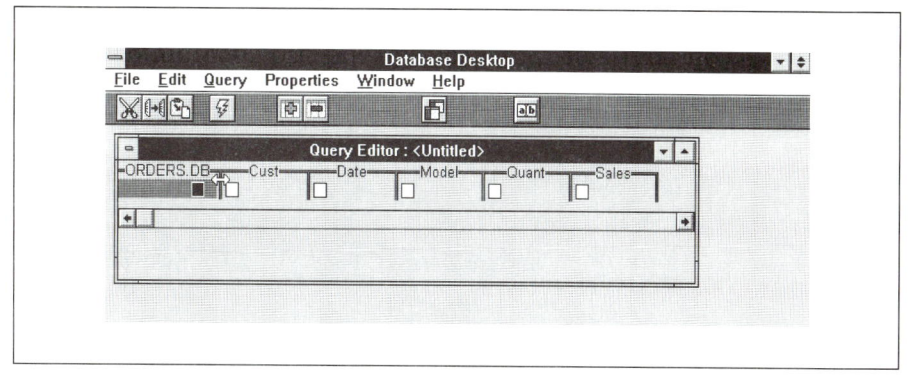

command. To select a field you click on the box. This displays a list of possible choices, as shown here:

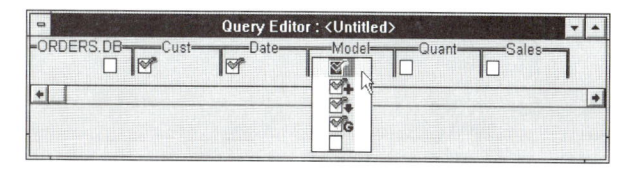

Note that the first few fields have been selected with a simple check mark, the first item on the list. This simply tells Database Desktop to include the field in the query. If you want to select all fields, you can use the check box below the table file name. Selecting a check mark from this box affects all fields in the table.

If you simply want to browse through a database file, you can check all fields and then issue the Query | Run command. The shortcut key for this is F8. Alternatively, you can click the appropriate button on the SpeedBar (the one with the lightning flash on it!). The effect of running a query at this point is to show you a table containing all fields and all records. You can see this in Figure 8-17. Note that the result of a query is always called ANSWER.DB. This is a special file used by Database Desktop to store the answer to, or results of, a query.

Note The name WORK, which precedes DATA\answer.db (Figure 8-13), is simply an alias for the QPW directory. Database Desktop uses aliases for directory names as part of its file management system. You can alter alias names through the File | Aliases command.

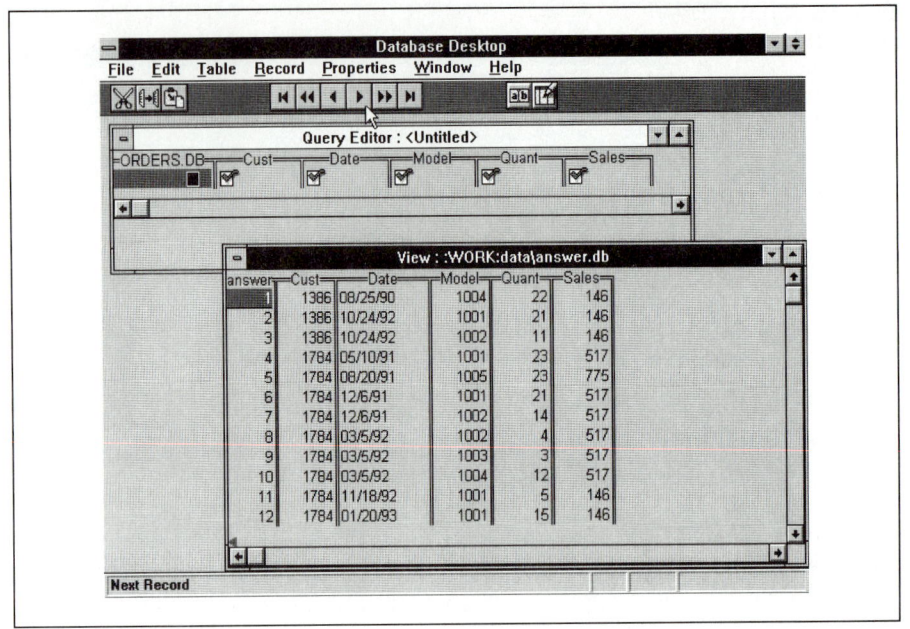

FIGURE 8-17 The answer table showing all fields and the first set of records

When an answer table is displayed, you can move between records with the arrow keys. The END key moves you to the last record, while HOME displays the first record. Use PGUP and PGDN to move between records one screen at a time. You can browse through records by using the VCR buttons that appear in the SpeedBar. These are, from left to right: First Record, Previous Set of Records, Previous Record, Next Record, Next Set of Records, and Last Record. A "set" of records simply means one screenful, and Next Set of Records is equivalent to pressing PGDN.

The answer table in Figure 8-17 lists all fields and all records in the ORDERS.DB file. The records represent individual orders placed by customers. The customers are identified by numbers and these are listed in the Cust field. For example, you can see that there are several orders for customer number 1386. Note that each record in the answer table has a record number assigned to it in the "answer" field. This field does not exist in the ORDERS.DB file but is added by Database Desktop to identify each record located by the query.

At this point you can do a number of things with the data in the answer table, including copy the contents to a Quattro Pro notebook. You can change the order of the columns and their width. You can also edit the data. To change the width of a column, you place the mouse pointer over the double dividing line on the right of the column. The mouse pointer changes to a white double-headed arrow, which you can drag the line left or right (to narrow or widen the column).

To move a column, you place the mouse pointer over the name of the field you want to move. The mouse pointer changes to a rectangular icon. You can then press and hold down the left mouse to get the black double-headed arrow that allows you to drag the column to the left or right. Note that you cannot move the "answer" column.

To edit data in the answer table, you can click on the piece of information you want to change and press F2 (the same key is used to edit cell entries in Quattro Pro). This activates EDIT mode and selects the entire item so that whatever you type next will replace the existing entry. Alternatively you can use the normal EDIT mode key to alter the entry. Press ENTER to leave the EDIT mode and confirm the change to the data. To leave the EDIT mode without recording changes, press F2. If you have made no change while in EDIT mode, pressing F2 will immediately exit EDIT mode. If you have made changes and want to cancel them, you must press ESC after F2 to leave EDIT mode.

Answers into Notebooks

When you have edited and arranged data in the answer table, you may want to copy it to a Quattro Pro notebook. The quickest way to do this is to use the Edit | Select All command on the Database Desktop menu, followed by Edit | Copy, switch to Quattro Pro, and use Edit | Paste. The Edit | Select All command immediately selects all records and fields in the answer table (indicated by a grey line around the selection). The Edit | Copy command copies the selected data to the Windows clipboard.

Now you can switch to Quattro Pro and prepare to paste the data into your notebook (use ALT-TAB to switch applications or press CTRL-ESC for the Windows Task List and select Quattro Pro from the list). Select the top-left cell of the section of the notebook page that is to receive the data and issue the Edit | Paste command. Figure 8-18 shows the results in this example.

FIGURE 8-18 An answer table pasted into a notebook

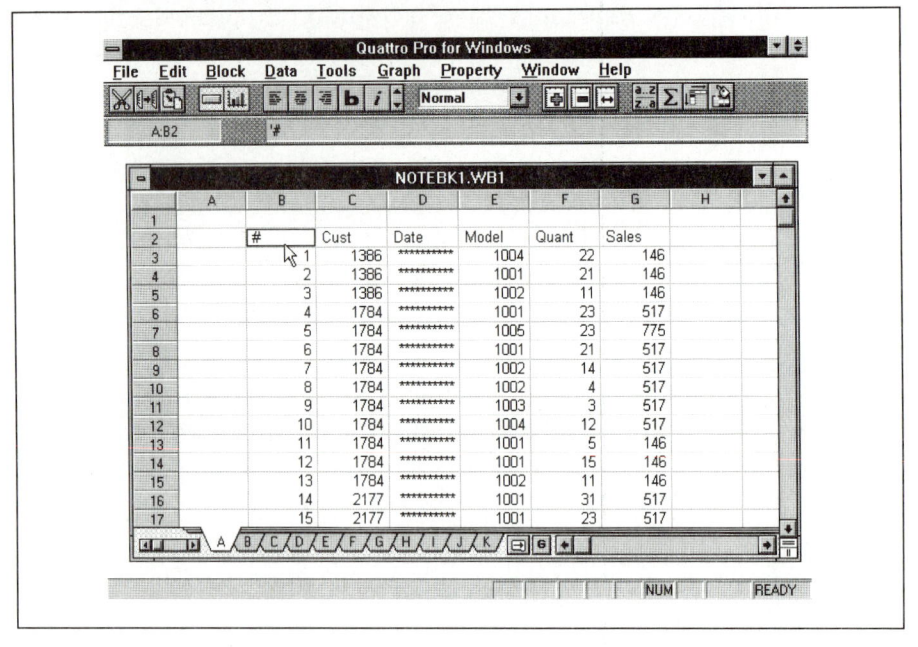

[Figure: Screenshot of Quattro Pro for Windows showing NOTEBK1.WB1 with an answer table pasted starting at cell B2, containing columns #, Cust, Date, Model, Quant, Sales.]

In this case, cell B2 of the notebook was selected before the paste operation was performed. Note that the pasted data does not affect the column widths of the spreadsheet, so the Date column is initially too narrow to display the date values. The first column, which contains the answer number, is simply labeled "#".

Bear in mind that the spreadsheet entries created by the above procedure are simply static data. Changes in the answer table will not be reflected in the notebook. If you want the notebook to reflect changes to the answer table, you should use Edit | Paste Link instead of Edit | Paste. This command creates a DDE link to the answer table. DDE stands for Dynamic Data Exchange, a Windows feature that allows documents from different programs to share the same data.

The results in Figure 8-18 would look much the same if Paste Link was used instead of Paste, however, the entry in the top left cell, B2, would not be a label but the following DDE formula:

@DDELINK([DBD|WORK:DATA\ANSWER.DB]"_TABLE")

This formula uses the DDELINK function, which takes as its arguments: the name of the application which created the document that provides the data, the name of the document providing the data, and the section of the document to be used. In this case the application is DBD (for Database Desktop). The doucment is WORK:DATA\ANSWER.DB. The section of the document required is known as _TABLE. This formula ensures that cell B2, and cells below and to the left of it, reflects any changes that are made to the answer table, such as a new or revised query.

Querying by Example

So far you have seen how to select fields to include in a query and how to view all records in a selected database. Now it is time to look at how you query a database for specific information. Suppose that you want to know which customers have ordered Model 1004. To create this query you can either open a new query window (using File | New Query) or edit the existing query.

To edit the existing query you simply deselect all fields except the Cust and Model fields. To do this you adjust the selection status for each field, or you can use the check box under the filename to deselect all fields and reselect Cust and Model. You can see these fields selected in Figure 8-19, which also shows the next step in the query, as well as the query result.

When you need to select records meeting certain criteria, you enter an example under the field name in the Query window. This means that to find records that have the entry 1004 in the Model field, you enter **= 1004** under Model, as shown in Figure 8-18. You can then issue the Query | Run command (you can do this by clicking the button in SpeedBar, indicated by the mouse pointer in Figure 8-19).

The answer table produced by this example is shown in Figure 8-19. Note that when the query window is active, the SpeedBar shows query-related buttons, as opposed to the record browsing buttons that appear when the answer window is active, as in Figure 8-17. Also note that Database Desktop shows you exactly what you asked for, a list of all customers who ordered Model 1004. You do not get every record in which the entry in the Model field is 1004. In other words, the result of the query

FIGURE 8-19 The edited query along with results in the answer table

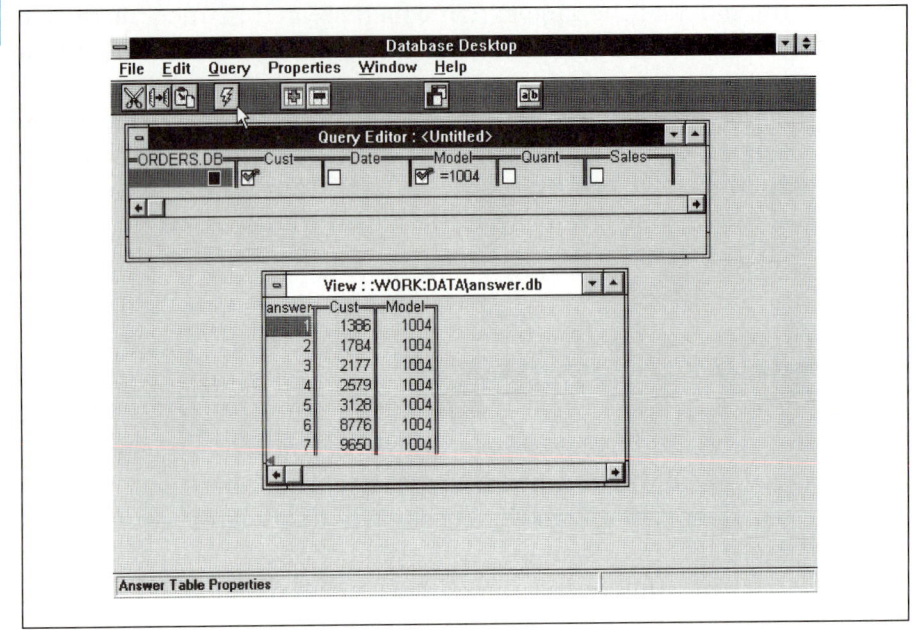

is similar to the operation of the Unique command in the Data Query dialog box, as opposed to the Extract command (see Chapter 6 for more about these two commands).

Querying Two Tables

Suppose that you want a list of the names of the customers who have ordered Model 1004. Such a list was seen earlier in Figure 8-13. As you may have noticed, the details about each customer are not stored in the ORDERS.DB database. In an arrangement quite typical of relational database managers such as Paradox and dBASE, details about the customers are stored in a different file. Programs like Paradox can establish relationships between two or more separate files, as long as there is common data within the records. In this case, the names and addresses of customers are stored in a file called CLIENTS.DB. Each record also includes the customer number and it is this common data that allows a relationship between the files to be established.

Chapter 8: Data Sharing and Transfer

So, in order to create a list of customers that ordered Model 1004, including the customer name, it is necessary to query two files at once. To add a table to a query you use the Add Table button, the one with the plus sign on it. This produces a Select File dialog box and you choose the file you need. In this case the file is called CLIENTS.DB. When you select OK, the field names from that file are listed in the current query window, as shown in Figure 8-20, which also shows the next step in the query process.

You can adjust the Query Editor window to view more of the fields if you want and you can scroll more fields into view. The first four fields of the CLIENTS.DB file are Cust, First, Last, and Company. You would like a list shows which companies ordered Model 1004 and how many they ordered. To do this you check the Model and Quant fields in ORDERS.DB and Company in CLIENTS.DB. The final step before running the query is to connect the two tables. You do this by entering an example of the common data in the respective fields of the two files in the Query Editor window.

As you can see from Figure 8-20, the example used in this case is 2177. This is one of the customer numbers that appear in both files. What you cannot see from Figure 8-20 is that 2177 appears in red to indicate that it is an example element and not a piece of data to be matched. To enter an example element you select the appropriate field, press F5, and then type the example data, in this case 2117. You then enter the same example in the same way in the second table. Note that the two fields do not have to have the same name, but they should contain similar data, including the exact data you supply as an example. With the query settings in Figure 8-20, the Query | Run command produces the answer table shown earlier in Figure 8-13. In Figure 8-21 you can see this data

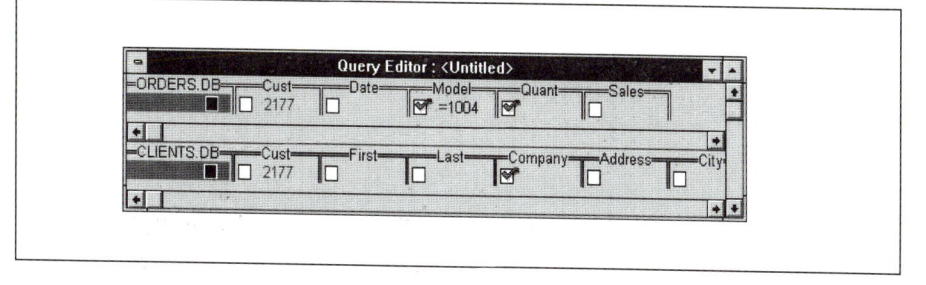

FIGURE 8-20 The second table added to the Query Editor window

as it might appear in a Quattro Pro notebook using the DDELINK function in B2.

Note that the Autowidth feature was used to adjust the width of the table columns and a descriptive label was added in A1. The rest of the information is supplied by the DDELINK formula. Also note that the data in the answer table was sorted in ascending order by Database Desktop. The sort order follows the order of the fields used in the table from left to right, that is, according to the Model and Quant field in the ORDERS.DB table then the Company field in CLIENTS.DB table.

Using Queries

So far you have seen part, but not all, of what you can accomplish with the very powerful Database Desktop. If you do a lot of work with database files, you will want to explore this feature further. Once you have created a query that you need to use on a regular basis, you can save it using the File | Save command from the Database Desktop menu (before issuing the command you should select the Query Editor window).

FIGURE 8-21 The Database Desktop answer table shared with a notebook using DDELINK

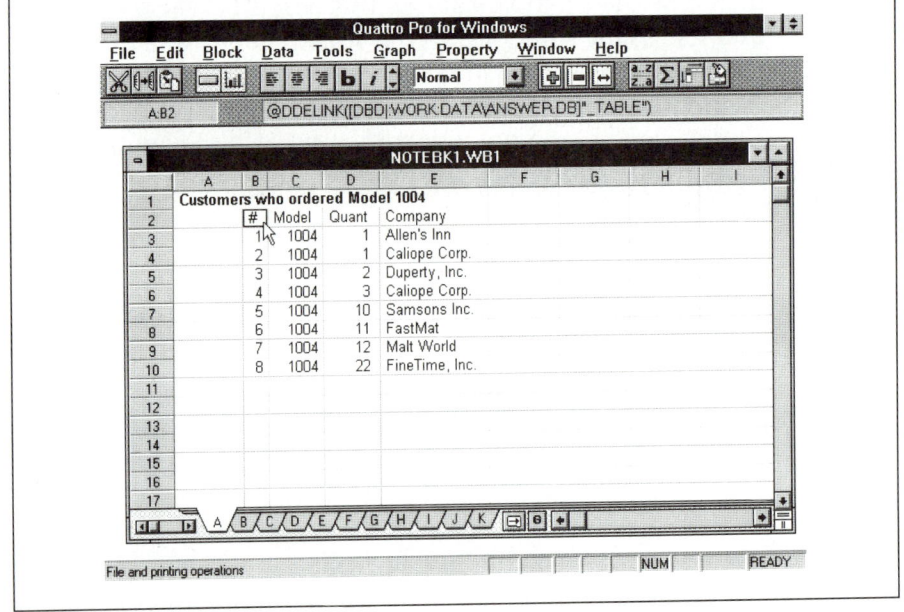

Chapter 8: Data Sharing and Transfer

Queries are saved with the extension QBE (for query by example). You can use File | Open to retrieve previously saved queries.

Queries created and saved by the Database Desktop or Paradox can be used within Quattro Pro by means of the Data | Table Query command. When you issue this command you get the following dialog box:

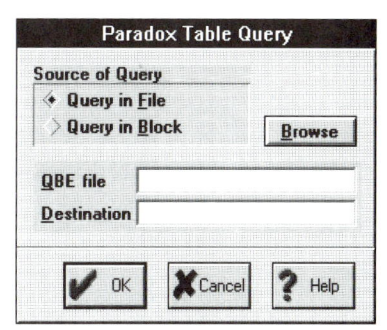

When you select Query in File, you can use the Browse button to locate the QBE file that you want to use. In the Destination field you enter the spreadsheet location for the results. When you choose OK, the answer table from the query you specified is pasted into the notebook at the location you indicated.

The Query in Block option in the Paradox Table Query dialog box allows you to define a query within a block of cells in a notebook instead of in a QBE file. The main advantage of this approach is that you can use spreadsheet formulas to create the query definition and thus change the definition very quickly, as well as incorporate it into macros. A query is defined in a spreadsheet by a column of label entries that begins with the label Query and ends with EndQuery, as shown here:

Query

ANSWER:C:\QPW\DATA\answer.db

C:\QPW\ORDERS.DB|Cust|Model|Quant|
|_2177|Check=1004|Check|

C:\QPW\CLIENTS.DB|Cust|Company|
|_2177|Check|

EndQuery

This series of labels defines the query used in the last example, that is, lists purchasers of Model 1004, showing company and quantity. Note the blank lines separating the various parts of the query definition. After the answer table is defined, the two database files are defined, along with the fields required and the status of each field. Thus the Cust, Model, and Quant fields of the ORDERS.DB field are required. The status is an example in the Cust field (_2177), a match in the Model field (Check=1004), and a simple listing in the Quant field (Check).

Although all of the entries in the query definition are labels, you can use string formulas to create these labels. Thus the number of the model you want to match could be stated in a separate cell and referenced in a formula, as shown in Figure 8-22. Here you can see that cell D2 contains the number 1004. This is referenced by cell A6 in the query definition:

+"|_2177|Check="&@STRING(D2,0)&"|Check|"

This formula means that the query entry in A6 will always reflect whatever model number is entered in D2 (see Chapter 12 for more on string formulas).

FIGURE 8-22 Using a query defined by spreadsheet entries

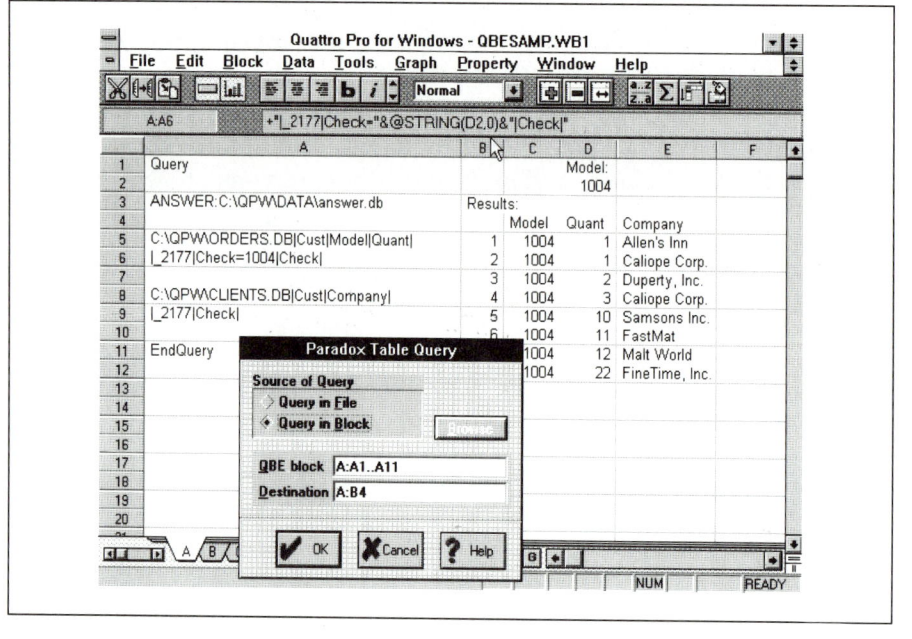

To perform the query, the results of which are visible in B4 through E12, the Data | Table Query command was issued and Query in Block was selected. Cells A1..A11 of page A were defined as the QBE Block, whose Destination was defined as B4. The OK button was then selected. Quattro Pro read the entries in A1..A11, interpreted them as a query, and used Database Desktop to find the results (you do not actually see the Database Desktop program at work, but it is used in this procedure). In this case the results are all of the entries in B4..E12, including the labels Model, Quant, and Company. The label Results: in B3 is purely ornamental, as is the label Model: in D1.

You can see that this arrangement allows you to change the model number in D2 and repeat the Data | Table Query command to get a different list of companies. This might be more convenient than using the query editor in Database Desktop, particularly if you want to incorporate the procedure in a Quattro Pro macro. Note that an easy way to create the initial entries required for a query definition is to create and test the definition with Database Desktop, save it as a QBE file, and use the Tools | Import command in Quattro Pro to read the QBE file into a notebook. You can then edit the entries if you want to change the query definition (for more on Tools | Import, see Chapter 12).

CHAPTER 9

Graphing Fundamentals

Graphs provide another way of looking at the data in your worksheet—a visual way. In a graph, you can see patterns in the data that may not have been obvious in a spreadsheet. In Figure 9-1, you see a record of year-to-date sales by the three agents at the Van Ness office of Quattro Vadis Travel. Can you see the patterns? Of course you can—as long as you're willing to spend some time examining all the numbers. For a quicker analysis, look at Figure 9-2, which shows the default graph that Quattro Pro for Windows constructs from the spreadsheet data. As you can see, that neat Fiji trip is selling pretty well, and Sue isn't doing badly in sales.

With Quattro Pro for Windows, creating graphs from spreadsheet data is exceptionally easy. You just select the data, as shown here:

Package	Joe	Sue	Sam
Riviera	56	61	53
Tahiti	35	39	24
Fiji	76	84	36
World Cru	27	45	43

Next, you click the Graph tool on the SpeedBar, and the pointer changes to a tiny graph. With this pointer, you select an unoccupied area of the

FIGURE 9-1 Numerical data in a spreadsheet

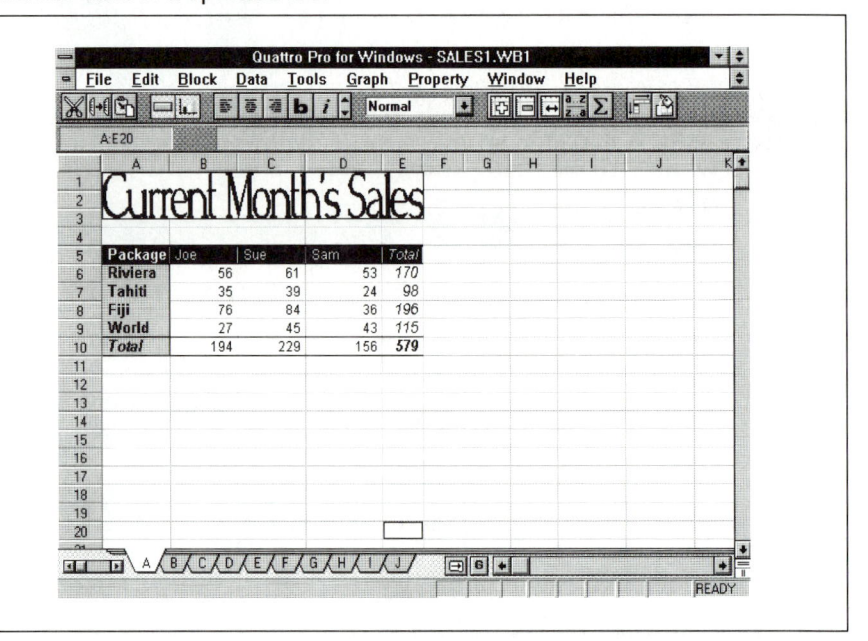

Chapter 9: Graphing Fundamentals

FIGURE 9-2 Bar graph of the numerical data

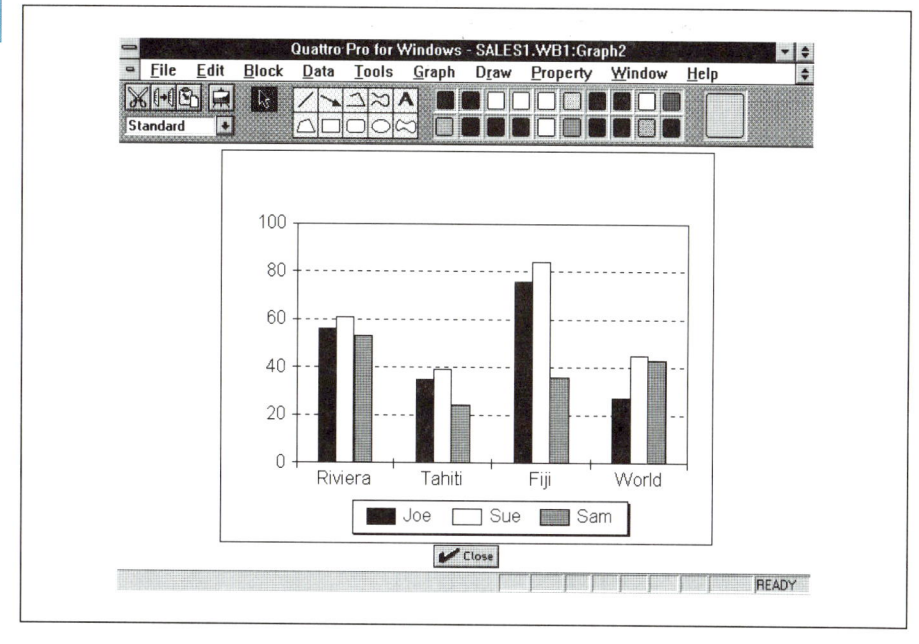

spreadsheet, and Quattro Pro automatically inserts the graph using the default graph settings.

A graph inserted in a spreadsheet in this way is called a *floating graph*. A floating graph is part of the spreadsheet; when you save the spreadsheet, you save the graph. Moreover, the floating graph is *dynamically linked* to the data in the spreadsheet. If you change the data, the graph changes.

Once you've created a floating graph, you will typically perform some of the following actions, which this chapter surveys in the following order:

- **Naming the graph** The *Graphs page* is always the last page of a notebook. It contains icons corresponding to all the graphs you have created in a notebook. You can use the Graphs page to rename graphs. The Graphs page is also used for presentation graphics purposes, such as creating a slide show. Chapter 10 discusses the many ways you can use Quattro Pro for Windows to create presentation-quality graphics.

- **Sizing and moving the floating graph** After you've inserted a floating graph into your spreadsheet, you can size the graph by dragging the handles or you can drag the graph to a different location. Using the graph properties menus, you can add a box (a border around the chart) and background colors.

- **Customizing the graph with the Graph window** The Graph window, shown in Figure 9-2, displays your graph in editable form and provides its own SpeedBar. From the Graph window SpeedBar, you can choose tools to dress up your graph with text, lines, shapes, arrows, colors, and patterns. From menus, you can choose commands to change the graph type, change the data series, and add titles. You can create a graph directly in the Graph window without making a floating graph, and you can later insert this graph into any notebook page.

- **Choosing a graph type** When you create a floating graph, Quattro Pro automatically creates a two-dimensional column chart, as shown in Figure 9-2. You can choose from many additional chart types, including bar charts, line charts, area charts, pie charts, and text charts. You can also choose three-dimensional charts.

- **Manually defining the data series** Quattro Pro makes certain assumptions about the location of data series when you create a graph using the Graph tool in the SpeedBar. If you created your graph from data that was typed in a format other than the one Quattro Pro expected, or if you wish to add or delete a data series, you can do so in the Graph window.

- **Adding titles** In the Graph window, you can add first and second titles, as well as axis titles.

- **Customizing your chart using graph properties** In the Graph window, you can modify your chart in many ways using Quattro Pro's properties menus, which appear when you right-click an object. Using these, you can add grid lines, annotate the data series, choose chart type options, modify the background, insert a legend, annotate the axes, add borders and fill patterns, and much more.

- **Managing charts** When you add a floating chart to a spreadsheet, Quattro Pro saves the chart along with the data. You can also create a chart that's not associated with a spreadsheet, and you can copy or move charts as you please.

Because Quattro Pro for Windows provides so many options for creating, editing, and managing graphs, illustrating every possible combination is beyond the scope of this book. The main options will be described, however, with suggestions for their application to your specific graphing needs. Note that the focus of this chapter is on the use of Quattro Pro graphs for analytical purposes—finding and understanding the patterns in your data. Chapter 10 discusses the customization of graphs for presentation purposes—conveying those patterns to your audience.

Understanding Graph Terminology

If you're new to graphics applications, learning a few basic terms will help you work with Quattro Pro graphs more effectively. Figure 9-3 calls your attention to some features of the graph that require special terms.

FIGURE 9-3 Parts of a Quattro Pro graph

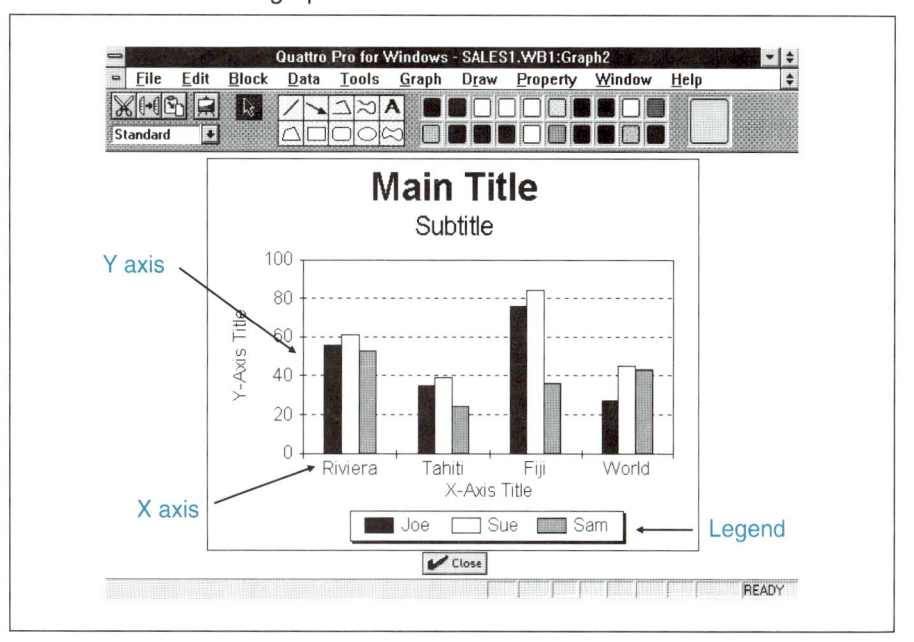

As you review this first graph, note that in graph terminology, the column of numbers for each travel agent (Joe, Sue, and Sam) constitutes a *data series*. A data series is a collection of numbers that all pertain to a single subject, such as Joe's sales or Sue's sales. Within a data series, each unit of data is called a *data point*. A data point lies at the intersection of a value (such as 61) and a category (such as Riviera). In Figure 9-1, the values 56, 35, 76, and 27 in Column B make up a single data series (Joe's data). Within Column B, there are four data points. The data point 35, for example, is Joe's sales data for the Tahiti trip.

In the chart shown in Figure 9-3, each data point corresponds to a column. The *Y axis*, which is sometimes called the *value axis*, measures the data points' values. Each of the categories—the various trip packages, such as Tahiti or Fiji—is listed across the *X axis*, also called the *category axis*. The box that explains the shading is called a *legend*. Quattro Pro for Windows enables you to remove the legend if it is not required (for example, when only one series of data is defined). There are many changes and embellishments you can make to this basic graph, and they will be dealt with in the course of this chapter. Bear in mind, however, that making this first graph took just one command, and the results are very respectable. Furthermore, the graph you have made is dynamically linked to the data in the spreadsheet. For example, suppose that Sam actually sold 63 trips to Fiji rather than 36. You exit the Graph window and change cell B8 from 36 to 63. You see the difference immediately in the floating chart, as shown in Figure 9-4.

Viewing the Graphs Page

When you create a floating graph, Quattro Pro automatically adds an icon to the Graphs page, the last page of a notebook. The icon represents the graph you've added, and its design reflects the graph type you've selected (a bar graph, in this case). To view the Graphs page, click the TurboTab button (the button with the arrow next to the right of the notebook page tabs at the bottom of the screen). You see the Graphs page, which contains an icon corresponding to the graph you've created, as shown in Figure 9-5.

As you can see, Quattro Pro has automatically assigned a name to the graph, Graph 1. When there are many graphs represented as icons in

Chapter 9: Graphing Fundamentals 443

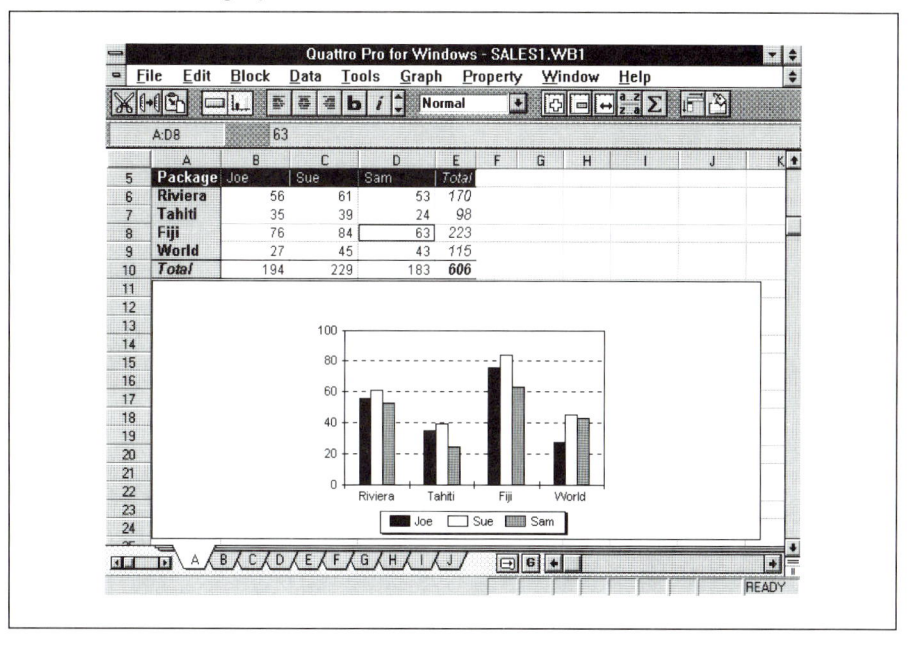

FIGURE 9-4 Corrected column graph

FIGURE 9-5 Graphs page containing a graph icon

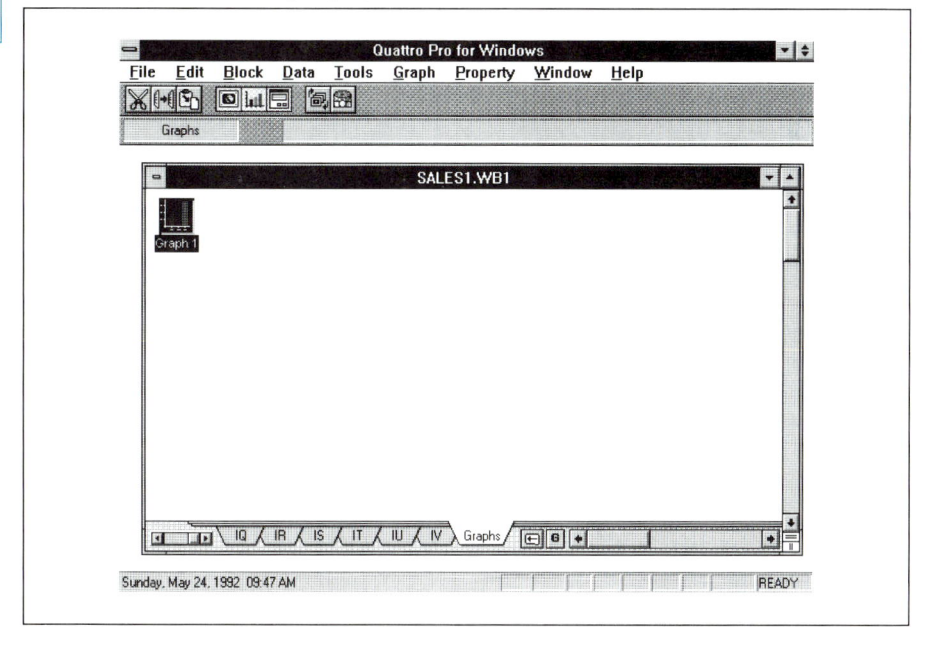

the Graphs page, you won't really be able to tell them apart unless you give them more descriptive names. To rename a graph, right-click the graph icon. You see the following dialog box:

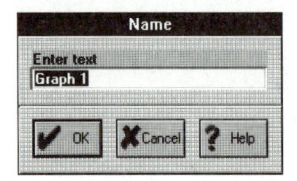

Type a name (**Van Ness Sales** would be a good choice for the example discussed here) and choose OK. Now you see the name under the icon.

A graph's icon on the Graphs page, rather than the original floating graph you created, is the graph's *source object.* This means you can delete the floating graph on the spreadsheet without wiping out the graph; if you click the TurboTab button, you'll still see the graph's icon on the Graphs page. To reinsert the graph anywhere within the notebook, move the cell selector to the place you want the graph to appear and then choose Insert from the Graph menu. You see a dialog box listing the graphs stored in the Graphs page, as shown here:

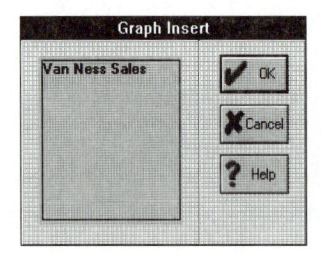

Select the graph name and click OK to insert the graph in the spreadsheet.

Note Bear in mind that the Graphs page contains the source objects for all the graphs you create in a notebook. The floating graphs that appear in spreadsheets are just copies of the source object. If you delete a floating graph from a spreadsheet page, you haven't deleted the source object. The source object still appears on the Graphs page. You can insert the graph anywhere in the notebook using the Insert command from the Graph menu.

Working with Floating Graphs

Once you have inserted a floating graph into your spreadsheet, you select it by clicking within it. A selected graph has eight *handles,* small black squares that appear on the graph's border. To move the floating graph, just drag the graph to its new position. To resize the height or width, drag one of the handles on the top, sides, or bottom. To scale the graph, drag one of the handles at the corners. If a gray border appears after scaling the graph, reset the aspect ratio to "inserted graph." For information on changing the aspect ratio of a graph, see the section titled "The Graph Window."

To change the floating graph's properties, right-click the selected graph. You see the Graph Object menu, as shown here:

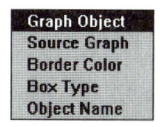

```
Graph Object
Source Graph
Border Color
Box Type
Object Name
```

From this menu you can change the source graph, change the color of the border (the frame surrounding the graph), change the box type (the thickness of the frame), and give the chart an object name for use in macros. You would change the name of the source graph only if you wanted to replace the currently displayed graph with another graph that is represented in the Graphs page. If you choose the Border Color option, you can select a color from a palette or create a different color using color scales. If you choose Box Type, you can choose from the following options: None, Thin (the default setting), Medium, and Thick.

Note You can size and move a floating graph, and you can also format its border, but most of the work you'll do to customize a graph will be done in the Graph window, the subject of the following section.

The Graph Window

The Graph window provides all the tools you need to annotate and edit your graph. To display a graph in the Graph window, you may use one of three techniques:

- Double-click a floating graph.

- Choose Edit from the Graph menu and select the name of the graph from the list box.

- Double-click a graph icon on the Graphs page.

The Graph window has the same menus as the Notebook window, with one exception: the Draw menu, which contains commands needed to arrange the elements of your graph. You also see the Graph window SpeedBar, as shown here:

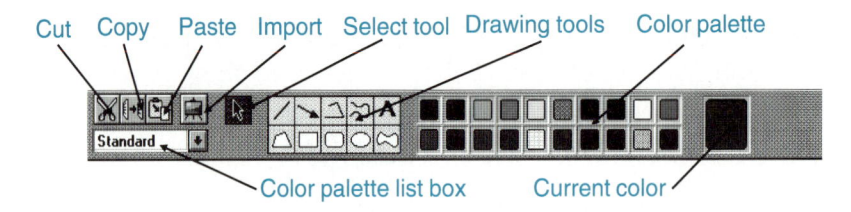

Like the Notebook window SpeedBar, it contains the Cut, Copy, and Paste buttons. In addition, you see a graphics file Import button. You can import graphics files in a very wide variety of formats, including Windows bitmap (BMP), Computer Graphics Metafile (CGM), Encapsulated PostScript (EPS), PCX, TIF, and more. Beneath the Cut, Copy, and Paste buttons, you see a list box that displays the name of the current color palette and lets you choose (or create) another palette. The default color palette is called Standard; other options are Summer, Fall, Winter, Spring, Monochrome, Washes, Blends, and ColorPatterns. To the right are the Select tool (for selecting individual objects within the Graph window), drawing tools, and the color palette. The large button at the right side of the SpeedBar shows the color of the currently selected object. In Chapter 10, you will learn more about dressing up your graphs with these tools.

Much of the initial work you will do in the Graph window involves the Graph menu, which you can use to change the graph type and data series settings, as well as add titles. By selecting properties and right-clicking, you can change additional aspects of the graph. The following sections explore these points in detail.

Chapter 9: Graphing Fundamentals

Choosing the Graph Type

When you create a floating graph by selecting a block and clicking the Graph tool in the SpeedBar, Quattro Pro creates a bar graph using its default settings. You may choose from many additional types of bar graphs, and you may also switch to another graph type.

To choose a graph type, select the floating graph or open the Graph window, and choose Type from the Graph menu. You see the Graph Types dialog box, shown in Figure 9-6.

In this dialog box, you select a graph by first clicking one of the five graph categories in the left column: two-dimensional (2-D), three-dimensional (3-D), rotated, combination, and text. By default, the 2-D option is selected. Then you choose a graph type within that category. The available graph categories are as follows:

- **2-D** Two-dimensional graphs show data in two dimensions, with the X axis aligned horizontally, and the Y axis aligned vertically.

- **3-D** Three-dimensional graphs are used to plot two or more data series against three-dimensional background walls and a base.

- **Rotate** Rotated graphs show the data with reversed axes: The X axis becomes the vertical axis, and the Y axis becomes the horizontal. You can rotate 3-D as well as 2-D graphs.

FIGURE 9-6 Graph Types dialog box

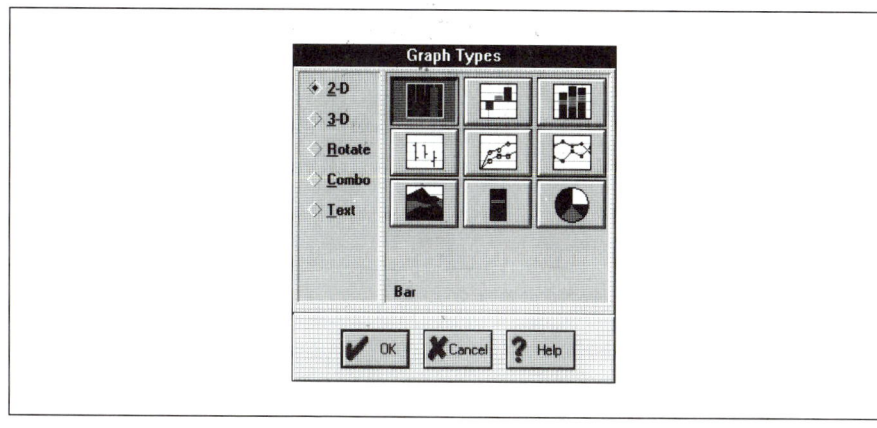

☐ **Combo** Combination graphs include more than one graph type, such as bars and lines. Three combination graphs are available automatically: line-bar, area-bar, and high-low-bar.

☐ **Text** Text graphs do not require numerical data. They are used for presentation graphics purposes, and are described in Chapter 10.

☐ **Multiple** Multiple graphs plot each data series as a separate graph. You can choose from multiple bars, multiple 2-D columns, multiple 3-D columns, and multiple pies (in both 2-D and 3-D versions). These are chosen with the Combo option.

When you choose a graph category other than 2-D, the Graph Types dialog box displays additional graph type choices. The 3-D option displays the following graph type choices:

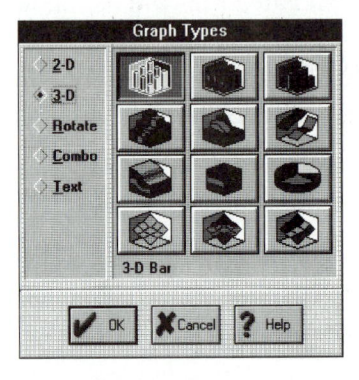

The Rotate option displays the following graph type choices:

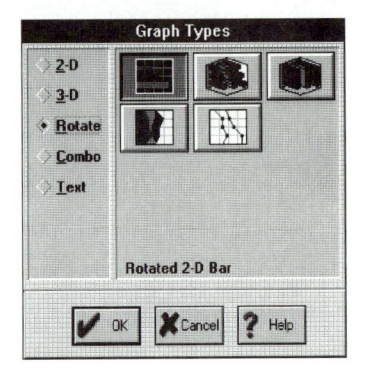

The Combo option displays the following graph type choices:

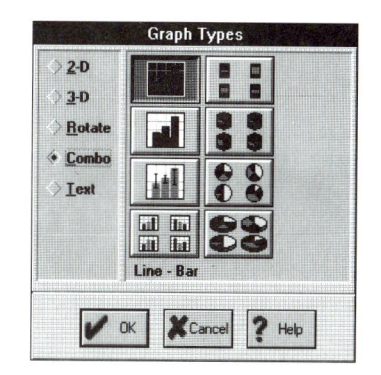

The Text option does not display any choices. You will learn more about text graphs in Chapter 10.

Two-Dimensional Graphs

Quattro Pro provides nine different types of two-dimensional graphs. Following are descriptions for each of these graph types. Examples are provided for some of the graphs in order to demonstrate the differences between the options.

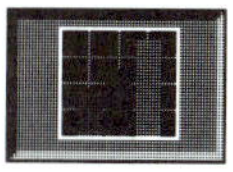

Bar graphs are the default graph type. Each bar represents a single data point in a data series. Values are plotted using the Y axis as a guide. If the source data includes more than one data series, Quattro Pro places the bars adjacent to one another, facilitating comparison, as shown in Figure 9-7.

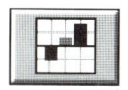

Variance graphs are bar graphs that show negative values by extending negative values below the X axis. Using the Y axis Property menu, you can set a baseline other than 0.

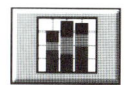

Stacked bar graphs display the values from all data series together in a vertical stack, showing how the values make up a whole. The first data series appears on the bottom, and the others are stacked in order. In Figure 9-8, you see how the values shown in Figure 9-7 have been stacked, showing the proportion each donor (individuals, corporations, and schools) made during the three years (1990, 1991, and 1992).

FIGURE 9-7 Bar graph (default graph type) facilitates comparison

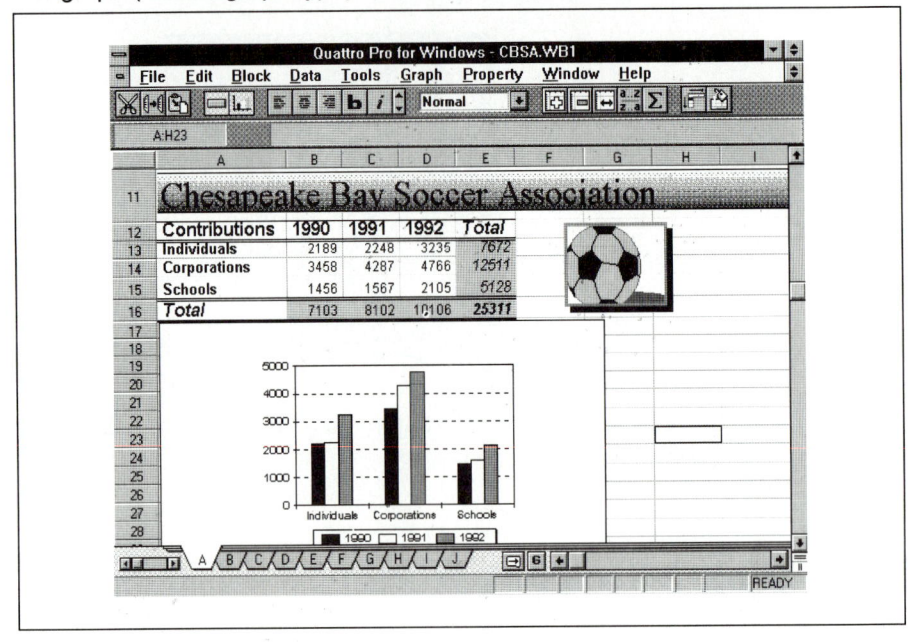

FIGURE 9-8 Stacked bar graph emphasizes proportion

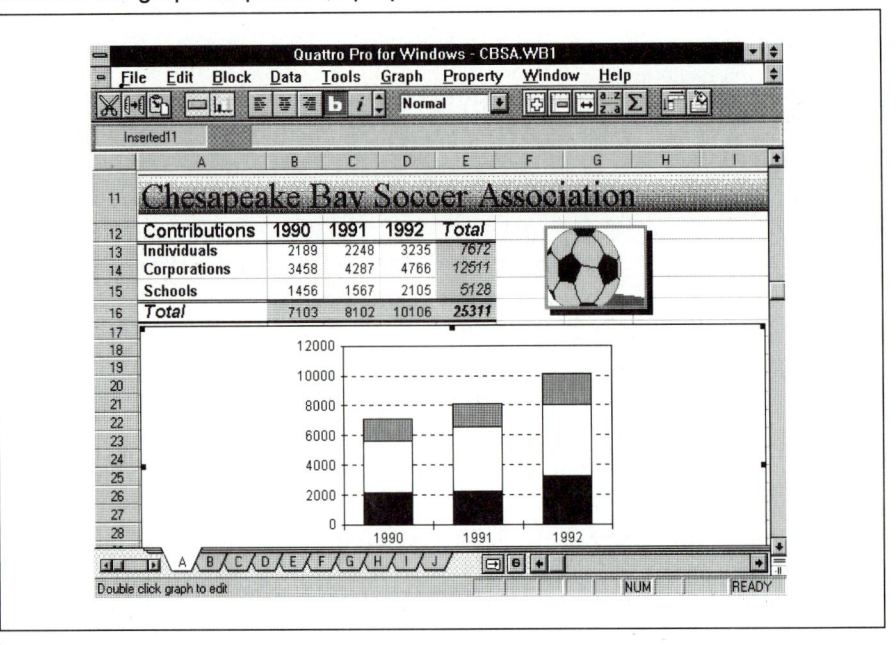

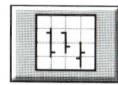

Chapter 9: Graphing Fundamentals 451

High-low graphs are used to display stock prices. They show a stock's highest and lowest prices for a period (such as a day, week, or month).

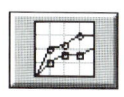

Line graphs show how values change over time, such as a chart showing the growth of market share over a ten-year period.

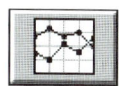

XY graphs plot values in one series in tandem with values in another series, showing a numerical relationship. Using an XY graph, for example, you can show how advertising expenditure relates to sales.

Area graphs also provide a way to show how a set of values make up a whole, but they are especially useful to show how the proportions change over time. Figure 9-9 illustrates an area graph.

FIGURE 9-9 Area graph

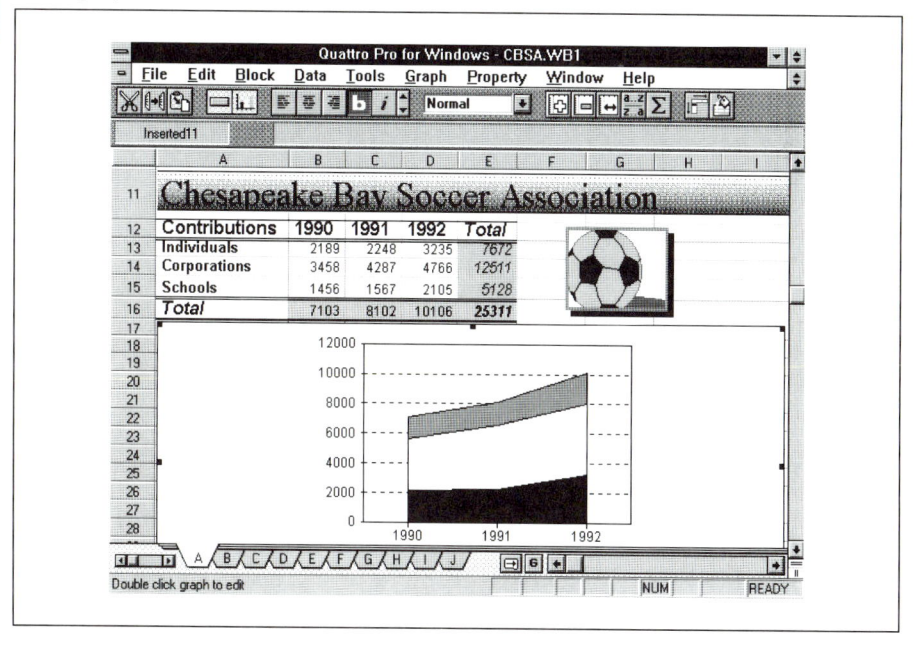

Column graphs show how a set of values make up a whole. A column graph uses only one data series or one data point in each series. If the selected data includes more than one data series, Quattro Pro uses only the first data series to construct the graph. Figure 9-10 shows a column chart that Quattro Pro automatically constructs from the data in B13..D15. The column graph shows the proportion given by each donor during 1990.

Pie graphs show how a set of values make up a whole, such as the contribution each salesperson made to the total sales for a month. A pie graph uses only one data series or one point in each data series. If the selected data includes more than one data series, Quattro Pro uses only the first data series to construct the graph. Figure 9-11 shows a pie graph that Quattro Pro automatically constructs from the data in B13..D15. Like the column graph in Figure 9-10, the pie graph shows the proportion given by each donor during the year 1990.

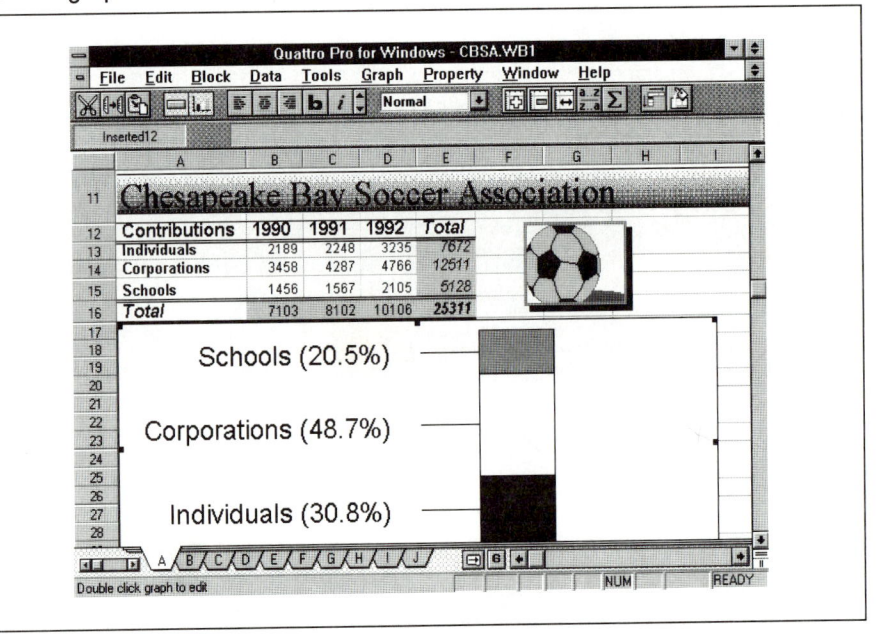

FIGURE 9-10 Column graph

Chapter 9: Graphing Fundamentals 453

FIGURE 9-11 Pie graph

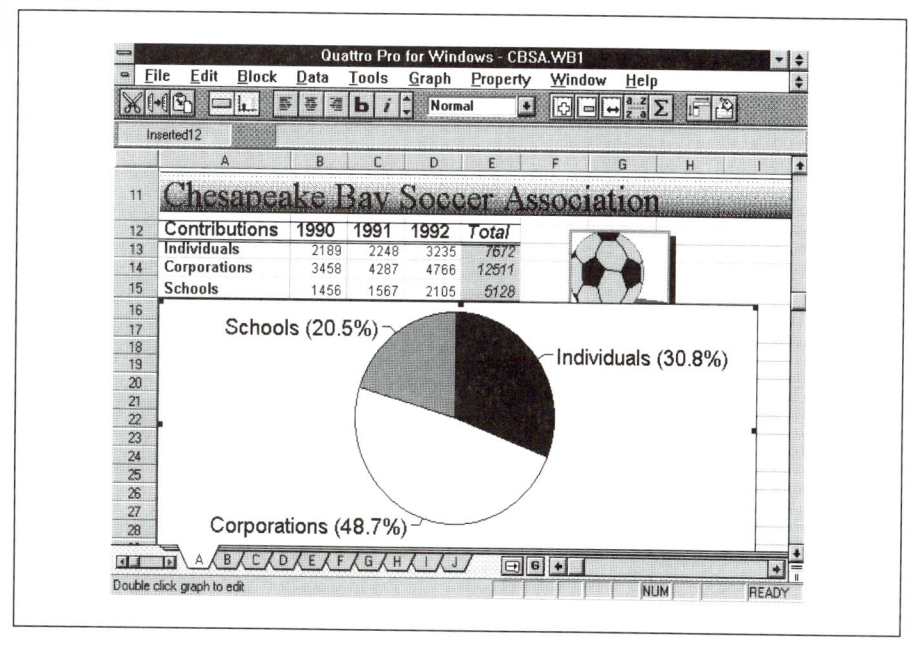

Three-Dimensional Graphs

Quattro Pro provides 12 different types of three-dimensional graphs. Following are descriptions for each of the 12 graph types. Examples are also provided for some of the three-dimensional graphs in order to demonstrate the differences between them.

3-D bar graphs display each data point as a three-dimensional column, as shown in Figure 9-12.

3-D stacked bar graphs show the cumulative values of all the data series, demonstrating how each data series contributes to the whole. Figure 9-13 shows a 3-D stacked bar graph.

2.5-D bar graphs place the series next to each other, rather than showing them in three dimensions.

454   Quattro Pro for Windows Inside & Out

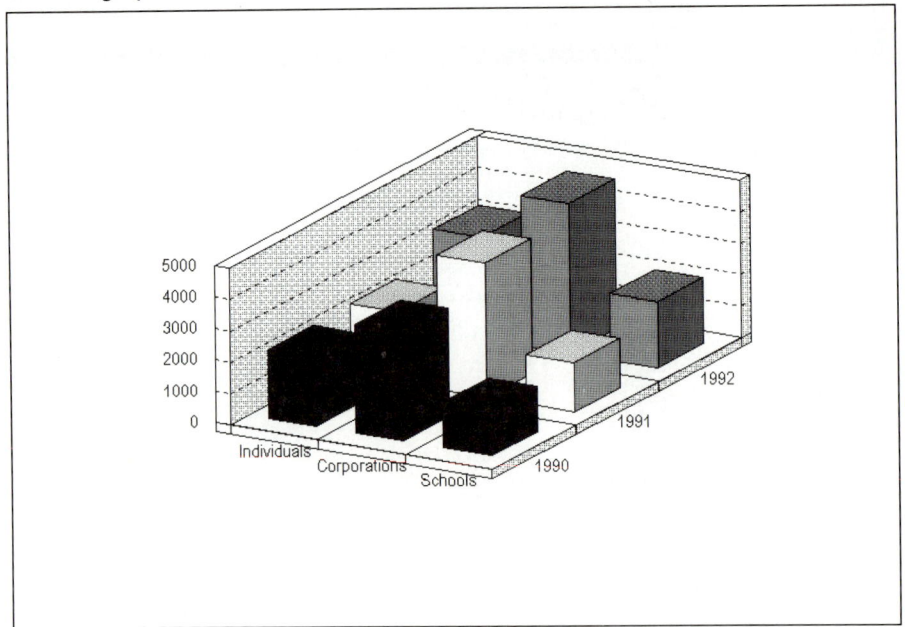

FIGURE 9-12 3-D bar graph

FIGURE 9-13 3-D stacked bar graph

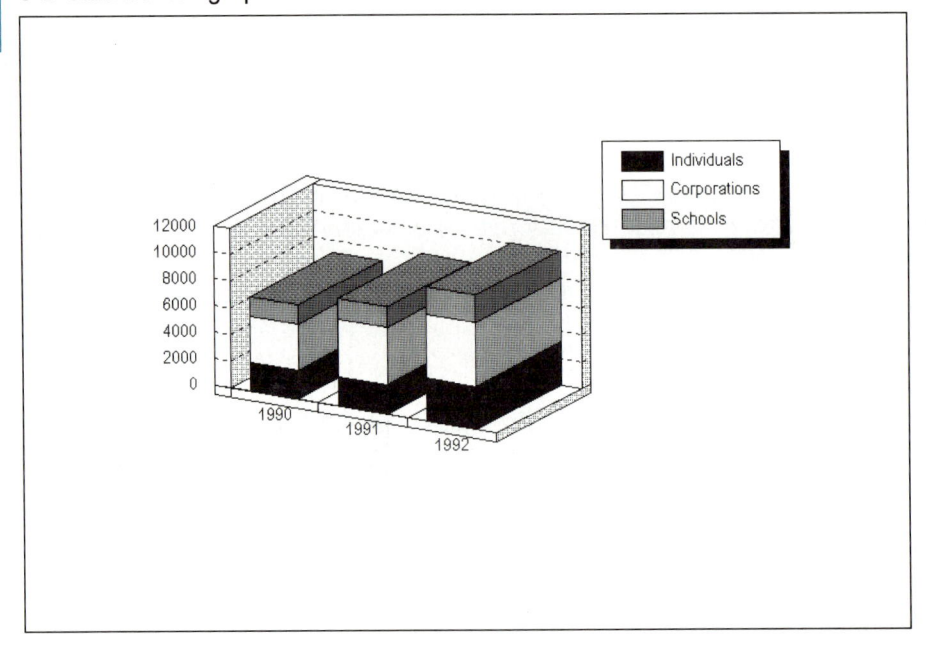

Chapter 9: Graphing Fundamentals

Stepped bar graphs closely resemble 3-D bar graphs, except that the bars touch. The effect is to emphasize the change that occurs from one step to the next, as shown in Figure 9-14.

3-D unstacked area graphs resemble 3-D bar graphs, except that they suggest cumulative change rather than a sharp, stepped gradation from one value to the next.

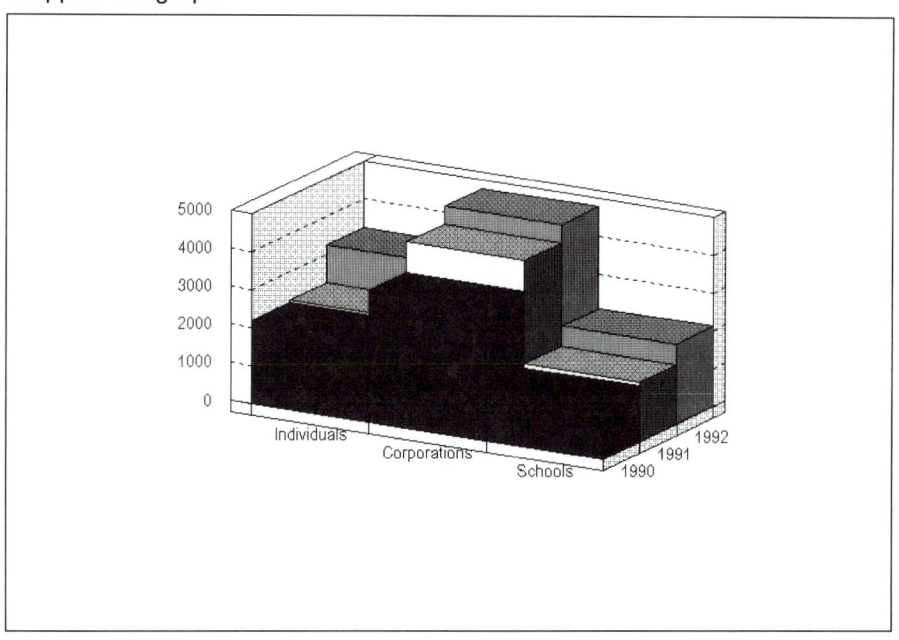

3-D ribbon graphs are three-dimensional line graphs; they show each data series as a floating ribbon, as in Figure 9-15.

3-D area graphs are identical to two-dimensional area graphs, except that the areas are shown in three-dimensional relief.

3-D column graphs are identical to two-dimensional column graphs, except that the column appears in three-dimensional relief. If more than one data series is selected, Quattro Pro displays only the first series.

FIGURE 9-14 Stepped bar graph

FIGURE 9-15 3-D ribbon graph

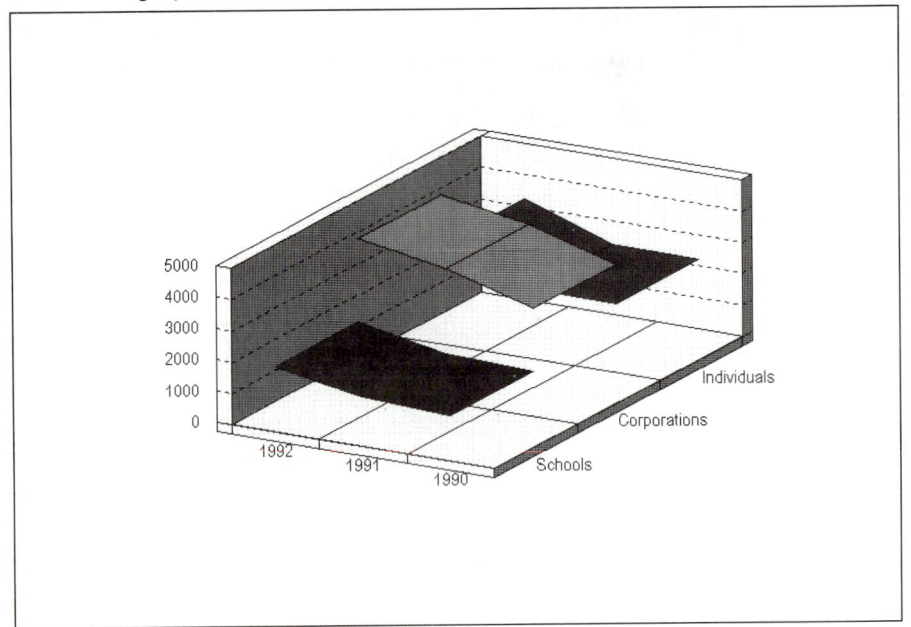

3-D pie graphs are identical to two-dimensional pie graphs, except that the pie appears in three-dimensional relief. If more than one data series is selected, Quattro Pro displays only the first data series.

3-D surface graphs plot data points as lines that form contoured surfaces on the screen, as shown in Figure 9-16. Values in columns form *mesh lines* that run from left to right in the graph, while values in rows form mesh lines that run from front to back.

3-D contour graphs resemble 3-D surface graphs, but shading is used to measure the shapes against the grid lines.

3-D shaded surface graphs also resemble 3-D surface graphs, except that the shapes are shaded as if a light were shining down on the shapes, as shown in Figure 9-17.

Chapter 9: Graphing Fundamentals 457

FIGURE 9-16 3-D surface graph

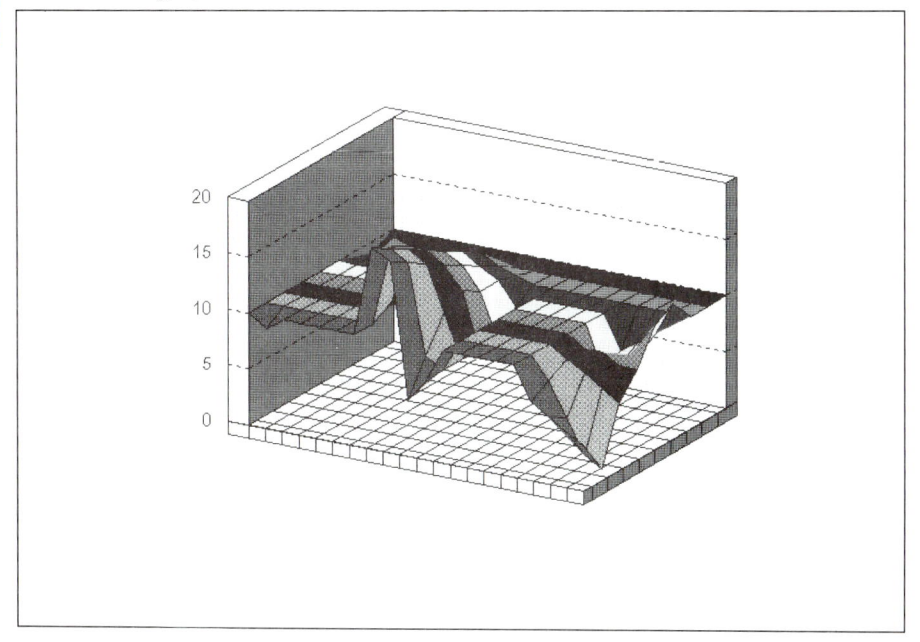

FIGURE 9-17 3-D shaded surface graph

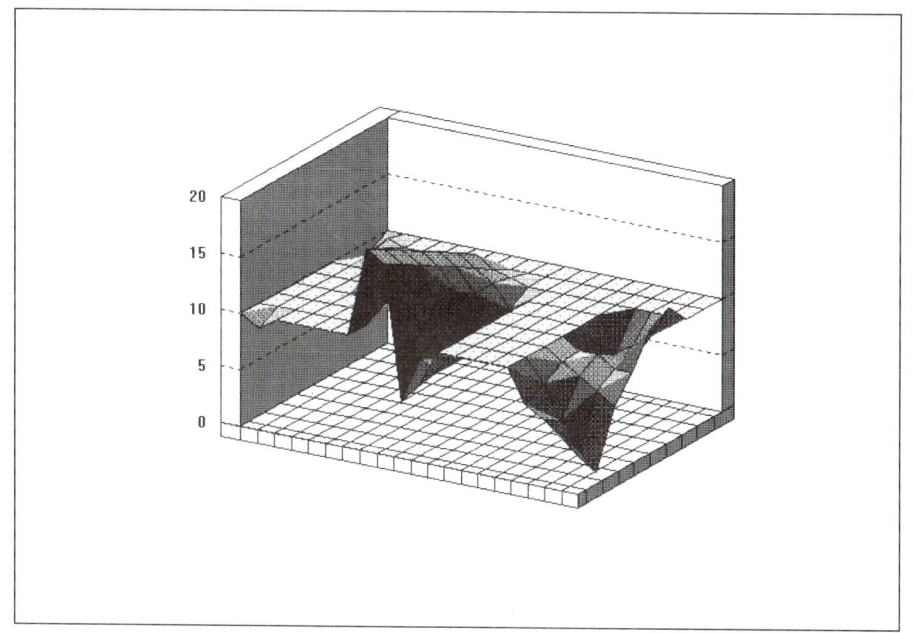

Rotated Graphs

If you choose the Rotated option, you can choose from five rotated graph types in which the X axis is displayed vertically (rather than horizontally, which is the default), as described in the following list. Rotated charts are often a good choice if you have long X-axis labels; there is more room for them along the vertical axis because your screen is wider than it is high.

Rotated 2-D bar graphs display the X axis vertically, producing the effect shown in Figure 9-18. Rotated bar graphs exaggerate the differences between the bars. Note the prominence of corporate contributions.

Rotated 3-D bar graphs closely resemble 3-D bar graphs, except that the X axis is displayed vertically. Rotated 3-D bar graphs have a legend box, unlike ordinary 3-D bar charts.

Rotated 2.5-D bar graphs closely resemble 2.5-D bar graphs; the bars of all series are drawn together (rather than shown in three-dimensional relief). However, the X axis is displayed vertically.

Rotated area graphs closely resemble area graphs, except that the X axis is displayed vertically. You can arrange the data series so that the prominent values appear to move forward.

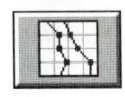

Rotated line graphs are line graphs with the X axis arranged vertically, as shown in Figure 9-19.

Combo and Multiple Graphs

Choosing the Combo option in the Graphs Types dialog box displays the eight combination and multiple graph types. Following are descriptions for each of these types. Examples are provided for several of the Graph Types to further demonstrate the differences between them.

Chapter 9: Graphing Fundamentals 459

FIGURE 9-18 Rotated 2-D bar graph

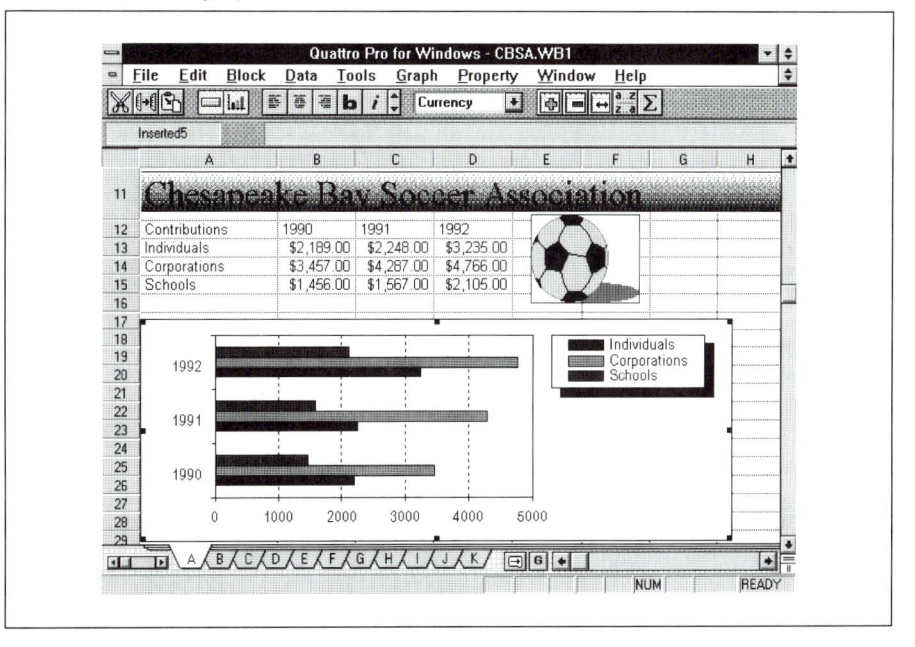

FIGURE 9-19 Rotated line graph

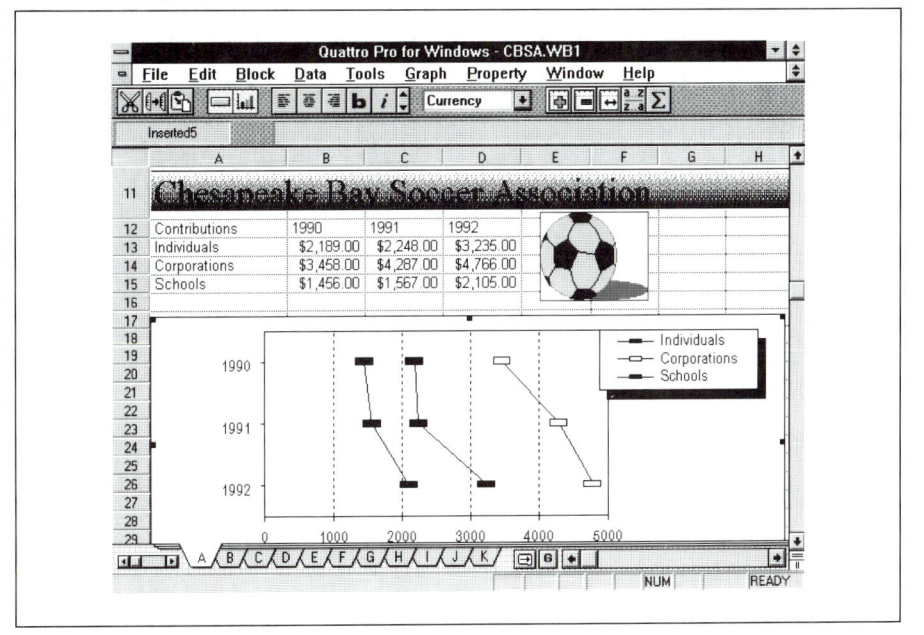

Line-bar combo graphs represent the first data series as a line and show additional data series as bars. A line-bar combo chart is a good choice if the first data series contains a different kind of data than the second and subsequent ones. Consider, for example, a line-bar combo graph in which the first data series (represented by a line) shows the Consumer Price Index, and additional data series (represented by bars) show house prices in three localities.

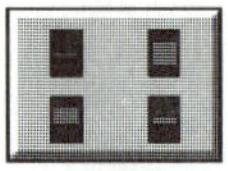

Area-bar combo graphs represent the first data series as a filled-in area and show additional data series as bars. Like line-bar combo graphs, these graphs are best used when the first data series differs from subsequent ones.

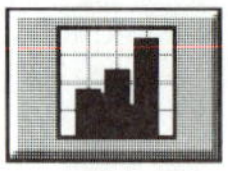

High-low-bar combo graphs display the first and second data series in tandem using high-low markers and show additional data series as bars. One use for this chart is to show a stock price's fluctuation (the first data series) against other data, such as the Dow-Jones index.

Multiple column graphs display each data series in its own stacked column, showing the percentages of each value as it contributes to the whole. Quattro Pro automatically constructs one column for each data series.

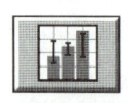

Multiple 3-D column graphs are identical to multiple column graphs, except that the columns are shown in three-dimensional relief.

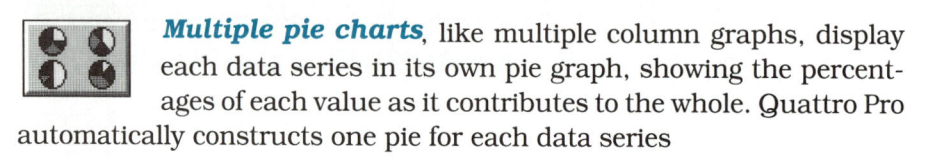

Multiple pie charts, like multiple column graphs, display each data series in its own pie graph, showing the percentages of each value as it contributes to the whole. Quattro Pro automatically constructs one pie for each data series

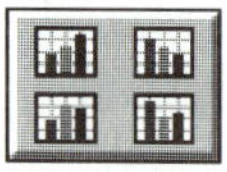

Multiple 3-D pie graphs are identical to multiple pie charts, except that the pies are shown in three-dimensional relief.

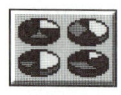

Multiple bar graphs display a separate bar graph for each data series, as shown in Figure 9-20. Quattro Pro automatically constructs one bar graph for each data series.

FIGURE 9-20 Multiple bar graphs

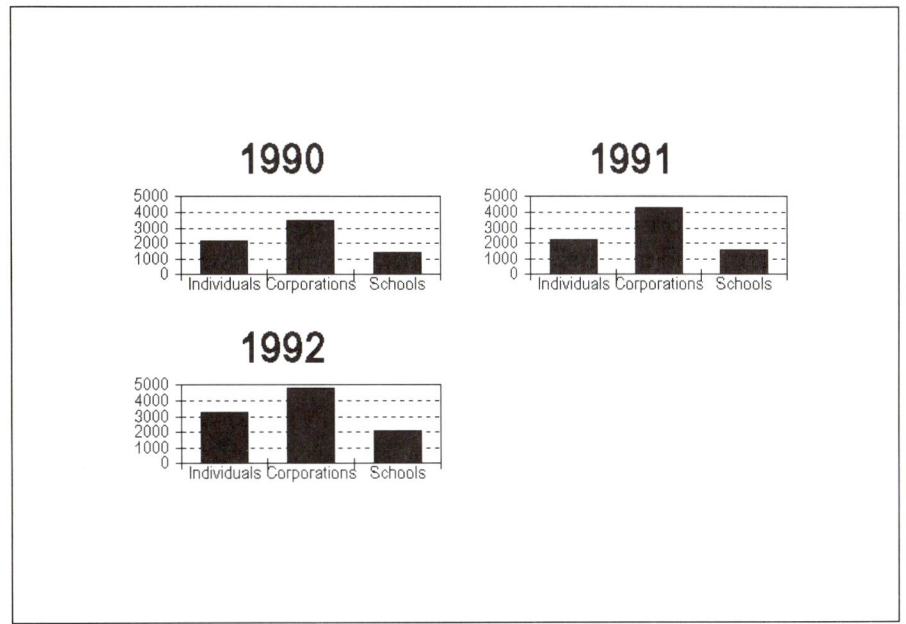

Data Series

When you create a graph by selecting data and clicking the Graph tool on the SpeedBar, Quattro Pro creates the graphs with certain assumptions. Suppose you type your data in tabular form, with text in the first column and across the first row, as in this example:

	1990	1992	1993
Individuals			
Corporations			
Schools			

Quattro Pro assumes that the first column (excepting the empty first cell) contains the X-axis data categories, while the first row (again excepting the first cell) contains the legend titles. The result is the default bar graph shown in Figure 9-21. Note the selected data, and note how Quattro Pro has used the A13..A15 titles as the X-axis categories and the B12..D12 titles for the legend.

FIGURE 9-21 Bar graph produced with row/column series settings

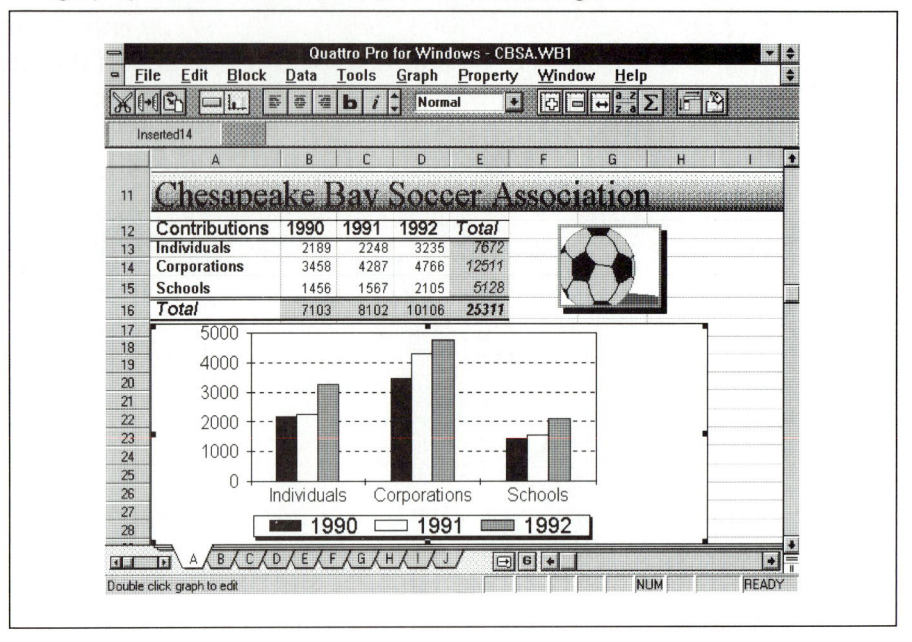

You can quickly swap the row and column settings, meaning that Quattro Pro will use B12..D12 for the X-axis categories and A13..A15 for the legend. To swap rows and columns, choose Series from the Graph menu. The Graph Series dialog box appears, as shown in Figure 9-22.

FIGURE 9-22 Graph Series dialog box

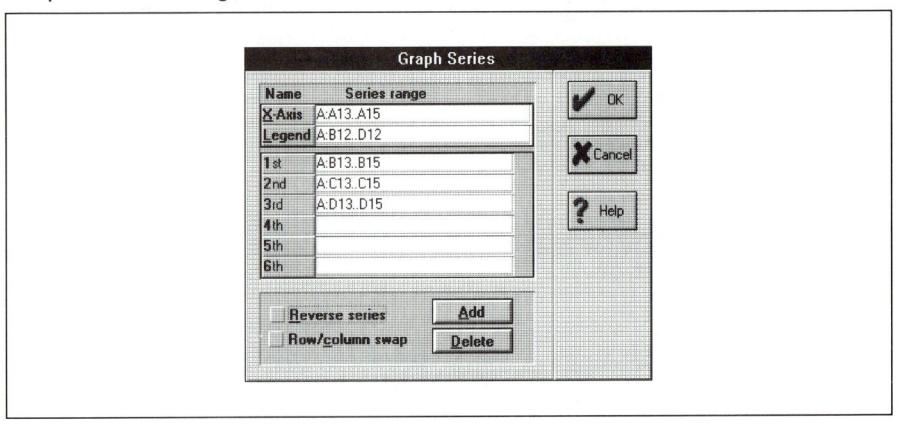

Chapter 9: Graphing Fundamentals 463

To reverse the series, click Row/column swap and choose OK. Figure 9-23 shows the result. Note that you can also reverse the order of the X-axis labels by clicking the Reverse series option in the Graph Series dialog box; in the present example, doing so would reverse the order of years (1992, 1991, 1990) in Figure 9-23. The Add and Delete buttons allow you to insert and cut data series, if you wish.

If your spreadsheet has been typed in a way other than the tabular format Quattro Pro expects, you can define the data series manually. To do so, start a new graph without creating a floating graph; this is done by choosing New from the Graph menu with no data selected. Quattro Pro automatically assigns the new graph a number, and displays the Graph New dialog box, as shown in Figure 9-24.

As you can see, this dialog box closely resembles the Graph Series dialog box. To define the X-axis labels, click the X-Axis button. Quattro Pro displays your spreadsheet. You then select the range of cells you want to define as the X-axis labels, and press ENTER to return to the Graph New dialog box. Repeat this step for the Legend and the data series buttons until you have defined your graph. Choose OK to complete the graph. When Quattro Pro displays your spreadsheet again, you see the

FIGURE 9-23 Bar graph with row/column settings reversed

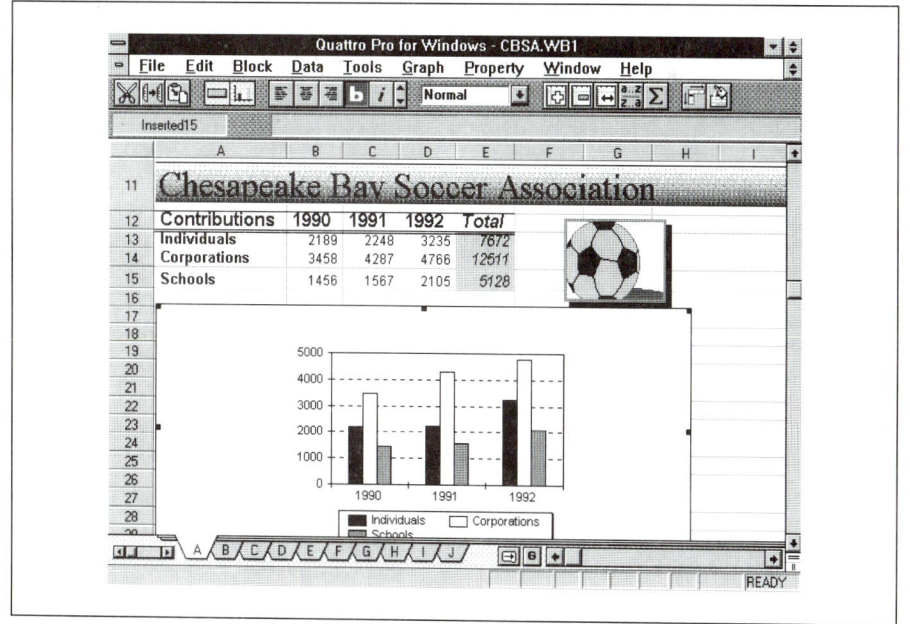

FIGURE 9-24 Graph New dialog box

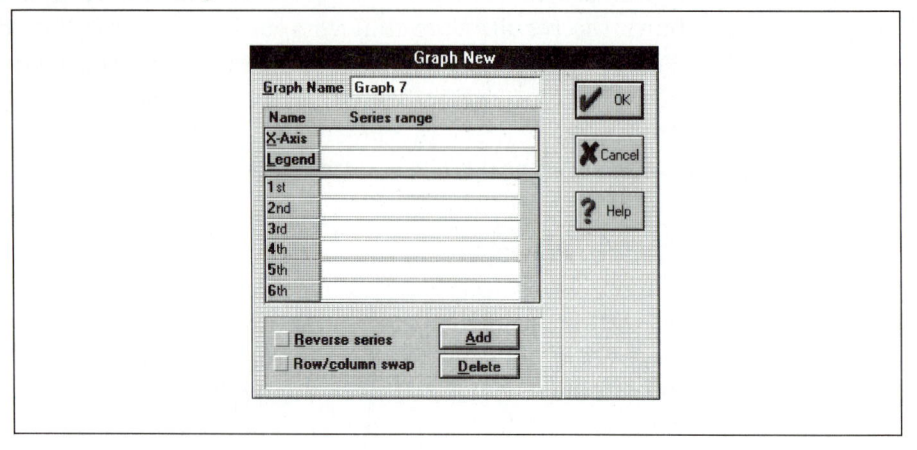

Graph window, displaying the new graph you've constructed. If you wish, you can change the graph type, add titles, or customize the graph in other ways. Click the Close button to complete the chart. To insert the newly created graph in your worksheet, display the spreadsheet page on which you want to insert the graph and then choose Insert from the Graph menu.

If you want to create a graph using data from more than one notebook page, you must use the Graph New procedure just described.

Special Series Considerations

If you're creating an XY graph or a high-low graph, you need to take into account the way Quattro Pro expects you to type the data.

An XY graph plots data against two numeric axes. Both the X axis and the Y axis must therefore contain data. (Normally, the X axis contains labels.) Chapter 11 discusses XY graphs in more detail.

High-low graphs are commonly used to track stock prices. To create a high-low graph, you must have an X-axis label series (which usually contains dates) and at least two data series. Quattro Pro expects the first data series to contain the high price, while the second contains the low price. If you wish, you can add one or two additional series. If you use a total of three series, Quattro Pro expects the third series to contain the closing price. If you use a total of four series, the third series should contain the opening price, and the fourth series should contain the closing price.

Titles

Every graph needs a title. With Quattro Pro, you can quickly and easily add titles using the Titles command on the Graphs menu. When you select a floating graph (or display a graph in the Graph window) and choose this command, you see the Graph Titles dialog box, shown in Figure 9-25.

To add text to the current chart, you simply type the text you want in the Main Title, Subtitle, X-Axis Title, Y-1 Axis Title, and Y-2 Axis Title text boxes and click OK. The Y-1 Axis Title box is sufficient unless you are creating a custom chart with two Y axes (for more information, see the section titled "Plotting Data on a Secondary Y Axis," later in this chapter). When you click OK, Quattro Pro creates the chart using the default formats for each of the titles you've requested, as shown in Figure 9-26. In the section titled "Defining Properties," you will learn how to change these formats.

FIGURE 9-25 Graph Titles dialog box

FIGURE 9-26 Titles entered with default formats

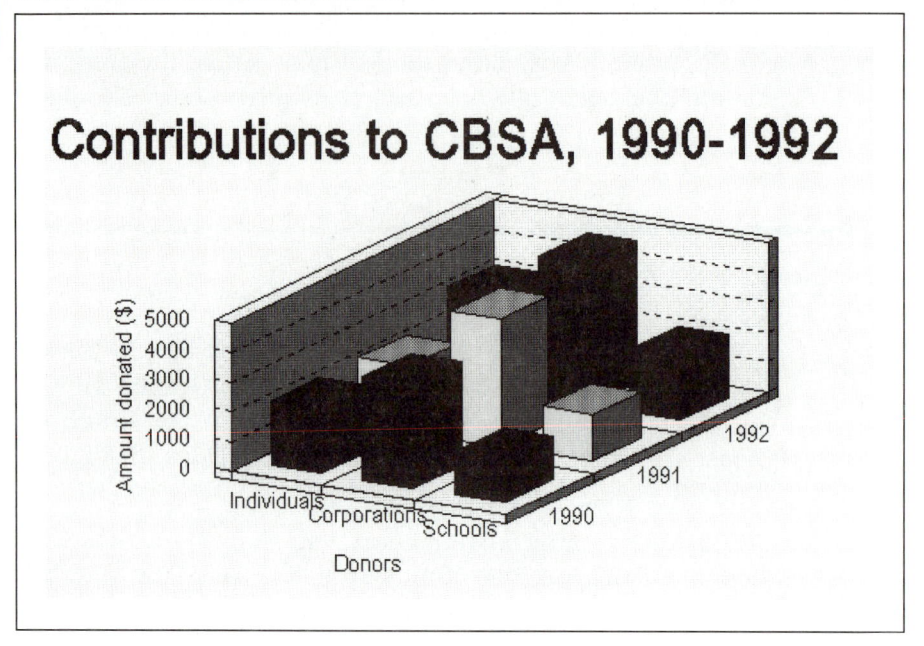

Customizing Your Graph with Properties

Within the Graph window, each of a graph's many components (called *objects* in Quattro Pro's nomenclature) can be individually selected and altered. You customize graphs in the Graph window by right-clicking an object, such as a title or legend, and using the Menus on Demand property menus. When you right-click the title area of a graph in the Graph window, you see the Graph Title Properties dialog box, shown in Figure 9-27.

To use the Graph Title Properties menu, you choose the category you want to customize from the list box on the left (Text Color, Text Bkg Color, Text Font, and Text Style). If you choose Text Font, new menu areas appear, as in Figure 9-28.

Once you've selected all the options you want in the Graph Title Properties box, click OK to confirm them, and you see the results in the Graph window. To customize other aspects of your graph, right-click

FIGURE 9-27 Graph Title Properties dialog box

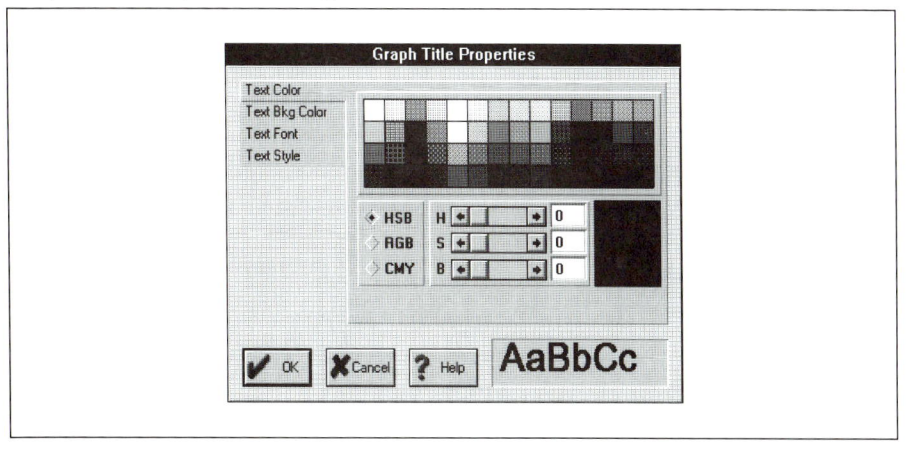

other areas to bring up additional property menus. Alternatively, you can select the object and choose Current Object from the Property menu, or just press F12.

Customizing graphs effectively requires that you learn where to right-click so that the correct property menu appears. (You can choose some of the property menus, but not all, from the Property menu in the Graph window.) Figure 9-29 shows the location of graph property menus for all types of charts. In 3-D charts, you can also right-click the graph's back

FIGURE 9-28 Text Font menu

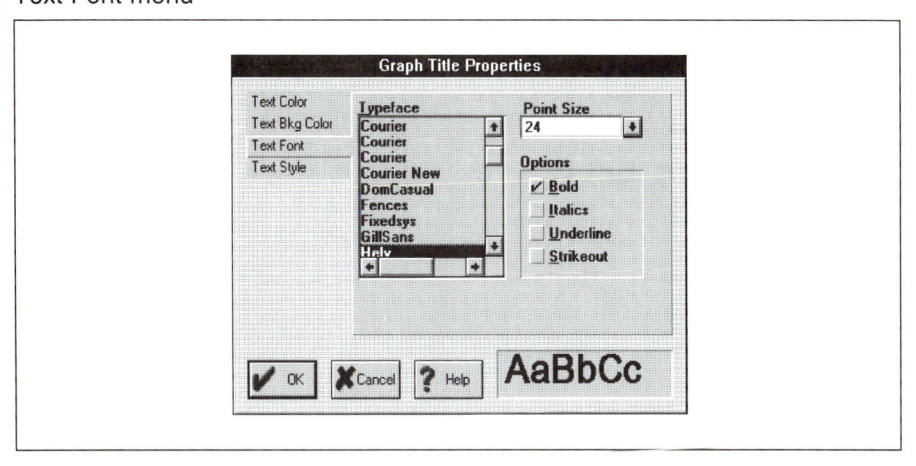

FIGURE 9-29 Where to click to call the graph properties menus (Graph window)

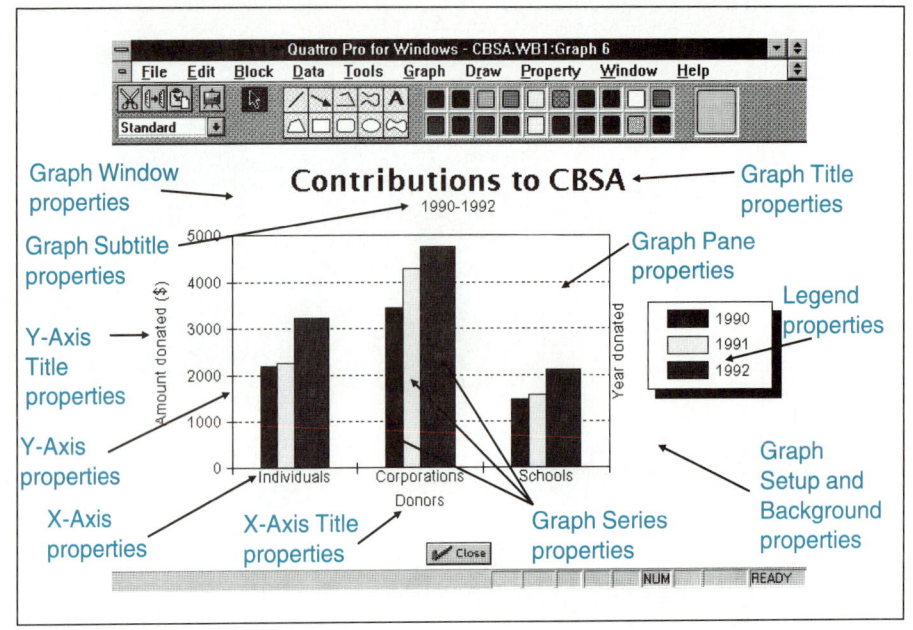

[Figure 9-29: Screenshot of Quattro Pro for Windows graph window showing "Contributions to CBSA 1990-1992" bar chart with labeled callouts pointing to: Graph Window properties, Graph Title properties, Graph Subtitle properties, Graph Pane properties, Y-Axis Title properties, Legend properties, Y-Axis properties, X-Axis properties, X-Axis Title properties, Graph Series properties, Graph Setup and Background properties]

wall to bring up the Graph Setup and Background properties (including 3-D view and 3-D wall options). In pie charts, you can right-click each slice of the pie separately to assign attributes to each.

Quattro Pro gives you so many graph customization options that an entire book could be devoted just to the program's graphics capabilities. Here, you find an overview of the graph properties menus, plus a more detailed discussion of the graph properties you're most likely to modify.

Graph Properties Menus

You can choose the following graph properties menus by right-clicking the appropriate area or by choosing the appropriate option from the Property menu. For example, to display the Graph Setup and Background menu, you can right-click the graph background or choose Current Object from the Property menu.

- **Graph Window** Use this menu to change the *aspect ratio* of your chart and to add grids. The aspect ratio is the ratio of the graph's horizontal and vertical measurements. You can choose from the following preset aspect ratios: Floating Graph (the aspect ratio of the graph as it is currently shown in your spreadsheet); Screen Slide (for an onscreen slide show), 35mm Slide (for presentation graphics), Printer Preview (shows how the graph will appear when printed using the current print settings), and Full Extent (fills the area designated for the floating graph). The grids you add with this menu are intended to help you place and size objects you add to your graph; the grids do not print. To add grid lines that print, you use the X-Axis and Y-Axis Properties menus, discussed later in this section.

- **Graph Setup and Background** This property menu controls settings that affect the whole graph, including the large frame that surrounds the graph. Use this menu to change the graph type, change the legend position (bottom, right, or none), adjust the 3-D view so that hidden objects become visible, choose 3-D options (you can selectively display or hide the left wall, back wall, and base), define the box type that surrounds the entire graph, choose fill and background colors for the box surrounding the entire graph, and choose fill styles (solid, pattern, wash, and bitmap).

- **Graph Pane Properties** Use this menu to control the frame that surrounds the graph itself (this frame includes the X axis and Y axis). You can selectively activate or deactivate all four sides of the frame. You can choose a fill color, fill style (solid, pattern, wash, or bitmap), background color, border color, and border style (line weights).

- **Legend Properties** This property menu controls the legend that Quattro Pro automatically creates with most graph types. Use this menu to choose the legend position (none, bottom, or right), text color, text background color, text font, text style (solid, wash, bitmap, or shadow), box type, fill color, fill style (solid, pattern, wash, or bitmap), and border color.

- **X-Axis Properties** Use this menu to control all aspects of the X axis (the categories axis, which is horizontal, except in rotated graphs). You can change the range from which the X-axis labels are drawn. You can choose *tick* (marker lines that go across an axis) options (ticks above, below, or across the axis), text color, text background color, text font, text style (solid, wash, bitmap, or shadow), major gridline style (line weights), and major gridline color.

- **Y-Axis Properties** Use this menu to control all aspects of the Y axis (the values axis, which is vertical, except in rotated graphs). You can use this menu to scale the Y axis by choosing logarithmic increments (10, 100, 1000, etc.), resetting the high and low values, and changing the increment interval. You can change the numeric format of the values displayed in this axis, choosing from all the numeric formats available in a spreadsheet cell. You can also change the tick style (left, right, across, or none) and set a length limit on the display of labels. Additionally, you can choose text color, text background color, text font, text style (solid, wash, bitmap, or shadow), major gridline style (line widths), and major gridline color.

The rest of the graph properties menus are accessed by right-clicking the appropriate area of the graph (or by selecting the area and choosing the Current Object option from the Property menu or pressing the F12 shortcut key).

- **Graph Title Properties** To access this menu, right-click the graph title. This property menu controls the first title's text. You can choose text color, text background color, text font, and text style (solid, wash, bitmap, or shadow).

- **Graph Subtitle Properties** To access this menu, right-click the graph subtitle (the second title). This property menu controls the second title's text. You can choose text color, text background color, text font, and text style (solid, wash, bitmap, or shadow).

- **Axis Title Properties** To access this menu, right-click the X-axis or Y-axis title. You can use this menu to change the axis title text. You can also choose text color, text background color, text font, and text style (solid, wash, bitmap, or shadow).

The following property menus are available only when you've selected the appropriate graph type. Using these property menus, you can selectively customize each individual data series.

- **Bar Series Properties and Area Series Properties** These menus are identical, except that one affects bars in a bar graph, and the other affects areas in an area graph. To access one of these menus, right-click one of the bars or areas in the graph. Your changes will affect the currently selected data series only. You can use these menus to choose a new spreadsheet block for the data series that the bar or area represents. You can define a block that contains series labels (values that appear at a specified location for each area), and you can change the label that appears in the legend for the currently selected series. To change the appearance of the bar or area, you can choose text color, text background color, text font, text style (solid, wash, bitmap, or shadow), fill color, background color, fill style, border color, and border style. To create a combination chart, you can select an *override type* (bar, area, or line), which changes the display of the currently selected data series.

- **Column Graph Properties** To access this menu, right-click one of the areas in a column graph. Your changes will affect the currently selected area of the column graph. You can use this menu to choose a new spreadsheet block for the data series that the column represents. You can also change the data label (currency, percent, value, or none). To change the appearance of the column, you can choose text color, text background color, text font, text style (solid, wash, bitmap, or shadow), fill color, background color, fill style, border color, and border style.

- **Pie Graph Properties** To access this menu, right-click one of the slices of the pie. Your changes will affect the currently selected slice. From this menu, you can explode the currently selected slice so that it stands out from the rest of the pie by a percentage you select (20% is the default). You can redefine the series used to create the pie, and change the data label (currency, percent, value, or none). You have the usual options for changing the text and color of the pie, including text color, text background color, text font, text style (solid, wash, bitmap, or shadow), fill color, background color, fill style, border color, and border style.

- **Area Fill Properties** To access this menu, right-click the walls or floor of a 3-D graph. You can choose a fill color, background color, fill style, border color, and border style.

If you want to customize a multiple graph, such as a multiple pie graph, switch to the single (nonmultiple) graph type first. For example, to customize a multiple pie graph, use the Graph Type dialog box to change the graph to a single pie graph. Then customize each data series as you wish (for example, by choosing fill patterns and exploding slices). When you switch to the multiple graph, each of the pies will have the options you've selected.

You will surely agree that Quattro Pro makes a wealth of customization options available! For analytical graphics, where the purpose is finding patterns in the data, you will typically use only a few of these options. The following sections discuss the options you are most likely to use as you seek to discover the patterns in your spreadsheet's numbers. In Chapter 10, you will learn how additional properties can be used to convey to others the patterns you have discovered.

Note Customizing a graph can be time consuming. However, Quattro Pro offers an advanced feature that lets you copy styles (all properties that affect the appearance of the graph, such as fonts, line styles, background colors, fill colors, etc.), the graph type, and series overrides to another chart. To copy styles, graph type, and series overrides to another chart, select the chart, and choose Copy from the Graph menu. When the Graph Copy menu appears, choose the name to assign the destination chart in the To list box, and activate the Style option. (Deactivate the Data option, unless you want the destination chart to use the same data as the source chart.) Choose OK to confirm the copy.

Plotting Data on a Secondary Y Axis

If your spreadsheet contains more than one type of data, you can plot the results on a graph with two different Y-axis measurement scales. In Figure 9-30, note the highlighted block. This block contains data that differs from the contribution data directly above it. Rather than listing donations in dollar amounts, it shows the organization's membership totals for the three years (1990, 1991, and 1992). Selecting all the data and clicking the Graph tool in the SpeedBar produces the default graph shown in Figure 9-31.

Chapter 9: Graphing Fundamentals

FIGURE 9-30 Spreadsheet range with two types of data: dollar amounts and membership totals

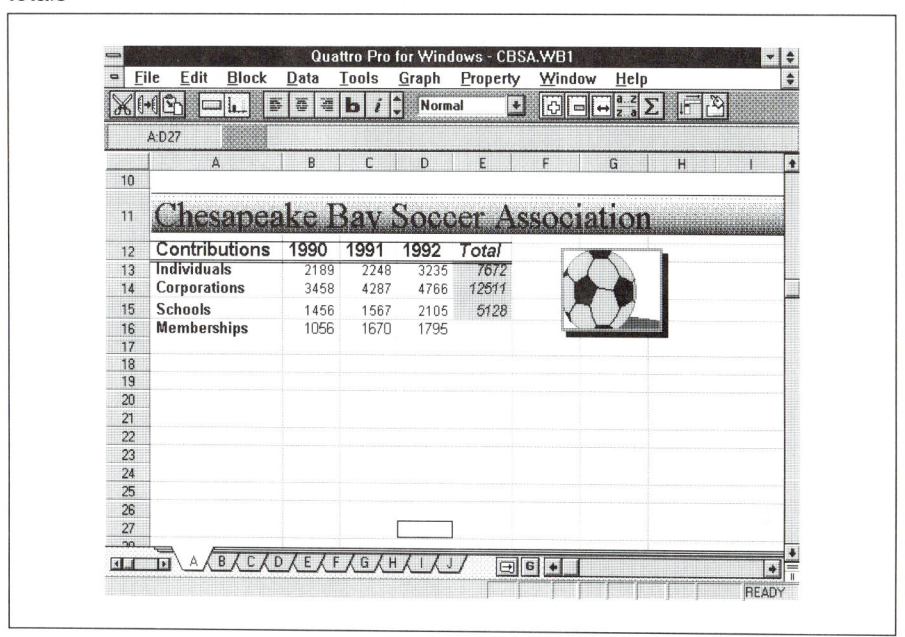

Contributions	1990	1991	1992	Total
Individuals	2189	2248	3235	7672
Corporations	3458	4287	4766	12511
Schools	1456	1567	2105	5128
Memberships	1056	1670	1795	

FIGURE 9-31 Default graph generated from data in previous figure

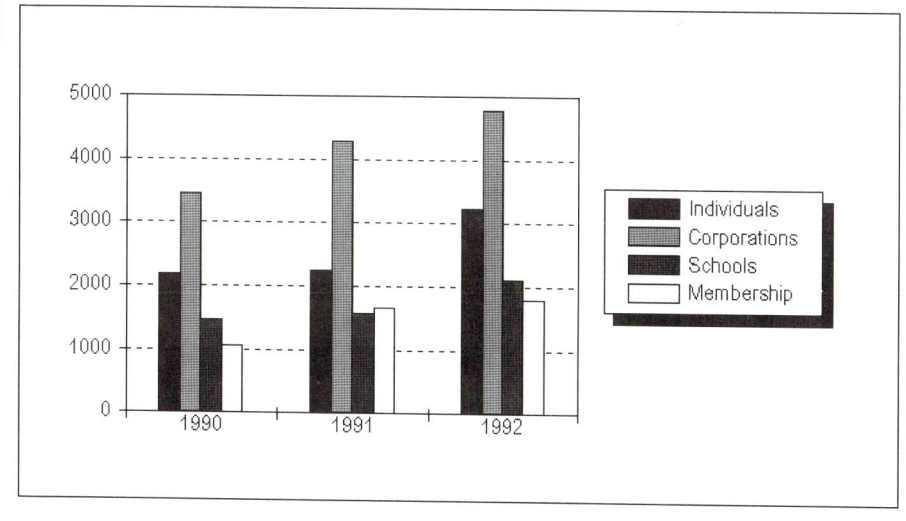

FIGURE 9-32 Bar Series Properties dialog box

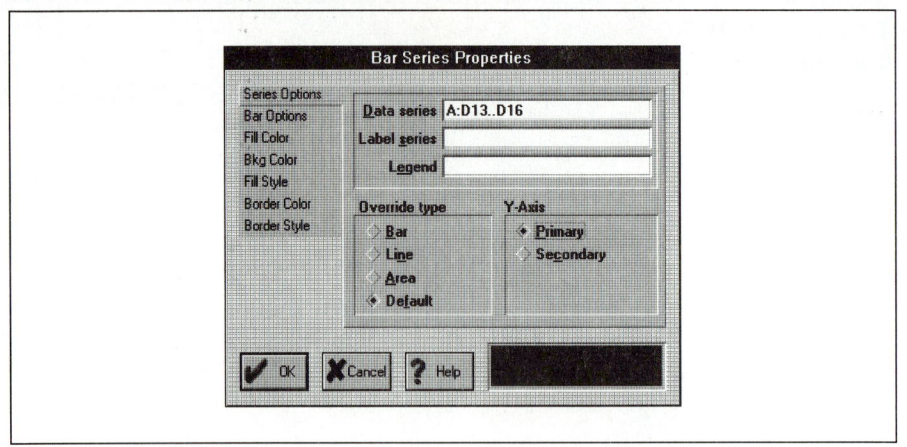

FIGURE 9-33 Combination chart with two Y axes

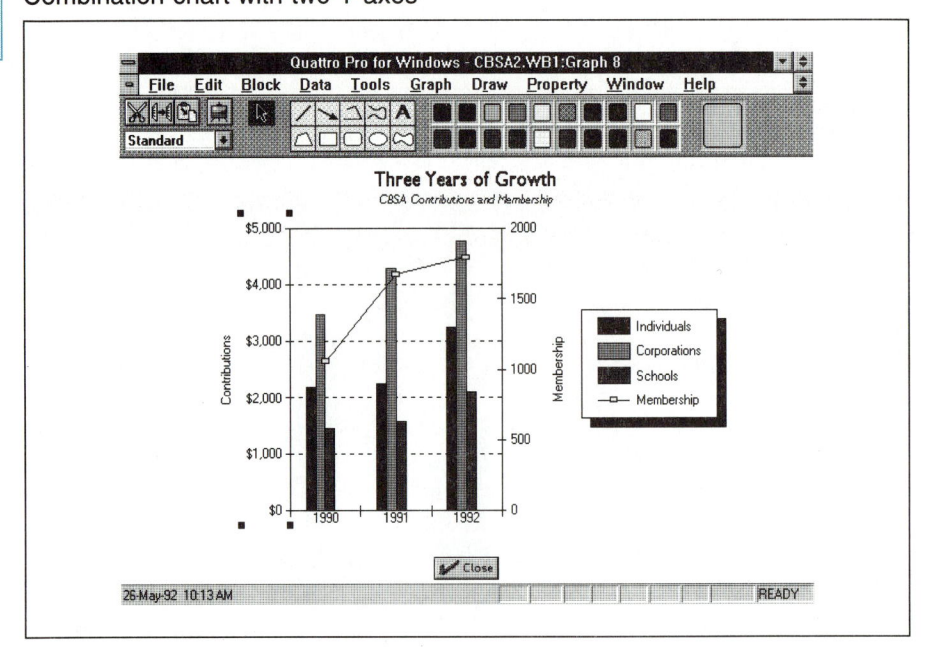

To fix this, switch to the Graph window and use the Y-axis property menu to change the Y-axis numeric format to currency. This measurement is appropriate for the contributions, but not for the membership totals. You need a second Y-axis measurement scale to measure the membership totals.

To create the second Y-axis scale, right-click the bar corresponding to the membership data series. The Bar Series Properties dialog box, shown in Figure 9-32, appears.

With Series Options selected, choose Secondary in the Y-Axis area, and to emphasize that a different type of data is being measured, choose Secondary in the Y-Axis area. Finally, choose Titles from the Graph menu, and define titles for each of the two Y axes. Figure 9-33 shows the result.

Using Logarithmic Scales

Suppose the financially strapped schools donated only a few hundred dollars, rather than thousands, to the soccer association. The result is an unattractive, difficult-to-read chart such as the one in Figure 9-34. This chart uses a normal Y-axis scale. The solution to this problem is to reset the Y axis to a logarithmic scale, as shown in Figure 9-35. A logarithmic scale, as you can see in this figure, exaggerates small values, making them much easier to read. In both figures, grid lines have been added to the Y axis (using the Major Grid Lines and Minor Grid Lines options in the Y-Axis Properties menu) to highlight the difference in the way the two charts measure values.

Adjusting the Y-Axis Scale

Ethical standards in professional graphics call for the strict use of 0 as the low value for the Y axis, unless there are very good reasons to do otherwise. If you use a low value other than 0, a graph exaggerates trends. A difference between 45 and 47 in a bar graph with a scale of 0 to 100 does not seem significant—but if you reset the scale with a minimum of

FIGURE 9-34 Chart using normal Y-axis scale

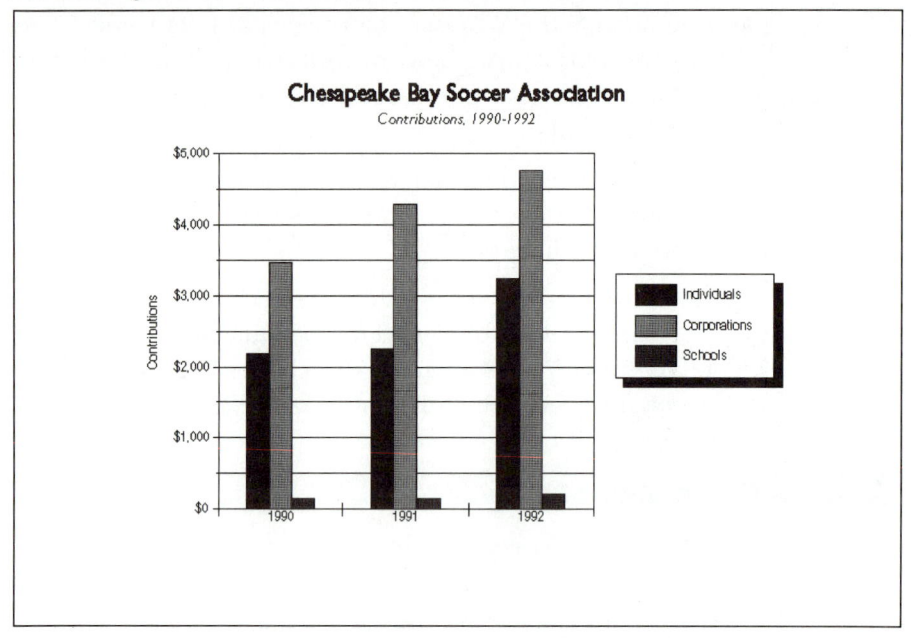

FIGURE 9-35 Chart using logarithmic Y-axis scale

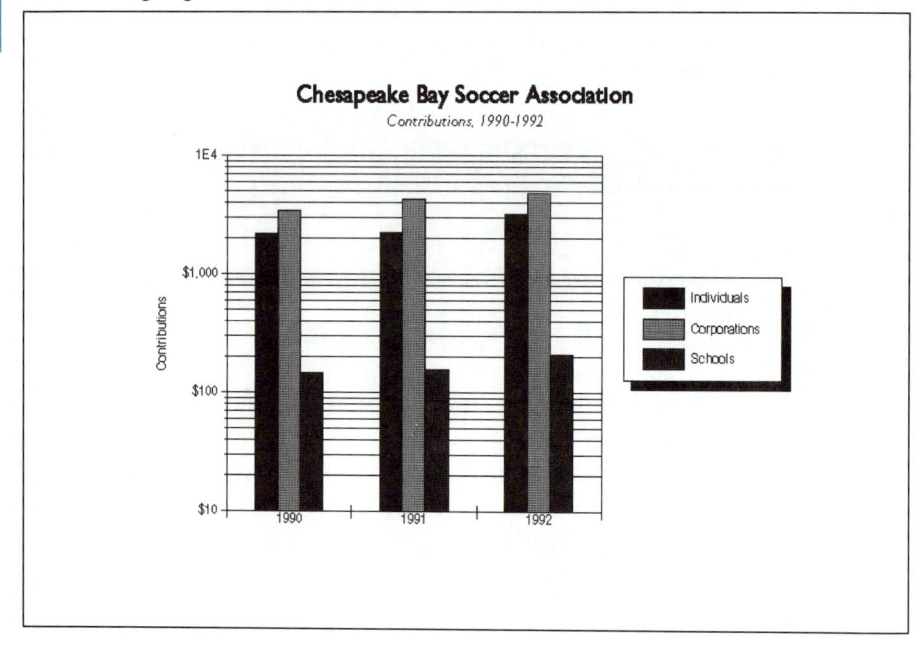

40 and a maximum of 50, the difference is very noticeable. This trick is commonly used in advertising to make a very small or insignificant difference between two quantities appear much larger than it is.

Still, there are sometimes good reasons for adjusting the Y-axis scale. The only real rule of analytical graphics is to tell the truth about the data, and sometimes adjusting the scale does a better job of telling the truth. In the high-low graph shown in Figure 9-36, for instance, the differences between the high, low, and closing prices are very hard to see. What is more, the slope of the rising prices is at too shallow a slope to truthfully convey this stock's impressive gains during this period. Figure 9-37 shows the same graph with the Y-axis scale reset as follows: minimum, 20; maximum, 45; step (interval), 5. The resulting graph more truthfully conveys the data.

FIGURE 9-36 High-low graph with automatically scaled Y axis

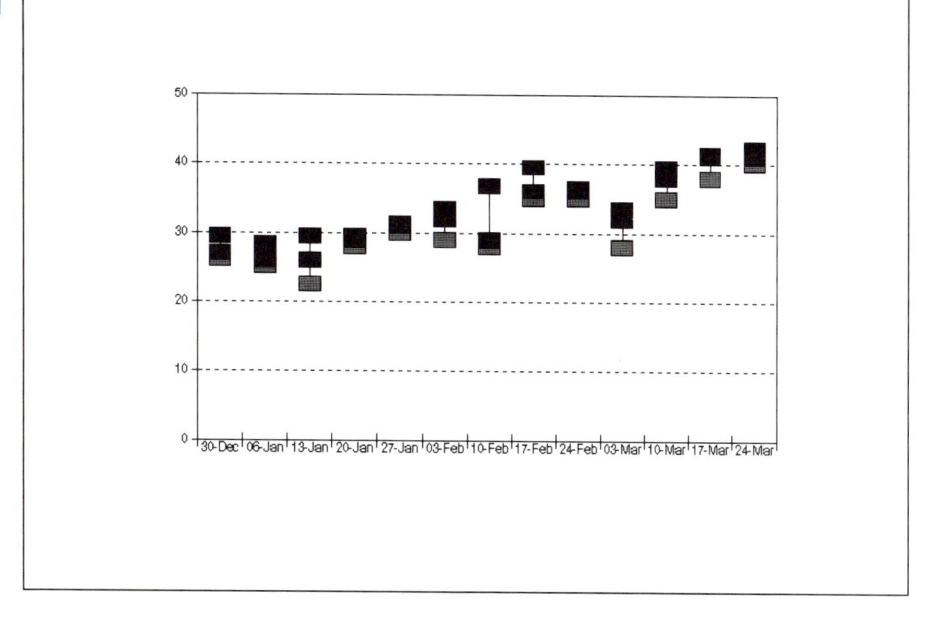

FIGURE 9-37 High-low graph after manually scaling the Y axis

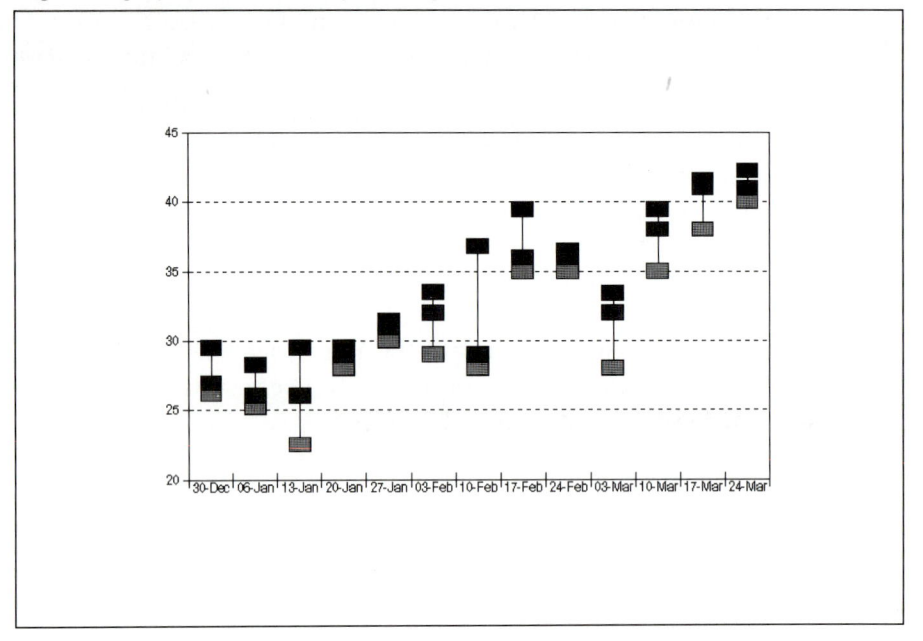

Managing Graphs

When you create a graph, Quattro Pro adds an icon to the Graphs page at the end of the notebook, as shown in Figure 9-38. You can perform the following actions with the Graphs page in view:

- **Printing graphs** To print one or more graphs, select the icons and choose Print from the File menu.

- **Naming and renaming graphs** To assign a name to a graph, or to change an existing name, right-click the graph icon and type the new name in the dialog box that appears. Choose OK to confirm the new name.

- **Editing graphs** To display a graph in the Graph window for editing or customization, double-click the graph. Alternatively, select the graph and choose Edit from the Graph menu.

Chapter 9: Graphing Fundamentals

FIGURE 9-38 Graphs page with several graph icons

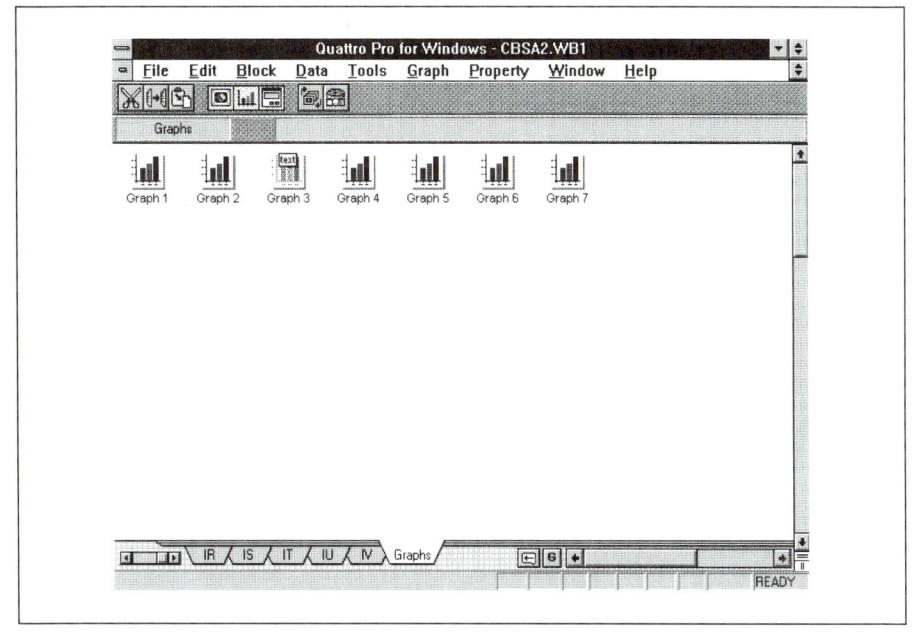

- **Viewing graphs** To view a full-screen display of the graph, select the graph and press F11 (or choose View from the Graph menu). To return to the Graphs page, press ESC.

- **Deleting graphs** To remove a graph permanently from the notebook, select the graph in the Graphs page and choose Cut from the Edit menu. *Deleting a graph from the Graphs page deletes the graph entirely and permanently,* so think twice before you delete graphs there. The graph icon is the source object for the graph.

Note You can retain a graph icon on the Graphs page without displaying the corresponding graph anywhere in your notebook.

This chapter has explored the use of Quattro Pro for analytical graphics. However, many of the program's graphics features can be used for presentation purposes. These features include some discussed here, such as the many properties that can be selectively customized, and others that have not been discussed here, such as the program's drawing capabilities. The next chapter, "Presentation Graphics," discusses ways you can enhance your Quattro Pro graphs so that they convey the desired message to your audience.

CHAPTER 10

Presentation Graphics

*I*n presentation graphics, your goal is to communicate to others the patterns you have discovered in the data. Chapter 9 introduced the basics of analytical graphics with Quattro Pro; the focus in that chapter was on the discovery of patterns. In this chapter, you learn how to emphasize the patterns you have discovered so that they are clear to your audience.

Quattro Pro for Windows is loaded with features that you can use to enhance your graphs for presentation purposes.

- **The aspect ratio** A few clicks of the mouse is all it takes to size all your graphs perfectly for a variety of presentation modes, including screen slides (for onscreen slide shows), 35mm slides (for professional presentations), printer (for handouts and transparencies), and floating graphs (for inclusion on a spreadsheet).

- **Properties** You can individually select every aspect of your graph: adding fonts, font styles, background colors, boxes, and many more effects.

- **Graph copying** Because you can so easily duplicate graphs within a notebook, you can focus your customization efforts on one graph, and then make many duplicates of it. You then assign a new graph type and data series to each duplicate. In this way, you quickly build a presentation with consistent properties throughout.

- **Text** You can add a text box anywhere to a chart, highlighting important information that your audience wants to know. To keep your text aligned perfectly, you can activate a grid that automatically aligns the text you enter.

- **Lines and shapes** With the Graph window's drawing tools, you can quickly add lines, circles, arrows, and many additional shapes.

- **Text charts** Charts with nothing but text are effective presentation tools. You can create and customize them easily with Quattro Pro.

- **Slide shows** A *slide show* is an onscreen presentation that you can create with Quattro Pro graphs. When you run the slide show, the viewer sees a series of full-screen views of your graphs. You can control how one graph replaces the other on the screen, using a variety of effects such as fade out/fade in. You can even insert buttons in graphs that allow the viewer to choose which graph to display next.

Quattro Pro's presentation graphics features are so extensive that they would be worthy of a presentation graphics program. This chapter could not cover all these features without taking over the book. However, you will find that this chapter covers the fundamental steps you take to develop an effective presentation, beginning with customizing a graph with properties, copying the graph, developing text charts, and creating a slide show.

Note Most of the presentation graphics modifications that you make to your graph require you to display the graph in the Graph window. To display a floating graph in the Graph window, select the graph and double-click it, or choose Edit from the Graph menu.

Choosing the Aspect Ratio

Before you expend time and energy customizing one or more graphs, be sure to choose the correct *aspect ratio* for the media you're planning to use. Aspect ratio refers to the ratio of the horizontal to the vertical measurement in a graphic. If you're planning to print your graph on paper or matte acetate, you will need an aspect ratio that fits the 8.5 × 11 inch page. (The term "matte acetate" refers to clear plastic sheets that you can load into your laser printer instead of paper. The printer prints directly to the sheets, producing transparencies that you can display with an overhead projector.) If you're planning to have your graph files converted to 35mm slides, you will need an aspect ratio that's appropriate for a horizontally oriented 35mm color slide.

It is important to choose the aspect ratio before customizing your chart because your choice affects the overall dimensions and layout of the graph. There's no point spending your time fussing with the position of text boxes and line drawings, for example, if you must repeat this work after choosing the aspect ratio. Choose the aspect ratio before customizing.

You can choose from five aspect ratios:

- **Floating Graph** The aspect ratio for the floating graph version of the current chart. This is the best choice if you're planning to include the graph on a printout of your spreadsheet.

- **Screen Slide** The aspect ratio needed to display a full-screen image of the graph on the computer display. This is the best choice if you're planning to create a slide show.

- **35mm Slide** The aspect ratio of a horizontally oriented 35mm slide (the horizontal dimension is longer than the vertical). This is the best option if you're planning to give your Quattro Pro graphics files to a graphics service bureau to be made into 35mm slides.

- **Printer Preview** The aspect ratio of printed page. By default, Quattro Pro prints in portrait orientation, so the vertical dimension is longer than the horizontal. If you choose Landscape in the Print orientation area of the Page Setup dialog box, this option displays the graph with a horizontal orientation that is longer than the vertical one. This is the best choice if you are planning to print your graphs on separate pages for handouts or transparencies.

- **Full Extent** This option displays the graph as large as possible in the Graph window without affecting the dimensions of the floating graph. You see graph elements at the largest possible size, but the floating graph may look different.

To choose the aspect ratio, display the graph in the Graph window and choose Graph Window from the Property menu. When the Graph Window menu appears, choose the aspect ratio.

Note No matter which aspect ratio you choose, you can preview the graph's appearance by choosing View from the Graph menu or by using the F11 shortcut. Quattro Pro displays a full-screen image of your graph, preserving the aspect ratio you have chosen.

Customizing a Graph with Properties

In Chapter 9, you learned that virtually every aspect of a Quattro Pro chart can be individually selected and modified with property menus. In

Chapter 10: Presentation Graphics 485

this chapter, with its focus on presentation graphics, it is appropriate to illustrate how a dowdy, default chart can be dressed up for presentation purposes. Figure 10-1, for instance, shows a default Quattro Pro pie chart, while Figure 10-2 shows the same chart after customization.

To customize this graph, the following property menus were used:

- **Graph Window Properties menu** The Screen Slide aspect ratio was chosen. The Screen Slide aspect ratio is designed so that the graphic will fill an entire screen when displayed in a slide show.

- **Graph Title Properties menu** In the Text Font menu, Utopia Black was chosen and formatted in 24-point bold.

- **Graph Title Box menu** A bold title box with rounded corners was chosen.

- **Graph Setup and Background menu** In the Box Type menu, a bold title box with rounded corners was chosen, repeating the box theme of the title box. In the Fill Color menu, a light color was chosen, and in the Fill Style menu, a wash effect was chosen.

FIGURE 10-1 Pie graph before customizing properties

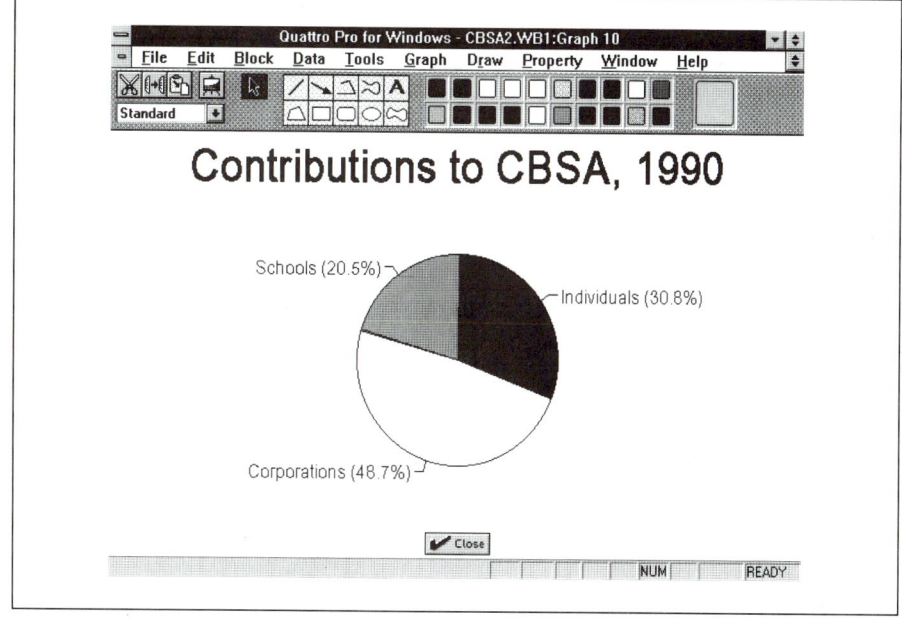

FIGURE 10-2 Pie graph after customizing properties

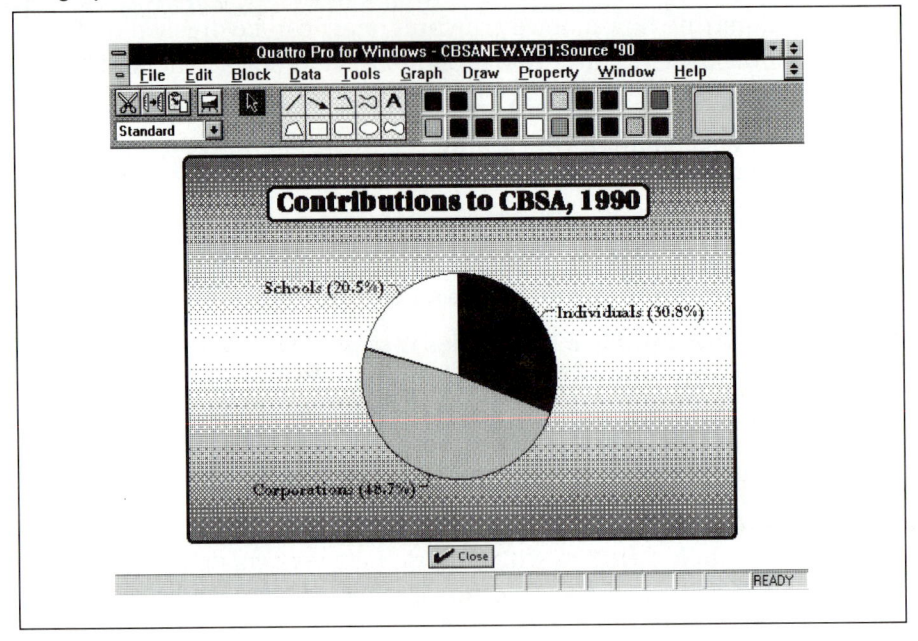

- **Pie Graph Properties menu** In the Text Font menu, the Perpetua font was chosen with 18-point bold formatting. For each data series, new fill colors were chosen to emphasize the contrasts among the slices.

You can choose so many effects from property menus that there's a real danger of overdoing the customization. Just remember a few simple rules of graphics good taste:

- **Be consistent** Use the same box styles, background colors, fonts, and font sizes throughout your presentation. Change one of these stylistic elements only when you want to call attention to something very important.

- **Use no more than two fonts** Because it's so easy to choose fonts with Windows, you may be tempted to go wild with font choices. But good graphic designers rarely use more than two.

☐ **Every graph should establish and develop just one basic point**
If you find yourself making two or more points in a graph, make new graphs.

Copying Graphs

Quattro Pro gives you powerful customization tools in its property menus, but this power comes at a price. The fact that each property can be individually selected and customized means that it takes some time to customize a graph properly. If you had to repeat all the customization steps for a dozen graphs, you'd probably give up the idea of creating a presentation with Quattro Pro.

Fortunately, there's a solution to this problem, but it requires a little advance planning. In essence, you create one chart and customize it. Then you make several copies of this chart, complete with the customized properties you've added. Then you modify each copy. Follow these steps:

1. Create and name the first graph for your presentation.
2. Customize this graph using property menus.
3. Switch to the Graphs page, and name the graph you just created.
4. Select the Graph icon.
5. Choose Copy from the Graph menu or click the Copy icon on the SpeedBar.

You see the Graph Copy dialog box, as shown in Figure 10-3. In the From list, Quattro Pro has highlighted the name of the graph you selected when you chose the Graph | Copy command.

6. Type the name of the second graph you want to create in the To window.
7. Choose OK.

FIGURE 10-3 Graph Copy dialog box

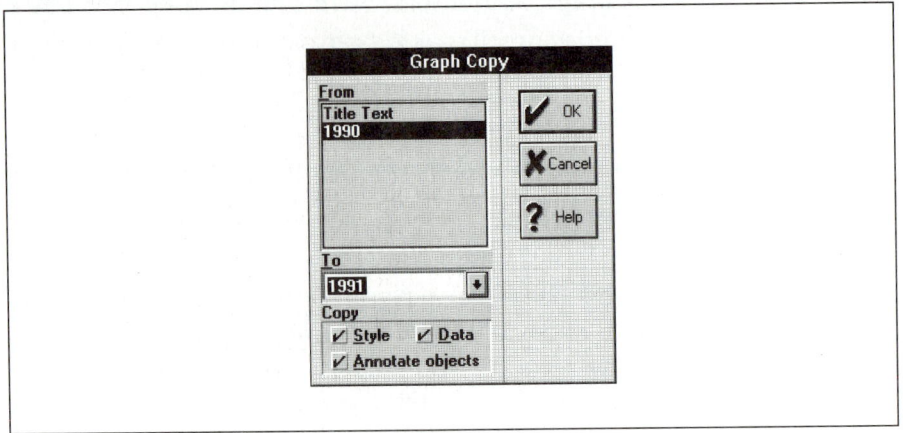

Quattro Pro creates a copy of the graph, and places the copy as an icon in the Graphs page, as shown in Figure 10-4.

FIGURE 10-4 Copied graphs in Graphs page

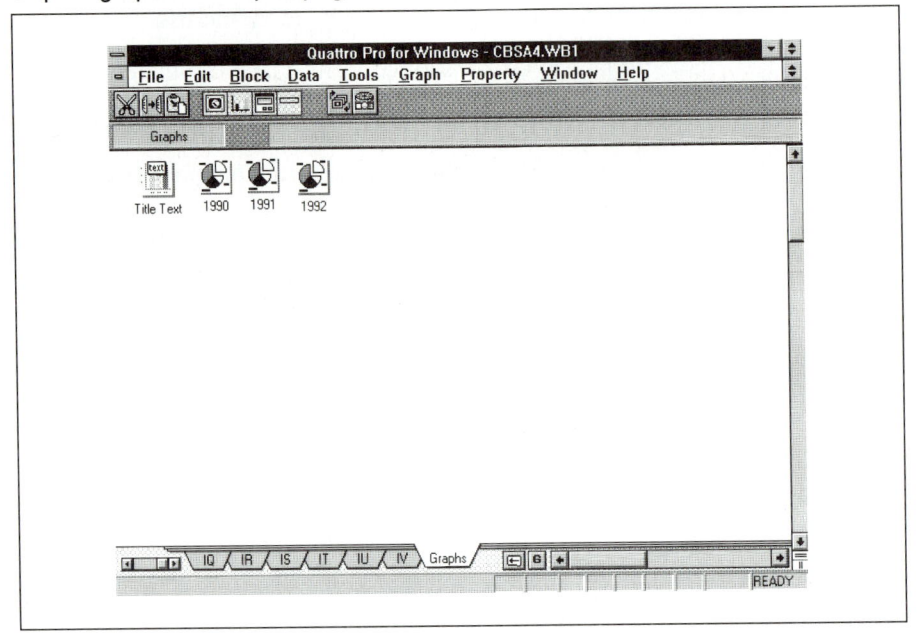

Chapter 10: Presentation Graphics 489

8. Repeat steps 5 through 7 to make as many additional copies of the graph as you need.

9. Double-click the first copy you made. Quattro Pro places the graph in the Graph window.

10. Use the Graph menu Type and Series commands to redefine the graph type and the supporting data series. In Figure 10-5, you see the Graph Series dialog box, where you redefine the data series. Quattro Pro redraws the graph but retains your formating choices.

In Figure 10-6, you see a graph that has been copied and modified in this way. The source of the graph was the graph shown in Figure 10-2. The copy was modified with the stacked bar data type, additional data series, a legend, and the Currency numeric format for the Y-axis labels.

As you can see, this shortcut method can save you a lot of time if you're developing a presentation with several charts.

In presentation graphics, you call attention to just one important fact about each slide, transparency, or handout—and that's true even if there's more than one point to make about it. In Figure 10-6, for example, two points could be made: Individuals contributed a lot more in 1992 than previously, and the trend of contributions is pleasingly upward. An

FIGURE 10-5 Changing the data series in the copied graph

FIGURE 10-6 Modified copy of the source graph

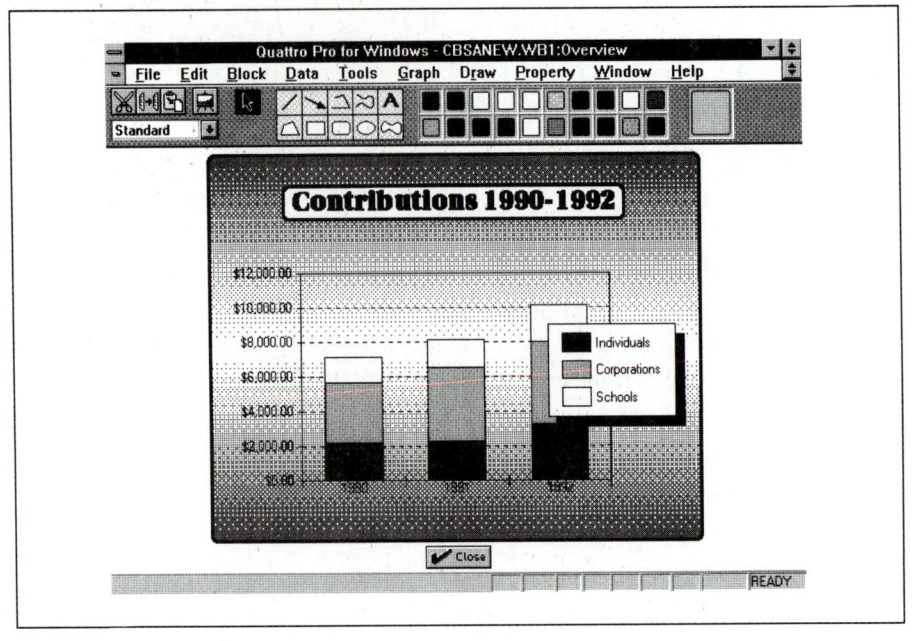

ideal presentation graph would use annotations to highlight just one of these points in each screen.

As you just learned, you can easily copy a graph. So you can have two graphs for this information, one emphasizing the increased contribution by individuals, and the other emphasizing the upward trend. Much of the work you'll do with presentation graphics involves highlighting the one point you want a chart to make. In the next section, you learn how to explode a slice of a pie chart, and in doing so, you learn one of several ways to make your key point.

Exploding a Pie Slice

An *exploded* pie slice has been separated from the rest of the graph for emphasis. In Figure 10-7, you see an exploded pie slice. One slice has been exploded for emphasis.

Chapter 10: Presentation Graphics 491

FIGURE 10-7 Exploded pie slice

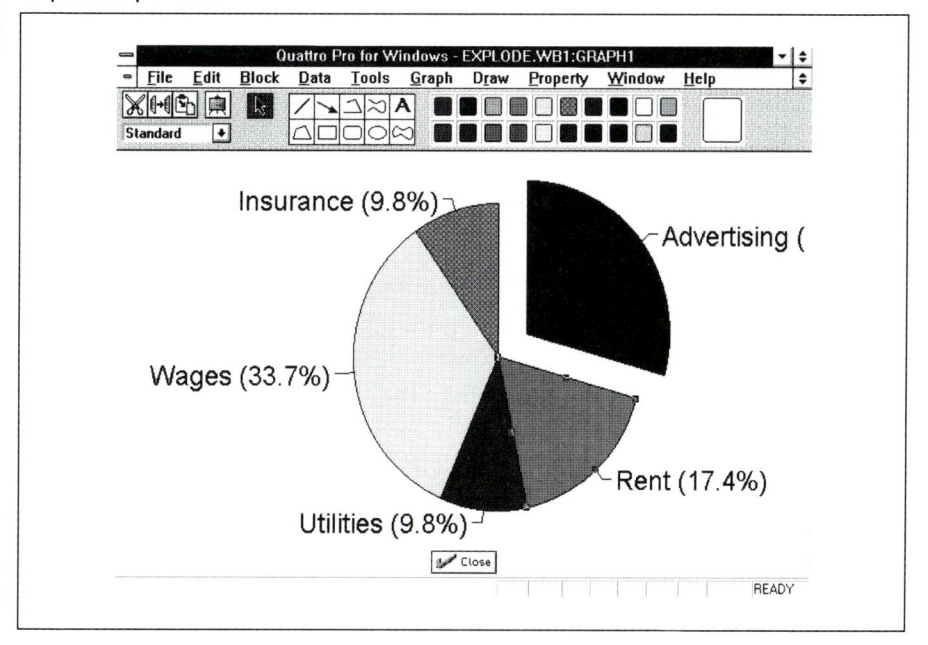

To explode a pie slice, double-click the slice you want to explode. You see the Pie Graph Properties dialog box, as shown in Figure 10-8.

FIGURE 10-8 Pie Graph Properties dialog box

Click the Explode option. If you wish, reset the Explode distance by dragging the slide box left or right. The greater the distance, the farther the slice will be positioned from the rest of the pie.

Adding Text

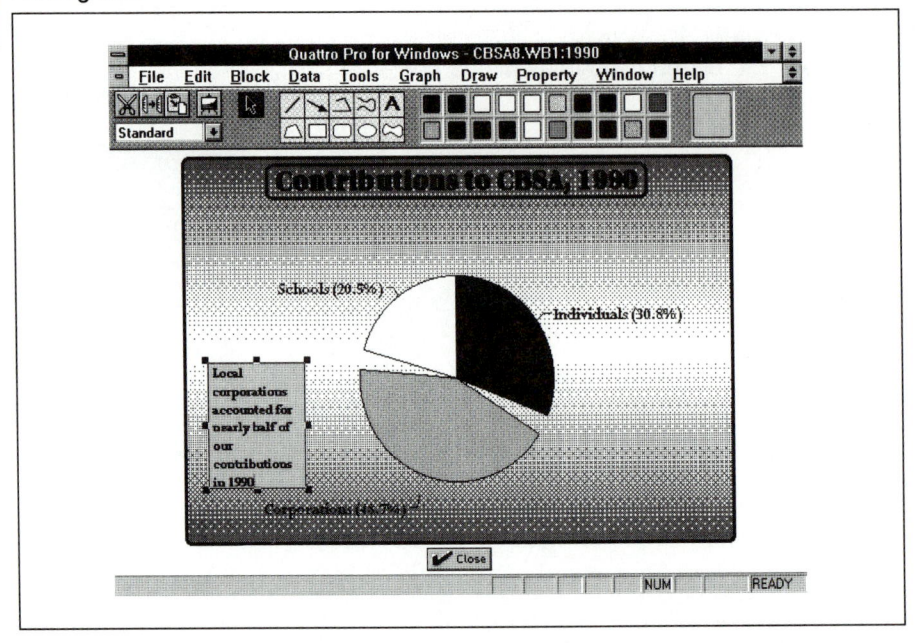

To make your point about a graph, you will find it helpful to add text annotations. To do so, simply click the Text tool in the drawing tools area of the Graph window SpeedBar, and then click in the document where you want the text to appear. A text box appears onscreen. You can then type the text you want to add, as shown in the lower-left corner of Figure 10-9.

Quattro Pro creates the text box using its default font, box, fill color, and other settings. You will probably want to customize the text box. In Figure 10-10, you see a text box customized with a bold rounded box (to match the rounded title box), the same font used in the pie chart series labels, and a light background to highlight the text box.

FIGURE 10-9 Adding text

Chapter 10: Presentation Graphics

FIGURE 10-10 Customized text box

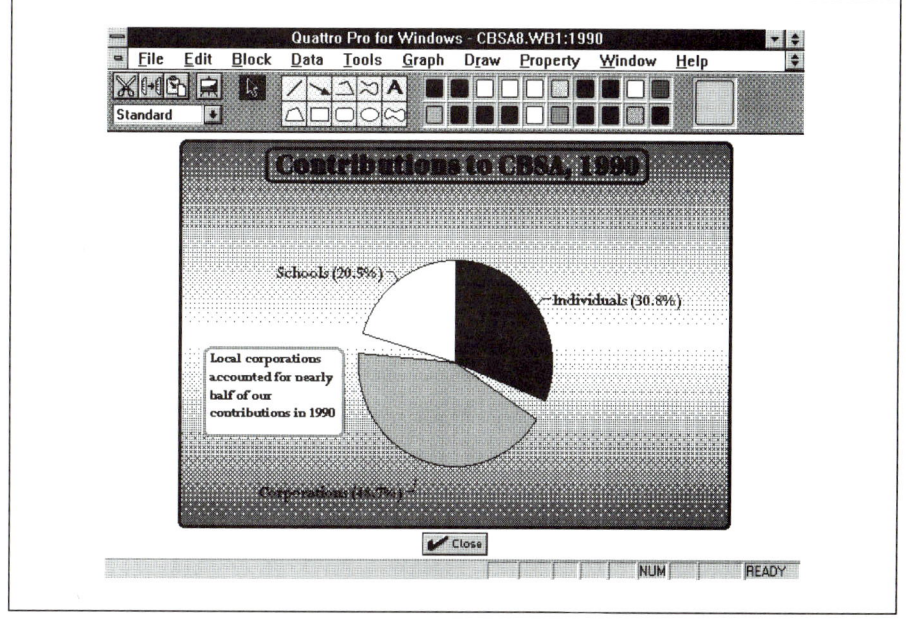

To customize the text box, right-click the text box background. You see the Box Properties menu, and you can pick from the Text Alignment options shown in Figure 10-11. Choose the box properties that you want

FIGURE 10-11 Box Properties dialog box

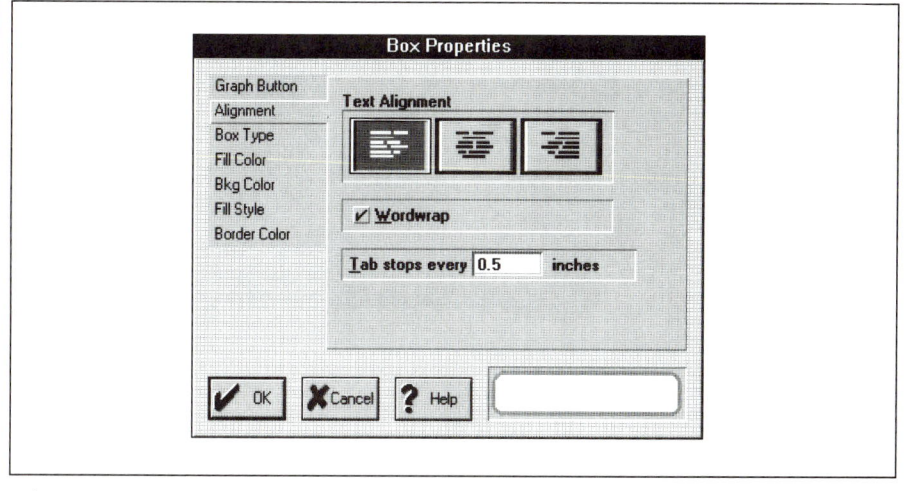

to change, and click OK. After choosing properties, you can still size and move the box as you please. Text box properties include alignment (flush left, centered, or flush right), wordwrap, tab stops, box border type, fill color, fill style, and border color.

Drawing Lines and Shapes

The drawing tools in the Graph window SpeedBar provide handy tools for adding a variety of lines and shapes to your graphs. Figure 10-12 shows the same graph that is displayed in Figure 10-10, with the addition of an arrow.

Note To expedite customization of lines and shapes, click the color you want from the color palette before you choose the drawing tool.

FIGURE 10-12 Graph with an arrow added

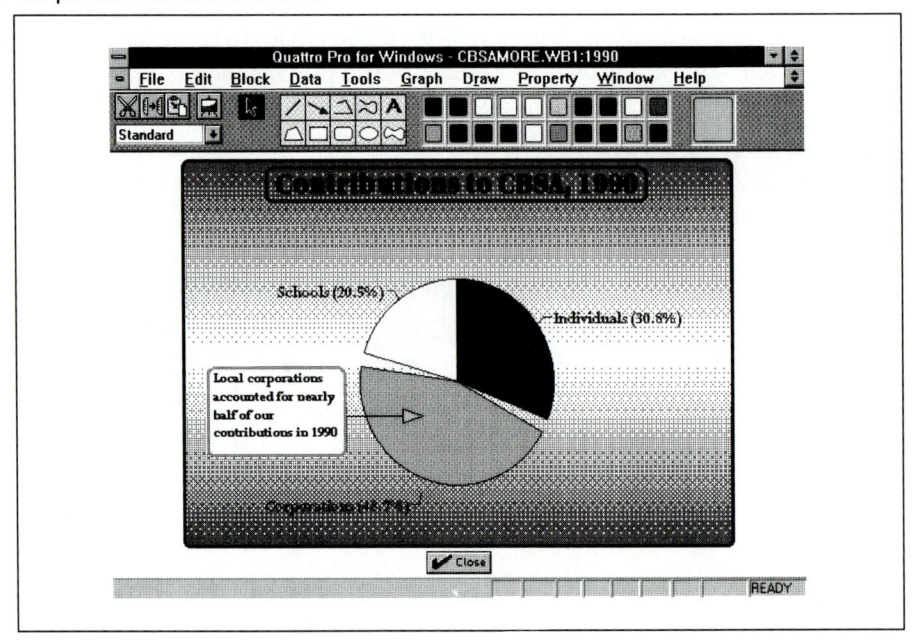

Chapter 10: Presentation Graphics

You may choose from the tools shown in Table 10-1.

TABLE 10-1 Quattro Pro's Drawing Tools

Icon	Tool	Description
	Line	Use the Line tool to draw straight lines anywhere on your graph. Click and drag to create the line.
	Arrow	Use this tool to draw a line that ends in an arrow. Click where you want the line to start, drag to create the line, and then release the button where you want the arrow to appear.
	Polyline	Choose this tool to draw a line that has more than one segment. To make a corner, click the mouse button. After you draw the last line segment, double-click to exit this tool.
	Freehand	Choose this tool to draw freehand shapes. Click and drag to create the shape.
	Text	Choose this tool and click in the Graph window to create a text box.
	Polygon	Choose this tool to draw a box with irregularly shaped sides (as many as you want). Click to turn corners and double-click to close the shape automatically. The polygon will have the currently chosen background color.
	Rectangle	Choose this tool to create a rectangle that has the currently selected background color.
	Rounded rectangle	Choose this tool to create a rectangle with rounded corners. The shape will have the current background color.
	Oval	Choose this tool to create a circle or oval. The shape will have the current background color.
	Closed freehand shape	Choose this tool to draw a freehand shape that has the current background color.

> **Note** To create perfect squares or circles, choose Graph Window from the Property menu and in the Graph Window dialog box, choose the Grid option. Then, activate the Display Grid option and the Snap to Grid option. Choose OK and then create the circle or square by dragging until the shape is symmetrical.

Creating a Text Graph

Text graphs are useful in any presentation. Figure 10-13 illustrates a text graph. With Quattro Pro, you can create a text graph easily by creating a graph with no data selected. You can position the text graph as a floating graph on your spreadsheet, or you can create the graph in the Graph window and store it separately. To create the text graph as a floating graph, select an empty cell and click the graph tool on the SpeedBar. To create the text graph in a Graph window, click an empty

FIGURE 10-13 Text graph created with Quattro Pro

cell and choose <u>N</u>ew from the <u>G</u>raph menu. Type a name for the graph, and choose OK.

Once you've created a text graph, you use the Text tool, one of the drawing tools on the Graph window SpeedBar, to create the text boxes. All the text in the text graph must be within text boxes. For this reason, creating a text graph is exactly like creating a text annotation in a chart. In Figure 10-13, the text box was modified to include a shaded fill color, a distinctive font, and a rounded rectangle border.

To add bullets to your text, you type codes, which are entered into the text surrounded by backslashes (\). Figure 10-14 shows the codes that underlie the bullets shown in Figure 10-13. The codes appear when the text box is active, but turn into bullets when you activate another part of your worksheet. Table 10-2 lists the codes you can use in Quattro Pro text charts. The text graph in Figure 10-13 uses the \bullet 2\ code, which produces the white box with check mark shown in the figure.

FIGURE 10-14 Bullet codes in the text graph

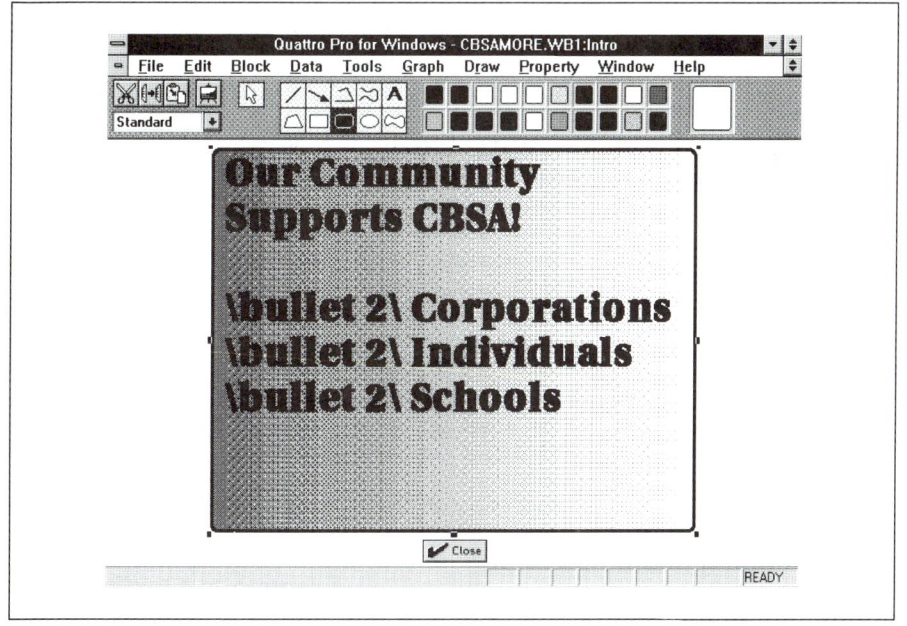

TABLE 10-2 Bullet Codes for Quattro Pro Text Charts

Code	Effect
\bullet 0\	White box
\bullet 1\	Black box
\bullet 2\	White box with check mark
\bullet 3\	Check mark
\bullet 4\	White box with black shadow
\bullet 5\	White box with black shadow and check mark
\bullet 6\	Black circle
\bullet 7\	White circle
\bullet 8\	White circle with check mark

Managing Graphics Objects

Once you've entered many graphic objects in the Graph window, including the graph itself, text boxes, and lines or shapes, you need to know how to select, move, and delete them. In addition, you can group and ungroup objects, arrange object layers, and align objects automatically. All these procedures are briefly described in this section.

Editing Objects

It's not necessary to select an object to change its properties. Just right-click the object. You need to select the object if you want to delete it, size it, move it, group it, or change its position in the object layer (above or below).

To select an object, click the arrow pointer tool, which is positioned left of the drawing tools on the Graph window SpeedBar, and click the object. To deselect the object, click another object or click the Graph window background. You can select more than one object at a time. To do so, hold down the SHIFT key as you click objects.

To delete a selected object, press DEL or choose Clear from the Edit menu. To size an object, drag one of the handles. To move an object, click on the selected object and hold down the mouse button until the pointer changes to a hand. Then drag the object to its new location.

Grouping and Ungrouping Objects

When you have grouped two or more objects, Quattro Pro treats them as if they were one object, which makes it easier to move them or delete them as a group. To group two or more objects, SHIFT-click them to select them, and then choose Group from the Draw menu. To ungroup the objects, select the group and choose Ungroup from the Draw menu.

Aligning Objects

Quattro Pro gives you two tools that you can use to keep objects aligned in your graph. The first tool is an onscreen grid, to which objects will snap into alignment when you drag them. To activate the grid, choose Graph Window from the Property menu. When you see the Graph Window menu, choose the Grid option. Choose Display Grid to activate the grid and Snap to Grid to make objects align to the nearest grid point, and choose OK. To turn off the grid, display this menu again and deactivate the Display Grid and Snap to Grid options.

The second alignment tool is the Align command in the Draw menu, which is used to align two or more objects. Before using the command, select the objects you want to align. Then, choose Align from the Draw menu. You see a submenu with six additional options: Left, Right, Horizontal Center, Top, Bottom, and Vertical Center. If you choose the Top option, for example, Quattro Pro aligns the top of the objects along an imaginary line across the screen. Figure 10-15 shows the effect of the Align commands.

Using Object Layers

Once you have added several objects (such as lines, arrows, and text boxes) to your graph, you may find that they overlap (as in Figure 10-16).

FIGURE 10-15 Alignment commands

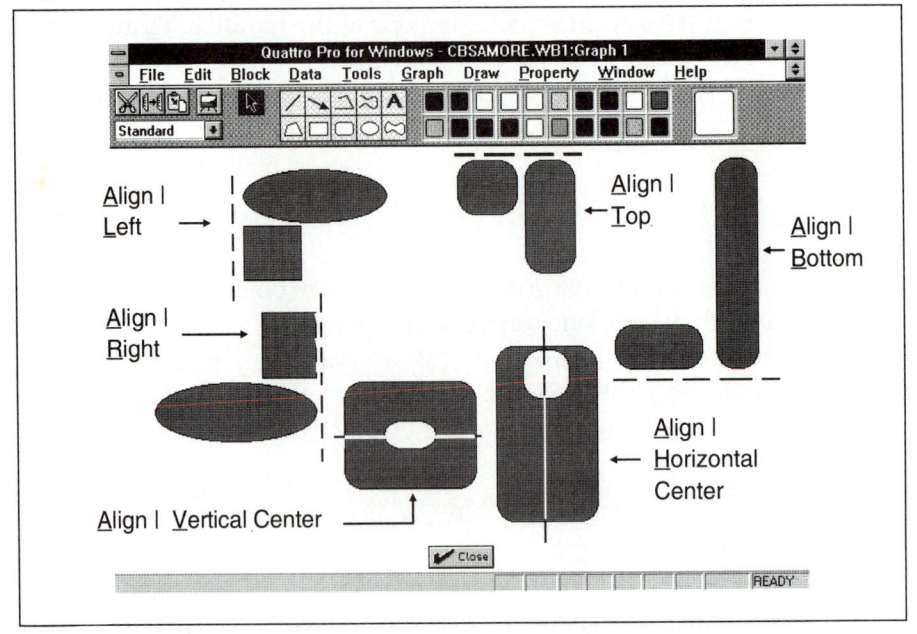

FIGURE 10-16 Overlapping objects

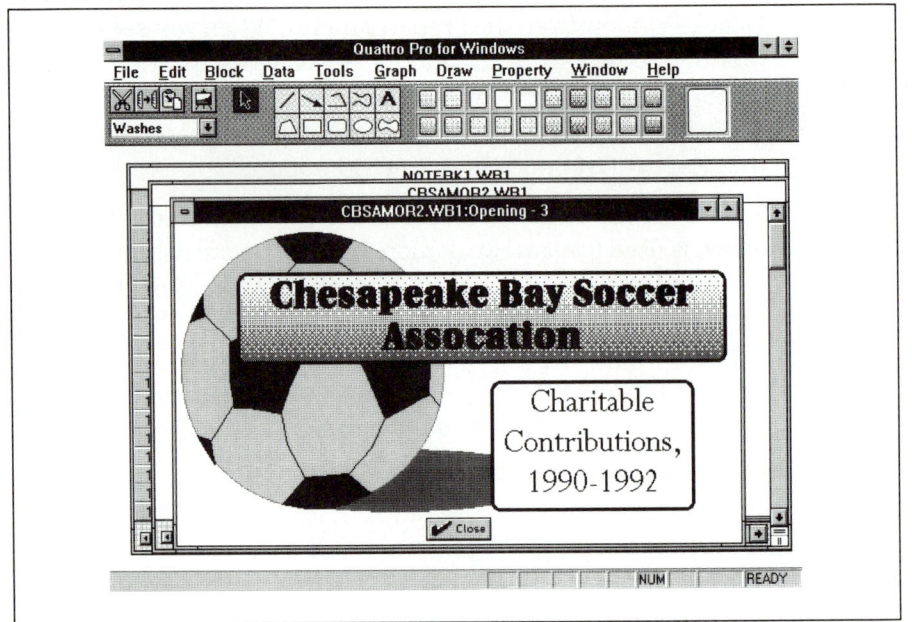

Objects are layered, with one object on top and others beneath. You can control the overlap using four commands on the Draw menu:

- Bring Forward moves the selected object forward one layer.
- Send Backward moves the selected object back one layer.
- Bring to Front moves the selected object to the top layer.
- Send to Back moves the selected object to the bottom layer.

Note To make a text box transparent so that the text seems to "float" above the background, use the Box Properties menu to choose a blank box type, and set the fill style to None.

Slide Shows

A *slide show* is a computer-based presentation in which the viewer sees a succession of full-screen graphs, including text graphs if desired. You can run the presentation on a desktop system, which is suitable for viewing by three or four people. Or if you equip your system with a display adapter for overhead projectors, you can turn this Quattro Pro capability into a sophisticated presentation device for larger audiences.

Creating Slide Shows

You use the Graphs page to create the slide show. The Graphs page contains icons that correspond to all the graphs you've created in the presentation. If you want to create a slide show, be sure to choose the Slide Show aspect ratio for all your graphs.

To create the slide show, display the Graphs page and click the Create Slide Show tool (this tool looks like a 35mm slide). You see the Create Slide Show dialog box, as shown here:

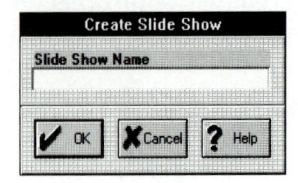

Type a name for the slide show, and choose OK. After you choose OK, Quattro Pro creates a new Graphs page icon that looks like a 35mm slide.

Creating the show is simplicity itself: You simply drag the graph icons to the slide show icon, one by one. Do so in the order you want the graphs to appear.

Displaying a Slide Show

To run a slide show you've created, choose Slide Show from the Graph menu. Choose the name of the slide show you want to display and choose OK. Quattro Pro displays the first graph. To advance to the next graph, click the left mouse button or press any key. To display the previous slide, click the right mouse button or press BACKSPACE. To cancel the slide show, and return to the Graph page, press ESC.

Editing a Slide Show

Once you've created a slide show, you can edit the order in which slides appear, remove slides from the show, and add special effects such as fixed delay times, wipes and fades between slides, and overlays.

To edit the slide show, double-click the slide show icon. You see the Light Table, as shown in Figure 10-17. To delete a slide, select it and press DEL. To move a slide, drag it to a new position. To choose an effect, drop down the Effect list box. You can choose from wipes (which simulate turning a page), tilts (which give the effect of one image pushing another off the screen), dissolves (one image fades out and another fades in), overlays (an image builds on the previous one), and a variety of cut effects (diamond in/out, curtain up/down, sides to center, center to sides). You can also control the speed of the transition (Slow, Med, Fast). You can

Chapter 10: Presentation Graphics   **503**

FIGURE 10-17 Light Table for editing slide shows

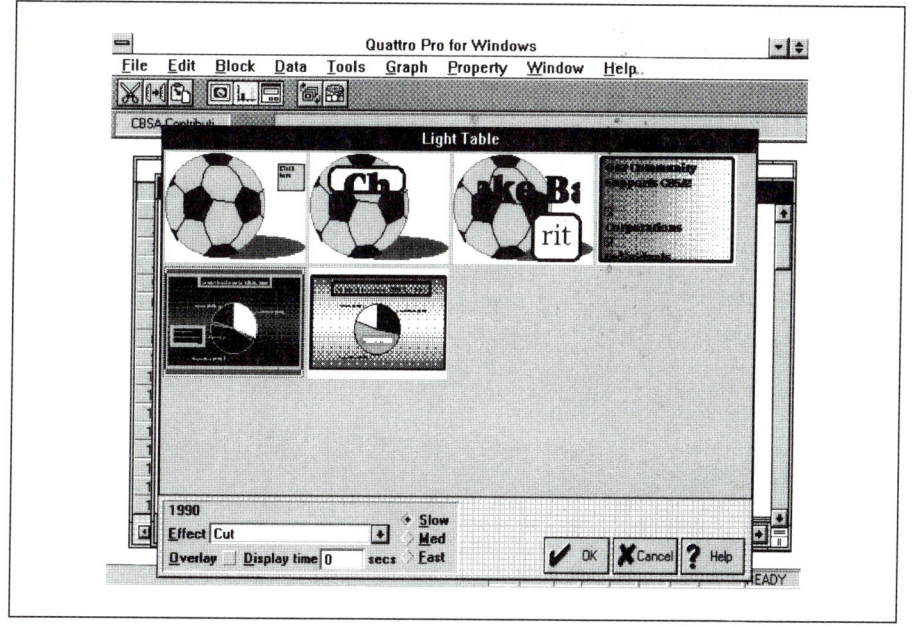

set a fixed display time for each slide by clicking the Display time option and typing a time in the secs box.

To choose a consistent default effect for the whole show, don't edit each slide individually. In the Graph window, right-click the slide show icon. You'll see the Slide Show property menu. When you choose Default Effect from the list box, you will see the Default Effect dialog box, as shown here:

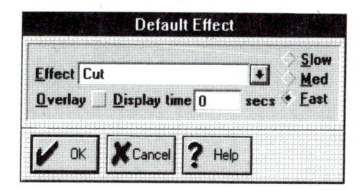

When you choose an effect from this dialog box, it applies to all the slides in your slide show. You can still add different effects to individual slides.

Creating an Interactive Presentation with Graph Buttons

Graph buttons provide an easy way to construct an interactive presentation, in which the user can select which slide is displayed next. A graph button is a text box that, when clicked, branches the slide show to a slide of your choice. To add a graph button to a graph, just enter a text box by clicking the text icon within the graph. Type the text you want to appear in the box, then right-click the box to display the Box Properties menu. Choose the Graph Button option. You see the Box Properties menu shown in Figure 10-18.

Activate the Select Graph option and choose the slide that you want displayed when the user clicks this button. Choose an effect, if you wish. Choose OK to confirm the button. The button looks like an ordinary text box on screen, so be sure to add directions to the user in text, as shown in Figure 10-19.

As you add buttons to your slide show, be sure to think of the user's convenience. Add buttons to return to branch points so that the user

FIGURE 10-18 Box Properties dialog box

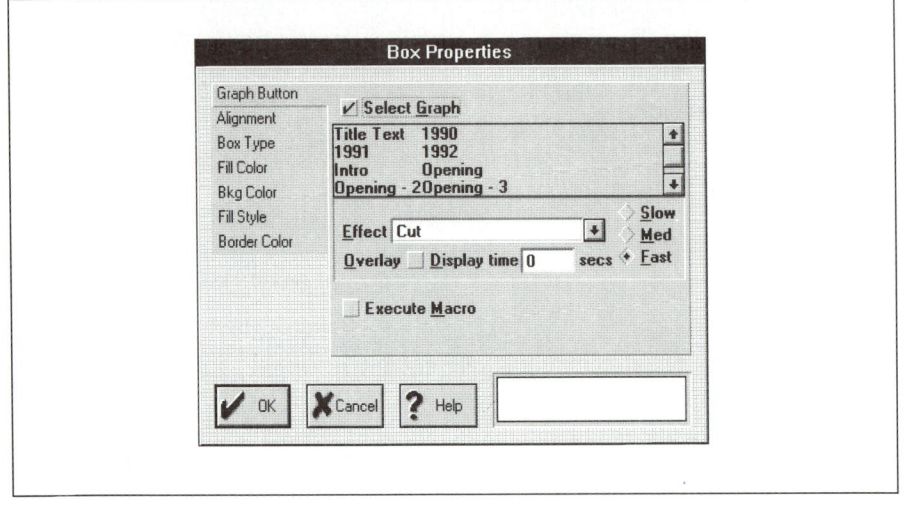

FIGURE 10-19 Graph buttons added to graph

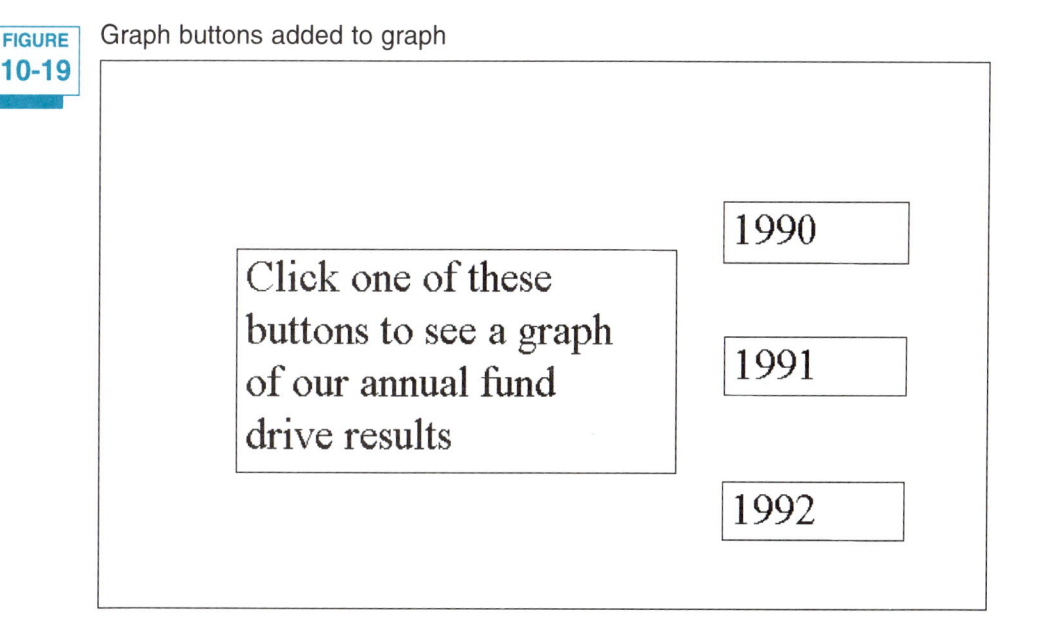

```
┌─────────────────────────────────────────────┐
│                                             │
│                                  ┌───────┐  │
│                                  │ 1990  │  │
│    ┌──────────────────────┐      └───────┘  │
│    │ Click one of these   │                 │
│    │ buttons to see a graph│     ┌───────┐  │
│    │ of our annual fund   │      │ 1991  │  │
│    │ drive results        │      └───────┘  │
│    └──────────────────────┘                 │
│                                  ┌───────┐  │
│                                  │ 1992  │  │
│                                  └───────┘  │
│                                             │
└─────────────────────────────────────────────┘
```

doesn't get lost, and perhaps add a button that takes you back to the first slide. Add a Quit button to end the show.

This chapter concludes the survey of Quattro Pro's impressive presentation graphics capabilities. In the next chapter, this book moves on to advanced data analysis capabilities.

CHAPTER 11

Advanced Data Analysis

*I*n the previous two chapters, you have learned how to make spreadsheet numbers reveal their patterns on screen—patterns that you may not have noticed had they not been displayed visually. In this chapter, you learn how to harness Quattro Pro's impressive data analysis capabilities, such as data frequency analysis, regression, optimization, and equation solving. As you learn in this chapter, these capabilities give you more tools to find patterns and meanings in your data—and even to make predictions—based on fixed assumptions. Many of these analytical procedures produce graphs such as XY graphs, so they are doubly useful—not only do they reveal the patterns in your data, but they also produce vivid graphs that visually show these patterns to you (and others).

This book isn't the place to teach the math and statistics that underlie the analytical procedures discussed in this chapter. However, you should take a look at its contents even if you don't understand terms such as "frequency analysis," "regression," and "optimization." The concepts aren't difficult to grasp, and this chapter illustrates all of them with easy-to-follow examples. Some of the thornier analytical capabilities, such as matrix arithmetic, are not covered because they are beyond this book's level. What's included is likely to be intelligible to the typical Quattro Pro user. So even if you're not a math whiz, give this chapter a try. Chances are that you'll find some very useful tools that you can apply to your business or profession.

Before you apply this chapter's material to business decision-making, though, be sure you fully understand the strengths and limitations of these tools. Consult a good statistics textbook or, better yet, you might consult someone with professional business management training to take a look at your work.

Regression: Finding Relationships Between Variables

When you have a large collection of related facts, you may want to see how strong the relationship is between them. For example, suppose your firm has increased its investment in employee training steadily over the past ten years. You also have data on productivity. Is there a relationship between the two? One method for answering such a question is called *linear regression analysis.* In brief, linear regression (or just regression for short) is a measurement of how strongly two variables relate to each other. Does productivity go up in proportion to your investment in employee training?

A common motivation for regression analysis is the need to make decisions. Employee training costs a lot of money. Is it paying off? Regression analysis is one way of finding an answer, but it's important to understand its limitations. Just because a regression analysis reveals two variables to be strongly related doesn't prove *a causal relationship* between them. In a causal relationship, one fact (employee training) *causes* another (productivity). Even if employee training and productivity are strongly related, no causal relationship is proven. The real cause may be a third, hidden factor, such as the reorganization of work into independent teams rather than the older, assembly line work procedure. All that regression can prove is that one variable, productivity, varies systematically with (and thus, seems to be *dependent* on) fluctuations in another variable (money spent on employee training). The actual reason for the dependent relationship may be very complex. In short, the results of any regression analysis should be viewed with a great deal of skepticism: It provides no answer, just a much more refined way of asking a question.

Linear regression is best used when there appears to be a strong *linear relationship* between two values—that is, as one value goes up, so does the other: The more money you spend on ice cream, the more you weigh! Linear regression is also useful for *inverse* relationships—for example, the more you exercise, the less you weigh. Linear regression isn't suitable when no such relationship is apparent. Bear in mind, too, that there's no guarantee that a well-established linear relationship will continue in the future. A third factor—such as exercise, in the ice cream/weight-gain scenario—may intrude and reduce the correlation.

A Regression Example

Imagine that you're managing the development office of a small charitable organization, and you're asking some fundamental questions about your office's performance. Your organization sends out direct mail solicitations to potential contributors—nothing fancy, just a few hundred letters cranked out with WordPerfect. Sometimes your office puts out as many as eight mailings a month, sometimes as few as four. Putting out more mailings seems to correlate with increased contributions, but you're not sure about this relationship. The extra mailings are stressful for your staff, though, and most of them are volunteers. Is it really paying off to push your staff to grind out seven or eight mailings per month? Or should you keep sending out as many mailings as you can?

Your impression is that the more mailings you send, the more money you get, so you decide to try a regression analysis. You have good data for the previous year or two, so you can create a spreadsheet to find out if the spreadsheet is really linear. You put together the spreadsheet shown in Figure 11-1. In column B, you type the number of direct mailings that went out each month. In column C, you also type the number of contributions that came in that are directly attributable to a given month's mailings. You name the B4..B15 range Mailings, and the C4..C15 range Contributions.

FIGURE 11-1 Figures for regression analysis

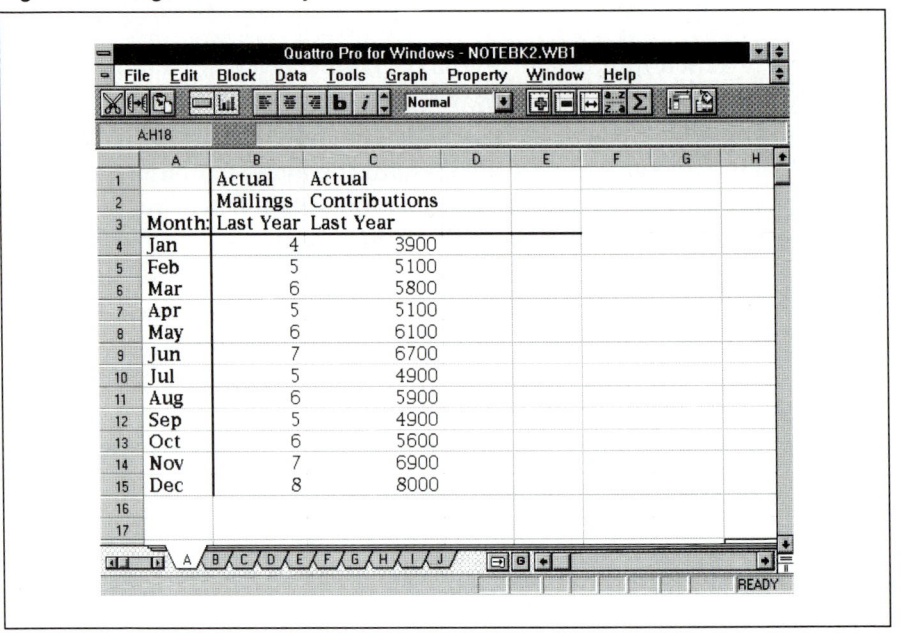

Month	Actual Mailings Last Year	Actual Contributions Last Year
Jan	4	3900
Feb	5	5100
Mar	6	5800
Apr	5	5100
May	6	6100
Jun	7	6700
Jul	5	4900
Aug	6	5900
Sep	5	4900
Oct	6	5600
Nov	7	6900
Dec	8	8000

Setting Up Regression

To perform a regression analysis with Quattro Pro, you need to learn a few terms. The number of mailings per month, which varies from month to month, is called the *independent variable*, while the amount of contributions received from these mailings is called the *dependent variable*. You're trying to find out just how strong this dependency is. The result of a regression analysis is a table of numbers, but ideally, you want to graphically plot the two values against each other to see whether increases in the independent variable correlate with increases (or decreases) in the dependent variable. For this reason, the independent variables are called the X-axis variables, and the dependent variables are called the Y-axis variables. That's how they will be plotted on the XY graph you'll make.

To carry out the regression analysis, you choose Advanced Math from the Tools menu, and Regression from the submenu that pops up. The Linear Regression dialog box appears, as shown in Figure 11-2.

The first two items on the Regression menu, Independent and Dependent, refer to the variable inputs to the regression calculation. Quattro Pro will calculate the correlation of the independent variable with the dependent variable. In this case, the Mailings block, in cells B4..B15, is the independent variable. Quattro Pro will determine whether increases in mailings leads to proportionate increases in contributions (in cells C4..C15). Both variables must be situated in matching columns and rows

FIGURE 11-2 Linear Regression dialog box

of the worksheet and must contain an equal number of data points, as is the case in this example.

Note: When working with linear regressions, you will find it helpful to name the independent and dependent variable ranges. For example, you can name the range B4..B15 Mailings, and the range C4..C15 Contributions. Doing so enables you to type these names instead of the ranges when using the Linear Regression dialog box. To name a block, select the cells and choose Names from the Block menu and then choose Create from the submenu (you can also use the CTRL-F3 shortcut). In the Create Name dialog box, type the block name in the Name box, and choose OK.

When you select Independent and Dependent, you can enter the cell coordinates either by typing them, typing a range name, or by pointing to them. (There can be more than one independent variable, as a later example shows.) The Output block is entered here as E3, although the results of the calculation will occupy four columns and nine rows. You need only define the upper-left corner of the cells of the Output block. When you've finished filling out the dialog box fields, your Linear Regression dialog box looks like the one in Figure 11-3.

Select OK to tell Quattro Pro to complete the regression calculation. The results are shown in Figure 11-4.

FIGURE 11-3 Linear Regression dialog box after it is filled out

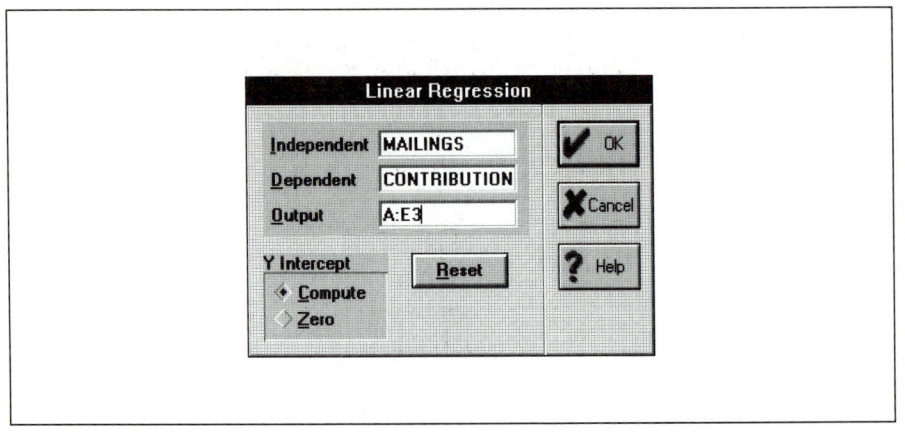

FIGURE 11-4 Results of linear regression analysis

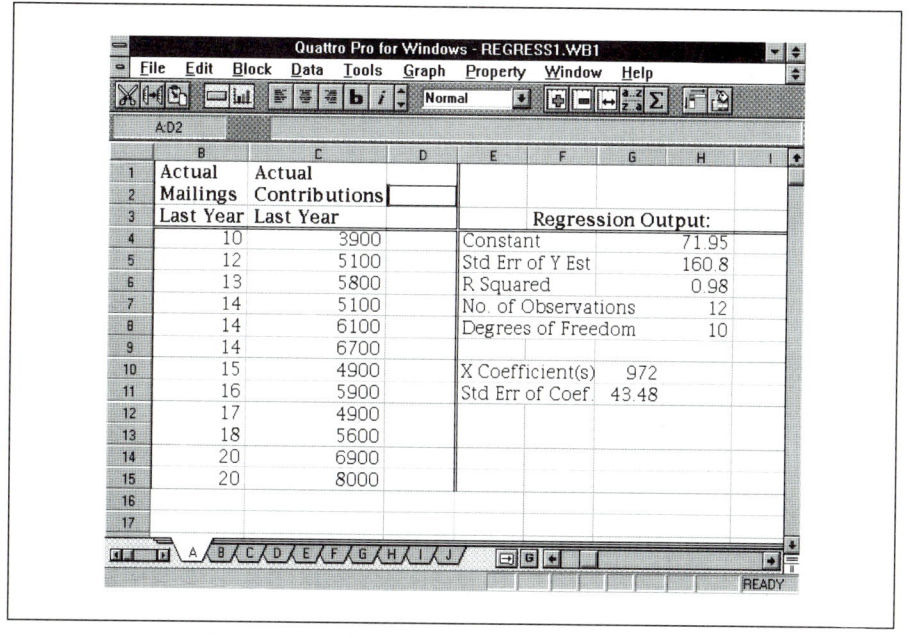

	Actual Mailings Last Year	Actual Contributions Last Year		Regression Output:	
1					
2					
3					
4	10	3900		Constant	71.95
5	12	5100		Std Err of Y Est	160.8
6	13	5800		R Squared	0.98
7	14	5100		No. of Observations	12
8	14	6100		Degrees of Freedom	10
9	14	6700			
10	15	4900		X Coefficient(s)	972
11	16	5900		Std Err of Coef.	43.48
12	17	4900			
13	18	5600			
14	20	6900			
15	20	8000			

Interpreting Regression Results

The result of a regression calculation is a column of numbers that represent the numeric relationships between the variables and labels describing these numbers. Interpreting these results involves understanding numerous statistical concepts. The No. of Observations, shown in Figure 11-4, is how many data points were observed for the variables—in this case 12, one for each month. Degrees of Freedom represents the number of observations minus one for each variable observed, in this case 10. The value R Squared, called the *coefficient of determination*, is a measure of the extent to which the variables are related, with 1 (or –1) being the maximum possible value. In this example, where the contributions are clearly very closely related to the mailings, the value of R Squared is nearly 1. In general, an R Squared value of .95 or greater (or, for an inverse relationship, of –.95 or *less*) is sufficient to suggest, even to the skeptical, a very strong relationship beween the two variables. The strength of this relationship is shown in Figure 11-5, which displays an XY graph of the data. You learn how to create an XY graph later in this chapter.

FIGURE 11-5 XY graph of the data shows a strong relationship

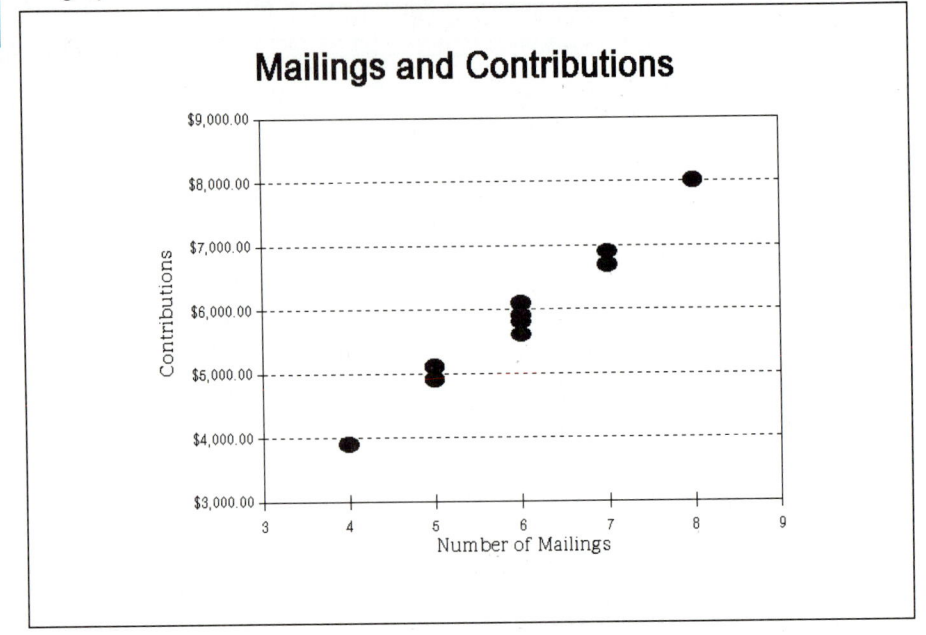

Mailings and Contributions

You'd need some background in statistics to understand most of the figures in the regression output. An exception is the X coefficient, which, apart from the coefficient of determination, is perhaps the most useful number in the regression output. The X coefficient tells how much the dependent variable, contributions, will change for a single unit increase in the independent variable, mailings. As you can see in the regression output block in Figure 11-4, this figure is close to 1000, and most of the sales figures are, in fact, about 1000 times the mailing figures. In short, every additional mailing is worth $1000 in contributions.

Using Regression Results

If every additional mailing brings in $1000 in additional contributions, how much would your office bring in if the number of mailings were doubled? Tripled? Would it be worth hiring a full-time WordPerfect whiz to crank out these mailings?

Chapter 11: Advanced Data Analysis

Now that you know every mailing brings in $1000, you can use the results of this analysis to predict how increasing the number of mailings might affect the amount of contributions you receive (bear in mind that this prediction will be accurate only if all the other conditions affecting contributions remain the same). To make this prediction, you can use the X Coefficient value, one of the regression output values you just learned about. This value tells how much contributions will increase with every increase in mailings. You can use this coefficient to predict how much a given increase in mailings is likely to produce in increased contributions.

First, you add formulas to column D that represent the predicted values for the number of mailings in column B. Figure 11-6 shows a calculation that has been entered in column D, representing the prediction formula

Constant + X Coefficient × Independent variable

In this case, cell D4 is $H$4+$G$10*B4. This formula was copied down the column to produce the predicted results, as shown in Figure 11-6, which are close to the real results.

FIGURE 11-6 Adding a prediction formula to column D

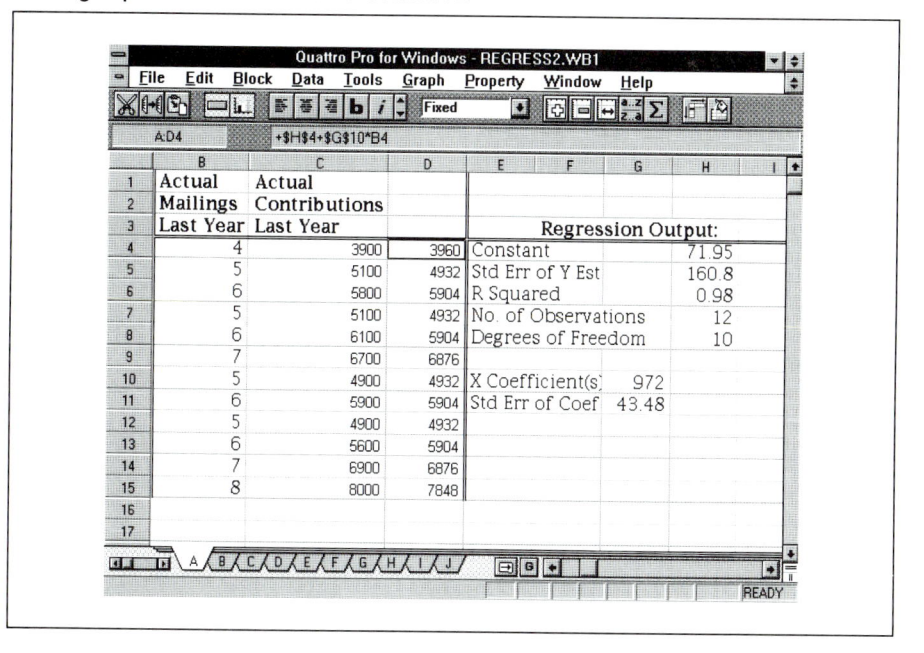

	B	C	D		F	G	H
1	Actual	Actual					
2	Mailings	Contributions					
3	Last Year	Last Year			Regression Output:		
4	4	3900	3960	Constant			71.95
5	5	5100	4932	Std Err of Y Est			160.8
6	6	5800	5904	R Squared			0.98
7	5	5100	4932	No. of Observations			12
8	6	6100	5904	Degrees of Freedom			10
9	7	6700	6876				
10	5	4900	4932	X Coefficient(s)		972	
11	6	5900	5904	Std Err of Coef		43.48	
12	5	4900	4932				
13	6	5600	5904				
14	7	6900	6876				
15	8	8000	7848				

Since you've added the prediction formulas to column D, you can proceed to the second step, which amounts to a "what-if" analysis: You replace the values in column B with the number of mailings that you think you can do *next* year, with increased staff on board. Figure 11-7 shows the impressive results.

Linear regression is a great tool, but this example suggests why its predictions should be taken with a grain of salt. The model really isn't complex enough to take the real development situation into account: When you bombard potential contributors with too many letters, they will get disgusted and quit contributing! This model's predictions would have some validity only if you were planning to expand the *geographical range* of the mailings, in addition to their frequency.

Regression with Multiple Variables

You can include more than one independent variable in the regression calculation. An example of this is the analysis of the results of a survey

FIGURE 11-7 Predicting next year's contributions

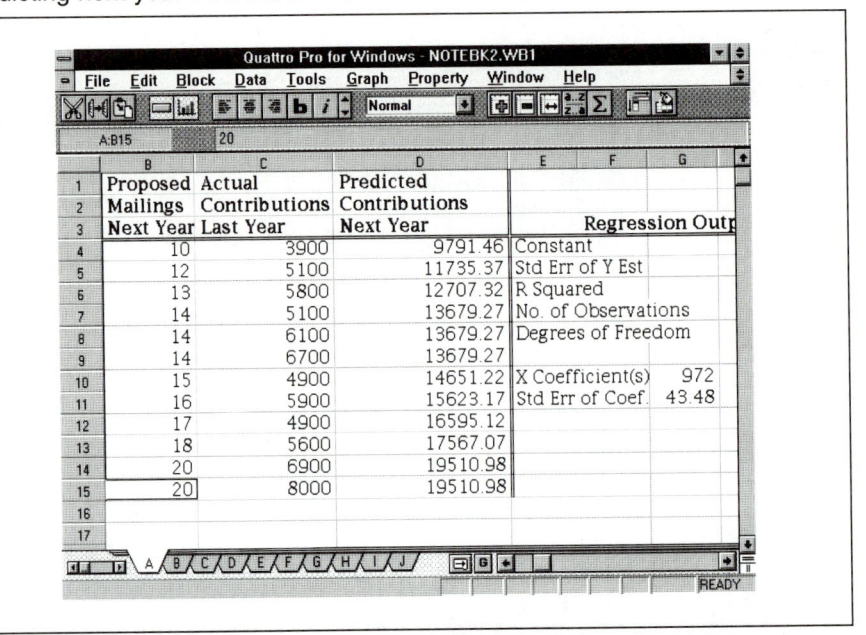

	B	C	D	E	F	G
1	Proposed	Actual	Predicted			
2	Mailings	Contributions	Contributions		Regression Output	
3	Next Year	Last Year	Next Year			
4	10	3900	9791.46	Constant		
5	12	5100	11735.37	Std Err of Y Est		
6	13	5800	12707.32	R Squared		
7	14	5100	13679.27	No. of Observations		
8	14	6100	13679.27	Degrees of Freedom		
9	14	6700	13679.27			
10	15	4900	14651.22	X Coefficient(s)		972
11	16	5900	15623.17	Std Err of Coef.		43.48
12	17	4900	16595.12			
13	18	5600	17567.07			
14	20	6900	19510.98			
15	20	8000	19510.98			

Chapter 11: Advanced Data Analysis

questionnaire. Ever curious about the fundamentals of its business, Take Over Airline sent a survey to all its corporate accounts, asking them a series of questions about the number of employees, the normal class of business travel, whether the firm's employees travel to Europe on business, and the number of trips to Europe they've made and are planning to make.

The results of the survey were entered into the worksheet in tabulated columns, as shown in Figure 11-8. The company names are in column A. Column B shows the number of employees at the company. The numbers entered in column C refer to a code for the company's type of business. There are just over a hundred responses to the survey. You could perform a simple regression analysis on any two values. For example, company size and European trips. However, the analyst wants to know whether there is a significant relationship among more than two values: the size of the company, as measured by the number of its employees; the type of business the company is in, as signified by the code; and the number of flights made to Europe in 1991, listed in column F. This means that the independent variables are columns B and C, and column F is the dependent variable.

FIGURE 11-8 Results of a survey include multiple variables

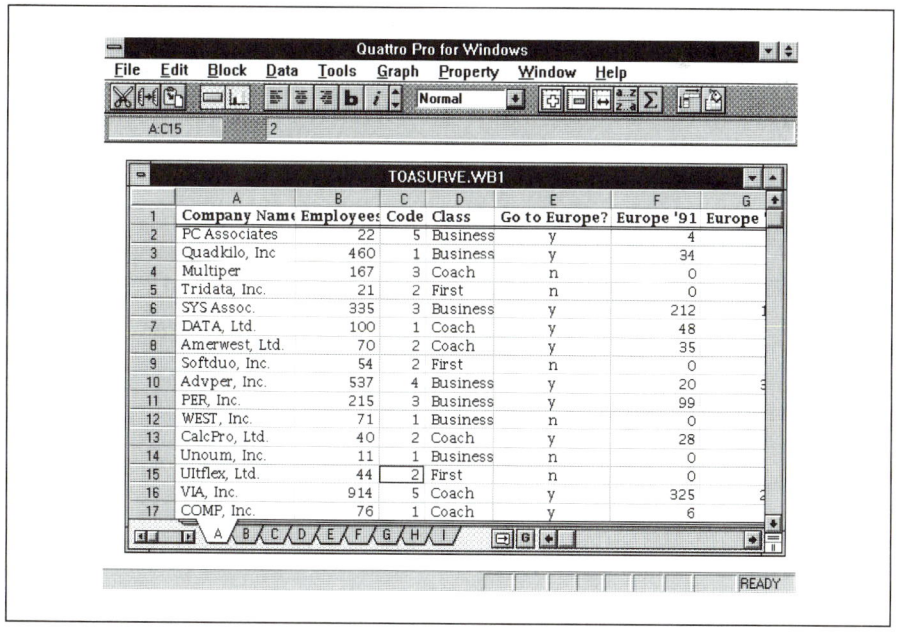

	A	B	C	D	E	F	G
1	Company Name	Employees	Code	Class	Go to Europe?	Europe '91	Europe
2	PC Associates	22	5	Business	y	4	
3	Quadkilo, Inc	460	1	Business	y	34	
4	Multiper	167	3	Coach	n	0	
5	Tridata, Inc.	21	2	First	n	0	
6	SYS Assoc.	335	3	Business	y	212	
7	DATA, Ltd.	100	1	Coach	y	48	
8	Amerwest, Ltd.	70	2	Coach	y	35	
9	Softduo, Inc.	54	2	First	n	0	
10	Advper, Inc.	537	4	Business	y	20	
11	PER, Inc.	215	3	Business	y	99	
12	WEST, Inc.	71	1	Business	n	0	
13	CalcPro, Ltd.	40	2	Coach	y	28	
14	Unoum, Inc.	11	1	Business	n	0	
15	Ultflex, Ltd.	44	2	First	n	0	
16	VIA, Inc.	914	5	Coach	y	325	
17	COMP, Inc.	76	1	Coach	y	6	

Note that *coded logical data*—data that has a "yes" or "no" answer, such as "Does your firm send employees to Europe?"—must be shown as numeric values if it is to be used as a variable. Also note that when you are using two or more independent variables, they should be in adjacent columns, as with the number of employees and business codes used in this example.

To perform the linear regression analysis, use the Tools | Advanced Math | Regression command, as before. Figure 11-9 shows the correct settings for the analysis (note that the output is directed to page B of the notebook).

The result of this regression example, using B:A1 as the Output block, can be seen in Figure 11-10. Note that there are two X coefficients, one for each of the independent variables. The measure of R Squared is 0.606, which shows only a moderate relationship between the two independent variables and the dependent one.

Note: If you try to duplicate this example, based on the data in Figure 11-8, your results will differ from those in Figure 11-10. This is because the example includes data through row 22 (as shown in Figure 11-9), but Figure 11-8 shows data only through row 17.

Generating a Frequency Distribution

When you are handling large quantities of data, such as the survey results discussed in the last example, you often need to analyze the

FIGURE 11-9 Linear Regression dialog box for the survey uses two independent variables

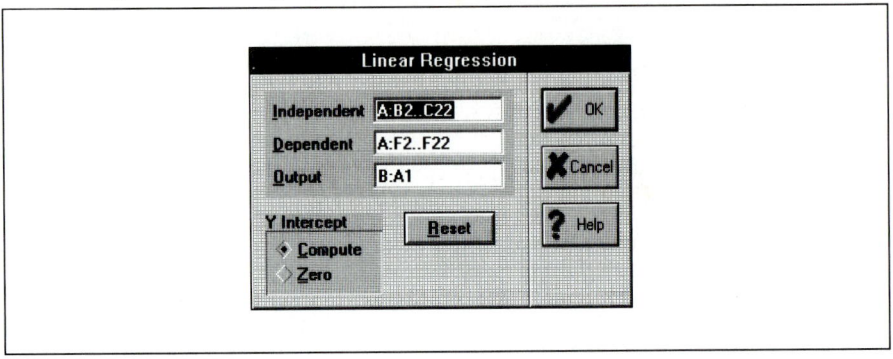

FIGURE 11-10 Regression analysis of the survey results

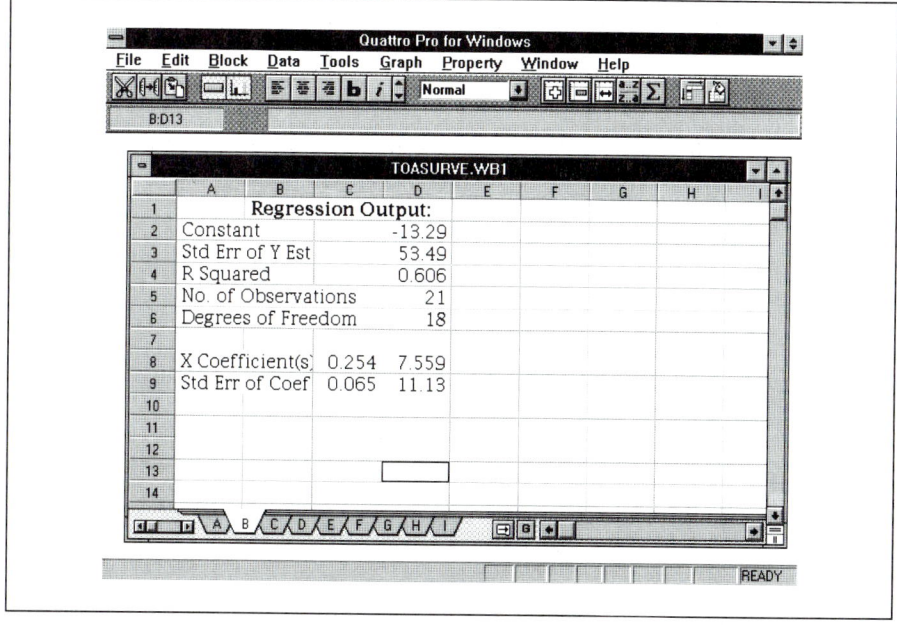

distribution of the data. For example, someone might ask "How big are the companies that responded?" Measured in terms of employees, you could say that they range from 22 to 914, which you could see from simply browsing column B. But this response would be rather vague. If you were to categorize the companies based on number of employees and count how many fell into each category, you would get a better understanding of the survey's respondents. This is the role of the Frequency command on the Data menu.

Performing a Distribution Analysis

To perform a frequency distribution with Quattro Pro, you need to supply two pieces of information. The first is the block of values to be categorized. The second is the column of numbers representing the range over which the values are to be distributed—the categories, as it were. The group of cells containing these category numbers is called the *bin block*, as though each number in the values block was tossed into the appropriate bin for counting. The result of the Data | Frequency command is a list of the totals of that count placed in the column to the right of the bin numbers.

To see this in action, consider the response to the TOA survey, which you want to analyze according to the number of employees at each company. First, a series of numbers for the bin block must be entered. You can do so on another page of the notebook in which the survey data is entered. The first number will represent from 0 to that number, so that 100 would represent companies with from 0 to 100 employees. For the employee numbers, you could use 100 through 1000 in intervals of 100. This series of numbers can easily be entered with the Block | Fill command. Begin by blocking the range A4..A13, which will hold the values. When you choose Fill from the Block menu, you see the dialog box shown in Figure 11-11.

If you type **100** in the Start box, **100** in the Step box, and **1000** in the Stop box, you get the results shown in Figure 11-12.

To generate the frequency distribution, choose Frequency from the Data menu with the values block still selected. You see the Frequency Tables dialog box, as shown in Figure 11-13.

When you select Frequency, you are first prompted for the values block, in this case, cells B2..B22 on notebook page A (A:B2..B22). The bin block is the block A4..A13 on page C. After you choose OK, Quattro Pro writes the results in the blank column adjacent to the bin block, as shown in Figure 11-14.

FIGURE 11-11 Block Fill dialog box

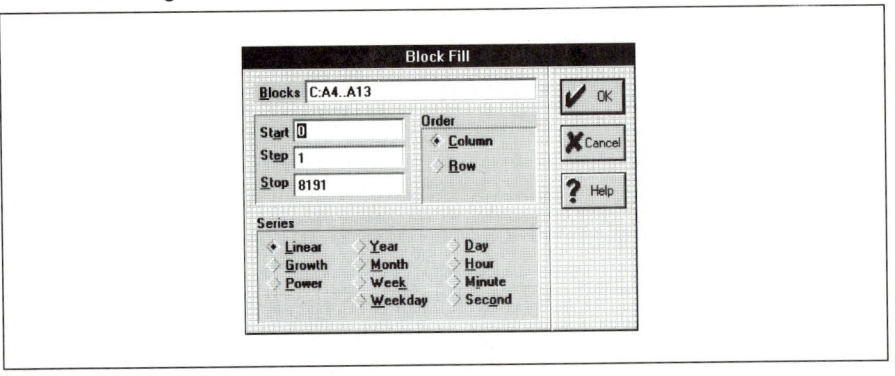

Chapter 11: Advanced Data Analysis

FIGURE 11-12 Block filled with values

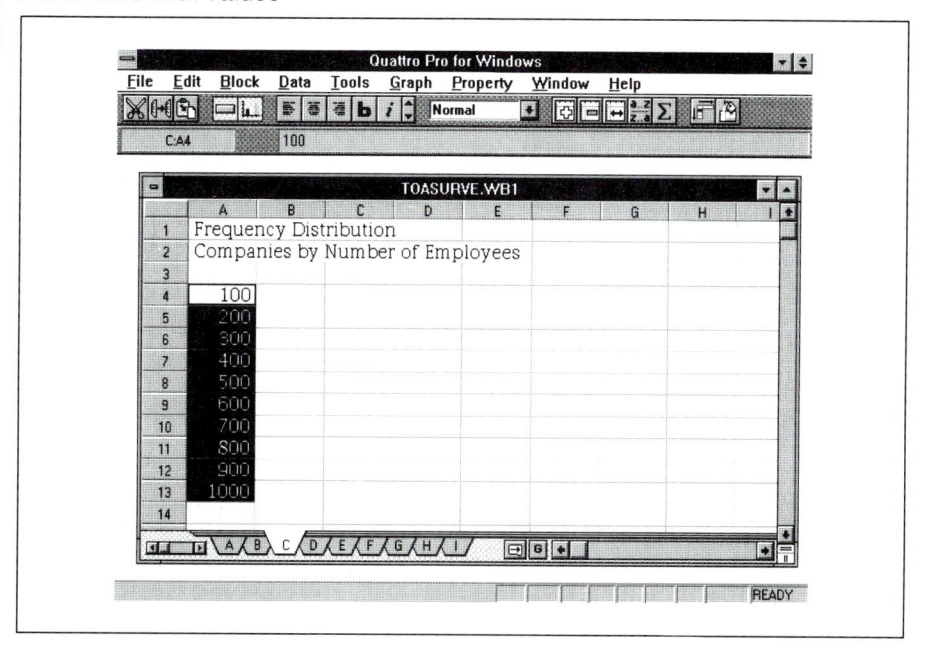

Generating What-If Tables

Arguably, the greatest value of spreadsheets lies in their potential to ask "What-if" questions, such as "What if I hired ten more employees? Would the increased work output be worth the increased expenses?" After

FIGURE 11-13 Frequency Tables dialog box

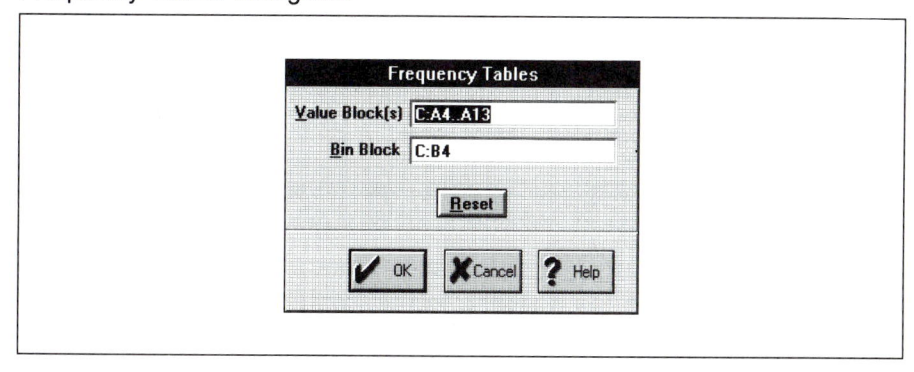

FIGURE 11-14 Results of frequency distribution analysis

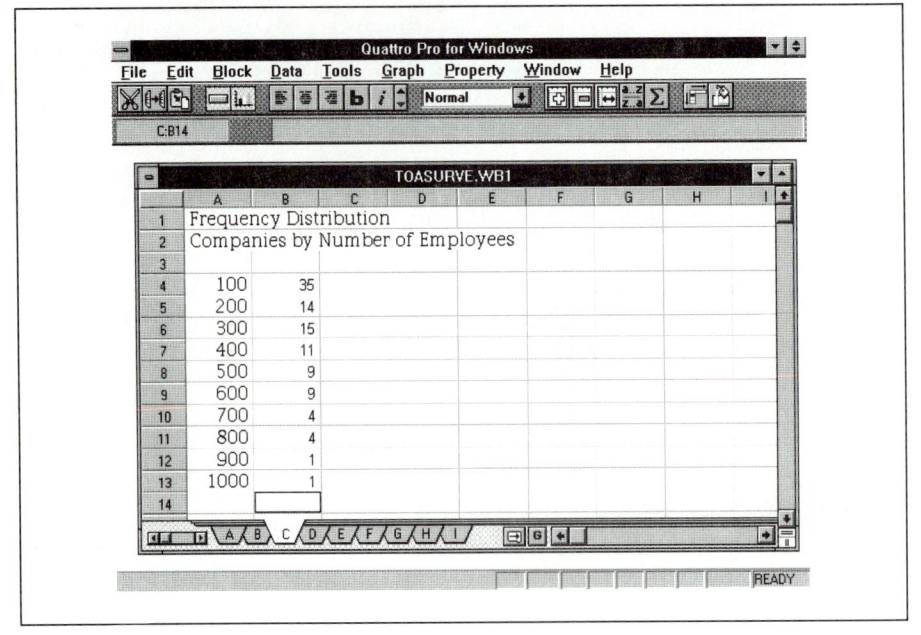

[Screenshot of Quattro Pro for Windows showing TOASURVE.WB1 with Frequency Distribution - Companies by Number of Employees:
- 100: 35
- 200: 14
- 300: 15
- 400: 11
- 500: 9
- 600: 9
- 700: 4
- 800: 4
- 900: 1
- 1000: 1]

you have established the formulas that relate the different cells in a worksheet to one another, you can change the numbers on which the formulas are based.

Here is another example of a *what-if analysis*. Suppose you set up a worksheet to calculate sales for the next 12 months, based on a starting volume of 2000 units increasing at 5 percent per month. By adding up the sales for the year, you can see what kinds of sales are possible with a 9 percent growth rate starting at 2000 units.

Most people do what-if analyses by typing in new starting values and looking at the bottom line. However, this procedure is time consuming and leaves no record of the alternative analyses. In this section, you learn how to create a *what-if table*, which lists all the alternatives in a handy and readable way. In essence, you get Quattro Pro to type in the alternative values, one by one, and create a table of the results. Why do it manually when this program can do it almost instantaneously—and give you output you can print or graph? To create a what-if table, you use the What-If command on the Data menu.

A What-If Scenario

Suppose you are thinking of buying a car. You've decided on the make and model, but you have a range of financing options available. The dealer has quoted you a 48-month loan at 8%, and you want to know how much you can save by shopping around. The spreadsheet shown in Figure 11-15 reveals the calculations involved. The cells in column B are formatted in the text format to show the formulas they contain. The total price of the car is calculated and the down payment subtracted to show the amount you would need to finance. The figures in B10, B11, and B12 show the principal, interest, and term of the loan.

You can perform what-if analyses just by typing new interest and term figures in cells B11 and B12. To create a what-if table, you could move to page B of the workbook and create the table shown in Figure 11-16. This table was created using the Block | Fill command, beginning with a start value of .005 and filling the cells A2..A14 with an increment (Step) of .0025. Then the column was formatted using the Percent option. Note that you must leave a blank cell above and to the right of the what-if values. In this cell (B2), you type a reference to the cell that contains the

FIGURE 11-15 Car cost analysis worksheet

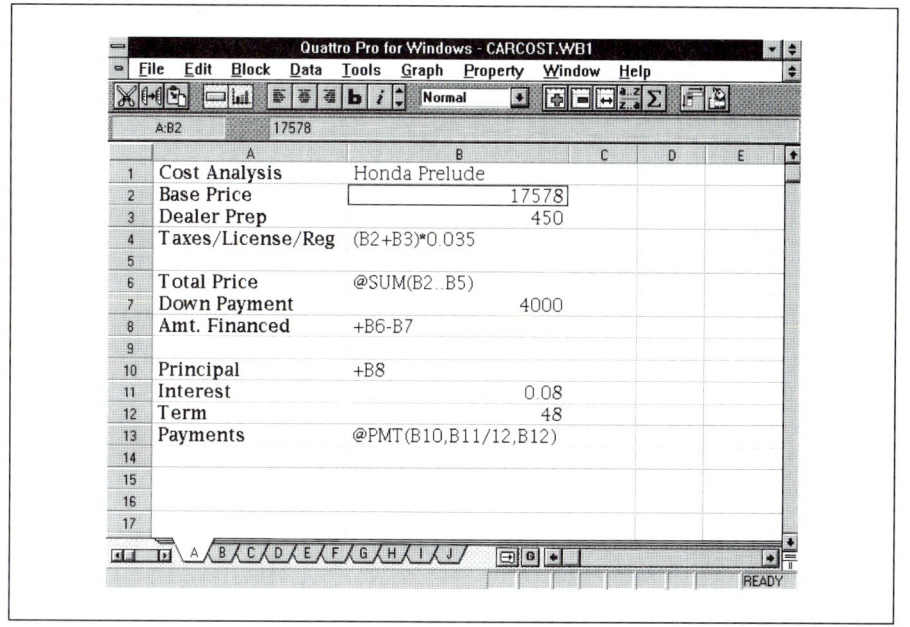

524 Quattro Pro for Windows Inside & Out

FIGURE 11-16 Starting the what-if table

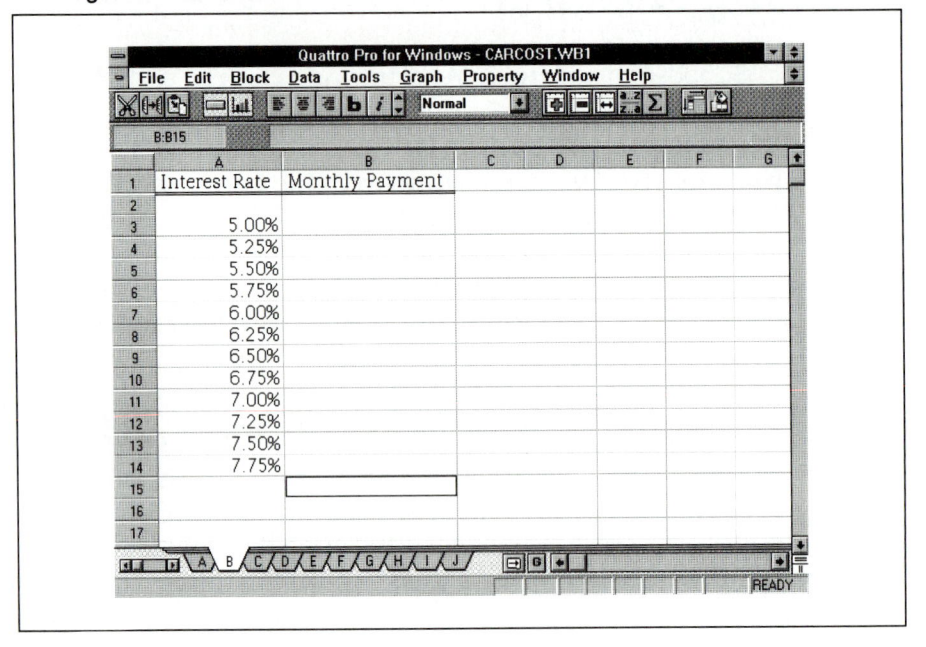

![Screenshot of Quattro Pro spreadsheet CARCOST.WB1 showing column A with "Interest Rate" header and values from 5.00% to 7.75% in rows 3-14, and column B with "Monthly Payment" header]

@PMT formula in A:B13. Quattro Pro shows the value produced by this formula with its current settings ($357.87).

The next step in constructing the what-if table is to choose the What-If command from the Data menu. You see the What-If dialog box, as shown in Figure 11-17.

FIGURE 11-17 What-If dialog box

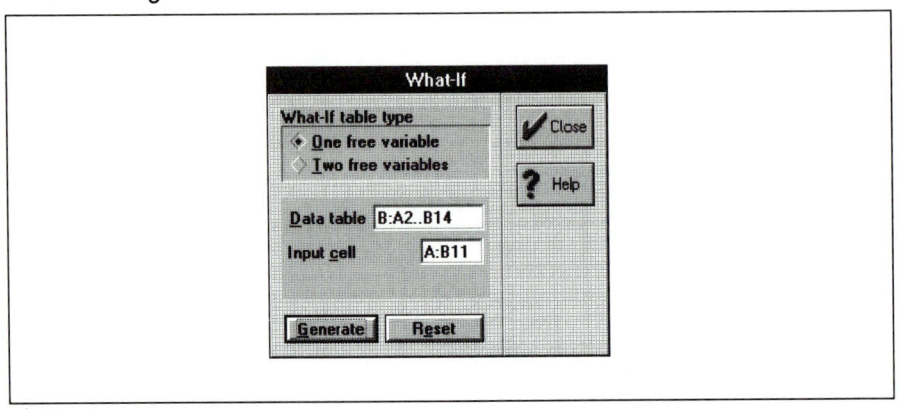

![Screenshot of What-If dialog box with options for "What-If table type" (One free variable selected, Two free variables), Data table: B:A2..B14, Input cell: A:B11, and buttons for Close, Help, Generate, and Reset]

In the Block box, you type or point to the range that contains the cell reference to the @PMT formula, the range of what-if values, and the range in which you want Quattro Pro to place the results. In the current example, this range is A2..B14 on notebook page B.

In the Input Cell 1 box, you type a reference to the cell that you want Quattro Pro to use for the what-if analysis. This is the cell you would use if you were performing the what-if analysis manually, typing in one value after another and seeing the results on the bottom line. For the current example, the input cell should be A:B11, the cell that contains the interest rate. With this cell identified as the interest rate, Quattro Pro will type in all the values you entered in A3..A14, one by one, and show the results in column B. To perform the analysis, you need only click the 1 Way Table button and then click OK. (In a moment, you will learn what a 2 Way Table does.) After choosing the Currency format for the data Quattro Pro generates, you see the results shown in Figure 11-18.

This output consists of numbers, not formulas, and so it is not interactive. Changing the terms of the loan on the spreadsheet would not cause any change in the cells of the data table. You must repeat the What-If command to take into account changes in the model. Just change

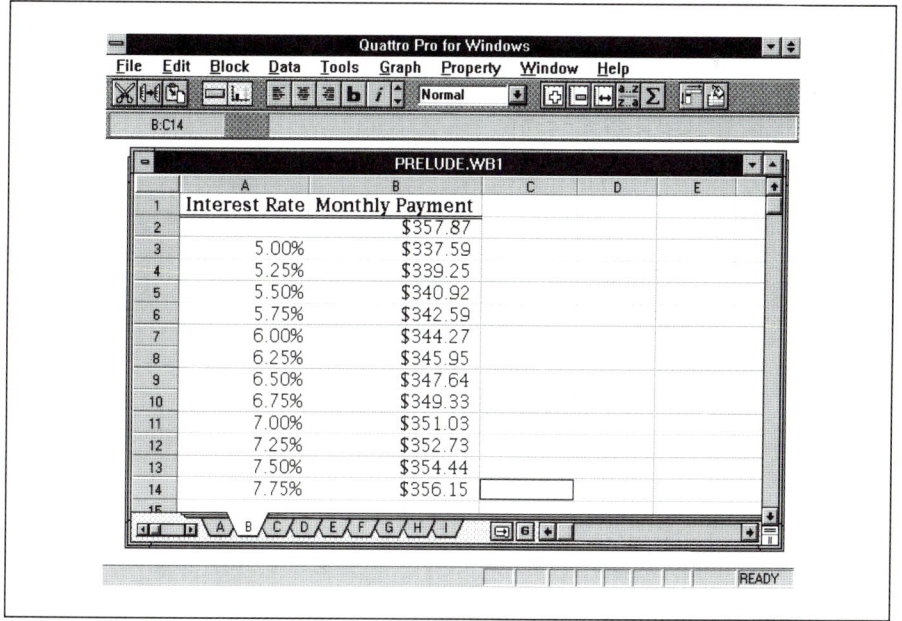

FIGURE 11-18 One-way what-if table generated by Data | What-If command

	A	B
1	Interest Rate	Monthly Payment
2		$357.87
3	5.00%	$337.59
4	5.25%	$339.25
5	5.50%	$340.92
6	5.75%	$342.59
7	6.00%	$344.27
8	6.25%	$345.95
9	6.50%	$347.64
10	6.75%	$349.33
11	7.00%	$351.03
12	7.25%	$352.73
13	7.50%	$354.44
14	7.75%	$356.15

the figures on page A of the notebook, turn to page B, and press the Table (F8) key to repeat the last table command.

Two-Way What-If Tables

The next step is a two-way data table, shown in Figure 11-19. This table shows the payments on the loan based on a variety of interest rates and five different payment terms. The table varies both the interest in A:B11 and the term in A:B12. The operation is performed by typing in cell B:A2 a reference to the formula to be used (here, you use the PMT formula in A:B13). Then you fill the interest rates down the side of the worksheet, as was done to create the one-way table, and, finally, you type the periods (in months) across the top. The What-If command is then selected from the Data menu. The data table is defined as the block formed by the column of variables and the row of variables, A2 through F14, in this case. You use A:B11 as input cell 1, and A:B12 as input cell 2.

FIGURE 11-19 Two-way what-if data table

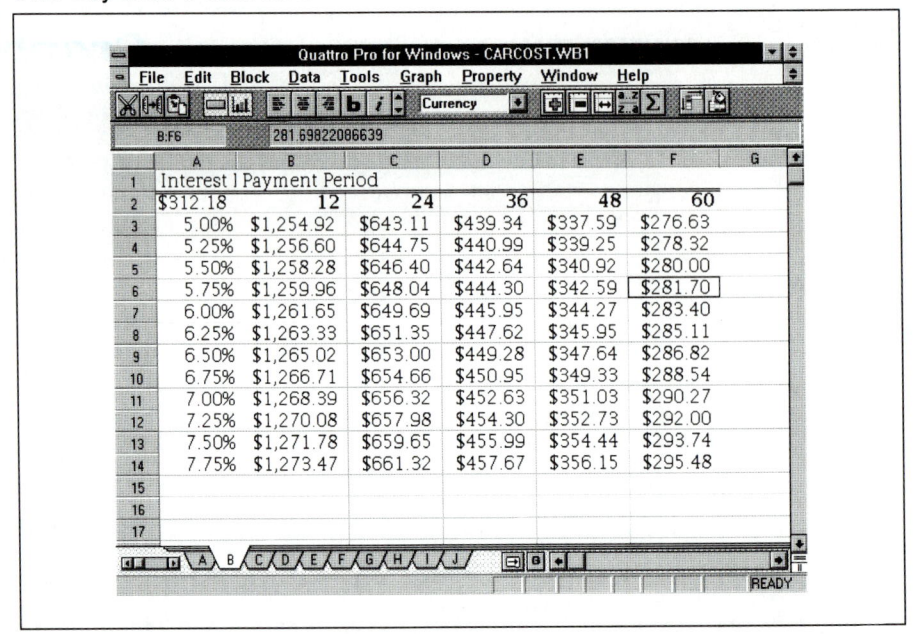

	A	B	C	D	E	F
1	Interest	Payment Period				
2	$312.18	12	24	36	48	60
3	5.00%	$1,254.92	$643.11	$439.34	$337.59	$276.63
4	5.25%	$1,256.60	$644.75	$440.99	$339.25	$278.32
5	5.50%	$1,258.28	$646.40	$442.64	$340.92	$280.00
6	5.75%	$1,259.96	$648.04	$444.30	$342.59	$281.70
7	6.00%	$1,261.65	$649.69	$445.95	$344.27	$283.40
8	6.25%	$1,263.33	$651.35	$447.62	$345.95	$285.11
9	6.50%	$1,265.02	$653.00	$449.28	$347.64	$286.82
10	6.75%	$1,266.71	$654.66	$450.95	$349.33	$288.54
11	7.00%	$1,268.39	$656.32	$452.63	$351.03	$290.27
12	7.25%	$1,270.08	$657.98	$454.30	$352.73	$292.00
13	7.50%	$1,271.78	$659.65	$455.99	$354.44	$293.74
14	7.75%	$1,273.47	$661.32	$457.67	$356.15	$295.48

As you can see from Figure 11-19, which shows the data for a different car, Quattro Pro can do a lot of what-if calculating for you! Cell B3, for example, calculates the PMT formula assuming an interest rate of 5% and a payment period of 12 months, while cell C3 calculates the formula with a rate of 5% and a term of 24 months. Manually, you would have to perform 50 what-if calculations to produce the same result—and you'd have nothing to show for your trouble unless you printed all 50 versions of the worksheet.

Creating XY Graphs

Because this chapter has discussed some advanced features of Quattro Pro for Windows for analyzing and determining relationships between collections of data, this is an appropriate place to address the subject of XY graphs, which were not extensively covered in the two previous chapters. Used to plot the relationship between data points that have two coordinates, XY graphing can be used for such tasks as analyzing measurements and displaying regression lines.

Plotting Data Series for an XY Graph

Figure 11-20 shows a worksheet of size and weight measurements for a number of packages. The weight is in kilos, and the size is the sum of the length plus the circumference of the package in centimeters. These packages were picked at random from the airport loading dock in an effort to learn more about the relationship between package size and weight. You decide to graph the size of these packages relative to their weight.

To create an XY graph, you follow a somewhat different procedure than that used to create other graphs. Begin by selecting the Y data range, which is the block C2..C14 in the current example. Then choose the New command from the Graph menu. You see the Graph New dialog box, as shown in Figure 11-21.

In the X-Axis box, type or point to the X-axis range (B2..B14) and choose OK. You'll see a bar graph. Choose Type from the Graph menu,

528   Quattro Pro for Windows Inside & Out

FIGURE 11-20   Data on package sizes and weights for an XY graph

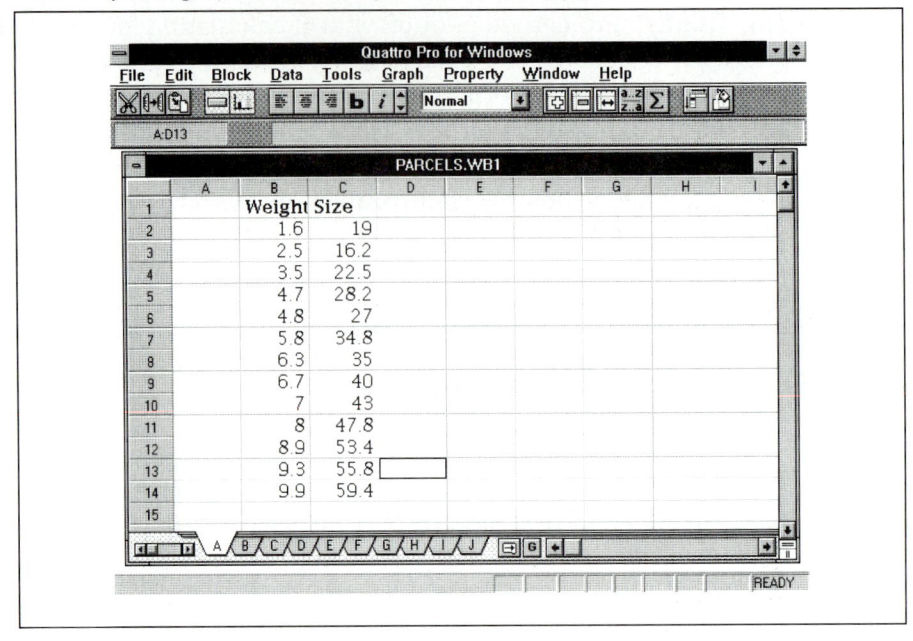

and then from the <u>2</u>-D submenu, choose the XY graph option, as shown in Figure 11-22.

These settings produce the graph shown in Figure 11-23.

FIGURE 11-21   Graph New dialog box

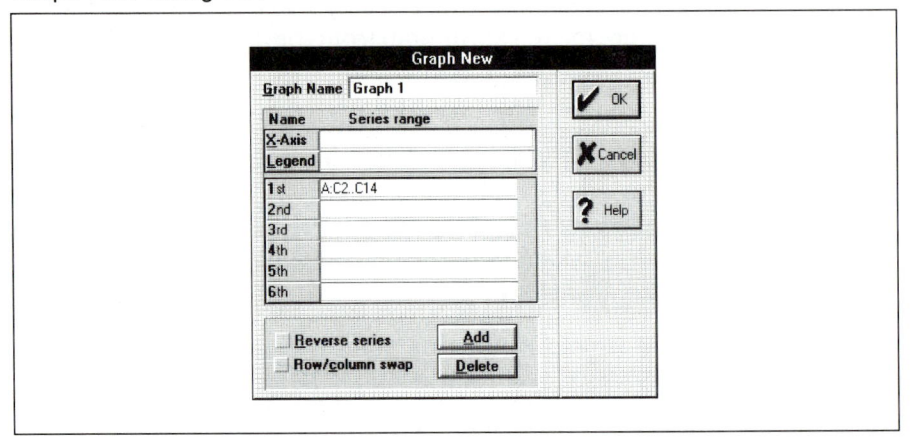

Chapter 11: Advanced Data Analysis 529

FIGURE 11-22 Graph Types dialog box

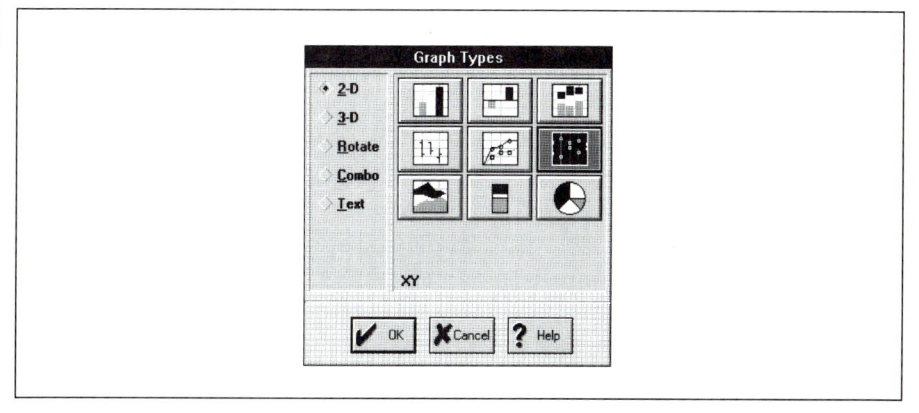

Each measurement is displayed as a point on the graph, a square box in this case. Note that the XY graph sorts the data on the X axis into order of magnitude. You can see a fairly strong relationship between the size and weight. As size increases, so does weight. If you were told a package weighed 6.5 kilos, you could guess that the size is probably 35 centimeters.

FIGURE 11-23 XY graph of package size versus weight

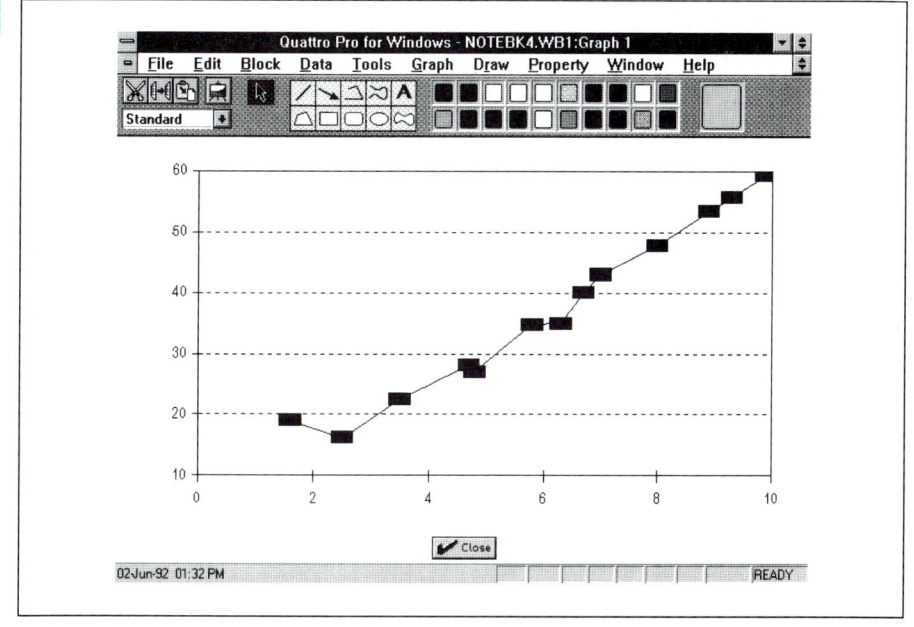

Goal Seeking with Solve For

In most mathematical problems, you start with the values, and try to get the answer—for example, if you're buying a house, and you want to know what the monthly payment will be if you finance $75,000 at 7.8 percent. Sometimes, though, you turn the usual problem on its head and start with the answer! Here's an example. Suppose you've decided you can afford to pay $1400 per month on a mortgage. You have saved $25,000 as a down payment on a house. The question is, how much can you afford to finance? In financial analysis, this question is called *goal seeking* because you start with the goal (you want to pay no more than $1400 per month).

To solve a problem when you know the result you want, you use the Solve For command on the Data menu. You begin by developing a spreadsheet that solves a typical problem, such as the mortgage analysis worksheet shown in Figure 11-24. This worksheet uses the PMT function.

To solve the payment formula for a given payment, choose Solve For from the Tools menu. You see the Solve For dialog box. You must provide

FIGURE 11-24 A mortgage analysis worksheet

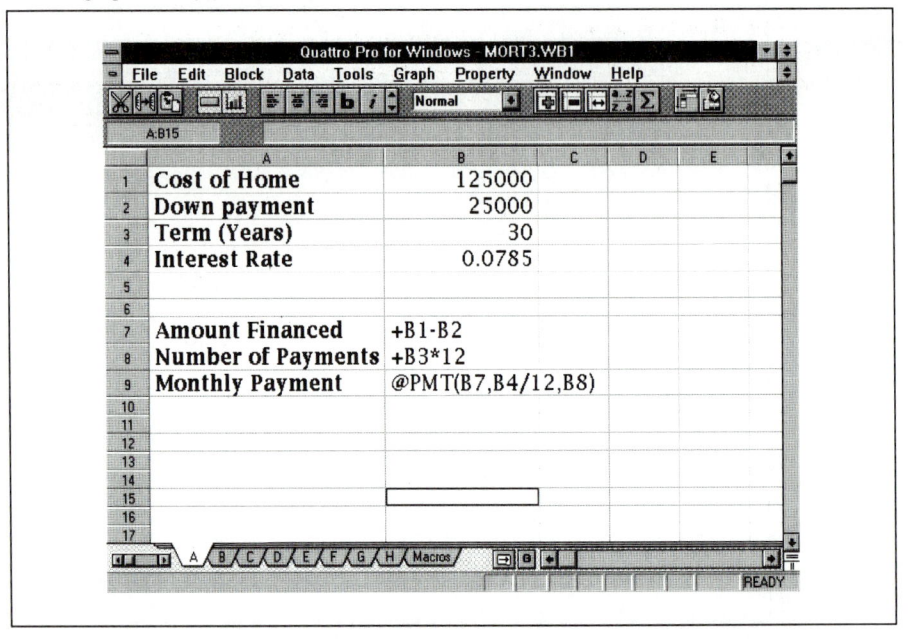

	A	B
1	Cost of Home	125000
2	Down payment	25000
3	Term (Years)	30
4	Interest Rate	0.0785
5		
6		
7	Amount Financed	+B1-B2
8	Number of Payments	+B3*12
9	Monthly Payment	@PMT(B7,B4/12,B8)

Chapter 11: Advanced Data Analysis 531

three pieces of information: Formula Cell, Target Value, and Variable Cell. Figure 11-25 shows how to fill in the Solve For dialog box to answer the question, "If I'm willing to pay $1400 per month, what's the most expensive house I can buy?" The formula cell contains the @PMT formula, while the *variable cell*, which contains the amount that Quattro Pro can vary to solve the problem, is cell B1, the cost of the home.

When you choose OK, Quattro Pro quickly finds the answer, as shown in Figure 11-26. If you want to restore the previous value, choose Undo from the Edit menu or press the ALT-F5 shortcut.

The Optimizer

The Solve For command gives you a way to find one unknown variable when you already know the outcome. But what happens when you want to find the solution to two or more variables? In this section, you are introduced to the Optimizer, a sophisticated analysis utility that was formerly available only with specialized financial analysis programs.

FIGURE 11-25 Filling in the Solve For dialog box

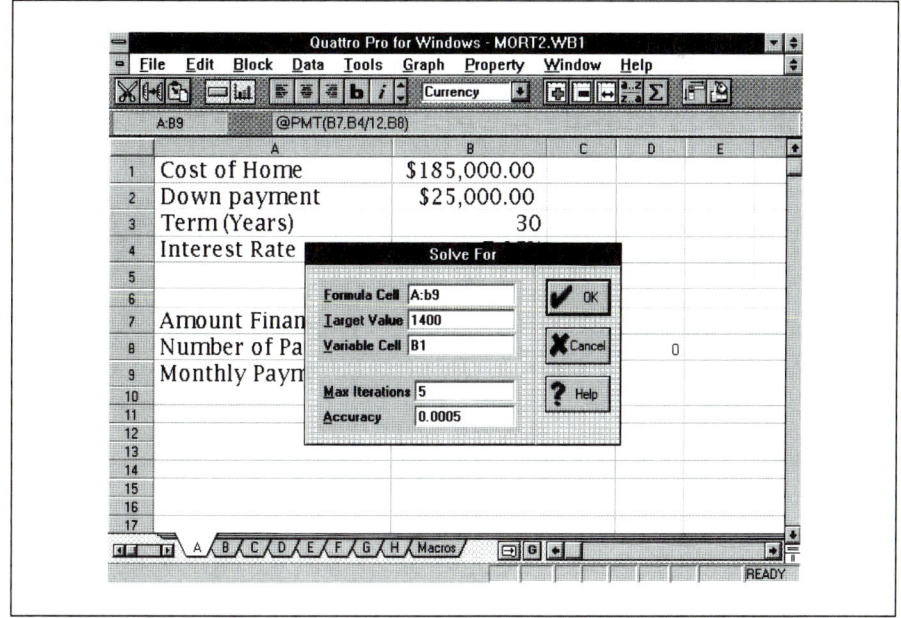

FIGURE 11-26 Solution found by Solve For

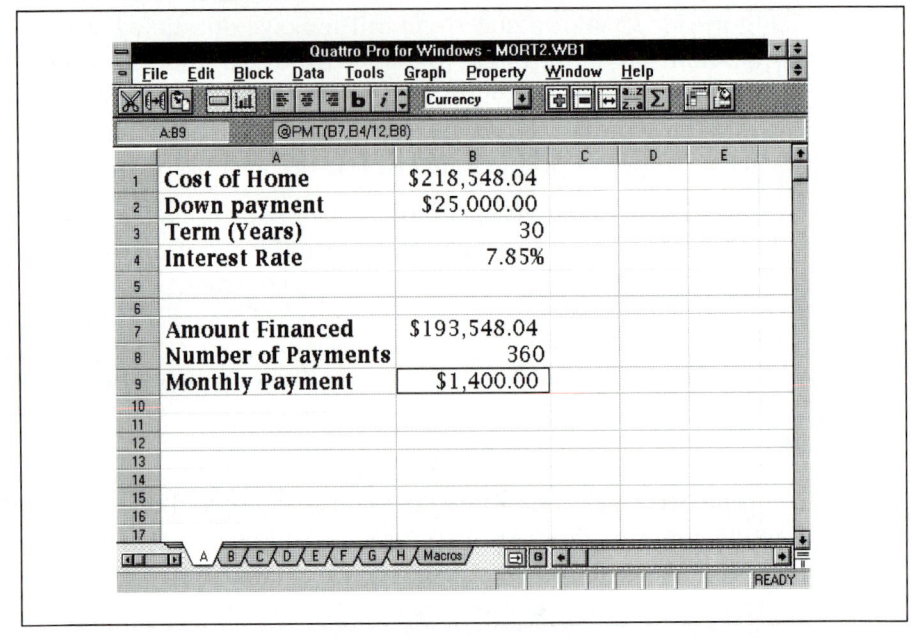

![Quattro Pro for Windows - MORT2.WB1 spreadsheet showing cell A:B9 with formula @PMT(B7,B4/12,B8). Cost of Home $218,548.04, Down payment $25,000.00, Term (Years) 30, Interest Rate 7.85%, Amount Financed $193,548.04, Number of Payments 360, Monthly Payment $1,400.00]

Among other things, the Optimizer can perform *multiple-variable goal seeking*—that is, it can change two or more variables as it tries to find a solution that gives you the result you want. This book only touches on Optimizer's capabilities, which—if fully exploited—put you in league with analytically oriented M.B.A.s

To illustrate a simple application of the Optimizer, suppose you run a mail order business that specializes in garden herbs and herb-related merchandise, including books, gardening tools, gathering baskets, and drying racks. On the basis of past experience, you know that every dollar you spend on advertising will bring in approximately $8.75, on average, in orders. However, your business is also subject to profound seasonal variations. You have decided that you would like to see $125,000 in orders next year, and you're wondering what you should spend on advertising.

The spreadsheet in Figure 11-27 shows your initial analysis. In Row 3, you see the seasonality adjustments, which range all the way from the

Chapter 11: Advanced Data Analysis   **533**

FIGURE 11-27   Initial analysis

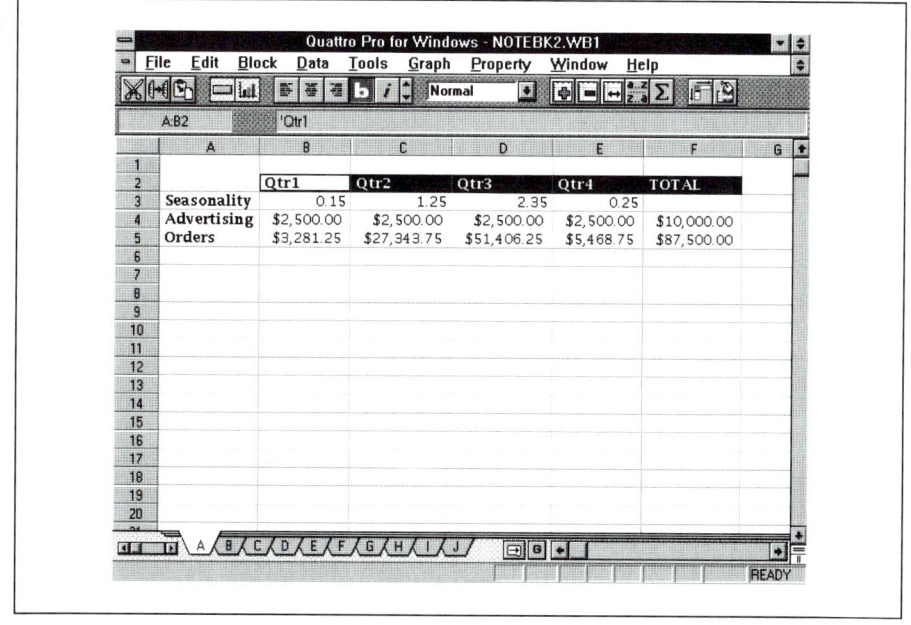

[Quattro Pro for Windows spreadsheet screenshot showing:]

	A	B	C	D	E	F
2		Qtr1	Qtr2	Qtr3	Qtr4	TOTAL
3	Seasonality	0.15	1.25	2.35	0.25	
4	Advertising	$2,500.00	$2,500.00	$2,500.00	$2,500.00	$10,000.00
5	Orders	$3,281.25	$27,343.75	$51,406.25	$5,468.75	$87,500.00

dismal 0.15 of winter to the heady 2.35 of summer. In Row 5, you see order predictions, based on the assumption that every dollar spent on advertising brings in $8.75 in orders. The following formulas are necessary to create this spreadsheet:

B5: **(+B4*8.75)*B3**

Copy the formula for B5 to C5 and E5.

F5: **@SUM(B5..E5)**

    To begin your analysis, you distribute a proposed advertising budget of $10,000 over each of the four cells in the range B4..E4. You want to find out how much you should spend on advertising to get $125,000 in orders.

    You can't solve this problem with Solve For, since Solve For can adjust only one variable. The Optimizer, however, is up to the task, as you'll see in this example. To solve for values in the range B4..E4, you choose Optimizer from the Tools menu, and you see the dialog box shown in Figure 11-28.

In the Solution Cell box, type or point to the cell that is to contain the target value—in this case, F5—and click Target Value so that you can enter **125000** in the text box. In the Variable Cell(s) box, type the range of cells you want the Optimizer to change: **B4..E4**. Choosing the Solve button produces the results shown in Figure 11-29.

In this solution, the Optimizer has tried to spread out the solution over all four cells in the range B4..E4. However, you might be able to spend less on advertising if you advertise more heavily during the peak season, and less during the off season. You can tell the Optimizer to take this fact into account by imposing a *constraint* on the Optimizer's analysis. A constraint tells the Optimizer to look for a solution that maximizes or minimizes a given variable. Figure 11-30 shows the Optimizer dialog box, which tells Quattro Pro to look for a solution that keeps the total advertising budget (cell F4) under $10,000.

You see the results in Figure 11-31.

This chapter has only scratched the surface of this powerful data analysis utility—but you'd need some training in mathematical analysis

FIGURE 11-28 Optimizer dialog box

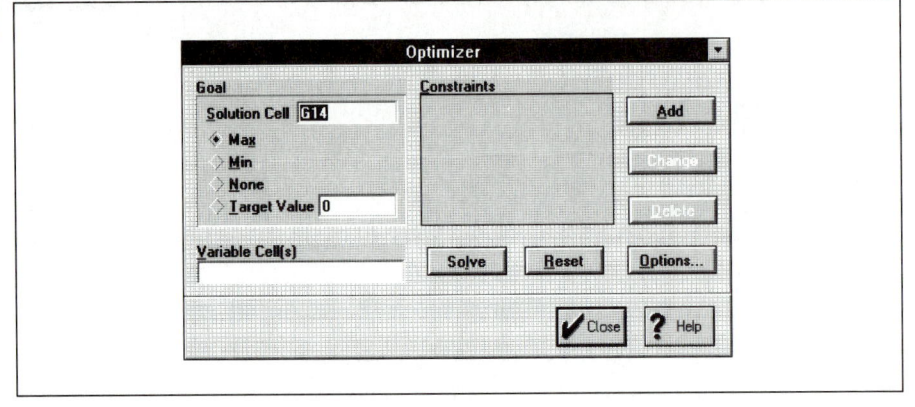

Chapter 11: Advanced Data Analysis 535

FIGURE 11-29 Optimizer solution

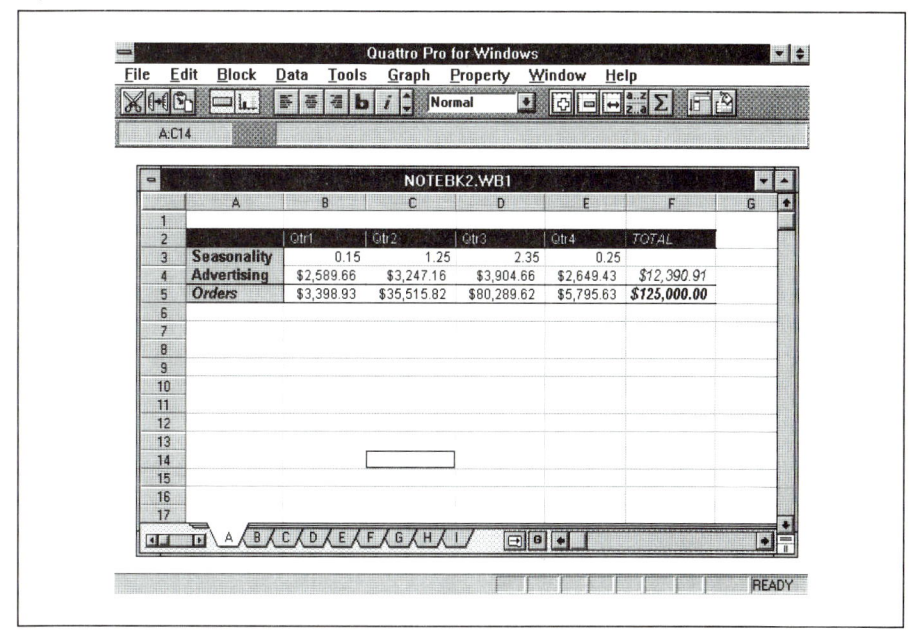

FIGURE 11-30 Optimizer dialog box with constraint shown

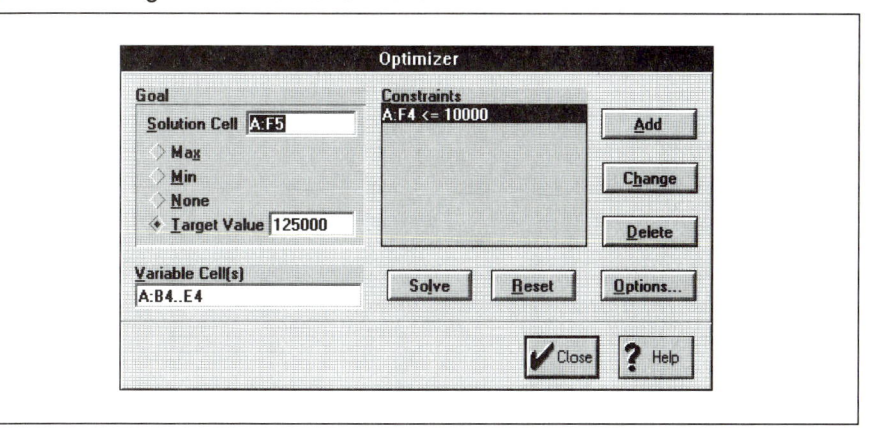

FIGURE 11-31 Optimizer solution with constraints on total advertising expenditure

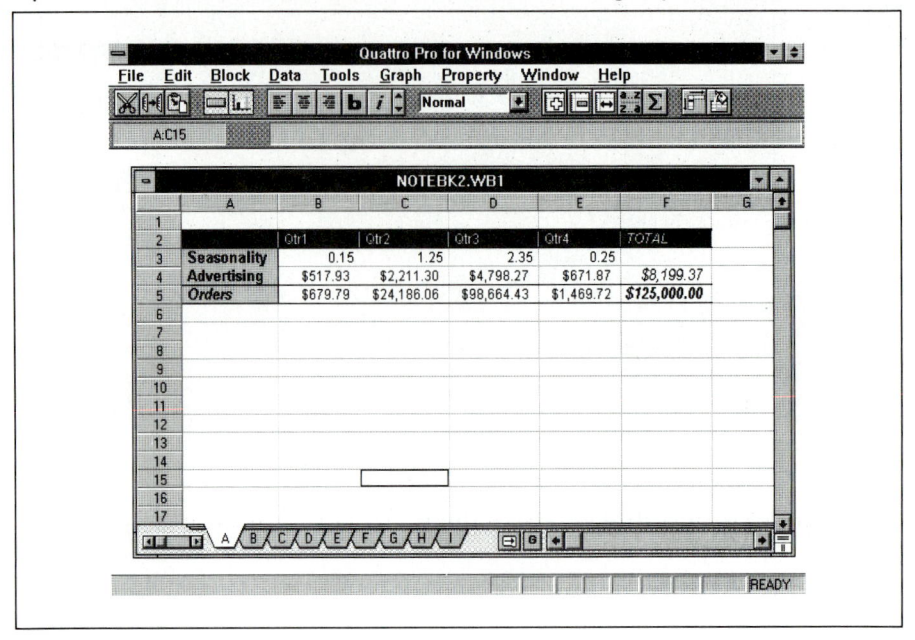

	A	B	C	D	E	F
1						
2		Qtr1	Qtr2	Qtr3	Qtr4	TOTAL
3	Seasonality	0.15	1.25	2.35	0.25	
4	Advertising	$517.93	$2,211.30	$4,798.27	$671.87	$8,199.37
5	Orders	$679.79	$24,186.06	$98,664.43	$1,469.72	*$125,000.00*

to grasp the impressive, advanced functions of the Optimizer. Even without that background, you can use the Optimizer as illustrated in this chapter for goal seeking with more than one variable.

CHAPTER 12

Managing Text

Quattro Pro is an electronic spreadsheet program, so numbers are its forté, but numbers without labels and text have little meaning. For this reason, Quattro Pro is designed to handle text—a fact you already appreciate, given that you've entered plenty of labels. However, Quattro Pro can do much more with text. In this chapter, you learn how to use Quattro Pro as text editor, including entering and formatting blocks of text. In addition, you learn how to parse incoming text data, such as stock quotes downloaded from an information service, so that the data is neatly divided among the spreadsheet's cells. You also learn how to use text functions in Quattro Pro formulas.

Entering and Reformatting Blocks of Text

Good spreadsheet design requires ample documentation of your spreadsheet. To document means to provide the user with ample instruction on the use of the spreadsheet, as well as the spreadsheet's limitations. And just who is the user? Is it you, or someone else in your office—someone who might not understand the assumptions built into your model? Even if you're the only user of the spreadsheet, bear in mind that you yourself may forget your own assumptions six months from now.

In Figure 12-1, you see a well-documented spreadsheet. The spreadsheet tells the user what to do. It clearly separates data entry from calculation areas. As you document a spreadsheet in this way, you can benefit from the text-entry tips and tricks that this chapter discusses. You'll learn how to enter blocks of text (and reformat them if they're too lengthy), link text generated by a word processing program with a Quattro Pro spreadsheet, parse incoming textual data, and use Quattro Pro's many text processing functions.

Entering a few words of text, like the first instruction in Figure 12-1, is simply a matter of typing a long label. You type the text and then press ENTER (or any of the other keys that complete a cell entry).

When you type a longer label, you must reformat the block so that it will fit within the space you allocate for it. In Figure 12-2, you see a long entry (instruction 4) that has just been placed into D6. As you can see, the label does not fit.

FIGURE 12-1 Spreadsheet with ample documentation

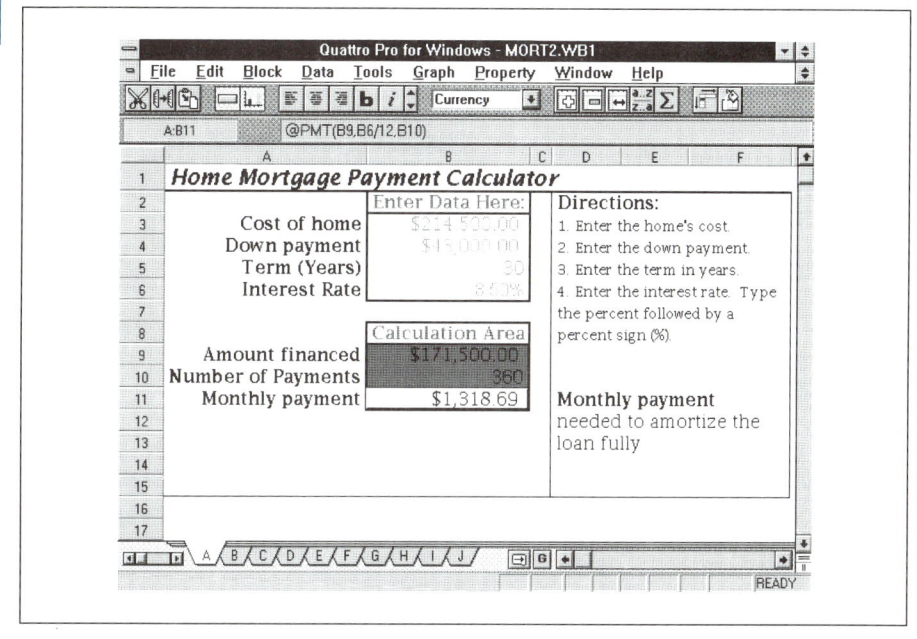

FIGURE 12-2 Long label before reformatting

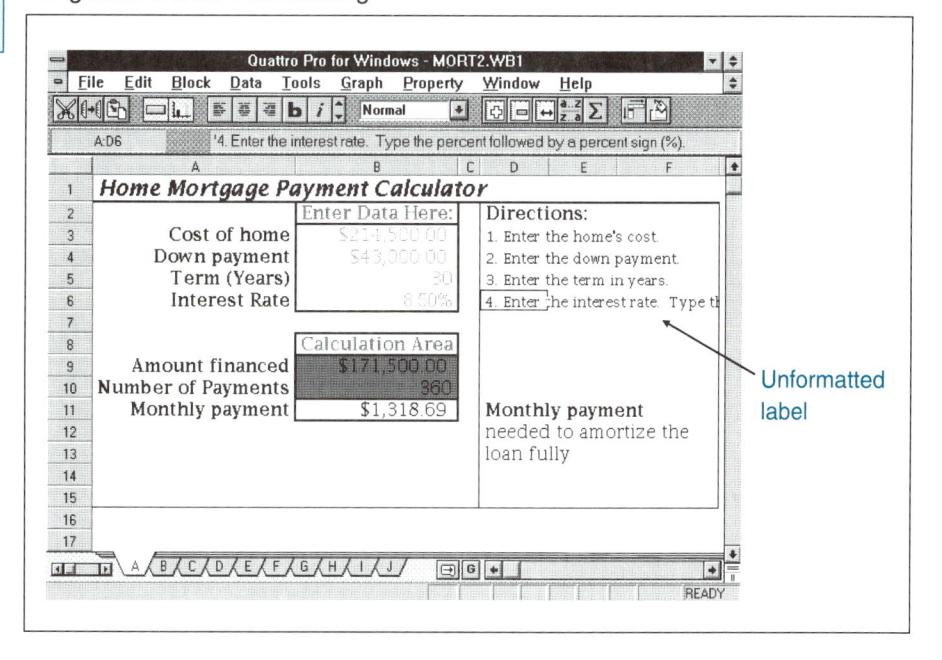

To solve this problem, select the block where you want the text to fit. (You must select enough space to accommodate all the text.) Then choose <u>R</u>eformat from the <u>B</u>lock menu. You see the Block Reformat dialog box, shown here:

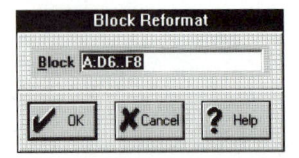

The dialog box shows the block you selected before choosing the command. If you wish to change the block, type a new block in the <u>B</u>lock text box. Choose OK to reformat the block. Figure 12-3 shows the result of reformatting this long entry.

To edit a reformatted block effectively, you will find it helpful to understand how Quattro Pro reformats a block. When you reformat a block, the program divides the text into equal parts, placing the parts in

FIGURE 12-3 Reformatted label

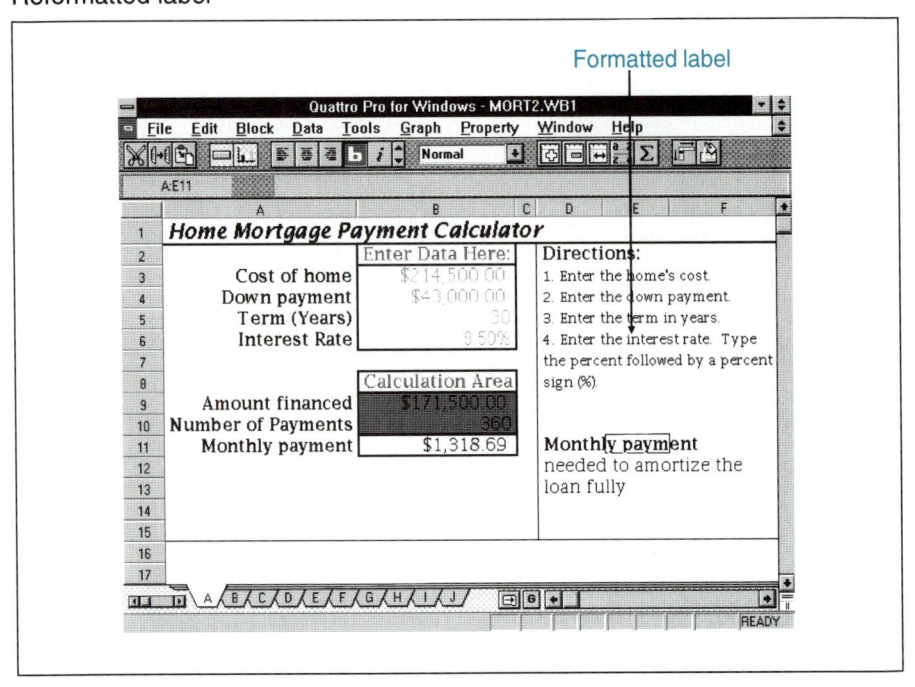

the first cell of each highlighted row in the block. The following shows how Quattro Pro allocates this entry:

D6:	4. Enter the interest rate. Type
D7:	the percent followed by a percent
D8:	sign (%).

If you need to edit the text that you have reformatted into shorter labels, highlight the cell containing the text to be edited and edit the entry using the usual techniques. However, if you make any line in the middle of a paragraph much shorter or longer than it was before editing, you must reformat the block.

Exchanging Data with Word Processing Programs

Despite the need to document worksheets, Quattro Pro for Windows is no word processing program. You might wish to prepare documentation text in a word processing program and then import it into Quattro Pro. Thanks to Windows, this task is so easy that it's worth doing. In the older DOS environment, exchanging data meant writing a word processing program's text document to an intermediary *ASCII file*, an unformatted text file containing nothing but standard characters, which DOS spreadsheet programs could read. With Windows, you have three options for data exchange that are much easier than the DOS techniques:

- **Copying with the Clipboard** The Windows Clipboard provides a temporary storage area for data exchange. You select the data you want to copy, and choose Copy from the Edit menu. Windows copies the data to the Clipboard. Then you switch to the destination document, place the cursor where you want the data to appear, and choose Edit | Paste.

- **Copying with hot links** Copy the data just as you would using the Clipboard technique. However, you paste the data into the destination document using a command named Paste Link (instead of the normal Paste). The pasted document is *linked* to the original—if you make changes to the source document, Windows automatically updates the copy that you have placed in the destination document. To copy with hot links, both applications must support Windows' dynamic data exchange (DDE) architecture. Many applications do.

- **Embedding objects** In this data exchange technique, you insert into your document an object—a unit of text or graphics—created by a *server application*, an application that is capable of creating objects for this purpose. The object contains all the information that the server application needs in order to edit the object. In this way, you can build a compound document consisting of data created by two or more applications. To edit an object, you just double-click it, and Windows starts the server application. Object embedding requires that applications support Windows' OLE (object linking and embedding) architecture. At present, only a fraction of Windows applications fully support OLE. Quattro Pro is capable of functioning as a *client application* for OLE purposes, which means that you can embed other applications' objects into Quattro Pro documents. However, Quattro Pro cannot function as a server application—you cannot embed Quattro Pro objects into documents created by other applications.

With Quattro Pro, you can use all three techniques: copying via the Clipboard, creating hot links, and embedding objects. To copy Quattro Pro data to other applications, you can use Clipboard copying and hot links. To copy other applications' data into your Quattro Pro document, you can use Clipboard copying, hot links, and embedding. The following sections detail these techniques, with emphasis on importing text into your Quattro Pro notebooks.

Data Exchange with the Clipboard

Windows' Clipboard provides a temporary storage area for data exchange, both within and between applications. You cut or copy data to the Clipboard, switch documents, and then paste the Clipboard contents at the cursor's location. You can use this technique to import text into your Quattro Pro notebook.

Chapter 12: Managing Text 543

To copy text from a word processing program into a Quattro Pro notebook, begin by creating the text in the word processing program (Microsoft Word for Windows is shown here). Select the text, as shown in Figure 12-4, and choose Copy from the application's Edit menu. Windows copies the text to the Clipboard. Switch to Quattro Pro, and select the cell where you want the text to appear. Then choose Paste from the Edit menu, use the SHIFT-INS shortcut, or click the Paste button on the SpeedBar. Quattro Pro pastes the text into the document, as shown in Figure 12-5. When you paste text from the Clipboard, Quattro Pro automatically reformats the text to preserve the line lengths from the source document.

Note When you import text into Quattro Pro via the Clipboard, you lose the formatting and font choices you made in the source document. Quattro Pro imports the text as unformatted text, using the default font. To format the text, use the Active Block properties menu.

FIGURE 12-4 Copying the text in the word processing document (in Microsoft Word for Windows)

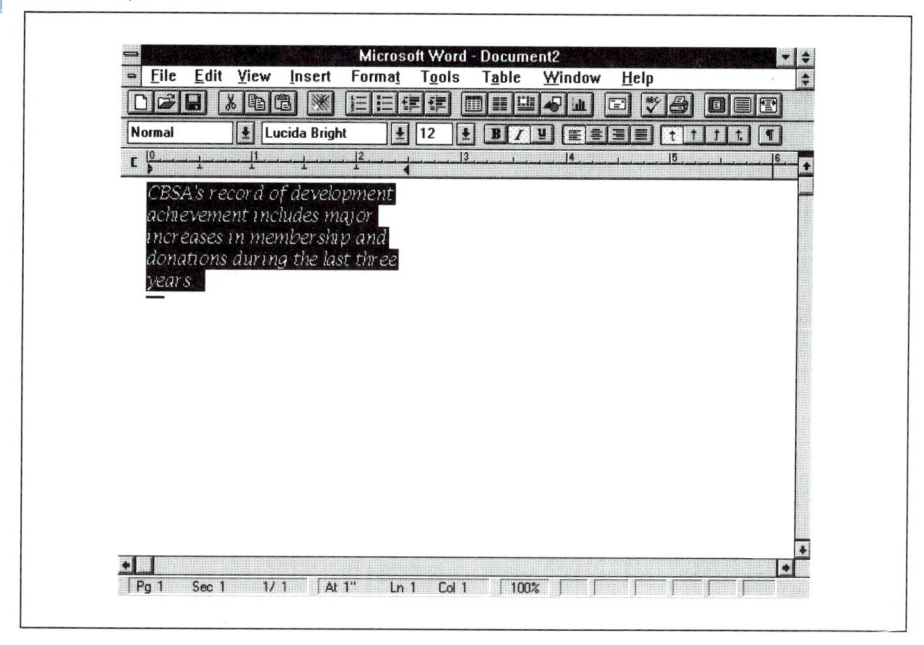

FIGURE 12-5 Text pasted into a Quattro Pro notebook

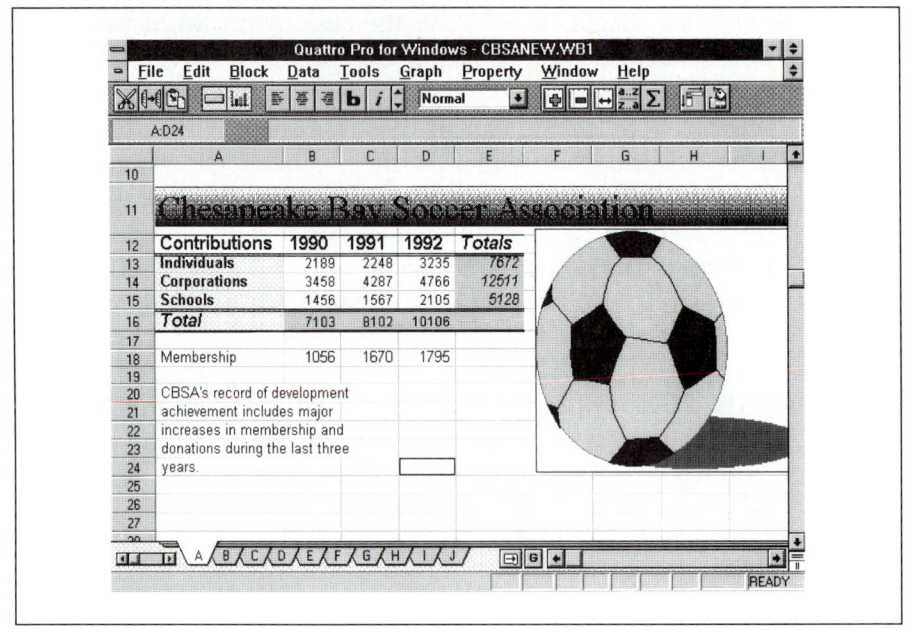

Importing Text with Hot Links

Copying via the Clipboard is easy, but it has one major drawback: If you make changes to the source document (the word processor), you must recopy the data (or manually change it in Quattro Pro) if you want it changed in the Quattro Pro document. If you don't, the copy is inaccurate. In some cases, this drawback of Clipboard copying can cause embarrassing errors to creep into your work. Consider, for example, a Quattro Pro report in which you must include a standard organizational description, such as the one beginning at A20 in Figure 12-6. This description is official and must be accurate. To make sure it's accurate, you create the text in a word processing document and save it there. Each time you use it, you copy the text to the Quattro Pro notebooks you create.

After copying this text a number of times, your boss takes a look at one of the reports and exclaims, "Hey, you can't say donations *are* tax deductible. You're supposed to say they *may be* tax deductible. We can get in a lot of trouble if we say the wrong thing here!" Now you must find and change all the copies to make sure they have the correct wording.

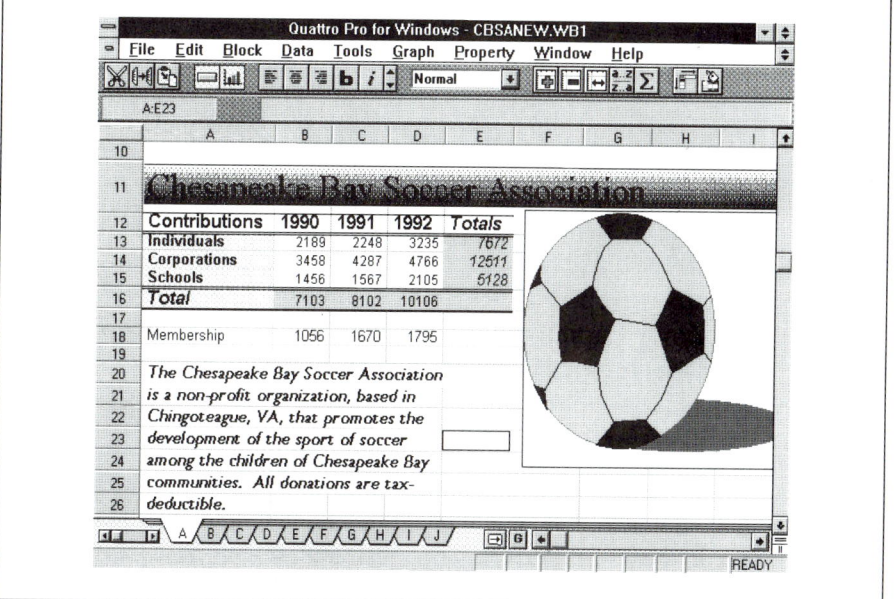

FIGURE 12-6 Standard organizational description copied into a Quattro Pro spreadsheet

Had you copied the text using hot links, also called dynamic links, it would not be necessary to track down and change every copy you made of this text, because Windows would do the updating automatically. In a hot link, every copy you make of data from a source document is automatically updated when you make changes to the source document.

Creating a hot link with the source document is almost as easy as copying with the Clipboard. In the source application, make sure the document has been saved to disk. You cannot establish a hot link to a source document that has not been saved. Having made sure the document has been saved, select the text in the source document and choose Copy from its Edit menu. Switch to Quattro Pro, position the cursor where you want the text to appear, and choose Paste Link from the Edit menu.

What happens after you choose Paste Link is a little more complicated than Clipboard copying—happily, the process is not more complicated for you to initiate. In the spreadsheet, Quattro Pro inserts the text as if you copied it at the keyboard or pasted it with the normal Clipboard techniques. In fact, the text is really being generated by an @function—

specifically the DDELINK function—as you can see on the entry line of Figure 12-7. To accomplish the DDE link, you could write this function yourself, but it's much easier to let Quattro Pro write the function for you. The program automatically writes the function when you paste using the Paste Link command.

Once you have established a hot link, any changes you make to the source document are automatically reflected in all the copies you have made. This very impressive Windows feature is best seen in action. Try it by switching to the source document, making a change, and saving the source document. (*Don't forget to save the changes:* the link is to the disk file, not the file in memory.) Switch back to the Quattro Pro notebook into which you have pasted the linked text, and *save this document* (you need to save this as well). You'll see the updated text in your Quattro Pro notebook.

Pasting linked data ensures that the changes you make in the source document will be automatically reflected in the destination document, as you have just seen. This has an additional advantage that greatly facilitates the task of editing the source document. You can initiate the

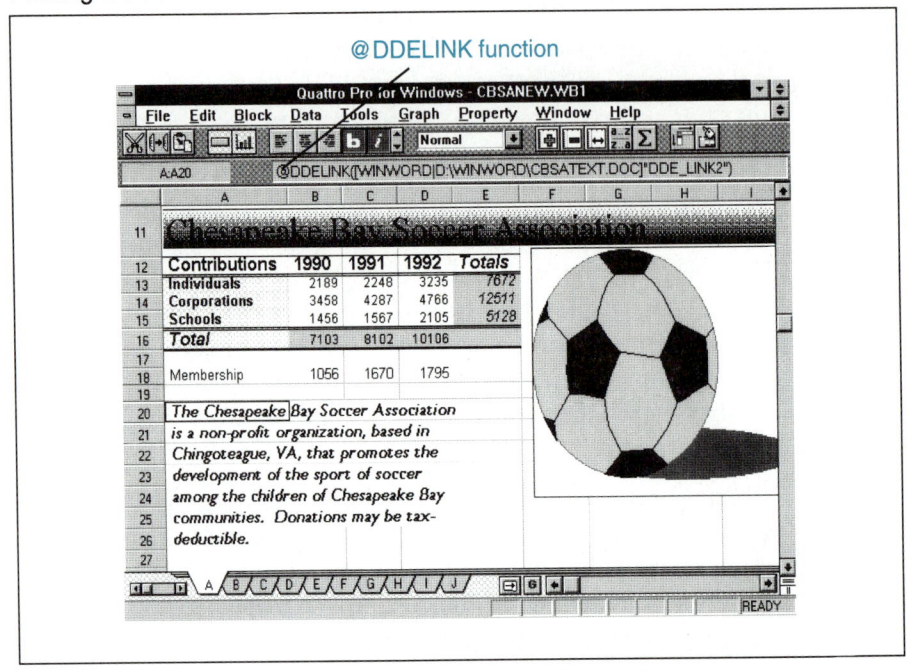

FIGURE 12-7 Pasting linked text into Quattro Pro with DDELINK function

editing process from within Quattro Pro, and Windows will find and display the source document (and application) for you automatically. Suppose you are looking at the linked text you have pasted into the Quattro Pro spreadsheet, and you see a mistake or want to make a change. To do so, you choose Update Links from the Tools menu, and then Open Links from the submenu that appears. You see the Open Links dialog box, as shown here:

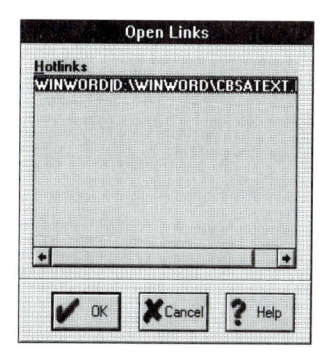

[Open Links dialog box showing Hotlinks: WINWORD|D:\WINWORD\CBSATEXT, with OK, Cancel, Help buttons]

Highlight the link you want to open and choose OK. Windows starts the application that created the source document, if it isn't already open, and displays the source document. Make the change, save it, and switch back to Quattro Pro. To see the change, save your Quattro Pro notebook.

Once you have hot-linked text into your notebook, you will see the following dialog box the next time you open the notebook:

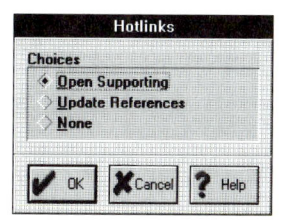

[Hotlinks dialog box with Choices: Open Supporting, Update References, None; OK, Cancel, Help buttons]

Quattro Pro is asking you whether you want to refresh the links before proceeding. If you choose None, Quattro Pro doesn't refresh the links at this time. (You can refresh the links later, if you wish, by choosing Tools | Update Links | Refresh Links.) If you choose Open Supporting, Quattro Pro tells Windows to open the source document and to start the source document's application, if it isn't already running. If you choose Update

References, Quattro Pro locates the source document file and updates the imported text.

Note Do not move the source document to a different subdirectory. If you do, Quattro Pro will be unable to locate the source document when you request updating.

Importing Data by Embedding It

Importing text with linking has many advantages over the Clipboard technique, as you have just learned. The changes you make in the source document are automatically reflected in the copies, and should you need to edit the source document, Windows will find and open this document for you automatically.

If your word processing program is capable of functioning as a server application for OLE purposes, you can import text into Quattro Pro as a *free-floating object*. A free-floating object is very much like a floating chart: You can size it, move it, and delete it without affecting the underlying cells. In Figure 12-8, you see a free-floating object in a Quattro Pro notebook (note the frame and handles). This object was created by Microsoft WordArt, an OLE-capable server application that is packaged with Microsoft Word for Windows.

Note As Figure 12-8 suggests, embedding has a very significant advantage over hot-linking: Embedding preserves formatting. Use embedding if you want to insert into your Quattro Pro notebook an object that preserves its appearance from the application that created it.

Embedding differs from hot-linking in two important ways. First, the embedded object is part of your Quattro Pro notebook. There is no connection to a source document—in fact, there might not be a source document other than the object you have placed in the Quattro Pro file. Embedding isn't a good choice if you need automatic updating from a source document. Second, embedding preserves the object's formatting as you applied it in the object's native application. Embedding is a very good choice, then, if you want to include objects that have attractive formatting.

Chapter 12: Managing Text 549

FIGURE 12-8 Free-floating text object embedded in Quattro Pro notebook

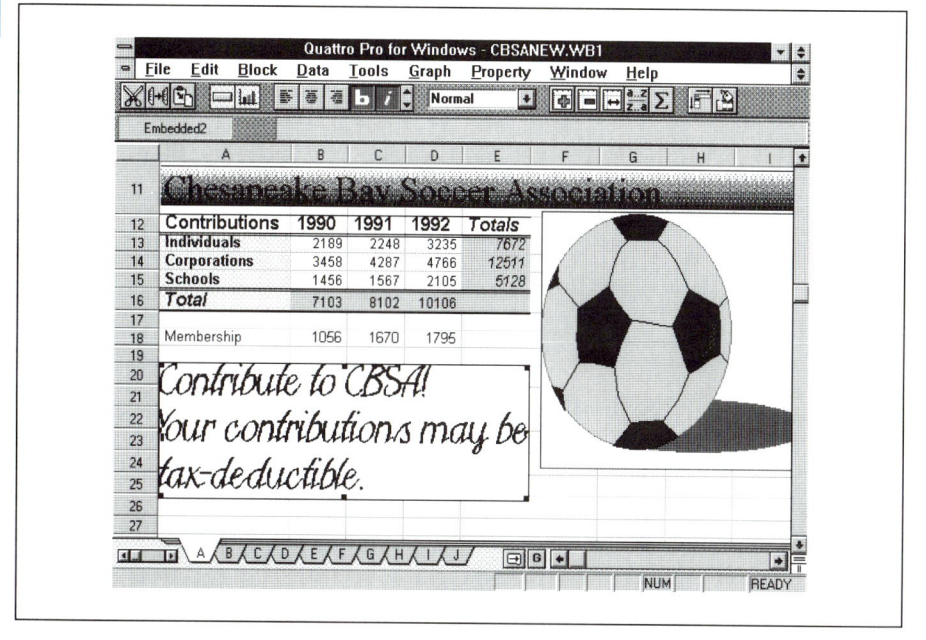

Embedding is an exciting and useful feature. It is very easy to use. In effect, it gives Quattro Pro all the advantages of all the OLE-capable applications on your system. To find out which applications on your system are capable of functioning as OLE servers, just choose Insert Object from the Edit menu. You see the following dialog box:

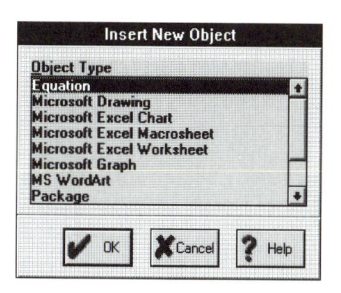

To insert an object at the cell selector's location, just choose one of the server applications on this list. Windows starts the server application and displays a blank document. This document's filename indicates that it is part of the Quattro Pro worksheet you are creating. In Figure 12-9, you

550 Quattro Pro for Windows Inside & Out

FIGURE 12-9 Word document opened by choosing Word Document option in Insert Object dialog box

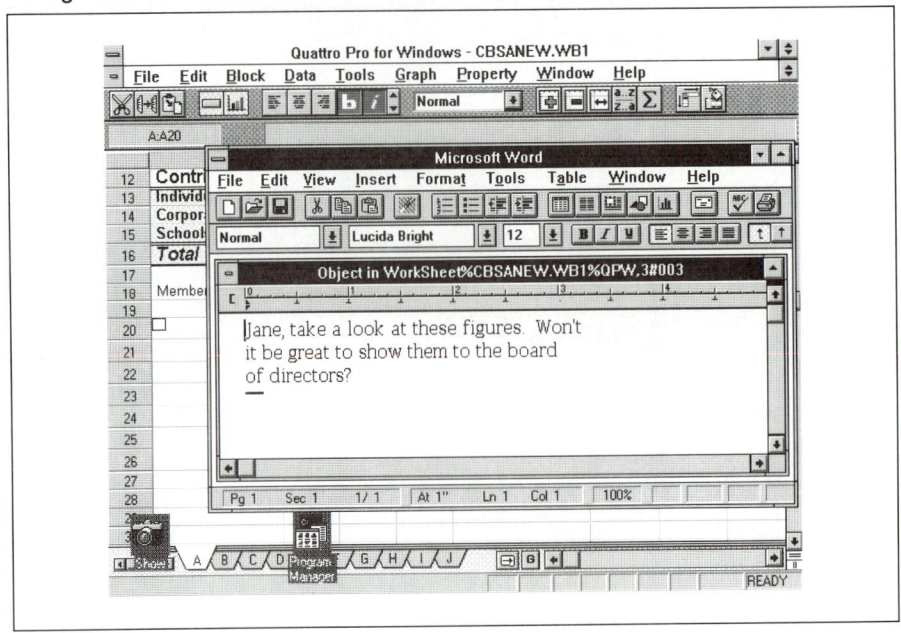

see a Word document that has been opened by choosing Microsoft Word document in Quattro Pro's Insert Object dialog box. Note the filename. This name refers to the file that you are creating with Quattro Pro. After creating the document and choosing Update from the server application's File menu, this application creates the object and Windows inserts the object into your Quattro Pro document.

Once you have inserted an object, you can resize or move it. Click the object to select it so that handles appear around the borders. To resize the object, drag one of the handles. To move an object, drag the object anywhere except by the handles. If you would like to change the properties of the floating object, right-click the object to display the Property | Current Object menu. You can change Border Color, Box Type, and Object Name settings. For OLE objects, you can also change the object settings. To do so, choose Object Settings from the Object properties menu. You see the Object Settings dialog box, as shown here:

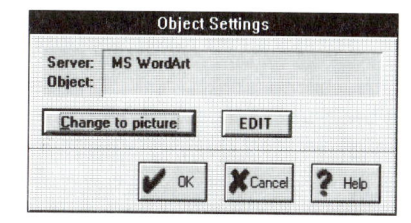

This dialog box allows you to convert the object into a picture, if you wish. If you do so, you will not be able to edit or alter the object, but it will consume less space on disk. You can also click EDIT to view the object in the server application. To edit the object, make the changes you want and then choose Update from the server application's File menu.

Note To edit an OLE object quickly, just double-click the object. Windows starts the server application and displays the object. Make the changes you want, and then choose Update from the server application's File menu.

Parsing Text

The previous sections have discussed the use of text in Quattro Pro notebooks. You've learned how to import text via the Clipboard, including importing with hot links, and you've learned how to embed free-floating objects. Sometimes, however, the text you're importing consists of data that you want to place in a block of cells. Suppose your company has a DOS accounting program for accounts receivable. The accounting program can print an ASCII text file of this data. You would like to create a spreadsheet of accounts receivable data and import it as spreadsheet data so that you can analyze it. To do so, you must allocate all of the data in the text file to corresponding cells in a Quattro Pro spreadsheet. Thanks to Quattro Pro's Data Parse command, you do not need to do this manually.

The Data | Parse command takes a block of text that you've imported into your Quattro Pro spreadsheet and allocates this text to a block of cells. This command doesn't use magic to accomplish this trick; it looks for tabs or spaces in the text data that serve as guidelines for separating the data cell by cell. Sometimes the command makes mistakes. But it's better than typing the data by hand. You can quickly fix the errors, if any appear.

To import data and *parse* it (make sense of the words), choose <u>I</u>mport from the <u>T</u>ools menu. You see the Import File dialog box, which is shown in Figure 12-10.

Note   The Import File dialog box assumes that you're going to import a file with the extension PRN. Many applications assign the PRN extension automatically when you print a file to disk. If the application does not do so automatically, type the extension yourself when you save the text file so that the file will show up in this dialog box's file list. Make sure you save the data in a monospace font such as Courier, and make sure the file contains data that is aligned in neat columns. If you are trying to open a file that doesn't have the PRN extension, you must type *.* in the <u>F</u>ile Name box.

Choose the <u>A</u>SCII Text File option and choose OK to import the text. Quattro Pro places the text into a single-column block of cells, as shown in Figure 12-11.

The information in cell A4 of Figure 12-11 looks a lot like a spreadsheet entry arranged in cells, but if you carefully observe the contents of cell A4, you will see that it is one long label. There is no data in columns B, C, D, and so on.

FIGURE 12-10   Import File dialog box

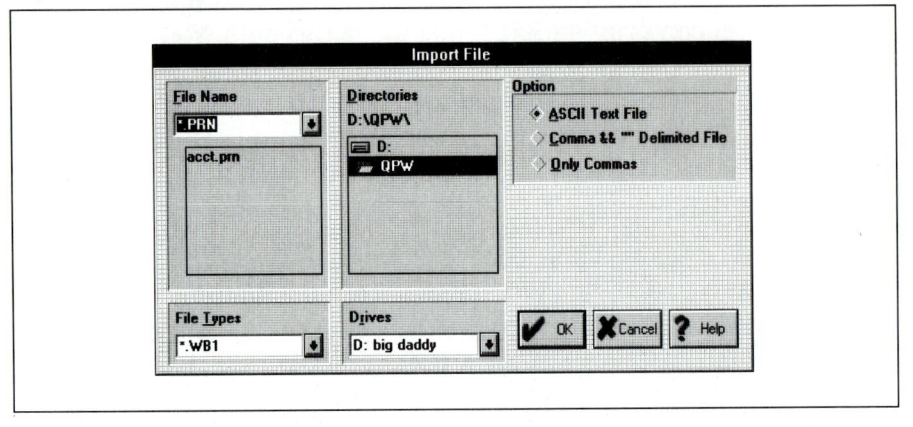

Chapter 12: Managing Text 553

FIGURE 12-11 Imported text in a single-column block of cells

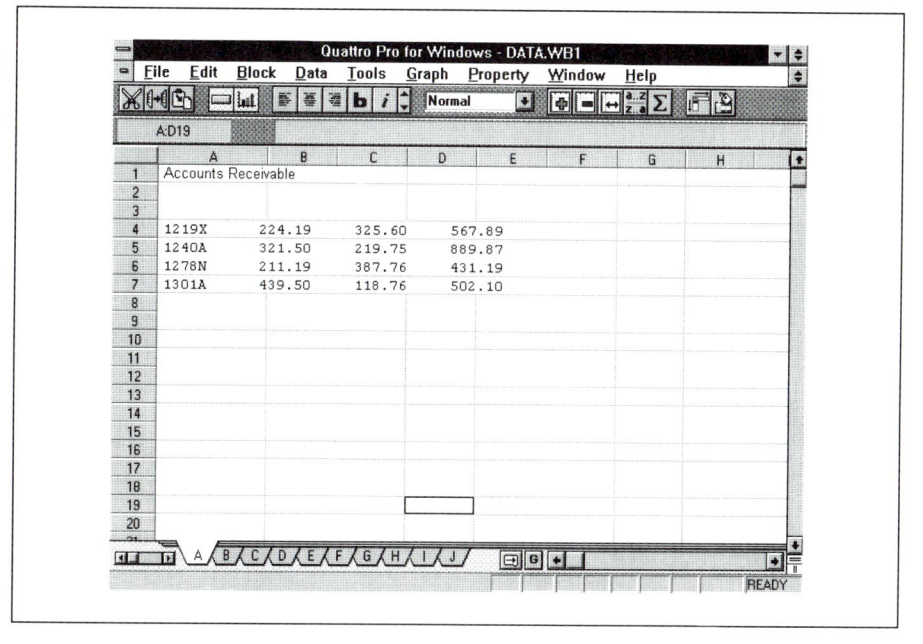

[Screenshot of Quattro Pro for Windows - DATA.WB1 showing cell A:D19 selected. Column A contains:
Row 1: Accounts Receivable
Row 4: 1219X   224.19   325.60   567.89
Row 5: 1240A   321.50   219.75   889.87
Row 6: 1278N   211.19   387.76   431.19
Row 7: 1301A   439.50   118.76   502.10]

To give Quattro Pro a set of rules by which to break up the long labels of data into separate cells of information, place your cell selector on the first cell containing a label to be parsed. You then choose Data | Parse. This will display the Data Parse dialog box, which is shown in the following illustration.

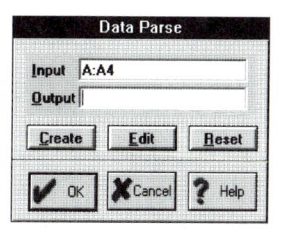

[Data Parse dialog box with Input: A:A4, Output field, and Create, Edit, Reset, OK, Cancel, Help buttons]

Choose Create. The Data Parse dialog box remains on screen, but Quattro Pro inserts a row of symbols above the current row, as shown in Figure 12-12. This line of symbols is called the *parse line*. It tells Quattro Pro how to make sense out of the data beneath the line.

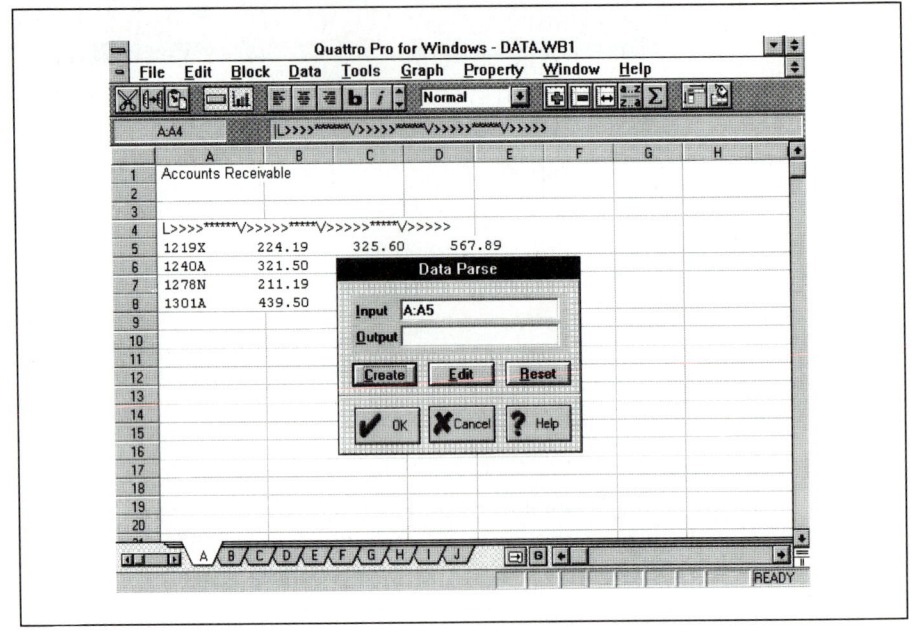

FIGURE 12-12 Line of symbols inserted by Data | Parse command

The parse line contains a mixture of different characters, which can include D, L, V, *, and >. These symbols stand for the type of data that Quattro Pro thinks the cell should contain: L for label, V for value, D for date, and T for time. After the type character comes a number of > signs. Quattro Pro uses the > signs to show how wide it thinks the entry will be. Add the type character to the number of > signs to get the total number of characters. The asterisks in the parse line simply fill in the spaces between entries.

After Quattro Pro enters the parse line, choose Cancel to return to your notebook, and highlight the whole block, making sure to include all the data as well as the parse line, and choose a monospace font such as Courier from the Block properties menu. Doing so will ensure that Quattro Pro parses the lines correctly. Choose Parse from the Data menu again to display the Data Parse dialog box; you'll see the settings you previously used.

To parse the data, you must type the correct input range in the Input box, and an output range in the Output box. The input range should include the format line and the cells containing the data (in this example, A4..A8). The output range must differ from the input range, and should be large enough to accommodate the parsed data (for example, you could use the output range A10..D14). You can use a different notebook page, if you wish, for the output range. In Figure 12-13, you see the parsed data below the imported text.

Quattro Pro does not always parse the data correctly, and it is sometimes necessary to edit the parse line symbols. For example, Quattro Pro may propose to break up a value among two cells if the imported data contains an extraneous space. To edit the parse line, choose Edit in the Data Parse dialog box. In this dialog box, you can edit the symbols until they work correctly.

Once data has been converted from text to cell entries, you can delete the imported text and add further formatting, such as lines, and descriptive labels, such as column headings, as shown in Figure 12-14. Although the text file you import may include headings and even column totals, it is not worth parsing them. Column headings are easy to add after parsing. Column totals will not parse into formulas, so you will have to re-create the necessary formulas anyway.

FIGURE 12-13 Successfully parsed data

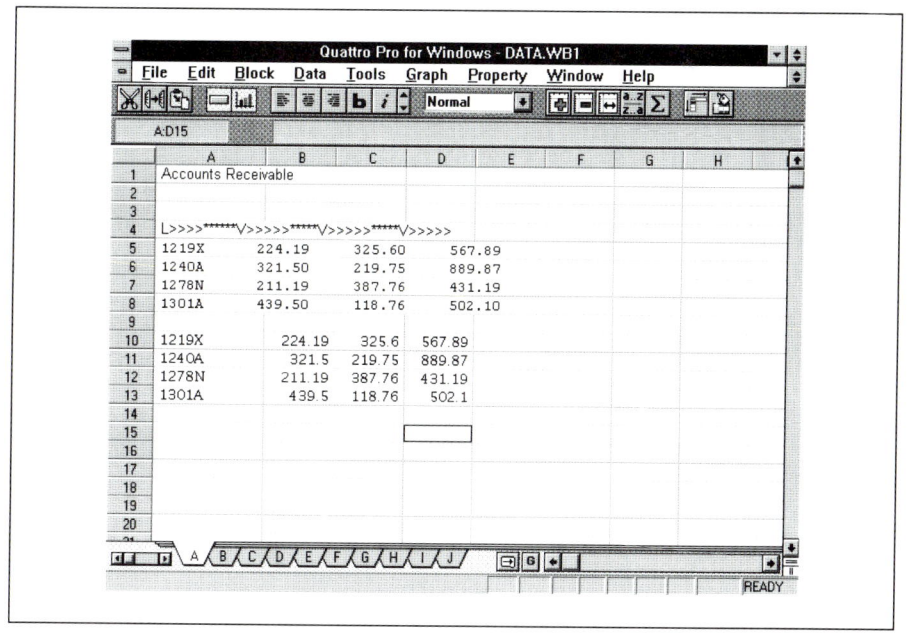

FIGURE 12-14 Parsed data with headings, formatting, and formulas added

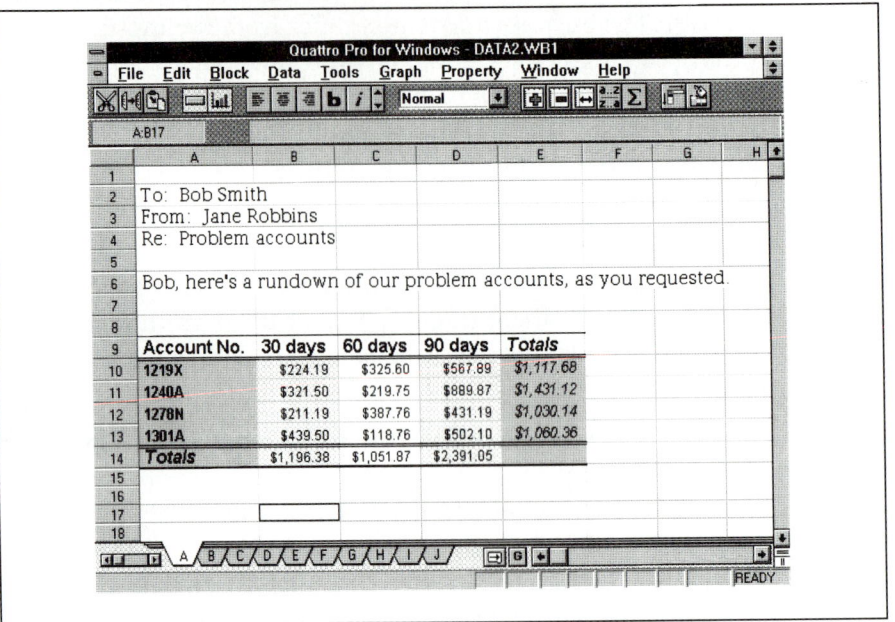

Text in Formulas

Text entered into a cell in Quattro Pro is a label and has no numeric value. However, the program can still use labels in many formulas. This means that you can handle a variety of data in your spreadsheet. Text formulas are particularly useful when you are developing macro commands, as described in Chapter 13. For example, you can write a macro that examines the results of a formula and returns the text "High Risk" if the value exceeds an amount you specify.

Labels in Logical Functions

You can use text in several of the @functions. Quattro Pro can enter a label in a cell by means of an IF formula. The formula

@IF(A1>1000,"Expensive","Cheap")

Chapter 12: Managing Text 557

returns the answer "Expensive" if the contents of A1 are greater than 1000, or "Cheap" if not.

You can use text in the CHOOSE function to supply a label for a number. As with the IF function, text in a CHOOSE statement must be enclosed in quotes. For example, the formula

@CHOOSE (A1,"Bill","Fred","Sue")

returns "Bill" if cell A1 is empty or contains 0. The same formula returns "Fred" if cell A1 contains 1 and "Sue" if A1 contains 2.

Combining Labels with Concatenation

Quattro Pro formulas can reference values in other cells as you have already learned. You can also reference labels in other cells, as you can see in Figure 12-15. The formula +B15 has been placed in cell B23. This formula cross-references the name that is located at the top of the list of contributors, which has been sorted in descending order. There are a

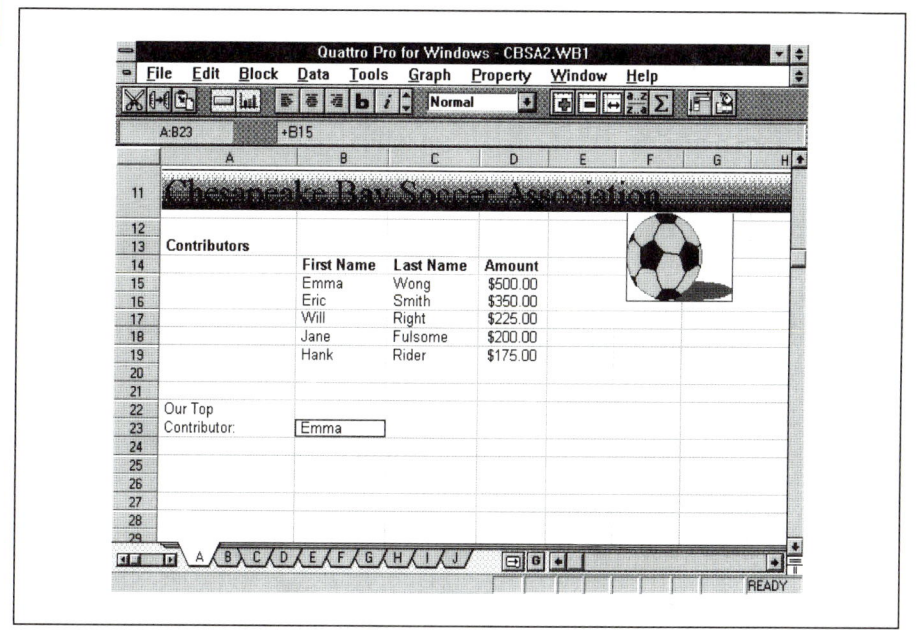

FIGURE 12-15 Text from another cell referenced in formula

number of situations where it is useful to relate label cells in this manner. Using the formula +C15 in cell C23, you could bring the last name (Wong) into the cell next to B23.

If you are preparing an information report from a spreadsheet, you may want to connect the two names with just one space between them, as in Emma Wong. You might be tempted to use the formula +B15+C15 to do this, but that formula results in 0 because Quattro Pro thinks you are trying to add two labels together, and labels have a value of 0. However, you can combine labels with the & sign. The formula +B15&C15 produces EmmaWong.

The & sign adds labels together. This process is called *concatenation*. However, +B15&C15 brings the two parts of the name together without a space between them. You can add a space and other text, such as words and punctuation, to a concatenated formula by enclosing the space (or whatever else you want to include directly) in quotes. You must add the text in quotes to the formula with an & sign. Thus,

+B15&" "&C15

produces the desired result, shown in Figure 12-16.

The & sign is not acceptable as the first character in a formula, but you can use it between cell references and strings of text in a formula. The previous formula is simply three pieces of information: a cell reference, B15; text placed in quotes, in this case, a space " "; and another cell reference, C15. The formula begins with a + sign to let Quattro Pro know this is a formula. The & sign simply works as an addition sign for text data.

String Functions

A specialized means of working with labels in formulas in Quattro Pro is through the use of @functions specifically designed for manipulating text. These functions are called the *string functions*, because a string in Quattro Pro is a series of characters that results in a label and not a value. String functions are valuable when you are working with data imported from other programs in the form of text files. They can also be used effectively with some advanced macro commands.

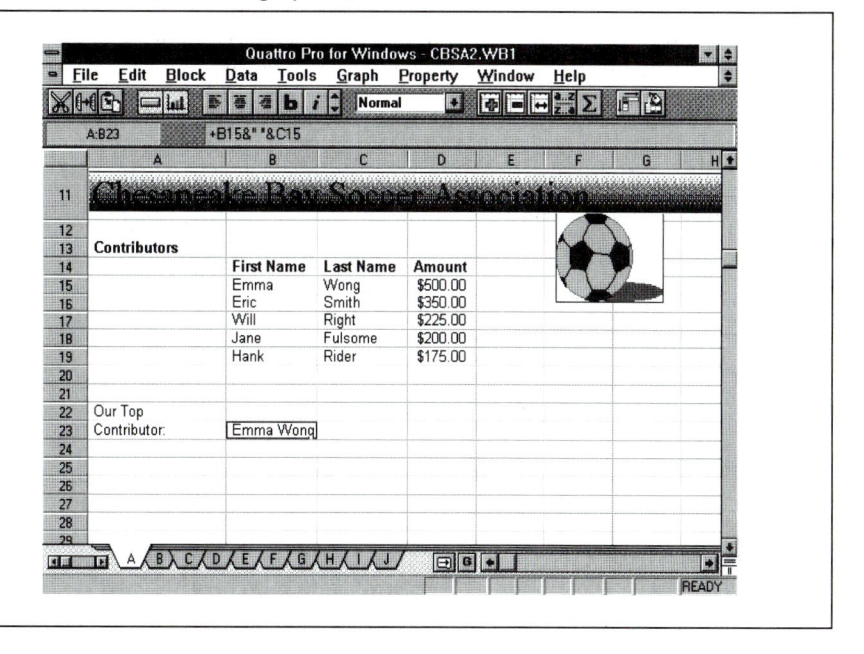

FIGURE 12-16 Concatenated text, including space, in cell B23

CHAR

Earlier you saw that many programs can share information by using ASCII characters. There are 256 ASCII characters, numbered from 0 to 255. Many of them are symbols not found on the keyboard, such as graphics characters. The CHAR function can display these codes in Quattro Pro. CHAR returns the ASCII character corresponding to a given ASCII code. Its syntax is

@CHAR(*code*)

where the argument, *code*, is a numeric value between 0 and 255 or the address of a cell containing the numeric value. Since Quattro Pro will truncate any decimal values entered as arguments, you should always enter the code argument as an integer.

REPEAT

The REPEAT function repeats a string of characters a specified number of times. Its syntax is

@REPEAT(*string,number*)

where the argument *string* is a string value (like the letter A) in quotes or a cell address containing a string, and *number* is a numeric value greater than or equal to 0 or a cell address containing the numeric value. REPEAT returns as many copies of the *string* as you specify with *number*. The result is a label.

Although this function is somewhat similar to the repeating label prefix (\) that is used to produce dashed lines in a cell, the main difference is that with REPEAT you can specify exactly how many times you want the string to be repeated. Also, the label prefix adjusts the number of repeated characters to fit the column, even when the width is changed. The REPEAT function can display a fixed number of characters that does not change. When you specify a text string with REPEAT, you must surround it with quotes.

The *number* argument in the REPEAT statement can be a formula or a cell reference. This argument can be used to repeat a character or characters according to a variable factor.

CODE

A reverse of the CHAR function, the CODE function tells you the ASCII code of a special character. Why would you want to know this? Sometimes data that you import from another program is corrupted by odd characters. Identifying them with the CODE function could help you determine their origin. Its syntax is

@CODE(*string*)

where the argument *string* is a string value in quotes or cell address of a string value, the first letter of which is evaluated by CODE to return the ASCII code.

FIND

The FIND function uses three arguments to find characters within a string. Its syntax is

@FIND("*substring*",*string*,*startnumber*)

where the argument *substring* is a string value representing the target value to search for, *string* is a valid string value (or cell address of one) representing the source value to search within, and *startnumber* is a numeric value of 0 or greater (or cell address containing such a number) representing the character position to begin searching with. The FIND function returns the character position at which the first occurrence of the target was found.

The number 0 represents the first character in the string, the second is 1, and so on. Thus, @FIND("t",A1,0) returns the value 3 if A1 contains "Quattro Pro", because the letter t first occurs at position 3. Note that the *startnumber* value tells the program to begin the search at that number of characters into the string. You will receive an error if the value of *startnumber* is more than the number of characters in the string minus 1. You will also get an error if FIND fails to find any occurrences of the substring.

Note FIND won't accept a cell value for *substring*, and will return ERR if you try it.

EXACT

Another way to compare labels is to use the EXACT function. This function has the syntax

@EXACT(*string1*,*string2*)

where the argument *string1* is a string value (in quotes) or a reference to a cell containing a string, and *string2* is a second string value (in quotes) or cell reference.

The EXACT function compares the values of *string1* and *string2*. If the values are exactly identical, including capitalization, it returns a value of 1. If there are any differences, it returns a 0 value. The text strings that you are comparing must be surrounded by double quotes unless the argument is a cell or block reference.

To compare strings or cell contents without regard for capitalization, you can use the IF function. The IF function is not case sensitive. For example, @IF(A1=A2,1,0) will return a 1 value, meaning true, if the contents of the cells are the same but capitalized differently (for example, if A1 contained YES and A2 contained Yes).

You can also ignore capitalization by using the following formula to refer to a string in cell A1

+A1="Yes"

which returns 1 for both "Yes" and "YES".

REPLACE

You can use the REPLACE function with four arguments to replace a string of characters within a label. The syntax is

@REPLACE(*string,startnumber,num,newstring*)

where the argument *string* is a string value in quotes (the label to be worked on) or its cell address; *startnumber* is the character position to begin with (or the cell address containing the number); *num* is the number of characters to delete; and *newstring* is a string value in quotes or the cell address of the *newstring*, the characters to insert at the position marked by *num* (which can also be an address). You could use the REPLACE function, for example, to update the spelling of "Sq." to "Square". Remember, REPLACE puts the result in the current cell, which might not be the cell of the original string.

LEFT, RIGHT, and MID

The LEFT, RIGHT, and MID functions are used to find strings of characters within labels based on the position of those characters. These functions follow the same basic syntax:

@LEFT(*string,number*)

where the argument *string* is a string value in quotes and *number* is a numeric value of 0 or greater.

The LEFT function returns the leftmost characters of *string*, the number of characters returned being that specified by the *number* argument. RIGHT does the same for the rightmost characters.

The MID function requires another argument, *offset*, to describe the point at which to start counting *number* (from the left)

@MID(*string,offset,number*)

where the first letter in the string is position 0.

Cell address can be used for *string*, *offset*, and *number*.

TRIM and LENGTH

The TRIM function has the syntax

@TRIM(*string*)

It is used to remove any extra spaces from a string (you can use the address of a cell containing a string). These extra spaces include the trailing spaces following the last nonspace character. It can also mean spaces preceding the first nonspace character plus duplicate spaces between words. Normal strings (those without leading or trailing spaces, and without duplicate spaces between words) are not affected. If the cell contains no string or numeric value, the TRIM function returns ERR. This function is particularly useful when you are working with data from other programs that pad some data to equal lengths by using trailing spaces.

The LENGTH function is used to measure the length of a label. It uses the syntax

@LENGTH(*string*)

Thus, @LENGTH(A1) returns 23 if A1 contains the words "Quattro Pro for Windows", and @LENGTH("five") returns 4.

LOWER, UPPER, and PROPER

The LOWER, UPPER, and PROPER functions change the case of a string. Their syntax is as follows:

@LOWER(*string*)
@UPPER(*string*)
@PROPER(*string*)

You can use LOWER to turn a string into all lowercase characters. The UPPER function returns all uppercase characters; that is, it capitalizes the string. The formula @UPPER(B4) returns "YES" if B4 contains either "yes" or "YES".

The PROPER function converts the first letter of every word in the string to uppercase and the rest of the characters to lowercase. In Quattro Pro, a word is defined as an unbroken string of alphabetic characters. The PROPER function considers any blank spaces, punctuation symbols, or numbers as marking the end of a word. You can use the PROPER function to produce better-looking text from uniformly capitalized text entries. Thus @PROPER(B4) returns "William Shakespeare" if B4 contains "WILLIAM SHAKESPEARE".

In all three functions, numbers and symbols within the string are unaffected by the function. If the string is blank or is a numeric or date value, the result is ERR.

STRING

Used to convert numbers to labels, the STRING function has the syntax

@STRING(*x*,*decplaces*)

where the argument *x* is a numeric value and *decplaces* is a numeric value between 0 and 15 representing the number of decimal places to the right of the decimal point. Thus, for example, @STRING(A1,2) converts 2.001 to a label, rounding it and using the number of decimal points indicated by *decplaces* (which can be the address of an integer)—2 in this case. The label returned is 2.00.

VALUE

The VALUE function converts a label to a numeric value. The syntax of the VALUE function is

@VALUE(*string*)

where the argument *string* is a string value (or cell address) that can contain numerals and/or any of the arithmetic operators, but must not contain dollar signs, commas, or embedded spaces. One period, interpreted as the decimal place, is permitted, and leading and trailing spaces are ignored.

The VALUE function is useful—together with DATEVALUE and TIMEVALUE—for converting data that was imported as text with the Tools | Import command but was not automatically converted into values. You can also use this function to return values for numbers that have been turned into labels.

This chapter has surveyed many ways you can work with text with Quattro Pro for Windows. In the next chapter, you begin your exploration of shortcuts and macros, the tools you use to create custom Quattro Pro applications.

CHAPTER 13

Macros

As you work with Quattro Pro, you may find yourself repeating tedious actions, such as choosing formats for a series of charts. To be sure, Quattro Pro provides many tools to reduce the tedium of spreadsheet use. However, you could still find yourself repeating the same actions, such as splitting the window into panes and locking titles, every time you open a notebook. This is when Quattro Pro's *macros* can perform the action (or series of actions) for you at a single command and save you a lot of time and effort.

In brief, macros give you a way to store and retrieve a series of keystrokes, mouse actions, and command choices. Running a macro is like having an obedient robot that effortlessly and rapidly repeats the actions you have recorded. For example, you could create a macro that places the cell selector where you want the window to split and then choose the Window | Panes command. This simple macro eliminates the need for you to position the cell selector yourself prior to choosing Window | Panes. Once you have created and used a macro, you will surely agree that this feature is one of Quattro Pro's biggest productivity boosters.

Anyone can learn to create a Quattro Pro macro. As you will learn in this chapter, you can easily create a macro using the *recording technique*: You simply perform the actions you want the macro to perform, and Quattro Pro records these actions. After you stop recording and name the macro, Quattro Pro "plays back" the macro when you wish, repeating just the actions you performed.

If you wish, you can delve more deeply into macros by learning how to write macros in Quattro Pro's command language. Doing so gives you many benefits. For example, written macros can pause and ask the user, by means of a dialog box, to supply needed data or carry out an action. In Chapter 14, you will see how written macros can be used to develop custom Quattro Pro applications, in which the program's normal user interface is replaced by menus, SpeedBars, and dialog boxes of your own design.

This chapter presents an introduction to recorded and written Quattro Pro macros. Beginning with recorded macros, you learn how to run macros, attach a macro to a key, and assign a macro to a notebook button. You'll learn where and how to store your macros. Progressing to written macros, you'll learn how to type your first written macro, how to name macros, and how to understand macro command syntax. You'll learn how to prompt the user for input, and how to create macros that branch different ways depending on a condition you specify. Finally, you'll learn how to track down *bugs*—programming errors that keep your macros from working correctly. Chapter 14 surveys Quattro Pro's macro commands.

Note Quattro Pro for Windows can run Quattro Pro for DOS macros without modification, as long as the macros were written using menu-equivalent commands (rather than keystrokes to select command options). If your Quattro Pro for DOS macros use keystrokes to select commands, right-click the application title bar to display the Application properties menu. Choose the Macro | Macro options, and choose Quattro Pro—DOS in the Slash Key menu. If you want to run Lotus 1-2-3 macros, activate the KeyReader option in the Macro options menu.

Using Macros

By far the easiest way to create a macro is to record your actions. As you do, Quattro Pro interprets them and writes macro commands that are actually placed in your notebook. Because you should keep the macro commands separate from the rest of your work, it's a good idea to create a Macros notebook page to store your macros. The macros you store in this page will be available throughout the current notebook. (Later, you will learn how to create a macro library that contains macros available to all notebooks.)

Recording Your First Macro

To create a Macros page in a new notebook, right-click the index tab for Notebook page I (the last page tab that is visible in a new notebook). You see the Active Page dialog box, as shown in Figure 13-1. In the Page Name text box, type **Macros**, and click OK. You see the new page name you've defined, as in Figure 13-2.

Clear macro-writing practice dictates the use of three columns for macros: You use Column A for names, Column B for commands, and Column C for explanations of what the commands do. Just why this

FIGURE 13-1 Naming Page I in the Active Page dialog box

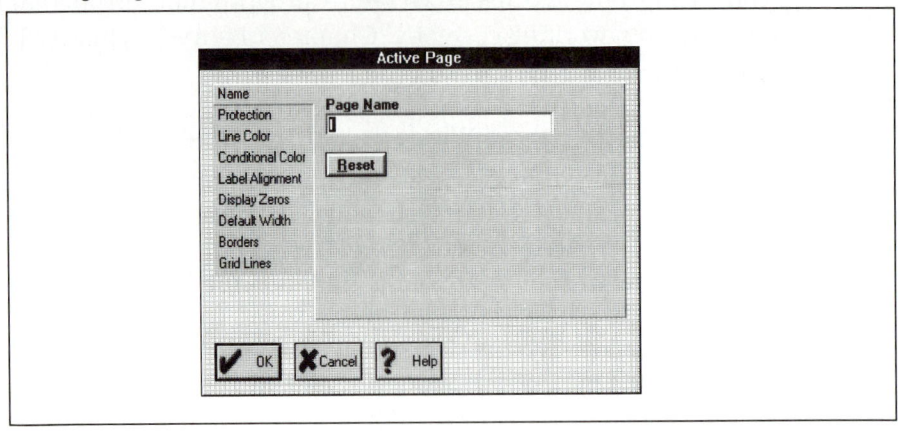

FIGURE 13-2 Macros page defined in new notebook

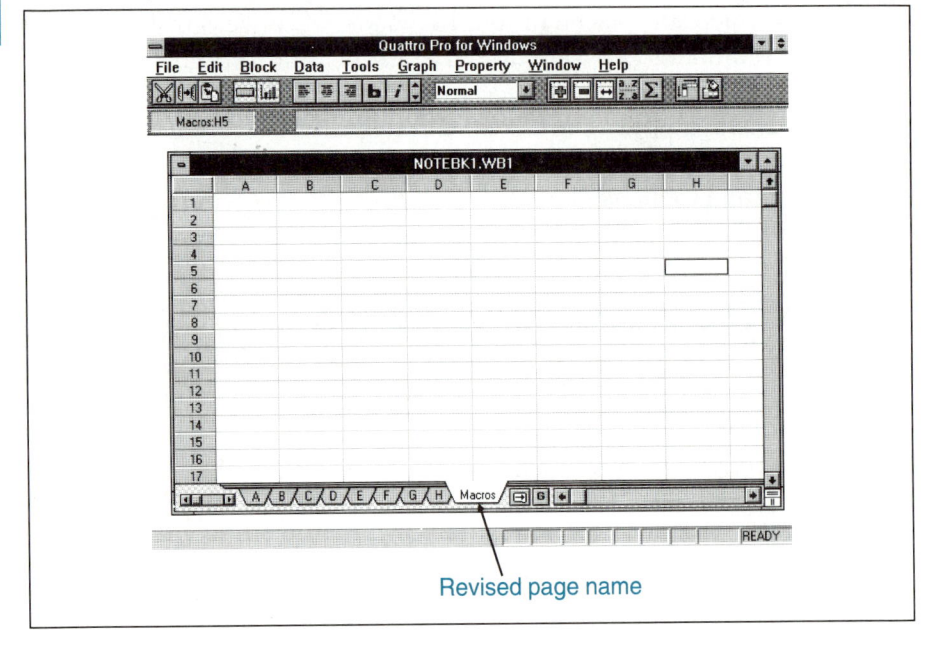

Revised page name

practice is a good one will become clear later. For now, though, begin your macros by placing the cell selector in Column B of the macros page.

In the following brief exercise, you create a macro that splits the window into two panes. To begin, place the cell pointer in cell B1 of the Macros page in your new notebook. Choose Macro from the Tools menu, and when the submenu appears, choose Record. You see the Record Macro dialog box:

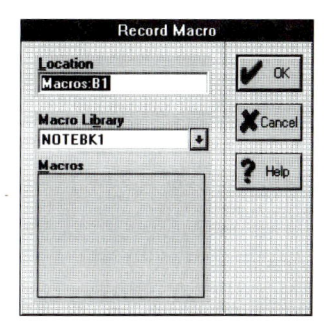

Note that the Location box contains the active cell's location: cell B1 on the Macros page. If you forgot to position the cell pointer before choosing the command, you can retype this cell address. The Macro Library text box contains the name of the current notebook. This setting indicates that the macro you record will be available only when this notebook is active. Choose OK to begin recording the macro. Note that the status bar contains the code REC, indicating that Quattro Pro is recording your keystrokes.

Note While recording a macro, you can use any method you like to choose commands, including the keyboard, shortcut keys, or the mouse. The technique you choose makes no difference in the macro's efficiency. Also note that it doesn't matter how quickly you choose the commands. Even if you take a long time to choose them, the macro will execute as quickly as Quattro Pro will allow.

Now click the cell pointer in cell A10 and choose Panes from the Window menu. When the Panes dialog box appears, choose Horizontal.

Then choose OK. Quattro Pro splits the screen. To stop recording, choose Macro from the Tools menu again, and choose Stop Record from the submenu.

Since you don't need split panes here, restore the window by choosing Panes from the Window menu again, choosing the Clear option, and choosing OK.

Your Macros page now contains two macro commands for your new macro, as shown in Figure 13-3. Note that the commands are each surrounded by curly braces. This is how Quattro Pro identifies macro commands. Now you name the macro.

Naming the Macro

Although you can run a macro without naming it, the names make macros easier to locate and choose.

Naming a macro is as easy as naming a block: You use exactly the same commands. Begin by selecting the block B1..B2 on the Macros

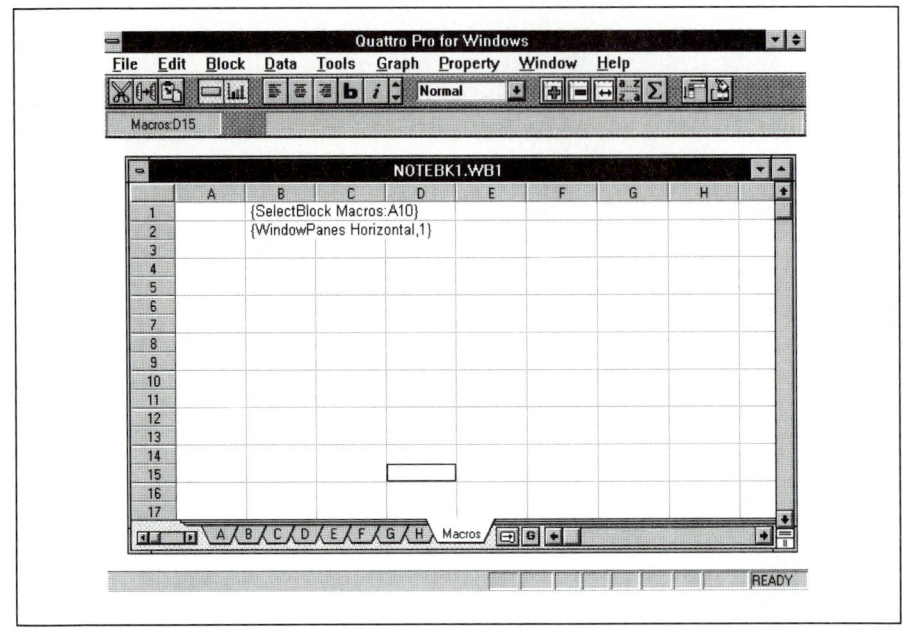

FIGURE 13-3 Macro commands automatically created by Quattro Pro

page. This block contains the two macro commands. Then choose <u>B</u>lock | <u>N</u>ames and choose <u>C</u>reate from the submenu. You see the Create Name dialog box. In the <u>N</u>ame box, type **SplitWindow**, as shown here:

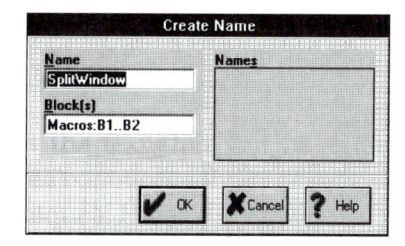

You can use any uppercase or lowercase pattern that you want, because Quattro Pro ignores case when naming blocks, but make sure the name is all one word, with no spaces. When you are sure the block is accurately defined (Macros:B1..B2), choose OK. You have now named your macro. As you will see in the next section, you run the macro by choosing its name from a list.

Running the Macro

To run the macro you've created, select notebook page A. Then choose <u>M</u>acro from the <u>T</u>ools menu, and when the submenu appears, choose <u>E</u>xecute (run). (You can skip all these steps by using the ALT-F2 keyboard shortcut.) You see the Run Macro dialog box:

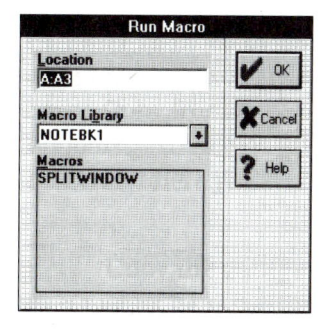

As you can see, the macro you named now appears on the list. To run the macro, choose SPLITWINDOW in the Macros list and choose OK.

The macro works, but it does something you don't want—it goes to the Macros page, and splits the window there! Why? Clear the window panes, and choose the Macros page. You can see why when you examine the macro. The first instruction looks like this:

{SelectBlock Macros:A10}

It tells Quattro Pro to select a block consisting of cell A10 on the Macros page, and Quattro Pro did just that. As you can see from this example, Quattro Pro takes its macro instructions very literally. To get this macro to work correctly, you must edit it, as discussed in the next section.

Note Don't run new macros on notebooks that contain your work; use a test notebook instead. Remember, you can halt the execution of most macros by pressing ESC. If your macro doesn't seem to be running properly, press ESC immediately (before it does any damage, which is possible if the macro started in the wrong place or contains instructions with implications you didn't foresee). Some macro commands disable the ESC key, however. If you're running a macro that won't stop even after you press ESC, press CTRL-BREAK. This key will halt any macro.

Editing a Recorded Macro

You can edit a macro just like any other cell entry. To edit the new macro, place the cell selector in cell B1 of the Macros page. You see the offending Select Block instruction in the formula bar. To fix the macro, delete "Macros:" (don't forget to delete the colon, too). When you have finished editing, the macro command in cell B1 should look like this:

{SelectBlock A10}

This instruction tells Quattro Pro to select the block A10 on the notebook page that is active when the macro is run.

Now turn to notebook page A, and try running the macro again. It should work fine. If you see the message "Unknown key/command," you probably didn't leave a space between "SelectBlock" and "A10" when you finished editing. Add the space, and try again.

Note Macro commands must begin and end with curly braces.

Recording Another Macro

By now, you're probably getting tired of choosing Window | Panes | Clear every time you test your macro. Why not create a pane-clearing macro? Position the cell selector in cell B5 of the Macros worksheet, choose Tools | Macro | Record, and choose OK to begin recording the macro. Choose Window | Panes, and when the Panes dialog box appears, choose Clear. Choose OK, and then choose Tools | Macro | Stop Record to stop recording the macro. You see the following instruction in cell B5:

{WindowPanes Clear,1}

Now use Block | Names | Create (or the CTRL-F3 shortcut) to name the macro CLEARSPLIT.

Run SPLITWINDOW to split the screen. To run CLEARSPLIT, choose Tools | Macro | Execute, or press ALT-F2 and choose CLEARSPLIT from the Macros list. The window is restored to its original condition

At this point, you have some work worth saving. Save your notebook using a name such as FIRSTMAC.

Assigning a Macro to a Key

You can see that using macros is easier than issuing all of the separate commands, but it's tedious to choose the macro names from the Run Macro dialog box, even if you use the ALT-F2 shortcut. To save time, you can assign frequently used macros to keys (specifically, CTRL-A through CTRL-Z), as you will learn in this section. If you create many macros in a notebook, bear in mind that you can only assign these 26 keys—but that should be enough for most users.

To assign a macro to a key, you name the macro using a backslash and the letter (A through Z) that you want to press to set the macro in motion. You will be wise to choose *mnemonic keys*—letters that remind you of the macro's function. CTRL-S would be a good choice for SPLITWINDOW, and CTRL-C would be a good choice for CLEARSPLIT.

If you are naming a macro for the first time, you can give the macro its CTRL-key name directly: Just name the macro using the backslash key and a letter from A to Z, such as \C or \S. (It doesn't matter whether you use uppercase or lowercase letters; Quattro Pro doesn't distinguish between them for key-naming purposes.) To assign an existing macro to a key, select the macro block and choose Block | Names | Create to assign the CTRL-key name. The following dialog box will assign the CTRL-C key to the CLEARSPLIT macro:

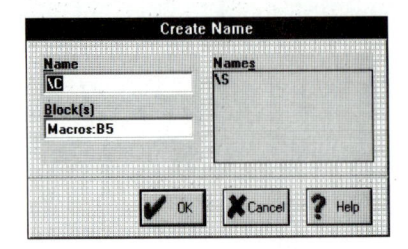

Now that you have assigned SPLITWINDOW and CLEARSPLIT to CTRL-S and CTRL-C, try pressing CTRL-S to split the window and CTRL-C to clear the split. Even dedicated mouse users will probably agree that this is a very convenient feature. And mouse users, read on.

Assigning a Macro to a Button

If you like using the mouse, you can add buttons that execute your macros to your notebook. In this section, you learn how to assign the macros you've created to two buttons that will appear on page A of the current notebook.

First, click on the tab for page A to make it active. Then, click the button tool on the SpeedBar, and move the cell selector to cell F3. Click and drag so that the selection covers four cells (F3..G4), and release the mouse button. You've created a button. To assign properties to the

Chapter 13: Macros

button, including a macro name, right-click the button. You see the Button Object menu, as shown in Figure 13-4.

To assign the macro to the button, choose the Macro Text option. You see the Macro Text dialog box, as shown here:

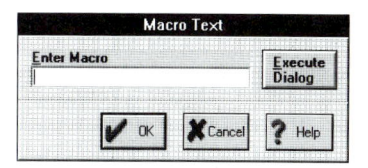

Unfortunately, you can't just type the name of a macro in this box. Quattro Pro expects you to type the text of the macro itself, with all the funny curly braces and strict syntax. However, there's a way you can trick the program into running a macro you have already created and named. (This is why programming is so much fun, incidentally.) The key to this trick is the {BRANCH} command.

FIGURE 13-4 Creating a button

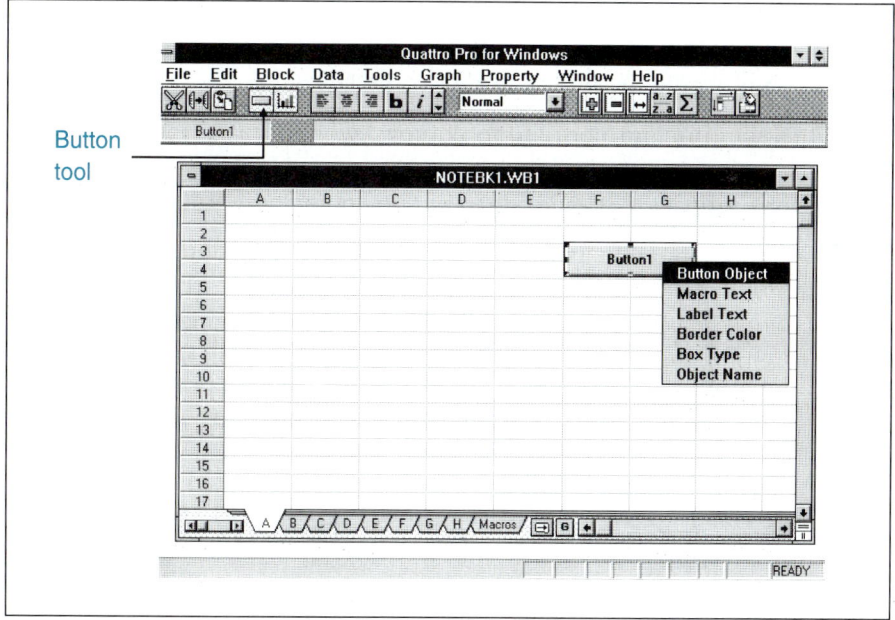

The {BRANCH} command is a macro command that tells Quattro Pro to jump to a macro that is located somewhere else, or to one that has a different name. In the Enter Macro box, type the following, exactly as you see it here:

{BRANCH \S}

Don't forget *both* curly braces, and don't forget to leave a space between "BRANCH" and the backslash (*not* a forward slash). You must type the command perfectly, or else it won't work. When you're sure it's correct, choose OK.

What you've done is to assign the \S macro (the SPLITWINDOW macro that you earlier assigned to CTRL-S) to this button. Now try clicking the button. The screen splits! (Press CTRL-C to clear the split.)

The button needs a label that tells what it does, so right-click the button again and choose Label Text. In the Label Text dialog box, type **Split Window** and choose OK. You see the named button in your notebook, as shown in Figure 13-5.

Repeat the above steps to add a macro button that runs the \C macro, and name the button Clear Split. In the Macro Text dialog box, enter **{BRANCH \C}**. When you're finished, you have two buttons in your notebook, as shown in Figure 13-6.

Organizing the Macros Page

When you create a lot of macros in a notebook, the Macros page can become hard to read. It's a good idea, therefore, to add explanatory text and formatting that will help you remember what your macros do. In Figure 13-7, you see a good plan for a well-organized Macros page. Each macro has a title, formatted with the Heading 2 style. The columns are widened to accommodate the longest entries. In Column C, notes are added that explain what each macro command does. If you organize your Macros page this way, your future work in Quattro Pro macros will be a lot easier.

Chapter 13: Macros 579

FIGURE 13-5 Label added to macro button

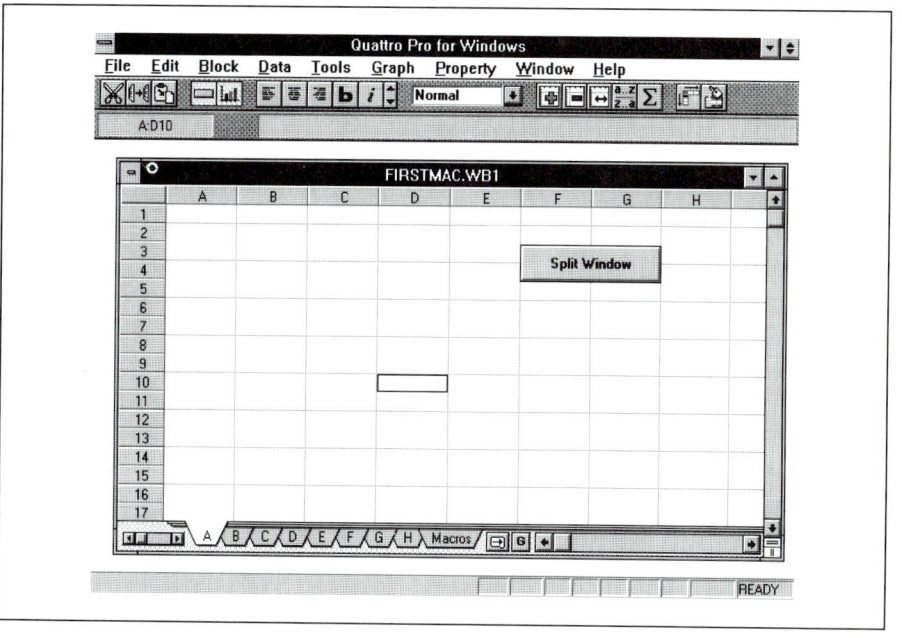

FIGURE 13-6 Buttons for both macros

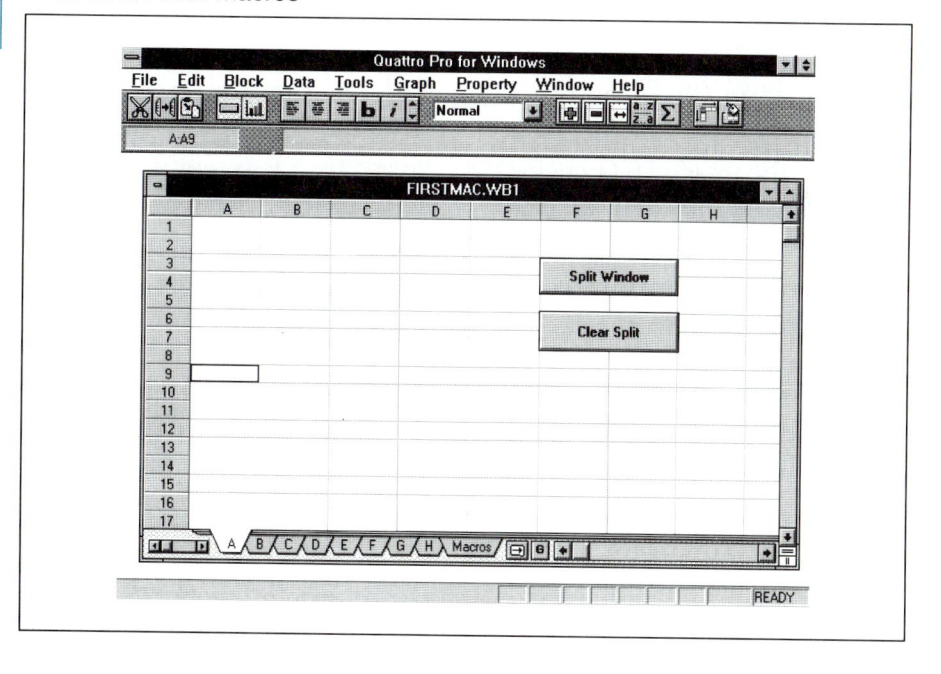

FIGURE 13-7 Well-organized Macros page

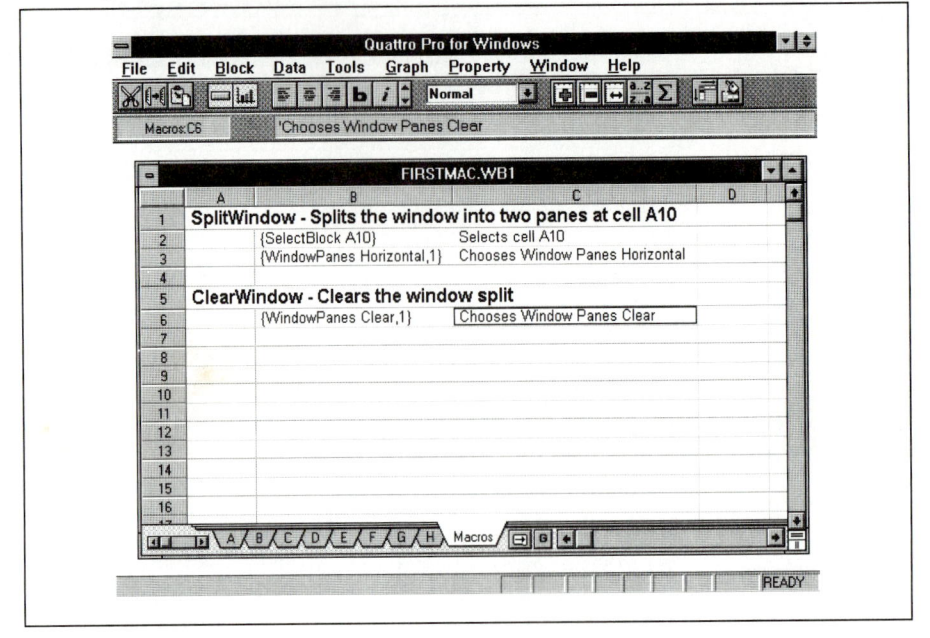

[Screenshot of Quattro Pro for Windows showing FIRSTMAC.WB1 with macros:

Row 1: SplitWindow - Splits the window into two panes at cell A10
Row 2: {SelectBlock A10}   Selects cell A10
Row 3: {WindowPanes Horizontal,1}   Chooses Window Panes Horizontal
Row 5: ClearWindow - Clears the window split
Row 6: {WindowPanes Clear,1}   Chooses Window Panes Clear]

Creating an Autoload Macro

Would you like your macro to run automatically every time you open the notebook that contains the macro? You can do so easily. Just name the macro \0 (a backslash followed by a zero, not the letter O). The next time you open the file, the macro will run automatically.

You can also start a macro as you load Quattro Pro. Just choose Run from the Program Manager's File menu, and type **QPW** followed by the notebook name and the macro name (QPW is the name of the Quattro Pro program file). To run Quattro Pro using the Run dialog box, you type **QPW** and all required path name information, just as if you were starting the program from the DOS prompt. The following example includes the path information Windows would need to find QPW.

The path information of the following example includes the name of QPW's directory (\QPW), the name of the Quattro Pro program file (QPW), the name of the file you want to load (MORTGAGE), and the name of the macro you want to run (SPLITWINDOW).

C:\QPW\QPW MORTGAGE SPLITWINDOW

Tips for Recording Macros

The macros you have created thus far in this chapter, {SPLITWINDOW} and {CLEARSPLIT}, are simple. As you have probably guessed, you can create much more complex macros. For example, you could record a macro that performs the following actions, once you've displayed a graph in the Graphs window:

- Chooses the 3-D step graph option for a floating graph (use the Graph | Type command)

- Chooses the 35mm Slide aspect ratio for the graph (use the Property | Graph Window command)

- Chooses a bold oval box (use the Property | Graph Setup command, and choose Box Type)

- Chooses a light gray fill pattern (use the Property Graph Setup command, and choose Fill Color)

- Chooses a wash pattern for the fill style (use the Property | Graph Setup command, and choose Fill Style)

Try recording this macro now in a notebook that contains a graph. As you learned previously, give page I the name Macros and store your macro beginning in cell B3. The resulting macro, which is fairly long, is shown in Figure 13-8.

Creating a successful macro of this length requires some forethought. For example, the macro in Figure 13-8 will not run correctly unless you display the graph in the Graphs window before running the macro. If you try to run this macro after selecting a floating graph, you see the Alert box shown here:

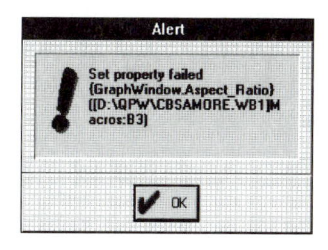

FIGURE 13-8 Recorded macro for formatting graphs

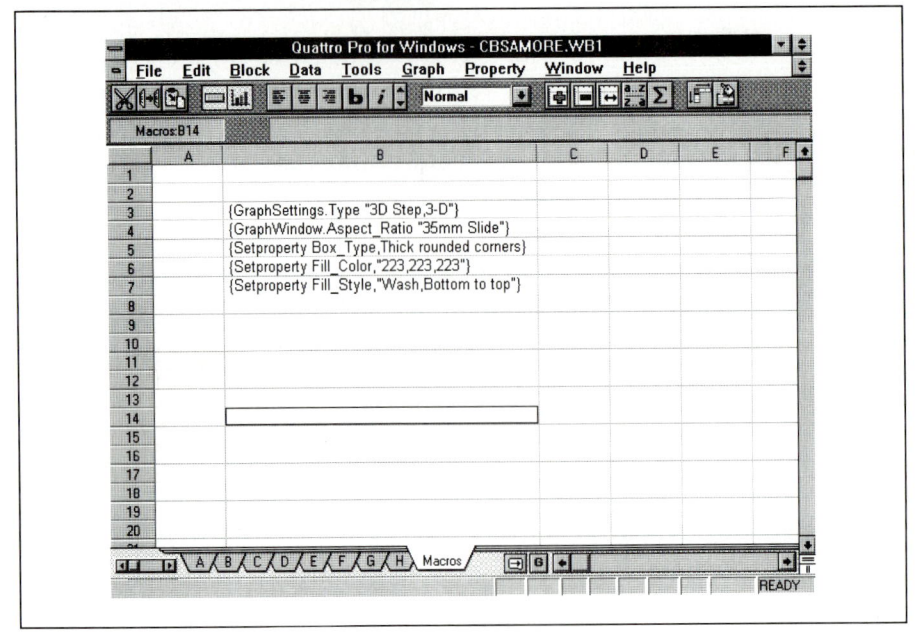

[Screenshot of Quattro Pro for Windows - CBSAMORE.WB1 showing the Macros:B14 page with the following contents:]

- B3: {GraphSettings.Type "3D Step,3-D"}
- B4: {GraphWindow.Aspect_Ratio "35mm Slide"}
- B5: {Setproperty Box_Type,Thick rounded corners}
- B6: {Setproperty Fill_Color,"223,223,223"}
- B7: {Setproperty Fill_Style,"Wash,Bottom to top"}

Why do you see this Alert box? Because there's no Graphs Window Aspect Ratio command in the Notebook window. This command appears on the menu bar only when you display the Graphs window. This macro won't work unless you display the graph in the Graphs window before executing it. You must either manually open the Graph window or add a missing instruction.

Note Here's a quick way to add a missing instruction to a recorded macro without having to repeat all the actions. Choose Tools | Macro Record, and when the Record Macro dialog box appears in the Location text box, type a reference to an unoccupied cell in your Macros page. Be sure to pick a cell with blank cells below it. Then record a one-action macro that performs the action that's missing from the macro you've created. After stopping recording, switch to the Macros page, select the new instructions, cut or copy them, and paste them within the existing instructions. (You may need to insert one or more rows.) Rename the macro so that it will include the new instructions.

Writing Macros

It's easy to record macros—but the results may not be satisfactory. For example, when you record macros, there's no way to remind the user to display the graph in the Graphs window before proceeding. That's because recorded macros can't pause for user input or action. Sooner or later, you will find it very helpful to learn how to write macros by typing macro commands directly.

This statement may sound imposing, especially if you've browsed through Quattro Pro's Developing Spreadsheet Applications manual and seen page after page of complicated-looking macro commands, each with its own peculiarities. But you don't have to learn all the nuances of Quattro Pro's macro language to be able to write macros successfully. In fact, you have already edited some of your recorded macros. You can learn on a need-to-know basis.

Note Quattro Pro can do much of the work for you when you create written macros. Build your macro by recording most of the steps. Quattro Pro will record the macro commands, written perfectly, in the specified range of your Macros page. To add macro commands that perform additional tasks such as pausing for user input, insert rows within the commands so that there's room for the commands you can add only by typing them directly.

In the following section, you will see how recorded macros can be significantly improved by adding just a few written instructions.

A major drawback of the graph-formatting macro just discussed is that you must remember to display the graph in the Graphs window before launching the macro. Otherwise, the macro may have unpredictable results. To help you remember to display the graph in the Graphs window, you can use the {MESSAGE} command. This command displays a dialog box on screen that contains a message you specify. You can follow the {MESSAGE} command with the {?} command, which pauses the macro until the user presses ENTER or chooses OK in a dialog box. Using the {MESSAGE} and {?} commands, you can display a dialog box that gives the user a chance to display the graph in the Graphs window, if it isn't there already. But before you use these commands, you need to know more about Quattro Pro's syntax.

Note Macro commands won't work unless you type them perfectly. They must be surrounded by curly braces, spelled correctly, and contain the correct punctuation. If you need help typing these commands, press SHIFT-F3. You'll see a menu listing Quattro Pro's macro command categories (such as "Keyboard," "Screen," "Command Equivalents," and so on). When you choose one of these categories, you see a list of macro command names. When you choose one of these names, Quattro Pro enters the correct macro command in the current cell. You may have to add arguments, as explained in the next section. For more information about the Macro command menu, refer to the section called "More About Written Macros."

Macro Command Syntax   *Syntax* refers to the rules you must follow to type the command correctly. These rules are very strict. If you make just one little tiny mistake, such as typing a period instead of a comma, the whole macro may not work. Fortunately, Quattro Pro can help you track down mistakes of this sort. You learn more about this feature in the section called "Debugging Macros."

The following shows the syntax of Quattro Pro macro commands:

{COMMANDNAME Argument1,Argument2,Argument3...}

The *COMMANDNAME* is simply the macro command's name. There must be a space between the *COMMANDNAME* and the arguments. As for the arguments, these specify additional information that Quattro Pro may need to carry out the macro command. Some macro commands don't have any arguments. Some have two or more. In the above example, the ellipses (...) indicate that there might be more than three arguments. Don't type three dots at the end of the argument list. Here's a command with one argument:

{BEEP 3}

This command makes your computer beep. The argument 3 makes the beep tone high and squeaky. The higher the number, the higher and squeakier the beep.

Sometimes arguments are optional. The BEEP command doesn't actually need an argument. If you put the command {BEEP} in your macro, you get a medium-pitch beep, equivalent to BEEP 1. To show that

Chapter 13: Macros

an argument is optional, Quattro Pro's printed documentation surrounds the optional argument in angle brackets, as in the following example:

{BEEP <number>}

You don't need to type the angle brackets in your command, though. In Quattro Pro's manuals, they're provided just to remind you that the argument is optional.

In this book, the command would read

{BEEP *number*}

If there's more than one argument, separate the arguments using commas, and don't forget that you must place commas *outside* quotation marks. Quotation marks are needed if the argument contains spaces or punctuation as shown here:

{GETLABEL "Don't worry, be happy", A4}

There are different kinds of arguments. When you look up commands such as {BEEP} or {MESSAGE} in Quattro Pro's documentation, you see that some of the arguments are categorized as *number, string, location,* or *condition.* For these arguments, you must use the correct type of information. For a number argument, you must use a value. For a string argument, you must use text. For a location, you must use a block or a block name. For a condition, you must specify a logical formula (such as >25). You'll learn more about logical formulas later. For now, just remember that the command description tells you what kind of information you must supply when you type an argument. If you include the wrong type of argument, you get an alert box informing you that there's an invalid number or expression in your macro—a pretty common mistake.

As you read about commands in Quattro Pro's documentation, you will see other arguments besides *number, string, location,* and *condition.* For example, the {MESSAGE} command's arguments are called *Block, Left, Top,* and *Time.* These are special arguments, which may be unique to this particular command, and they are explained in the text that follows the command name.

The only other fact you need to know about macro command syntax is that you must place the whole command in one cell—you can't split it up over two or more cells. You may, however, put more than one command in a single cell.

Now you know enough about macro command syntax to understand Quattro Pro's macro command documentation, which, you can see on screen by choosing *Macros* from the *Help* menu, and clicking Macro Command Index. Scroll down to MESSAGE, and click it. You see the {MESSAGE} help screen, as shown in Figure 13-9.

As you can see, the {MESSAGE} command has four required arguments. *Block* specifies the block where the text that you want the dialog box to display is stored. *Left* and *Top* let you specify the screen coordinates where you want the box to appear. (You can try 15,20 initially.) *Time* lets you specify how long the dialog box should remain on the screen. If you type **0**, Quattro Pro keeps the box on screen until the user presses a key.

In the next section, you will use {MESSAGE} and {?} to customize the previous graph-formatting macro.

FIGURE 13-9 {MESSAGE} Help screen

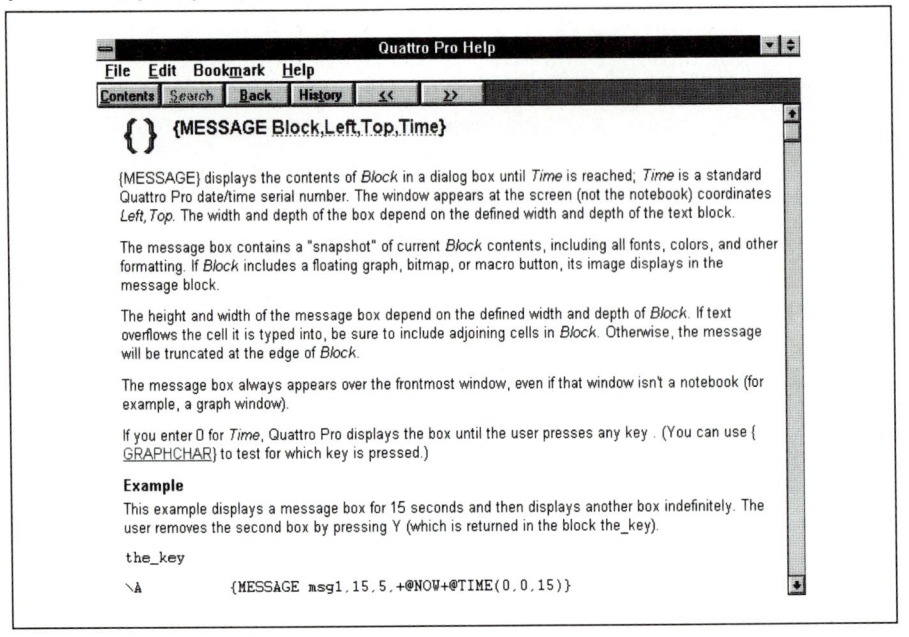

Pausing a Macro for User Action

To add the {MESSAGE} command to your macro, open the Macros page, and display the graph-formatting macro you previously created. In cell B2, type the following:

{MESSAGE Macros:D2..G6,15,20,0} {?}

Double-check your typing to make sure you've entered both commands—{MESSAGE} and {?}—correctly. In the block D2..D6, type the following:

Please display the graph in the Graph window. Press any key to hide this message. Then choose Graph Edit if necessary, or press ENTER if the Graph window is already open.

Because the block D2..D6 will appear on screen with any formatting you've chosen, you may wish to format the block with a box, fill color, and font, as shown in Figure 13-10.

This macro runs well whether you start it from a floating graph or the Graphs window. If you start from a floating graph, you press a key to hide the dialog box and then choose Graph | Edit. When you choose OK in this dialog box, Quattro Pro resumes the macro. If you start from the Graphs window, you press a key to hide the dialog box and press ENTER to resume the macro.

Prompting the User for Input

A common use for spreadsheet macros is to prompt the user for input. With the {GETNUMBER} command, you can create a macro that prompts the user to supply the needed values and then inserts these values into the correct cells. When Quattro Pro executes the {GETNUMBER} command, you see an onscreen dialog box that prompts you to type the required value.

FIGURE 13-10 {MESSAGE} instruction added to graph-formatting macro, and message displayed

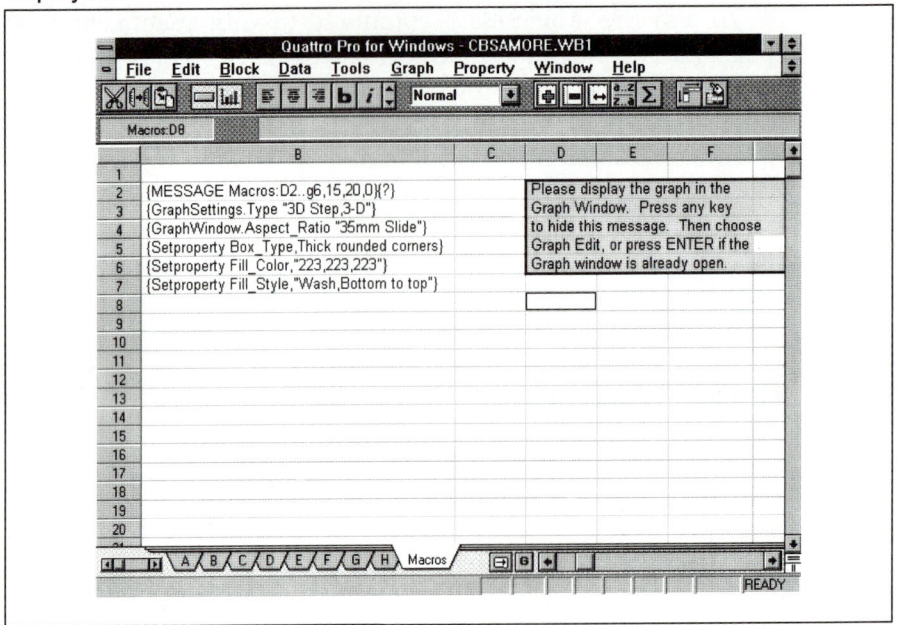

The {GETNUMBER} command requires two arguments: the prompt (the message you want to appear in the dialog box) and the location where Quattro Pro will place the value after you've typed it and chosen OK. In Figure 13-11, you see four {GETNUMBER} commands that include prompts and locations. Note that this macro is named \0 (zero, not a letter O), so that it executes automatically when you open the notebook. Figure 13-12 shows this macro in action.

Using Conditional Instructions

In the previous section, you learned how to prompt the user for input. In this section, you learn how to ask the user to make a decision and how to write a macro that branches to different outcomes depending on the response the user makes. This example illustrates many additional aspects of written macros. For example, you will also learn why good macro planning requires leaving room in column A, next to the macro commands.

Chapter 13: Macros

FIGURE 13-11 {GETNUMBER} commands in an autoload macro

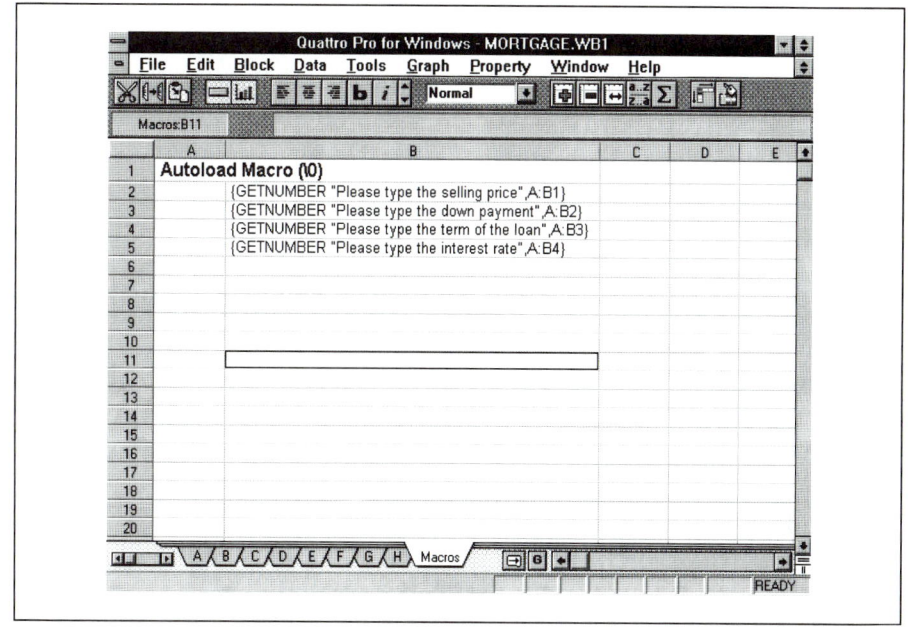

```
Autoload Macro (\0)
    {GETNUMBER "Please type the selling price",A:B1}
    {GETNUMBER "Please type the down payment",A:B2}
    {GETNUMBER "Please type the term of the loan",A:B3}
    {GETNUMBER "Please type the interest rate",A:B4}
```

FIGURE 13-12 {GETNUMBER} values inserted in proper places

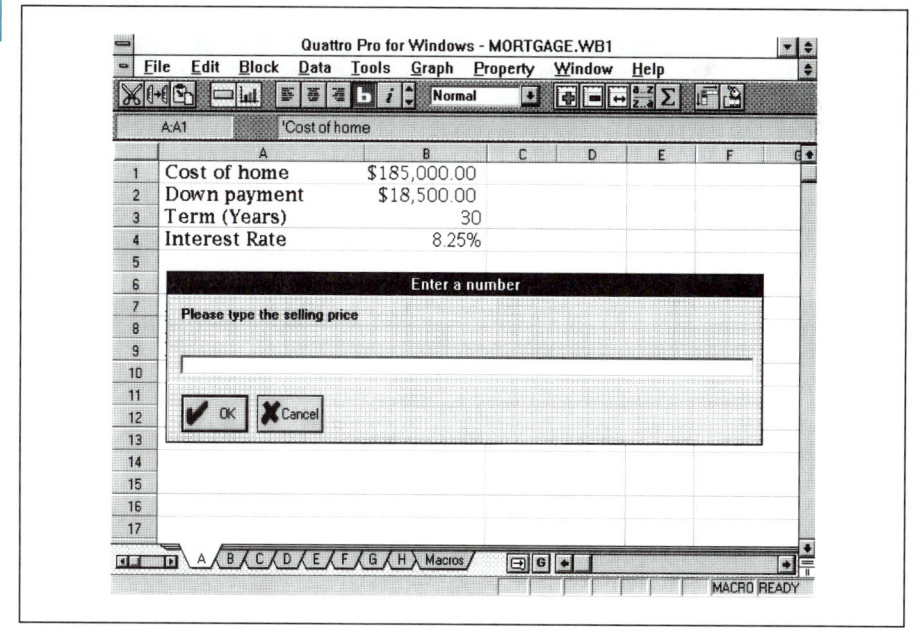

	A	B
1	Cost of home	$185,000.00
2	Down payment	$18,500.00
3	Term (Years)	30
4	Interest Rate	8.25%

Enter a number

Please type the selling price

The key to this useful branching capability is the {IF} command, which has only one argument: *condition*. If the condition is true, Quattro Pro can branch to instructions that wouldn't otherwise come into play. Figure 13-13 shows how the Autoload macro for the Mortgage notebook can be expanded with conditional instructions. In brief, this modified macro asks the user to supply the needed values. It then asks the user whether the notebook page should be printed, and if the user agrees, prints the page. Finally, it asks the user whether the notebook should be saved, and if the user agrees, saves the notebook.

Cells B2 through B5 contain the {GETNUMBER} instructions added previously. New to this figure are the commands in B6 through B19.

The {CALC} command in B6 tells Quattro Pro to recalculate the notebook. It's necessary because recalculation is suspended while a macro is executing. The {GETNUMBER} commands change the values, so without {CALC}, the printout of the results won't be accurate.

The {GETLABEL} instruction in B7 closely resembles {GETNUMBER}, in that it presents a dialog box on screen. But instead of accepting a number, it accepts a string (characters). This command prompts the user

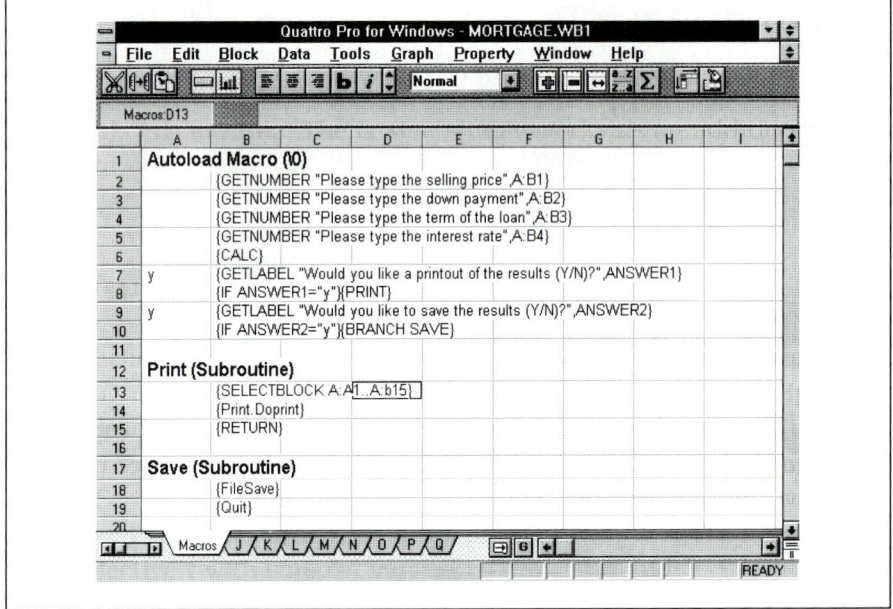

FIGURE 13-13 Conditional instructions added to Autoload macro

to type **Y** or **N** (case doesn't matter) in response to the prompt. The command stores the answer in a location called ANSWER1.

To make sure there is a location called ANSWER1, you must define a block with that name. It's convenient to place this block to the left of the command—which is why you've been leaving Column A blank. With cell A7 defined as ANSWER1, Quattro Pro has a place to store your response to the {GETLABEL} prompt.

The instruction in cell B8 says, in English, "If the user typed **Y** or **y** in response to the prompt about printing the results, carry out the next command (which happens to be {PRINT}) in this cell. If the user typed anything else, don't {PRINT}."

The {PRINT} command, which executes only if the ANSWER1 contains Y or y, is a *subroutine* call. A subroutine is a named subsection of a program that comes into play only if it's referenced in a macro command. In this reference, the name of the subroutine must be surrounded with curly braces. A subroutine call tells Quattro Pro, in effect, to locate the macro with the indicated name and execute its instructions as if they were part of the current macro. At the conclusion of the subroutine, Quattro Pro resumes executing the current macro starting with the next instruction. The {PRINT} command, then, calls the PRINT subroutine. You can see this subroutine in B13..B15.

Skipping down to the {PRINT} subroutine, the first instruction selects the block A:A1..B15, a necessary prelude to printing. The next instruction, {Print.DoPrint}, is a *command equivalent*. You've already seen lots of these; Quattro Pro enters them automatically when you choose commands while recording a macro. You can type them, too, as long as you know what to type. Command equivalents aren't available in Quattro Pro's online help; you have to look them up in Appendix A of the program's manual, "Building Spreadsheet Applications."

Note If Quattro Pro's manual isn't handy when you need to type a command equivalent, don't despair. Use the trick of recording the one-cell macro that chooses a command. Quattro Pro will enter the necessary command equivalent in the cell, and you can copy the cell's contents into your macro listing.

The {RETURN} command in B15 is important. It tells Quattro Pro to go back to cell B8 and continue executing the macro from that location.

Subroutines that are referenced with a subroutine call, such as {PRINT}, should always end in {RETURN}.

Back in the autoload macro, cell B9 contains another {GETLABEL} instruction. Cell A9 is the location of ANSWER2. In cell B10, the final IF instruction tests to see whether the user typed **Y** or **y** in response to the prompt about saving the notebook. If the string stored in ANSWER2 (that is, cell B9) matches Y or y, the next command in the cell—{BRANCH}—is executed. If the user typed anything else, the macro stops at this point.

The {BRANCH} command tells Quattro Pro to jump to the indicated location, SAVE, which is a block name for the macro in B18..B19. Unlike a subroutine call, the {BRANCH} command tells Quattro Pro to go to the indicated macro but does not require the program to return to the main macro. Macros referenced by a {BRANCH} command must end with the {QUIT} command. In cell B18, you see a command equivalent for choosing Save from the File menu. In cell B19, you see the {QUIT} command, which should always be used at the end of a branch (otherwise, Quattro Pro will keep looking down the column for any additional commands, and may stray into another macro listing).

Pausing for Dialog Box Entries In the previous section, you learned that you can type command equivalents such as {Print.DoPrint} to initiate tasks that you would choose from the menus if you were performing the actions manually. The command equivalents initiate the command directly and provide you with a very efficient means of writing macro instructions. If it were not for the command equivalents, you would have to write instructions mimicking all the keys the user would press to access a menu command, to choose options from a dialog box, and to confirm the options by choosing OK.

Sometimes, however, the macro should include the dialog box options. In the previous example, the macro could present the user with the Print dialog box, which would give the user the option of printing more than one copy of the mortgage analysis. In a macro that presents a dialog box, you can use the {PAUSEMACRO} command, which pauses the macro when a dialog box appears. When the user presses ENTER or chooses OK, the macro continues executing.

The following print subroutine displays the Print dialog box and waits for the user to choose options,

{PRINT!}
{PAUSEMACRO}
{RETURN}

allowing the user to choose print options such as multiple copies. When the user presses ENTER or chooses OK, the macro resumes execution.

Note You can assign written macros to keys or buttons, just as you can with recorded macros.

More About Written Macros   The above examples survey commonly used macro techniques. You've learned how to pause a macro for user input, prompt the user to type values or text, incorporate conditional instructions, and pause while the user carries out actions in a dialog box. As your knowledge of macros grows, you will want to explore more macro commands and features. In this section, you learn more about macro commands that this chapter has not yet mentioned, or has mentioned only briefly.

Quattro Pro's macro commands fall into 13 categories. To help you understand and use the many Quattro Pro macro commands, Quattro Pro provides the Macro menu, which you can access by pressing SHIFT-F3. You can enter the command you want into the current cell's input line by simply choosing it. This can save a lot of frustrating typing problems. The macro categories are as follows:

- **Keyboard** Keyboard commands give you a way of emulating the action of keys on the keyboard, such as SHIFT, ENTER, and ESC. To repeat a keyboard command, type a number after the command name ({LEFT 5} or {DOWN 2}). Use a tilde (~) to indicate the ENTER key. To indicate "holding down" a key while pressing another, use a plus sign between keys. For example, to simulate the SHIFT-F3 key combination that calls up the Macro menu, enter **{SHIFT+F3}** as the macro command.

Note You can't simulate key combinations that initiate Windows task switching, such as CTRL-ESC, because Quattro Pro will ignore such macro commands.

- **Screen** Screen commands perform functions such as beeping, displaying text in the mode indicator, disabling menus and prompts, controlling screen updating, and zooming the window. You can use the {INDICATE} command to change the message on the status line.

- **Interactive** Interactive commands help you create macros that interact with the user. You can allow the user to choose from the list of open windows, display a dialog box, pause the macro to accept user input, create custom menus, pause to accept dialog box entries, and more.

- **Program flow** Program-flow commands structure the sequence in which macro commands are executed. Normally, execution proceeds from the top cell downward. However, you can instruct Quattro Pro to branch to another macro or to a subroutine, to keep executing an instruction until a condition is met, and to execute a command conditionally (depending on whether a specified condition has been met).

- **Cell** Cell commands deal with cell contents, such as erasing a cell, copying the contents of a cell to another cell, placing a value in a cell, storing values in a block, recalculating formulas in a block, and SpeedSumming the values in a block.

- **File** File commands handle disk operations, such as opening and closing files.

- **/ Commands** / (Slash) commands let you write macros that older spreadsheet programs, such as Quattro Pro for DOS and Lotus 1-2-3 for DOS, can read.

- **Command Equivalents** Command equivalents provide a way to access menu commands and dialog box options easily and quickly. Without them, you would have to type a long series of commands that mimicked the keys the user would press to choose the same option. Even if you did so, the macro might not work correctly if you started it when a different menu (such as the Graphs window menu) is on screen. Always use command equivalents to access menu options.

- **DDE** DDE commands allow you to initiate dynamic data exchange (DDE) conversations with other DDE-capable applications. A conversation between DDE applications allows Quattro Pro to receive data that is automatically updated, should you later change the source document. With Quattro Pro's DDE commands, you can initiate a DDE conversation, request data from the other application, send data to the other application, and terminate the conversation.

- **UI**   User interface (UI) building commands give you the tools to build custom applications, complete with their own menus.
- **Positioning**   Positioning commands provide tools for moving the cell selector, as well as grouping or ungrouping objects.
- **Object**   Object commands provide tools for dealing with Quattro Pro's floating objects, such as floating graphs and objects embedded into Quattro Pro from other applications. These tools allow you to size, move, and select objects and obtain their property settings
- **Miscellaneous**   Miscellaneous commands allow you to insert punctuation, scroll the window, and control slide shows.

You can find documentation for each of these commands in Quattro Pro's help screens. There's much more to learn about Quattro Pro's macro capabilities—in fact, these capabilities deserve a book-length treatment of their own. But you've learned enough already to give you a good start. In Chapter 14, you will extend your macro knowledge by learning how to create applications that change Quattro Pro's user interface and present custom dialog boxes.

Creating a Macro Library

The macros you have created so far are only available in the notebook within which you have placed them. If you create macros that are useful in many notebooks, you can place them in a *macro library*. A macro library is a special notebook that contains nothing but macros.

To create a macro library, open a new notebook. Right-click the notebook title bar. You'll see the Active Notebook dialog box. Choose the Macro Library option, and select Yes under Macro Library. Choose OK to exit the dialog box.

If you wish, copy macros from other notebooks into the macro library (you will need to redefine their names). You may also create new ones.

To save the macro library, choose **S**ave from the **F**ile menu, and name the library with a name such as **MACROS**. (You can name the library anything you want, but MACROS is a logical choice.)

To use the macros in your macro library, the macro library must be open, but it doesn't have to be visible. You can use the **H**ide command in the **W**indow menu to hide the macro library so it doesn't clutter up your screen. You can create more than one macro library, but only one should be open at a time.

Note You can add an autoload (\0) macro to your macro library that consists of just one command: {WindowHide}. This macro tells the macro library to hide itself when you open it. To view the window, choose **S**how from the **W**indow menu, and choose the macro library from the list.

When you execute a macro, Quattro Pro looks first in the current notebook. If the program does not find the macro in the current notebook, it looks in the macro library you've opened.

Note Don't open more than one macro library at a time. If you do, and if two libraries contain a macro with the same name, you can't predict which one Quattro Pro will run.

Debugging Macros

Quattro Pro macros execute quickly, so it may be hard to tell what goes wrong when a macro misbehaves, and it may be hard to stop the macro before it is completed. For this reason, Quattro Pro provides a *debugger* that helps you track down problems (*bugs*) in your macros. With the debugger, you can run macros step by step, to see what each step does. You can set *breakpoints* that pause the macro at a given point. You can also trace changes to specific cells as the macro runs.

To run the debugger, choose **M**acros from the **T**ools menu and choose the **D**ebugger option, or press SHIFT-F2. This command turns on the debugger, but it doesn't do anything until you run a macro. When you run a macro, the Macro Debugger dialog box appears, as shown here:

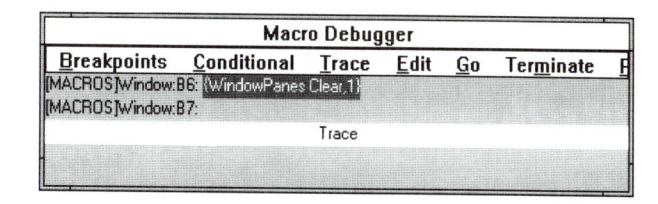

Chapter 13: Macros

```
                    Macro Debugger
  Breakpoints  Conditional  Trace   Edit   Go   Terminate
  [MACROS]Window:B6: {WindowPanes Clear,1}
  [MACROS]Window:B7:
                        Trace
```

At the top of the window, you see the first macro command highlighted. The next command is shown, as well. At the bottom of the window is the Trace indicator. If you want to see what happens to cells the macro affects, choose Trace from the debugger window menu, and choose the trace cell to set (you can choose from 1st Cell through 4th Cell). After you choose the cell, the trace indicator shows what happens to the cell as the macro runs through its steps. To choose the 5th through 9th cells, choose Trace again.

To step through the macro one line at a time, click the dialog box window or press SPACEBAR. Each time you click the mouse, the macro advances one step. When you want to resume running at full speed, choose Go or press ENTER.

If you've written a lengthy macro, you may not want to step through the whole macro just to reach a troublesome spot. In such a situation, set a breakpoint in the macro. A breakpoint is a cell where full-speed macro execution stops, allowing you to run the macro step by step from that position on. To set a breakpoint, choose Breakpoint from the debugger menu, and choose the 1st Breakpoint option. You see the Break Point dialog box, as shown here:

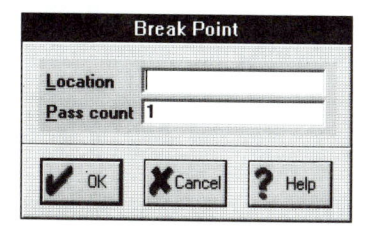

```
              Break Point
  Location    [          ]
  Pass count  [1]

     [✓ OK]  [✗ Cancel]  [? Help]
```

In the Location box, type the address of the cell containing the macro command above the one that's causing you trouble. The Pass Count option lets you specify whether the debugger should stop at this cell every time you run the macro (the default, Pass Count value of 1), or every other time (Pass Count value of 2). Choose OK to confirm the breakpoint. You can set additional breakpoints, if you wish.

If you've set breakpoints, choose Go to run the macro at full speed until the breakpoint is reached. Then click the mouse to advance the macro step by step.

You can also set *conditional breakpoints*. A conditional breakpoint stops the macro if a logical formula you supply becomes true. Suppose you know that the macro goes haywire after "$185,000" appears in cell B1. To set the conditional breakpoint, type the formula **B1=185000** in any empty cell, choose Debugger, and choose Conditional from the debugger menu. Choose 1st Cell, and type the location of the cell that contains the logical formula you just typed. Choose OK and then Go to begin execution with the conditional breakpoint. The debugger will halt macro execution when the formula in the specified cell becomes true (that is, in this example, when Quattro Pro places "$185,000" in cell B1). From that point, you can execute the macro step by step.

If you would like to clear all the trace points and breakpoints, choose Reset from the debugger menu.

When the macro finishes running, the debugger is still turned on (as indicated by the DEBUG indicator on the status line). To turn off the debugger, choose Macros from the Tools menu, and choose Disable Debugger.

As you have seen in this chapter's discussion of Quattro Pro's macro capabilities, macros give you powerful tools for automating your work with spreadsheets. But there's even more to Quattro Pro's capabilities. In the next chapter, you will learn how you can use Quattro Pro's macro features to create a custom application. A custom application hides Quattro Pro's normal user interface, presenting the user instead with custom dialog boxes and menus that you have designed.

CHAPTER 14

Creating Applications

Every time you create a Quattro Pro spreadsheet, you're creating a tool that helps you in some way. For example, the mortgage analysis spreadsheet developed in previous chapters is a useful tool for figuring out the monthly payment on a mortgage, given the home's selling price, the down payment, the term of the loan, and the interest rate. You can turn a well-developed spreadsheet such as this one into an *application*, if you wish. An application temporarily transforms Quattro Pro into a special-purpose program, designed to perform just one function (such as determining a mortgage payment or analyzing heat transfer) with the maximum convenience to the user.

If a Quattro Pro application is to be convenient, it should have two characteristics: First, it should mask Quattro Pro's complexity, showing the user only those Quattro Pro commands and tools that are directly useful for the task at hand. Second, it should provide custom menus, SpeedBars, and dialog boxes that allow easy and quick manipulation of the application.

Quattro Pro for Windows provides application development tools that meet both these criteria. These tools go very far beyond anything previously available in a spreadsheet program. An entire book could easily be devoted to Quattro Pro application development—in fact, an entire book would be needed to cover all the program's application development tools! This chapter seeks to provide only a conceptual introduction to Quattro Pro application development, a firm foundation that you can use on your own to explore application development more fully.

Introducing Quattro Pro's Application Development Tools

Applications make extensive use of macros, which were introduced in the previous chapter. Any application will involve a lot of macros, but it would be very tedious to build an application out of macros alone. For this reason, Quattro Pro includes advanced application development tools that free you from the tedium of writing line-by-line commands for everything that happens. These tools include the following:

- **Macros** In Chapter 13, you learned how to write macros that automatically start when you open a notebook. You can use such macros to remove some of Quattro Pro's default command names on the menu bar, simplifying your application for the user's benefit. You can also use macros to add new command names and menus to the menu bar.

- **UI Builder** This Tools menu command stands for User Interface Builder. It displays a dialog box that contains nothing but the OK and Cancel buttons. It also displays a new SpeedBar, which contains new icons. These icons correspond to dialog box controls, such as check boxes and text boxes, which you can add and position in this new dialog box by clicking and dragging. Using UI Builder, you can very quickly create a custom dialog box for your application. If you had to write macros to create the dialog box and position all the controls, you would be spending hours writing literally hundreds of instructions. With the UI Builder, you can accomplish the task within minutes.

- **Link commands** After you have chosen UI Builder from the Tools menu, a new command appears on Quattro Pro's menu bar: Dialog. From this menu, you choose Links to display the Object Link dialog box, in which you can link each control in your new dialog box to a corresponding action. When you create a link, you specify the event—such as a changed value or a mouse click—that sets the action in motion. Then you tell Quattro Pro what action you want carried out. You can tell the program to execute a macro, or you can just write a macro command directly in the Object Link dialog box.

- **Custom SpeedBars** When the Dialog menu is displayed, you can choose New SpeedBar to create a custom SpeedBar for your application. Like the UI Builder, the SpeedBar builder presents a blank SpeedBar, to which you can add bitmap buttons (buttons that display an icon in them).

In addition to these advanced application development tools, you can also use macro commands that hide Quattro Pro's normal menus, selectively display existing menu commands (such as Print and Save), and include custom command options of your own devising.

If all this sounds confusing, read on: Chapter 13, "Using Macros," has taught you much of what you need to get started in application development. For example, a Quattro Pro application is nothing more than an ordinary notebook that contains an Autoload macro, which comes into play automatically every time you open the notebook. An application's Autoload macro typically hides Quattro Pro's normal menu bar, displays a custom menu, and tells the user what to do from that point on. Creating dialog boxes, building links, and adding SpeedBars is easy, too. If you've learned all the material in this book thus far, you can develop your own applications.

Using Macros to Hide Quattro Pro's Complexity

A good application reduces the amount of information with which the user must cope down to the minimum that is needed. For example, suppose you create an application that helps a real estate agent prequalify house hunters for a home in a given price range. To use such an application, the agent will probably not need any of the commands in the Block, Data, Tools, Graphs, and Property menus. The first step in creating a good application, then, is to write an autoload macro that hides unnecessary menu items temporarily.

Figure 14-1 shows two macros, an AutoLoad macro that removes unneeded menu commands, and a RestoreMenus macro that restores the default menu bar. The RestoreMenus macro will be run when the user quits the application. In the AutoLoad macro, the {DeleteMenu} command is used to hide the unneeded menu items. Note that, despite the name DeleteMenu, this command does not really delete the menus. It just hides them. You can restore the menus by running the RestoreMenus command. In addition, you will see the default menus the next time you start Quattro Pro.

The RestoreMenus command makes use of just one macro command line, which contains the {SETMENUBAR} command. This command tells Quattro Pro to consult the default menu bar file, QPW.MEN. This file contains the default menu bar settings for Quattro Pro. When you run

Chapter 14: Creating Applications   603

FIGURE 14-1   AutoLoad macro for hiding unneeded menu names

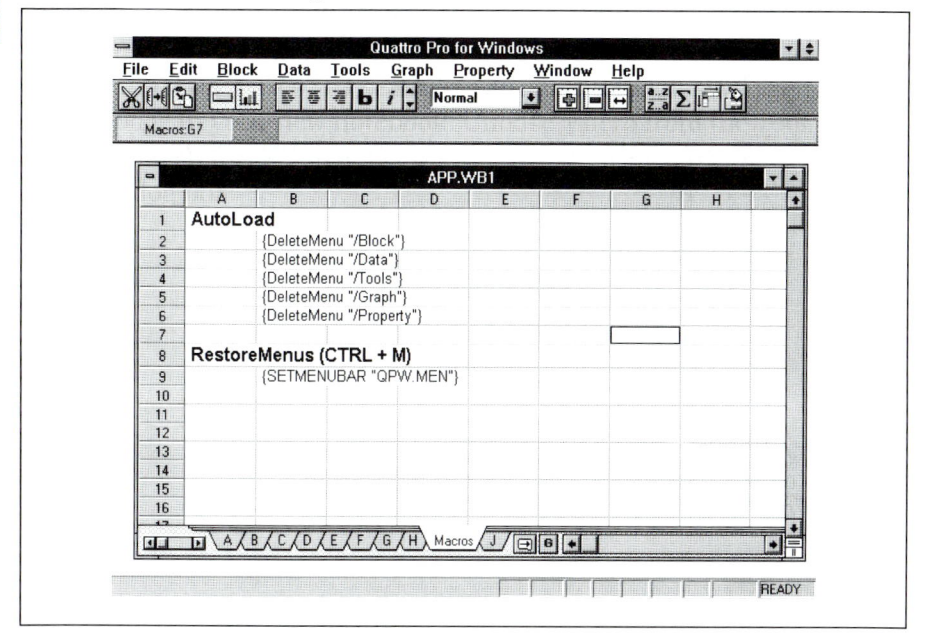

[Screenshot of Quattro Pro for Windows notebook APP.WB1 showing:]

```
AutoLoad
          {DeleteMenu "/Block"}
          {DeleteMenu "/Data"}
          {DeleteMenu "/Tools"}
          {DeleteMenu "/Graph"}
          {DeleteMenu "/Property"}

RestoreMenus (CTRL + M)
          {SETMENUBAR "QPW.MEN"}
```

this macro, you restore the default menu bar, just as you see it when you start Quattro Pro.

Introducing UI Builder

Unquestionably, Quattro Pro's UI Builder command (on the Tools menu) is one of the program's most useful and attractive features. Using this command, you can easily and quickly create custom dialog boxes that take full advantage of an application's features. Given the fact that Quattro Pro's Database Desktop provides excellent access to data stored in Paradox and dBASE databases, UI Builder is very likely to become the development platform of choice for database application developers who must now write hundreds of lines of programming code to perform simple operations. Instead, they will create Quattro Pro notebooks with dialog boxes that provide database and spreadsheet access simultaneously.

The purpose of the UI Builder command is to allow you to create a dialog box, add dialog box controls such as radio buttons and list boxes, and size and format these controls. However, the controls you add cannot do anything until you use *link commands*. A link command specifies what a dialog box control is supposed to do. Link commands can place a value in a cell, run a macro, and perform other actions. In this section, you learn how to use UI Builder to design your dialog box; link commands are covered subsequently.

When you choose UI Builder from the Tools menu, you see a blank dialog box, as shown in Figure 14-2. The dialog box contains an OK and Cancel button, but nothing else. In addition, you see a new SpeedBar: the dialog window SpeedBar. This SpeedBar contains buttons that you use to add controls to your dialog box. In Figure 14-3, for example, you see a variety of controls: option buttons in a group, edit fields for data entry, a spin control box (containing arrows you can click to increase or decrease the box's value), and a check box. All these controls, and more, can be added by choosing tools from the UI Builder SpeedBar.

FIGURE 14-2 Blank dialog box

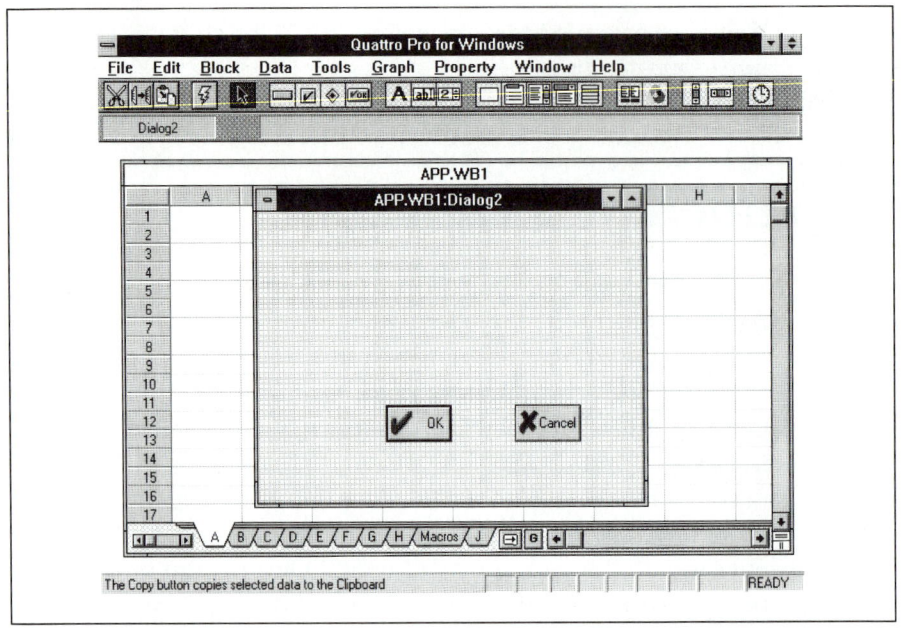

Chapter 14: Creating Applications

FIGURE 14-3 Dialog box with controls

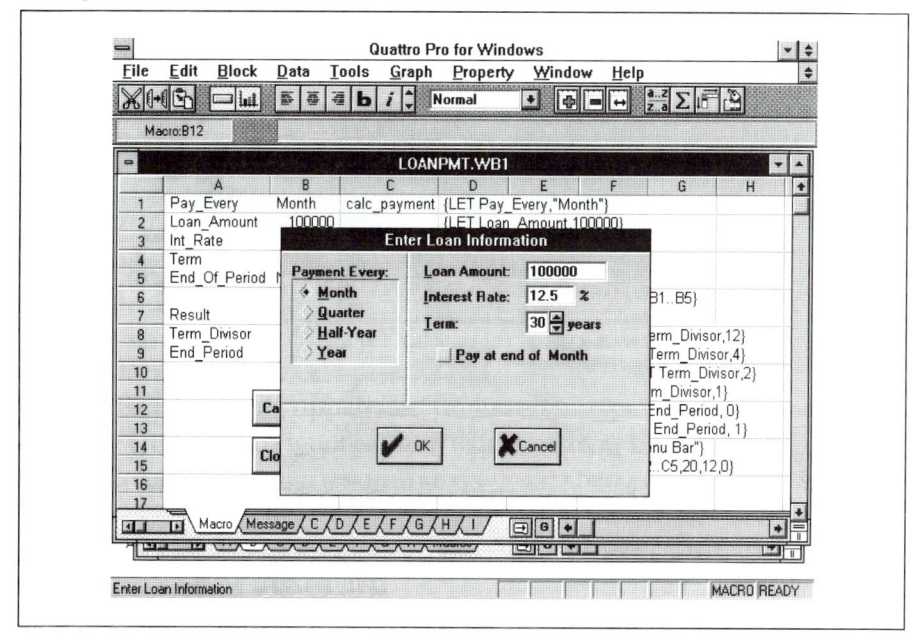

[Screenshot of Quattro Pro for Windows showing the LOANPMT.WB1 spreadsheet with an "Enter Loan Information" dialog box containing Payment Every radio buttons (Month, Quarter, Half-Year, Year), Loan Amount, Interest Rate, Term fields, a "Pay at end of Month" checkbox, and OK/Cancel buttons.]

In Figure 14-4 you can see the UI Builder SpeedBar and the buttons and tools it makes available. In addition to the Cut, Copy, and Paste buttons, which you see in other SpeedBars, this SpeedBar contains tools that add controls to your dialog box, in very much the same way that the Graph tool adds a floating graph to your spreadsheets. After you choose the tool, the pointer changes shape to indicate which tool you've chosen. To add the control to your dialog box, click and drag to where you want the control to appear. When you release the mouse button, the control is still selected, so you can move and resize the control as you wish by dragging its handles. You can also define its properties, as explained later.

Following is a brief overview of the buttons and tools on the UI Builder SpeedBar:

Test button Press the button to test the operation of the dialog box. In the test mode, the dialog box performs as it will when manipulated by the user. To exit the test mode, choose the OK

FIGURE 14-4 Grid Options dialog box

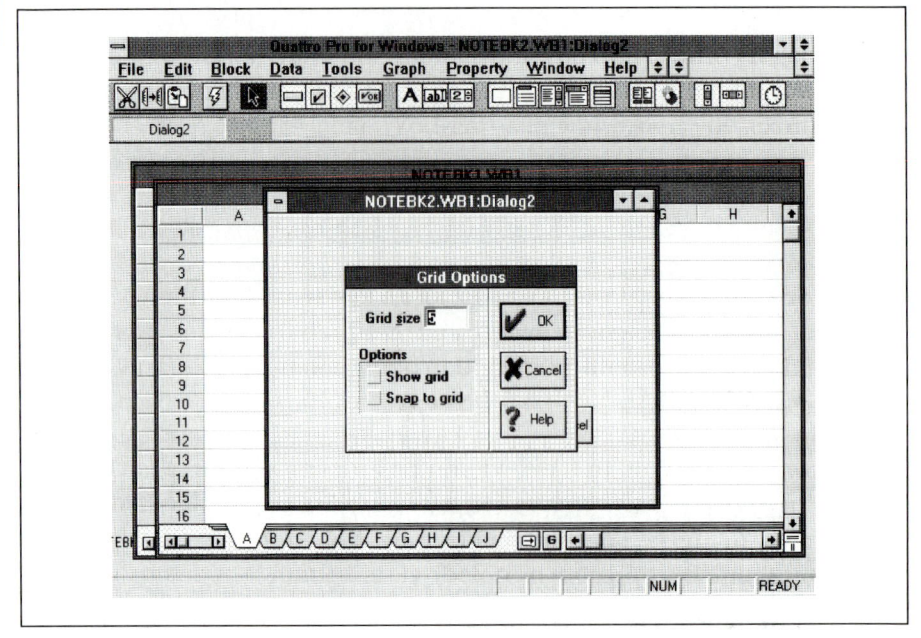

button in your new dialog box. Quattro Pro will return to the UI Builder mode.

Pointer tool Press this button to move or resize any control in the dialog box, as well as to change the properties of these controls.

Pushbutton tool Press this button to add a pushbutton to your dialog box.

Check Box tool Press this button to add a check box to your dialog box.

Radio Button tool Press this button to add a radio button to your dialog box.

Bitmap Button tool Press this button to add a *bitmap button* to your dialog box. A bitmap button contains a picture. By default, the bitmap is the OK check. After adding the button, you right-click it to display the Bitmap Button properties menu. When you select the

Chapter 14: Creating Applications   607

Bitmap option in this menu, you see a list box with dozens of bitmaps you can use. These bitmaps include all the bitmaps used in Quattro Pro's SpeedBars and dialog boxes, including pictures of printers, alert symbols, bold characters, italic characters, preview icons, and many more. You can also add your own bitmap, if it has been saved to a BMP (Windows Bitmap) file.

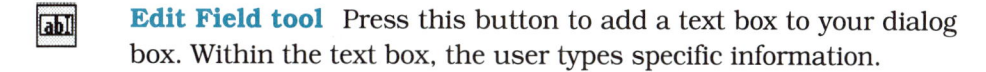

Label tool Press this button to add text to your dialog box.

Edit Field tool Press this button to add a text box to your dialog box. Within the text box, the user types specific information.

Spin Control tool Press this button to add a *spin control* to your dialog box. A spin control lets the user click an up or down arrow to increase or decrease the value that is displayed in the spin control text box.

Rectangle tool Press this button to add a rectangle to the dialog box for aesthetic purposes. To group radio buttons or check boxes, use the Group Box tool.

Group Box tool Press this button to group radio buttons or check boxes and surround them with a rectangle. The group box has a title at the top.

List Box tool Press this button to add a list box to your dialog box. To add items to the list, paste the list into the box from the Clipboard or use the List option in the ListBox properties menu to specify a spreadsheet block that contains the list.

Combo Box tool Press this button to add a combo box to your dialog box. A combo box is a list box that has a text box at the top. When the user chooses an item from the list, the combo box places the user's choice in the text box. However, the user may also type a choice in the text box. To add items to the list, paste the list into the box from the Clipboard, or you can use the List option in the ComboBox properties menu to specify a spreadsheet block that contains the list.

Pick List tool Press this button to add a pick list to your dialog box. A pick list button displays a drop-down list of choices when the user points to the list and holds down the left mouse button. To add items to the list, paste the list into the box from the Clipboard.

File Control tool Press this button to add a file control button which, when pressed by the user, displays a version of the Open dialog box. Using this dialog box, the user can choose a document to open.

Color Control tool Press this button to add color control options to the dialog box.

Scroll Bar tools Choose one of these tools to add vertical and horizontal scroll bars to your dialog box. These scroll bars let the user pick a value, which must be an integer, from a fixed range of values. To determine the minimum and maximum values, use the ScrollBar properties menu.

Time tool Choose this tool to add a time control to your dialog box. This control shows the user the current time. You can also use the Time tool to specify the time at which the control automatically retrieves values from a specified cell in an open window. Additionally, you can use the Time tool to create an alarm that sounds at a specified time.

Note There's a fast way to create a group box filled with radio buttons. Use the Group Box tool to enter a group box. Then hold down the CTRL key and drag the lower-right handle of the group box. When you release the button, Quattro Pro will fill the group box with radio buttons. By adjusting the size of the group box while holding down CTRL, you can change the number of radio buttons that have been entered.

When you right-click a control that you have added to your dialog box, you see its properties menu. The control properties options are too numerous to list here. In general, they include options that assist you in positioning the control, adding text to buttons, formatting text, determining whether the control is hidden or displayed under certain conditions, adding a brief line of help text that will appear on the status line when the control is selected, and determining whether the control will act as a tab stop when the TAB key is pressed. A common reason for using the control properties menu is to add label text that appears on the face of a button or next to a check box or option button.

Example: Creating a Dialog Box

After you choose UI Builder from the Tools menu, Quattro Pro creates a new dialog box that contains nothing but the OK and Cancel buttons. The dialog box is named Dialog1. (You can create additional dialog boxes for your application, and each will have its own number.)

Right-clicking the dialog box background reveals the Dialog properties menu. You can use this menu to give the dialog box a new title and adjust its size and position. Most importantly for your dialog box's neat appearance, you can choose a grid that temporarily appears on the screen and allows you to position your controls in precise alignment. Choosing Grid Options displays the Grid Options dialog box, as shown in Figure 14-4.

Once you've added the grid to the dialog box, you can easily position and align your controls so that your dialog box looks as if it had been professionally prepared. In Figure 14-5, you see a dialog box to which have been added a group box, two edit fields, two spin controls, a rectangle, and a check box. All these controls, as well as the text, have been aligned using the grid.

When you've laid out your dialog box to your satisfaction, you can test the controls you've entered by clicking the Test button on the SpeedBar. In the test mode, shown in Figure 14-6, you can manipulate the controls as the user would: you can type text in text fields, click the arrows to change the values that appear in the spin controls, and activate or deactivate the check box. However, manipulating these controls does not perform any action. The controls are not yet linked to link commands or macro commands. When you are finished testing the controls, choose the OK button to return to the UI Builder mode.

After testing the dialog box's controls, you can close the dialog box by clicking its minimize button. After you do so, Quattro Pro stores your dialog box on the Graphs page, as shown in Figure 14-7. To perform additional work on your dialog box, you open the Graphs page and double-click the dialog box icon, just as you would open a graph for additional customization.

FIGURE 14-5 Dialog box with controls aligned with the grid

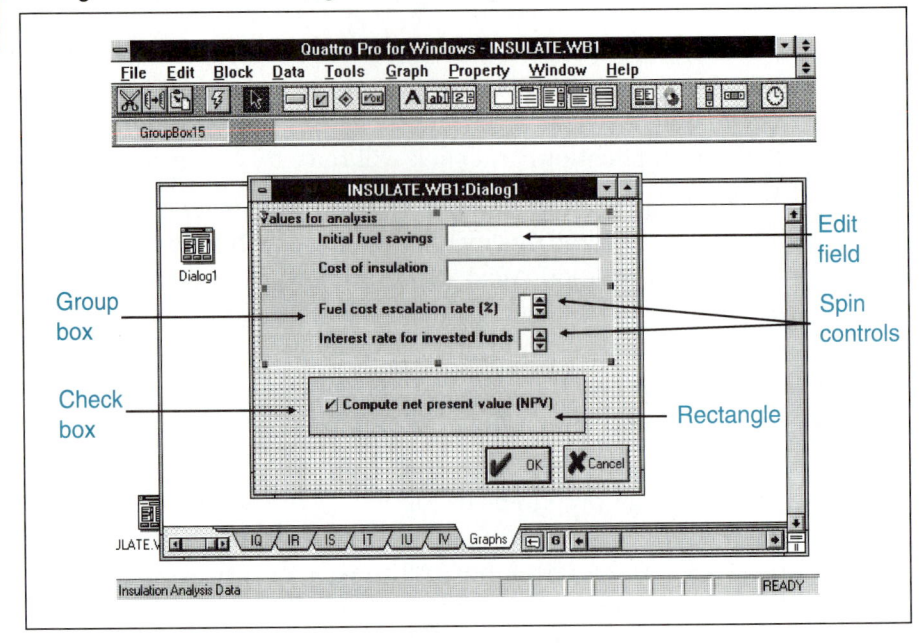

FIGURE 14-6 Test mode

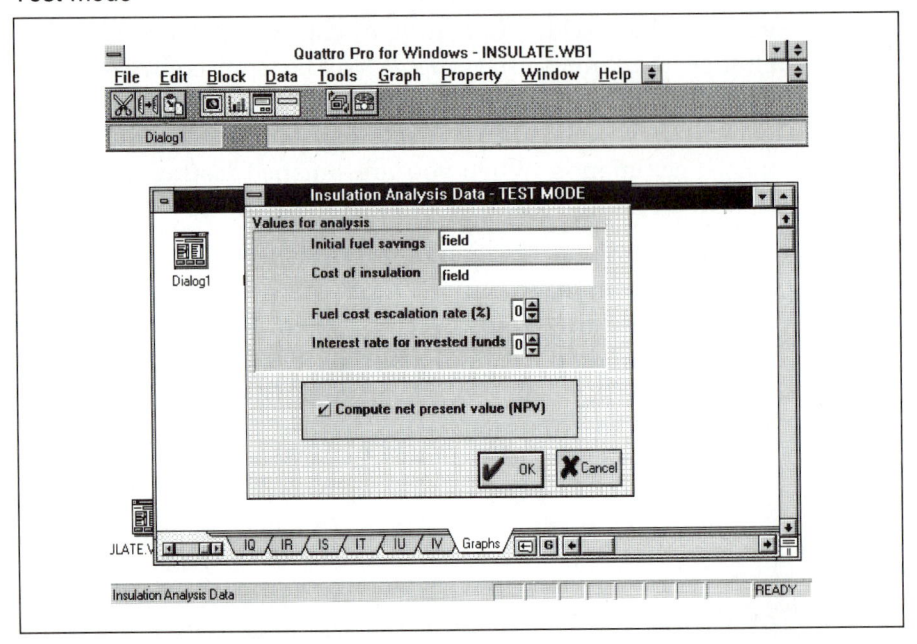

FIGURE 14-7 Dialog boxes stored on Graphs page

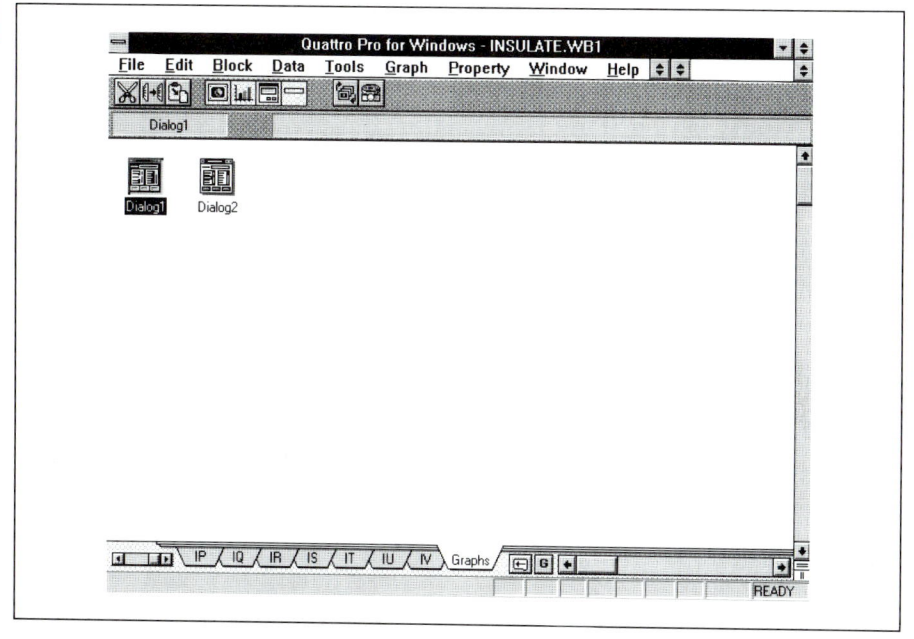

Linking Controls to Commands

Once you've created a dialog box such as the one shown in Figure 14-6, you add link commands to make the controls perform actions. Link commands differ from the macros you learned to write in Chapter 13. To write link commands, you do not need to learn any complicated command syntax. In contrast, you build the link command by choosing options from pick lists and by pointing.

To build link commands, you select the dialog box control that you want to affect, and then you choose the Dialog | Connect or the Dialog | Links command. The Dialog | Connect is the best choice when you want to link a value in a dialog box control to a specific cell on a worksheet. The Dialog | Links command lets you perform more complex actions, such as running a macro when the user presses a button.

Using D<u>i</u>alog | <u>C</u>onnect

By far the easiest link commands to create are the connections you can create between dialog box controls and spreadsheet cells. You create these connections by selecting the control and choosing the D<u>i</u>alog | <u>C</u>onnect command. In Figure 14-8, you see a Connection dialog box with the entries needed to establish a connection between EditField7 (the edit field next to the text "Initial fuel savings" in Dialog1) and the spreadsheet cell C3 on notebook page A. With the <u>D</u>ynamic Connection check box activated, as it is by default, the connection amounts to a hot link: it is instantly updated, whether you make a change in the dialog box or in the spreadsheet cell.

Using D<u>i</u>alog | <u>C</u>onnect commands, you can easily and quickly connect the second edit field and the two spin controls to spreadsheet cells. When you fill out the dialog box, Quattro Pro enters the data you've supplied into the cells. If you've entered formulas that reference these cells, the program will carry out the calculations.

FIGURE 14-8 Creating a link command with the Connections dialog box

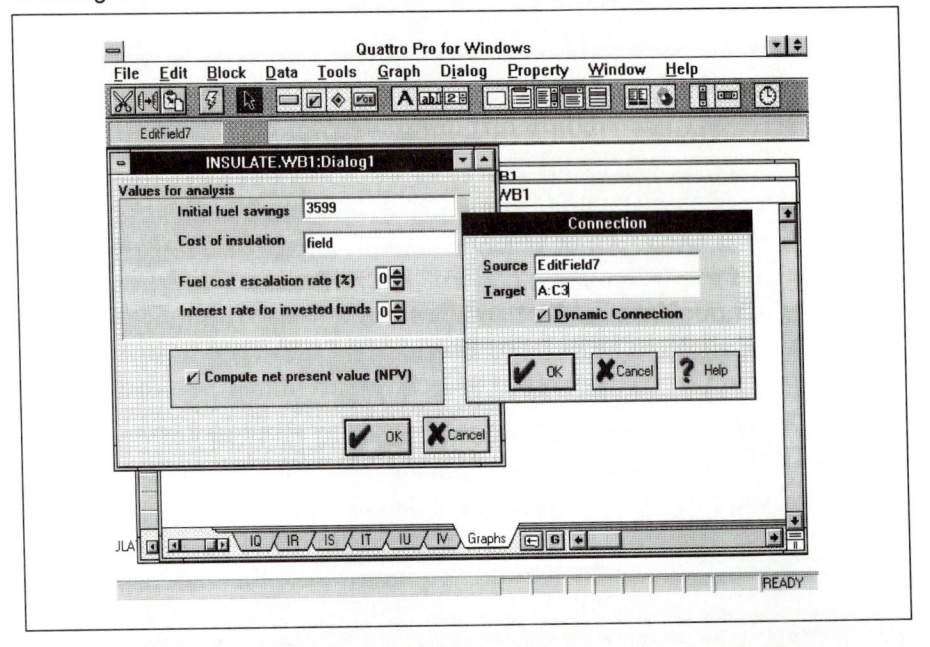

Using D̲ialog | L̲inks

You can also create a link command using D̲ialog | L̲inks, which provides many more options than D̲ialog | C̲onnect. With D̲ialog | L̲inks, you create a command with the following general form: "When *x* occurs, do *y*," or "When *x* occurs, do *y* to *z*." For example, you can create a command that says, in effect, "When the user activates this check box, run the macro named NPV."

To create a link command with L̲inks, select the control you want to affect and choose L̲inks from the D̲ialog menu. You see the Object Link dialog box, as shown here:

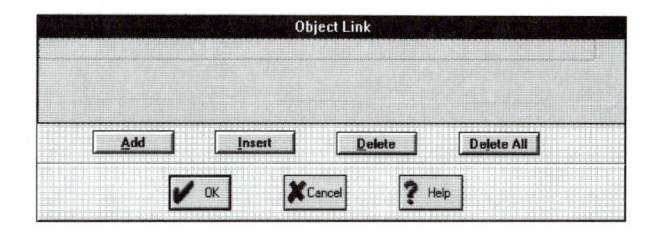

After pressing the A̲dd button, you see the default link command, as shown in this Object Link dialog box:

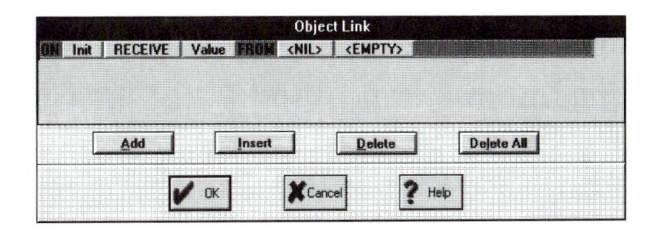

Included within the command are a series of buttons that activate pick lists. By choosing an item from the pick list that appears when you click the button, you can create literally hundreds of different commands.

Following is an explanation of the second and third items in the row of buttons that appear after you activate the default link command (the first item, On, is not a pick list; it stays the same no matter which option you pick).

Event (default: Init)

In the pick list controlled by the second button, you choose the event that you want to serve as the trigger for the command. You can define the command so that the link command is activated (triggered) in many different ways, such as when the dialog box opens or when the user changes the value in a text field.

Since the purpose of this chapter is to introduce Quattro Pro's User Interface Builder, rather than to survey every last option exhaustively, it is not possible to describe all the pick list options in detail. To provide an illustration of the Dialog | Link command's impressive flexibility, though, consider the following list of events that can trigger link commands. All these options and more can be chosen from the Event pick list (some options, like Thumb, require a relevant element, like a scroll bar, to have already been dragged into the dialog box before appearing on the list):

- **Init** Triggers the command when the dialog box is opened
- **Init_Complete** Triggers the command when any command started by Init has finished running
- **OKExit** Triggers the command when the OK button is pushed
- **CancelExit** Triggers the command when the Cancel button is pushed
- **Clicked** Triggers the command when the user clicks the control
- **Right_bdown** Triggers the command when the user right-clicks the control
- **Left_bdown** Triggers the command when the user left-clicks the control
- **Doubleclick** Triggers the command when the user double-clicks the control
- **Valuechanged** Triggers the command when the user changes the value of the control by typing a new value in a text entry field box
- **Dynamic** Triggers the command when the user changes the control's value by manipulating a scroll box or spin control

Chapter 14: Creating Applications 615

- **key:***keystroke* Triggers the command when the user presses the standard Quattro Pro key combination (such as CTRL-F5) given in *keystroke*

- **Activate** Triggers the command when the user chooses the control (for example, by clicking an edit field)

- **Deactivate** Triggers the command when the user chooses another control

- **Lineup** Triggers the command when the user increases the scroll bar's value by clicking the scroll arrow up

- **Linedown** Triggers the command when the user decreases the scroll bar's value by clicking the scroll arrow down

- **Pageup** Triggers the command when the user increases the scroll bar's value by clicking between the up scroll arrow and the scroll box

- **Pagedown** Triggers the command when the user decreases the scroll bar's value by clicking between the down scroll arrow and the scroll box

- **Thumb** Triggers the command when the user clicks or drags the scroll box

- **Editdynamic** Triggers the command when the user is inserting or deleting characters in a combo box field

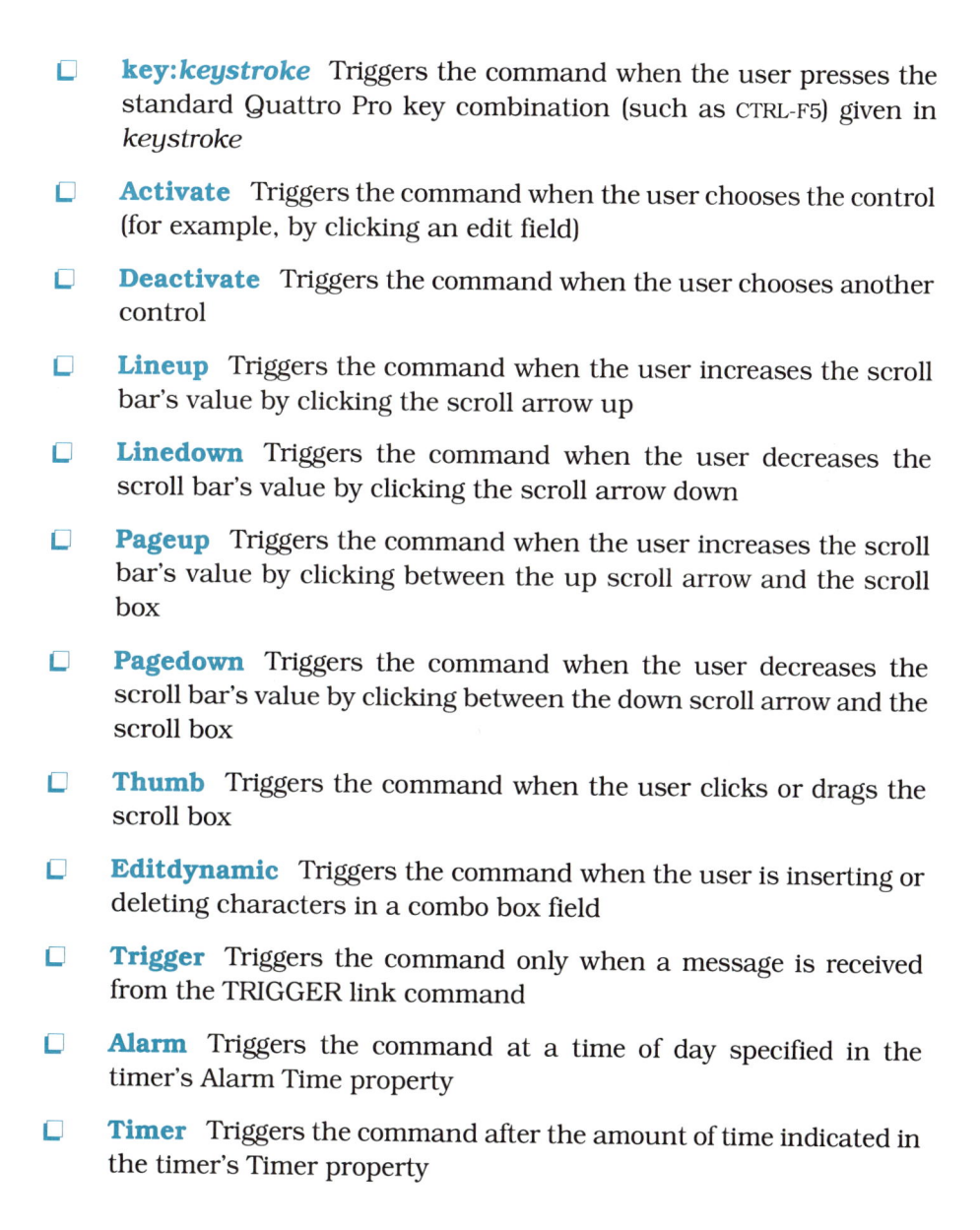

- **Trigger** Triggers the command only when a message is received from the TRIGGER link command

- **Alarm** Triggers the command at a time of day specified in the timer's Alarm Time property

- **Timer** Triggers the command after the amount of time indicated in the timer's Timer property

Command (default: RECEIVE)

In the pick list controlled by the third button, you choose the link command you want to execute. You can choose from a list of commands that includes the following items:

- **SEND** Sends a value to a cell
- **RECEIVE** Receives a value from a cell
- **DOMACRO** Executes a macro you have created
- **EXECUTE** Initiates one of seven possible actions, including duplicating the selected object, removing the object, or deactivating the object
- **CONNECT** Establishes a dynamic connection to a cell
- **SET** Sets the object to a value you specify
- **TRIGGER** Activates a link command in another control

When you choose a command, the rest of the default link command changes to reflect the choices available for the current command. For example, if you choose DOMACRO, the rest of the default link command buttons disappear, and you see an edit field in which you can type the name of the macro you want executed.

The link command appears when you choose Activate in the Event pick list and DOMACRO in the Command pick list as shown here:

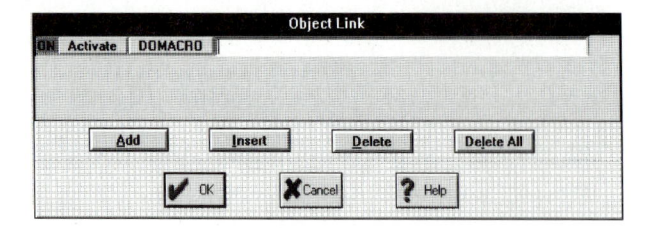

When you type the name of a macro in the text field, Quattro Pro will carry out the macro when the check box has been activated and the user has choosen OK.

Opening a Dialog Box

Once you've created dialog boxes and linked their controls to commands, you need a way to display the dialog box. You can do so in two

Chapter 14: Creating Applications

ways. The first way is to create an autoload macro that opens the dialog box when you start the program. The second way is to create a new menu command that opens the dialog box. Both techniques are discussed here.

Opening a Dialog Box with an Autoload Macro

In Figure 14-9, you see the AutoLoad macro, discussed earlier in this chapter, which removes unneeded menus. An added line (Row 11) contains a {DODIALOG} command, which tells Quattro Pro to open a dialog box. This command has the following syntax:

{DODIALOG "*DialogName*",*OKExit?*,*Arguments*,*MacUse?*}

In this command, *DialogName* refers to the name you have given the dialog box, and this name must be typed in quotes. (As with charts, you can assign a name to a dialog box by right-clicking the dialog box icon

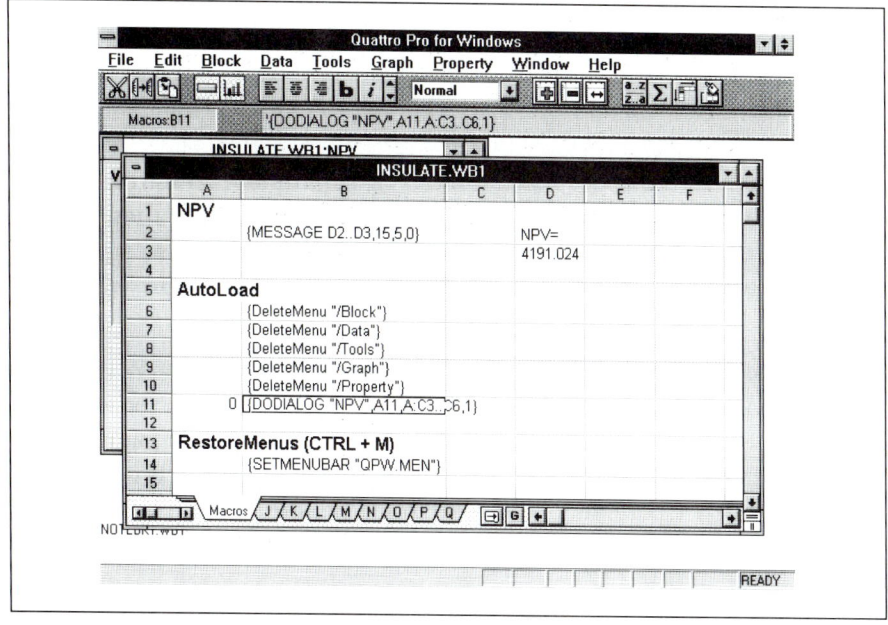

FIGURE 14-9 The Autoload macro containing the {DODIALOG} command

in the Graphs menu. The dialog box activated by this macro has been named NPV.) *OKExit?* is an argument that specifies how the dialog box closes. You must type a cell reference that contains the controlling value (1 to exit with OK, 0 to exit with Cancel). In this example, the cell is A11, the cell just to the left of this macro command. *Arguments* refers to a block containing the values you want to display in the cell initially. In this example, this block is A:C3..C6. *MacUse?*, finally, is a control that specifies whether the user may modify the dialog box. If not, the macro controls it. 1 indicates that the user may modify the box; 0 specifies macro control. The completed command appears as follows:

{DODIALOG "NPV",A11,A:C3..C6,1}

When you open this file, since this is an autoload macro, Quattro Pro will immediately hide the Block, Data, Tools, Graph, and Property menus and display the NPV dialog box.

Opening a Dialog Box with a Menu

As you have already learned, you can delete (hide) Quattro Pro's default menus. You can also add new menus. Such deletions and additions aren't permanent; they're lost when you exit Quattro Pro, so don't worry about ruining Quattro Pro's defaults. A very good reason for adding a new menu is to provide the user with a way to access the dialog boxes you have created.

In Figure 14-10, you see an additional menu, the Analysis menu, which is positioned before the Help menu. This menu contains only one option, Enter Data, which displays the NPV dialog box. (You can create menus with many options, if you want.) The commands shown under the Analysis menu heading (cell A16) in Figure 14-10 are the ones needed to display a new Analysis menu on the menu bar. Figure 14-10 also shows the menu command that this macro creates.

In Row 11, you see a change to the AutoLoad macro that automatically runs when you open this notebook. In place of the {DODIALOG} command just discussed, you see an {ADDMENU} command. This command tells Quattro Pro to create a menu and add it to the menu bar.

The {ADDMENU} command's syntax is as follows:

FIGURE 14-10 Analysis command added to menu bar

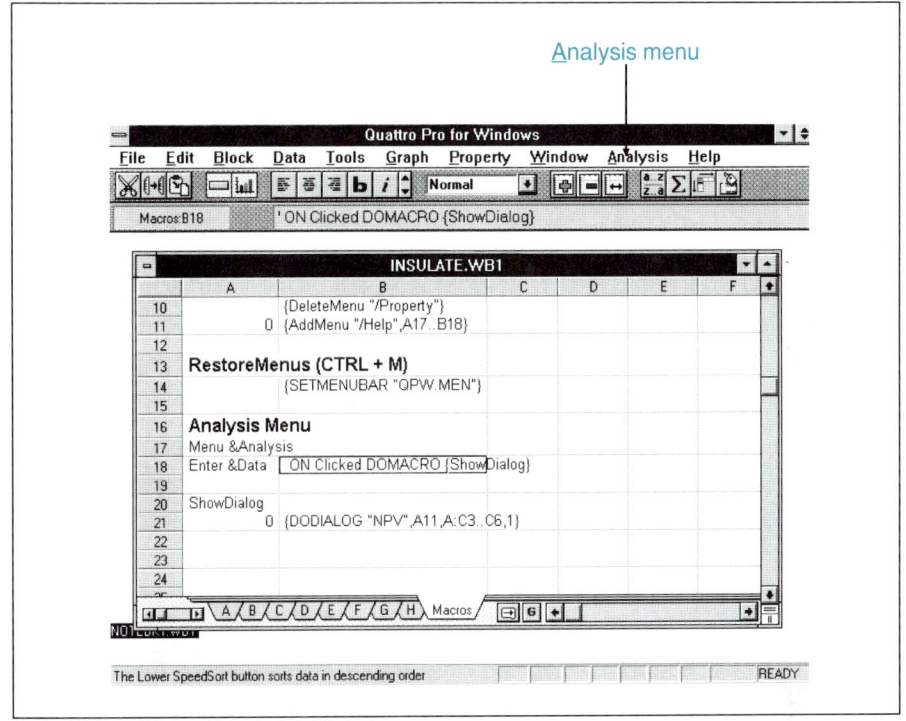

{ADDMENU /*MenuName,Block*}

In the *MenuName* argument, you indicate the placement of your new menu on the menu bar by typing the name of the menu that will follow it. In the example you see on Row 11, this menu name is /Help. This argument tells Quattro Pro to create the new menu just before the existing Help menu.

Block refers to a block of cells containing the menu definition. Cells A17..B18 contain the menu definition for the Analysis menu. In Cell A17, you see the name of the new menu: Analysis. The ampersand (&) tells Quattro Pro to underline the character immediately following the symbol. In cell A18, you see the name of the first option on the menu (Enter Data). In cell B18, to the right of the Enter Data option, you see a typed version of a link command (On Clicked DOMACRO {ShowDialog}). This command tells Quattro Pro to execute the macro {ShowDialog} when the user chooses this command. Cell B21 contains the {ShowDialog} macro, which is identical to the {ShowDialog} command that was included in our AutoLoad macro (discussed in the previous section).

Developing Your Own Applications

Quattro Pro's User Interface Builder is without question one of this program's most impressive features, and this chapter has only scratched the surface of its capabilities. Still, the material that has been discussed should prove sufficient to allow you to begin to explore these powerful capabilities.

When you contemplate creating your own applications, bear in mind the major lesson that computer programmers have learned: There isn't much point in starting application development until you have a clear idea of just how you want your application to work. In short, you need to do a lot of planning.

To plan your application, carefully consider just who is going to use the application. Will users know Quattro Pro well? How much guidance will your application need to provide?

Also consider just what tasks users will need to perform with the application. Will they need to save files? Will they need to print?

As you develop your application, keep these points in mind. Simplicity should be your keynote. Don't bombard the user with huge, complex dialog boxes, with dozens of options. Eliminate menu commands that aren't needed. Anticipate what users will want to do at each step. And be sure to document your macros—later, you may wish to expand your application and you may have forgotten what a particular command does.

APPENDIX A

Working with Windows

The main purpose of this book is to help you learn and make the most of Quattro Pro for Windows. To accomplish this goal as efficiently as possible, we have made a couple of assumptions. The first is that you already possess a basic knowledge of Windows, the operating environment on which Quattro Pro depends. Also, we have assumed that Windows and Quattro Pro are installed on your computer. If you need to know more about installing Quattro Pro, see Appendix B. This Appendix is for readers who are new to Windows and need pointers on working with the world's most popular GUI.

GUIs and CLIs

A GUI is a Graphical User Interface, a means of helping computer users to command and control software. Windows is a GUI designed by Microsoft to run on what used to be called "IBM-compatible computers" or "IBM PC clones." These days such computers are better described as Intel-based PCs, since they use processing chips based on the Intel family of processors. This family started with the 8088 chip used in the first IBM PC introduced in 1981. The next member was the 80286 that IBM used in the IBM PC AT. Since then we have had 80386 and 80486 chips, followed by the 80586.

To understand the role that Windows plays on your computer it helps to consider what happens when you switch on your computer and carry out work with a PC that does not use Windows. First consider the following steps, which take place whether or not you are using Windows:

1. Turning the machine on initiates a short diagnostic routine (including a test of the memory chips) and loads the most basic level of software, the BIOS (Basic Input/Output System). The BIOS is permanently stored on chips inside your computer.

2. The BIOS tells the computer to look for the operating system, a set of programs that organizes data into files, arranges the files on disk, and controls the flow of information between the various parts of the system, the screen, printer, disk drives, and so on.

3. The operating system is stored on a disk and is known as the Disk Operating System, or DOS. When the BIOS finds DOS, it reads it

Appendix A: Working with Windows

from disk into the Random Access Memory, or RAM, the electronic work area within your computer.

4. When DOS is loaded, it looks for certain files that tell it how to behave and how to relate to the various parts of the computer system. These are the CONFIG.SYS file and device drivers, such as HIMEM.SYS.

5. DOS then looks for a batch file called AUTOEXEC.BAT. A batch file is simply a list of commands that DOS carries out one after another when given the name of the batch file. The AUTOEXEC.BAT file lists the commands that you want DOS to execute whenever the computer is started.

At this point, most PCs present what is called the *DOS prompt*. This consists of a letter, indicating which disk drive is being used, a greater-than sign, and a flashing line or cursor, like this:

C>_

Some prompts are more elaborate (you can customize your DOS prompt in your AUTOEXEC.BAT file) and include such information as the date and the directory or area of the disk that is being used. However, operation of the DOS prompt is the same, no matter what the prompt displays. To get DOS to do anything, you have to type the name of a command and press ENTER.

If, for example, you want a list of files on the disk, you type **DIR** and press ENTER. The letters DIR are actually the name of a program that is part of DOS. The main purpose of DOS is to look after the basic workings of the computer so that you can use applications. An *application* is a piece of software designed to apply the power of the computer to a practical task, such as word processing. These days applications can be divided into those that require Windows, known as Windows-based, and those that do not, known as DOS-based.

To use a DOS-based application such as the DOS version of Word-Perfect, you type the program name (in this case, **WP**) at the DOS prompt and press ENTER. When you exit the program, you are returned to the DOS prompt, where you can enter the name of the next application you want to use. This method of controlling a computer is known as a CLI, that is, a Command-Line Interface. There are several disadvantages to a

CLI. For example, you need to know what programs are installed and what commands you use to load them, because you are staring at a blank (except for the DOS prompt) screen. This information has to be gathered by a knowledgeable user. It is not immediately obvious. It is possible to create a menu to simplify loading programs, but there are other disadvantages to this pre-Windows state of affairs.

When you want to exit WordPerfect, you press F7. When you want to leave another DOS-based program, such as 1-2-3, you have to use different keystrokes to leave the program (in this case / and then Q and then Y). To print a document in WordPerfect, use SHIFT-F7. In 1-2-3, it is /PPG. You have to learn different keypresses to do the same job in different programs.

In Windows-based programs, quitting the program is always File | Exit. Printing is always File | Print. This makes life a lot easier.

A Role for Windows

When you switch on your computer and load Windows, it provides a "graphical user interface and mouse-driven operating environment" instead of a command-line interface. This means that all actions and operations are represented visually, using *icons* (small pictures that represent the command or group) and dialog boxes, and you can use a mouse to issue commands. The basic visual metaphor is the desktop. You can see the basic Windows desktop in Figure A-1. Your screen might look different, depending upon the options you have selected and the programs you have installed.

The programs you use with Windows are represented by icons, such as the one labeled File Manager. If you want to run a program you use its icon (double-click or click and press ENTER). You don't have to type a command-line instruction. You don't have to figure out how to start or finish a particular program, as they all start and finish in the same way.

All program icons are arranged in groups, like the one titled Main. You can see that Quattro Pro has been assigned an icon within its own group. This is done automatically during the installation process. Note that the title bar of the Main group is light text on a dark background, while the title of the Quattro Pro group is dark text on a light background. This is

Appendix A: Working with Windows 625

FIGURE A-1 A typical Windows desktop

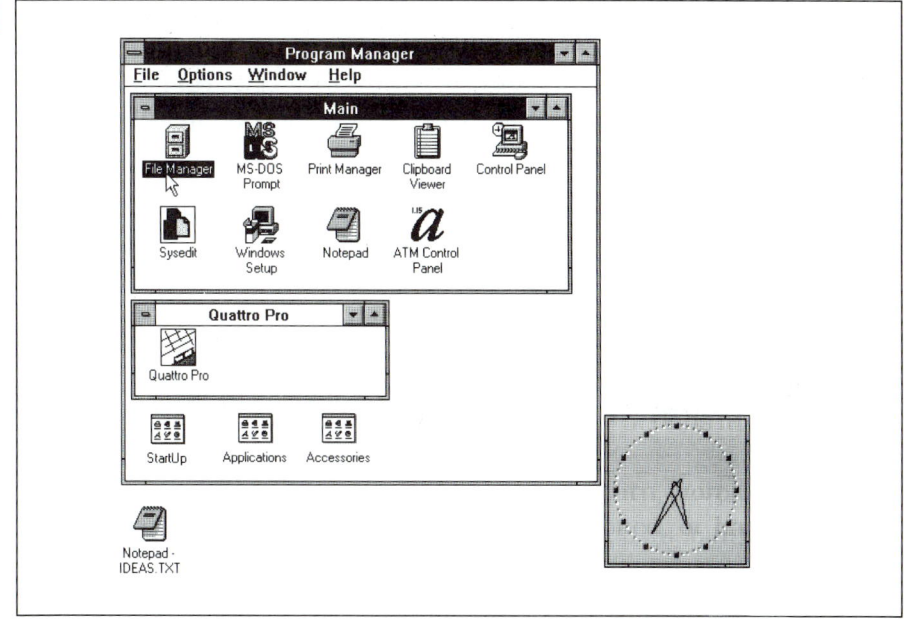

how Windows distinguishes between the *active window* and other windows that are said to be *inactive*.

The Main group window is active in Figure A-1 because the File Manager icon has been *selected* (you can tell by the shading around the name). When an item has been selected, the user can issue commands to affect that item. For example, pressing ENTER at this point will launch the File Manager program. An item that is selected is also said to be *current*. The Main window is the current window and the File Manager icon is the currently selected icon.

It is possible to operate Windows with keystrokes instead of a mouse, but you will find a mouse easier for many operations and essential for some. Mouse actions consist of pointing, clicking, dragging, and double-clicking. *Pointing* means moving the mouse pointer so that it is over a specific object on the screen. *Clicking* means pressing and then quickly releasing the mouse button when you are pointing to an object. For most commands you use the button on the left; however, Quattro Pro makes extensive use of the right mouse button as well. *Dragging* means pointing to an object, holding down the mouse button while moving the mouse, and then releasing the button. *Double-clicking* means pressing and releasing the mouse button twice in quick succession while pointing to an object. For example, one way to start a program in Windows is to point to the program icon and then double-click on it.

Using Windows

Most Windows-based programs run within a window that can be moved around the screen and made larger or smaller. If you make a window so small that all of the menu items won't fit across the top of the window, then they are wrapped onto two lines. You can actually shrink a window into an icon so that a program stays loaded but takes up very little space on the screen. Consider the view shown in Figure A-2. The Notepad program, still running, has been turned into an icon (minimized). You can see Quattro Pro running in a window, as well as File Manager. Windows allows you to load several programs at once. You can switch between them by pressing ALT-TAB or using the Task List, shown in Figure A-2.

Pressing ALT-TAB switches you from one program to another, rotating through all currently loaded programs. The Task List allows you to choose which program you want to switch to. You can call up the Task List by pressing CTRL-ESC or double-clicking anywhere on the Windows desktop. The box that appears is called a dialog box, because it allows the program to ask you questions. In this case you are asked to indicate which program you want to switch to. You can double-click on the name of the program in the list. Alternatively, you can use the arrow keys on your keyboard to move the highlighting bar to the program you want and then press ENTER.

Note that there are six buttons at the bottom of the Task List dialog box. The Switch To button has a heavier outline than the others. This means that pressing ENTER selects this button, as opposed to one of the others. The Switch To button is said to be the current button. Also, it is the default button, meaning that it is the one that Windows assumes you want to use. Also note that one letter in the name of each button is underlined (with the exception of Cancel). The underlined letter is the

Appendix A: Working with Windows

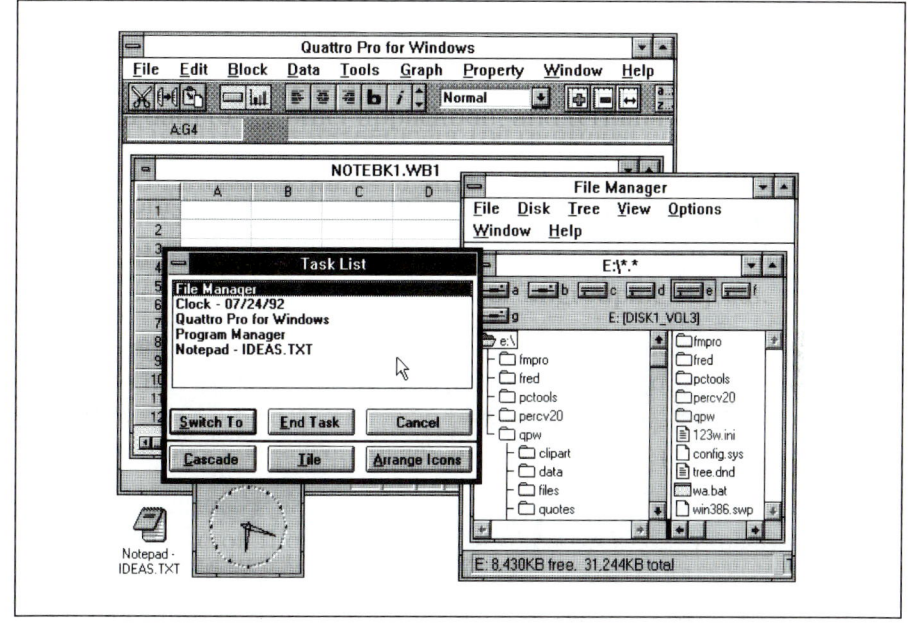

FIGURE A-2 Using the Task List to switch between applications

key letter, meaning that you can select that item by pressing ALT-*letter*, as in ALT-S to select Switch To.

You move a program window by dragging the title bar. You adjust the size of a window by dragging the window border. When you position the mouse pointer over a border the pointer changes to a double-headed arrow, allowing you to drag the border in the directions indicated by the arrow. The corners of windows allow you to adjust both side and bottom borders at once.

Program windows can be adjusted to fill the screen, giving you the maximum space possible for your work. To maximize a window, you click the upward arrow button on the right of the title bar (known as the Maximize button). If a Window is maximized, this up-arrow button changes to a double-arrow button (known as the Restore button). You click the double arrow to restore the program to a less-than-full-screen window (the double arrow then changes back to a single arrow). To turn a program into an icon without unloading it click the down-arrow button known as the Minimize button, which is next to the Maximize/Restore button. To restore a program from an icon, select the program from the Task List, mentioned earlier, or double-click on the icon.

Dialog Boxing

When issuing program commands in Windows, each action is a logical progression from the previous command. A variety of visual input devices are used, including radio buttons, sliders, check boxes, and pop-up lists. To see how this works, try adjusting your wallpaper, the background design that is displayed on the Windows desktop. You begin by double-clicking on the Control Panel icon in the Main program group, seen in the background of Figure A-3.

The Control Panel window opens, and you can double-click on the Desktop icon, also visible in Figure A-3. This produces the Desktop dialog box seen in the foreground of Figure A-3. There are numerous settings in this dialog box (there will be slightly fewer settings if you are using Windows 3.0). The design of sculpted dots in the background of Figure

FIGURE A-3 Using the Desktop dialog box, a typical Windows dialog box

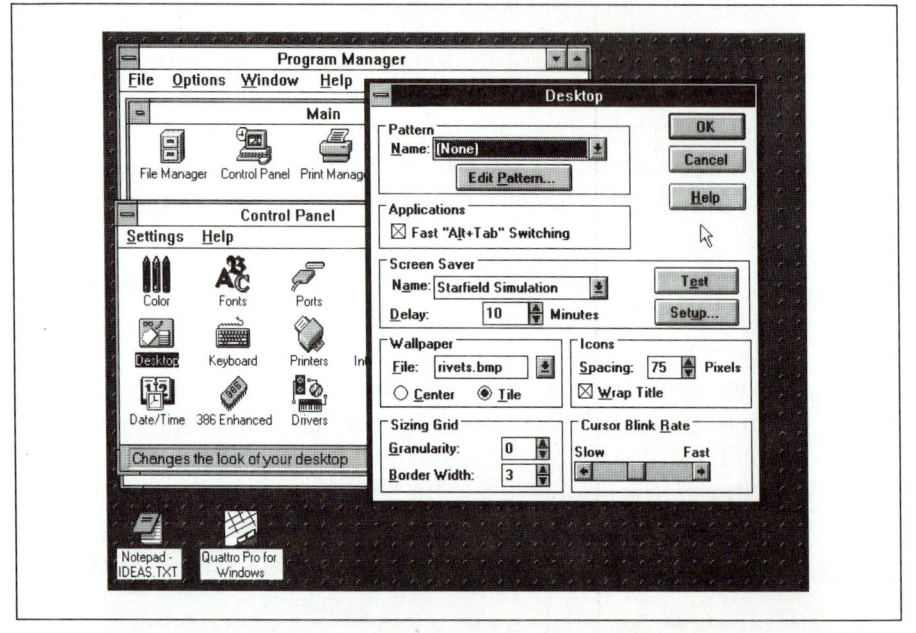

A-3 is created by the Wallpaper settings. These consist of File and a choice between Center and Tile.

The File setting is a *text field*, meaning that you enter text into the box provided. In this case, the text you enter is the name of a graphics file that will be used to create the wallpaper. The File setting also has a pop-up list that allows you to choose a file instead of typing the name. To pop up the list, you click the down-arrow button to the right of the field (you can also press ALT-DOWN ARROW). If there are a lot of graphics files available, the list will have a scroll bar that you can drag. Alternatively, you can click the arrows at either end of the scroll bar to scroll the list. Keyboard users can use the arrow keys to scroll the list. You press ENTER when you have highlighted the item in the list that you want. You can also click on the item to select it. In Figure A-3, the file called RIVETS.BMP has been selected.

The Center and Tile options are radio buttons, meaning that one or the other must be selected, but not both. If you select Center, then Tile will automatically be deselected, and vice versa. The RIVETS.BMP file is actually quite small, and the effect in Figure A-3 is achieved by repeating the design across the desktop with the Tile option. When the settings in the Desktop dialog box are the way you want them, you can select OK. This means clicking the OK button or pressing ENTER when the button is current, indicated by the heavier outline, as in Figure A-3.

The Desktop dialog box uses several other standard input devices. The Applications setting is controlled by a check box. This can either be selected or not (in this case, selecting the option means that you can use ALT-TAB to move between applications). In the Icons section of the Desktop dialog box, you can see another check box called Wrap Title. This determines whether the titles for icons are wrapped onto two lines, as is the case with the Quattro Pro for Windows icon in Figure A-3. To determine Spacing of icons on the desktop you can type a number in the box (the current setting is 75). Alternatively, you can use the increment arrows to the right of the box. Clicking the up arrow increases the value, and clicking the down arrow decreases it (for this particular setting a smaller value means the icons will be placed closer together when you use the Window | Arrange Icons command).

To leave a dialog box without registering any changes, you select the Cancel button and press ENTER or press ESC. Some dialog boxes have a Help button that will summon up an explanation of items in the current dialog box.

Conclusion

While it may take some time to get used to the way that Windows works, it is definitely time well spent. There is only one set of basic commands to learn for all applications designed to run under Windows. Learn to use Quattro Pro for Windows and you will have little trouble transferring your skills to Word for Windows, Windows Draw, or any other Windows-based program you care to use.

You have seen that there are usually several different ways to execute a command or register a choice. This is part of the flexibility of Windows, which allows you to develop a style of operation that you are comfortable with. Users more familiar with the keyboard will probably want to take advantage of keyboard shortcuts, while less accomplished typists will appreciate mouse control. Because there are often different ways of doing the same thing under Windows, you will find that as the text of this book progresses it tends to use general instructions, like "choose OK," rather than specific ones like "click on the OK button or press ENTER after moving the button highlighting to the OK button." This should make it easier for you to develop and use your preferred method of working with Windows.

APPENDIX B

Installation

This Appendix tells you how to install Quattro Pro. Because Quattro Pro is a full-fledged Windows product, installation is straightforward and mainly consists of copying files from the master disks onto your hard disk. As far as screen display, printers, and fonts are concerned, Quattro Pro uses your current Windows settings.

Basic Installation

Quattro Pro arrives on a number of floppy disks that contain compressed files. You install Quattro Pro by using the INSTALL program on the first master disk. This is a Windows program and so you must be running Windows before you start the installation. You should also check that you have more than 10 megabytes (10,240Kb) of free hard disk space before installing Quattro Pro. You can use the Windows File Manager to check free disk space. As you can see from Figure B-1, this is listed in the bottom-left corner of the File Manager window. In this case, there are

FIGURE B-1 Using the File Manager to assess disk space

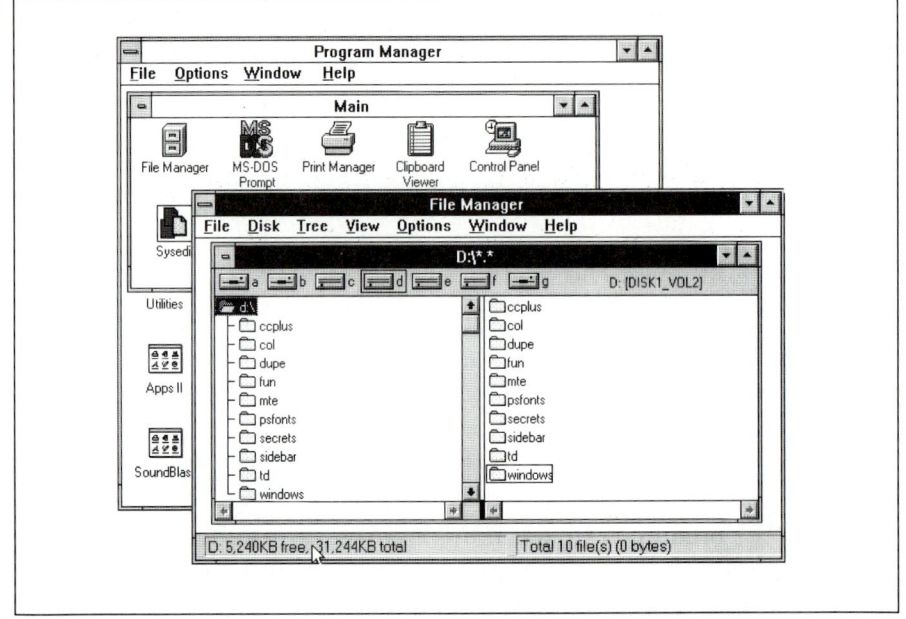

Appendix B: Installation

only 5240Kb worth of free disk space on this drive—not enough to install Quattro Pro for Windows.

To begin the installation, first make sure that you are running Wiindows. Then place the first disk in your floppy disk drive. From the Program Manager menu, select File | Run, type **A:INSTALL** in the Command Line field (if the installation disk is in drive A), and choose OK. If the disk is in drive B, enter **B:INSTALL**. If you are using Windows 3.1 or later, you can use the Browse button in the Run dialog box to select the INSTALL program through a standard Windows file selection dialog box in the usual manner.

A few moments after you choose OK in the Run dialog box, a dialog box like the one in Figure B-2 will appear. You need to fill this in with your name, the name of your organization, and the program serial number (you can press the TAB key to move from one field to the next).

You also need to check that the Install To entry (a default is suggested) is correct and that the drive selected has enough space for the installation you want to perform (the space available should be greater than the space required, as in Figure B-2). Installing the Database Desktop is optional

FIGURE B-2 Complete this dialog box before continuing with Install

and, since it takes up quite a lot of room, you should not install it at this point unless you know you will be needing it (you can always use INSTALL to install the Database Desktop at a later date).

If you are installing Quattro Pro on a network, you should click the Network Installation button. This pops up a dialog box like this:

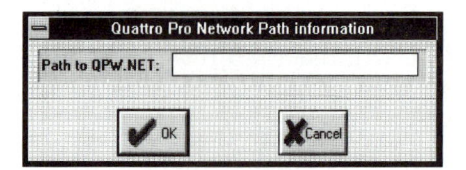

```
Quattro Pro Network Path information
Path to QPW.NET: [          ]
         OK        Cancel
```

Here you enter the drive and directory for the QPW.NET file that Quattro Pro installs when you are using the program on a network. This should be a directory with read/write access for all Quattro Pro users (see the network installation section of the manuals for more information on network installation).

When you have entered the information in the Quattro Pro for Windows dialog box, choose Install. The INSTALL program starts copying files to the hard disk while the screen displays a driver's eye view of a road through the desert, complete with "byte-o-meter" that shows the progress of the installation procedure. Several billboards also appear, offering information about the program and a useful reminder to register your copy of Quattro Pro. After the first disk has been installed, the program beeps and you are prompted to insert the second disk, as shown in Figure B-3, which also shows the registration reminder.

Insert Disk #2 and choose OK. Repeat this process until all of the original program disks have been copied. Note that you cannot simply use DOS or the File Manager to copy the original files to your hard disk, since the files on the original disk are compressed and unusable in this compressed form. When the installation is complete, place the original disks in a safe place.

After installation, you are returned to the Windows desktop. You will find that a new group called Quattro Pro for Windows has been created. This contains an icon for Quattro Pro and, if you have chosen to install it, an icon for Database Desktop. Double-click on the Quattro Pro program icon to make sure that the program runs (keyboard users can

Appendix B: Installation   **635**

FIGURE B-3 You are prompted to insert the next disk—then choose OK to continue

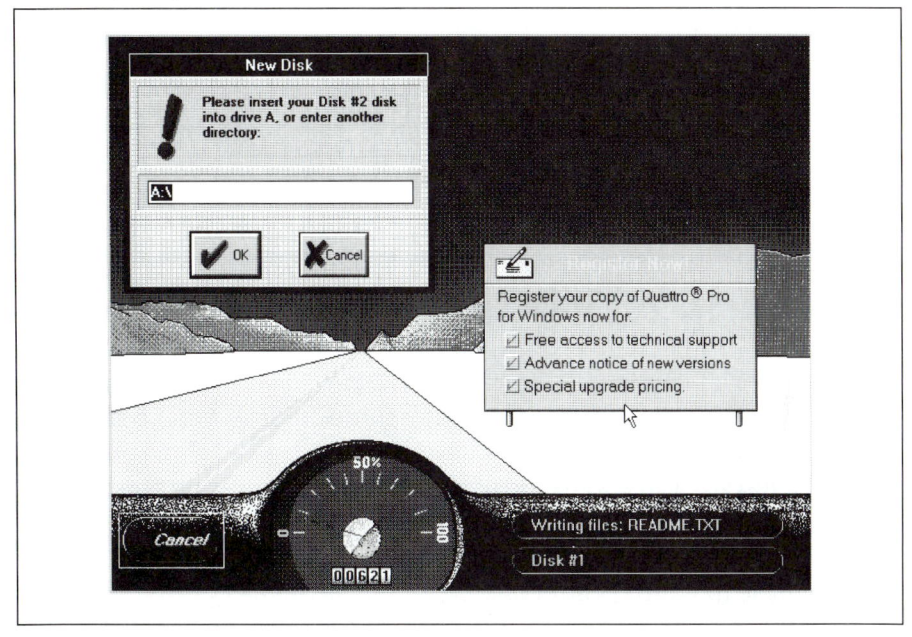

use the arrow keys to highlight the icon and then press ENTER to load the program).

The Big Screen

Since all screen and printer activity is handled by Windows rather than Quattro Pro, the installation procedure for Quattro Pro makes no mention of screen settings or printers. When you installed Windows, you had to tell it the type of display being used. With some display systems you can choose between several different screen resolution and color settings. The resolution setting determines how sharp the screen appears and is measured as lines and rows, as in 640×480, which is the basic VGA setting. A higher resolution, such as 800×600, means that objects on the screen can be drawn smaller while retaining legibility. This allows Windows to "zoom out" and show you a larger work area.

The color setting is often stated along with the resolution, as in 800×600×16, meaning that 16 colors are used. Many display systems can show more colors, as in 800×600×256. However, the more colors you use, the longer it takes Windows to draw the screen. Windows 3.1 comes with an 800×600×16 driver that is particularly fast and can be used with a wide range of Super VGA cards.

Choosing a Printer

You can install a printer for Windows at any time, using the Printers tool in the Control Panel, a program that is usually found in the Main program group. You can see the Control Panel and the Printers dialog box in the background of Figure B-4. Whatever printer models you install through the Printers dialog box will be available in Quattro Pro. If you want a particular printer to be the default printer, highlight the model in the Installed Printers list and use the Set as Default Printer button. This

FIGURE B-4 Setting up a printer for use with Windows

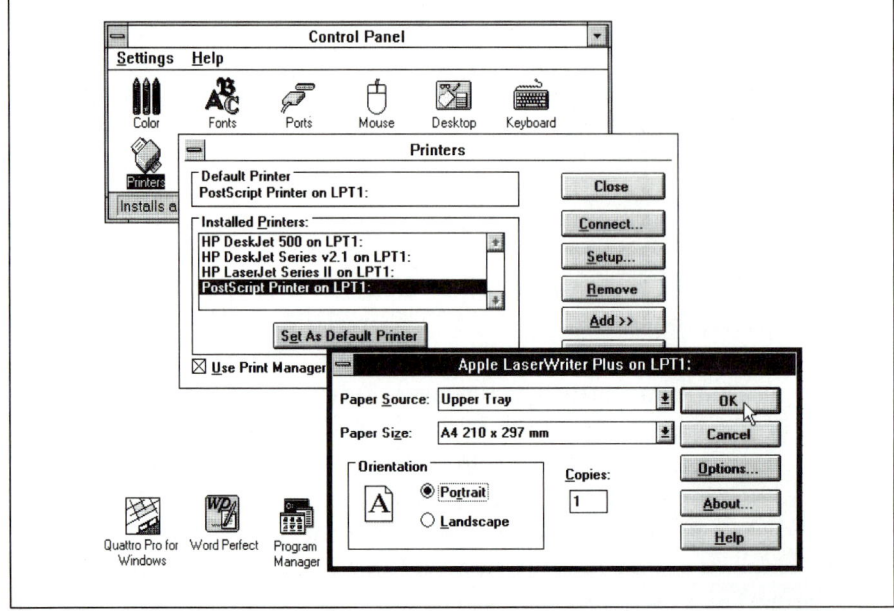

printer will then be the default printer in Quattro Pro as well as any other Windows applications.

Note You can use the File | Printer Setup command within Quattro Pro to select a different printer.

You can use the Setup button in the Printers dialog box to adjust the default settings for each printer. In Figure B-4, the Setup button was chosen while the PostScript Printer was highlighted in the Installed Printers list. Windows responded with the dialog box shown in the bottom right of the screen. This allows you to adjust Paper Source, Page Size, Orientation, and Copies. Changes you make here are also reflected as the default settings for this printer when you use it in Quattro Pro. Note that the setup dialog box differs from printer to printer in order to accommodate features unique to that model.

As you probably know, one of the great advantages of Windows is that it can display text in a variety of different styles. A specific shape and size of characters and numbers is referred to as a *font*. A font consists of a typestyle or letter shape, such as Times or Helvetica; a point size, usually between 6 and 72; and an optional attribute, such as bold or italic. Quattro Pro can use all of the fonts you have installed in your version of Windows, including those supplied by Adobe and BitStream, and you can mix and match as many fonts as you like. Bear in mind that scalable fonts will give you a closer match between what you see on the screen and what is printed out. Examples of scalable fonts are the TrueType fonts supplied with Windows 3.1 and those supported by Adobe Type Manager and BitStream Facelift.

The Data Directory

When Quattro Pro is successfully installed, you might want to think about where you will store your notebook files. A good place to use is a subdirectory of the QPW directory. The Quattro Pro installation program creates two subdirectories for you. One is called CLIPART and contains graphics files that you can use when editing charts. The other subdirectory is SAMPLES, which contains sample notebook files. You can see these subdirectories displayed by File Manager in Figure B-5, which

FIGURE B-5 Creating a directory with the File Manager

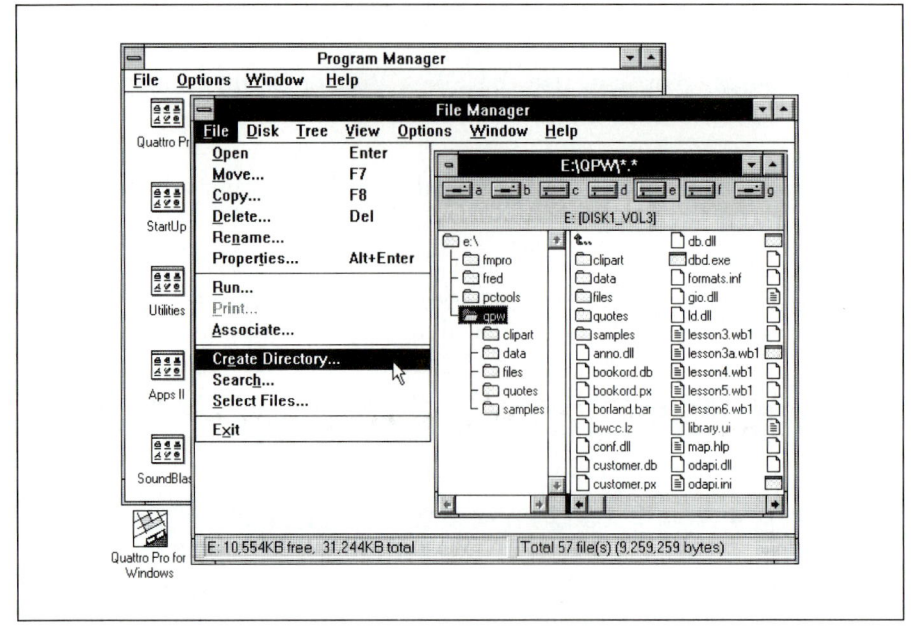

shows a typical directory arrangement for Quattro Pro. The QPW directory was created during installation, as were CLIPART and SAMPLES. The DATA, FILES, and QUOTES directories were created by the user to store notebook files.

In addition to the sample notebook files in SAMPLES, the Quattro Pro installation program copies other data files to your hard disk. These are files used in the tutorial that comes with the program and they are copied to the QPW directory. You might want to use File Manager to move these files to your data directory.

To create a subdirectory of the QPW directory, highlight it on the left of the file window, as shown in Figure B-5, and then issue the File | Create Directory command. In the dialog box that is presented, type the name, such as DATA, and choose OK. To use this directory as the normal or default directory for your notebooks, switch to Quattro Pro and press ALT-F12 to display the Application dialog box. Move to the Startup page and use the Directory setting to record the name of the directory.

Appendix B: Installation   **639**

If you do not make an entry in the Directory field but leave it blank, Quattro Pro will use the program directory (QPW) or the directory you specify as the Working directory in the Program Item Properties setting for the Quattro Pro program icon (this is possible in Windows 3.1 and later).

In fact, you can set up several different program icons for Quattro Pro and set different working directories for each one. To set a working directory for a Windows program, select the program icon and press ALT-ENTER. This produces the Program Item Properties dialog box shown in Figure B-6.

The title that appears under the icon is entered in the Description field. The program path and name are entered in the Command Line field. The Working Directory field is where you put the name of the directory that you want Quattro Pro to use as the default directory when this icon is used to load the program. Note that if you later enter a directory in the Directory field on the Startup page of the Application settings in Quattro Pro it will override the Working Directory setting in the program icon settings.

FIGURE B-6 Using the Program Item Properties dialog box

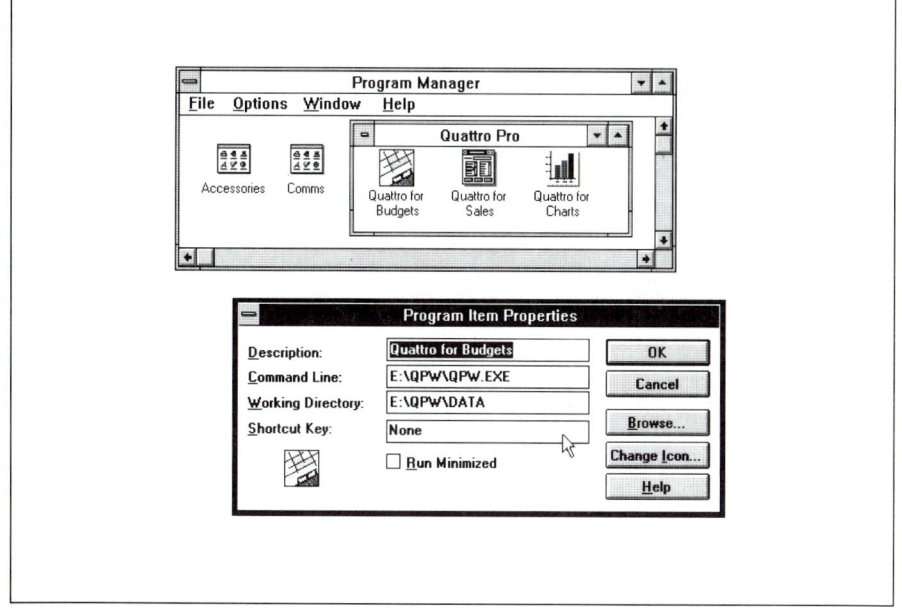

To create a new icon for Quattro Pro, open the program group in which you want the icon to appear and then use the File | New command on the Program Manager menu. Check that Program Item is checked and then choose OK. A blank Program Item Properties dialog box will appear. When you have entered the program name in the Command Line field, you can select Change Icon to select one of the many icons that are stored in the QPW.EXE program file.

An Autoload File

If there is a notebook that you use every time you work with Quattro Pro, you can have the file loaded automatically whenever Quattro Pro is launched. There are several ways to do this. You can enter the name of the file in the Autoload File field of the Startup page in the Application settings. Alternatively, you can leave that setting as QUATTRO.WB1 and save your autoload notebook with this name. If the autoload file is stored in the working data directory set on the Startup page, you need only enter the name of the file. If the file you want autoloaded is not in the working directory you must include the full path to the file.

You can also get a file autoloaded by including it in the Command Line field of the Program Item Properties dialog box, described in the previous section and shown in Figure B-6. For example, to load BUDGET.WB1 stored in E:\QPW\DATA\BUDGET.WB1, the entry in the Command Line field would be

E:\QPW\QPW.EXE E:\QPW\DATA\BUDGET.WB1

This approach requires that the full path to the file be stated. For an explanation of file paths see the next section.

The PATH Statement

Installation of Quattro Pro is usually quite straightforward. However, there is one area that might present problems: the PATH. If you have used DOS before, you will know that when you type the name of a

Appendix B: Installation 641

program file at the DOS prompt and then press ENTER, DOS looks for a file in the current directory that has the name that you have entered, plus one of the valid program file extensions (COM, EXE, and BAT). For example, if you enter **Q**, DOS looks in the current directory for a file called Q.COM, Q.EXE, or Q.BAT. If such a file is found in the current directory, DOS loads it. If such a file is not found in the current directory, DOS returns the rather unfriendly message "Bad command or file name," *unless* your system has a PATH setting in effect.

The PATH setting is created by the PATH command, which you issue at the DOS prompt. The PATH setting tells DOS which directories should be searched for a program file when it cannot be found in the current directory. For example, the following command tells DOS to look in the root directory of drive C, the Windows directory, and the \DOS subdirectory, as well as the current directory:

PATH = C:\;C:\DOS;C:\WINDOWS

Note that the three directory statements are separated by a semicolon. The following statement tells DOS to look in the same directories, plus the Quattro Pro program directory:

PATH = C:\;C:\DOS;C:\WINDOWS;C:\QPW

This means when DOS is looking for program files, it will look in C:\QPW, as well as the other directories. Adding the Quattro Pro program directory to the PATH helps to ensure smooth running of the program.

You can use the PATH command at the DOS prompt at any time. If you simply enter **PATH**, DOS tells you what the current setting is. If you enter **PATH** followed by the equal sign and one or more directory names, then those directories become the current path setting, superseding the previous setting. Typically, a PATH statement is incorporated in the AUTOEXEC.BAT file to set the various paths required for the programs you normally run.

If you want to check that your Quattro Pro program directory has been correctly added to the PATH statement in your AUTOEXEC.BAT file (this is a good idea), use the System Configuration Editor program, otherwise known as Sysedit. This is a small program that comes with Windows and is usually stored in the \WINDOWS\SYSTEM directory. To use Sysedit, you first issue the File | Run command from the Program Manager menu.

In the Command Line field you type **\WINDOWS\SYSTEM\SYSEDIT** or use the Browse button to find the SYSEDIT.EXE file. When you have completed the Command Line entry, select OK. Windows loads a special version of the Notepad program and opens the four files that control how your system works: SYSTEM.INI, WIN.INI, CONFIG.SYS, and AUTOEXEC.BAT.

After you have made the necessary changes to these files, you can select File | Exit, and the program will prompt you to save any changes you have made. You will need to exit Windows and restart your computer before any changes to AUTOEXEC.BAT take effect.

APPENDIX C

Questions and Support

*T*echnology as powerful as that used by today's personal computers is not always easy to understand and is bound to give rise to questions. This appendix provides some suggestions for when you run into problems using Quattro Pro, along with answers to some frequently asked questions.

Getting Support

When you are facing a problem using Quattro Pro, one of the first things to do is take a break. Give yourself a few minutes away from the computer to relax. You can then return to the problem in a better, and often clearer, frame of mind. If that does not help, trying asking fellow workers for their suggestions. Describing the problem to someone else can often help you see the solution. Be sure to check relevant sections in the manual. Check the spelling and syntax of any formula, functions, or macro commands you are using. Refer to the index of this book for the relevant subject. If you still do not have an acceptable answer, consider the following sources of support.

Written Support

Don't underestimate the venerable process of putting the problem into words and putting those words on paper. This can sometimes solve the problem as you think it through. If you still need help, send the problem, together with any printouts, screen prints, plus the software version and the serial number from the front of the original program disk to the following address:

Borland International, Inc.
1800 Green Hills Road
P.O. Box 660001
Scotts Valley, CA 95066-0001
1-408-438-5300

Although this is not the fastest way of finding support, it is sometimes the best way, particularly if you feel you need to present printed data from the program.

Online Support

If you have a modem and communications software, you should consider subscribing to CompuServe, the online information bank. Here you will find the Borland Applications Forum (accessed with GO BORAPP from the CompuServe prompt). The Forum contains answers to many common questions about Quattro Pro, as well as useful Quattro Pro notebook files that you can download. There is also a message and discussion system for exchanging views and news with other Quattro Pro users. Many computer stores and bookstores sell sign-up packages for CompuServe, or you can write to

CompuServe Information Service, Inc.
P.O. Box 20212
Columbus, OH 43220

Note that CompuServe is available via a local phone call in many countries, so although it is operated from somewhere in the United States, it is a valuable support system and forum for users all around the world.

Registration

If you have just bought Quattro Pro, be sure to fill out and return the user registration card in the front of the manual. Registering your software protects your investment in it and ensures that you will hear of upgrades and related product announcements.

Questions

This section contains several tips and questions that have cropped up while working with Quattro Pro.

Can I drag-and-drop a single notebook entry?

Quattro Pro does not allow "single cell drag-and-drop," meaning that you cannot use the mouse alone to move or copy one cell at a time. You have to select at least two cells before you can drag with the mouse pointer to move cells, or CTRL-drag to copy them. The reason for this is safety, since it would be easy for careless movement of the mouse to accidentally move the wrong cell. However in most circumstances, you can move or copy a single cell entry by selecting an empty cell adjacent to the cell entry you want to move.

Consider the entry in A1 of Figure C-1. To move this large label using drag-and-drop, select A1..B1, point to the selected cells, press and hold down the left mouse button, and drag the cells to their new location.

Note that if completion of your drag-and-drop action will overwrite existing entries in the spreadsheet, you get the message shown in Figure C-1 in the Alert dialog box: "Overwrite non-blank cells in destination block?" You can press ENTER to choose OK or press ESC to choose cancel. The same technique can be used to move the label First Quarter in B3. You could select B3..B4 before dragging. The label Chicago in B2 can be dragged by first selecting B1..B2, since B1 is actually an empty cell. With a little ingenuity you can use drag-and-drop in many situations, and Quattro Pro will help you avoid overwriting valuable data by mistake.

Can I change the color of the Quattro Pro work area?

You will note that the workspace around the notebook in Figure C-1 is black. You can make this area any color you like by using the Color

Appendix C: Questions and Support 647

FIGURE C-1 Sample notebook

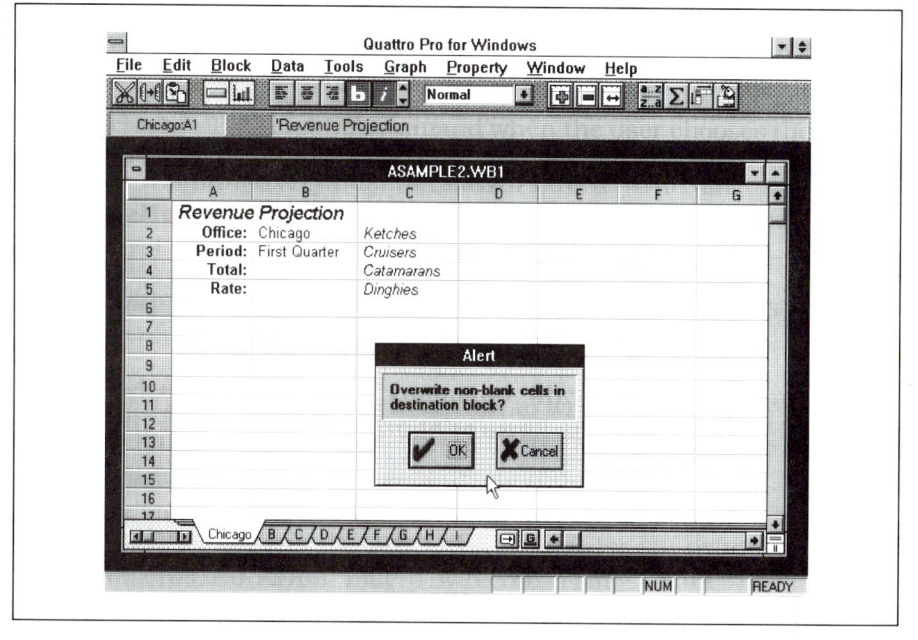

settings in the Windows Control Panel. The Screen Element you want to change is known as Application Workspace.

How do I display the names of days of the week for dates?

Virtually any unit of measure can be accommodated in a custom format in the User defined option of the Active Block dialog box. There are symbols for creating custom date formats, such as TWeekday Month D YYYY, which would display the last day of the century as Friday December 31, 1999.

To create a new custom format, you can edit the entry in the Formats defined field. Type the symbols that you want and when you choose OK, the format you have defined is applied to the cells in the active block. See Chapter 7, the section entitled "User-Defined Numeric Formats," for more details on custom formats.

Can I load Quattro Pro notebooks from the File Manager?

If the file has the WB1 extension, it is already associated with Quattro Pro for Windows. All you need to do is double-click the filename or icon in the File Manager (or select it and press ENTER), and Quattro Pro will launch with the file you have chosen.

If the file is not already associated with Quattro Pro, you will get a message that no association exists for this file. The process of association is very straightforward. Choose Associate from the File menu, and the Associate dialog box appears. In the Files with Extension box, type the extension, such as WK1, that you want to associate to Quattro Pro. In the Associate With box, type **QPW**. Choose the OK button, and the file is associated with Quattro Pro. Now when you double-click it, it will launch Quattro Pro—provided, of course, that it is a type that Quattro Pro can read. See Chapter 8 for details on which files Quattro Pro can read. Windows will remember this association, and you will be able to launch directly from the File Manager in future sessions.

Index

2.5-D bar graphs, 453
2-D graphs, 447, 449-453
3-D graphs, 447, 453-457, 471
& (ampersand), **58**, 233, 557-558
<> (angle brackets), **58**, 233, 335
' (apostrophe), **33**, **58**, 81
* (asterisk), **36**, **58**, 233
@ (at sign)
    in formulas, 43, 243
    on SpeedBar, 32, 242
    as value indicator, 84
@Functions, 103-104
  See also Functions
\ (backslash)
    as cell fill character, 64-65
    in DOS syntax, 179
    as label indicator, 58
    in macros, 575
    versus REPEAT function, 560
    text graphs and, 497
^ (caret)
    as exponent operator, 233

    labels and, 33-34, 58
: (colon), **58**, 179
, (commas), in numbers, **35**, 41-42, 85-86
{} (curly braces), 32, 575, 578
$ (dollar sign), 84, 124-125
= (equal to operator), 233, 335
! (exclamation point), 58
> (greater than operator), 233, 335
>= (greater than or equal to operator), 233, 335
< (less than operator), 233, 335
<= (less than or equal to operator), 233, 335
– (minus sign), 165, 233
<> (not equal to operator), 233, 335
() (parentheses), 58, 84, 231, 233-234
% (percent sign), 58
. (period), 182
+ (plus sign), **37**, 103, 233
# (pound sign), 84, 336
" (quotation mark), **33**, **58**, 336

649

? (question mark), 58
; (semicolon), 58
/ (slash), **26**, 81, 233
    slash commands, 594
[] (square brackets), 58
~ (tilde), 58
_ (underline symbol), 58
| (vertical bar), 58, 212

A

ABS (absolute value) function, 252
Absolute cell references, 123-127
Absolute key (F4), 125-127
Absolute page references, 124-125
Accelerated cost recovery calculation, 284-285, 293-294
Access control. *See* Passwords
ACOS function, 297
Active Block dialog box, **39-42**, 394-400
    Alignment setting, 58-61
    Auto Width setting, 68-69
    Data Entry Input option, 81, 344-345
    default levels and, 368-369
    Define Style command and, 394
    Font settings, 219-221
    formatting with, 92-95
    Line Drawing setting, 221-223
    Shading setting, 223-224
    Text Color settings, 221
    type style settings, 220-221
    User defined option, 396-400
    See also Blocks
Active Notebook dialog box, **382-388**
    default levels and, 368
    Display settings, 368, 388
    Macro Library setting, 388, 595-596
    Palette settings, 386-387
    Recalc settings, 382-385
    Zoom Factor setting, 118-119, 204-205, 354, 360, 385-386
    See also Notebooks
Active Page dialog box, **388-393**
    Border settings, 393
    Conditional Color settings, 390-392
    default settings and, 54-57, 368
    Default Width settings, 393
    Display Zeros setting, 392-393
    Grid Line settings, 367-368, 393
    Label Alignment setting, 58-61, 392
    Line Color setting, 390
    macros and, 569-570
    Name setting, 389
    Protection setting, 390
    See also Pages
Addition operator (+), 233
{ADDMENU} command, 618-619
Adobe Type Manager, 10, 21
Advanced Math option, Tools menu, 511, 518
Aggregate functions, **245-251**
    AVG (average value) function, 249-250
    COUNT function, 249
    MAX (maximum value) function, 250
    MIN (minimum value) function, 250-251
    STD (standard deviation) function, 251
    SUM function, 104-107, 245-247
    SUMPRODUCT function, 248
    VAR (variance) function, 251
    See also Functions
Aliases command, File menu, 425

Index

Alignment
    in cells, 32, 84
    changing, 40
    of graphic objects, 499
    of headers and footers, 212
    of labels, 33-34, 58-61, 392
    of numbers, 84
Allways files, 408
ALT key
    + F3 key, 45, 242-244
    + F4 key, 48, 195
    + TAB key, 626
    international characters and, 400
    key letters and, 26
    menu bar and, 27
Ampersand (&), **58**, 233, 557-558
#AND# operator, 233, 336
Angle brackets (<>)
    as label indicators, 58
    as not equal to operator, 233, 335
ANSI codes, for international characters, 400
Answer tables
    copying to notebooks, 427-429
    generating, 425-427
    Query By Example and, 429-430
Apostrophe ('), 33, 58, 81
Application command, Properties menu, 181, 369
Application development tools, **600-620**
    custom SpeedBars, 601
    dialog box creation example, 609-611
    Link commands, 601, 611-616
    macros, 601-603, 617-618
    types of, 600-602
    UI Builder command, 601, 603-611
Application dialog box, **369-382**

3-D Syntax option, 370-371
Clock Display option, 370
default levels and, 368
Display Options, 368, 370
International settings, 371-374, 400
Macro settings, 380
SpeedBar settings, 381-382
Startup settings, 181, 374-379
Applications
    data exchange and, 542
    defined, 623
Area graphs, **451**, 455, 458, 471
Arithmetic functions, **251-256**
    ABS (absolute value) function, 252
    EXP (exponent) function, 255
    INT (number as integer) function, 252
    LN (natural log) function, 256
    LOG function, 256
    MOD (remainder) function, 252-253
    RND (random number) function, 253
    ROUND function, 127-129, 254-255
    SQRT (square root) function, 255-256
    See also Functions
Arithmetic operators, 230, 233-234
Arrange Icons command, Window menu, 358
Arrow keys
    cell navigation with, 29, 49
    in dialog boxes, 50
    in EDIT mode, 75
    entering data with, 34
    menu system navigation with, 26-27

ASCII codes, 559-560
ASCII files, 541
ASIN function, 297
Aspect ratio, of graphs, 482-484
Asterisk (*), **36**, **58**, 233
At sign (@)
    in formulas, 43, 243
    on SpeedBar, 32, 242
    as value indicator, 84
ATAN function, 297
ATAN2 function, 297
Auto Width command, 67-69
AUTOEXEC.BAT, 641-642
Autoload File option, 377
Autoload macros, 580, 590
Automatic recalculation feature, 382-385
AVG (average value) function, 249-250
Axis, graph, **442**, 469-470

B

Background printing, 200
Background recalculation feature, 382-385
Backslash (\)
    as cell fill character, 64-65
    in DOS syntax, 179
    as label indicator, 58
    in macros, 575
    versus REPEAT function, 560
    text graphs and, 497
BACKSPACE key, 33, 74
Bar graphs
    properties of, 471, 474
    rotated, 458-459
    three-dimensional, 453-454
    two-dimensional, 449-450
Bar symbol (|), 58, 212
{BEEP} command, 584-585

Beep setting, 378
Bitmap Button tool, UI Builder SpeedBar, 606
BitStream FaceLift, 10, 21
Block arguments, 242
Block coordinates, 131-133
Block Copy dialog box, 135-136
Block Fill dialog box, 520
Block menu, **129-170**
    Copy command, 135-140
    Delete menu, 151-152
    Fill command, 156-159
    Insert Break command, 215
    Insert Columns dialog box, 143-144
    Insert menu, 140-141, 144-146
    Insert Rows dialog box, 141-143
    inserting pages with, 146-149
    Insert | File command, 417-418
    Model Copy option, 137-139
    Move command, 130-135
    Move Pages command, 149-151
    Names command, 161-165, 236-238
    Names | Labels command, 166-167
    Reformat command, 540
    reverse copying with, 139-140
    Transpose command, 168-169
    Values command, 169-170
    See also Edit menu commands; EDIT mode
Block Move dialog box, 131-132
Block names, **161-165**
    creating, 161-162
    deleting and tracking, 163-165
    in formulas, 164-165, 236-238
    navigating with, 165
    rules for, 163
Block Reformat dialog box, 540

Index

Blocks
    changing properties of, 39-42
    compound, 61, 104
    formulas and, 103-107, 234-235
    printing, 196-199
    selecting, 38-39
  See also Active Block dialog box; Cells
Bold setting, **67**, 220-221
Borders
    and maximizing windows, 367-368
    printing, 210-211
    settings for, 393
Borland International, 644-645
Brackets. *See* Angle brackets; Curly braces; Square brackets
{BRANCH} command, **577-578**, 592
Breakpoints, in macros, 596-598
Bullet codes, for text graphs, 497-498
Button tool, SpeedBar, 576-577
Buttons, creating, **576-578**, 606-607

C

{CALC} command, 590
Calc key (F9), 236, 304
Calculations. *See* Formulas; Functions
Capitalization
    in criteria tables, 334
    passwords and, 405
    string functions for, 564
CAPS LOCK key, 28, 32-33
Caret (^)
    as exponent operator, 233
    labels and, 33-34, 58
Cascade command, Window menu, 358-359
Case sensitivity. *See* Capitalization; Lowercase
Cell blocks. *See* Blocks

Cell commands, Macro menu, 594
Cell fill character (\), 64-65
Cell formulas option, Print Options dialog box, 209-210
Cell identifier, 28-29
Cell references
    absolute, 123-127
    and deleting cells, 151-152
    relative, 122-123
    SpeedFill button and, 155
Cells
    alignment in, 32, 58-61
    changing properties of, 39-42
    defined, 4, 29
    editing, 35-36, 74-80
    formatting, 35, 38-42
    moving, 130-135
    navigating between, 29-30, 49-50
    selecting, 111, 171
  See also Block menu; Blocks; Labels; Values
Centered alignment, **33-34**, 212
CHAR function, 559
Characters Unit setting, 56-57
Charts. *See* Graphs
Check Box tool, UI Builder SpeedBar, 606
CHOOSE function, 293, 303-304, 557
Circles, drawing, 496
Circular references, in formulas, 240
Clear command, 76-79, 102
Clear Contents command, 76-79, 102
Clicking, 17
Client applications, 542
Clipboard
    data exchange via, 541, 542-544
    versus Paste Link copying, 545-546

Clipboard buttons. *See* Copy command; Cut command; Paste command
CLIs (Command-Line Interfaces), 403-404
Close All command, File menu, 194
Close command, File menu, 48, 192, 360
CODE function, 560
Coefficient of determination, 513
Colon (:), 58, 179
Color Control tool, UI Builder SpeedBar, 608
Color settings
    Active Block Shading property, 223-224
    Active Page dialog box, 390-392
    Edit Palette Color dialog box, 386-387
    Print Preview screen, 204
    for Quattro Pro work area, 646-647
Column graphs, 452, 455, 471
Column Width settings
    changing, 40-42, 47, 62-64
    changing default for, 53-57
    in databases, 323
Columns
    cell references and, 125
    deleting, 151-152
    fields and, 12
    inserting, 143-146
    printing and, 224-226
    selecting entire, 69-70
    setting width of, 69-70
    See also Rows
Combination graphs, 448-449, 458-460
Combine command, Tools menu, 413, 415-417

Combo Box tool, UI Builder SpeedBar, 607
Command equivalents, Macro menu, 594
Command-Line Interfaces (CLIs), 403-404
Commas (,), in numbers, 35, 41-42, 85-86
Comparison operators, 233, 334-336
Compatible Keys option, Application dialog box, 378-379
Compound blocks, 61, 104
Compound growth rate functions (IRATE and RATE), 277-278
CompuServe support, 645
Concatenation of text, 557-559
Conditional breakpoints, in macros, 598
Conditional Color settings, 390-392
Constants, in formulas, 232
Contract key, 165
Control button
    notebook title bar, 28-29
    program title bar, 24-25
Control Panel icon, 17
Controls. *See* Buttons; Dialog boxes; SpeedBar
Copy command
    Block menu, 135-140
    data exchange via, 541
    formulas and, 235-236
    Model option, 137-139
    and Paste command, 97-101
    reverse copying with, 139-140
    SpeedBar and, 27
COS function, 297
COUNT function, 249
CPUs, 16-17
Criteria formulas, 334-336
Criteria Tables

cross-tabulations and, 348-351
defining, 326-328
locating, 329-330
multiple criteria in, 330-332
techniques for using, 332-333
See also Queries
Cross (X) button, 71
Cross-referencing labels, 557-558
Cross-tabulations, in databases, 348-351
CTERM (number of periods) function, 270, 271
CTRL key
+ BREAK key, 574
+ F4 key, 360
mouse operation and, 69, 87, 105
navigating with, 49, 50
Curly braces ({}), 32, 575, 578
Currency style, 92, 93
Current Object option, Properties menu, 39
Cursor keys. *See* Arrow keys
Cut command
and Paste command, 102-103
SpeedBar and, 27, 79

D

Data
combining, 415-417
exporting, 409-413, 415
extracting, 413-415
extracting from foreign files, 418-421
importing from foreign databases, 342-343, 418-421
recovery of, 406-407
Data analysis. *See* Frequency distribution analysis; Goal seeking; Optimizer feature; Regression analysis; What-If tables; XY graphs
Data entry, **34-35**
correcting errors in, 71-73
for databases, 343-345
of dates, 81
error messages and, 80
in Group mode, 116-118
reentry and, 75
of text with numbers, 81
Data Entry Input option, Active Block dialog box, 81, 344-345
Data exchange
with Clipboard, 541-544
with embedded objects, 542, 548-551
with hot links, 8, 428-429, 541-542, 544-548
overview of, 342-343
See also Foreign files
Data extraction, **413-415**
from foreign files, 418-421
Data menu. *See* Database commands
Data Parse dialog box, 553
Data points, 442
Data protection. *See* Security
Data Query dialog box, **327**
Delete button, 340-341
Extract button, 337-340
Extract Unique button, 339-340
Field Names option, 333-334
Data recovery, 406-407
Data series
defined, 442
graphs and, 440, 461-465
Data types, 30-34
See also Labels; Values
Database Blocks, 326-328
See also Queries
Database commands

Database Desktop command,
    422-423
Frequency command, 519-521
Parse command, 551-556
Query command, 418-421
Restrict Input command, 343-344
Sort command, 314-319
What-If command, 5, 346-351,
    524-526
Database Desktop, **421-435**
    copying query data from, 427-429
    creating queries in, 422-427
    overview of, 421-422
    Query By Example in, 12, 422,
        429-430
    querying two tables in, 430-432
    Table Query command and,
        433-435
Database functions, **256-260**
    DMAX (maximum value)
        function, 258
    DMIN (minimum value) function,
        258-259
    DSTD (standard deviation)
        function, 259
    DSUM (sum value) function, 259
    DVAR (variance) function,
        259-260
    syntax of, 256-258, 345-346
    What-If command and, 348-351
    See also Functions
Database management software,
    320-321
Databases, **319-325**
    column widths and, 323
    creating, 322-323
    cross-tabulations of, 348-351
    data entry techniques for,
        343-345
    defining, 319-320

extracting data to, 415
fields and records in, 321-322
formulas in, 324-325
importing data from foreign,
    342-343
limits of Quattro Pro, 322
problem data in, 323-324
Quattro Pro features for, 2, 11-12
See also Foreign files; Queries
Date Format settings, international,
    373
Date functions, **299-304**
    CHOOSE function and, 303-304
    creating date series with, 301-302
    DATE function, 299-300
    DATEVALUE function, 300-301
    DAY function, 302
    IF function and, 304
    MONTH function, 302-303
    NOW function, 301
    performing math with, 301
    TODAY function, 301
    YEAR function, 303
    See also Functions
Date key, 81
Date part functions, 302-304
Dates
    converting to values, 299-300
    days of the week and, 647
    Fill command and, 159-161
    formats for, 81, 95-97
Dates Only setting, 345
DATEVALUE function, 300-301
DAY function, 302
Days of the week, 647
.DB files, 424
dBASE, 418-422, 424, 430
.DBF files, 424
DDB (double-declining-balance
    depreciation) function, 283-284

Index

DDE (Dynamic Data Exchange), 8, 428-429, 541-542, 544-548
DDE commands, Macro menu, 594-595
DDELINK function, 428-429, 545-546
Debugging macros, 596-598
Decimal places
    ROUND function and, 127-129
    setting display of, 41-42, 86-88
    value indicator for, 36
    See also Numbers
Default settings
    changing, 53-57
    hierarchy of, 368-369
    for label alignment, 34
Default Width settings, 393
    changing, 53-57
    Unit setting for, 55-57
DEGREES function, 295
Degrees of Freedom, 513
Delete button, Data Query dialog box, 340-341
Delete menu, Block menu, 151-152
{DeleteMenu} command, 602
Depreciation functions, 282-285
    accelerated cost recovery and, 284-285
    DDB (double-declining-balance) function, 283-284
    SLN (straight-line) function, 283
    SYD (sum-of-years') function, 283-284
    See also Functions
Desktop dialog box, 17-19
Desktop publishing features, Quattro Pro, 10-11
Dialog boxes
    compound, 54
    creating, 603-616
    displaying custom, 616-620
    exiting, 26
    in macros, 592-593
    navigating in, 50
    in Windows, 18, 628-629
Dialog menu commands
    Connect command, 611-612
    Links command, 611, 613-616
    New SpeedBar command, 601
    Object Link dialog box, 601
Direct Drive technology, 27
Directories
    changing, 185-187
    creating, 179
    file structure and, 177-179
    installation and, 637-640
    saving files in, 48-49
Directory option, Startup settings, 375-376
Disk drives
    changing, 185-187
    requirements for, 15-16
Display settings, Active Notebook settings, 368, 388
Display Zeros setting, 392-393
Distribution analysis. *See* Frequency distribution analysis
Divider tabs. *See* Tabs
Division operator (/), 233
DMAX (maximum value) function, 258
DMIN (minimum value) function, 258-259
Documenting spreadsheets, 538-541
{DODIALOG} command, 617-618
Dollar sign ($), 84, 124-125
DOS
    PATH statement, 640-642
    Quattro Pro and, 17, 19
Double quotation mark ("), **33**, **58**, 336
Double-clicking, 17

Double-declining-balance depreciation function (DDB), 283-284
Drag-and-drop feature
    CTRL key and, 87, 105-106
    moving files with, 179-180
    overview of, 71-73
    for single cells, 646
    See also Mouse
Dragging, 17
Draw menu commands, 501
Drawing Tools, Graph window, 494-496
Drives. *See* Disk drives
DSTD (standard deviation) function, 259
DSUM (database sum value) function, 259
DVAR (database variance) function, 259-260
Dynamic Data Exchange (DDE), 8, 428-429, 541-542, 544-548
Dynamic values, 236

E

Edit Field tool, UI Builder SpeedBar, 607
Edit key (F2), 35, 75-76
Edit line. *See* Input line
Edit menu commands
    Clear command, 76-77, 102
    Clear Contents command, 76-79, 102
    Copy command, 97-101
    Cut command, 27, 79, 102-103
    data exchange via, 541
    Define Style command, 394-395
    for labels, 34
    mouse and, 36
    Paste command, 97-103

Paste Link command, 541-542, 545-548
Paste Special command, 101-102
Search and Replace command, 170-173
SpeedBar and, 27
See also Block menu
EDIT mode, **35-36**, 75-80
    customizing keystrokes for, 378-379
    Edit key (F2) and, 35, 75-76
    error messages and, 80
    insert mode in, 76
    keyboard functions in, 75, 77-79
    overstrike mode in, 76
    SPACEBAR in, 79-80
    See also Block menu
Embedding objects, 8, 542, **548-551**
Encrypting files, 403-406
END key, 30, 49, 75
Equal to operator (=), 233, 335
ERR function, 307
Error messages
    CIRC message, 240, 385
    data entry and, 80-81
    for formulas, 237-241
    "Invalid reference," 80-81, 237-238
    for queries, 328
    "Syntax error," 80
    "Unknown function," 80
    "Unknown key/command," 574-575
ESC key
    data entry and, 71
    halting macros with, 574
    menus and, 26
EXACT function, 561-562
Exclamation point (!), 58
Exit command, File menu, 48, 195-196

Index

Exit Preview button, Print Preview screen, 204
EXP (exponent) function, 255
Explode option, Pie Graph Properties dialog box, 491
Exponent operator (^), 233
Exporting. *See* Data exchange
Extend key (SHIFT-F7), 39
Extensions. *See* File extensions
Extract button, Data Query dialog box, 329, 337-340
Extract command, Tools menu, 413-415
Extract Unique button, Data Query dialog box, 339-340
Extraction, data, 413-415
  from foreign files, 418-421

F

F1 key, 26
F2 key, 35
F3 key, 45
F4 key
  + ALT key, 48, 195
  as Absolute key, 125-127
F5 key, 49
F7 key
  + SHIFT key, 39
  queries and, 330, 338-339
F9 key, 236, 304
F12 key, 39
FALSE function, 307
Field Names option, Data Query dialog box, 333-334
Fields, 11, 321-322
File commands, Macro menu, 594
File Control tool, UI Builder SpeedBar, 607-608
File Extension option, 377

File extensions
  .DB and .DBF, 424
  .PRN, 552
  .WB1, 47, 82
  .WK1 and .WK3, 182
  .WQ1, 182
  for notebooks, 182
  setting, 377
  for workspace files, 194
File Extract dialog box, 414
File Manager, Windows, 178-180, 637-638, 648
File menu commands
  Aliases command, 425
  Close All command, 194
  Close command, 48, 192, 360
  Exit command, 195-196
  Named Settings command and, 199, 218
  New command, 189-190
  Open command, 190-192
  Print Preview command, 203-205
  Printer Setup command, 200, 217-219
  Retrieve command, 190-192
  Save All command, 193-194
  Workspace commands, 194-195
  See also Save As command; Save command
File specifications, 187-189
File Types option, Save File dialog box, **187-189**, 408
Filenames. *See* Naming conventions
Files
  Allways, 408
  automatic loading of, 377
  directories and, 177-179
  exporting, 409-413, 415
  inserting, 417-419
  moving, 179-180

naming, 47-48, 181-182
passwords for, 403-406
paths and, 181-182
Quattro Pro-compatible formats, **409**
selecting, 180
types of, 187-189
Wysiwyg/Impress, 408, 410
See also Foreign files; Save As command; Save command; Save File dialog box
Fill command, Block menu, **156-159**
dates and, 159-161
What-If tables and, 523-524
Financial functions, **260-285**
depreciation functions, 282-285
investment functions, 270-282
payment functions, 261-270
See also Functions
FIND function, 561
FIND mode, 328
Fit button, SpeedBar, 67-69
Fixed values, 236
Fixed-pitch printers, 57
Flat-file database managers, 321
Floating graphs
creating graphs from, 439-441
deleting, 444
displaying in graph window, 483
setting attributes of, 445
Font property settings, 40-41, 219-221
Fonts
in graphs, 486
monospaced, 57
printing and, 219-221
proportional, 57
scalable, 21
in Windows, 10, 21
See also Type styles

Footer settings, Page Setup dialog box, 212-213
Foreign files, **407-413**
data extraction and; 413-415, 418-421
opening, 407-409
saving, 407
writing to, 409-413
See also Data exchange
Formatting
with Active Block dialog box, 92-95
cells, 39-42
editing Normal style, 394-395
formulas, 85-88
long labels and, 538-541
named styles and, 88-92
user-defined numeric formats, 396-400
See also SpeedFormat button
Formulas, **103-110**, 230-241
blocks and, 103-107, 234-235
cell references and, 122-127
common errors in, 237-241
converting to values, 236
creating, 106-107
criteria, 334-336
in databases, 324-325
editing, 235-236, 240-241
formatting and, 85-88
formulas within, 231
versus functions, 103
IF functions in, 231-232
operators in, 230, 233-234
overview of, 36-38, 230-232
page references and, 124-125
in queries, 334-336
SpeedSum button and, 107-110
syntax of, 230-232, 240
values and, 230, 232

Index

See also Functions
Forward slash (/). *See* Slash
Free-floating objects, 548
Frequency distribution analysis, 518-522
Frequency Tables dialog box, 521
Function arguments, 43, 104, 241-242
Function statements, 241
Functions, **241-308**
    aggregate, 245-251
    arithmetic, 251-256
    blocks and, 103-107
    CHOOSE function, 293, 303-304, 557
    database, 256-260
    date, 299-304
    DDELINK function, 545-546
    depreciation, 282-285
    displaying list of, 242-244
    ERR function, 307
    FALSE function, 307
    financial, 260-285
    versus formulas, 103
    guidelines for using, 244-245
    IF function, 285-289, 304, 556-557, 562
    INDEX function, 284-285, 293-294
    investment, 270-282
    IS, 307-308
    logical, 285-294
    lookup table, 289-294
    NA function, 307
    overview of, 42-46
    payment, 261-270
    ROUND function, 127-129, 254-255
    special, 306-307
    string, 308, 558-565
    SUM function, 104-107, 245-247
    syntax of, 242-244
    time, 304-306
    in Tools menu, 245
    trigonometric, 294-298
    TRUE function, 307
    values in, 232
    See also Formulas; entries for above function types
Functions key (ALT-F3), 45, 242-244
Future value, 264-265
FV function, 281-282
FVAL (future value) function, 279-281

G

{GETLABEL} command, 590-591
{GETNUMBER} command, 587-589
Goal seeking, **530-531**
    multiple-variable, 531-536
Goto key (F5), 49
Graph Copy dialog box, 488
Graph menu
    Insert command, 444
    New command, 463
    Series command, 462
Graph New dialog box, **463-464**, 528
Graph Series dialog box, 462-463
Graph Title Properties dialog box, 466-468
Graph Titles dialog box, 465
Graph Types dialog box, 529
Graph window, **445-446**
    displaying floating graphs in, 483
    Drawing Tools, 494-496
Graphics buttons. *See* Graph menu
Graphics objects, **498-501**
    aligning, 499
    editing, 498-499
    grouping and ungrouping, 499
    layering, 499-501

Graphical User Interfaces (GUIs), 402-403
Graphs, **438-480**, 482-505
    2.5-D bar, 453
    3-D contour, 456
    3-D ribbon, 455-456
    3-D shaded surface, 456-457
    3-D surface, 456-457
    3-D unstacked area, 455
    area, 451, 455, 458, 471
    aspect ratio and, 482-484
    bar, 449-450, 453-454, 458-459, 471, 474
    column, 452, 455, 471
    combination, 448-449, 458-460
    copying, 487-490
    customizing, 440, 466-472, 484-487
    data series and, 440, 461-465
    deleting, 444, 479
    displaying in Graph window, 445-446
    drawing lines and shapes in, 494-496
    editing, 478
    exploded pie slice in, 490-492
    floating graphs and, 439, 440, 444, 483
    fonts in, 486
    graphic objects and, 498-501
    high-low, 451
    inserting, 444
    interactive presentations and, 504-505
    line, 451, 458-459
    logarithmic scales in, 475
    managing, 478-480
    moving, 440
    multiple, 448, 458-461, 472
    naming, 439, 443-444, 478
    overview of, 12-14, 438-441
    parts of, 441-442
    pie, 452-453, 456, 471, 486, 490-492
    printing, 478
    properties of, 468-472, 474, 482, 484-487
    rotated, 447-448, 458-459
    with secondary Y-axis, 472-475
    sizing, 440
    slide shows and, 482-483, 501-503
    source objects of, 444
    stacked bar, 449-450, 453-454
    stepped bar, 455
    text, 448, 496-498
    text in, 492-494
    three-dimensional, 447, 453-457, 471
    titles of, 440, 465-468, 470
    two-dimensional, 447, 449-453
    types of, 440, 447-449
    variance, 449
    viewing, 479
    X axis of, 442, 469-470
    XY, 451
    Y axis of, 472-478
    See also Presentation graphics
Graphs page, viewing, 442-444
Greater than operator (>), 233, 335
Greater than or equal to operator (>=), 233, 335
Grid Lines setting
    Active Page dialog box, 367-368, 393
    Print Options dialog box, 210-211
Grid Options dialog box, 606, 609
Group Box tool, UI Builder SpeedBar, 607
Group mode, **110-118**

Index

Copy command in, 135, 140
data entry in, 116-118
editing cells in, 138
inserting columns and rows in, 146
named groups in, 115-116
printing in, 197
temporary groupings and, 110-114
GUIs (Graphical User Interfaces), 402-403

H

Handles, graph, 445
Hard disk drives
    changing, 185-187
    requirements for, 15-16
Hard page breaks, 215-217
Header settings, Page Setup dialog box, 212-213
Headings settings, Print Options dialog box, 206-208
Help, technical, 644-645
Help button, 26
Hide command, Window menu, 356
Hiding columns and rows, 224-226
High-low graphs, 451
HLOOKUP function, 289-292
HOME key
    in EDIT mode, 75
    navigating with, 29-30, 49
    selecting cells with, 111
Hot links, 428-429, 541-542, 544-548
HOUR function, 306

I

Icon, for Quattro Pro, 640
Iconized display, 23-24
{IF} command, 590
IF function, 285-289, 304, 556-557, 562
Import File dialog box, 552
Importing. See Data exchange
Impress files, 408, 410
INDEX function, 284-285, 293-294
Input forms, for databases, 343-344
Input line, 28, 33
INPUT mode, 344
Inquiries. See Queries
Insert button, SpeedBar, 144-146, 148-151
Insert Columns dialog box, 143-144
Insert menu, Block menu, **140-149**
    inserting columns with, 143-144
    inserting pages with, 146-149
    inserting rows with, 141-143
    moving pages with, 149-151
    tips on using, 144-146
Insert mode, in EDIT mode, 76
Insert Object dialog box, 550
Insert Rows dialog box, 141-143
Insert | File command, Block menu, 417-418
Installation, 21-22, 632-642
Instructions. See Formulas
INT (number as integer) function, 252
Interactive commands, Macro menu, 594
Interactive presentations, 504-505
Interest payment function (IPAYMT), 268-269
Internal rate of return function (IRR), 278-279
International settings, **371-374**, 400
    Date Format settings, 373
    Language settings, 374
    Punctuation settings, 372-373
    Time Format settings, 373-374

Inverse trigonometric functions, 297
Investment functions, **270-282**
    FV function, 281-282
    FVAL (future value) function, 279-281
    IRATE (compound growth rate) function, 277-278
    IRR (internal rate of return) function, 278-279
    NPV (net present value) function, 274-277
    present value and, 271-272
    PV function, 274
    PVAL (present value) function, 272-274
    RATE function, 278
    See also Functions
IPAYMT (interest payment) function, 268-269
IRATE (compound growth rate) function, 277-278
IRR (internal rate of return) function, 278-279
IS functions, 307-308
Italic setting, 67, 220-221

K

Key letters
    in menus, 26
    in Windows, 19, 626-627
Keyboard commands, Macro menu, 593
Keyboard shortcuts
    copying with, 87-88
    creating formulas with, 45, 106-107
    defining criteria tables with, 328
    in EDIT mode, 77-79, 378-379
    for exiting, 48

    macro commands for, 593
    in POINT mode, 132
    in Quattro Pro, 49-50
    selecting blocks with, 39
    for selecting cells, 111
    in Windows, 19, 626-628
Keys, assigning macros to, 575-576

L

Label Alignment setting, Active Page dialog box, **58-61**, 392
Label indicators, 58, 81
Label tool, UI Builder SpeedBar, 607
Labels
    alignment of, 33-34, 58-61
    cell fill character and, 64-65
    changing case of, 564
    comparing, 561-562
    converting numbers to, 564
    converting to numbers, 565
    cross-referencing, 557-558
    documenting spreadsheets with, 538-541
    editing, 34
    entering, 34-35
    finding characters in, 561, 562-563
    formatting, 39-42
    long, 62-64, 538-541
    measuring length of, 563
    naming, 166-167
    overview of, 30, 32-34
    replacing characters in, 562
    versus values, 81
    width of, 62-64
    See also String functions
Labels Only setting, 345
Landscape orientation, 207, 215
Language settings, 374

Index

LEFT function, 562-563
Left-alignment, 33-34, 212
Legends, graph, 442, 469
LENGTH function, 563
Less than operator (<), 233, 335
Less than or equal to operator (<=), 233, 335
Line Color setting, 390
Line Drawing property, 221-223
Line graphs, 451, 458-459
Linear regression analysis. *See* Regression analysis
Linear Regression dialog box, 511-512
Lines
    in graphs, 494-496
    and maximizing windows, 367-368
    See also Grid Lines setting; Grid Options dialog box
Link commands, 601, 604, **611-616**
Links, data exchange via, 428-429, 541-542, 544-548
List Box tool, UI Builder SpeedBar, 607
LN (natural log) function, 256
Loan payment calculation, 43-46
Loan payment functions. *See* Payment functions
Loan tables, 266-268
Locate command, Data menu, 328-330
Locked Titles command, Window menu, 365-367
LOG function, 256
Logarithmic scales, in graphs, 475
Logical functions, **285-294**
    CHOOSE function, 293, 303-304
    HLOOKUP function, 289-292
    IF function, 285-289, 304
    INDEX function, 284-285, 293-294

lookup table functions, 289-294
    VLOOKUP function, 289-292
    See also Functions
Logical operators, 233, 334-336
Long labels, 62-64
Lookup table functions, 289-294
Lotus 1-2-3
    file extensions for, 182
    multiple-sheet spreadsheets and, 6
    versus Quattro Pro, 8, 240
LOWER function, 564
Lowercase
    in criteria tables, 334
    passwords and, 405
    string function for, 564

M

Macro commands
    {ADDMENU} command, 618-619
    {BEEP} command, 584-585
    {BRANCH} command, 577-578, 592
    {CALC} command, 590
    {DeleteMenu} command, 602
    {DODIALOG} command, 617-618
    {GETLABEL} command, 590-591
    {GETNUMBER} command, 587-589
    {IF} command, 590
    {MESSAGE} command, 583, 585-587
    {PAUSEMACRO} command, 562-563
    {PRINT} command, 591
    {QUIT} command, 592
    {RETURN} command, 591-592
    syntax of, 575, 583-586
    types of, 593-595

{WindowHide} command, 596
Macro Debugger dialog box, 596-597
Macro Library option, 388, 595-596
Macros, **568-598**
    application development and, 601-603, 617-620
    assigning to buttons, 576-579, 593
    assigning to keys, 575-576, 593
    Autoload, 580, 590
    breakpoints in, 596-598
    conditional instructions in, 588-595
    creating libraries of, 388, 595-596
    customization settings, 380
    debugging, 596-598
    documenting, 548-550
    editing, 574-575
    halting, 574
    naming, 572-573
    overview of, 568-569
    pausing for dialog boxes in, 592-593
    pausing for user action in, 587
    prompting for input in, 587-588
    recording, 569-572, 581-582
    running, 573-574
    startup setting for, 377
    syntax of, 583-586
    text in formulas and, 556
    written, 583-586, 593-595
MACRS (modified accelerated cost recovery system), 284-285, 293-294
Manual recalculation feature, 382-385
Margin settings, Page Setup dialog box, 214
Math coprocessors, 17
Maximize button, **23-24**, 28-29, 356-357
Maximum value function
    aggregate (MAX), 250
    database (DMAX), 258
Menu bar, Quattro Pro, 25-27
Menus
    in customized dialog boxes, 618-620
    hiding with macros, 602-603
    navigating in, 25-27
    saving with, 47-48
{MESSAGE} command, 583, 585-587
Microsoft Windows, 622-630
    Clipboard, 541-544
    data exchange in, 541-551
    dialog boxes in, 628-629
    Dynamic Data Exchange (DDE), 8, 428-429, 541-542, 544-548
    File Manager, 178-180, 637-638, 648
    fonts in, 10, 21
    keyboard shortcuts in, 19, 626-628
    monitors and, 20
    Object Linking and Embedding (OLE), 8, 542, 548-551
    overview of, 17-19, 622-630
    Print Manager, 200-201
    printers and, 20-21
    Task List, 24, 196, 626-627
MID function, 562-563
Minimize button, **23-24**, 28-29, 356-357
Minimum value function
    aggregate (MIN), 250-251
    database (DMIN), 258-259
Minus sign (–), 84, 165, 233
MINUTE function, 306
Miscellaneous commands, Macro menu, 595
MOD (remainder) function, 252-253
Mode indicator box, 28

Models
- copying, 137-139
- creating sample, 52-53
- defined, 4
- three-dimensional, 6

Modified accelerated cost recovery system (MACRS), 284-285, 293-294

Monitors, 20-21, 23, 635-636

MONTH function, 302-303

Mouse
- changing default settings with, 54-55
- creating formulas with, 107
- CTRL key and, 69
- data entry and, 71-73
- defining criteria tables with, 327-328
- editing with, 36, 75-76, 79
- moving pages with, 150
- operation of, 17, 19
- selecting blocks with, 235
- selecting columns with, 69-70
- setting decimal places with, 86-87
- SHIFT key and, 69
- *See also* Drag-and-drop feature

Move command
- Block menu, 130-135
- Window menu, 358

Multiple graphs, 448, **458-461**, 472

Multiplication operator (*), 36, 233

N

NA function, 307

Name setting, Active Page dialog box, **55-56**, 389

Named Settings command, File menu, 199, 218

Named styles
- copying to new notebook, 95
- creating, 88-92
- numeric formats and, 93-95

Names command, Block menu, 161-165, 236-238

Names | Labels command, Block menu, 166-167

Naming conventions
- for blocks, 163
- for files, 47-48, 82, 181-182

Negation operator (–), 165, 233

Net present value function (NPV), 274-277

Networks, installing Quattro Pro on, 634

New command, File menu, 189-190

New SpeedBar command, 601

New View command, Window menu, 360-361

No. of Observations, regression analysis and, 513

Noncontiguous blocks. *See* Blocks, compound

Normal style, editing, 395

#NOT# operator, 233, 336

Not equal to operator (<>), 233, 335

Notebook title bar, 28-29

Notebooks
- automatic loading of, 377
- closing, 192, 194
- copying styles to new, 95
- creating new, 189-190
- data exchange and, 541-551
- navigating in, 28-30
- opening, 190-192
- overview of, 3-8
- pages in, 5, 30
- retrieving, 191-192
- Zoom Factor and, 118-119, 204-205, 354, 360, 385-386

See also Active Notebook dialog box; Active Page dialog box; Graphs page; Pages
Notepad program, 23
NOW function, 301
NPER (number of payments) function, 269
NPV (net present value) function, 274-277
NUM LOCK key, 28
Number as integer function (INT), 252
Number of payments functions (NPER and TERM), 269-270
Number of periods function (CTERM), 269-270
Number symbol (#), 84, 336
Numbers
    alignment of, 84
    commas in, 35, 41-42, 85-86
    converting labels to, 565
    converting to labels, 564
    decimal places in, 41-42, 86-88
    formatting, 39-42, 85-88
    function for random, 253
    long, 85
    as percents, 46-47
    rounding, 127-129, 254-255
    value indicators and, 84
    See also Values
Numeric arguments, 241-242
Numeric Format settings
    customizing, 396-400
    for dates, 95-97
    formulas and, 85-88
    named styles and, 92-95
    overview of, 39-42
    for percent, 46-47
    rounding and, 127-129, 254-255
    for time, 305
Numeric operators, 230, 233-234

O

Object commands, Macro menu, 595
Object inspector
    changing default settings with, 54-57
    overview of, 38-42
Object Link dialog box, 601
Object Linking and Embedding (OLE), 8, 542, 548-551
    versus hot-linking, 548
Objects, free-floating, 548
OLE-capable server applications, 542, 548
Online support, 645
Open command, File menu, 190-192
Operators
    in formulas, 230, 233-234, 334-336
    order of precedence of, 234
Optimizer dialog box, 534, 535
Optimizer feature, 531-536
#OR# operator, 233, 336
Order of precedence, of operators, 234
Output Block, for Extract command, 338
Overstrike mode, in EDIT mode, 76

P

Page breaks setting
    Page Setup dialog box, 215-217
    Print dialog box, 202-203
Page Guides button, Print Preview screen, 204
Page references, **124-125**
    cell coordinates and, 132
Page Setup button, Print Preview screen, 204
Page Setup dialog box, **211-217**

Index

Center blocks setting, 217
footers and, 212-213
headers and, 212-213
margin settings, 214
page break setting, 215-217
paper type setting, 214
print orientation setting, 215
Print to fit setting, 216
scaling setting, 217
See also Print Options dialog box; Printing
Page tabs. *See* Tabs
Pages
cell references and, 125
deleting, 151-152
inserting, 146-149
moving, 149-151
naming, 237
overview of, 6-7
See also Active Page dialog box; Graphs page; Group mode; Tabs
Palette settings, 386-387
Panes command, Window menu, 361-365
Paper type setting, Page Setup dialog box and, 214
Paradox, 411-412, 421-422, 430, 433
Paradox File Structure dialog box, 412
Paradox for Windows Made Easy (Jones), 422
Paradox Table Query dialog box, 433
Parentheses
in formulas, 231, 233-234
as label indicator, 58
as value indicator, 84
Parsing text, 551-556
Passwords, 403-406
Paste command
and Copy command, 97-101

and Cut command, 102-103
data exchange via, 541
SpeedBar and, 27
Paste Link command, 541-542, 545-548
Paste Special command, 101-102
PATH statement, DOS, 640-642
Paths, files and, 181-182
{PAUSEMACRO} command, 562-563
Payment calculation, creating, 43-46
Payment functions, **261-270**
CTERM (number of periods) function, 270, 271
IPAYMT (interest payment) function, 268-269
loan tables and, 266-268
NPER (number of payments) function, 269
PAYMT (sophisticated loan payment) function, 263-266
PMT (basic loan payment) function, 261-263
PPAYMT (principal payment) function, 268-269
TERM function, 270
See also Functions
Percent sign (%), 58
Period (.), 84, 182
PGDN key, 29, 49
PGUP key, 29, 49
PI function, 295
Pick List tool, UI Builder SpeedBar, 607
Pie graphs, **452-453**, 456, 471, 486
Pie slice, exploded, 490-492
Plus sign (+), 37, 84, 103, 233
PMT (basic loan payment) function, 261-263
POINT mode, 131-133
Point size, 40, 220

Pointer, changing column width with, 69-70
Pointer tool, UI Builder SpeedBar, 606
Pointing, 17
Portrait orientation, 207, 215
Positioning commands, Macro menu, 595
Pound sign (#), 84, 336
PPAYMT (principal payment) function, 268-269
Present value, 271-272
Present value functions (PVAL and PV), 272-277
Presentation graphics, **482-505**
    interactive, 504-505
    slide shows and, 482-483, 501-503
    See also Graphs
Presentation programs, 2
Principal payment function (PPAYMT), 268-269
Print block(s) setting, 197-199
Print button, Print Preview screen, 204
{PRINT} command, 591
Print command, 197-199
Print dialog box, **199-201**
    Copies setting, 201
    page breaks and, 202-203
    Print pages setting, 201-203
Print Manager, Windows, 200-201
Print Options button, Print Preview screen, 204
Print Options dialog box, **205-211**
    Cell formulas option, 209-210
    Gridlines option, 210-211
    Headings options, 206-208
    Row/Column borders option, 210-211
    spacing options, 208-209
    See also Page Setup dialog box

Print orientation, 207, 215
Print Preview screen, 203-205
Print queues, 200
Printer Setup command, File menu, 200, **217-219**, 637
Printers
    fixed-pitch, 57
    installation and, 636-637
    overview of, 20-21
    proportional fonts and, 57
Printing, **196-219**
    background, 200
    Copies setting and, 201
    graphs, 478
    Line Drawing property and, 221-223
    Named Settings command and, 199, 218
    Print dialog box and, 199-201
    Print Manager and, 200-201
    Print Pages setting and, 201-203
    Print Preview command and, 203-205
    Printer Setup command and, 200, 217-219
    Reveal/Hide property and, 224-226
    selecting cells for, 196-199
    Shading property and, 223-225
    SpeedFormat button and, 226-228
    terminating jobs, 200-201
    See also Fonts; Page Setup dialog box; Print Options dialog box
.PRN files, 552
Processors, requirements for, 16-17
Program flow commands, Macro menu, 594
Program Item Properties dialog box, 639

Index

Center blocks setting, 217
footers and, 212-213
headers and, 212-213
margin settings, 214
page break setting, 215-217
paper type setting, 214
print orientation setting, 215
Print to fit setting, 216
scaling setting, 217
See also Print Options dialog box; Printing
Page tabs. *See* Tabs
Pages
cell references and, 125
deleting, 151-152
inserting, 146-149
moving, 149-151
naming, 237
overview of, 6-7
See also Active Page dialog box; Graphs page; Group mode; Tabs
Palette settings, 386-387
Panes command, Window menu, 361-365
Paper type setting, Page Setup dialog box and, 214
Paradox, 411-412, 421-422, 430, 433
Paradox File Structure dialog box, 412
Paradox for Windows Made Easy (Jones), 422
Paradox Table Query dialog box, 433
Parentheses
in formulas, 231, 233-234
as label indicator, 58
as value indicator, 84
Parsing text, 551-556
Passwords, 403-406
Paste command
and Copy command, 97-101
and Cut command, 102-103
data exchange via, 541
SpeedBar and, 27
Paste Link command, 541-542, 545-548
Paste Special command, 101-102
PATH statement, DOS, 640-642
Paths, files and, 181-182
{PAUSEMACRO} command, 562-563
Payment calculation, creating, 43-46
Payment functions, **261-270**
CTERM (number of periods) function, 270, 271
IPAYMT (interest payment) function, 268-269
loan tables and, 266-268
NPER (number of payments) function, 269
PAYMT (sophisticated loan payment) function, 263-266
PMT (basic loan payment) function, 261-263
PPAYMT (principal payment) function, 268-269
TERM function, 270
See also Functions
Percent sign (%), 58
Period (.), 84, 182
PGDN key, 29, 49
PGUP key, 29, 49
PI function, 295
Pick List tool, UI Builder SpeedBar, 607
Pie graphs, **452-453**, 456, 471, 486
Pie slice, exploded, 490-492
Plus sign (+), 37, 84, 103, 233
PMT (basic loan payment) function, 261-263
POINT mode, 131-133
Point size, 40, 220

Pointer, changing column width with, 69-70
Pointer tool, UI Builder SpeedBar, 606
Pointing, 17
Portrait orientation, 207, 215
Positioning commands, Macro menu, 595
Pound sign (#), 84, 336
PPAYMT (principal payment) function, 268-269
Present value, 271-272
Present value functions (PVAL and PV), 272-277
Presentation graphics, **482-505**
    interactive, 504-505
    slide shows and, 482-483, 501-503
    See also Graphs
Presentation programs, 2
Principal payment function (PPAYMT), 268-269
Print block(s) setting, 197-199
Print button, Print Preview screen, 204
{PRINT} command, 591
Print command, 197-199
Print dialog box, **199-201**
    Copies setting, 201
    page breaks and, 202-203
    Print pages setting, 201-203
Print Manager, Windows, 200-201
Print Options button, Print Preview screen, 204
Print Options dialog box, **205-211**
    Cell formulas option, 209-210
    Gridlines option, 210-211
    Headings options, 206-208
    Row/Column borders option, 210-211
    spacing options, 208-209
    See also Page Setup dialog box

Print orientation, 207, 215
Print Preview screen, 203-205
Print queues, 200
Printer Setup command, File menu, 200, **217-219**, 637
Printers
    fixed-pitch, 57
    installation and, 636-637
    overview of, 20-21
    proportional fonts and, 57
Printing, **196-219**
    background, 200
    Copies setting and, 201
    graphs, 478
    Line Drawing property and, 221-223
    Named Settings command and, 199, 218
    Print dialog box and, 199-201
    Print Manager and, 200-201
    Print Pages setting and, 201-203
    Print Preview command and, 203-205
    Printer Setup command and, 200, 217-219
    Reveal/Hide property and, 224-226
    selecting cells for, 196-199
    Shading property and, 223-225
    SpeedFormat button and, 226-228
    terminating jobs, 200-201
    See also Fonts; Page Setup dialog box; Print Options dialog box
.PRN files, 552
Processors, requirements for, 16-17
Program flow commands, Macro menu, 594
Program Item Properties dialog box, 639

Program title bar, 23-25
PROPER function, 564
Properties
    Application command and, 181
    changing, 39-42
    changing default settings for, 53-57
    of customized dialog boxes, 608
    of graphs, 466-472, 474, 482, 484-487
    Label Alignment property, 58-61
    Line Drawing property, 221-223
    Reveal/Hide property, 224-226
    Shading property, 223-225
    See also Fonts; Formatting
Property menu
    Active Notebook command, 382
    Active Page command, 388-389
    Application command, 369
Proportional fonts, 57
Protection setting, Active Page dialog box, 390
Publishing features, Quattro Pro, 10-11
Pull-down menus, 25-27
Punctuation settings, international, 372-373
Pushbutton tool, UI Builder SpeedBar, 606
PV function, 274
PVAL (present value) function, 272-274

Q

QBE (Query By Example), 12, 422, 429-430
Quattro Pro
    autoloading, 640
    Clipboard, 541-544
    color of work area in, 646-647
    database features of, 11-12
    dBASE and, 418-422, 424, 430
    DOS and, 17, 19
    DOS PATH statement and, 640-642
    exiting, 25, 48, 195-196
    foreign file formats and, 407-413
    graphics features of, 12-15
    hardware requirements for, 15-17
    icon for, 640
    installing, 21-22, 632-642
    installing on networks, 634
    limits of databases in, 322
    loading, 21-22
    versus Lotus 1-2-3, 8, 240
    navigating in, 28-30, 49-50
    overview of, 2-14
    Paradox and, 411-412, 421-422, 430, 433
    publishing features of, 10-11
    questions and answers about, 646-648
    registration of, 645
    software requirements for, 17-20
    spreadsheet features of, 10
    technical support for, 644-645
    See also Microsoft Windows
Queries, 12, **325-343**
    cross-tabulations and, 348-351
    Database Desktop, 421-422, 424-427, 429-435
    defining database blocks, 326-328
    deleting records with, 340-341
    extracting data in, 337-340
    formulas in, 334-336
    importing data with, 418-421
    locating data with, 328-330
    logical operators in, 334-336
    multiple criteria in, 330-332

multiple spreadsheets and, 341-342
naming fields in, 333-334
repeating, 330
searching text in, 336-337
of two tables, 430-432
use of, 432-435
See also Criteria Tables; Data Query dialog box; Database Desktop; Databases
Query By Example, 12, 422, 429-430
Query command
importing data with, 418-421
overview of, 326-328
Question mark (?), 58
Questions and answers, about Quattro Pro, 646-648
Queues, print, 200
{QUIT} command, 592
Quotation mark ("), 33, 58, 336

R

R Squared value, regression analysis and, 513
RADIANS function, 295-296
Radio Button tool, UI Builder SpeedBar, 606
RAM, 15-16, 177
Random number function (RND), 253
RATE function, 278
READY mode
data entry and, 71
Status line and, 28
Recalculation settings, 382-385
Record Macro dialog box, 571
Records, database, 11, 321-322
Rectangle tool, UI Builder SpeedBar, 607
References

absolute, 123-127
cell, 122-127, 151-152, 155
circular, 240
"Invalid reference" error message, 80-81, 237-238
page, 124-125, 132
relative, 122-123
Reformat command, Block menu, 540
Registration, Quattro Pro, 645
Regression analysis, **508-519**
example of, 509-510
explained, 508-509
interpreting results of, 513-514
with multiple variables, 516-519
performing, 511-512
using results of, 514-516
Regression command, 511, 518
Relational database managers, 320-321
Relative cell references, 122-123
Remainder function (MOD), 252-253
REPEAT function, 560
REPLACE function, 562
Replacing and saving files, 83
Reports. *See* Printing
Restore function, 23-24
Restrict Input command, Data menu, 343-344
Retrieve command, File menu, 190-192
{RETURN} command, 591-592
Reveal/Hide property, 224-226
Reverse copying, 139-140
RIGHT function, 562-563
Right alignment, **32-34**, 212
RND (random number) function, 253
Rotated graphs, 447-448, 458-459
ROUND function, 127-129, 254-255
Row/Column borders option, Print Options dialog box, 210-211

Index

Rows
    cell references and, 125
    changing height of, 70, 224
    deleting, 151-152
    inserting, 141-146
    printing and, 224-226
    records and, 12
    See also Columns
Run Macro dialog box, 573, 575

S

Save All command, File menu, 193-194
Save As command, File menu, 118, **193**
    exporting files and, 413
    passwords and, 403-406
Save command
    data protection and, 406-407
    foreign files and, 407
    links and, 546
    passwords and, 405
    replacing with, 83, 118
    use of, 46-49, 81-83, 182-185
    Workspace, 195, 358-360
Save File dialog box, 47-48, 182-187
Scalable fonts, 21
Scientific notation, 85
Screen commands, Macro menu, 594
Screens, 20-21, 23, 635-636
Scroll Bar tool, UI Builder SpeedBar, 608
Scroll bars, 30, 388
SCROLL LOCK key, 28
Search and Replace command, Edit menu, 170-173
Search criteria. *See* Criteria Tables
Searches. *See* Queries; Search and Replace command
SECOND function, 306

Security, 402-407
Semicolon (;), 58
Server applications, 542
Shading property, **223-225**, 386-387
Shapes, in graphs, 494-496
SHIFT key
    + F7 key, 39
    + TAB key, 29, 50
    capitalization and, 33
    mouse operation and, 69
    selecting and, 111
Shortcut keys. *See* Keyboard shortcuts
Show command, Window menu, 356, 357
SIN function, 297
Size command, Window menu, 358
Slash (/), **26**
    in dates, 81
    in formulas, 233
Slash (/) commands, Macro menu, 594
Slide shows, 482-483, **501-503**
    creating, 501-502
    displaying, 502
    editing, 502-503
    See also Graphs
SLN (straight-line depreciation) function, 283
Soft page breaks, 215-217
Solve For command, Tools menu, 530-532
Solve For dialog box, 531
Sorting, 310-319
    Data | Sort command, 314-319
    rules for, 316
    SpeedSort button, 310-314
    tips for, 316-319
Source objects, of graphs, 444
SPACEBAR, 79-80
Spaces
    in formulas, 240

removing from strings, 563
Spacing options, Print Options dialog box, 208-209
Special functions, 306-307
SpeedBar
    Button tool, 576-577
    customizing, 381-382, 601
    Fit button, 67-69
    Graph tool, 438-439
    Graph window, 446
    Insert button, 144-146
    overview of, 2, 27-28, 65-66
    Style buttons, 67
    Style Selector, 88
    UI Builder, 604-608
SpeedFill button, 66, **152-156**
SpeedFormat button, 66, **226-228**
    See also Formatting
SpeedSort button, 66, **310-314**
SpeedSum button, 28, 66, **107-110**
Spin Control tool, UI Builder SpeedBar, 607
Spreadsheet features, Quattro Pro, 2-11
Spreadsheet Page Setup dialog box. See Page Setup dialog box
Spreadsheet Print dialog box. See Print dialog box
Spreadsheet Print Options dialog box. See Print Options dialog box
SQL commands, 12
SQRT (square root) function, 255-256
Square brackets ([]), 58
Squares, drawing, 496
Stacked bar graphs, 449-450, 453-454
Standard deviation function
    aggregate (STD), 251
    database (DSTD), 259
Standard Query language. See SQL commands

Startup Macro option, 377
Startup settings, **374-379**
    Autoload File option, 377
    Compatible Keys option, 378-379
    Directory option, 375-376
    File Extension option, 377
    Startup Macro option, 377
    Undo Enabled option, 378
    Use Beep option, 378
Statistics. See Frequency distribution analysis; Goal seeking; Optimizer feature; Regression analysis; What-If tables; XY graphs
Status line, 28
STD function, 251
The Stephen Cobb Complete Guide to Personal Computer and Network Security, 402
Stepped bar graphs, 455
Straight-line depreciation function (SLN), 283
Strikeout setting, 220-221
String arguments, 242
STRING function, 564
String functions, 308, **558-565**
    CHAR function, 559
    CODE function, 560
    EXACT function, 561-562
    FIND function, 561
    LEFT function, 562-563
    LENGTH function, 563
    LOWER function, 564
    MID function, 562-563
    PROPER function, 564
    REPEAT function, 560
    REPLACE function, 562
    RIGHT function, 562-563
    STRING function, 564
    TRIM function, 563
    UPPER function, 564

Index

VALUE function, 565
    See also Functions
Style buttons, SpeedBar, 67, 88
Style Selector, SpeedBar, 88
Styles
    editing Normal, 394-395
    named, 88-92
    numeric formats and named, 92-95
Styling reports. *See* Printing
Subdirectories, 177-179
    See also Directories
Subtraction operator (–), 233
SUM function, 104-107, 245-247
    database (DSUM), 259
    SpeedSum button and, 107-110
    See also Functions
Sum-of-years' depreciation function (SYD), 283-284
SUMPRODUCT function, 248
Support, technical, 644-645
SYD (sum-of-years' depreciation) function, 283-284
Symbols
    settings for international, 371-374, 400
    SHIFT key and, 33
    in user-defined numeric formats, 397-400
System requirements, Quattro Pro, 15-17

T

TAB key
    + ALT key, 626
    navigating with, 29, 49-50
Table Query command, 433-435
Tabs, page
    defined, 5
    moving pages with, 150
    navigating with, 30
    turning on/off, 388
TAN function, 297
Task List, Windows, 24, 196, 626-627
Technical support, 644-645
TERM function, 270
Test button, UI Builder SpeedBar, 605
Text, **538-565**
    concatenation of, 557-559
    entering blocks of, 538-541
    in graphs, 492-494
    importing as embedded objects, 8, 542, 548-551
    importing with Clipboard, 541-544
    importing with hot links, 541-542, 544-548
    in logical functions, 556-557
    parsing, 551-556
    reformatting blocks of, 538-541
    searching in queries, 336-337
    See also String functions
Text Color settings, Active Block dialog box, 221
Text graphs, 448, **496-498**
Three-dimensional graphs, 447, **453-457**, 471
Tilde (~), 58
Tile command, Window menu, 358-359
Time Format settings, international, 373-374
Time functions, **304-306**
    HOUR function, 306
    MINUTE function, 306
    SECOND function, 306
    TIME function, 305
    TIMEVALUE function, 305-306
    See also Functions
Time part functions, 306

Time tool, UI Builder SpeedBar, 608
Title bar
    notebook, 28-29
    program, 23-25
Titles, in graphs, 440, **465-468**, 470, 485
TODAY function, 301
Tool icons. *See* SpeedBar
Tools menu
    Advanced Math option, 511, 518
    Combine command, 413, 415-417
    Execute command, 573
    Extract command, 413-415
    Macro Record command, 582
    Macros command, 571
    Solve For command, 530-532
    UI Builder command, 601, 603-611
Totals, calculating, 37
Transpose command, Block menu, 168-169
Trigonometric functions, 294-298
    ACOS function, 297
    applications for, 297-298
    ASIN function, 297
    ATAN function, 297
    ATAN2 function, 297
    COS function, 297
    DEGREES function, 295
    inverse, 297
    PI function, 295
    RADIANS function, 295-296
    SIN function, 297
    TAN function, 297
    See also Functions
TRIM function, 563
TRUE function, 307
TrueType fonts, 10, 21
TurboTab button, 442, 444
Two-dimensional graphs, 447, 449-453

Type styles, 40, 67, 220-221
Typefaces. *See* Fonts

U

UI Builder command, Tools menu, 601, 603-611
UI commands, Macro menu, 595
Underline setting, 220-221
Underline symbol (_), 58
Undo command, 73-74, 76
Undo Enabled option, 378
Unit settings, Default Width, 55-57
UPPER function, 564
Uppercase. *See* Capitalization
Use Beep option, 378
User interface (UI) commands, Macro menu, 595

V

Value axis, 442
VALUE function, 565
Value indicators, 36, 84, 103
Values
    converting formulas to, 236
    converting to dates, 299-300
    dynamic versus fixed, 236
    formulas and, 230, 232
    in functions, 232
    versus labels, 81
    overview of, 30-32
Values command, Block menu, 169-170
Variance function
    aggregate (VAR), 251
    database (DVAR), 259-260
Variance graphs, 449
Vertical bar (|), 58, 212

Index

Viewing options. *See* Window menu commands
VLOOKUP function, 289-292

W

.WB1 extension, 47, 82
.WBS extension, 194
What-If command, 5
    database functions and, 348-351
    overview of, 346-348
What-If tables, 521-527
    example using, 523-526
    explained, 521-522
    two-way, 526-527
Width settings. *See* Auto Width command; Column Width settings; Default Width settings; Fit button
Wildcard characters, 187-189
Window menu commands, **355-368**
    Arrange Icons command, 358
    Cascade command, 358-359
    Hide command, 356
    Locked Titles command, 365-367
    Maximize command, 356-357
    Minimize command, 356-357
    Move command, 358
    New View command, 360-361
    Panes command, 361-365
    Show command, 356-357
    Size command, 358
    Tile command, 358-359
Windowed display, 23

{WindowHide} command, 596
Windows. *See* Microsoft Windows
.WK1 extension, 182
.WK3 extension, 182
Word processing, data exchange and, 541-551
Workspace command, File menu, 194-195, 358-360
.WQ1 extension, 182
WYSIWYG, defined, 8-11
Wysiwyg/Impress files, 408, 410

X

X coefficient, 514-515
X axis, 442, 469-470
XY graphs, 451, 513-514, 527-529

Y

Y axis, 442, 470
    modifying scale of, 475-478
    secondary, 472-475
YEAR function, 303

Z

Zeros, display setting for, 392-393
Zoom Factor
    Active Notebook dialog box, 118-119, 354, 360, 385-386
    Print Preview screen, 204-205

▷ Expand Your Skills Even More

with help from our expert authors. Now that you've gained greater skills with **Quattro Pro for Windows Inside & Out,** *let us suggest the following related titles that will help you use your computer to full advantage.*

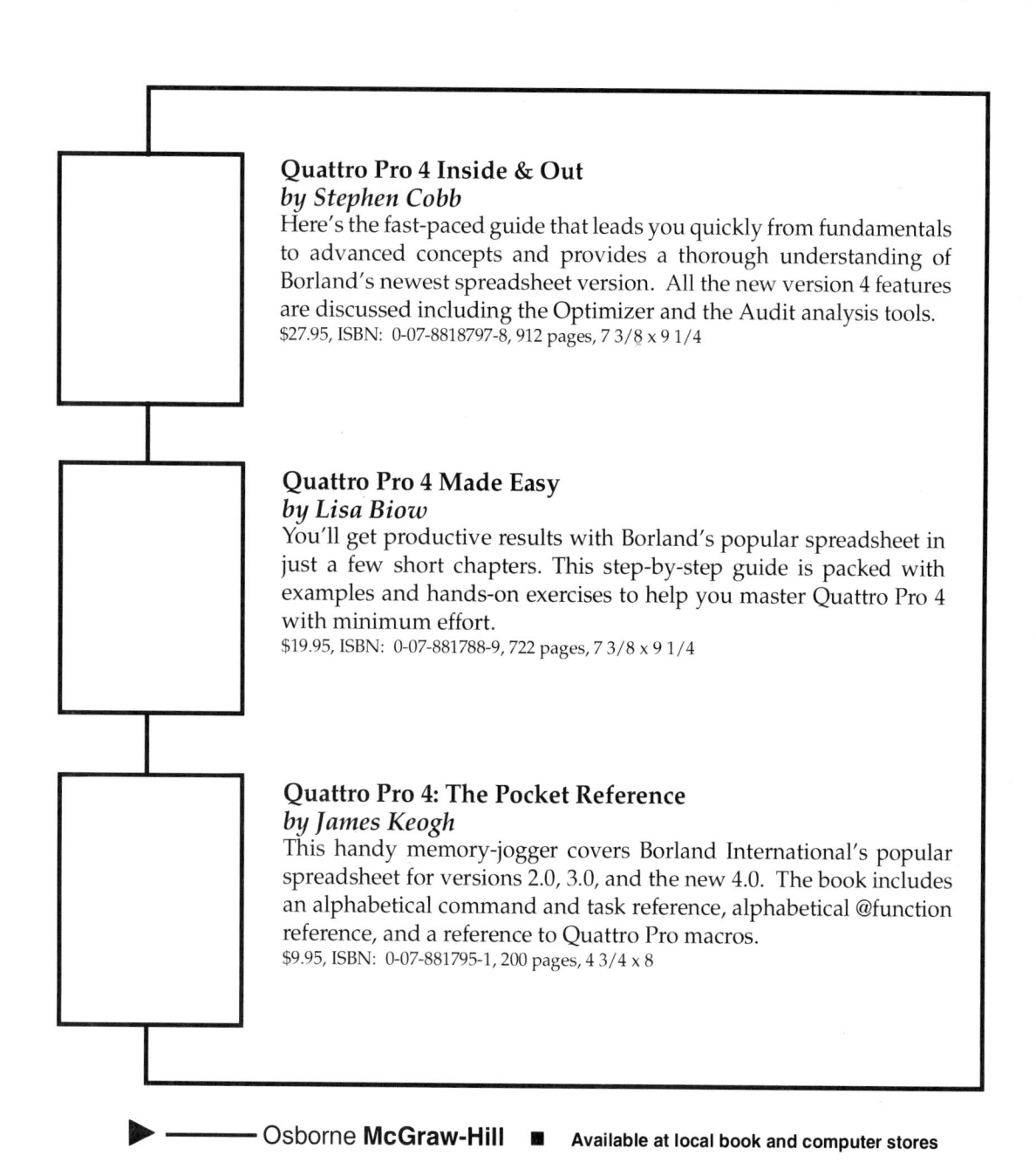

Quattro Pro 4 Inside & Out
by Stephen Cobb

Here's the fast-paced guide that leads you quickly from fundamentals to advanced concepts and provides a thorough understanding of Borland's newest spreadsheet version. All the new version 4 features are discussed including the Optimizer and the Audit analysis tools.
$27.95, ISBN: 0-07-8818797-8, 912 pages, 7 3/8 x 9 1/4

Quattro Pro 4 Made Easy
by Lisa Biow

You'll get productive results with Borland's popular spreadsheet in just a few short chapters. This step-by-step guide is packed with examples and hands-on exercises to help you master Quattro Pro 4 with minimum effort.
$19.95, ISBN: 0-07-881788-9, 722 pages, 7 3/8 x 9 1/4

Quattro Pro 4: The Pocket Reference
by James Keogh

This handy memory-jogger covers Borland International's popular spreadsheet for versions 2.0, 3.0, and the new 4.0. The book includes an alphabetical command and task reference, alphabetical @function reference, and a reference to Quattro Pro macros.
$9.95, ISBN: 0-07-881795-1, 200 pages, 4 3/4 x 8

▶ ——— Osborne **McGraw-Hill**   ■   Available at local book and computer stores

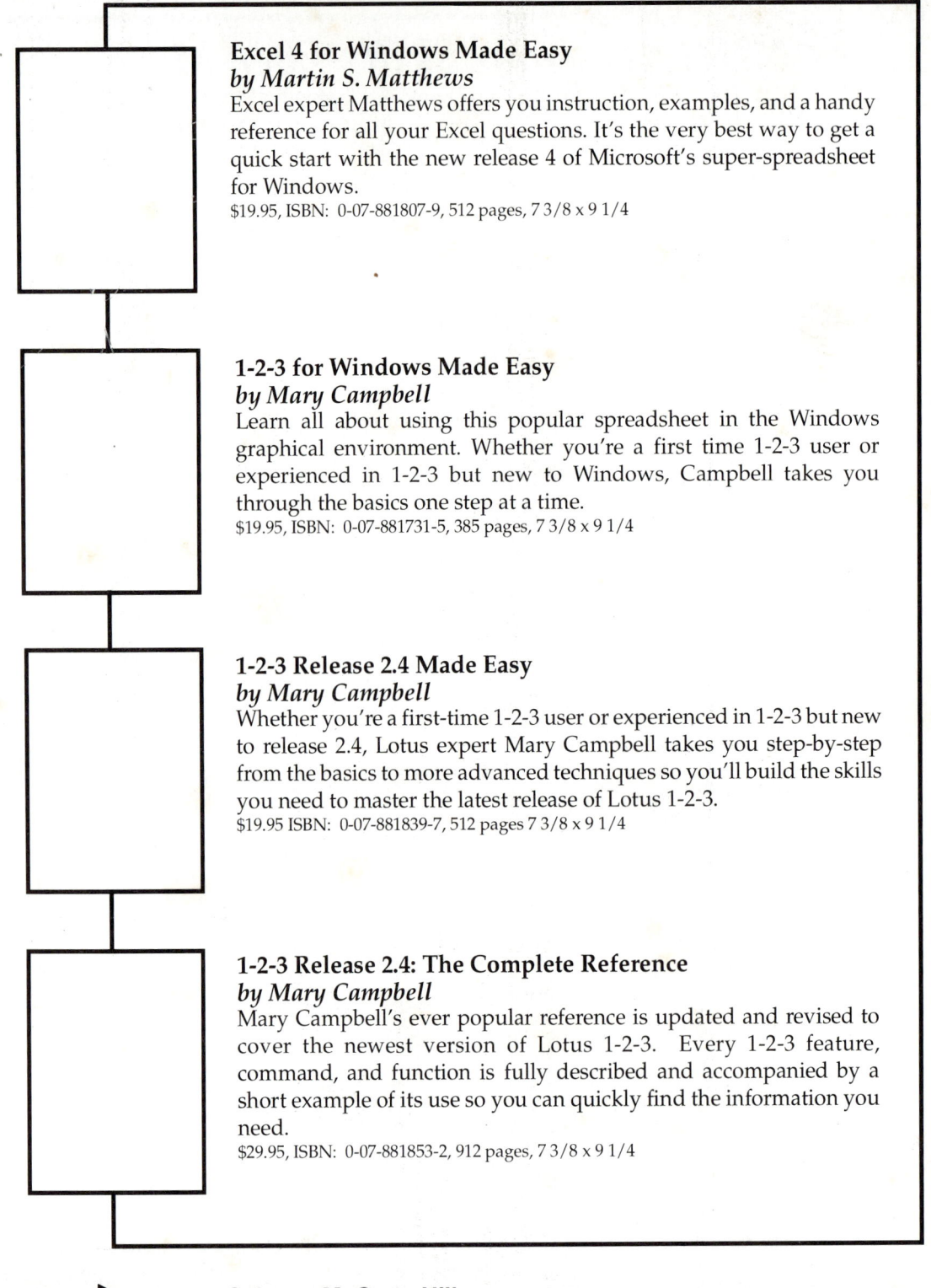

Excel 4 for Windows Made Easy
by Martin S. Matthews
Excel expert Matthews offers you instruction, examples, and a handy reference for all your Excel questions. It's the very best way to get a quick start with the new release 4 of Microsoft's super-spreadsheet for Windows.
$19.95, ISBN: 0-07-881807-9, 512 pages, 7 3/8 x 9 1/4

1-2-3 for Windows Made Easy
by Mary Campbell
Learn all about using this popular spreadsheet in the Windows graphical environment. Whether you're a first time 1-2-3 user or experienced in 1-2-3 but new to Windows, Campbell takes you through the basics one step at a time.
$19.95, ISBN: 0-07-881731-5, 385 pages, 7 3/8 x 9 1/4

1-2-3 Release 2.4 Made Easy
by Mary Campbell
Whether you're a first-time 1-2-3 user or experienced in 1-2-3 but new to release 2.4, Lotus expert Mary Campbell takes you step-by-step from the basics to more advanced techniques so you'll build the skills you need to master the latest release of Lotus 1-2-3.
$19.95 ISBN: 0-07-881839-7, 512 pages 7 3/8 x 9 1/4

1-2-3 Release 2.4: The Complete Reference
by Mary Campbell
Mary Campbell's ever popular reference is updated and revised to cover the newest version of Lotus 1-2-3. Every 1-2-3 feature, command, and function is fully described and accompanied by a short example of its use so you can quickly find the information you need.
$29.95, ISBN: 0-07-881853-2, 912 pages, 7 3/8 x 9 1/4

▶ ──── Osborne **McGraw-Hill** ■ Available at local book and computer stores